Family Devotions

for

Every Day in the Church Year

––––––––

Gathered from the writings of
Dr. Martin Luther

by

Geo. Link

Evangelical Lutheran Pastor to St. Louis, Missouri – 1877

Translated from the German

by

Joel Baseley

Evangelical Lutheran Pastor to Dearborn, Michigan – 1996

Published by:
Mark V Publications
2000 North York
Dearborn, MI 48128

Fifth Printing, revised

Library of Congress Catalog Card Number: 96-77109

International Standard Book Number 0-9652403-0-4

Printed by Sheridan Books, Inc., Chelsea, Michigan

The Rev. Georg Link, 1829–1908

The Editor of this work is the Rev. Georg Link, who was born in Thalmessing, Bavaria, Germany in 1829. Rev. Link graduated from the Lutheran Seminary in Ft. Wayne, Indiana, in 1851. In that year he was ordained at Salem Lutheran Church, Black Jack, Missouri, on August 24 by Dr. W. Sihler. He served eight congregations during his fifty-two years in the ministry. He and his wife raised twelve children.

Pastor Link was serving Zion Lutheran Church, St. Louis, Missouri, when he gathered this collection from Luther's writings as he was also serving as Vice-President of the Western District of the Lutheran Church—Missouri Synod.

(Photo kindly provided by the Concordia Historical Institute, St. Louis, Missouri)

Editor's Forward.

The undersigned came upon the contents of this book unexpectedly. He had the same mission; to seek the sources in Luther as did the *Evangelical House Blessings*, offered by Dr. J. L. Pasig, and to unite with Pasig in his effort to distribute his book. But as the undersigned took up this work, it was soon evident that in his book Pasig had not given Luther as he is. Not just in a few sentences, but on every page his citations are changed. Luther's flow of speech will not suffer that. So it was resolutely decided to produce a similar edifying book according to Pasig's plan, but not to arbitrarily mutilate Luther. The dear reader will find, therefore, our Luther in his *Daily Family Devotions* completely unchanged, so far as he is cited.

The plan of this book will be apparent to the eyes of the reader. So much as amenable, the quoted verses of the Holy Scriptures, the contemplation of it and the hymn verses were adapted, generally, to the customary order of the church year. That this must be of great worth, especially to a Lutheran, needs no proof. It is pleasant for the father of a family, when he is with his household on the morning of a Sunday or holy day, to read a devotion which is introduced into the heart by the appointed gospel or epistle. With an even greater benefit he will be able to hear a good preacher in his church. Yes, it is written into the spirit of us Lutheran Christians that it is almost a necessity to use meditations like the *Family Devotions* on holy days.

The dear reader will not object that at the top of each devotion of the book stands a passage of Holy Scriptures that is masterfully clarified with Luther's words and with a hymn verse copied, which can be sung. In this way a daily spiritual meal is prepared for the dear reader, that he can eat with blessing and pleasure.

Those who know Luther's writing will easily see that the meditations are all, without exception, good, very good. That the selection could be better, that there could be much better things that have been left out, are gladly conceded, yet with the modest comment: It is easier said than done.

May the true God set Luther's daily home devotions as a blessing for many families!

St. Louis, 25 April 1877

Geo. Link

Translator's Forward.

The strength of this work is in its fine selections from the writings of Luther. From this we gather the strength and vibrance of the devotional life of those who went before us in the nineteenth century. Many printings of this book enriched the faith and confession of Christ around the family altar.

This work is intended to fill many purposes in your library. For pastors, this work, linked with the historical readings for the church year, can provide not only valuable aids in textual interpretation and application, but it can also be a doorway into the solid sermon resources available but often overlooked due to the switch to the three-year cycle of readings (post Vatican II). By all means purchase and read Lenker's *Sermons of Martin Luther*, the Church Postil, and also Klug's recent translation, *Sermons of Martin Luther: The House Postils* (both from *Baker*). Perusing these treasures, I believe that any preacher humble enough to seek good guidance in his preaching will be compelled by the quality of these resources to revive preaching the historical series once again. More is not always better.

For those who want a daily devotional aid, these writings were gathered to fill that need, especially towards the concerns of the late nineteenth century, which are amazingly contemporary. Enjoy the depths of Luther's treatments and his uncovering the core of the gospel as the work and gift of Christ given through faith to you. With Luther battle the enemies of this single faith and of his undefeatable reliance in the Lord against all competing faith.

For anyone looking for a small volume that can be used as a "Luther says" resource, the indices in back list Bible references, names and topics for your enjoyment and use.

With respect for Link's concern to leave Luther unchanged, Luther in this work is unabashedly Luther. He freely praises what is the Lord's and condemns all that would overshadow this Lord. His concerns are Christian concerns; for the faith and confession of his Lord.

Dearborn, Michigan 1996

Joel Baseley

Some Notes on the Text:

Hymn verses cited at the end of each devotion are from *The Lutheran Hymnal* (TLH), copyright 1941, CPH and *Lutheran Worship*, copyright 1982, CPH. In a few instances, where noted, a verse was found in *The Evangelical Lutheran Hymn Book* (ELHP), CPH 1927. In yet a few instances it was found desirable to translate the verse quoted in Link when no appropriate substitute was found.

Please note that within the text of this volume certain words and phrases appear in ( ) parentheses and others in square brackets [ ]. Words in the (parentheses) come directly from Link (which also occur in the original sources so far as they were verified by this translator). Words in the [brackets] have been added by the translator in order to supply antecedents of indefinite nouns or to complete the thought to make it read well in English.

Translations of Bible verses are literal translations from the German in Link. This will account for differences with modern English translations with which the reader will be familiar.

The Luther sources are listed with their abbreviations below:

STANDARD SCHOLARLY SOURCES

> Altb. — Altenburg
> Erl.   — Erlangen
> Walch

LESS FAMILIAR SOURCES

Hauspost. or Hauspost. NY Ausgabe: *Dr. Martin Luther's Hauspostille,* Heinrich Ludwig Buchdruecker, NY. 1854.

Kirchenpostille or Stutt: *Dr. Martin Luther's Kirchen-Postille*, in two volumes, Stuttgart, 1845

Conversion: 3YL Festivals to Family Devotion (FD) Festivals

If your church currently uses the 3 Year Lectionary (3YL), convert that liturgical calendar (as the Sundays are named in your church bulletin) to *Family Devotion* Festivals (as named in this book) to use this *Luther's Family Devotions* in an orderly way and in the proper season.

3YL Festivals	Family Devotion Festivals
Advent through Epiphany	No Conversion necessary
Fourth Sunday before Ash Wed.	Skip to Epiphany VI (p. 122)
Third Sunday before Ash Wed.	Septuagesima (p. 134)
Second Sunday before Ash Wed.	Sexagesima (p. 144)
Transfiguration	Quinquagesima (p. 154)
Lent I	Invocavit (p. 165)
Lent II	Reminiscere (p. 175)
Lent III	Oculi (p. 186)
Lent IV	Laetare (p. 195)
Lent V	Judica (p. 206)
Palm/Passion Sunday	Palmarum (p. 216)
Easter	Easter (p. 226)
2nd S. of Easter	Quasimodogeniti (p. 237)
3rd S. of Easter	Misericordias Domini (p. 247)
4th S. of Easter	Jubilate (p. 258)
5th S. of Easter	Cantate (p. 270)
6th S. of Easter	Rogate (p. 281)
7th S. of Easter	Exaudi (p. 292)
Pentecost	Pentecost (p. 301)
1st S. after Pentecost	Trinity (p. 311)
2nd S. after Pentecost	1st S. after Trinity (p. 323)
3rd S. after Pentecost	2nd S. after Trinity (p. 336)

In general in converting Sundays after Pentecost to Sundays after Trinity, subtract one from the number of Sundays after Pentecost and that will give you the Sunday after Trinity, or, if you are algebraically minded:

'x' th S. after Pentecost	'(x-1)' S. after Trinity
Third last Sunday of the church year	25th S. after Trinity (p. 630)
Second last Sunday of the church year	26th S. after Trinity (p. 640)
Last Sunday	27th S. after Trinity (p. 650)

With Special Thanks. . .

The translator and publisher would be remiss if he did not extend special thanks to those to whom he is deeply indebted.

Many thanks to the Rev. Dr. Karl Barth, a father in the faith, and to the Rev. Dr. Norman Nagel for his kindness, guidance and encouragement in the Lord.

Thanks to the Rev. Jon Vieker whose help in the area of editorial style for publication was invaluable.

And last but far from least, thanks to my parents, Robert and Marjorie Baseley, to Mr. and Mrs. Verne and Betty Symer and to Mrs. Polly Symer for their help in proof reading and for their enthusiasm towards the goal of making Dr. Luther's writings available to a wider readership.

First Week in Advent

Sunday

Behold, your king is coming. Matthew 21:5

"He comes." Without doubt, you do not come to him and catch him. He is too high and far from you. You will not reach him by your might, striving and work. You cannot brag as though you had brought him to yourself through your service and worthiness. No, dear man, here lay aside all service and worthiness. For in your possession is nothing that deserves his coming, but only unworthiness. What is his is pure grace and mercy. The poor and the rich come here together, as in Proverbs 22:2.

And with this, all the scandalous, unchristian teachings about free will, that come from the papacy and are taught by the exalted institutions of learning and the cloisters, will be cursed. For all their teaching is that we should begin and lay the first stone. We should, from the power of the free will, in the first place seek God, come to him, and run after him and earn his grace. Guard yourself! Guard yourself against such poison. It is only the doctrine of the devil. By this he can be spotted in all the world. Before you could call upon God or seek him, God must already have come and found you, as Paul says in Romans 10:14-15, "How can they call upon God unless they first believe? How can they believe, unless first they hear preaching? How can they preach, unless first they are sent?" etc. So God must lay the first stone and begin in you so that you seek and pray to him. He is already there if you begin and seek. But if he is not there, then you do not begin anything but pure sin; and you sin even more so long as you undertake greater and holier work and become a more hardened hypocrite.

But, you ask, how then do you begin to become good? Or, what must you do that God begins to do it in you? Answer: Didn't you hear that in you is no deed or starting point to become good? So you have just as little ability to grow or complete it. God alone is the beginning, advancement and end. All that you begin is sinful and remains sinful, as beautifully as it is done in hypocrisy. You are capable of nothing but sins, do what you will. For this reason all the teaching of the schools and cloisters is seduction when they teach: begin, pray, do good works, give, sing, become spiritual and serve God by this.

But you say, "So, must I sin by necessity when I act and live without God by following pure free will, and can I not avoid sins no matter what I do?" Answer: To God it is obvious that you must remain in sins no matter what you do and you must sin when you act purely out of your free will. For if you yourself, out of free will, were able not to sin, or do what is not sinful, what necessity would you have of Christ? He would have been a fool to shed his blood for the sake of your sins if you yourself were so free and mighty that you could do something that was not sinful.

Therefore learn here from the gospel what happens when God begins to make us good. [Learn] what is the beginning of being made good. There is no other beginning but that your king comes to you and begins in you. It happens this way: The gospel must be the very first thing. That must be preached and heard. In this gospel you hear and learn your situation. What you do and begin is nothing but sin before God unless your king is before you first and reigns. Behold, there he begins your salvation. There let your work fall away and deny yourself because you hear and see that your whole situation is sinful and nothing, as the gospel tells you. Get up and cling to your king through faith. Hang on him, praise his grace and trust only upon his goodness. But even the fact that you hear and receive it is not because of your power, but God's grace, which the gospel makes fruitful in you while you believe him.

Erl. 10, 8–10: Sermon for Advent I on Matthew 21:1–9

Hail to the Lord's Anointed, Great David's greater Son!
Hail, in the time appointed, His reign on earth begun!
He comes to break oppression, To set the captive free,
To take away transgression, And rule in equity. (*TLH* 59: 1)

Monday

Behold, your king is coming. Matthew 21:5

"Your king." Here he distinguishes this king from all other kings. He is your king, he says, who was promised you. This one, and no other, is your own, who will reign for you. Yet this is by the Spirit and not according to a human government. This is such a comforting word to a believing heart. For outside of Christ a person is trampled by many raging tyrants who are not kings, but rather fine murderers under whom he suffers great necessity and trouble; as there are the devil, the flesh, the world, sins, and also the law and death with hell. By all these a person's miserable conscience is smothered. He has a difficult prison, and leads a sour anxious life. For where there are sins, there is no good conscience. Where there is no good conscience, there is only an unsure manner and unrelenting fear of death or hell, over which no joy or pleasure of the heart can conquer. But, as Leviticus 26:36 says, such a heart is even terrified by a smoking leaf.

But when a heart receives this king with a strong faith, he is safe, fears neither sins, death nor hell, nor any misfortune. For he knows already and doesn't doubt that this king is a Lord over life and death, over sins and grace, over hell and heaven. All things are in his hands. For this is the reason that he has become our king and comes to us. He frees us from all those terrible tyrants and he himself alone reigns over us. So whoever has come under this king and holds him with firm faith cannot be harmed by either sins, death, hell, devil, people or any creature. But rather, just as his king lives without sins and is blessed, so also must he through Christ be preserved without death, without sins, alive and blessed.

See what great things these poor words have in them. "Receive your king." Such a poor donkey-riding and despiseable king brings such overwhelmingly great wealth. Reason does not see such things and nature does not comprehend it, but only faith. So it is well that he is called king. But "yours." "Yours" who are driven and plagued by sins, devil, death and hell, flesh and the world. "You" would be ruled and led by him sweetly in grace, in the Spirit, in life, in heaven, in God. This also happens to you when you only believe.

So he preserves faith with these Words, that you hold it as sure that he is that kind of king unto you; that he has this kind of an administration and also comes and is preached. For if you do not believe this of him, then apart from this you will nevermore encounter it [such surety] with any works. As you regard him, that's how you have him. In the way that you expect him to be, that's what you will find about him and as you believe, so it will be to you. Yet he remains who he is, indestructible, a king of life, grace and salvation, whether or not that is believed.

Erl. 10, 6–8: Sermon for Advent I on Matthew 21:1-9

He comes with succor speedy
To those who suffer wrong;
To help the poor and needy
And bid the weak be strong;

To give them songs for sighing,
Their darkness turn to light,
Whose souls, condemned and dying,
Were precious in His sight. (*TLH* 59: 2)

Tuesday

Behold, your king comes to you humbly. Matthew 21:5

"He comes to you." What does this mean "to you"? Isn't it enough that he is your king? If he is yours, what should he say to you when he comes to you? For everything to be said is already established by the prophets. They portray Christ as the most desirable one and he allures people to faith. It is not enough that Christ free us from the tyranny and lordship of sins, death and hell and is our king. Rather, he also gives himself to us to own, that everything he is and has is ours. St. Paul speaks of this in Romans 8:32, "He has not withheld his own son, but rather gave everything for us; will he not also, then, give us all things with him?"

So the daughter of Zion has a two-fold wealth from Christ: The first is faith and the Spirit in her heart, by which she is pure and free from sins. The other is Christ himself, so she is able to praise the wealth given from Christ, as if all that Christ himself is were also her own. She can depend on everything from Christ as a wedding present to her.

See what this means: He comes to you, for your good, for you to own. Because he is your king, you receive his grace in your heart, by which he helps with sins and death and becomes your king and you his subject. But because he comes to you, he would be your own that you also are made mighty by his wealth, as a bride is made mighty by her husband's wealth, more than by the jewelry that he places upon her. Oh, that is a dear and comforting saying. Who would despair or be frightened by death or hell, when he believes these Words and has won Christ as his own?

"Your king comes to you humbly." It is wonderful to mark this passage that comforts the sinful conscience in such a loving way. For sins naturally result in a fearful, fugitive conscience, as Adam fled in paradise, and could not stand God's coming. For it knows and naturally feels that God is the enemy of sins and punishes them terribly. Therefore a sinful conscience flees and is frightened when it only hears God call. It troubles itself that he would quickly beat those sins with a club. So now he does not hunt us with such thoughts and cringing. In a comforting way he promises that this king comes humbly.

It's as if he would say: Don't run away and do not cringe, he is not coming now as he did to Adam, Cain, to Babylon, to Sodom and Gomorrah; also not as he came to the nation of Israel on the Mountain of Sinai. He does not come in wrath. He will not judge you or promote guilt. All wrath is laid aside. Pure humility and goodness is there. He will immediately deal with you so that your heart's desire, love and all confidence shall have him; that you, from now on, will regard him as much greater and seek refuge in him more than you did when you previously had been terrified and run away. See, he is now always purely humble towards you. He is totally a different man. He presents himself as one who is sorrowful that he had once made you frightened and flee because of his punishment and wrath. Therefore he would now again make you bold and confident and bring you to himself as a friend.

Erl. 10, 11-13: Sermon for Advent I on Matthew 21:1-9

He shall come down like showers Upon the fruitful earth,
And joy and hope, like flowers, Spring in His path to birth.
Before Him on the mountains Shall peace, the heralds, go
And righteousness, in fountains, From hill to valley flow. (*TLH* 59: 3)

Wednesday

You are the most beautiful of the children of men. Psalm 45:2

The prophet describes the king according to his person (who he is) and says: I will write about the kind of king who is the most beautiful among the children of man; yes, who, alone among the people is beautiful. But in no way is he speaking here about the physical beauty of the body as if we believed that Christ had beauty from nature, a comely shape and weight in all his members. The prophet doesn't deal with these things. Rather his Words treat the spiritual beauty of this spiritual and eternal king.

So this is the first beauty that this king has. Christ was born true God and man, pure, without any fault and impurity of original sin, and without God's wrath, unlike we people. For no person is without sins, but we all are born without righteousness and wisdom. We also live and die in that condition if Christ does not come to help. But other kings, that even appear wiser and more beautiful before the world, are ever more foolish and hateful before God by such an appearance.

Thus we understand this beauty, first in a spiritual way concerning the self evident manner and nature of our king, Christ. He is without any sins, pure, conceived by the Holy Ghost and born of the virgin Mary. Because he was without any stain of sin, he was full of grace and truth (John 1). Both flesh and spirit were completely holy throughout, so that even one hair or a drop from Christ is more beautiful and purer than the whole sun. It is surely possible that one may become more beautiful, bodily, than Christ, as Luke writes about Stephen, that his appearance looked like the appearance of an angel. Also, it is possible, perhaps, that in his day others were more beautiful than Christ, for we do not read that the Jews had been amazed at all by the beauty of Christ.

But we speak here, as said above, not about the natural beauty of Christ, but rather of the spiritual. That beauty is of such a form that he not only far surpasses the beauty of all men, but he is also the only one who is and remains beautiful. Other people are all hateful and filthy from blasphemy and sins which fill human nature. It still adheres. But because we are so hateful and misshapen, we could not see mankind as it is. We do not have the ability to create/shape it for we do not even see spiritual beauty or pay attention to it. Since we are flesh and blood, we only see the outward, natural beauty of the body which physical eyes see. But if we had spiritual eyes, then we would see what a horrible thing it is that a person strives against God's will, blasphemes God, stands against God's honor and majesty, despises God and is his enemy, begrudges his neighbor anything good, is full of evil desire, pride and avarice, etc. That is the terrible misshapeness which even the heathen see in part. They have also said that righteousness would enlighten better than the morning star if one could see it with the bodily eye.

So now this is the first honor and loveliness of this song, or psalm, that the poet heard and by which he feeds the reader hope. He wants to sing of that kind of kingdom in which a king shall rule and reign who will be pure and beautiful throughout, in whom is no fault or anything impure. But he shall be all comfort, the highest wisdom, the greatest love to all poor troubled sinners. This king is full of mercy, grace and truth, friendly, affable, overall lovely and sweet. As Isaiah says, he does not call out on the way, etc., but rather is patient and long-suffering. Yet he finally punishes the godless and the evil, but shows mercy to the sinner who repents.

Altb. VI, 377: Commentary on Psalm 45, 1534

Kings shall bow down before Him And gold and incense bring;
All nations shall adore Him, His praise all peoples sing;
To Him shall prayer unceasing And daily vows ascend,
His kingdom still increasing, A kingdom without end. (*TLH* 59: 5)

Thursday

Lovely are your lips. Psalm 45:2

After the prophet had described the person and outstanding, beautiful form of this king, he now also speaks of his wisdom. He praises it as highly as his beautiful appearance, and says it is placed in him so that he has a sweet mouth and lips. But it is apparent to me as it was also to Luke. He had these words, "Sweet are your lips," in mind, when he writes of the Lord Christ in Chapter 4, "All eyes that were in the congregation beheld him. Soon thereafter they all gave witness to him and wondered about the lovely Words that went out of his mouth."

The Holy Ghost, again here secretly considers Moses, who also had lips. But they were hard, uncompromising and wrathful lips in which was no loveliness, but pure wrath, terror, sins and death. Now bundle together in a heap all wisdom, both of Moses and all the heathen and philosophers. You will find that before God they are idolatry or falsely fashioned wisdom. Even wisdom by which land and people are ruled is only a wisdom of wrath and punishment.

Because of the beauty of this king, Christ alone has the true and right beauty, compared to which all other royal appearance is black and hateful. So also his wisdom alone is the true and right wisdom. For it is a sweet comforting wisdom, that is, a wisdom of divine promise. His Word is loving and full of every comfort and confidence in the grace of God. So we see that the writer of this psalm gladly read the promises of God and had seen that his lips are the loveliest and sweetest, which draw all troubled hearts to himself.

Therefore, you should not portray Christ on the rainbow carrying a sword in his mouth as some try. For you desire to understand it spiritually. It is his true form and color that only milk and honey are under his tongue and out of his mouth and lips flow nothing but sugar and noble perfume. Whoever portrays this mouth, tongue and lips in another way, definitely errs. Therefore, we will much more readily believe the poet of this psalm then Satan and the papists who have conceived this terrifying picture. The prophet surely does not deceive us when he portrays Christ as having sweet lips, that is, that by his Words he does not deceive or frighten the heart, but rather comforts and strengthens it.

Therefore, all who terrify and trouble those under Christ who have a dull, despairing conscience, who feel their sins and would gladly be free of them, are not from Christ, but are sent by the devil. Let me say that to you and mark it well. For that is described regarding Jesus' name also in Isaiah, when he says in chapter 42: "He will not cry out or shout, and you will not hear his voice on the highway. The bruised reed will he not break and the smoking flax he will not quench." He is not an unfriendly, harsh and angry man, like Moses, who looks horrible like the devil and says that he would like to take someone's heart away. Then his lips would spill over with gall and wrath and would be bitter through and through with choking and dragon's poison and, yes, also with hell fire. Therefore, always go back to Moses for the stubborn and wicked people and proud saints, whom he should frighten and humble. But our king has gentle saving lips. That means that his Word is a Word of forgiveness of sins that also comforts the poor struck conscience, a Word of life and salvation which enlivens and restores those buried by the weight of their sins and that feel death and damnation.

Altb. VI, 379–380: Commentary on Psalm 45, 1534

O'er every foe victorious, He on His throne shall rest,
From age to age more glorious, All blessing and all-blest.
The tide of time shall never His covenant remove;
His name shall stand forever That name to us is Love. (*TLH* 59: 6)

Friday

The peoples fall before you. Psalm 45:5

A praiseworthy king and chief is also successful, as Cicero says in praise of Pompeii. That is why this psalm gives Christ the praise that he is successful and says: It is a difficult war. Our king goes forth with his chariot. We follow him in our chariot (for he speaks according to the way kings were) or we ride next to him where there are also many great victories. So even if our enemies are very numerous and mighty, yet we hold the field. In such a battle, one servant of God can battle ten thousand, even if the whole papacy with pope, bishops, princes, kings and countless sects assail him. One should be very cowardly if he had to battle against such great wisdom and might alone, if he did not have the support of Christ. Yes, not only does he battle against the wisdom and might of the world but rather also the devil and the gates of hell. For this reason, that is a very hard war, not only because of our weakness, as you can observe, and that our numbers are small, but also because of the great might, wisdom and multitudes of the enemy. For Christ himself says in Luke 16:8 that the children of this world are wiser than the children of light.

So it would not be a wonder even if some who are weak and pusillanimous under us left the preaching office because so many things happened to them. Holy and powerful people infuriate them. Yes, the whole world along with the gates of hell are heaped upon them. I will not speak of the unthankfulness of the common people and their great despising and weariness towards the Word. In short, you see all sorts of plain misfortune. The enemies persecute the Word. They despise what is ours and are becoming weary of us so our pastors must die of hunger and win no better reward for their work, their true and bitter service, than unthankfulness, envy and hatred. So where is that success and happiness that he speaks of here? Without doubt, it is nowhere but in the Spirit.

Therefore, be comforted and undaunted. Let no misfortunes drive you back, but rather go to them lively and joyfully in plain sight and hold fast. Also, do not let all the despising and unthankfulness of our own people nor the murderous attack and rage of the bloodthirsty papists move you to walk away from your office. Take comfort, as St. Paul says, in 2 Corinthians 12, "When I am weak, then I am strong. When I am overcome, then I first appraise myself rightly," as a palm tree striving against the heavy storm. So everyone thought that we all must be ruined and crushed by the Council at Augsburg in 1530. But it was our affair of power. We are mighty in weakness by the grace of Christ unto the present day. So when we think in melancholy and weariness that there is no council or comfort, you must not doubt that God is there giving hope and comfort. So then also, after the Word of God is despised to the utmost and everyone is sated, appropriate honor of the Word is the first to go.

So let us rightly understand this verse by the unseeable, ungraspable happiness, growth and increase; for our king prospers and suffices even if we do not see it. It also would not be good that we see such increase, for we would become proud by it.

Altb. VI, 384–385: Commentary on Psalm 45, 1534

With might of ours can naught be done Soon were our loss effected;
But for us fights the Valiant One, Whom God Himself elected.
Ask ye, Who is this? Jesus Christ it is, Of Sabaoth Lord,
And there's none other God; He holds the field forever. (*TLH* 262: 2)

Saturday

And I will put enmity between you and the woman and between your seed and her seed. He shall trample your head and you will strike his heel. Genesis 3:15

God does not say this for the sake of the devil. God doesn't consider him worth the effort of proclaiming his damnation. On the contrary, it would be enough that God damned him in his own will.

But this is said for the sake of Adam and Eve. They hear Satan's judgment and are comforted, because they see that God is his enemy by nature and against him because he had inflicted on mankind such trouble and harm. So they view God's grace and mercy even here commencing in the midst of God's wrath awakened by sin and disobedience. Under the supreme threats of the Father, his heart breaks open. He is not so angry that he would cast away his son for the sake of sins, but he would reveal help. He foretells of victory against the enemy who had deceived and conquered human nature.

So there is not a unified judgment against Satan and mankind though man fell into sin through Satan. God did not place them together in their punishments. He is not able to act as if they had done good, which would contradict justice, but he separates them far from each other. He would yet be angry with man. But man had not listened to Satan because he wanted to. So the greater anger is against Satan. So he damns [Satan] harshly and punishes him so Adam and Eve could see and hear it. By this they can be encouraged and trust that it won't go so harshly in their case. Their first consolation was that the snake, and with him Satan, was accused and cursed for the sake of Adam and Eve.

In these words is also THE comfort. Before them, the ominous clouds were darkened. Then the bright sun lifted itself above the clouds. With loving splendor, God lights up their frightened hearts. Adam and Eve would not hear the kind of judgment against them as made against the snake. Rather, they would stand against the damned foe as on a mountain top in time of war. They would stand in the hope that help would come, the Son of God, the Seed of the woman. So the forgiveness of sins is shown here to Adam and Eve. They were taken completely in grace as they were declared free from sin and death, from hell and this terror and fear, which had strangled them right to death before the face of God. Then this comfort comes. God did not curse Adam and Eve as he did the snake. They would be left together in war with the snake. In this war they would be useless but it would turn out for the greatest good of man. This is the main comfort. Although this enemy converts them and disputes with them by cunning and deceit, yet there would be born a Seed who would crush the snake's head. Here the eternal destruction of the tyranny of Satan is revealed.

Altb. IX, 90–91: Commentary on Genesis, 1535; cf. AE vol. 1–8

Though devils all the world should fill, All eager to devour us,
We tremble not, we fear no ill, They shall not overpow'r us,
This world's prince may still Scowl fierce as he will,
He can harm us none, He's judged; the deed is done;
One little Word can fell him. (*TLH* 262: 3)

Second Week in Advent

Sunday

But when all of this begins to happen, look up and lift up your heads, for your salvation is approaching. Luke 21:28

You would like to respond, "Who could lift up his head here in such horrid wrath and judgment?" All the world will be terrified on that day and duck their heads way down and stare at the ground with fear and terror. So how will we look up and hold up our head, which certainly means that we would have joy and anticipation? This can only be said of the Christian who is a true Christian and not of the heathen or the Jews. But true Christians remain under such great tribulation and persecution by sins and all kinds of evil that this life becomes sour and hateful to them. For that reason they wait and have longings. They pray to be free of sins and every evil. The Lord's Prayer also rings out "Thy kingdom come." "And deliver us from evil."

If we are true Christians, we pray these same things ardently, from the bottom of our hearts. If we do not pray this from the depths of our hearts and earnestly, then we are not yet true Christians. But if we truthfully pray this, then it must also truly abide in us. So we behold these signs of the end (recorded in Luke 21) with joy and anticipation no matter how terrifying they are. It is as Christ exhorts and speaks here, "When these things happen, look up." He doesn't say to be afraid or to duck your head under. What is coming is what we have been praying for!

St. Paul also says this in 2 Timothy 4:8, "He will give the crown of righteousness not only to me but also to all who have loved his appearing." What will he give those who hate and fear his appearing? Without doubt (he will give them) hell as to his enemies. And Titus 2:13, "We shall wait for the appearing of the majesty of God, which is great." And in Luke 12:36, "You shall be as the people that wait upon their master when he comes from a business trip."

But those who fear and don't desire him to come, what are they doing when they pray, "Thy kingdom come, Thy will be done. . . deliver us from evil?" Do they not approach God and lie to him against themselves? Do they not also strive against the will of God who would bring this day for the sake of freeing his saints? So it is very easy to grasp this so that hatred and enmity will not be found in us against this day. For such a reaction is an evil sign that belongs to the damned. The same hard head and impenetrable heart must be moved and broken with this kind of jolt and terror if it would ever be improved.

But to the believers, he will be faithful and loving. That day will be for the believers both the highest joy and safety and for the unbelievers the highest terror and rout. Just as it is also in this life [true that] the gospel truth is by far the sweetest thing to the pious and the most hateful thing for the evil. Why should the believers fear this and not rejoice in the highest? For they trust in Christ and the judge comes for the sake of their salvation. He is their portion.

Erl. 10, 66–68: Sermon for Advent II on Luke 21:25-36

The humble heart and lowly
God lifteth up on high;
Beneath His feet in anguish
The haughty soul shall lie.
The heart, sincere and right,
That heeds God's invitation
And makes true preparation,
It is the Lord's delight.

Prepare my heart, Lord Jesus,
Turn not from me aside,
And grant that I receive Thee
This blessed Adventide.
From stall and manger low
Come thou to dwell within me;
Loud praises will I sing Thee
And forth Thy glory show. (*TLH* 75: 3–4)

Monday

Father, I desire that where I am, these whom You have given me also may be with me. That they see my glory which you have given me. John 17:24

This is the last, but the most comforting part of this (high-priestly) prayer. We and all who cling to Christ may be sure and secure in our final hope, where we find peace and where we will remain while we suffer here in the world. Here we are excluded and have no enduring country. We have heard that whoever is a Christian must forgo all the world's favor, grace, safety, power and rest and be the devil's footstool. The Christian must constantly be in danger of body and life and await death every hour. This is utterly terrifying and horrible because of death, especially since death is always before our eyes and you don't know where you might place that first step that will send you on your one-way path into that night. Therefore, Christ acts as a kind, true savior who cares about us. He informs us that he has set us in a shelter so that we will always be with him and have what is good, just as he has this from his Father. He says to be comforted and not to be concerned about where you might stay or how you should go. Just let the world and the devil rant and rage, murder, burn and push you out of the world. You shall be well cared for and enter where you desire to go and where you can be safe and have peace and remain there on account of the devils and all the world.

Where would that be? What is that place called? "Where I am," he says. That is, in the Father's arm and bosom, where all the angels must run to lift and carry us. Apart from this it has no name. It doesn't allow itself to be pointed to with fingers or described. It must rather be grasped in this world through faith. So we will receive this text as our chief happiness and as a fluffy featherbed for our souls. With joyous hearts we go there. When the precious little hour comes when we are free of our sins and misfortune and from the power of the world and the devil, with these Words we are taken to eternal rest and joy.

What Christ means by these Words, "whom you have given me," is often stated. Namely, these Words give us worth and are given for our great comfort. Those who cling to and retain his Words will not doubt that Christ will take us to himself in his glory, even if we are yet sinners, weak and broken. This is especially so in need and affliction when the world, for the sake of these Words, lords over and persecutes us and takes our goods, honor, body and life. Then we boldly cling to such promises. These Words are spoken to us as we live upon earth with flesh and blood, not to the angels in heaven or the saints who have died. Especially note in this Word that he says, "I desire." He speaks to his Father so excellently, since he would not leave it unsaid. By this, the promise he establishes is made sure, spoken by the one who cannot lie. All this is for the sake of his awakening us who are weak and foul to believe so we are established with no doubt at all. We hold it as so sure that we might already see it before our eyes.

Altb. VI, 256: Lecture on the 17th Chapter of John, 1534

Jesus comes in joy and sorrow,
Shares alike our hopes and fears;
Jesus comes, whate'er befalls us,
Glads our hearts, and dries our tears;
Alleluia! Alleluia!
Cheering e'en our failing years.

Jesus comes on clouds triumphant
When the heavens shall pass away;
Jesus comes again in glory.
Let us, then, our homage pay.
Alleluia! Ever singing
Till the dawn of endless day. (*TLH* 56: 4–5)

Tuesday

Righteous Father, the world knows you not. John 17:25

This is a needed addition, a remarkable text. With it, Jesus turns his eyes to the world and speaks from the desires of his heart. "O, dear

Father, how is it that you do not allow the world to speak and preach so that they also would acknowledge your name?" Why does he start to praise his Father here, at the end of the prayer, by calling him "Righteous Father" instead of the better, more merciful title "Holy Father" as he did previously? Doesn't he know what he had said before?

Answer: As said above, he has yearned in his heart in this hour. He looked back on the world that unfortunately would not hear or suffer the Word. The more one preaches the more thoughtless they become. As unwise children they run from it barefoot, yes, they even crawl barefoot from it to the ends of the world. They are borne as a great emptiness. Yes, they are borne (by God) as one bears a bad habit. By this they earn pure wrath and eternal punishment. Yet this should not be accepted as a reason to give thanks, in blasphemy and profanation. So Jesus must be temperate and say: You are truly a great God who does what is good and right because you differentiate between those who are from the world and those you have given me, that is, between those whom you have shut out and these whom you brought to me so that they stay where I am. You let the others go where they belong as those who refuse to be informed or helped.

So now we must also be against the world. For the sake of that world we bear the gospel publicly and generously. By doing that we have done all that we can. We have not stopped doing anything that might help them be converted by preaching, exhortation, loving, serving, bearing, warning, frightening, drawing and after that in all things we suffer, forgive and pray for them. In short, in every way we have tried, by our stringent courage and work, cost and danger, and fighting for no higher wages than unthankfulness, scorn, blasphemy, and persecution by the public for the revealed truth. How could anyone help but say that he does the right thing when God punishes such a horrid, hardened vice and blasphemy with constant pestilence, war, Turks, devil and all kinds of plagues? Practically all of this mercy is lost on them. Nothing good or gracious will help them. So it would be too bold to ask it and it should overwhelm us that God could and would peek from behind his fingers and pour himself out and shower us with all good things while at the same time his truest, dearest, highest treasure must suffer from the world when it sets him aside and, yes, spits in his eye and tramples his Word with their feet.

So he concludes here and says: Dear Father, the world does not know you and doesn't want to know you, even if your Word is publicly preached and clearly presented. By that it pokes you in the eye and it cannot lie about it since that is the truth. Therefore, you do rightly when you let them go to the devil in their impenitent darkness.

Altb. VI, 256: Lecture on the 17th Chapter of John, 1534

What though the foes be raging,
Heed not their craft and spite;
You Lord, the battle waging,
Will scatter all their might.
He comes, a King most glorious,
And all His earthly foes
In vain His course victorious
Endeavor to oppose.

He comes to judge the nations,
A terror to His foes,
A Light of consolations
And blessed Hope to those
Who love the Lord's appearing.
O glorious Sun, now come,
Send forth Thy beams most cheering,
And guide us safely home. (*TLH* 58: 8–9)

Wednesday

And as many as receive him he gives the power to become God's children. John 1:12

Hear what a great and mighty wonder and what an unspeakable eternal treasure is bestowed through the coming of God's Son on those who receive him, believe on him and regard him as the man sent by God to help the world. Namely, this will be the new work and method by which he will give the power and right to become children of God unto all who believe on his name. When we believe that he is the eternal Word of the Father by whom all things are made, as the life and light of mankind and the Lamb of God who bears the sins of the world, takes them away and drowns them in the depth of the seas; and who is also called upon in every kind of need and in thanks for his unspeakable grace and mercy, we are by this brought to the great glory. He makes known to us his excellent justice and gives us the glorious power and freedom of having a gracious Father in heaven. Yes, we are his dear children and heirs of his eternal heavenly goods. As Paul says in Romans 8, we are brothers of Christ and co-heirs of eternal life and salvation.

How? Has he given all mankind this might and freedom so that they still are all children of wrath? No, says the evangelist. Rather, those who believe on his name, without exception, who receive his Word with faith and hold it fast, call upon him. You hear mentioned also here that we come to this high honor, wondrous freedom and power in no other way, means and manner, than by the confession and thorough faith on Jesus Christ (excluding the strength of life, joining the order of Carthusian monks or the Franciscans, by free will, human skill, devotion, holiness, by what you can take from the earth, by angelic spirituality and humility or even by God's law). Throughout the year and daily we are taught of this glory and brought to worship. This glory is so great that no man, no matter what he would call it, would be able to consider it adequately, much less express with words that we poor maggot sacks and accursed miserable sinners by the birth from the first Adam, should come to this high honor and highest nobility; that God, who is eternal and almighty, is our Father and we his children; that Christ is our brother and we his co-heirs; that the dear angels like Michael and Gabriel will not be our lords, but rather our brothers and servants, for they also call God their Father as we do. Oh, this is great and overwhelming. Whoever reflects upon him (children of the world are not free to do so, but Christians do this, but also not all of them do), must also be jarred by the fact that this has caught ahold of him. Friends, is it both possible and true? Therefore, the Holy Ghost here must be the master and write this confession and faith upon our hearts and witness to our heart that it is sure and "amen." We have become children of God by faith and remain eternally. St. John did not bring forth this gospel by human intention. John is rather borne by the Holy Ghost, who is the Spirit of Truth. So he is surely not deceiving us. It is an astounding thing that a man should be God's Son and heir.

Altb. VI, 1161–1162: Commentary on John, 1537

My heart for very joy doth leap,
My lips no more can silence keep;
I, too, must sing with joyful tongue
That sweetest ancient cradle-song;

Glory to God in highest heaven,
Who unto us His Son hath given!
While angels sing with pious mirth
A glad new year to all the earth. (*TLH* 85: 14–15)

Thursday

If anyone desire to do his will, he will know if this teaching is from God or if I speak from myself. John 7:17

This is the will of the Father: that you value and hear what this man, Christ, says and heed his Word. You will not be clever enough to master or dispute about his Word, but hear it directly, so the Holy Ghost will enter and enrich your heart that you believe from your heart the preaching of the divine Word and say: That is God's Word and the whole truth. That is also the Word by which your life is preserved. But if you want people to listen to you and by your reason you would strike out Christ from his Word, understanding yourself to be the master of that Word, and if you would use it to master other people and after that purpose investigate how it is to be understood in order to mince and mix it so the Words must sound as you desire them to sound, if you bring it to your mind primarily because you doubt it and want to come up with reasons for it out of your head, then that is not in keeping with being a student, but with being a master. In this manner you will nevermore come to it and experience what the Lord's Word is or who his heavenly Father is.

Because of this it is impossible for people that want to master it with their thoughts to understand God's Word. This is what the pope and the heretical spirits do. They take any passage from the Holy Scripture and then drivel, prattle, play and make out of it whatever they want to until they become completely blind. So close your reason and trample your wisdom under foot. Don't let them probe into the sack that treats of your salvation with feeling or thinking, but only hear the plain speaking of the Son of God which is his Word and remain with that. That is called *"hunc audite."* Listen! Listen! For that is our Lord God's will purely and finely presented as he promised. He who hears the Son, is given the Holy Ghost. He will enlighten and kindle him so he rightly understands what the Word of God is. God will make of him a man according to all God's mercies. God will also do that!

On the other hand, whoever wants to do his own will by his own opinions and his experience, preaching and hearing only what he himself recommends and desires, has closed and barricaded heaven and that one will nevermore taste or smell a little bit or a dot of what a passage or Word of Scripture is.

Altb. V, 716–717: Sermons on John 6-8, 1530-1532; cf. AE 23

Precious Jesus, I beseech Thee, May Thy Words take root in me;
May this gift from heaven enrich me So that I bear fruit for Thee!
Take them never from my heart Till I see Thee as Thou art,
When in heav'nly bliss and glory I shall greet Thee and adore Thee. (*TLH* 296: 4)

Friday

Lord, to whom shall we go? You have the Words of eternal life; And we have believed and known that you are Christ, the Son of the living God. John 6:68-69

This is the true preacher! In this way you will know a true preacher. St. Peter, as a true pope and a truthful preacher acts upon this, uses his office and speaks, "Where should we go?" He looks around and says, "I can find no other teaching that gives life. But we have experienced that you have the Word of life. You are a truthful teacher for these people." There you also will arrive at the fact that Jesus is called this (Word of life). He along with his every doctrine is also purely exalted above the earth. Moses and his law will not help us. Also, all the wisdom of the earth doesn't count. All doctrines that you desire to preach and exhort [from one's own ideas] will be damned and we want none of them.

We still say this also about the pope and his adherents. We know nothing of their ways and we don't know how to walk in their streets. For they want to lead us out of the only Word that the Lord Christ has taught, which Word is life and spirit. They want to speak to us something else that we do not [desire to] approach. For no other doctrine will be confirmed without this. They will be damned because you can only be informed by the one man, Christ, and by his doctrine. So a Christian can say: How can you speak as a wolf and devil by saying that you have the Holy Ghost and that you are permitted to change the Word of Christ by an appeal to the Holy Spirit and that what you command in this way must be retained and obeyed? Do you want to present more than what Christ himself has taught; as if it should be commanded and inspired by the Holy Ghost that you ought to distribute communion in one kind, that priests should have no wife, etc., and so one must follow the church?

But the Christian church acts as does St. Peter speaking here in this passage: Where shall we go? What shall we hear? I know nothing but you, Lord! I know of no preaching, but "You have the Words of eternal life." This preaching that is pure and untainted has marrow and bone and helps against eternal death, sins and all misery. Of all the crowd, St. Peter preaches here that he is the first to mark and reject all doctrine that is not Christ's Word. So if we deal with eternal life and salvation, then we let St. Peter and all godfearing doctrines have free course. We know of no other doctrines than those that the one man, Christ, has. Of these St. Peter says: You have Words of life. Upon that Word I will be satisfied. It is well given in all its parts. He will not cling to the bodily person of Christ. Rather he will cling to his Word. We also desire to remain in these for the Words give eternal life. That is rightly compelled and such people as grasp this about Christ and his Word always find themselves there, bound to the Word. And even if the seventy-two should fall away, yet those like St. Peter and the other apostles remain and say, "We know of no one or anything else that endures, except for your Word."

Altb. V, 701: Sermons on John 6-8, 1530–1532; cf. AE 23

I thank Thee, Jesus, Sun from heaven Whose radiance hath bro't light to me;
I thank Thee, who hast richly given All that could make me glad and free.
I thank Thee that my soul is healed By what Thy lips revealed. (*TLH* 399: 3)

Saturday

The night is gone, the day is come. Romans 13:12

As I've mentioned, this is often repeated: "Our salvation is near." By the day of the gospel, Paul means the day when the heart or soul is enlightened. So since the day is breaking, our salvation is near us. That is, Christ and his grace, promised to Abraham, is now going forth, is preached in all the world, enlightens all mankind, awakens us all from sleep and shows us true eternal kindness. With this day we will have to get up and behave worthily in the day. On the other hand, you must understand that all doctrine, which is not the gospel, belongs to the night. There is no saving doctrine outside of the gospel. All else is night and darkness.

Attend to the Words of Paul. He describes the dearest and most enlivening part of the day: the dear happy dawn of the morning and the arrival of the sun. For the dawn is when the night is over and the day approaches. We see that at dawn all the birds sing. All the animals stir. All the people arise. He sees that the world also appears to be new. All things are lively when the day breaks and the dawn comes. So many places in the Scriptures compare this comforting preaching of the gospel to the dawn and the coming of the sun. Sometimes it is done figuratively and sometimes with plain words. Here, with clear words, Paul calls the gospel the breaking day.

This day means the most beloved sun, Jesus Christ. As Malachi calls him a "sun of righteousness"and says in chapter 4:2, "You, who fear my name, shall come upon the sun of righteousness and salvation is under his wing." So all who believe in Christ receive the brilliance of his grace and righteousness from him and become saved under his wing. Psalm 118:24 also says, "This is the day the Lord has made, let us rejoice and be encouraged." He is saying, "The living sun makes a living day, but the Lord himself makes this day. He is himself the sun, from whom the splendor and the day, that is, the gospel, goes forth and shines in all the world." John 9:5, "I am the light of the world. . . ."

But what does this light reveal to us? Who can relate it all? He teaches us all things: What God is, what we are, what has happened, what will happen, of heaven, hell, earth, angels, devils. He reveals it so we see how we should regard all of these and in relation to all of them, [he reveals] where we come from, where we are and where we are going. Yet the devil has deceived us that we forsake the day and seek the truth from the philosophers and heathen who have not yet known a single part of all these things. The devil has us mix them with human teaching to lead us into the night again.

20

It must be a great plague of divine wrath that we seek these other secondary lights against such bright clear passages of Scripture. The Lord calls himself the light of the world and the sun. If we ask if there might be any other truth signs by which people should like to learn, then we point out that the high scholars of the papacy were the most horrid of the devils, heretics and fools. It should be abundant enough (proof to note that) they raise (the heathen) Aristotle without a bit of shame as a secondary light. They also boast of him more than they do of Christ. Yes, they use nothing from Christ, and everything from Aristotle.

Erl. 7, 29: Sermon on the Epistle, Advent I

Lord Jesus Christ, my Life, my Light
My Strength by day, My trust by night,
On earth I'm but a passing guest
And sorely with my sins opprest.

Far off I see my fatherland
Where thro' Thy blood I hope to stand.
But ere I reach that Paradise,
A weary way before me lies. (*TLH* 148: 1–2)

Third Week of Advent

Sunday

Fill us early with your grace, so we will rejoice and be joyful our whole lives. Psalm 90:14

This text and the understanding of it in the context of the Psalms compels us not to regard that little word "grace" as some trivial, poor, isolated mercy to one or two people. But it is a general universal grace against the horrid tragic death of mankind, namely, against original sin, God's wrath and eternal death.

It means: "O, you merciful, kind God! You have let us be as the grass that blooms in the spring that is withered and dies by your wrath and anger. Our life is shortened and your displeasure is spilled out over us. We pray you, dear merciful Father, to turn again to us. Fill us early with your grace. Not with a trivial, poor, isolated grace by which you will preserve the household, or the worldly kingdom, or the preaching office or the body's health, but rather give us a rich, overwhelming eternal grace by which we are eternally preserved and saved from the devil, death, sins and hell."

We Christians must have a greater grace, help and comfort than food, drink, a healthy body, money and goods, and what the world has to comfort and give joy. You can comfort a greedy person with money, an ill person with medicine, a beggar with a slice of bread. But nothing helps the Christian. A Christian has no joy or trust except when he hears that God the Father has wiped out the ancient sin by his promised seed, his dear Son, Jesus Christ; that he has satisfied God's wrath, taken away eternal death and on the last day he will raise his believers and redeem them from death and hell and every tragedy to bring them to eternal life. That is the comfort we have through Jesus Christ. Satan is overcome. Death is strangled, sins wiped away, hell destroyed, guilt paid for and the Father has called us acquitted, rid of and freed from them. The inheritance is prepared. Life is brought. Heaven is open. Our dwelling is ready. Out of the bleeding wounds of Christ flows all of our grace, salvation and blessedness.

So we do not pray for an isolated or a temporal, passing grace. We pray rather for the general, universal grace that makes us acquitted, free and loosed from all sins, be they inherited or committed, common or mortal and that makes eternal life safe and sure. Only that kind of grace brings eternal comfort, eternal joys and thanksgiving; and after this troublesome life, eternal life. Amen!

Altb. VIII, 195–196: Commentary on Ps. 90, 1541

Hence, all fear and sadness!
For the Lord of gladness,
Jesus enters in.
Those who love the Father,
Though the storms may gather;

Still have peace within.
Yea, whate'er I here must bear,
Thou art still my purest Pleasure,
Jesus, priceless Treasure!
(TLH 347: 6)

Monday

Show your servants your works and your glory to their children. Psalm 90:16

Moses wants to say, "O, you dear God! We have become guilty, plagued our whole lives by the devil and by sins, hell and death. We are miserably worried and tortured. Satan has made us his work place and exposed us to all his mischief. So, dear Lord, show your servants your works. Make us your workshop that we eternally enjoy your works and rewards."

In his first epistle St. John says in chapter 3 concerning the devil's work, "Dear children, by this we see that the Son of God has destroyed the works of the devil." The devil's work is his evil deception of our father Adam and leading him from grace to sins, from integrity to guilt, from life to death by this devilish cunning. So the devil is called a master, inventor and the cause of death also in Hebrews 2. It also says, "Just as the children have flesh and blood, Christ has also become entirely the same. By death he has taken away the one who had the power of death, that is, the devil. And he freed those who were slaves their whole lives because of the fear of death."

Jesus came against such works of the devil with his Word and destroyed sins, death and hell. He gave his servants only grace, life and salvation. That is God's own work; that he makes sinners good, right, alive and holy. So he also works death and the death of the flesh in us as we hear in the law of Moses. Scripture also plainly says that God wounds and heals. He makes dead and alive, places into hell and helps again to escape. So the dear Hannah prays to God in 1 Samuel 2. "The Lord puts to death and gives life, leads into hell and out again. The Lord makes poor and rich. He lays low and raises up. He lifts the needy out of the dust, etc. . . . ."

So this is the meaning of this verse, where Moses would say, "O good, merciful God! Show your servants that truly serve you, who hope and trust in you from the heart, who seek you according to your goodness, according to your works. You have mortally wounded us with original sin; save us again. With death you have disheartened us. Comfort us again and make us alive. You have stranded us in hell, help us again to heaven. You have damned us by sins, receive us again through grace. Make us right and blessed."

Altb. VIII, 198: Commentary on Ps. 90, 1541

The load Thou takest on Thee, That pressed so sorely on me,
It crushed me to the ground. The cross for me enduring,
The crown for me securing, My healing in Thy wounds is found. (*TLH* 171: 6)

Tuesday

I am the Light of the World. John 8:12

By this doctrine, "I am the Light of the world," he informs everyone what is to be preached. For there are many kinds of doctrine upon the earth. When they are profitably preached, the highest teaching is Moses' law, the Ten Commandments. Yet they do not bring people out of the darkness into the light. The law doesn't teach how man can live forever or become saved. You hear in that doctrine what we should do. The Ten Commandments preach of our works. But no one can do them. If this doctrine alone remained, people would not be brought into the light. They teach performing good works well, but people cannot bear them. So, by necessity, there is another doctrine, namely, the gospel, which then says, "I, Christ, am the light." It is still impossible that you could be blessed because you are a sinner and therefore remain stuck in darkness. The law makes you more desolate than it helps. But the gospel says, "If you believe in me, you see that I, Christ, died for you and have taken away your sins. There is your help." See that hereafter you do not teach the doctrine of what you should do for God, but rather what you have received and found.

This law doctrine is the moon and teaches [what] the fruits of a good tree [are, that is], what we shall do. The other light is the sun that teaches of new people who are fruits of another tree when they find the gospel from Christ. From this we hear how you become good from that time on. It occurs through faith. So the gospel is not a teaching of our works, but of grace and a gift, i.e., what good God does and gives us through Christ. The Ten Commandments say what we shall do unto God. Now the moon shines well in the night, but does not make it day by shining. It yet remains night. But Christ is the true sun who makes the morning and the day break. He teaches us how we will be saved and freed from sins and death. So he also says, "I am the Light, which lights the whole world." For he also helps from sins, death, devil and hell.

The Jews and the whole world have not known this glory and confession. But now it proceeds and lights up not only the Jews, but the whole world. It will be preached that through Christ all sins are damned and we are freed from sins without works, without our assent or our action, but only through the death of Christ. That is the preaching of the gospel, the light and the true glow of the sun, through whom the whole world shines and glows. So the Lord Christ now acts rightly, so this doctrine concerning himself is true. He is the light of the world, no other. He rightly boasts of himself. He does not shy away and stay in the background. Rather he says, "I am it." He testifies to the whole world of himself. He will alone be that. He will alone teach and be the teacher, master and leader of the world. The others will remain students. All these people must go to school and acknowledge this school master and say that they have been in darkness, but now they see the sun.

Altb. V, 760: Sermons on the Gospel of St. John Chapters 6–8, 1530-1532; cf. AE 23

Thou, O Christ, art all I want; More than all in Thee I find.
Raise the fallen, cheer the faint, Heal the sick, and lead the blind,
Just and holy is Thy name; I am all unrighteousness,
False and full of sin I am; Thou art full of truth and grace. (*TLH* 345: 4)

Wednesday

Whoever follows me will not wander in darkness but will have the Light of the world. John 8:12

Who is able to do this? You can witness by his works and his example how good it is being called a follower of Christ. But it is Christ who draws the disciples to him, saying, "Follow me. Hold my doctrine." So following Christ means heeding his Words that preach that he suffered and died for us. This is called "heeding his Words" with faith. Whoever follows Christ with faith grasps the light. He would not cast himself upon saints or follow heretics. Then he would follow jack-o-lanterns and erring lights, flattering spirits who seduce the people in fields at night. But this is right following; following in faith. We count on him. Thereafter is another following so that you follow his example, do his works and suffer as he suffered. He teaches that but not especially in this passage. Here he desires that you see the doctrine, hold it, and forsake all other teachings that do not preach the Light that is Christ. So, whoever believes on Christ does not remain in darkness but will have the Light of life.

Now he makes it clear that whoever follows him will see the kind of Light by which he lives. So he says, "He does not wander in the dark." See what this following is. With his works one does not receive that kind of Light by which he lives. One cannot grasp the Light by his meditation. Rather one sees it only with his eyes. When one then follows the Light and splendor, then Christ will also not be taken out of the picture by good works. Rather, you must open the eyes of faith, perceive, hear, let the Word shine in your heart and acknowledge it. By the Light we shall live. The Word will not let us die. By that Light we will live forever.

Now these are lies and heresy to the world and the Jews. "Oh," they say, "should then our ancestors and forefathers be eternally lost and be in eternal darkness? Do you think they have all become fools?" Now all those who have come to Christ are saved. They are (and were) all preserved by this Light, as the Lord Christ said: "Abraham is dead but he saw my day and was glad." That is, he saw my Light, my shining. This sun enlightened him which also now enlightens and shines on us.

Altb. V, 760: Sermons on the Gospel of St. John Chapters 6–8, 1530-1532; cf. AE 23

Plenteous grace with Thee is found, Grace to cover all my sin.
Let the healing streams abound; Make and keep me pure within.
Thou of life the Fountain art. Freely let me take of thee;
Spring Thou up within my heart, Rise to all eternity. (*TLH* 345: 5)

Thursday

You judge according to the flesh. I judge no one. John 8:15

Here Jesus reveals his office and says, "You do not judge rightly, but I have true judgment. Yet I judge no one." The world has its method. It brags, judges, avenges itself as Matthew records in chapter 7. Christ has not come to judge but to make us all alike so that one is like all the others. He wants to say, "Even if you are all damned, yet I have not come to damn. It is not a duty of my office to pronounce this verdict over you. Rather I desire to commute the sentence so you all remain unjudged and unsentenced." So he praises his office and departs from the fleshly judges who quickly go out and sentence. He says, "I have not come according to the flesh to judge. I judge no one. I already had that power. I could have and should have already done that. But I do not do that. I am not come for that. I commute the sentence, so that I bring others to me and they all become enlightened."

This is a beautiful text. By it you do not grasp Christ as a judge, as the papacy had depicted him to us, that he would judge on the last day. They think that Christ sits above only because he wants to judge and sentence. Those are my thoughts and your thoughts concerning the papacy now. You cannot lie about that. There all good works, all cloisters and religious orders are formed in order to appease the judge. For this [purpose] you take Mary to help, who had suckled Christ. Thereafter come all the places of pilgrimages and all the calling upon the saints.[1] The gospel is laid low to the ground by this. It is exterminated and makes Christ a mortal enemy. I would gladly have seen him [Christ] put away before all the devils. Everyone fled from him and became his enemy. We and our fellow hearers would have gladly heard this preaching if Christ were not the one from whom we fled. But Christ is not only a judge whom the guilty must fear and hate and that the evil doer must regard as his judge, hangman and gallows, yet this judge will only help everyone that seeks comfort from him.

Now we have had such preachers who completely turned Christ around, who have made light darkness and made a judge and ruler out of the savior. These came because of our great unthankfulness for what we ought to give thanks. On the last day he will judge, but as a savior who will deliver me from my enemies and overturn all those who have made me sorrow. He will not be terrifying to me, but comforting. For I have a good case even if we are plagued by the devil. A good citizen who suffers need is not afraid of the mayor or judge, but calls on the authorities in need, seeks help, advice and comfort. The judge will be fearful and threatening to the guilty and the evil doer, but not to the troubled.

Altb. V, 764: Sermons on the Gospel of St. John Chapters 6–8, 1530-1532; cf. AE 23

Lord, on that day, that wrathful day, When man to judgment wakes from clay,
Be Thou the trembling sinner's Stay, Though heav'n and earth shall pass away. (*TLH* 612: 3)

Friday

All whom my Father gives come to me. John 6:37

---

[1]Luther refers to the Roman Catholic penance system in which merits of saints could be recieved and applied to one's sins through prayers and pilgrimages to sacred sites.

There is a lot to say about this text if one wanted. It sounds as if the Lord is first saying, "You (godless Jews) see and hear me, yet you don't believe in me. For you are not the crowd whom my Father gave me. By this you show that you have not only graduated beyond him and are foreigners, but you also are cast away from your fathers and completely rejected from the gospel." They would not even flail against this but treated it as the wind, as if it were a slight thing that they did not believe in him or heed him. So he says by all this, "It is a weighty matter that they do not hear me for they also don't hear the Father." By this he would with clear words point out their punishment to the despisers of the gospel and God. For they saw and heard Christ and his Word and did not believe it. They are cut off and pushed aside by God from Christ and his Words. They are against God for they do not believe in this man. This is their ban and sentence. This verdict is spoken and this thunderclap has gone over them. Now they could fast or do whatever they wanted and yet they do not belong to the Father for they don't believe in Christ. So the Father does not give them to him. For whoever doesn't believe in Christ, even if he were also the most holy, does not please God.

This text is just as comforting to others who are pious and believe to the same extent as it is terrifying to the godless, as he first says to the Jews. "On the other hand this preaching will not remain useless and without fruit because of you. Since you will not, someone else will. If you will not believe, another will. Your wisdom and cleverness don't approach me, for you know a better way that I could not show you. But still, there is a little group of poor, afflicted, frightened consciences. This little group comes to me and receives my Word and believes in me. They eat my flesh and drink my blood and have eternal life. They are called those 'whom my Father gives me.' "

So we must now trust this so we believe in and preach of Christ. The world does not ask after it, nor does she dance, even if we flatter her and sing and play the flute. She does not weep if one complains about her. If you promise and flatter as much as the world does so that you become tired of doing it, yet it does not help at all. They will not believe. They are like an actor in a play who cannot act, though in his own opinion he can do it altogether better than you. So there are many who want to and feel they can do it better than me (says Christ). Yes, the more they act that way in order to help themselves the more stubborn and twisted they become than they were before. But what should I do? I must say, "Walk in my place and do it as well as you can," and then let him walk off. Christ himself speaks here. Yet that same Word will have its result. It will yet come daily to those that will receive it as he says, "Whom the Father gives me." That must happen.

Altb. V, 635–636: Sermons on the Gospel of St. John Chapters 6–8, 1530-1532; cf. AE 23

The Savior kindly calls Our children to His breast;
He folds them in His gracious arms, Himself declares them blest. (*TLH* 302: 1)

Saturday

And whoever comes to me I will in no way send away. John 6:37

It says, "Comes to me." My Word will not be grasped by human understanding as we see in heathen and philosophical books and teaching. They have figured God out according to reason. They taught about God as if he were a man, like Cicero and Homer taught. They portray God as they would a man. That is also how the spirit of the sects speaks of God, as it desires, as reason thinks good. By that God's Word is forced to say what they want it to say. But God does not think as we people think or as our reason would like. Reason will not speak altogether of Christ. Everything that my reason and that the clever, wise people of the world bring me. . . . Heaven forbid! That is excluded. Reason cannot do it. Kingdoms and human wisdom and everything that is not God hinders the effort and is of no use. But only come to this bread and spiritual meal where we eat the food and the bread of life. Only God must act! What people do, as natural as it seems, is all a great hindrance. When a clever, learned, experienced person comes, when he wants to master this, he falls [away from it] with his clever reason. He is vexed and stuck on the gospel. For it is not that kind of people that God can teach. But Christ wants to have students who are simple and humble themselves and who fall to the Words of God and let themselves learn. When they hear it, they do not judge and master the doctrine, but they let themselves be re-formed, mastered and taught. They submit to it.

One could say a lot about this. It is a comforting doctrine to those who know and feel that they will there come to Christ. Such a person has comfort from this. He feels that Christ's Word pleases him from the heart. He wants to also receive all that Christ has. Such a person can say, "I who will come to Christ, am the one being given to."

Altb. V, 636: Sermons on the Gospel of St. John Chapters 6–8, 1530-1532; cf. AE 23

Abide with Me! Fast falls the eventide; The darkness deepens; Lord, with me abide.
When other helpers fail and comforts flee, Help of the helpless, oh, abide with me! (*TLH* 552: 1)

Fourth Week of Advent

Sunday

John said, "I am the voice preaching in the wilderness, 'Make straight the way of the Lord,' as the prophet said." John 1:23

He is saying, "Your salvation is much nearer than a prophet would normally say. Do not strain your eyes so far in time. The Lord of all the prophets himself is here. Here you have no need of a prophet. The Lord follows and I am the forerunner. He follows in my footsteps. I do not prophecy of him like a prophet does, but I speak as a forerunner so that you give place and make room for him so that he can approach. I do not say, 'Behold, he is in the future,' as the prophets spoke. But I say, 'Behold he comes and is here.' I do not speak words about him, but point to him with my finger. For as Isaiah had previously prophesied that before him such a cry should come to make way for the Lord, so I am that one and not a prophet. Therefore, step to the side. Give room and let the Lord himself now walk among you. Do not look for any more prophecy about him."

This is the answer that no learned, wise, holy man can stand. John must have a devil and be a heretic in every letter of it. For only sinners and fools regard him as a holy, good man and give room to his cry and make a place for the Lord, repenting of what hinders his path. But all who throw wood, stone and mud in response to him kill both the forerunner and the Lord himself when such people say, "How so?" John says they should make straight the way of the Lord. He is saying, "You have neither the Lord nor his way. What do you have then? Whoever is not of the Lord or of his way must be on their own way and be of the devil and all evil." Now see if the holy wise people are not rightly angry because of John. They curse his Word and thereafter strangle him with his Lord. Should he be so audacious to consign such holy people to the devil with all their knowledge? Should he call them godless and cursed and allege that their ways are not the ways of the Lord so that they should therefore make straight the way of the Lord; that the "holy" life they've led is fruitless?

If he would secretly write it on a tablet they would probably have patience with him. But now he brings voice to it and not only a voice, but he cries out loud. There is no single corner unfilled by it. It is free under heaven, in the wilderness, before all the world and public. Before all the people he makes the holy ones sinners and disgraceful with all their walk and way. No longer would the people regard them according to outward appearances. The honor and affirmation which they had previously for their "holy" lives departed.

Erl. 10, 113: Sermon for Advent IV

On Jordan's bank the Baptist's cry Announces that the Lord is nigh;
Come, then, and hearken, for he brings Glad tidings from the King of Kings. (*TLH* 67: 1)

Monday

And he shall be called . . . Wonderful. Isaiah 9:6

This first name shows what manner the king has in ruling his kingdom. He makes it "wonderful" so that all reason, nature and cleverness will not understand it. How does he do this? He reigns over us as he himself was ruled by the Father. As Psalm 118:22f says, "The stone the builders rejected has become the cornerstone. That is done by the Lord, and is a wonder before our eyes." Was it not a wonderful thing that desiring to enter eternal life he went into death; and so that he would go to the Father in his glory, he came into all shame; also that he hung on the cross under the sentence of a murderer in the most graceful way; that he should make many people and the whole world humble even as his own people strayed from him and they not only lied about him, but also betrayed, sold, gave over, crucified and blasphemed him? Now is that not an odd and wonderful thing that the stone, hurled so far and deep, should become a cornerstone? In short, on earth nothing is named or seen that is more foolish, undesirable, and doubtful than that a man who has died should not only be alive, but also become the Lord and author of life by the resurrection from the dead; that death should come under [the rule of] the one who died and that death would even be made eternally dead by him; that this Lord should be the king of glory whom his own people forsook, betrayed, persecuted, murdered, blasphemed and shamed. So in its every aspect this pure unspeakable wonder goes on. But we are used to hearing about this everyday so we no longer wonder about it. We do not give thanks for it and so do not believe it zealously. Otherwise we would be wondering about this constantly!

So he works in this way among his own, that is, in his kingdom. One who is worldly reigns so that he holds his people to himself and with himself while foreigners and enemies are cast away from him. This king turns that [the manner of ruling] around. He lets his own people, the Jews, go and takes the heathen, his enemies. He breaks and destroys Judaism to the ground and builds the gentiles into a kingdom as wide as the world. How well should one praise that prince who leaves his people and takes his enemies into his land, pretending thereafter that his reign would be precious? One would regard him as nonsensical, crazy and silly as one would [rightly do] if an earthly power used such a plan. Also, those he desires to make good are doubtful sinners. Those whom he wants to make wise are those he makes into fools. Those he wants to make strong he makes weak. Those he would make alive are those he places in the sentence of death. Those he would lead up to heaven are those he sticks in the bottom of hell. Those that he will lead to glory, salvation, to lordship high and great he brings them all to shame; curses them to be a servant, lowly and small. It is named and goes forth in this way in this passage. The first are the last and the last are first, Matthew 19:30. Who would be great, let him be least. Who would go ahead, let him be behind.

Now that is the wondrous and unusual king. He is then nearest when he is furthest. So the more distant, the nearer he is. Now that should, indeed, seem wondrous to us. That means we don't experience it and are also under trial in this. But we hear and daily are covered by the Words until we become full and satiated and yet never come to the experience of the wonder. But those who are in it and become practiced see and feel what a wonderful method this is, and why he is justly called wonderful. This is it in a nutshell: He is wonderful because his method, rule and reign is established in the suffering and death of the Old Adam and lets nothing that he (that is, sinful nature) knows or is be capable of being considered good.

Erl. 15, 93–95: Christmas Sermon on Isaiah's Prophecy on the Kingdom of Christ

Then cleansed be every Christian breast And furnished for so great a Guest.
Yea, let us each our hearts prepare, For Christ to come and enter there. (*TLH* 63: 2)

Tuesday

And he will be called . . . Counselor. Isaiah 9:6

The first name shows how he stands by us in sufferings, death and cross so we do not doubt or become ruined under them. His standing by us is also wonderful. For he does not stand by us the way the world and the Old Adam do, as he says in John 14:27 and 16:33. "Peace I leave you, my peace I give you, not as the world gives. For in the world you will have trouble, but in me you have peace." The world stands by you so that you flee troubles and suffering or you defend yourself with might so that you might be free. So you use bodily strength against it, or suffer it unwillingly if you must. But Christ allows his own to remain under it. He stands by them without physical strength but with his Word, as he says in Isaiah 50:4, "The Lord has given me a wise tongue so I can strengthen those who are weary with the world." Such a Word, by which we are comforted in suffering, is a good counsel. Whoever can do that is a good counselor. He counsels the apostles in John 16:33, "Be comforted, I have overcome the world" and 14:26, "Let your heart not be terrified and do not fear. You have heard that I said to you, 'I go forth and will return to you.' If you had loved me you would have rejoiced that I said to you that I go to the Father. For the Father is greater than I am, etc." This whole discourse is nothing but pure counsel and Words of comfort in suffering. So the Lord Christ also says especially to his own in Psalm 16:7, "The Lord has counseled me," or Proverbs 2:6, "The Lord gives me understanding," etc. That is, he lets me suffer presently in weakness. But he does not forsake me with counsel and understanding how I will remain in it.

So in Christ's kingdom we are only ruled by God's Word, which Isaiah here praises as having the virtue to give counsel and comfort. No other king or lord is able to do that. For when they are physically overcome or their land is ruined, the advice and comfort they give are gone. Their counsel and comfort are only there when the table is full and they are in power and while their honor remains intact. But here, when all is ruined and doubtful, this is called the best counsel and comfort. Therefore this belongs to faith. It is a counsel for faith because it comes when nothing is left and there is only the unseeable to hope in. Who else could then lead us if the Lord, according to his first name, leads us so wonderfully that we have nothing to hold on to? Then there must be at least a Word that counsels and comforts us. In short, he is called "Counselor" for that reason. He comforts his own in the world, who are persecuted and in all kinds of affliction, with the gospel.

Erl. 15, 95–96: Christmas Sermon on Isaiah's Prophecy on the Kingdom of Christ

For Thou art our Salvation, Lord, Our Refuge, and our great Reward.
Without Thy grace our souls must fade And wither like a flow'r decayed. (*TLH* 63: 3)

Wednesday

And he shall be called . . . Mighty. Isaiah 9:6

The word "El" is used only of God. Many times in (Hebrew) Scripture it is also the name of God. By this fact one can refute the

Jews with the fact that Christ is God by using this passage from Isaiah. So the Jews defend themselves and evade this fact as well as they can. To put it briefly, (they say that) just because the word "El" is dedicated only to God in Scripture, that doesn't define the essence of the deity. So one may not convince anyone from this fact that this word will and must name God. Just as when God is called good and right, one cannot imply from that that such words, "good" and "right," when found in Scriptures, must name God. Both words are used to describe God as well as others.

But Isaiah speaks here of the kind of names that do not reveal the person but the office of Christ and the method employed in his kingdom. We must have even surer passages, which we also have, to prove Christ's deity. So I will stay with the natural meaning of these words, that inform about the ways of his kingdom. This does not speak about his essence but of his might or ability, as we have in Exodus 28:32 where Moses speaks of the misfortune of the Jews, "And there will be no 'El' in your hand," where you read, "There will be no 'might' in your hands to defend or save yourself from such tragedies." So in the German speaking lands we have names that simply denote "might (Kraft)" as in "craftsman," which are formed or borrowed from the Hebrew. So "mighty" or "craftsman" is this king's third name. . . .

Now "mighty" shows how the counsel is mighty, just as in the German we also set the two words together and say, "counsel and aid." For where there is only counsel in words, but they have no consequence and nothing comes of it, what good is it? But Christ, because he gives us counsel and aid in the gospel, gives might so that we believe it and remain in it and persist. He finally brings us through so we obtain the victory and hold the field. For it is not the intention of Christ, when he leads us wonderfully and brings us into suffering and the cross, that we should always stay in it and be satisfied only to have counsel and Word and that's all. No, not so. The counsel and Word shall be there so long as the misery fights us and it preserves us that we not sin in the weakness nor that through it our patience is overwhelmed and spent.

An example from Paul: How often was he placed before the roar of the lion, that is, into all kinds of trouble? But how was he counseled and comforted? By the counsel and Word of God. But he came through it and finally won as he richly describes all of it in the second epistle to the Corinthians, Chapter 11. So even if we have many troubles, always one after another and all at once; now sins, now death, now world, now devil, etc., yet that is all a Word of "wonder." Under all of this is the mighty one with his counsel and Word. He comforts us so that we can endure. Finally, he leads us out and again brings good weather. We hold the field as Paul says in 2 Corinthians 1:3, "Praised be God who lets us hold the field through Christ." So he is called "mighty" and can not only counsel and comfort but also deliver and cast the suffering under us. He controls the outcome and is a rock, that not even the gates of hell can overcome. Matthew 16:18.

Erl. 15, 96–98: Christmas Sermon on Isaiah's Prophecy on the Kingdom of Christ

Lay on the sick Thy healing hand And make the fallen strong to stand;
Show us the glory of Thy face Till Beauty springs in every place. (*TLH* 63: 4)

Thursday

And he shall be called . . . Hero. Isaiah 9:6

How well the names follow one another and hang upon each other. In every way they act [to show how] things happen in the kingdom of Christ. For the first is putting to death the Old Adam by all kinds of suffering and cross. But comfort and counsel are heard through the Word. It is not enough to have counsel and the Word, but might must also be there that we come through it. That is half of the names. We see that all three are meant for us and for our sake to serve us and for us to use and not for the sake of the one being named here.

With the three names we are ruled, renewed, preserved and defended. He, the king, has three offices. In them he creates his own. But the fourth name now reveals how he also engages the enemies and deals with them. So this is a true Lord, who cares for his land and his people. He prepares them and rules. By that he engages the enemies and increases his kingdom. But that happens wonderfully. For all of it must be wonderful, that is, from this king that the first name proclaims. He died wonderfully. He counsels and comforts wonderfully. Wonderfully he helps win and triumph, all in suffering and without apparent might. He also punishes and fights and wonderfully brings the people under him. For he is a hero and a man of valor; yes, a giant without sword and armor as Paul says in 2 Corinthians 10:4-6, "The weapons of our redemption are not fleshly, but rather mighty before God to destroy fortifications; by which we destroy plots and all high things which exalt themselves against the knowledge of God. We take captive every thought under the obedience of Christ and are ready to avenge all the disobedient." So also Psalm 110:2 says, "He shall rule in the midst of your enemies." And in Psalm 45:5, "Your arrows are sharp in the belly of the enemies of the king. The nations shall work under you."

He does all these things with the holy gospel which is his sword, his arrow and his weapon. By this he casts away and shatters all cleverness, wisdom, reason, might and holiness. Is it not a wonderful thing? Nothing leads the Word and with it the world is won without sword play. Yet it is with suffering and cross. It not only conquers, but it also defends and sets itself against all heresy and error and finally throws them under and gains the victory. No king on earth can do that, for his word is too weak. He must act with might and strength. Now here it is like the parable where he says in Matthew 12:29, "As a strong man he sits in peace within his house until a stronger one comes over him and overcomes him, and takes from him all that he has and divides the spoils." That is the victorious, strong hero to whom Isaiah here refers. He should be called "*gibbor*" [in Hebrew] and is in truth a true master of this fighting and winning. First he grasps the heart with the Word. Then he allows preaching that works in such a way that all wit and reason are nothing but pure sin before God. There [against such preaching] all holiness, wisdom, might, kingdom and what the world has fails. So man's presumption is banished. There man must despair of himself and yield and acknowledge that it is so. But where the heart despairs and is won, how can a person defend himself or argue? But those who are not yet desperate are not yet won. With them the hero yet fights through his Word till they are won or until the justice of God comes forth.

Erl. 15, 98–100: Christmas Sermon on Isaiah's Prophecy on the Kingdom of Christ

All praise, eternal Son, to Thee Whose advent sets thy people free,
Whom, with the Father, we adore And Holy Ghost forevermore. (*TLH* 63: 5)

Friday

And he shall be called . . . Everlasting Father. Isaiah 9:6

The fifth and sixth names show the reward and wealth enjoyed by those who are in the kingdom of Christ. I would rather have translated it: "Eternal Father," as could also be done, but using it this way it would sound as if God the Father and not Christ would be understood by this name. The same God/Father is also called Eternal Father. This is because his person, his being, is eternal and lives eternally. But this king shall be called Everlasting Father because he is eternally disposed and makes himself known to us as a Father and begets and nourishes us who are his children. It is necessary, if he will always and eternally preserve us as a Father, that he himself must also live eternally. For a mortal father, although he also regards himself as a father of his children, cannot do this for long. For he must die and leave his children behind so someone else eventually commands them. Therefore, he cannot become or be called "forever father." He could be called father only for a blink of an eye, for his life is certain for no longer than a moment.

But this king dies nevermore. He doesn't leave his children behind him. He always beholds them before him. They must live eternally with him. That he is here called "Father" shows how he not only conceives his own but also nourishes, clothes, teaches, corrects, provides and readies them as an heir. So when they sin, he punishes as a father, but does not cast them away. He is like a mortal father who conceives, punishes, corrects, loves and preserves and does not cast them away if the child is unclean, scabby or especially if he is weak. So Christ does much more with his own and does it eternally. Here they start in faith and there [in eternity] by sight. In short, this name will accomplish what St. Paul says of it in Romans 5:3–5, "We boast in trial because we know that trials bring patience, but patience brings experience and experience brings hope, but hope does not disappoint." So as the Christians become well practiced by the previous names with suffering, with comfort, with victory and strife against sins, they win the definite hope towards God from all this, that they are the children and will never be forsaken. This hope is now the work and fruit of this name; that by so much practice they win a child-like heart to God and that God alone is so sweet and lovely to them in their hearts that no fruits remain in them but only praise and comfort of God. This will be given out through Christ in his kingdom. So he is simply called "Forever Father."

Erl. 15, 100–102: Christmas Sermon on Isaiah's Prophecy on the Kingdom of Christ

When sinners see their lost condition And feel the pressing load of sin,
And Jesus cometh on His mission To heal the sin-sick heart within,
All grief must flee before his grace, And joy divine will take its place. (*TLH* 65: 1)

Saturday

And he shall be called . . . Prince of Peace. Isaiah 9:6

Not as the world gives peace! Especially since the first names are not a nothing, where he is called Wonderful, Counselor and Mighty. But [it is peace] before God in the conscience. It has received peace. When it [the conscience] is stirred up so much, its suffering is that much greater. Peace comes from our feeling we are children and knowing the eternal Father. By that we are secure and sure of his grace and have a comforting access to our dear Father. How well the six names follow one another. First, just as Christ rules us by suffering for us himself, on our behalf, the first three names show how Christ governs us to fight mightily against his opponents as shown in the fourth name. But the last two show how he rules us towards himself. In the first part [name, that is] is only trouble, in another only work. But in the third is only rest, peace and joy. For who suffers has rest, who fights has work, but who rests has peace. That is the true Prince of Peace and free kingdom, that is not composed of temporal goods or joy, but in spiritual and eternal peace. So we are rich even in the midst of discord. So these six names with their work go together with each other in one Christ. None of them are separate from the others.

He is not merely called "kingdom of peace" as Solomon (means in Hebrew), but Prince of Peace, *Shar-Shalom*. That peace is established in his authority, as a prince and Lord who is so mighty in peace in his kingdom that he gives peace to his own. No one then can break or take them. They rather hold the finest and safest escort against the devil, death, sins and all of the gates of hell; that sins not terrify us before God. His justice and wrath do not trample us. The devil and death cannot lay us siege. He is called a true Lord of Peace, or Prince of Peace. Worldly princes are also considered safe escort and peace. But they often fail, for they cannot be in all places and defend in every hour and moment. Therefore, they would like to be called peaceful rulers, but they cannot be a prince of peace even in their external rule before the people not to mention in the spiritual realm before God. For in peace they are not so lordly and mighty. They are sometimes broken and taken, even in the strongest kingdoms. But our Lord is in every corner and watches every moment and can preserve peace mightily as Psalm 121:4 says, "Behold, he who guards Israel neither slumbers nor sleeps." In short, Christ's kingdom is pure peace. For God always acts towards him for good and never for ill. So do not act to harm one another but rather always for their good. Then the enemies can do no harm, for the Christians gladly suffer it. Completely turned around, they mightily hold on [because of their enemies] through peace from Christ, the Prince of Peace.

Erl. 15, 103–104: Christmas Sermon on Isaiah's Prophecy on the Kingdom of Christ

When Jesus enters meek and lowly To fill the home with sweetest peace;
When hearts have felt His blessing holy And found from sin complete release,
Then light and calm within shall reign And hearts divided love again. (*TLH* 65: 2)

Christmas Week

First day of Christmas

Behold, I proclaim to you great joy, which will be for all people. For a Savior is born to you today, who is Christ, the Lord, in the city of David. Luke 2:10,11

Clearly you see in these Words that he is born to us. He doesn't only say, "Christ is born"; but rather: "to you," "to you, he is born." And he doesn't say, "I proclaim a great joy"; but, "to you"; "to you I proclaim a great joy." This joy does not remain in Christ, but it will be to all people. He doesn't have this faith alone, that some other cursed or evil man would not also have it. For this is the true basis for all salvation by which Christ would purify the believing heart. All is shared between Christ and those who believe. But what do they share? Christ has a pure, sinless, holy birth. People have an unclean, sinful and cursed birth as David says in Psalm 51:7, "Behold, I am made in sin in my mother's womb, and in sin my mother conceived me." Such a person could not be helped, but through the pure birth of Christ. So if the bodily birth of Christ were not given, then no one could be helped. Therefore this birth is spiritually handed out to everyone through the Word, as the angel here says that all who believe firmly are also born by him and are not made guilty by their impure birth. This is the means and substance of becoming pure from our miserable birth from Adam. So Christ wanted to be born so that through him we would be born in a new way, as he says in John 3:3. This happens through the kind of faith that James describes in 1:18, "He has willingly given birth to us through the Word of truth, that we begin to be his new creature."

See how, Christ thus takes our birth from us to himself, and submerges it in his own birth. He gives us his [birth] so that we become pure and new in it as if it were our own. So every Christian would rejoice and praise this birth of Christ no less than if he also were bodily born of Mary, just as Christ was. Who does not believe it, or doubts, is no Christian. Oh, that is a great joy of which the angel sings! That is the comfort and the overwhelming goodness of God, that a person who believes this great treasure could boast that Mary is his true mother, Christ is his brother and God is his Father. These things all truly happened, so we believe. That is the chief part and greatest good in all the Gospels, before one takes up the doctrine of good works. Before all things Christ must be ours and we must be his before we consider good works. This shows that only through such faith the teaching of the Gospels is rightly understood and one begins at the right place. This is what rightly knowing Christ means. By this the conscience is joyful, free and at peace. Out of this, love and praise increase to God because it is such an overwhelming goodness that could not have been given to us except through Christ. A truly willing courage follows. Such courage acts, allows and suffers everything that God is pleased to give whether it is life or death, as I have often said. That is what Isaiah says in 9:6, "Unto us a child is born and unto us a Son is given." To us, to us, to us is born, and to us is given. Therefore, see to it that you do not only take courage in the history by the gospel. That will not endure long. Also, not just the example, for that won't stick long without faith. But rather, see to it that you make this birth your own and grow with him, that you put your birth aside and his envelopes yours. This means, when you believe so, that you surely sit in the virgin Mary's lap and are her dear child. You will use such faith and pray because having such a faith, you live. It can never be strong enough to be satisfied. That is our basis and inheritance upon which good works are built.

Erl. 10, 134–136: Sermon on Christmas Day, Luke 2

Oh, rejoice, ye Christians, loudly
For our joy hath now begun;
Wondrous things our God hath done.
Tell abroad His goodness proudly
Who our race hath honored thus
That He deigns to dwell with us.

Joy, O Joy, beyond all gladness,
Christ hath done away with sadness!
Hence, all sorrow and repining,
For the Sun of Grace is shining!
(*TLH* 96: 1)

Second day of Christmas

Unto us a child is born, unto us a Son is given, and the government will be on his shoulders; and he will be called Wonderful, Counselor, Mighty, Hero, Eternal Father, Prince of Peace. Isaiah 9:6

Here Isaiah ascends and portrays the head or king of this kingdom. That fine carol is taken from this text and people now sing it at Christmas time. "To us a child of hope is born. . ." A wondrous king who is spoken of above, will take care of such great matters that he shall overcome death, sins, the law, reign without a sword, and make the world full of joy. For Isaiah clearly says here that all these things come because a child is born to us and unto us a Son is given. It is as if he would say: through the child and by the Son all such things come. He is the means by which they will be administered. So it is good to underline the little word US in this passage, as the place where its might lies. All children who are born are born to themselves or their parents. Only this one child bears a name that tells us that he is born for us. US, US, US, it says. To all of us and for our good he is born. For he had no need to be born for himself. For this reason all that he is, has and does, by birth or according to his humanity is called ours and is ours. By it our salvation and blessedness are served to us. Now the word US promotes steadfast faith. For if he were a thousand men or born a thousand times and yet he were not born for us and become our own we would not be helped at all. What help is it to us that many thousand such men be born if they were born daily since the beginning of the world?

So see in these words what kind of person this king is and how Isaiah masterfully sets forth and conceives his words. First, this is a child born, that is, a natural man. For *jeled* in Hebrew means "infant," a newly born child, as born of a woman. By this Christ is described as a true natural man, born of a woman; flesh, blood, bone, having head and hair, that lives, moves, stands, and does what others do, and yet he is born without sin, death or breaking the law. For it doesn't fit that the one who breaks and conquers sin should be born in sin. Otherwise, sin would have destroyed and conquered him much more than any other person ever born.

So now we hold that this child is a natural, but guiltless, holy child and that the same one is altogether ours, [along with] what he is, has, does and desires. So because he is holy and guiltless, we also will be holy and guiltless because he is born to us. Therefore, his holiness and innocence is ours, as if we had them ourselves, and we clothe and adorn ourselves in them before God. They are our jewels that are given us so that we believe in another that he is true. So we are innocent and holy in the innocence and holiness of this child.

He who is given us is the Son of another. He doesn't say here: The Son is born to us, but given. Those are his loving Words. He calls him Son, by which he makes known that this king is not only a man, but also by nature true God. He must be the Son of another than all the rest of mankind because he will do such things as is said: even if all sons were our own, yet it would not help us at all because there is no one who can break sins, death and the law. If he will now break the power of sins, death and the law, he must truly have divine power in himself, especially since he will not do it for himself but for us as he is given to us. For to help other people with sin, death and the law, nothing but God's might prevails.

Erl. 15, 87–89: Christmas Sermon on Isaiah's Prophecy on the Kingdom of Christ

Child of wonder, virgin born,
King of all creation,
On this happy Christmas morn
Come for our salvation!
Were this Child for us not born,

We should all be lost, forlorn,
No true hope possessing.
Dear Lord Jesus, thanks to Thee
Now and thro' eternity
For this grace and blessing! (*TLH* 78: 2)

Third day of Christmas

Glory to God in the highest, and on earth peace, good will to men. Luke 2:14

The angel arranges three things in this hymn; (1) the praise, or glory, (2) the peace and (3) the satisfaction, or good will. They give the praise to God, peace to the earth and satisfaction to men. The first is the glory or praise of God. One should also exalt because God will be given praise and honor in all things. He does, gives, and has all things. For no one ascribes anything to himself or receives a single thing from himself. For the glory belongs to no one but to God alone and he will not give it or share it with another. Adam had stolen the glory to himself by the evil spirit, so that every person from then on is under God's disfavor. It is still so deeply rooted in all men that there is no burden so deep in him as original sin. No one wants to be considered as or to be a nothing. Everyone experiences himself as good. From this, then, all tragedy, disturbance and war comes upon the earth.

Christ has now again brought the glory of God, his Father. By this he taught us that all our affairs are nothing but pure wrath and disfavor before God. We can in no way brag nor can we be satisfied with anything of ourselves, but rather must fear and be ashamed as being in the greatest danger and shame so we must shove our glory and self-satisfaction to the ground and become nothing. We become joyous that we are done with them so we can be found in Christ and be established.

But the angel sings, "praise to God in the highest," in Hebrew. God is called upon as if he alone lived on high. He is also called the most high, and what is high belongs to God.

The other is peace on earth. So just as where God's honor is absent, there must be a lack of peace, as Solomon says in Proverbs 13:10, "Under pride is always discord," so also again, where God's glory is, there must be peace. Why should you cause discord if you know that nothing is your own? Rather everything that you are, have and are able to do is of God. So let that govern you and be satisfied that you have a gracious God. For whoever knows that all his own affairs are nothing before God, he does not worry readily, and he thinks about another who is something before God, that is, on Christ.

From this it follows that where there are true Christians, there can be neither strife nor discord among them, as Isaiah foretold and said in chapter 11:9, "You will not murder nor injure one another on my holy mountain" (that is, in Christianity). The reason follows, "for the earth is full of the knowledge of God," that is, because if they know that all is God's and what is ours is nothing, then they could already have peace with each other. So this same Isaiah also says in another place, 2:4, "You will turn your swords into plowshares, and your spears into sickles; you will no longer raise your sword against another, nor persue strife."

Therefore our Lord, Christ, is called a king of peace, or a prince of peace. It is illustrated through "King Solomon," whose name in English would mean "king of peace," that Christ makes peace for us inwardly towards God in our conscience through faith which is built upon him and outwardly towards people in a physical walk through love. Through him is altogether peace on earth.

The third is the good will, or the satisfaction with mankind. This doesn't mean the good will, which good works do, but rather the satisfaction and peaceful heart, that lets everything happen that it encounters whether it is good or evil, sweet or sour. For the angels know well that the peace of which they sing strikes no further than among those who truly believe in Christ. Those definitely have peace among themselves. But the world and the devil have no quietness and allow themselves no peace. They persecute his disciples unto death, as Christ says in John 16:33, "In me you have peace; but in the world you will have fear and trouble."

Erl. 15, 130-132: Sermon on the Christmas Festival Gospel, John 1:1-14

We Christians may rejoice today,
When Christ was born to comfort
and to save us.
Who thus believes no longer grieves,
For none are lost who grasp the hope
He gave us.

Oh, wondrous joy that God most high
Should take our flesh and thus our
race should honor!
A virgin mild hath borne this child;
Such grace and glory God hath put
upon her. (*TLH* 107: 1-2)

The 28th of December

In the beginning was the Word, and the Word was with God and the Word was God. John 1:1

There he calls that child who lies in his mother's lap, a Word that was in the beginning of creation with God. This little child is so great that heaven and earth with all that is in them are called into being and made by nothing but through this child. Not only are they made through him, but also they are continually preserved through him, so that even his mother who carries, suckles and burps him is created by the child, and no drop of blood is in her that he does not make and preserve. These are the wonder and hiddeness of our faith that reason does not attend and derides as pure foolishness. Even that same eternal Word, concludes John, has become flesh by which that flesh itself is made. It is thus brought into the world. That is the crown and the sum of this gospel.

But first we must see why John calls him a Word, which is such a poor name in our ears compared to the high majesty. The Scriptures sometimes call Christ according to his divine nature God's Son, God's Word, as God's picture and likeness, so that through the gospel we know not just about the nature of angels, what they are and how they live, but more than that God has poured himself out and so completely revealed himself, though in faith, that we know how the highest majesty and most hidden nature is enclosed, which is completely higher than is revealed in his creation. Therefore we have a great mighty light and surpassingly rich knowledge. God grant that we learn it and be thankful for it!

Namely, first Christ is called an exact image or a "knock-off" of the Father that is like him in all things as Paul says in Colossians 1:15, "He is the living image of the invisible God." And to the Hebrews in Chapter 1:3, "an image of the Divine nature," that is, a picture that is even there God and has the same nature, more identical than a seal which presses itself into wax and makes an exact image. So with such images the prophets and the evangelists want to express the divine nature so that he is in every measure the same as the Father and with the Father. It is not like when someone describes a "knock-off" or a seal. For when these are used the seal conforms to it, but only the image remains. But in this "picture" of God everything God is inheres. If the seal itself could take on the wax unto the seal, and make one thing out of the two, then it would be a full comparison. It is as if a person could paint a picture of a man so the picture had flesh and blood but each kept its own nature.

The Scriptures would now reveal that this Son is completely like the Father in divinity, all power, knowledge, might and in all ways, none excepted. In all things he is the same God. He is not painted, nor made or formed, but born from eternity so that he brings that nature with him. The divine nature itself follows in this portrait. So far the Scriptures teach us. It also remains there and we cannot hold it in any better way. Therefore, it is settled for us: As the Father is God, in every way, so the Son is also God and yet there is only one

God. That could not be if he were a created image but he is born unceasingly and he remains in the same nature.

Erl. 15, 136-138: Sermon on the Christmas Festival Gospel, John 1:1-14

Now art Thou here, Thou Everblest!
In lowly manger dost Thou rest.
Thou, making all things great, art small;
So poor art Thou, yet clothest all.
Hallelujah!
(Original translation of verse in Link)

In foreign body you rest sublime,
Yet all in heav'n is truly thine,
You drink your milk at human breast
Yet angels serve on your behest.
Hallelujah!

The 29th of December

And the Word became flesh and dwelt among us and we saw his glory, the glory as of the only begotten of the Father, full of grace and truth. John 1:14

Here he resolves to do everything that has to be done for our sakes. Since we should become children of God through faith in the Word, he had need to reveal that Word to us and become flesh, that is, a natural man. He has dwelt with us, that is, he has come to us and taken on every human need and weakness. Yes, he poured out his divine majesty as Paul says in Philippians 2:7,8. But yet we have seen in the flesh that there is nothing more to be seen of such great majesty, even of the Father, himself. So He has made it [his majesty] known with his Words and his work and in addition it rang over him publicly through the Holy Ghost and the Father's voice and witness. This is also a wonder above all that he has done. Therefore, St. Peter also reveals it and majestically praises it in 2 Peter 1:16-18, "We beheld his majesty, that he received from God, the Father, glory and praise through a voice, which revealed him from the surpassing majesty, 'This is my beloved Son, in whom I am well pleased.' We have heard the voice brought from heaven when we were with him on the holy mountain." Through such majesty and glory, resounding through the world, the Word has become known to be full of grace and truth, that is, everything that is from him is agreeable and rightly fashioned, as everything that is in us is unacceptable and the wrath of God. It is all only flesh and foolishness so that he alone must rightly form us and establish us for good. He also makes us acceptable, dear children, as said, through faith.

So you see in this gospel how mightily and clearly St. John has presented the chief part of true Christian doctrine and has established the highest article of faith. First, how Christ is by nature truly God with the Father and additionally he is truly by nature a man. And we learn what we are and what we are able to do when he speaks pure lightning bolts against all our human teaching of free will, trusting in works, and all fictitious divine offices. Thirdly, [he presents] what we have from Christ and what our faith brings us, through which we receive all that is in Christ.

Erl. 15, 154–155: Sermon on the Christmas Festival Gospel, John 1:1–14

Fling wide the portals of your heart;
Make it a temple set apart
From earthly use for Heaven's employ
Adorned with prayer and love and joy.
So shall your Sovereign enter in
And new and nobler life begin.
To Thee, O God, be praise
For word and deed and grace.

Redeemer, Come! I open wide
My heart to Thee; here, Lord, abide!
Let me Thine inner presence feel,
Thy grace and love in me reveal;
Thy Holy Spirit guide us on
Until our glorious goal is won.
Eternal praise and fame
We offer to Thy name. (*TLH* 73: 4–5)

The 30th of December

To as many as receive him he gives the power to become the children of God, who believe in his name. John 1:12

Here are both our shame and glory with which he has endowed us. The shame is great, that we were previously the children of the devil. But the glory is much greater that now we have become children of God. So how could we have greater glory and comfort in heaven and earth than that we are called the children of the highest majesty and have everything that he has and is? As St. Paul wonderfully boasts, we have become partakers of the divine nature through Christ, 2 Peter 1:4. So, though we are not as Christ is by nature, yet we share of the same glory. But how do we come to that? Through faith (he says) in his name. There [in faith] all our manner and ways are off, all works and service thrown away. For so long as we are not God's children, we are completely stuck in the devil's kingdom, in death and darkness, as said above. Now what will a child of the devil and a flame of hell do or deserve if he would like to be a child of God? Christ must offer us his service and present grace out of undeserved goodness. So he must only be believed and received by us. All that we have in spiritual goodness is grasped in faith. For God rips us out of the smoke of sins and the devil and makes his dear children from children of wrath. If now we are God's children, then we have no sins, hell or death and all misfortunes are lost. But because these things happen through faith, then be mightily convinced that where there is no faith, there is no child of God, but rather only sins, disfavor and death remain, even if you also have done every holy service and you are martyred with your works to death. Therefore, it cannot be our act to repent of sins and do enough to overcome death and flee hell.

See that you have the right kernel of the gospel and all our comfort, bright and clear, as the sun at noon; nor that we become so completely stone-blind; that no one has considered such Words and passages, and not seized or considered it for what it is. How could one speak definitively and wonderfully about faith, if he [Christ] did not make us children of God, and handle death and the devil? Yet he transfigures himself further so one sees how he alone gives faith its honor, all works aside, lest anyone say that he accepts works in addition to it. That is how our lying preachers mix everything up.

Erl. 15, 151-152: Sermon on the Christmas Festival Gospel, John 1:1-14

He will on you the gifts bestow Prepared by God for all below,
That in His kingdom, bright and fair, You may with us His glory share. (*TLH* 85: 4)

The 31st of December

Give thanks to the Lord, for he is good, and his mercy lasts forever. Psalm 118:1

This verse is a general thanksgiving for every kindness that God the Lord provides daily, without ceasing, to all the world in all things to both good and evil people. That is the custom of the holy prophets. When they desire to praise and thank God for particular things, they begin with a higher and wider scope and praise him also in general, in all of his wonders and kindnesses. So here, when this psalm especially praises God for his most exalted kindness that he provided for the world, namely for Christ and his kingdom of grace, promised to the world and now provided, he begins with general praise and says, "Thanks be to the Lord." For he is surely a concerned, gracious, good, kind God, who is constantly showing his goodness and pouring it upon others in heaps.

So you must not read these (friendly and fine) words so coldly and crudely, nor pass them by, as the nuns read the psalter or as the choir master and choir may bleat or howl them in your church. But rather think of them as living, important, rich Words, which embrace and contain everything. Namely, that God is kind. Not like a person, but as the one who is always favorably inclined to help and do good from the bottom of his heart. He does not desire to be angry and punish, even if he must do it when he is also wholly compelled and forced to it by the unremitting, impenitent, hardened evil of mankind.

Yet if he must be angry and punish, then a person would not be able to have any hope. He could punish a hundred thousand times more harshly than he does.

He makes such kind and gracious favor richly and mightily known beyond all measure with his daily and eternal blessings, as he says here, "Thy goodness lasts forever." That is, without interruption he does the best things for us always. He forms our body and soul, defends us day and night, preserves us in life without fail, gives the sun and moon to shine on us, gives us the heavens, fire, air and water, wine, corn, fodder, food, clothing, lumber, and all necessities that grow from the earth, gives gold and silver, house and home, wife and child, beast, bird, fish. In summary, who can count all of it? He does all of this fully and overwhelmingly every year, every day, every hour, every instance. For who can reckon the good he does when only he gives and preserves a healthy eye or hand? When we are sick, or must dispense with some blessing, then one sees for the first time what a kindness it is to have a healthy eye, a healthy hand, foot, leg, head, nose, finger; or what a grace it is to have bread, clothing, water, fire, house, etc.

If we people were not so blind and tired of God's kindnesses and so careless with them, as is, surely, every person on earth, a person would see that he has so much wealth that if it came to exchanging it, he would not take any principality or kingdom for it and be robbed of his own blessings. For what kind of treasure can a kingdom be compared to a healthy body? What is all the world's money and goods compared to what the sun does daily for us in a single day? If the sun did not shine in a day, who would not rather be dead? Or what help would be all his goods and honor? What good is all the wine and cheese in the whole world if we should lack water for a day? What would all the beautiful castles, houses, velvet, silk, purple cloth, golden chains, jewels, all the splendor, decoration and arrogance count, if we should long be deprived of the desire the Father has for us?

Such blessings of God are the greatest and the most forgotten. Because they are so common no one thanks God for them. We take them and use them every day constantly, as we must, as if we had an absolute right to them and we need not once thank God for them. Meanwhile we proceed to complain, sorrow, hate, punish, wrestle and defend for the sake of the rest of the money or goods, for honor and desire, and, in summary, for the sake of such dispensable blessings that could not be reckoned as important as water, and are not one hundredth as necessary as water. This rather much more hinders us from happily and peacefully using the common blessings so we do not acknowledge nor can we thank God because of them.

48

The miserable devil makes it so we cannot be satisfied. So we can neither use nor acknowledge God's goodness and his rich daily blessings lest we also be blessed.

Erl. 41, 9–11: Commentary on Ps. 118, 1530

Well He knows what best to grant me;
All the longing hopes that haunt me,
Joy and sorrow, have their day.
I shall doubt His wisdom never
As God wills, so be it ever
I to Him commit my way.

If on earth my days He lengthen,
He my weary soul will strengthen;
All my trust in Him I place.
Earthly wealth is not abiding,
Like a stream away is gliding;
Safe I anchor in His grace. (*TLH* 425: 5–6)

New Year's Week

The 1st of January

And on the eighth day, when he would be circumcised, he
was named Jesus, the name given by the angel before he
was conceived in his mother. Luke 2:21

In German the name Jesus means, as we normally speak, about
the same as "savior" or "helper". Simply it means "one who makes
holy". But that is not good German. "Savior" sounds better. The
reason Christ carries this name is explained by the angel Gabriel,
when he says to Joseph in Matthew 1:21, "You shall call his name
Jesus, for he will save his people from their sins."

Let us learn and take notice of this name this little child Jesus
is called. He is a savior who delivers us from the highest and greatest
misery, namely from sin. Not [a savior] from the beggarly needs and
weak tribulations that accompany this life, such as the filth proper to
our bodily condition and wealth that somebody might experience.
God has ordained (solutions to such things) to the world. It has kings
and kaisers so that they will defend their subjects against foes. The
world has fathers and mothers so that the children are supported and
raised. It has doctors who can treat bodily illnesses and help. But
these are all poor saviors compared to the one who is a savior who
redeems his people from their sins.

Now whoever receives this little child and will let him be his Jesus,
or savior, will then see that he is a savior, not especially towards this
life, which he (as just said) has ordained to others, but rather towards
eternal life because he delivers from sins and death. For where sin
is taken away, then death must also be left behind. Therefore,
consider in your own mind whether you have anything more from
God than you have to hope from the kaiser and other earthly rulers.
Do you not wish to believe that there is another life after this life?
[Do you wish to believe] that (here) you have saviors enough in the
kaiser, in your father and mother and from the doctors? For these are
founded for this life and physical need, etc. But as you believe that
there is another life after this one, you have great need for this
savior. Apart from him no additional savior, neither kaiser, father,
mother, doctor nor anyone else, not even an angel, can help. It is
also good that it is true that if the kaiser, father and mother, and
other people don't want to or cannot help in physical need, then the
Lord Jesus will be there and stay with his own. But that is not his

peculiar and chief office, which is why we preachers do not make this the chief point when we inform the people.

But this is his peculiar office and here he wants his name seen over and against all sinners. He is named Jesus because he wants to deliver from sins, eternal death and the devil's kingdom. They [all], therefore need him. For if there were no such hell, no devil's kingdom, no eternal punishment and torture, what want or need could there be for the Lord Jesus? Then it would be the same if a man were to die as if a tree was felled, or as a cow when it died; it would make no difference. So you also see what a wild reckless servant he is that believes nothing about God and eternal life. But whoever believes that there is a God must also then be convinced that everything is not given out in this life but that another eternal life lies ahead. That is what we experience. God has not given this temporal life as the chief one; else he would not put up with the evil fools and their mischief for so long and let them have their fill here on earth. But God speaks to us in this life of another eternal one. For this reason this little child, Jesus, should be our savior and helper. If he has also delivered us to it, then he has helped us enough! There is nothing laying in wait that he would allow to swallow us up in this temporal life as if we had no God who desires us or can help us. For your help shall be an eternal help. Because of that we should be satisfied no matter what happens in this temporal life.

Erl. 1, 314–316: Sermon on the Circumcision of our Lord

Oh, joy to know that Thou, my Friend,
Art Lord, Beginning without end,
The First and Last, Eternal!
And Thou at length—O glorious grace!—
Wilt take me to that holy place,
The home of joys supernal.
Amen, Amen!
Come and meet me! Quickly greet me!
With deep yearning,
Lord, I look for Thy returning. (*TLH* 343: 7)

The 2nd of January

Seek first the kingdom of God and his righteousness, and all these things will be given you. Matthew 6:33

This [passage] depends on one already picturing in his heart what God's kingdom is like and what it gives. For if someone were able to describe it so that we might rightly consider it, and could judge and weigh in our hearts what a great costly treasure it is compared to mammon, or the earthly kingdom, that is, all that is on earth, then we would spit upon the mammon. For what would you have more if you had all the money and power of the king of France, and of the Turkish king's throne than a beggar before the gates with his crust of bread? Everthing there is for the purpose of daily filling one's belly. One cannot do more than that with all the world's goods and majesty. So the poorest beggar has just as much as the mightiest kaiser. To him his crust of bread probably tastes better and is more profitable than those who have a glorious and royal meal. Yet it remains true and bothers everyone equally that it only lasts a brief short time. We must let it all go and these things are not able to sustain our life for another hour when the last hour comes. That is why it is a poor, miserable, yes, a foul and smelly kingdom.

But what is it compared to the kingdom of God or of our Lord Jesus Christ? Figure it out for yourself. Tell me, what is the creature compared to his creator, or the world compared to God? For even if heaven and earth were altogether mine, what would I have compared to God? It is not so much as a drop of water, or a piece of straw compared to the whole sea. It is also such a treasure that it cannot be stopped or decreased and made poorer. It is such a treasure that both for the sake of its size and defense, it is not judged or grasped by human hearts or minds. Shall I let go of God and his kingdom so shamefully and leave it behind so that I take this unprofitable, deadly kingdom of the stomach in place of everything that is divine, imperishable, and that gives me eternal life, righteousness, peace, joy and salvation? Everything that I seek and desire here temporally, I will have in this kingdom eternally, only everything immeasurably more glorious and overwhelming than what I can gain here on the earth with great trouble, sorrow and work. And [here] even before I accomplish it and bring it to where I may possess it, I must [someday] leave it and let it lay. Is it not a great scandalous misery and blindness that we cannot see such things? Yes, isn't it a persistent evil in the world, which is possessed by the devil, that you will not be told, nor pay attention when someone preaches it to you?

Christ would gladly awaken us with these words, "If you would rightly worry and seek how you would always have enough, then seek after this treasure that is called God's kingdom. Don't worry anymore about the temporal, passing treasures which the moths and rust consume," as he had said above. "You have yet a much greater treasure in heaven, which I show you. If you would worry and seek after it [the heavenly kingdom] and think of what you have there then you would forget all about the other. For it is the kind of treasure that you retain eternally. It cannot pass away or be taken. So because the treasure remains and you hang upon it, then you must also remain, even if you had not a penny of the world's goods."

But what the kingdom of God is is often said. In the shortest way of saying it, it is not established by external things like eating and drinking, etc., nor in other works which you can do. Rather, it lies in your believing on Jesus Christ, who is the head and single king in this kingdom, in and through whom we have everything. Whoever remains in him cannot be harmed by any sins, death and misfortune, but has eternal life, peace and salvation. Here you begin with faith, but on the last day it all will be visible and eternally accomplished.

Erl. 43, 252-254: Commentary on the Sermon on the Mount, 1532; cf. AE 21

All that I am and have, Thy gifts so free,
In joy, in grief, through life, Dear Lord, for Thee!
And when Thy face I see, My ransomed soul shall be
Thro' all eternity Something for Thee. (*TLH* 403: 4)

The 3rd of January

Seek first the kingdom of God and his righteousness; and all these will be given you. Matthew 6:33

What does it mean to seek after this kingdom? Or how does one come to it? What is the street and the path which one must take? One directs here and another out there. So the pope also teaches: run up to Rome and get an indulgence, confession and penance, conduct or hear a mass, wear a hood, and practice great services to God and a hard disciplined life. There we ran on every path as they had recommended, as mad and foolish people, and all desired to seek the kingdom of God, but only found the devil's kingdom. For there are many ways, but only one, which is believing in Christ and the gospel, in which faith remains. This faith gladly practices and motivates itself with preaching, hearing, reading, singing, meditation and whatever can be done to receive it into the heart of faith and become stronger, and break out through much fruit, to progress ever further. So, many people are led to it. As we (God be praised!) presently do, there are also many, both preachers and other Christians, that are diligently motivated and contend that they would rather lose everything before they would let go of the Word.

No monks, nuns or priests know how to do such a thing even if they brag that they are God's servant and Christ's bride. For they are lacking the one true way and let go of the gospel. They know neither God nor Christ and his kingdom. For whoever wants to know and travel it must not seek it by way of his own head, but hear his Word, as the ground and cornerstone, and seek where he will direct him and how he describes it. Now this is his Word about his kingdom: Who believes and is baptized will be saved. That Word is not spun out of our head, nor did it grow out of the heart of a man. But rather is falls from heaven, and is revealed by the mouth of God, so that we would be sure and not miss the right road. When this is rightly carried on in the tradition, that people are readily compelled to the Word and Sacrament, that tradition is propagated and preserved, so that these [holy things] would be remembered among the people [as what] produce and teach the young people. That is what it means to seek and promote the kingdom of God. In this way, it will be regarded with appropriate zeal.

What, then, does it mean that he adds, "and his righteousness"? This kingdom also has a righteousness. But it is another righteousness than what is in the world, as it is also another kingdom. This is now called a righteousness that comes from faith, which is creative and is active through good works. It also means that I will think about the gospel with all seriousness and diligently hear it or demand it and thereafter live after it with actions. I will not be a lax watcher or a hypocrite who lets it go in one ear and out the other, but rather make it known with deeds and power, as St. Paul says in I Corinthians 4, "The kingdom of God remains not in Words, but in power." That means we act on the faith with its fruits, that is good works. We wait in faith's callings or offices and suffer all kinds of things because of it. For he calls righteousness, in general, the whole life of a Christian in respect to God and people, as the tree with its fruits. But not in a way that it is completely perfected, but that it [this righteousness] constantly proceeds. So he here calls his disciples to always seek after it, as they have not yet completely grasped it, nor already have perfectly completed their training and lived according to it. For in the kingdom of Christ we are half sinner and half saint. For that which is the faith and Christ in us is pure and complete, for it is not ours but from Christ. It is ours through faith. This lives and works in us. But what is yet our own, that is pure sin. Yet under and in Christ, it is covered and consumed through the forgiveness of sins. Also, these are daily put to death through the same grace of the Spirit until we have completely died off to this life.

Behold, this righteousness of this kingdom proceeds rightly and has no hypocrisy. For it is set against those who can speak and brag well about the gospel but do not live because of it.

Erl. 43, 254–256: Commentary on the Sermon on the Mount, 1532; cf. AE 21

I am content! Lord, draw me unto Thee And wake me from the dead
That I may rise forevermore to be With Thee, my living Head.
The fetters my body sever, Then shall my soul rejoice forever.
I am content! I am content! (*TLH* 196: 5)

The 4th of January

Behold the birds in the heavens, they do not sow, they do not reap, they do not store in barns, and yet your heavenly Father nourishes them. Are you not much greater than they? Matthew 6.26.

Here he admonishes us by an example and analogy to mock, deride and put to shame our terrible avarice and self indulgence in order to take it away from us. He shows what we, in ourselves, are so we must be ashamed to the heart. We are surely much higher, nobler and better than the birds, since we are their lords, and all things are given us to serve. They were made for our sakes. Yet not many believe that or provide what those creatures need, though God has entrusted and given them to us. Yet, without their [the birds'] worrying or thinking he daily gives nourishment and food to the littlest bird, yes, even to the lowliest worm. These store absolutely nothing nor do they produce by a plan. They neither sow nor gather.

Now it is a murderous scandal that we cannot trust our bellies to God without worry and avarice, when God has given and entrusted us with all creatures and when every year he lets so much grow that we yearly have enough to sow and much more than that to harvest. For if anyone should worry and gather, the little birds should. Since they cannot do such things, they ought to think this way when summer comes, "Look, now all the world is sowing its corn, so that they can gather it again after summer. Now, or in the fall, everyone is harvesting and gathering, and we don't even have a little kernel of corn to sow or to gather. When it is all gathered in at the end of the year and there is nothing in the field, especially in the cold winter, where will we get something to eat?" What would we people do if we had nothing to sow some summer? Surely, if we did not have provisions stored that would last for fourteen days, would not we worldly people despair as if we must all die of starvation? Now the dear little birds fly in the air in the summer and winter and they sing and are happy. They do not worry or complain about anything at all, even though they do not know where they should eat or hunt tomorrow. We complaining, greedy bellies cannot stop worrying even when we have our fields and sheds full and we see the corn grow so richly in the field.

So see how he makes the little birds our masters and teachers. A weak sparrow becomes our great eternal shame and is placed in the gospel as the wisest doctor and preacher of man. Our eyes and ears must daily consider this. It is as if he wanted to say to us, "Look, you miserable man, you have house and home, money and goods, and every year you have a field full of corn and all kinds of crops, more than you need. Yet you cannot have peace and always worry as if you would starve to death. When you do not see a store of provisions, you think that you cannot trust God to give you food to eat for a day." Yet what we have is so much that it is uncountable, not at all because it is worried over in life's day, but because God daily provides for us. In short, we have so many masters and preachers, like the birds of the air, that put us to shame with their living examples. We ought to be ashamed and bow our heads when we hear the birds sing while God's praise and our shame are cawed up to heaven. Yet we are so hard-hearted that we do not once turn ourselves around if we hear them preach and sing such things to us daily with our great stores.

Erl. 43, 243–245: Commentary on the Sermon on the Mount, 1532; cf. AE 21

Almighty Father, heav'n and earth
With lavish wealth before Thee bow;
Those treasures owe to Thee their birth,
Creator, Ruler, Giver, Thou.

The wealth of earth, of sky, of sea,
The gold, the silver, sparking gem,
The waving corn, the bending tree,
To us Thou lendest them. (*TLH* 438: 1–2)

The 5th of January

Therefore you shall not say, "What will we eat? What will we drink? With what shall we clothe ourselves?" The heathen seek such things. For your heavenly Father knows that you need all this. Matthew 6:31,32

Since you see this example daily, in everything that lives and grows upon the earth, how God nourishes and feeds everything and clothes and adorns them in the most majestic way, then he would move you to put aside your worry and disbelief. You are Christians and not heathen. Such worry and greed belong to the heathen who do not know God or pray to him. It is true idolatry, as Paul says, and it is also said above where he calls it "serving mammon."

For that reason, no greedy belly is a Christian, even if he is baptized. Rather, he has definitely lost Christ and become a heathen. For the two, greed or worry and believing, cannot stand together; one must expel the other. To the Christian, who hears and knows the Word, there is no greater shame before God and all creatures, than to become like the heathen. They do not believe that God provides and gives all things. To fall away from God like this, to deny the faith, and not turn either to his Word or to this obvious example is truly a good reason for everyone to fear. For it is quickly determined that a Christian thinks this way and forsakes the worry of avarice. Or he knows that he is no Christian but is rather ten times more wicked than a heathen person.

For this reason (he speaks) to you because you are a Christian, so that you may not doubt that your Father already knows that you need all these things. He knows that you have a stomach which eats and drinks and a body that must have clothes. If he did not know it then you would have reason to worry and plan how you could provide for yourself. But now he must know so that God will not abandon you. For he is surely so good that he gladly does this and especially for you Christians. For he (as said) also concerns himself with the birds of the air. So let your worry go, for you do not gain anything by it. Your help does not depend on your worry, but on his knowledge and concern. If something in the field should not grow before we worried about it, then we would all die in the cradle and it must not grow in any night that we lay down and sleep. Yes, even if we should all worry ourselves to death, no stalk in the field would grow because of our worry. Yet we are such hopeless people that we do not want to let go of such worry and greed, nor let God alone worry, to whom alone this belongs, as a Father worries on behalf of his children.

Erl. 43, 249-250: Commentary on the Sermon on the Mount, 1532; cf. AE 21

To Thee, as early morning's dew, Our praises alms, and prayers shall rise
As rose, when joyous earth was new, Faith's patriarchal sacrifice. (*TLH* 438: 3)

The Week of Epiphany

Festival of Epiphany

Arise and shine, for your light is coming and the glory of the Lord is rising over you. Isaiah 60:1

So now the light and the splendor of God himself is come, as Christ says in John 8:12, "I am the Light." We have heard this above in the epistle for Christ's day, how Christ is the appearance of divine splendor. From this it is evident that Isaiah is not speaking here about the future or acknowledgment of the birth of Christ, but of the understanding of the gospel by the ascension of Christ. Through this, Christ is spiritually and blessedly acknowledged and is clarified in the hearts of all believers in the world. The Scriptures speak more of this acknowledgment than of the birth of Christ. For in this also lies the power [of the gospel]. It is also the reason that he was born, as St. Paul concludes and says, "The gospel is promised by God through the prophets in the Holy Scriptures, by his Son. . . ."

From this it is also evident what the gospel is and of whom it speaks. It is a promise of light and a procession of divine splendor. It says nothing more than what concerns divine splendor, honor and praise. That is, it boasts of nothing more than God's Word, his grace, his goodness to us and that we shall and must have his work, his grace and his goodness and he himself, if we would become holy. This does two things in us.

First, it buries our natural reason and light, convincing us that they are nothing and only darkness. For if there were light and not only darkness in us, then God would bring his light to us for nothing. Light does not enlighten light, but rather [it enlightens] darkness. Therefore in this epistle all natural wisdom, all human reason, all heathen skills, every human teaching and statute are mightily thrown aside and accursed. They are certified as pure darkness, while this future light is necessary. This is so that you guard against every human teaching and all the pleasant thoughts of reason. They belong to darkness that is accursed of God and depraved. We are only to arise and awaken to receive this light as true, to follow him alone.

The other work is that it buries all praise and the splendor of our works, wealth and free will so that we are not able to trust any of them or have honor for them, but only pure disgrace and shame before God. For if there were anything in us that was somewhat worthy of honor or praise, then this divine honor and splendor would

58

have gone over us for nothing. But since they have gone over us, they make it certain that there is nothing in us for which we do not have shame and disgrace. Paul says of this in Romans 3:23, "All people are sinners and are devoid of divine splendor or glory." He says, "You can certainly have, by nature, your own human righteousness and have glory, praise and splendor from it before people temporally on earth, as if you were not transgressors. But before God you are sinners and do not have his splendor and cannot boast of his pleasure or even of [having] him."

Therefore if anyone would become holy, God's splendor must be in him so that he can be comforted and praise only God and his divine favor, as in Jeremiah 9:24 and 2 Corinthians 10:14, "If any man boast let him boast in the Lord." See, that is called divine splendor rising. That is also what the gospel does. It excludes every thing that is ours and only praises divine grace and favor, that is, [God] himself, so that we will find comfort only in him and praise, as Psalm 144:15 says, "Blessed are the people whose God is the Lord," and no one else.

Erl. 7, 332–334: Sermon on the Epistle for New Years, Gal. 3:23-29

A pledge of peace from God I see
When Thy pure eyes are turned to me
To show me Thy good pleasure.
Jesus, Thy Spirit and Thy Word,
Thy body and Thy blood, afford

My soul its dearest treasure.
Keep me Kindly
In Thy favor, O my Savior!
Thou wilt cheer me;
Thy Word calls me to draw near Thee. (*TLH* 343: 4)

Monday

Awake, O sleeper, and rise from the dead for Christ would enlighten you. Ephesians 5:14

Without doubt Christ is this light, of whom Isaiah also speaks (Chapter 60). He illuminates all the world through the gospel and enlightens all who there arise and desire him. Now who are these sleepy and dead people? Without doubt, all who are under the law, for they are all dead through sins. But especially, the dead are those that do not regard the law and openly live free of it. But the works-righteous people are the sleepers who do not sense it flooding upon them. Neither of these think much of the gospel and always sleep and die because of it. Therefore the Spirit must awaken them that they see and are aware of this Light. But the third [type of people], who feel the law and whose conscience bites them, are worthy of grace and sigh after the gospel. They also see that the gospel will be brought forth and be given. They also are diligent that the sleepers and the dead awaken and receive the light. Isaiah is one of these.

Therefore, he says, "Be enlightened," or "become light." See that you walk in the light. Crawl, you dead person, not in the grave of your stinking life. That is, stop living and following the evil life so that you walk in the gospel light and find praise. Wake up, you sleeper. Do not creep in the bed of your inadmissible and drowsy security and the presumptuousness of your own righteousness so that the true Light may have its rightful place in you. So to both of these, many exhortations are needed. For the free life stops the dead mightily and their own presumptuous righteousness makes it difficult for the sleepers to acknowledge and receive this blessed Light.

"For your light comes." Why does the prophet say "your light" [addressing the people] when it is God's light? Answer: It is God's light and also our light. It is God's, who gives it. It is ours because it illuminates us and we are used [by it]. Just as Christ says that the sun is the Father's, in Matthew 5:45, "He lets his sun shine on the good and the evil." He says in John 11:9, "Whoever walks in the day is not hidden, for he sees the light of the world," that is, the same sun of God, that illuminates the world. For he says of himself in John 8:12, "I am the light of the world." And yet he alone is God's light. Above all he is Jerusalem's and the Israelite nation's own particular light for the sake of the promise. For he is only promised to Abraham and his seed, as Mary sings in Luke 1:55, "As he has spoken to our fathers, Abraham and his seed forever." To this degree he is not the heathen's light, to whom he is not promised and yet he has said they would receive it, as the Words of his promise say.

Erl. 7, 328–329: Sermon on the Epistle for New Years, Gal. 3:23-29

How lovely shines the Morning Star! The nations see and hail afar
The light in Judah shining. Thou David's Son of Jacob's race,
My Bridegroom and my King of Grace, For Thee my heart is pining,
Lowly, Holy, Great and glorious, Thou victorious Prince of graces
Filling all the heav'ly places. (*TLH* 343: 1)

Tuesday

And the Lord our God befriends us. Psalm 90:17

Here Moses prays that God would show his works to his servants, that is, to all who are faithful and believing. They would then see his divine grace, righteousness, holiness and salvation, the highest good, eternal life. [Moses also prays] that he not only would reveal this after this temporal life, after death, but rather also in this poor miserable life that he give a foretaste of his divine grace and eternal life, that we taste and sense how sweet and kind the Lord is. Here we are already invested with the penny[2] of God, his divine grace, that we are safe and sure of eternal life and our heart not doubt it. God's grace is the penny of God of eternal majesty. Whom God bestows his grace, he also calls to heaven. Whoever now already invests the penny of God, the bestowed grace of God, is safe and sure that the deal will precede him and he will surely receive eternal salvation.

We practice giving the penny of God which he has already spent on us for the sake of God. So we will also never turn from divine grace, bestowed on us by God, but only die to self and live to God's glory and for the help and comfort of our neighbor. Where that happens the eternal glory must accompany it. Christ previously gave Peter a foretaste of his glory on Mount Tabor, where he says in Matthew 17, "Lord, it is good to be here. If you wish we will make three booths." And St. Paul is told by him in 2 Corinthians 12, "My grace is sufficient for you for my power is mighty in weakness." Then St. Paul also says in 2 Timothy 4, "Henceforth the crown of righteousness is reserved for me, which the Lord, the righteous Judge will give to me on the latter day." God gives such a divine penny to all who are baptized. But since they do not all invest it, the majesty and eternal life also do not come to them.

As God gives his saints and elect here on earth a foretaste of heaven and eternal majesty and gives them a little drink of heavenly joy and salvation, so he also gives them a foretaste of hell's anxiety and damnation. This happened to Christ's parents. They surely had in Christ, in his birth, a true heavenly joy when the shepherds came from their fields and told them the angels' proclamation, and when the wise men came from the east and gave Christ gold, frankincense and myrrh. This joy should have surely preserved them when they lost Christ for three days. The dear virgin also experienced this. She had pure joy while he was with her, but when he was taken from her only fear and despair.

Altb. VIII, 200: Commentary on Ps. 90, 1541

---

[2]"Penny" here refers to a small deposit on a great fortune. Thus grace through faith is the promise that tells us we possess the coming Lord and all that is his. This "penny" cannot be separated from God and all that is his.

Finish, then, Thy new creation; Pure and spotless let us be.
Let us see Thy great salvation Perfectly restored in Thee,
Changed from glory into glory, Till in heav'n we take our place,
Till we cast our crowns before Thee, Lost in wonder, love and praise. (*TLH* 351: 4)

Wednesday

Jesus answered him and said, "Truly, truly, I say to you, you do not seek me because you have seen the miracles but because you have eaten the bread and were filled." John 6:26

In this text we hear Jesus tell the Jews why they were seeking him, not because of his miracles and doctrine, but because of their dear pitiful bellies. For they thought, "That is a good teacher for us. He will bring us a bodily freedom so that everyone will be filled and satisfied and can do what he wants." By this the Lord shows what kind of students the teacher of the gospel has. For even today the gospel also finds people that think it is the kind of teaching that gives nothing but what fills the belly and satisfies every kind of desire and serves only for this temporal life.

This dream goes on with such strength and might even to this day that I have become completely weary of preaching and teaching. For the people come to the preaching of the gospel just as if they were these same voracious students. But under this appearance they seek nothing but a full belly and their own needs. They regard the gospel as a belly-teaching from which you learn how to eat and drink. These are all purely human thoughts that come from below and rise up to rule. For among the princes, earls, nobility and officials, city dwellers and farmers, the people regard the preaching of the gospel as belly-preaching.

But this doctrine, that everyone should seek his own and should suck from it what pleases him, or that it should fill our belly and preserve all fleshly desire, is not sent from heaven. Christ did not shed his blood for that. Rather the gospel is a preaching of the honor, praise and majesty of God which shows how God would be praised by us. For God would be honored and praised by us so that we do what pleases him. So first we seek the honor and kingdom of God. Thereafter he will also give us not only everything that we need for this temporal life, but also eternal life.

For God had previously given the world what they need for their bellies. It would not be necessary that we should now preach the gospel for the sake of the belly. For in the first chapter of Genesis he had given to man all the animals of the field, the fish in the sea and the birds in the air and set him as lord over them. He made the earth subject to him so that it would bear corn, wine, sheep, oxen and clothing. Thus they should farm the land so that they would be able to eat and would be nourished. He richly fills their cellar and kitchen so they would have joy and pleasure. Finally, he gives them also the sun so the day would be lightened, and the moon of the night so that the people and animals could sleep and rest when they were tired of their work and satisfied. Thus he gave them everything that they should have.

So Christ had no need to come to teach these things. For temporal goods are also given those that ask nothing of Christ but are godless. Yes, these probably have most of the kingdoms of the world, just as we see that the Turks have many kingdoms under them. Now how do we come to think that the gospel is that kind of doctrine that gives lessons how to scrape, scratch and skim off everything and under the glow and cover of the gospel want to be usurers, misers and pretend kings? But that isn't what it means. So the people persist in such thoughts of the gospel that in its place they say, "Hey, Christ proclaims freedom for us in the gospel! Isn't it true? Oh, then we do not want to work, but to eat and drink." And then each one gathers into his sack only what will fill his belly.

Altb. V, 615–616: Sermons on the Gospel of St. John Chapters 6–8; 1531, cf. AE 23

May we in faith its tidings learn Nor thanklessly its blessings spurn;
May we in faith its truth confess And praise the Lord our righteousness! (*TLH* 297: 6)

Thursday

Jesus answered him and said, "Truly, truly, I say to you, you do not seek me because you have seen the miracles but because you have eaten the bread and were filled." John 6:26

But this is our comfort. When it happens to us today that we preach the gospel and our opponents, the tyrants, persecute this doctrine and will not let it be preached, and we also fall into this sorrow, "Oh we must die of hunger!", such things do not happen without reason. For this persecution will be necessary for us to face. It works in us an even greater zeal for the gospel. For if we had a prince who did not confess the gospel, but rather set himself against it and persecuted it, we would hear this preaching with much greater love, fruit and longing. We would give up two cooks that we might have one good preacher. For in the homeland one would give ten guldens so that he could hear God's Word the whole year through.

But our farmers say, "I wouldn't give a penny for it." If we weren't being persecuted, then we would be as bad and wicked as our opponents. For even now we would gladly let the pastors in the villages starve to death. We are greedy and scratching. See now what the citizens and farmers, princes, officials and the governors do to me. But only rally some comfort. It will become a pleasure to have hungry bellies and poor purses and the guldens will gladly be paid and shared and be plundered and robbed. As I have often said, all of a sudden it will happen that you will seek a good preacher and the gospel for a hundred miles. But it will be lost and not be found. And as you now would not give three pennies for a preacher, then you would gladly give him three guldens. But you won't believe it. Rather you want to experience it. For the Jews now would give a king's treasure that they should hear the preaching of an apostle or a prophet. But they must not hear one any more.

Now, a preacher must be comforted by this. For where the gospel is preached, there sows and hounds will be his listeners, students that will not be anything else. They seek nothing else from the gospel than their own pleasure. And when it happens to you, then say, "Why do you get so upset about that? You are no better than the Lord Christ. As it was towards him, it will be to you. It's only right."

So what does the Lord Christ do? He would gladly turn them away from such false dreams and seeking after their own needs. He would deliver them and lead them from their bellies by the Spirit. For the gospel is not preached to them so that they would have temporal nourishment and bodily goods from it, but so that it gives them something better than food, drink, house and home, wife and children. Above all it should not teach avarice, being safe and becoming lazy. For such [teaching] would even be against the first creation where God commanded Adam to till the garden, but after the fall [he said that] the work would be unpleasant so that he would eat bread by the sweat of his brow.

So whenever you hear the gospel you must direct your heart, [telling it] that the gospel gives much more than the whole world is able, or that all kaisers, kings, princes and lords possess.

Altb. V, 616: Sermons on the Gospel of St. John Chapters 6–8; 1531, cf. AE 23

This lamp through all the tedious night Of life shall guide our way
Till we behold the clearer light Of an eternal day. (*TLH* 285: 6)

Friday

Seek food that does not perish but which remains in eternal life, which the Son of Man will give you. For God the Father has certified him. John 6:27

As he says, "I want to give you different food. You poor beggars, why do you want to seek and crave these meager crumbs and beggar's portions from me? I want to give you a different food that doesn't spoil; a bread that will last forever, which also will not let you die but rather preserves you to eternal life."

But when they hear that he would direct them from bakers and money to the gospel and from field and from the earth up to heaven, it did not please them and they deserted him. For flesh and blood ask no one for anything but for bodily nourishment. For the breath of the common rabble stinks only of greed. The whole world seeks after nothing but money and goods, food and drink. But Christ speaks only for the sake of a few good hearts who accept this Word and think further than of bread and beer, money and goods. The other things can be left behind. Who even asks about them?

But here he sets the two kinds of food next to each other, the one being perishable, the other, eternal. When these two types of food are offered together to hearts, then such a heart would be comforted by the eternal food and not cling so to the temporal goods, but say, "I hear that Christ says there is a perishable and also an eternal food." So Christ wants to say, "Even if I were to give you what you already have now, like bread that the baker bakes, and give you enough for the whole world, how would that help you? Even if I had so much wheat, barley, oats, money and goods as the Turkish kaiser or the Roman kaiser, how would that be better?" He lets that be food, but only a perishable food that does not last forever. This addition, that it is perishable, makes such food despicable. Since these foods will spoil, they become worse and consume themselves and do not help. They even condemn a healthy body and life if they are misused. How then do they help your troubles? The perishable bread only preserves temporal life. It cannot be said enough, that even if someone had all the world's wealth, yet it all passes away. So then what would it help that you despise and refuse the imperishable food and eternal life for the sake of this perishable bread and life? Are you not foolish and stupid?

There is no farmer so silly that he would give a hundred bushels of corn for a torn piece of paper, or a citizen [who would give] a hundred barrels of beer for a drink of water. Rather the citizens would rather trade a drink of beer for a hundred guldens or the farmer a bushel of corn for a hundred guldens. But Christ says here, "It is perishable," and whoever wants to have this imperishable food, he might give all that he has. But that's what happens in the world. Unfortunately, they take what is perishable and ignore the eternal; they take a hand full of corn and always let the gospel pass by. Thus we unthinking fools defy God. But who is hurt by it will easily be discovered in the end.

Christ gladly wants to take our trouble and ruin away from us. He warns us not to act so foolishly and exhorts us to receive the eternal food. For this food does not pass away. If it is taken away, then you must die in eternity. All the more you should be drawn towards this food and not despise it but rather let it be the most important food, eternal food that gives eternal life. You should ask after this food. For when the perishable food ceases, you will be eternally preserved and then have eternal life.

Altb. V, 617: Sermons on the Gospel of St. John Chapters 6–8; 1531, cf. AE 23

Let our prayers each morn prevail That these gifts may never fail;
And as we confess the sin And the Tempter's pow'r within,
Feed us with the Bread of Life; Fit us for our daily strife. (*TLH* 537: 3)

Saturday

Seek food that does not perish but which remains in eternal life, which the Son of Man will give you. For God the Father has certified him. John 6:27

Now the gospel has the kind of students that only seek after this eternal food and wealth. St. Peter and the beloved apostle, also other pious Christians, have gladly grasped and held this preaching as St. Peter says hereafter, "You have the Words of eternal life," that is, Words that give eternal life. They remained with this preaching and would not shy away from Christ. But the others had despised it as crude and godless people still say, "What's all this heaven, heaven! Who has enough flour here?!" Or what can you say about eternal life to those who have altogether enough in this world? And yet these want to be considered good evangelical people!

But here the Lord shows them not to consider temporal goods and nourishment that adhere to this life as if God had not already richly provided these. They are already free to use them in their need and in the service of God. But they should think further and say "Seek food that does not spoil." That is a Hebraism. He would say,

"You only worry about having food for your belly. But consider that he bakes you true bread, and creates bread and corn or grain for you that is imperishable. Sow from such corn, cut from such ears, also gather such counsel into the barn to thresh, toil and keep on pursuing this work so that you fashion imperishable bread, a food that will not let you die and that fetches a price that does not run out."

But someone always asks, "Should one not then plow, disk and work?" He does not forbid this, for in Genesis God has commanded it. But he forbids altogether that one should seek these things as if one only needs them, while despising the doctrine and miracles of Christ, as he then complains and says, "You do not seek me because of the miracles you have seen, but rather because you have eaten bread. You should not seek me for the sake of what is passing away. For I (he would say) am a different teacher, who does not preach concerning perishable food, how one should sow, bake and plough, for you know about that all too well and Moses has previously taught how one should work. My doctrine is not ruled by that and you should not come to me for that, but that I give you eternal food."

So he leads them on another discourse about food. But when one preaches this to human flesh and blood then this teaching is soon dismissed. For everyone would rather have the bread that he sees and holds, as when the farmer also keeps his corn and says, "I hear well enough that you would feed me and give me bread, but I do not hear any money jingling, nor see a sack full of corn. Where do you have it? Are you yourself a beggar? Where do you have your corn crib? Where then is this food?" So he [Christ] says, "It is that which the Son of Man will give you." With these Words he tears all of our hearts and eyes from all the houses of bakers and corn cribs and from all the cellars, cribs, fields and bags; yes, from all works and he draws them to himself. For he is a generous Baker. He wants to give what no other field or bag can carry.

Altb. V, 617–618: Sermons on the Gospel of St. John Chapters 6–8; 1531, cf. AE 23

Jesus, be endless praise to Thee, Whose boundless mercy hath for me,
For me, and all Thy hands have made, An everlasting ransom paid. (*TLH* 371: 7)

The First Week after Epiphany

———

Sunday

For God the Father himself has set his seal on him. John 6:27

This says in a lavish way that God wants his Son, who is a man, the one who is this food as well as the corn-miller, the baker, waiter and supplier, that is, Jesus Christ, marked with a seal. He is the one whom I desire. He is given by God as if impressed with his seal and marked by his initials. He is the one. But this is a "Hebraic" phrase, in which our Lord God has a writing finger, a signet ring and seal on his thumb with which he seals things when he writes letters and sends them. Christ shall be sealed and no other. By this he discards and curses every other seal. That is a strong Word which grasps him with immeasurable breadth. Whoever would live eternally must have this food which the Son gives and must be found in this Son, who is here sealed. Otherwise, whoever does not have him will lose eternal life. We are pressed by this seal and witness to this very place. With this Word, "sealed," he would subjugate everything that is proud, holy and wise in this world under this doctrine and this single master, Christ. People dispute even to this day if one might be made righteous and gain eternal life through our own preparations and good works, through our own love, action and services. But compare the two with each other. See if the work that you do or your service, fasts, prayers, pilgrimages or if the flesh and blood of Jesus Christ is the food that the Son of Man gives. Set them next to each other: my body, effort and work and the body of Christ. Even if I fasted all the time and called on the saints and walked on pilgrimages, gave up sleep, did this or that work; then taking it all together in a heap and throwing it in a sack, see if such works are the body and blood of Christ. It would fall completely short. So how can someone boast that he will become holy through his own works? We could not give ourselves this food but you will receive it from the Son of Man. That is why Christ shall be impressed with this seal; so that I know that my dear God is gracious to me. For he does not say, "You will give and set before me food so that you are eternally preserved." Rather he says, "I will give it to you." From the Son of Man whom you see before you you will share it. From him you will receive the food, his flesh and blood. For this reason see to it that you grasp this food that he, Christ, himself, is, namely where his body and blood are given. For that is surely not your work. I have not done or made it. It is only God's work. It is done without any works of our hands. Just as

Christ is also conceived by the Holy Ghost and born of the virgin Mary and she, the mother, had also not made him, but the Holy Ghost did, by whom he was conceived. She had only added her body and limbs so that he would be born from her to the world. So why, then, am I so foolish that I would want to obtain such things with my works?

Altb. V, 619–620: Sermons on the Gospel of St. John Chapters 6–8; 1531, cf. AE 23

He who craves a precious treasure Neither cost nor pain will measure;
But the priceless gifts of heaven God to us hath freely given.
Tho' the wealth of earth were proffered, Naught would buy the gifts here offered:
Christ's true body, for thee riven, And His blood, for thee once given. (*TLH* 305: 3)

Monday

Everything that my Father gives comes to me; and whoever comes to me, I will by no means cast away. John 6:37

These are the finest Words, "Whoever comes to me, I would not cast away. Whoever believes in me must be given me by the Father and I will not cast him away. This is true even if you worked a long time and were holy, fasted, prayed, and didn't trouble yourself about me, but regarded me as a fool. But whoever believes in me, has that from the Father. Such a person is given to me by the Father so that he comes to me. And whoever comes to me eats in comfort and drinks safely. For my sake he will not be thrown away."

"Whoever believes on me. . ." He is thinking deeper than on mere eating and drinking. Namely, whoever receives his Word and follows and believes in him will be sealed and confirmed so that he will not cast him away. He says, "You will ask me for nothing, I will already be by you before you come to me. I am more willing and ready to give then you are to ask. So you can come to me. Do not be afraid of me. I will not be your executioner or judge."

And as he says the Words he also is thinking, "False prophets and preachers will come in my name who will cast away the people who come to me and their conscience. But whoever believes that I can give life will not be cast away." They have acted against the kingdom of Christ to cast away those who believed on Christ. But Christ has previously established a flock and said, "If you will come believing, then there is nothing lacking. Your infirmities and failures will not harm you," as is said in Romans 14 and 15. He has forgiveness of sins. Christ will not quickly throw him away. "Whoever once comes to me and believes, I will also steady him as though he were stumbling (as then the sins remain in the flesh of the Christian, as an evil affliction, as it is said in Romans 6, 7, and 8)." That will not harm him. That is, the sins in his flesh will not rule. For there is nothing condemnable in those who are in Christ, even if they are not completely clean, nor is the flesh in them completely put to death.

But the Jews do not understand that whoever believes and comes to me has the sure benefit that I will not cast him out. I will not throw him away.

These are words that are self-evident. If there were a servant who was obedient and served his master well, then it is no great virtue if his lord would say, "I will not cast you away from me." The master is merely indulging himself. But if the good servant would be cast out of the house, that would not be a lack of virtue or a derision accounted to the servant, but to the master. But if he were evil and the master kept him in the house, that would be an indulgence on the part of the master. So if you also in the same way were to fall and sin, thereafter Christ will not cast you out. A mother also does not throw out a soiled, scabby and sick child. A son or daughter in the house often does what is not right and is not for that reason disinherited and cast out. Rather, the father says, "If you would be my son and daughter and I remain your father, then do this or that. This time I will be gracious to you."

That's also what the Lord Christ does.

Altb. V, 634–635: Sermons on the Gospel of St. John Chapters 6–8; 1531, cf. AE 23

"And whosoever cometh, I will not cast him out."
O patient love of Jesus, Which drives away our doubt,
Which, tho' we be unworthy Of love so great and free,
Invites us very sinners To come, dear Lord, to Thee! (*TLH* 276: 4)

Tuesday

Whoever comes to me, I will not cast him out. John 6:37

But this coming is not bodily, as if one would climb into heaven and over the clouds. This coming also doesn't happen by hands and feet, but rather the heart comes to God through faith. When you hear his Word and it pleases you so that you cling to it, your heart goes to him. There you eat this food. So it is a gift and grace of God for faith. It is not a human skill nor our work.

So he says here also, "What the Father does not draw comes not to me. No one can hear me in this way unless the Father gives it to him." This is said to the proud, clever, highly learned, wise people and sharp minds who talk a lot and know how to rule and be masters. Do not take it by your mind. You should not be so muddled that you think you would come to this by your reason. You will not master Christ. Your haughtiness and pride will be thrown away just at that point.

So the Jews also thought, "There Christ stands and preaches. We could do it much better than him." They thought they would come to the food and Bread of Life without his preaching. But Christ would then say, "I will bolt the door so that you will not come in, not that I would not gladly have you, but you seem to need to enter by another way. If you would desire to come to Christ and receive this drink and food, then your reason and wisdom must be left behind. But if you would come to me, then the Father must give you to me. And you would give me nothing. There is nothing in you or your skills. Therefore the Father should give you to me. You should not come to me with your great understanding and cleverness for you would be bringing yourself then and would need absolutely nothing from the Father. If you would want to teach God how he should rule the world, this would be the same wisdom of the miserable devil in the world and it belongs in the depths of hell. So if you bring yourself the Father doesn't need to bring you." But these are near-sighted and troublesome people who stand on their head and want to master God. When they have heard but one sermon and have looked over the New Testament but once, they think they know it all and want to lead themselves as if they needed no preacher. But when they breathe their last and their bones are laid out then you will learn well what this Word is, "Every one that the Father gives me. . .", and then we will know great thanksgiving and actually see if your beggar's head or skill has gotten you there and if you come to me because of what you are or if not.

In summary, he wants to say, "The Jews don't ask after it and they also don't respect me at all. And I also ask nothing of them. I would gladly give them the food and drink but they don't want it. So be it, I don't want you either. You are not hungry or thirsty, poor and unholy. So then remain learned, holy, safe, wise and clever people who want to master everything, you will discover it when everything is swept away. My little bunch, whom my Father gives me don't know how to help themselves and allow themselves to learn and bear it, to hear the Word, learn it, and are never satiated by the food, nor are they able to slake their thirst. With zeal these remain hungry and thirsty. They know that their righteousness and goodness, and sorrow are nothing. For the Holy Ghost works in them and they are directed by his power. They will be drawn to me and the Father also gives them the Holy Ghost so that the Word is mighty in them. For they do not stay in their own holiness and do not build on their own wisdom."

Altb. V, 630–631: Sermons on the Gospel of St. John Chapters 6–8; 1531, cf. AE 23

Thou, Lord, alone
This work hast done
By Thy free grace and favor.
All who believe
Will grace receive
Through Jesus Christ, our Savior.

And tho' the Foe
Would overthrow
Thy Word with grim endeavor,
All he hath wrought
Must come to naught,
Thy Word will stand forever. (*TLH* 266: 3)

Wednesday

Believe in God. Believe also in me. John 14:1

Now if you believe and depend upon God, then also believe on me. If your faith rightly expects everything good from God, then also expect the same of me. Whatever you seek and await from his comfort and help, await that also from me. I will surely not fail you, so little as God himself would. Until now I have helped you and done everything with you that you needed. I have revealed myself with Words and works so that you have been able to trust me and boldly rely on me. I have not yet let you down. I will do the same from now on. I will not leave you even if I do not remain with you bodily. For I have the same power and might with and from God so that I can and want to do it. Only do not doubt and be timid as if you had lost both God and me, but remain steadfast in the faith. Do not let your confidence sink or weaken, even if you see me suffer and die and you are left alone behind me.

As previously you have physically seen and experienced my assistance and protection, so also now believe even if you might not see it before your eyes. So that you will be my disciples and true Christians, you must not ever remain clinging to what you see and experience as outward comforts. Rather you must go forth and learn the attribute which is Christ's attribute; that you believe without doubt that I can and will help you. You cannot see or sense it. Rather you sense and see the opposite in the middle of suffering and all kinds of needs. At all times this remains your comfort: you have God and me even if everything rejects and forgets you.

Here you see clearly how Christ speaks of himself. He insists that he is the same God, the Almighty. He desires that we should believe on him as we believe on God. If he were not true God with the Father then this faith would be false and idolatry. For, in short, the human heart should not trust in or entrust itself except to the only God. Whatever you trust or depend on apart from that one is pure idolatry. So when a rich person trusts and builds on his wealth, he knows that he has a treasure behind him. Because of this he is confident and bold. Another trusts someone as a good friend or a gracious prince and thinks that when all else fails yet he would still have his powerful friend. That is called in Scripture *confidere*, trust. But in trusting a person or a prince you make an idol out of the person by such trust. You become bold and safe, as if you had God and everything and as if you needed nothing besides.

Now you see and learn what this and similar idolatry is. The two things, trust and God, belong together. What a heart trusts and depends on is definitely its God. Should it be a false god then there definitely is idolatry reigning in all the world. Christ calls it mammon except where the true, only, great God would be revealed, as St. Paul calls him in Titus 2. Not all idolatry is crass idolatry, though whoever practices it is proud and feels safe. He doesn't ask anything. That is because if there can be any boldness or boasting and safety, it must be established on a God. If now the God is true, then the trust is also true and on the other hand. . .

Now our trust and comfort, since we are Christians and not of the world, are also set upon God. Thus they stand. I am in the world. It is my enemy along with the devil. My own conscience bites and troubles me and makes all of me terrified and timid, so what should I think? I will think thus: "I see how a rich belly trusts and believes in his idol, and when someone gets too close to him, or would attack him, then he readily has comfort and pride because of this mammon. He surely hopes there is no need so long as he has it. Should I, then, not have more trust and confidence in my true eternal God?"

Altb. VII, 51: Sermons on the Gospel of St. John Chapters 14-16, 1537; cf. AE 24

Draw us to Thee That also we Thy heavenly bliss inherit
And ever dwell Where sin and hell No more can vex our spirit. (*TLH* 215: 4)

Thursday

In my Father's house there are many rooms. If it were not so I would have told you. I go to prepare a place for you. John 14:2

St. Augustine has expounded most precisely about the dwelling in heaven. Each will have his own prepared and provided for him where he will dwell. But that Christ would go back and prepare these, he explains so precisely, means nothing else than that we also are prepared. That is truly a fine sharp exposition and a good *Chatachresis*[3]. But we do not wish to travel so high as he traveled. We treat it rather in the most simple way, as the text itself delivers it. Just here he comforts his dear disciples and Christians in a three-fold manner. First, they will know that with his Father there are many dwellings for them. Here he compares two kinds of houses or dwellings with one another. On earth you will not have many houses or sure dwellings, for here the devil has his kingdom, his house and dwelling. He sits there as lord in his household. Therefore, since you strive against him and his kingdom he will not let you dwell and find housing here. For he is, as the Scriptures give him his title, a liar and a murderer. You also observe in the world that his administration is nothing but these two. He misleads people with false teaching and thoughts by which he seduces their souls. Then he also fills everything with death, war and all kinds of misfortune and heartache. It is as if he has nothing else to do but to kill physically and spiritually. That is his nature and office. We must observe this and nothing else while we are in his property. But Christ says, "Do not be afraid of this. It will not harm you if you cannot have a house and dwelling here and if the devil hunts you with his tyranny out of the world. Nevertheless, you will have rooms enough where you will dwell. If you will not be liked by citizens and neighbors or even by your guests, and you are isolated because of the Word, then so be it. You know that you will also afterward abide and have much."

This is the simplest meaning, as he says in another place: "Whoever loses houses, brother or sister, or father, or mother, or wife, or child, or fields for my sake and the sake of the gospel, he will receive a hundred-fold in this life and in the coming world eternal life." So also here the meaning is: If one drives you out of a house, then you will have many houses for it. If one takes one sort of thing from you, then you will receive back many times [what you lost]. It will not make you evil. They can not take so much from you that you will not have it back a hundred times as good and much better. If you have nothing here, then you will definitely receive it there richly. For he has so much supply that he can give each one a hundred dwellings for one. So here for comfort and refreshment you are told what the world can take from you. The dwellings of the

---

[3]Greek for 'condemnation', indicating that Augustine's writing delineated the true exposition and condemned 'sharply' false interpretations of the matter.

living are far more extensive than the dwellings of the dead. If they have stuck you here in jail and prison, or also chased you out, don't let that bother you. These are only houses that belong to the world. Look up to another for which you have waited which you will receive and possess there.

So this text is for the direct comfort of the Christian. They do not become disturbed if the world lays on them every plague and if they are not only robbed of this dwelling but the world takes everything that they have here; wealth, honor, life. Even if it casts them into misery, sadness, nakedness, shame, disgrace and death. But compare that to what they will win after this paultry loss. When they now are robbed of a dwelling, they will receive a much better dwelling for it, namely at the place that is called "in my Father's house." Where that is and remains, there will you and I also remain. As he says further on, you will have no temporal or human dwellings, but heavenly, divine dwellings and houses. In place of the filthy, perishable, unsafe, unstable dwelling that you and all the world must soon let go of, [you will receive] only beautiful, glorious, expansive, eternally safe and sure dwellings which cannot be taken from you. These will be preserved in peace before everyone.

What is accomplished, even if they take everything now and expell you completely from them? But stay on your guard against this trouble and misery. Be cheered by these same eternal dwellings, where you will no longer be under the devil's kingdom, nor separated from me, but will dwell eternally with me and the Father. Then they will nevermore rule or have pleasure. Since now they persecute you and here they have what is in the world, sitting safe and sure in their desires and they live in luxury, they will eventually not have any room or place here or there. It will be so terrible in eternity that they will not be settled and have peace for a split second.

Altb. VII, 54: Sermons on the Gospel of St. John Chapters 14-16, 1537; cf. AE 24

There rest and peace in endless measure Shall be ours through eternity;
No grief, no care, shall mar our pleasure, And untold bliss our lot shall be.
Oh, had we wings to hasten yonder— No more o'er earthly ills to ponder
To join the glad, triumphant band! Make haste, my soul, forget all sadness;
For peace awaits thee, joy and gladness, The perfect rest is nigh at hand.
(*TLH* 615: 4)

Friday

If it were not so I would have told you.
I go to prepare a place for you. John 14:2

That is, even if the dwelling were not yet prepared there, as you believe, I have the power to finish and prepare it for you. Even for that reason I am leaving you, that I prepare them. I will put them in order so that you do not worry or doubt where you will live. In summary, you will undoubtedly have dwellings. And if they were not already enough, I will make enough for you. If it were too little that you receive one hundred [dwellings in exchange] for one, I would create a hundred thousand for you and even more. There will be no deficiency or defect in any dwelling as your heart may fear.

He speaks to them here in a most simple way and at the same time in a child-like way according to their thoughts (as one must attract and allure the simple). By this he charms them so that they take comfort and retain these thoughts. What is it then? Now if one takes my house and home and this perishable dwelling and someone sticks me in a dark jail, I will have greater ones; more majestic, fairer, more expansive and safer dwellings and fortifications than my foes and all the world have now because my Lord Christ has promised. He has gone there to prepare them. They are sure by him. I will always find them ready.

But that is the art of those who believe, for it is certainly true that every Christian will confess the Word either by preaching or else before the judge. He is in an evil position on earth. Every hour is unsafe. In danger they drive him from wealth, wife and child while the others have everything in the fullest, living in comfort and good pleasures. But when we also look on to what is awaiting us and where we will end up, then we should also be joyous, and put up all the more with the poor miserable world. For what of it if they tread us under their feet and plague us by their best efforts and make us sorry. We still can lose nothing. The treasure still remains in any event. We will receive both. What we lose we receive again richly and also much more; we receive eternal divine wealth.

On the other hand they have the shells and the husks. They have already lost the kernel and the true treasure. They must also leave the husks here so that they are completely naked and miserable. Everything will be turned topsy turvy for them since they will have nothing, whereas now they have everything in abundance. And as we suffer a little misery, sadness and need now, then they have to suffer eternal misery, fear and sadness. I don't know how I could avenge the world more than by their being plagued with blindness, despising and persecuting the gospel. Can they be cursed any more terribly and horribly? We would much rather pray for them if they could be helped out of that misery.

Altb. VII, 54: Sermons on the Gospel of St. John Chapters 14-16, 1537; cf. AE 24

So I must hasten forward – Thank God, the end will come!
This land of passing shadows Is not my destined home.
The everlasting city, Jerusalem above,
This evermore abideth, The home of light and love. (*TLH* 586: 5)

Saturday

*Jesus said to him, "I am the Way, the Truth and the Life.
No one comes to the Father but through me." John 14:6*

So now learn to understand this beautiful passage. He says, "I
am the Way. . ." This is not about some kind of path or street that
you walk upon and traverse with your feet. Rather one walks and
traverses through the faith of the heart upon this path which only
holds onto the Lord Christ. For there are many kinds of going and
wanderings upon the earth. There are also many kinds of paths and
footbridges, first physical or natural ones connecting one place to
another, as also the cows and herds with everything that lives
traverse. They go and travel upon them to preserve their natural lives
and for their necessities. The Scriptures and God's Word teach
nothing concerning them.

There are other paths and walkways that also belong to this life,
which one calls temporal, or common ways and life where we walk
relative to each other outwardly before the world in a good honorable
walk, in morality and virtue to preserve this temporal authority,
peace, honor and chastity through which one comes to wealth and
honor, etc. The philosophers teach well about this from their reason.
The rulers place all kinds of ordinances and laws for this path. These
are all still the kind of paths and walkways that belong to and remain
in this perishable life.

But over all this is yet another going and traveling of which only
the Holy Scriptures and Christ speak just here. It tells how one
procedes from this life into another coming life. This is a much
different way and foot-bridge. So when one lies on his death bed and
his body and soul will now be severed, or even when he is
condemned and is driven out so he will be hanged, or beheaded or
drowned, a person in such a state also has a path before him that he
must take. He can never remain here. There is a path which he does
not see nor can he walk it with feet or travel it in a cart. And yet one
says, "He is departed, he has gone on. . .," but not bodily or in a
physical manner. For there the eyes and ears are closed, all sense has
fallen; hands and feet are bound. Then nothing is done by his works
and abilities. Therefore, there is also no path or foot bridge as we

would call it, nor is it conceived by us or foreseen. Yet, as said, just here all our reason ceases and nothing of how one goes from this life to another is known or understood. Much less is it known to whom or through what such a path will traverse.

Therefore, one must not think, hear or follow any human reason or teaching of the law, nor what man is able to do, as what will reveal the way. For even if reason should think a lot about it and try, even if it tried using all kinds of ways by which it would think to come up to heaven, yet it would all be vain and lost, as I have said. A Cartusian monk builds that kind of a path by which he would go up to heaven. "I will abandon the world since it is evil and unclean and will creep into a corner, fast every day and eat no meat to martyr my body. God will behold such a strong spiritual life and make me holy." That is also a path spiritually made and traveled. For he would not go on it with feet, but rather with the heart, which thinks that if he lives and acts this way, then he is on the true highway up to heaven. But a different monk or brother who would also live spiritually makes another path: "If I hold so many private masses and pray, go forth in woolen clothing and barefoot, then I go on the true street. As soon as I close my eyes, I will go from my mouth up to heaven."

These are all called ways, made from human efforts and opinions and based on our actions and works, that do not belong to anything further than to this life. Therefore, they are not ways to heaven but pure error and seduction when their intention is understood. For what will and can my hood, tonsure, barefooted journey and the like do to help my soul, when I make the jump through death into that eternal life? These are all fleshly things and the kind of works that unbelievers are also able to accomplish. And even if they do it with the best intentions and thoughts, it is still a most offensive thing by which everything is completely ruined. Otherwise you would need nothing at all. These Words would be complete lies, when he says that he is the Way, the Truth, etc.

Altb. VII, 59: Sermons on the Gospel of St. John Chapters 14-16, 1537; cf. AE 24

Grant that Thy Spirit's help
To me be always given
Lest I should fall again
And lose the way to heaven;
That He may give me strength
In mine infirmity
And e'er renew my heart
To serve Thee willingly.

Oh, Guide and lead me, Lord,
While here below I wander
That I may follow Thee
Till I shall see Thee yonder.
For if I led myself,
I soon would go astray;
But if Thou leadest me,
I keep the narrow way. (*TLH* 417: 5-6)

The Second Week after Epiphany

Sunday

I am the truth and the life. John 14:6

We want to treat these words in the simplest way and let go of the sharp *Speculationes*[4] of others. To speak of it in a coarse German way, this is all one matter. But here is another name telling what is accomplished when [that way or path] is walked over or traversed. For this all refers to the one Christ, and yet he has many kinds of names according to the many experiences of those who cling to him and finally come to the end with him. So first, as said, according to what our senses and understanding think, one goes this way to the Father and travels up to heaven only through cross and death. We see neither the path nor bridge, neither counsel nor help for the soul. Everyone is drowned and frightened before going over and no one knows how he will proceed to get over it since he has a wide grave or deep water before him that he must cross, and yet he sees no path and no bridge. Just as the children of Israel were frightened at the Red Sea before the wild wide flood when they heard that they could cross nowhere else, and could not go back, or stay where they were in the hands of their enemies. They might have said, "Should that be called a way out of death and slavery? We are closed in on every side with great mountains and before us by only waves and water. Yes, if we were fish or birds, we could fly over or swim through it." Yet there had to be a way because of God's Word. The sea separated and they went in its midst on dry land.

Here also there is nothing to see or feel that should be the way and path into eternal life when a person feels nothing but the fear of death and terror. But against this stands Christ with his Word, where he says, "I am the Way. . ." By this he makes a "yes" out of "no" and a way out of ruin; a way and bridge. A person should walk upon him lively and trusting and through him he will come through it just as all of them went unhindered and with dry feet physically through the sea. They journeyed on God's Word where otherwise there was no path. That is one [important aspect of this Word].

The other, now, is that when one comes on the Way and has plunged in and begun to believe, then it is thereafter necessary that one be sure of the matter and remain steadfast and not let himself be

---

[4]Latin for speculation or pious guess.

drawn back or frightened away from it. For here, even more, the devil has directed his cunning and tricks to mislead this kind of people and even does that with the Words of Scripture and under the name of Christ. So all the sectarian spirits and heretics come with their sheep's clothing, even using the same Word, wisdom and customs as if they were true teachers of the Word. They praise nothing but the glory of Christ and faith in Christ and by this they mislead the people who want to cling to Christ and would gladly walk the true Way.

It is like someone walking on the highway to the right gate, but he comes to a place where two or three ways intersect and some rascal comes to him who persuades him to go the wrong way. Therefore, this passage belongs to what is called *probatio et perseverantia fidei*, a testing, so that one becomes completely sure and remains on the original way.

That, I think, is just here called, most simply, the other part, *veritas*, that is, the Truth. Christ is not only the beginning of the Way, but he is the true sure way, and remains the way to the very end. Upon him one must finally remain and not let wrong ways mislead him so that we think there is something to seek other than Christ that should also help us to salvation. This is what those do who first acknowledge Christ by faith and then fall away from him again through works-righteousness, as was done to this time under the papacy. Or some give up and turn around and look back as sticks and stones come against us when the devil sends so many kinds of contrary teaching, sects and divisions, troubling evil examples, also persecution, trial and danger that we begin to doubt the Way or become weary and drowned.

Altb. VII, 63: Sermons on the Gospel of St. John Chapters 14-16, 1537; cf. AE 24

But Christ, the second Adam, came To bear our sin and woe and shame,
To be our Life, our Light, our Way, Our only Hope, our only stay. (*TLH* 369: 4)

Monday

No one comes to the Father, but by me. John 14:6

He takes the three parts in one pile and takes hold of everything at once. He explains with clear, unflowery words, what he means and for what purpose he has called himself the "Way, Truth and Life." Namely, that one should come to the Father. In summary, "it must only be done by me, beginning, middle and end." But what is "coming to" the Father? Nothing but, as is now often said, coming out of death to life, out of sins and damnation to guiltlessness and goodness, out of trouble and heartache to eternal joy and salvation. "No one," he says, "can be brought before him in any other way but through me." That is said clearly and definitively enough. This completely shuts out and lays aside every doctrine of the service of works and our own righteousness, and harshly negates and denies every other comfort and trust through which one would suppose that they could come up to heaven. For it says curtly, "No one, no one comes to the Father, but by me. There is no other boat or passage."

So we say that a person receives such things only through faith which clings to Christ. Neither our work, nor that of all people and the saints will have that glory and praise. That doesn't mean that one should not do good works, but that to receive grace before God and eternal life, one must first have only this Christ through faith. After and next to him [Christ] he [the believer] also does good works and makes his love known. But let this difference be rightly maintained [between Christ's good works and ours]. One should not account to our life and works the power and value to bring us up to the Father. Rather they are judged as that which praises God here on earth for the betterment of the neighbor and as helpful to all people.

But when it comes to receiving life before God, then I must have another treasure in my heart so that I could definitely conclude: "When I lose everything and I must pass on, yet I have the treasure which remains there forever, and which cannot be taken away or fail me. This is not mine or a person's work or reward. Rather he himself is called the Way, the Truth and the Life and the only one through whom one can come to the Father. I will stay with him and live and die to him. So I want to neither hear nor know of all the works teachings of all the monks and fanatics. These are all soundly condemned here. It is sure that what a person trusts to bring him up to heaven outside of Christ, is definitely not the way up to heaven. Rather it is pure death and grave; not the truth, but pure falsehood and lies; not the life, but the devil and death.

And what could be said that is a greater dishonor, blasphemy and denial of the Lord Christ and his Word than that one would lay such power and praise for our works against such a clear passage, and rob and darken Christ's honor? Friend, it is not brought about by our own works that we receive such great things. Why would you still brag of your work or abilities when you will go through a wide wild sea, between some great swells and waves on both sides, where you will see nothing but sure death before you and will know no counsel or help to pull back from it, even if you should be martyred to death with your works. We are just as the people of Israel who had to doubt without any human wisdom, help and counsel, and had no way to pull back if they would not cling to God's Word and had not held to faith. They would have had to walk, jump and dance with their feet a long time before they would be able to part the waters and go through it if the Word and their faith in it had not been there.

Much less is the path or gangway for the journey by which you should overcome and safely come through completed by works and our powers. For this journey is much more difficult and dangerous than someone bodily going through the Red Sea when sins's load, God's wrath, eternal death and the devil and all of hell fall upon our neck and overwhelm us. It takes more than red shoes can accomplish at the dance. Therefore, faith must rule and it alone does everything.

But thereafter, if you have such faith, good works will also follow as that which must flow and follow from faith. For they will be good and God-pleasing and so they cannot and will not be done if faith is not there first. Just as with the Children of Israel, even if they did go through the Red Sea on foot, yet previously faith must have been in their hearts, which would carry their feet and upon which they could go through the sea. Without it they never could have gone through, even if they beat the water with their feet forever. (Altb. VII, 66)

Altb. VII, 66: Sermons on the Gospel of St. John Chapters 14-16, 1537; cf. AE 24

In faith, Lord, let me serve Thee;
Tho' persecution, grief, and pain
Should seek to overwhelm me,
Let me a steadfast trust retain;
And then at my departure
Take Thou me home to Thee
And let me there inherit
All Thou hast promised me.
In life and death, Lord, keep me
Until Thy heav'n I gain,
Where I by Thy great mercy
The end of faith attain. (*TLH* 381: 3)

Tuesday

Philip, whoever sees me sees the Father. John 14:9

Do you hear what I say? "Whoever sees me sees the Father, himself, and you don't believe that I am in the Father and the Father in me. For the Words that I say are not my thoughts, but the Father's Words." These are good friendly Words, but also earnest Words of the Lord. For he will not suffer people gaping in vain and unsurely here and there and turning from him in a fickle way. He would have us bound completely to him and his Word, that we seek God nowhere but in him.

In previous times a good hermit, St. Anthony, said this of the young inexperienced saints, when they wanted to be clever and establish their thoughts and everything on God's hidden counsel. He exhorted his brothers: If they wanted to crawl up to heaven and look around, they should just as soon leave him behind. He would not go with them. They were people who must crash down upon their heads. That is well said against such fickle spirits who like to speculate about high matters. They want to bore a hole through to heaven and see everything that God is and does. In the meantime they let go of Christ as if they had no need of what is his.

So guard yourself against such thoughts that proceed without Words and that separate and rip Christ away from God. For he has not commanded you that you should so crudely go off and gape at what he does in heaven with the angels. He rather calls out his command, "This is my beloved Son in whom I am well pleased, listen to him." There I come down to you so that you see, hear and can grasp me. Here and to no one else all who belong to me and would gladly be free of sins and be saved, will go and find me. There you will quickly find him and conclude, "God himself says that. I will follow him. I will hear no other Word or preaching and take note of and learn nothing else about God." "For in this person," says St. Paul, "dwells truly the whole Godhead and outside of him there is no God that I could go to or come to even though he is everywhere." Now wherever one hears this man's Word, or sees his works he definitely hears and sees God's Word and work there.

Now when Christ further gives his apostles his command to proclaim and to perform his Word and work, there one also sees and hears Christ himself and also God, the Father. For they speak and compel no other Word but what they have received from his [Christ's] mouth and only point to him. In the same way this follows further from the apostles after them to us through true bishops, pastors and preachers, who have received it from the apostles. So all preachers in Christianity must proceed from and show this one Christ, so that their Word and work, as they act in the office of Christianity (God grant, whether in their person they are good or evil), are the Word and work of the Lord Christ. They all teach this: You should not behold me or follow me, but rather only the Lord Christ, and what he said or revealed through me. For this is not mine, but Christ's Word. The Baptism and Sacrament which I give out are not mine, but his Baptism and Sacrament. This office that I perform is not mine but the Office of Christ. But since it is Christ's Word and Baptism, then it is also the Father's Word and Baptism, for he says, "What I say and do, I do not do on my own, but the Father, who dwells in me."

Altb. VII, 72: Sermons on the Gospel of St. John Chapters 14-16, 1537; cf. AE 24

I know my faith is founded
On Jesus Christ, my God and Lord;
And this my faith confessing,
Unmoved I stand upon His Word.
Man's reason cannot fathom
The truth of God profound;

Who trusts her subtle wisdom
Relies on shifting ground.
God's Word is all sufficient,
It makes divinely sure,
And trusting in its wisdom,
My faith shall rest secure. (*TLH* 381: 1)

Wednesday

Do you not believe that I am in the Father and the Father in me? The Words which I speak to you I do not speak from myself. But the Father, who dwells in me, he does the works. John 14:10

Therefore, where you hear the gospel being rightly taught, or you see a person being baptized, the Sacrament being handed out or received, or one being absolved there you can boldly say, "Today I have seen God's Word and work, yes, heard God himself and seen his preaching and Baptism. The tongue, voice, hands, etc., are of men, but the Word and office are actually the divine majesty itself." So it should also be observed and believed as if one heard God's voice ringing from heaven above, or saw his hands baptizing or giving out the Sacrament so that one make no separation or distinction between God and his Word or office given us through Christ, or seek God or think about him in any other way.

When we come up to heaven then we will see him otherwise without means and cover, but here on earth you will not see him or receive him with your senses or thoughts, but rather, as St. Paul says, we see him in a dark Word or a veiled image, namely in the Word and Sacraments. It is just as [if they were] his mask or clothing under which he is hidden. But he is present there without a doubt so that he himself does wonders, preaches, gives the Sacrament, comforts, strengthens and helps. And thus we see him, as one sees the sun behind the clouds. For now we could not stand to see the bright sight and glow of that majesty. So he must clothe and veil himself in that way, as behind thick clouds. So it is sure, that whoever wants to see and cling to both the Father and Christ, after he is revealed and sits in his majesty, he grasps him through the Word and the works that he does in Christianity through the preaching office and other stations.

Therefore, we should not be lacking understanding about his body that we let God, Christ, and his Word be divided and partitioned, and dispute about God as the heathen, Turks, Sophists or the others do concerning his naked majesty. In that we would depart from the way that he speaks and acts towards us here on earth through preachers, fathers and mothers, etc.; and meanwhile travel into the clouds and concern yourself with what God himself does or thinks. That is what the devil tells you to ask and think. It is no good spirit. But if you would rightly know how it is between you and God, and whether your way pleases him, then pay attention to this Word, so that it quickly tells you, "Whoever sees or hears me, also sees and hears the Father." So, if that pleases your heart, only look at what Christ preaches and does towards you through his christianity, as through your preacher, father, mother and other good people. Listen to that from your heart and keep clinging to that so that you are already sure of the matter. You should and must not doubt about it. For what these say to you God, himself, is actually saying to you.

But if you want to go on as a wicked person and do not want to pay attention to this, and through your own head inquire and establish how you are with God in heaven, then you are lost. What then happens to you is right because you will not receive it, since you call God a liar, and seek him in another way. For he is there so that he tells and shows you these will give you assurance of his attitude towards you and he has so ordered every office and station in life in Christianity so that the whole world is full of God's work. You let all of that be put off as if it were nothing and you think, "God is up in heaven behind the angels and has other things to do; how could a preacher, father or mother, help me? If I could only hear and see him myself. . ." That is called separating and dividing God and his work from each other, Christ and his Word, which one should most solidly hold and bind together.

Therefore, every one should guard himself against ever again inquiring after God with his own senses and thoughts, but rather learn only to fasten and cling to his Word and act and decide only on that basis so that he will not fail. Now don't pay attention to anything else but believe that I, for Christ's sake, forgive you all your sins and am gracious and upon this you are baptized. Be obedient to your mother and father and do what your office and station in life ask. Then you have everything including God. "Oh," you say, "is that called seeing and hearing God? I thought he was up there in heaven and that I had to have some special revelation from him." No, not so. Rather, if you want to meet him then first see him in the Word under his mask so that hereafter you will see him in his majesty. For he will not do anything special for you outside and against his command, which he has given in his Word.

Altb. VII, 73: Sermons on the Gospel of St. John Chapters 14-16, 1537; cf. AE 24

Now I have found the firm foundation Which holds mine anchor ever sure;
'Twas laid before the world's creation In Christ my Savior's wounds secure;
Foundation which unmoved shall stay When heav'n and earth shall pass away. (*TLH* 385: 1)

Thursday

Be diligent to present yourself to God as a rightly fashioned, guiltless worker, rightly dividing the Word of Truth. 2 Timothy 2:15

If I did not know that I should divide the law and gospel, then there would be no need for me to say, "Has God then given only one kind of Word, namely, the law? Hasn't he also commanded the preaching of the gospel of grace and the forgiveness of sins?" Yes, says the conscience, if there is not faith in the promise, there the law soon presses hard, "This and that is commanded you, and you have not done it, so you must pay." In that kind of battle and the fear of death it is high time and a necessity that faith exhorts and breaks forth with all power, and treads the law out of sight and speaks comfort, "O, dear law, are you the only Word of God? Is the gospel not also the Word of God? Has the promise now ended? Has God's mercy stopped? Or are the two, law and gospel, or reward and grace, now mixed and cooked together so that they are now one thing?" We would not have a God who can give nothing more than the law, or who knows nothing more. So we also do not want to have the law mixed with the gospel. Therefore, let this division go freely, unopposed and unhindered; so that if you are pressed by duty and justice, the gospel informs us of pure grace and gift.

Therefore, when the law condemns me: "I have done this or that; I am unrighteous and a sinner, written up in God's book of debts," then I must acknowledge that it is all true. But what is said after this: "Therefore you are accursed," I must not submit to, but you must defend me with strong faith and say, "According to the law, which tells me my guilt, I am surely a poor, damned sinner, but I appeal from the law to the gospel. For God has given yet another Word over the law, that is called the gospel. This bestows on us his grace, forgiveness of sins, eternal righteousness and life. It also declares me free from your terror and damnation and comforts me. For all guilt is repaid through the Son of God, Jesus Christ, himself." Therefore, there is a great need that one know to use and handle both Words rightly and readily so that they do not become mixed up with one another.

So God has given these two sorts of Words, law and gospel, one as much as the other and each with its purpose: The law, that demands complete righteousness from every person; the gospel, that those from whom the law required righteousness and do not have it (that is all people), are given it by grace. Now whoever has not fulfilled the law, laying destroyed in sins and death, but turns from the law to the gospel, believes the preaching of Christ, that he is truly the Lamb of God who bears the sins of the world, satisfies his heavenly Father, and gives eternal righteousness, life and salvation to all who believe it by pure grace. He holds only to this preaching, calls on Christ, asks for grace and the forgiveness of sins, firmly believes (for only though faith will this great gift be held), so he has it as he believes.

Now this is the true differentiation. The whole power lies in rightly dividing the two. It is easy in preaching, or dividing the Words, but to use it and bring it into practice is a high art and hard to do. The papists and fanatics know nothing of it. I also see in me and others who know best how to speak how difficult this differentiating is. The skill is common. It is soon told how the law is another Word and doctrine than the gospel, but *practice* to divide it and the art of applying it is an effort and work.

Erl. 19, 241–243: Sermon on the Differentiation of Law & Gospel; Gal. 3:23–24, 1532

As by one man all mankind fell And, born in sin, was doomed to hell,
So by one Man, who took our place, We all received the gift of grace. (*TLH* 369: 5)

Friday

Put on the armor of God that you can stand against the cunning attack of the devil. Ephesians 6:11

As he has said that we should be strong and have such power with us to slay the foe, he now will explain and clarify how, and by what means, we must do the same. In other words, he speaks of our armor and defense. He tells us to diligently put on our armor as warriors who are armed for war and shall stand to make defense. He does not show the kind of armor that one uses here on earth to protect the body, but what is called "God's armor." That will be a unique armor. Where will we get it, or where is the artisan who will craft such armor? He will hereafter tell what it is and list what belongs to it.

But here he says in general that the armor must not be from a person, but from God, himself. For here on earth one could not find an artisan who could craft such armor which could serve against the devil. For here no human strength, power, or wisdom and understanding can withstand this foe. He can pulverize all of these to ashes when he blows with his desolations. So since they are different battles (he wants to say) and you oppose different foes, then you must also have another armor than the world has or can make.

But he also calls it God's armor in order to show what kind of matter it is over which we must battle. Namely, it is God's own war and we are his soldiers, as those who fight for him and his interests. Therefore, we must also use his armor, by which he battles. He would say, "You have a Lord of whom the devil is a foe and you stand behind his crown and deity. Therefore, if you will have him as Lord and remain with him and will be a partaker in his wealth, then you must also have a foe against you and stand against him in battle and defence." For whoever wants to be under a Lord must also walk under his banner and have his enemies as enemy. Now since the devil is God's foe and he wants to destroy his kingdom, then do not think that you will always be safe before him, but rather be prepared for battle, even with the armor by which he himself will battle through Christianity.

So he would encourage us by this. If in the world we must stand in war and strife our whole life, and suffer so that everything rages and storms against us, then we know that such things are not for our sakes, but rather it is done because of God and our war is not ours, but God's own. We stand there in his service and we have an even surer comfort that he will not forsake us. But he truly stands with us and helps so that we do not work alone. Rather, he will be mightily victorious through us.

Erl. 19, 258-260: Sermon on the Christian's Armor & Weapons, Eph. 6:10, 1532

Stand, then, in His great might,
With all His strength endued;
But take, to arm you for the fight,
The panoply of God,

That, having all things done
And all your conflicts past,
Ye may o'ercome through Christ alone
And stand entire at last. (*TLH* 450: 3–4)

Saturday

Dear brothers, I exhort you as strangers and pilgrims, put away from you fleshly desires that war against the soul. 1 Peter 2:12

He calls us strangers and pilgrims to show what our life is on earth and how we should regard it. A stranger is what an alien or foreigner is called who is not a citizen by origin and birth in the place where he lives. He has his origin somewhere else. In brief, one is called a stranger who is not a native as the children of Israel were strangers and not native in Egypt, where they had come from the land of Canaan because of the famine. So Moses reproaches them and says in Exodus 22:21, Leviticus 19:34, "You were strangers in Egypt." A pilgrim is a wanderer who travels through a land and is not in his city, nor in the place where he belongs. But he only lodges in a strange place as one passing through. He is not only an alien, a stranger, he is also a guest and has nothing of his own. Nor does he desire to think [much] about the place but only to pass through.

As the children of Israel were pilgrims in the wilderness, so the Christian is a stranger and pilgrim in this world, 1 Peter 2:11 and Hebrews 11:13. They are strangers because according to their fleshly birth they come from God into this world, which was created out of nothing. They do not remain in this world, but must leave this world, as do all people on earth. As Job says in 1:21, "I have come naked from my mother's body, and naked I will go forth again." They are pilgrims because they, according to their spiritual birth, where they are born again by the washing of water in the Word by the Holy Ghost, are as guests upon the earth. Their life is only a pilgrimage as the Patriarch Jacob calls it in Genesis 47:9.

So now St. Peter wants to show that we should not consider this life but as a stranger and pilgrim considers the country in which he is an alien and guest. A stranger cannot say, "Here is my homeland," for he is not a native. A pilgrim does not consider staying in the country where he sojourns and in the lodging where he stays overnight, but rather his heart and thoughts remain elsewhere. In the lodge he only takes his meal and bed and always travels on to the place where he is at home. "So also are you Christians," he says, "only strangers and guests in this world. You belong to another country and kingdom where you have an eternal lodging and an abiding city."

So also present yourself as strangers and guests in this foreign country and guest house, out of which you take nothing more than eat, drink, clothing, shoes and what you need in this overnight lodge. Only consider what lies ahead in your homeland where you are a citizen.

We will note this passage well so that we rightly confess our Lord Jesus Christ, learning rightly to become acquainted with him and his gospel and Holy Baptism. Not that we build ourselves an eternal life here in this world, pursuing and clinging to it as if it were our chief treasure and the kingdom of heaven, as if we wanted to have the Lord Christ, his gospel and Baptism in order to become rich and mighty in this life. Rather, while we must live on this earth so long as God desires, that we eat, drink, marry, plant, build, have house and home and use what God provides as strangers and guests in a foreign country and in a guest house. Remember that all of that will be left. Rather take your staff out of the strange land and out of the evil unsafe guest house into the true homeland where only safety, peace, quiet and joy will be forever. So we are accustomed to life in heaven and the kingdom of God by the Lord Christ, by the gospel and Baptism.

Erl. 19, 333–335: Sermon on our Blessed Hope, Titus 2:13, 1531

Therefore I murmur not, Heav'n is my home;
Whate'er my earthly lot, Heav'n is my home;
And I shall surely stand There at my Lord's right hand.
Heav'n is my fatherland, Heav'n is my home. (*TLH* 660: 4)

The Third Week after Epiphany

Sunday

I will not die, but live, and proclaim the work of the Lord. Psalm 118:17

This verse embraces the two parts previously mentioned in verses six and seven, comfort and help, by which God benefits the good and righteous. For here you see how the right hand of God comforts the heart. In the middle of death, he [the psalmist] is comforted so mightily that he can say, "And even if I die, then nevertheless I will not die. Even if I suffer, yet I am not harmed by it. Even if I fall, I still will not be laid under. Even if I am shamed, I do not remain in shame." That is the comfort. Further he says of the help, "Rather I will live." Is it not a wonderful help that the dying one lives, the suffering one is happy, the fallen arise, the shamed are in glory? So Christ also says in John 11, "Whoever believes in me does not die, and even if he should die, he yet will live." St. Paul also speaks in this way in 2 Corinthians 4, "There is trouble for us but we are not defeated. We suffer, but we are not overcome. We are laid low, but we are not ruined. . ." These are all words which no human heart understands.

Note here that this comfort and help is eternal life, which is the true eternal comfort of God. The whole psalm also presents this. Since he separates the good bunch from the other three, and yet gives these same three everything that is in this life on earth, namely: worldly rule, spiritual administration, and all created wealth, necessities and their use, then of necessity there must be another life for the sake of the little pious heap's comfort, namely, the eternal one. For the three begrudge and do not allow them their comfort in this life. Therefore, this comfort must be the eternal comfort and this help eternal. And how can it be otherwise, for the psalmist himself sings that his boast is of the Lord himself above and outside all the wealth of princes and people who have the other kind? For the Lord is surely an eternal wealth. So every one can also count it the same way. When the heart experiences a gracious God, forgiveness of sins must be there. If the sins are taken away, then death is also taken away and there must be the comfort and confidence of eternal righteousness and of eternal life, which cannot fail.

Therefore, let us note in this verse a masterpiece. How mightily he punches death in the eye and will know nothing of death or sins. He portrays life as being unshakable and will know nothing but life.

Whoever does not see death lives eternally, as Jesus says in John 8, "Whoever keeps my Word will never see death." So he submerges himself completely in life so that death is gobbled up in life and completely disappears. So he clings to the right hand of God with solid faith.

All saints have sung this verse and must sing it to him without ceasing unto the end. But we have especially seen this in the dear martyrs who die before the world. Their heart speaks with firm faith: "Yet will I not die, but live. . . ."

Erl. 41, 63–65: The Good Confession of Psalm 118, 1530

All depends on our possessing
God's abundant grace and blessing,
Tho' all earthly wealth depart.
He who trusts with faith unshaken
In his God is not forsaken
And e'er keeps a dauntless heart.

Many spend their lives in fretting
Over trifles and in getting
Things that have no solid ground.
I shall strive to win a treasure
That will bring me lasting pleasure
And that now is seldom found.

If on earth my days He lengthen,
He my weary soul will strengthen;
All my trust in Him I place.
Earthly wealth is not abiding,
Like a stream away is gliding;
Safe I anchor in His grace. (*TLH* 425: 1,3,6)

Monday

Open to me the doors of righteousness that I may enter and thank the Lord. Psalm 118:19

This verse is a passionate prayer for the kingdom of Christ and the gospel and it desires the end of the heavy burden of the law of Moses, of which Peter says in Acts 15, "which neither we nor our fathers were able to bear." But he calls the New Testament a door of righteousness after the Hebrew manner [of speaking], where one calls townhalls, schools, synagogues, courthouses and such public places "doors," where one administers public affairs of the congregation, as in Proverbs 31, "Your man is honorable when he sits in the door under the counselors in the land." This same usage is found all over the place in the Old Testament. Therefore, the doors of righteousness are nothing else than the churchly acts or bishoprics in which one publicly carries out the offices of Christianity, as preaching, praising God, thanksgiving, singing, Baptism, the administration and reception of Holy Communion, chastising, comforting, praying and what belongs to salvation. For there are seated the counselors of the spiritual kingdom of Christ, that is, pastor, preacher, bishop, teacher and others entrusted with soul care [*Seelsorger*].

But he calls them doors of righteousness contrary to the Old Testament. For in the New Testament is only the teaching of forgiveness of sins, of grace, of faith, which make one righteous and holy, and absolutely nothing about works of the law or of one's own works. But the law, in his gates and schools, compels only works and makes sinners, increases sins and wrath, as St. Paul says to the Romans and Galatians. It cannot help for righteousness. It might well be called the gate of sin or unrighteousness. For law is not grace. But now grace alone can make one right. It is impossible that the law should make one right, but rather must make sinners and administer wrath. Romans 4. For this reason St. Paul also in 2 Corinthians 3 can boldly call the law of Moses an office of death, and in Galatians 2 an office of sins; and in 1 Corinthians 15 he says, "The law is the power of sins and sins are death's sting." So also now our works-teachers (that the world is full of), almost all the bishops and spiritual estate, belong in the Old Testament and have also again closed the gates of righteousness and instead opened the gates of sin. And yet there is no one so good as those who encumber and confuse the conscience with purely human laws, with false, unnecessary, made-up sins, as Christ and his apostles warned would happen. But yet still there are a few gates of righteousness.

Erl. 41, 69–71: The Good Confession of Psalm 118, 1530

The pastors of Thy fold With grace and power endue
That, faithful, pure, and bold, They may be pastors true.
O Lord, stretch forth Thy mighty hand And guard and bless our Fatherland. (*TLH* 580: 6)

Tuesday

I thank you, that you have humbled and helped me. Psalm 118:21

These are the offerings and services of God that in the New Testament, in the gate of the Lord, will be used by the righteous and the Christians. Namely, they thank and praise God with preaching, doctrine, singing and confessing. The same offerings are two: one is our humility, of which David says in Psalm 51, "The sacrifices of God are a broken spirit, and broken and a contrite heart, O Lord, you will not despise." That is a great, extensive, long, daily, and eternal offering, when God chastises us with his Word in all our works and lets our holiness, wisdom, power be nothing, so that we must be guilty sinners before him, as Romans [says] in strongest terms. Such are driven back by the Word with a frightened conscience and are deeply plagued by all kinds of troubles. For we become cooked and done according to the old sinful Adam, whose life will be over in the end, until our pride, comfort and confidence in our work and wisdom are completely dead. See, whoever can suffer, endure and hold fast and yet persist in this, can also praise and thank God for it, as does the one who sings this verse heartily thinks and sees it as good, "I thank you, that you have humbled me." He doesn't say, "The devil has humbled me, but rather, you, you, it is your gracious will for my good. Without your will the devil would just as well not bother with it."

The other offering is when God also again comforts and helps us at that point so that the spirit and the new man increases as much as the flesh and the old man decreases. He gives us even more and more greater and richer gifts. He always helps us overcome and prevail so that we are joyous before him and in him; as he says in Psalm 50, "Call upon me in the time of trouble and I will help you so you will praise me. Offer a thank offering to God, and pay your vows." Whoever does that sings this verse: "I thank you, that you are my salvation, helper and savior." This is also an eternal, great and daily offering by the righteous in the gate of the Lord. With this he disposes of and lifts away all the offerings of the Old Testament which were pictures and figures of this thank offering and which could be made by both the good and the evil. But this thank offering can be performed by no one but only the pious, the righteous, the Christian. You also see this easily in experience, how the Jews in the apostles' time were enraged just as now our works-saints are, that one would cast away their works and wisdom. They did not want to be humbled. They blasphemed instead of thanking. They chided, hunted, murdered [the apostles] and thought these same fantasies of theirs were the most acceptable offerings to God. John 16.

So now this verse is joyous and sings with a full voice, "Are you not a wonderful, dear God, who reigns over us so wonderfully and kindly? You lift us up when you bring us down. You make us upright when you make us sinners. You bring us up to heaven when you cast us into hell. You give us victory when you let us be struck down. You make us lively when you let us perish. You make us joyous when you let us wail. You make us sing as you let us cry. You make us strong when we suffer. You make us wise when you make us a fool. You make us rich when you give us poverty. You make us as lords when you let us serve." And countless wonders of the same sort are all embraced in this verse and will be praised in Christianity in one heap with these short words: "I thank you that

94

you have humbled me, but also you help me again."

Erl. 41, 74–76: The Good Confession of Psalm 118, 1530

Increase my faith, dear Savior,
For Satan seeks by night and day
To rob me of this treasure
And take my hope of bliss away.
But, Lord, with Thee beside me,
I shall be undismayed;

And led by Thy good Spirit,
I shall be unafraid.
Abide with me, O Savior,
A firmer faith bestow;
Then I shall bid defiance
To every evil foe. (*TLH* 381: 2)

Wednesday

The stone which the builders rejected has become the cornerstone. Psalm 118:22

Now Christ comes here to the head of holy Christianity and presents this as an example for us. For as much and more than all the saints, he also is humbled and raised up. So we should not think it strange or a wonder if we also suffer trials and troubles. Haven't those who belong to their father, Beelzebub, become many more than those belonging to your household? A servant is not better than his lord. But he quickly embraces the suffering and resurrected Christ in this verse. For in that he is rejected, he shows his suffering, death, disgrace and scorn under which Christ was placed. In that he becomes the cornerstone, he shows his resurrection, life and eternal Lordship. He compares it with buildings. So when some stone is not used in a wall because it doesn't match the other stones, but rather changes the whole pattern, it is an unworthy, useless stone. One must throw it away. But another alien master builder could come and know how to use the same stone very well. He might say, "Wait, you great fool. You are a master builder and you don't want that stone? It is good to me. I will not use it to fill the gap nor to chip a filler stone off it. It is also not so poor a stone to be used as a piece of the work. Rather, it will be a cornerstone which does not support one, but two walls. It will do more than any other stone and more than all the stones in the whole building."

So Christ would never fit with the manner and holiness of the pharisees, or with the whole world. They could not stand him. He ruined their walls, punished and chided their good, outwardly holy manner. Then they were angry, cursed and rejected him, the true master builder. From this he made a cornerstone to found the whole of Christianity upon, assembled both from Jews and Gentiles. So he does evermore. For the stone is rejected, is declared rejected and remains rejected. But yet he is no less and remains for the righteous and believers costly, noble and worthy. This is not built upon our own human work, nor upon the power of princes, but upon this stone.

But note who they are that reject this stone. They are not terrible people, but rather the very best, namely, the holiest, the cleverest, the most learned. The greatest, the most noble must reject this stone. For the poor miserable sinners who have become troubled, erring, despised, poor and unlearned are glad and heartily desire to have him.

Erl. 41, 76–78: The Good Confession of Psalm 118, 1530

Lord Jesus Christ, Thy pow'r make known, For Thou art Lord of lords alone;
Defend Thy Christendom that we May evermore sing praise to Thee. (*TLH* 261: 2)

Thursday

That is done by the Lord, and is a wonder before our eyes.
Psalm 118:23

"The Lord himself," he says, "is this strange master builder, who makes all worldly wisdom and builders as fools, choosing and exalting what they throw away." St. Paul also says in 1 Corinthians 1, "What is foolish before the world, God has chosen so that he makes the wise dishonored." And Habakkuk 1, "Look among the heathen and be amazed, for I will do a work in your time that you will not believe even if someone would tell it." As this verse says, God always does works that no godless person believes and they must be made fools, especially here. He makes this discarded stone an unsurpassable cornerstone. This is such a great, strange work that not only every heathen, with all their wisdom and reason, was made foolish by it, but also his own people (the Jews) stumbled and were toppled. It has completely rolled them to the ground. They have lost both kingdom and priesthood and also heaven and earth. They have no wondrous signs no matter how many and tangible they once were. But even through such enduring punishment and plagues, they cannot be brought back again.

Why in these days also among us Christians is there now such strife, so many heretics and sects? What makes the papacy so enraged, wanton, blind, wild and foolish now that they cannot suffer the teaching that faith without works makes one good, saved, alive and free of sins, death and the devil? Though they acknowledge with their mouth that Christ is this rejected and elevated cornerstone, yet they will not let it be put into practice. By their practice they put such things away from them. Is it a wonder that fleshly people and false hypocrites kick against such things? Yet here David says that it is also a wonder before our own eyes. For although the dear saints and Christians are not troubled by it, they also have enough to learn of it their whole lives so they believe it. What others experience [as opposed to what Christ teaches] is what they know best, but nevertheless they consider themselves Christians. But I know well how sour and hard it has become for me and will yet daily be, that I cling to and hold to this cornerstone. People want to call me "Lutheran." But they do me an utter injustice, for am I just a poor weak Lutheran? God strengthen me!

Yes, these Words: Christ is our salvation, he is our righteousness, our works do not help us from sins and death, the one rejected cornerstone must do it, etc., are soon learned and said; and how fine and well I can also show and compel them in my little books. But when I go out for a walk so that I am bitten by the devil, sins, death, need and the world, then there is no help, comfort and advice there without the one cornerstone. There I quickly find what I can do and what kind of a skill it is to believe on Christ. Then I quickly see what David means by these words: "It is a wonder before our eyes." Yes, it immediately seems wondrous to us and completely aggravating and nothing else. But my papists sing them this way, "And it is trifling and trivial before our eyes." What faith, faith! They say: "do you think that we are heathen or Jews?" No one can speak this verse so quickly but in that very instance when they have fallen out of faith with him. Yes, unfortunately, being all too pure, they will allow nothing to be given them from us or anyone.

Erl. 41, 79–81: The Good Confession of Psalm 118, 1530

O Lord, look down from heav'n, behold And let Thy pity waken;
How few are we within Thy fold, Thy saints by men forsaken!
True faith seems quenched on ev'ry hand, Men suffer not Thy Word to stand;
Dark times have us o'ertaken. (*TLH* 260: 1)

Friday

The Lord is with me, therefore I will not fear. What can men do to me? Psalm 118:6

Now he does spiritual leaps and eternal rejoicing. He shows what it is like when his prayer is heard. He says, "This is what happens. First he gives me inward comfort in my heart." This verse speaks of this and it is further expressed in the eighteenth verse.

Thereafter, he also gives help externally and frees us from need. Of this the following verse speaks. For comfort he says, "The Lord is with me," as if he would say, "My prayer will be heeded. So even if the need is not yet abated, yet I receive a mighty, powerful, strong supporter who is with me and stands by me. That makes it sweet and easy for me to bear such a yoke," Matthew 11. Who is he? Oh, it is the Lord himself to whom I cry. He fills my heart with his eternal Word and Spirit in the midst of my need, so I barely feel it. Then we must not, as the sectarians, assume that God would comfort us without means and without his Word in our hearts. It doesn't happen without the external Word. For the Holy Ghost knows well how to remind the heart [of it] and fan it to flames, even if it were heard ten years before.

From such comfort, see how he becomes bold and courageous. He shines forth and boasts, "Do not fear. I am not afraid or dismayed. I have no problem. I am of good cheer and regret nothing. For it is true that trouble and lamentation are at hand. They look at me with disdain and would gladly have me fear before them and beg them for grace. But I know these cowards and say, 'Dear dunce, do not devour me. You truly look hideous enough to those who would be frightened by you. But I have another sight, which is all the more lovely, which illumines me like the dear sun all the way to eternal life. I pay no attention to you little, temporary, dark clouds and wrathful little winds.' "

Thereafter he is comforted in the solace of God. He wraps the whole world in the presence of its great courage and insolence and says, "What could man do to me?" That is speaking comfort upon comfort. By this kings, princes and lords become justly mad and foolish that a poor sinner respects them so lightly. If such as they were thrown all together in a heap and he walked up to them, went on and looked over them, they would lie on the road as nothing but straw. He would gape his mouth open and say, "Who is laying there?" For do you not know what all mankind is called? All the world, everything that is of people, Tartars, Turks, Roman kaisers, popes, kings, princes, bishops, lords with all their might, wisdom, kingdom, land and people, etc., and, in summary, the whole world with their god, the devil and his angels and what they are able to do truly look horrible. It is right that they look so horrible. Yes, before one of them you should rightly take your seat as a miserable, lost person. Yet you can speak against them, all of them, "Friend, what can you do to me?"

They would slay you. What will they do after that? Perhaps they will wake you up and kill you again? Or perhaps they would eat you alive, a tasty bite? They cannot and will not even put you to death, unless my Lord first allows them to do it. He forewarns me that he will allow it, else they should take counsel for a year and a day, draw their knife, show their teeth, bite with their mouth and look sour and nevertheless hear Psalm 112, "The godless must see to it and vex him, and show their teeth and nothing will come of it. For what the godless desire must not happen." They are secure in their might and wealth. Those are their god and comfort. But my comfort is called: "The Lord." I will let them argue with him. I think they will capture Rome and reject the Cornerstone so that they will stagger and be shattered while I sing, "What could man do to me?"

Erl. 41, 29–30: The Good Confession of Psalm 118, 1530

If God Himself be for me,
I may a host defy;
For when I pray, before me
My foes, confounded, fly.

If Christ, my Head and Master,
Befriend me from above,
What foe or what disaster
Can drive me from His love? (*TLH* 528: 1)

Saturday

The Lord is my might and my song, and he is my savior.
Psalm 118:14

See how well he grasps everything and divides it into three parts. The Lord is my might, my song, my salvation. The first is that he trusts in God purely and well, for God works everything and all that is in him, and all that he speaks and lives. He does not boast of his own power, abilities, reason, wisdom, holiness or works. He wants to be nothing so that God is everything in him and does everything. Oh, that is an exalted song and a strange melody on earth. So he also neither trusts nor counts on any men or princes, or in the might of the world, kingdom, friends, societies, counsel, wisdom, work, comfort or help. But [he trusts] solely in God and so never in himself, nor all the might, wisdom, and holiness of the world. Then again, since he cannot be silent about such things, he makes a song out of it. He sings it, preaches it, teaches it, confesses and says of God what he believes. For his faith doesn't depart. He confesses from faith what he believes: Romans 10. But then the world cannot suffer or hear that their might, wisdom, holiness, work, counsel and works should be damned and nothing; that human and princely salvation and comfort will be discarded and despised; that their doctrine should be nothing and false. So the singer of this psalm must stand the racket and suffer that [they say] his psalm does not praise God and his preaching is not the glory of God; that his confession is not the truth, but rather blasphemy, heresy, error, lies, disturbing the peace and seduction of the world; that there is no more shameful song in the earth and nothing is preached more shamefully under the sun. Just as quickly will they deliver him [the psalmist] to the jailer, to fire, to exile, condemned, accursed, condemned by God to great slavery, burned, drowned, hanged, or murdered in some other way and ambushed by all misfortune. Then there follows the third part, that God is his salvation, who finally does not forsake his singer and his psalm. He helps him out, whether through death or life, and gives the victory. Should all of the hellish gates and all the world become wild and mad, then finally God will be our salvation. We and our psalm or doctrine remain and all the opponents go to ruin. For God's Word remains forever where no dreams, or rage, or blasphemy or curses can prevail.

Erl. 41, 51–53: The Good Confession of Psalm 118, 1530

Lord, my Shepherd, take me to Thee.
Thou art mine; I was Thine,
Even ere I knew Thee.
I am Thine, for Thou hast bought me;
Lost I stood, But Thy blood
Free salvation brought me.

Thou art mine; I love and own Thee.
Light of Joy, Ne'er shall I
From my heart dethrone Thee.
Savior, Let me soon behold Thee
Face to face — May Thy grace
Evermore enfold me. (*TLH* 523: 7– 8)

The Fourth Week after Epiphany

Sunday

The right hand of God is exalted; the right hand of God retains the victory. Psalm 118:16

From the 14th verse, which is explained above, one can understand almost this whole song of the righteous. For it is one in the same thought; namely, that the righteous in their assembly do not sing, teach, preach, confess or praise human works, holiness, wisdom, nor the prince's might, comfort, and help, as do the hypocritical, proud and self-made saints and the godless, who defect from the works of Christ in their assembly. They [the righteous] rather cast aside and despise such stinking self-righteousness, and such undependable help and comfort of men, princes and the world. They live alone by God's grace, work, Word and might, revealed in Christ, which is their preaching, hymn, praise and song. For this verse sits: *Dextra domini*, at the Lord's right hand, for the purpose, *contra dexteram hominum*, contrary to the hand of men, that one should know that before God what human hands can accomplish does not help. Human works also do not serve as righteousness, do not efface sins. They do no good works. It [human action] knows and understands nothing of truth and the true way of salvation, much less can it advise and help deliver from needs, danger, death and hell, nor does it give life and salvation.

But the right hand of God is what does it. First it [this verse] makes that might known to you. This might is also spoken of above which gives comfort. But here it will be described a little better. This is the might of God, that whoever believes on him and trusts him, will be freed from all sins, evil conscience, error, lies, deception, and freed from all the power of the devil and brought to grace, righteousness, truth, knowledge, comfort and to the true light. So thenceforth God is our might and we live not in ourselves, but rather in him. He does everything in us and he speaks. But those are all great, mighty, divine works and wonders which no human understanding, power and might understands at all. Rather these are silent because they will do nothing to add to it to help. But rather, much more, through their false comforts, teachings and promises they run from it and compel their errors evermore. Although before the world their matters have a great, important appearance and they let themselves appear as if they were pure skill and would quickly help all the way to heaven, yet whoever believes in God's might sees that it is purely the work of man and a lazy, loose, vain deceit. Whoever trusts in it digs his own hell.

For the other [part], the right hand is exalted, goes way up, lies above, and always triumphs. That is, the believers not only have the comfort of God that they are free of their sins and are righteous before God, but they also have help from him so that they finally are victorious against the devil, mankind and the world. So they are freed from death, hell and from every evil. They need no human or princely help to add to this. They also have no need to be able to do such high, great works and wonders. Rather, the high glorious hand of God goes forth there in such exalted wonderful works and helps in every need. But if we should even die for this then it truly brings us immediately to life that has no end. For this right hand is so high that neither trouble nor fear, neither sword nor hunger, neither angel nor prince can tear us from it, Romans 8. If we cling to it with steadfast faith, as all the righteous do, then we are also just as exalted. Neither troubles, nor fear, nor prince, nor devil, neither fire nor water, nor any other creature will pull us down. The victory will be ours. Then again, whoever clings to human works and is comforted by the prince's power, must go down to the bottom of hell even if he were to travel over the clouds or were to sit in heaven.

Erl. 41, 57–58: The Good Confession of Psalm 118, 1530

Ye who confess Christ's holy name, To God give praise and glory!
Ye who the Father's power proclaim, To God give praise and glory!
All idols under foot be trod, The Lord is God! The Lord is God!
To God all praise and glory! (*TLH* 19: 5)

Monday

Then you will see your desire and exalt, and your heart will be amazed and be magnified, when the multitude on the sea are converted to you and the strength of the heathen comes to you. Isaiah 60:5

Now this passage of Isaiah is fulfilled for the most part through St. Paul, who is our apostle. Through his preaching, the multitude of the seas was converted and so many of the heathen came to faith. All of this is said as a clarification of who the sons and daughters are that come from afar; namely, the crowd of paganism on the great Mediterranean converted through Paul.

But from this it is clear that such a gathering can not be understood as a bodily coming. For how would such a crowd and glut of gentiles be assembled in one city, Jerusalem, to say nothing of dwelling or staying? He says, "The crowd of the sea will be converted" or turned around, just as one moves and turns his face or body. This also shows that the heathen will not bodily come to Jerusalem, but rather their turning around is their coming. Previously, they were converted to the world, now they are turned and converted to the church.

He also calls the crowd of the sea in Hebrew, *Hamon*, that is, a tribe or people. Without doubt he is referring to God's promise to Abraham, that he should be a father of many nations. For God said this to him in Genesis 17:5, "You will henceforth not be called Abram, but your name shall be Abraham. For I have made you father of many nations."

Just here God writes the first letter of the *hamon* into Abram and makes Abraham out of it. He gives the reason for it and says, "Because he will be a father *hamon*, that is of the crowds of the gentiles." Just as he says with Isaiah, "He will be a father *hamon*, of the seas, a father of the multitudes of the gentiles." As St. Paul brings out in his epistles, the gentiles through faith are Abraham's children and seed according to the promise of God. Isaiah just here also refers to this, describing the fulfillment of the promise, "Previously he was named Abram, a father who is exalted, or exalted father. Now he is named Abraham, a father of the multitudes of the gentiles, so his exaltation and elevation is completed in the gentiles."

What does it mean, though, that he writes such overflowing words and says, "Then you will see and exalt, and your heart will be amazed and magnified."? These are all words of comforting promise. The Hebrew language has the way [of speaking] that it is called "seeing" when our will or desire is accomplished, as in Psalm 54:9, "And my eyes will see my foes," that is, I will see what I dearly wanted to see, namely, they are subdued and the truth is established. Or in Psalm 37:34, "When the godless are cut off, then you will see," that is, then you will see what you want to see, that is, "Oh, how good it is that we finally get to see it." So here also, "Then you will see," that is, "you see now that you are the poor miserable little people seeing your foes. What you want to see and you would gladly see is that you are great and many; but you do not see that yet and must see what you don't want to see for a little while. Thereafter you will also see what you desire and they will not. When the multitude of the seas are turned to you, then you will see what you so wanted to see. They will not see what they desired to see. You must bear patiently for a while and not see as a few things pass, [while you] bear the cross."

Erl. 7, 348–350: Sermon on the day of the Three Holy Kings, Isaiah 60:1–6, 1523

Waft, waft, ye winds, His story,
And you, ye waters, roll,
Till like a sea of glory
It spreads from pole to pole;

Till o'er our ransomed nature
The Lamb for sinners slain,
Redeemer, King, Creator,
In bliss returns to reign. (*TLH* 495: 4)

Tuesday

Since, then, you are his children, God has sent the Spirit of his Son into your hearts, who cries, "Abba, dear Father." Galatians 4:6

There we see that the Holy Ghost is given not through works, but through faith. For he says here that the Spirit is given so that you are children and not servants. Children believe. Servants work. Children are free of the law. Servants are under the law. From the previous explanations, all that is easy to understand. One should therefore become used to the Pauline usage and the point of what is a child versus a slave, what is free versus what is compelled. Compelled works belong to the slave. Free works are of the child.

But why does he say that the Holy Ghost is given them because they are children, when the Holy Ghost makes children out of servants and must be there before they are children? Answer: He speaks in the manner as he says above in verse 3, "We were under the elements until the time would be fulfilled." So they were going to be children before God. Therefore, the Holy Ghost was sent to them, who makes them into children, as they were previously ordained.

And he calls the Spirit a Spirit of God's Son. Why not his Spirit? Because he remains on the course. He calls them children of God so he sends them the same Spirit which Christ has, who also is a child, so that they call out just like him, "Abba, dear Father!" As if you should say, "God sends you his Spirit, which dwells in his Son, that you will be his brother and co-heir, just as he pleads, 'dear Father.' " But by this the inexpressible wealth and grace of God will be praised, that we through faith sit with Christ in pure wealth and we have all that he has and is, even his Spirit.

Along with these words he also makes known the third person of the Godhead, the Holy Ghost. He is not only in Christ as he would dwell in a person, but he is also the one who is from him and has the divine nature as he has from the Father. Otherwise the words that Paul says would be false, "He is the Son's Spirit." No creature can say, nor can it be said of it, that the Holy Ghost is his. He is only God's own Spirit. The creatures are only of the Holy Ghost.

Then one would be able so say, "My Holy Ghost!" as we say, "My God, my Lord, etc." So he must be the Son of God since God's Spirit is his Spirit.

Now here each is to take this as true and test if he also experiences the Holy Ghost. Is his voice perceived in him? For St. Paul says here: When he is in the heart, he calls out, "Abba, dear Father!" as he also says in Romans 8:15, "You have received the Spirit of the gracious adoption of God, through whom we cry out, 'Abba, dear Father!'" So one feels that crying, then, when the conscience is steadfastly encouraged without any wavering or doubt and is also sure that not only are his sins forgiven him, but that he also is a child of God and salvation is secure. With a joyous, sure heart he desires to call God his dear Father and pray in sure confidence. That must be sure for him, that even his own life is not so sure to him as this. So he should rather suffer every death and hell on top of it before he lets that go and doubts it. For if Christ's action and suffering would be near and we were not believing that he had earned everything in unsurpassing measure by them, then we would be allowing his great work and suffering to pass us by and not to strengthen us to confidence. Then sins or trials would make us terrified and draw back [from Christ].

It can surely be a conflict when a person feels worried that he is not a child and lets himself think this way. He would then also perceive that God is over him as a wrathful stern God, as it happened to Job and many others. But in the war this childlike confidence must prevail, even if it trembles and shakes; else all is lost.

Erl. 7, 273-275: Sermon for the Sunday after Christmas on Galatians 4:1-7

For He can plead for me with sighings That are unspeakable to lips like mine;
He bids me pray with earnest cryings, Bear witness with my soul that I am Thine,
Joint heir with Christ, and thus may dare to say: O Heav'nly Father, hear me when
I pray! (*TLH* 21: 4)

Wednesday

But what does not come from faith is sin. Romans 14:23

The apostle wants to say, "what proceeds from faith is pure grace and righteousness." That is quickly established. Therefore, man may not say, if man should do a good work, that they do it themselves, unaided. That's what the passage in the 25th Psalm says, "Every way of the Lord is grace and truth." That is, when God works and creates faith in us so it is purely by grace that we also do the truth, that is, that we proceed on a true ground and not as a hypocrite. But on the other hand it must also be true that all the ways of man are not grace, but rather pure wrath; not truth, but rather only a show and hypocrisy because it comes out of disbelief.

Therefore, you should not make this gloss by a gut reaction and say: faith alone doesn't do it, but rather works also are necessary to make one good. For it says clearly enough that the works add nothing. No one comes to harm except by disbelief, because works are not enough, for if faith is there then everything will be good. Therefore, as little as good works help, since they are evil in the unbelievers, so little do they also help those in faith to make them good. Rather, disbelief only ruins all works, but faith makes them all good.

Therefore, set these next to each other so that you can rightly decide. Where there is faith, there are not so many sins that they are not weakened and effaced through faith. Where there is unbelief, there you can never do so many good works that you weaken the most paltry sins. As little as sins can now remain in the presence of faith, so little could good works remain with unbelievers. So it follows, whoever believes has no sins, and only does good works. On the other hand, whoever doesn't believe actually does no good works, but rather everything is sin. So I say again, you cannot have committed so many sins that still make God so hostile to you that all of it cannot be put away and forgiven when you begin to believe. Then, through faith, you have Christ as your own, who is given to you that he take away your sins. So who will then be so bold that he curses him? Therefore, no sins can remain, no matter how big they are. If you believe, then you are a dear child even if things are difficult and what you do is all right. If you do not believe, then you are accursed even if you do everything that you want to. For since you do not have Christ, it is impossible for you to exterminate sins, since there is no other means to take away sins than Christ. So you say, "Why is it then that one must do good works when it all depends on faith?" Answer: where faith is right, it cannot be without good works. Just as, on the other hand, where there is disbelief, there can be no good works. So if you believe, then from faith only good works must follow. For as faith brings you salvation and eternal life, so it also brings you good works and they are irrepressible. So just as a living person cannot help but move, eat, drink and work and it is not possible that such works can be omitted while he is alive, such that one does not compel or command him to do such works, but rather if he is living he does them, even so one is not obligated to do any more good works. Thus you could say: "Only believe, and you will do them all yourself."

Altb. VIII, 923: Sermon on the Day of Christ's Ascension, Mark 16

Create in me a new heart, Lord, That gladly I obey Thy Word
And naught but what Thou wilt, desire;
With such new life my soul inspire. (*TLH* 398: 3)

Thursday

But now the righteousness that holds before God without
the works of the law is revealed and witnessed through the
law and the prophets. Romans 3:21

This righteousness is completely hidden and buried more than
anything. The world knows and understands nothing of it. Even to
the Christian himself it is hard to grasp and can never be grasped
well enough. Because of that, one always teaches about it and must
exercise himself in it constantly and well. It is sure that whoever
doesn't have this righteousness nor has soon grasped it when his
conscience needed it, and when he was earnestly terrified of God's
judgment because of his sins, then it is also entirely impossible that
he could be established and remain. For it is sure that there is no
other established and sure comfort for the poor frightened conscience
than this righteousness which our Lord God has created and worked
in us without our works and preparations for his own sake.

We people on earth have such a poor, mean, pitifull nature that
in these terrors of conscience and death pangs we can find nothing
better to help than our own works, worthiness, service and the
teachings of the law. And since we can find nothing in ourselves but
pure sin and guilt, we merely gloss over our life, as we have led and
spent it in the past. Because of that, then, a poor sinner groans in
great pain and heartache and in himself must think and lament, "O
God my great sorrow, how I have so evilly spent my life; woe is me
a poor sinner! Oh that I might yet live on a little while, then I will
do much better and lead my life well. . ." This unblessed misfortune
is so deeply rooted in our hearts that it is not possible that human
reason, so long as it beholds the righteousness of its own works, can
silence such thoughts, grasp the righteousness of Christ and be able
to preserve itself. Rather, it only stays clinging firmly to its own
work.

And when Satan, who has such great and numerous advantages
against the weak human nature, compels such thoughts so mightily
and swiftly into the human heart, it never fails that the conscience
must become ever more timid, shy and fearful. So long as one feels
this terror of sins and has to deal with it, the human heart itself does
not desire comfort, does not expect grace. Satan acts to stir up so

many kinds of arguments over the works in order to not put away this consistent attitude, much less to despair completely of itself. For this is an art that easily surpasses all human skills and desires, thought and understanding, yes, even God's law itself, and is utterly much, much too high. Even if God's law is the highest art and the most precious doctrine in all the world, yet it is not possible that it can comfort and bring peace and quiet to a troubled, terrified conscience. Yes, it only makes it more troubled until in the end it must completely be filled with doubt. Through the law, sins are only made bigger, greater and mightier, as St. Paul shows in Romans 7.

For this reason, a poor troubled conscience has no help or medicine to cling to against the doubting and eternal death but grace which is presented to it through Christ, which is Christ or the righteousness of faith, which God himself works in us without any of our works or preparations. Whoever has this can then freely say in comfort, "Even if I am not right by my own works, that will not make me doubt." (No citation in Link)

By grace! Oh, mark this word of promise When thou art by thy sins opprest,
When Satan plagues thy troubled conscience, And when thy heart is seeking rest.
What reason cannot comprehend God by His grace to thee doth send. (*TLH* 373: 3)

Friday

Through the law comes the knowledge of sins. Romans 3:20

Again, one must compel the law and the teaching of works in the world as if there where altogether no promise or grace. That is for the sake of the stubborn, high-handed, wild people to whom one can place, present and set nothing before their eyes but the law so that they also become frightened and humbled. For that very reason the law is given; that the secure and hardened become terrified and put to death. It will only seize, quickly plague and murder the old Adam. In this way, both kinds of Word and preaching, of grace and wrath, should be rightly divided, according to the counsel of the apostle. 2 Timothy 2.

This skill needs a true and clever teacher, who knows how much of the law to compel and to use it so that it goes no further than is proper and good. For if I would preach the law to the people as though they became righteous and good before God through it, then I have already used it all too much and have kicked over the traces and mixed these two kinds of righteousness, as namely, the righteousness that comes out of the law and is my own doing, with the other righteousness that comes without the law out of grace and is given and bestowed without any of my works and preparations from God, for the sake of Christ. Because of this it would be a gross ungifted preacher, who, without distinction, would add the hundreds to the thousands [columns] and mix them with each other.

But if the teaching of the law and works is to the old Adam, the promise and grace are presented and preached to the new man, so it is divided rightly. For the flesh, or the old Adam, belongs together with the law and works just as to the spirit, or new man, promise and grace, belong together. So when I note that the person is broken sufficiently by the law and suffers need under it, that he is tortured with his sins and craves grace, then it is truly high time and of necessity that I rip away from his eyes the law with the righteousness of his own doing and show him through the gospel the other righteousness which God makes and gives without him, without his own work, service and preparation, only through grace for the sake of his Son. This righteousness is the one that calls one from Moses [and the law] with his weak righteousness and presents to the one terrified by the law the promise of Christ, the one who came for the sake of those miserable consciences and poor sinners. Then the poor people would be helped rightly so that God creates a true comforting hope and good confidence. For he is no longer under the law, but under grace. But how is he no longer under the law? Answer: according to the new man, which does not at all receive anything from the law, but rather is only directed by Christ, as St. Paul hereafter also says: "The law stood guard until Christ." When that one comes, Moses must stop and demure with the law, circumcision, offerings, Sabbath, etc. and with him all the prophets. (No citation in Link)

It was a false, misleading dream That God His Law had given
That sinners could themselves redeem And by their works gain heaven.
The Law is but a mirror bright To bring the inbred sin to light
That lurks within our nature. (*TLH* 377: 3)

Saturday

But we know that the law is good, if anyone use it rightly.
1 Timothy 1:8

Now this is our theology in which we teach to distinguish between these two kinds of righteousness with special effort. The one is established by our own doing; the other God himself works and makes in us without our doing. One must not mix up what is to be taught in distinguishing between the honor of outward life and faith, between works and grace, between world authority and of the spiritual service of God. So although one must needs teach and compel both kinds, yet they should also be differentiated as to where each is useful and used. For the Christian, righteousness pertains only to the new man, but the righteousness of the law pertains to the old man, to which, as it is born of flesh and blood, one must lay on the law just as one places his load and burden on an ass. He should not be allowed to use anything of the Spirit and the freedom of grace until he has also put on the new man through faith in Christ (which yet, though, in this life cannot completely be done). When this is done, then he can also receive and use the inexpressibly great grace of the kingdom and its gifts.

This I say so that no one think we would cast aside or forbid good works, as the papists lay on us and falsely give us guilt. Yet they themselves do not understand either what they themselves say or much less, what we teach. For they know nothing to speak of definitely other than only of the righteousness of the law and yet they also dare to decide and judge doctrine so that theirs is so immeasurably higher than the law, that no person on earth can decide and judge them, even if he had the Holy Ghost. Therefore, it never fails that they must be stuck and aggravated on it so they come to no higher knowledge or understanding than only as much as the law teaches. Therefore, to them everything that is higher than the law must be [for them] the highest aggravation.

But we steadfastly teach as if there were two worlds, the one heavenly, the other earthly, in which we divide these two kinds of righteousness so that each of them has their own place. The righteousness of the law is an earthly righteousness, that concerns earthly matters, and through that we do good works. But just as the soil does not bear fruit, you receive it as a blessing from above (for the soil surely cannot master, renew, and rule heaven but must much more be mastered, renewed, and ruled by heaven so that it becomes fruitful and does what God wills): so we also do much according to the law. Yet nothing is done. We fulfill much, and yet it remains unfulfilled, if we are not made right previously through the righteousness of Christ apart from all our work and service, all of which has nothing to do with the righteousness of the law as something that is completely an earthly thing and our own doing. So this is a heavenly righteousness that we do not have from ourselves, nor can we bring it to action by our doing, but we must receive it apart from our works from heaven, namely, through faith by which we are raised and ascended above all laws and works. So now, as we have worn the image of the earthly Adam, according to St. Paul's

Word, so we should also wear the image of the heavenly Adam, which is a new man in a new world, where there is absolutely no law, no sins, no conscience, no death but rather only pure joy, righteousness, grace, peace, life, salvation and glory. (No citation in Link)

Faith clings to Jesus' cross alone And rests in Him unceasing;
And by its fruits true faith is known, With love and hope increasing.
Yet faith alone doth justify, Works serve thy neighbor and supply
The proof that faith is living. (*TLH* 377: 9)

The Fifth Week after Epiphany

Sunday

*Grace to you and peace from God the Father and our Lord
Jesus Christ. Galatians 1:3*

This is a greeting which the apostle uses often. Apart from this
[usage] it is completely alien to the world. Before the on-going
preaching of the gospel it was unheard of. In those two short little
words, "grace" and "peace," are embraced the sum and substance of
the whole Christian doctrine and essence. Grace forgives sins and so
helps the conscience to be still, for the two devils that want to vex us
are sins and the conscience. Christ has conquered both of these
horrible and frightening tyrants and put them under his feet in this
contrary and present world. But since the world knows nothing about
this, it can also teach nothing to the conscience of how one will
overcome sins, an evil conscience and death. This doctrine is only
with the Christian. This teaching is useful to overcome sins, doubt
and eternal death. It is the kind of doctrine that certainly has nothing
to do with free will or human reason and wisdom, but is given
directly by our Lord God himself.

So grasp these two parts, grace and peace, containing the whole
Christian essence. The grace is forgiveness of sins, peace, a joyous
and liberated conscience. No one can ever have peace except by the
forgiveness of sins. Now if the sins were not forgiven so that one had
to keep the law, since no one does the law enough, then the law
would always accuse the conscience. It would terrorize us for the
sake of sins, earning God's wrath, and driving the conscience to
despair. Now these sins will not be forgiven through the law, so they
certainly will be much less forgiven through human works which are
only blasphemous misuses and idolatrous service. Yes, they only
become more and greater, and sourer and heavier than the works-
saints allow themselves to become. To overcome and lay aside sins
with works makes them even more horrid. But through grace, we
would make them free and by grace is the only way. Therefore, St.
Paul customarily desired grace and peace for all the world in the
greeting of his epistles. By these, one can be established against sins
and an evil conscience. Surely, one must learn to do this well. The
words are easy, but to bring it and hold surely to it while the heart

is being tried, so that we will have forgiveness of sins and peace with God in heaven and in earth only through pure grace without doing any kind of work and means, is the difficult thing for the masses.

It is sure that the world doesn't know or understand a single bit of this doctrine. Because of that, it also will not and cannot suffer it. Yes, the world also curses this doctrine, through which we can receive and gain grace and peace, that is forgiveness of sins and a happy conscience, as the most grievous heresy and godless error. Instead, the world praises free will, natural enlightenment, our own powers and good works. But it is impossible that the conscience can become peaceful and happy ever again unless it receives peace through this grace, that is, through the forgiveness of sins that is promised us in Christ.

Altb. VI, 533–536: Commentary on Galatians, 1535, cf. AE, 26 & 27

Oh, how great is Thy compassion, Faithful Father, God of grace,
That with all our fallen race And in our deep degradation
Thou wast merciful that we Might be saved eternally. (*TLH* 384: 1)

Monday

I am amazed that you have so quickly turned away from that to which you were called through the grace of Christ to another gospel. Galatians 1:6

There you see St. Paul complain how they stumbled and fell from faith so quickly and easily. Therefore he warns and exhorts the Christians here and in other places and says, "Let he that stands be careful that he doesn't fall." We also daily encounter what crude and miserable things happen when a human heart wants to grasp and retain faith, or how troublesome it is when one prepares a militant nation for the Lord. If one even had ten whole years with doctrine, exhortation and discipline, he would have his hands full to bring forth a church or congregation in a single place that would run in an orderly and Christian manner. If he finally did pull it off after a great effort, then, afterwards, some unholy fanatic would sneak in, a great coarse ass who has only the skill to contradict and blaspheme the true preachers, overturning the congregation again. Whose heart would not ache over such a tragedy?

Now by God's grace we have accomplished this. Here in Wittenberg [the church runs] in the manner and form of a true church or Christian congregation, for one preaches the pure gospel and God's Word, so one uses the Sacrament rightly, one exhorts and prays for all stations in life, etc. In summary, God be praised, it goes well and fine as it should. Yet it is sure that if the profane fanatics could come, those who presently act according to their own traditions, they would ruin it at once and (so to speak) subvert and throw what we have been able to establish in so many years with such great effort into a junk heap, in the twinkling of an eye.

This was encountered also by St. Paul, the chosen instrument of God. He had established the congregations in Galatia with great care and work. The false apostles came after he left. In a short time they overturned everything, as this battling epistle, along with the others, also give abundant witness. This, our life on earth, is a totally poor, miserably, weak, uncertain, tenuous thing. So Satan has arranged things everywhere for us, and everywhere he has laid so many trip wires for us that whenever we turn around, a single fanatic overthrows and ruinously tramples what the good, right and true servants of Christ have produced over a long period of time with great labor day and night. That is what we must (unfortunately) experience at this time with trouble and great heartache. We hold it inside and are unable to help or counsel in such miserable trouble.

For this reason also, since Christianity is such a fragile and tender thing, which is why this happens so quickly and painfully, one must always have a good ready eye out for such fanatics and sectarian spirits. They are so sneaky that they think that when they have heard a sermon or two, or read a pamphlet or two, then they are already accomplished masters over all masters and disciples, even if no one has also ordained, called or sent them. Some uneducated laborers can also be so stupidly bold, and they appraise and understand this great, high, difficult and dangerous office [the Office of the Holy Ministry] so lightly, that they disregard it even though their whole lives long they [the fanatics] were never in a true trial before God's wrath and judgment, nor heartily and earnestly terrified, much less had they tasted God's grace.

But since they are only godless windbags, they teach according to their own opinions what pleases themselves and what the people want to hear. Since the people gladly hear only what is strange and new, such new tricks also please them well and he gathers a swarm in the hive. While they dream that they correctly have the teaching of the Father, and are even practiced in a few afflictions and trials, in this they are drawn and misled by crazy fanatical spirits.

Altb. VI, 547-548: Commentary on Galatians, 1535, cf. AE, 26 & 27

Lord, Jesus, help, Thy Church uphold, For we are sluggish, thoughtless, cold.
Oh, prosper well Thy Word of grace And spread its truth in every place! (*TLH* 292: 3)

Tuesday

*I am amazed that you have so quickly turned away from
what you were called to through the grace of Christ to
another gospel. Galatians 1:6*

Saint Paul does not use any hard, wrathful, unfriendly words
here. He does not say, "I am amazed that you have apostatized so
quickly; that you are so disobedient, careless, fickle and unthankful."
Rather, he only says, "I am amazed that you have so quickly turned
away," as if he would say, "You are still good people who
yourselves do not want to act wrongly, but only they have done
wrong and you have been deceived and misled." So he doesn't scold
the poor people who were injured, but the false apostles and
deceivers who had done the mischief. Yet he also chastises them
civilly and mildly because they were so forgetful and unwary and had
let themselves turn away. As if he would say, "Although I have
loved you as a father [does] his children, and I know well that it is
not your own fault, but the fault of the false apostles that you are
misled and in error, yet I might well sorrow and would (if I could)
dearly wish that you were better grounded in the saving doctrine of
Christ, and were standing more steadfastly and stubbornly.
Unfortunately you have not grasped the Word so surely and well, as
you rightly should have. For if it were rightly grasped and well
rooted, then you would not have let yourselves be turned by such
light winds so quickly and suddenly."

St. Heironymous interpreted this as if St. Paul with these words
(turned away) wants to illustrate this using the Galatian's name,
which sounds the same as the Hebrew word "*GALAH*" (meaning
turned). Its as if he wanted to say, "You are just like you are named,
true Galatians, that is, good people that are easily turned away."

Some think that we Germans must be descended from the
Galatians and will now soon fail under the right conditions. For we
Germans are like that (if the truth be told). It would be well to wish
that our dear Germans were a bit more steadfast and brave. For it is
our way, when first something new comes along, that we are very
ardent and passionate for it and follow it doing handsprings. We want
to go to it like a blind horse through fire and water. But so soon as
this same first passion is a little extinguished, then we let it ebb,
become tired of it, and as easily as we had desired it in the
beginning, so easily we again soon let it go again. Yes, we have
become satiated over time with what in the beginning only pleased us
very much, so that we neither want to see nor hear it.

I'll give an example of that: In the beginning, when in the most horrible darkness of the papistic unholy human teaching, the dear saving gospel of God's grace was published, God help us, with great effort, zeal and eagerness, many people heard the preachers and regarded them with such great honor. But now that the Christian doctrine is so well purified and has gone out so abundantly, many who have received the doctrine not only despise it, but also have become its foe along with [becoming foes of] those teaching and preaching it. They not only despise the holy Scriptures, but also every other writing and good art. So they become true sow bellies and filthy folk who could well compare with the undiscerning Galatians.

Altb. VI, 548–549: Commentary on Galatians, 1535, cf. AE, 26 & 27

O Lord, look down from heav'n, behold And let Thy pity waken;
How few are we within Thy fold, Thy saints by men forsaken!
True faith seems quenched on ev'ry hand, Men suffer not Thy Word to stand;
Dark times have us o'ertaken. (*TLH* 260: 1)

Wednesday

I am amazed that you have so quickly turned away from what you were called to through the grace of Christ to another gospel. Galatians 1:6

These Words (of Christ, who has called you in grace) have something special and important behind them. They must be well founded, as is self-evident, since they concern grace, to which Christ had called the Galatians. This is against the law, which the false apostles push in order to make them both the same. St. Paul wants to say, "Oh, how easily you let yourselves be turned from Christ, who has not called you to the law, nor works, nor under sins, wrath nor damnation as Moses does, but rather to pure grace and mercy."

So in these times we must also complain with St. Paul that there is still a horrible, terrifying blindness and a wrong attitude in the world. For absolutely no one will accept the doctrine of grace and salvation. Or, when a few receive it, they again fall away from it so quickly and tragically. So this doctrine brings all kinds of kindnesses, physical and spiritual, like the forgiveness of sins, actual righteousness, peace of the heart and eternal life. Further, it also brings a light and sure knowledge of all things, makes us sure of worldly government and all kinds of stations in life which God has ordained and established, as those in the household, and other similar ones. It [makes us] secure because God is pleased by them and so we can use the same [established orders] blessedly with a good conscience. This teaching pursues all kinds of harmful doctrine through which one comes into error, sins, death, trouble and shame. It reveals and destroys all works of the devil. Through Christ, it gives us knowledge, informs us through Christ of God's gracious will, mercy and love towards us and comforts us all by God's Word. What kind of pity and mean foolishness is it when the world is such a bitter foe of this Word and the gospel of Christ which brings us only eternal comfort, grace, life and salvation? With such devilish wantonness the world blasphemes and persecutes it.

But St. Paul has sufficiently answered this question above. He says this present world is a wicked world, that is, only a foolish, evil and true kingdom of the devil. For if such were not the case, they would surely also acknowledge God's charity and mercy, which they, if it is in the devil's power to do it, cannot stand at all. Rather, they hunt and persecute it away from themselves. They would much rather have darkness, error and the devil's kingdom than the light, truth and the kingdom of Christ. Therefore, it is also not error nor a case of their misunderstanding it. Rather, it is only pure devilish trouble-making and evil, which one can easily recognize. For Christ, God's Son, even though he gave himself for all sins into death, will earn no other thanks in the world. The world blasphemes such inexpressible charity, persecutes his saving Word and if they could, they would be even more glad to crucify him now than before. So the world not only acts and wanders in darkness, but it is the darkness itself as John 1 describes it.

That is why St. Paul makes these Words so great (of Christ, who has called you in grace) and implicitly also insists that they stop making the preaching of grace the same as the preaching of the law. It's as if he is saying, "I have not encumbered you in my preaching office with the difficult and unbearable law of Moses nor ever taught you how you should work and serve under the yoke of the law, but I have preached to you only grace and freedom from the law and sins. Namely, how Christ out of compassion has called you to grace that you should be free children under him and not a slave under Moses, whose learners and disciples you have become again through the additional advice of your false apostles. Through Moses' law and not at all through grace, they have called you much more under God's wrath so that you have become God's foe and must be ruined in sins and eternal death. But Christ called those who believe his Word to grace and salvation. He helps you from the law to the gospel, from wrath to grace, from sins to righteousness, from death to life. How does it happen, then, that you should so quickly and tragically turn away from such a lively and abundant wellspring of grace and salvation? So if Moses calls us through God's law under God's wrath and under sins, where does the pope then call us with his unholy, yes, devilish laws?"

Altb. VI, 549–550: Commentary on Galatians, 1535, cf. AE, 26 & 27

With fraud which they themselves invent The truth they have confounded;
Their hearts are not with one consent On Thy pure doctrine grounded.
While they parade with outward show, They lead the people to and fro,
In error's maze astounded. (*TLH* 260: 2)

Thursday

I am amazed that you have so quickly turned away from what you were called to through the grace of Christ to another gospel. Galatians 1:6

Here he lets us learn to recognize at once the devil's fraud and treacherous character. No heretic comes with the appearance or reputation that he came from the devil and would mislead us into error. Even the devil himself comes not as a devil when he is just the opposite; the good looking, white and good devil. Yes, even the black and nasty devil, when he would move the people to coarse and open evil, sins and shame, masks the matter in such a mantel that the sins that one will do or has already done never look so big, but much smaller than they really are. A murderer, while he is in his madness and rages, does not see or know that murder is a great and horrible sin, as it is of itself, for the devil has hidden it so that he cannot know or see it. Adulterers, thieves, greedy bellies, and drunkards, etc., all have something that they love and that blinds them to their burden. Also, the true black and nasty devil has his special masks and face paints in all his works and plots to dress himself up and deceive the people so they cannot know how evil and horrible their sin is. Rather they dream that it is not dangerous and shameful.

But in spiritual sins, Satan is neither black nor nasty, but rather comes sneaking in all in white and beautiful, as if he were an angel, yes, God himself. He can masterfully disguise himself and hide the rogue. So in skulduggery he is the general. He then preaches his deadly pestilent poison as pure grace and gives it out as God's Word and the gospel of Jesus Christ. So then St. Paul takes the erring doctrine of the false apostles and servants of the devil and says, "The Galatians have turned to another gospel." Yet he does not take pains to say that the devil's doctrine is a gospel. He is rather only mocking and scoffing it. Its as if he would say, "Well now, dear Galatians, you now have another new gospel and new gospel preachers. So I must be converted by you and be despised with my gospel. It is good for nothing now, etc."

From all this it is easy to note and review how the false apostles have discarded and condemned the gospel of St. Paul among the Galatians. They said that Paul had made a good beginning to teach, but what good is that? One must not only begin but also carry on; there are yet far higher and greater parts further on that one must know and have for salvation, of which St. Paul knows nothing. They also said this in Acts 15, that it is not nearly enough that one believes on Christ, is baptized, etc. You must also have yourself circumcised, for if you are not circumcised according to the law of Moses, you cannot become saved. Bottom line, this is as much as saying, "Christ is truly a good carpenter, since he has begun the building well, but he cannot complete it. Rather, if it will be complete, then Moses must prepare it for completion."

This is also what our fanatics and sectarians do today; since they cannot publicly condemn us, they say that the Lutherans have a much too timid and troubled spirit. If we would let the truth be freely proclaimed and break through, then we must go further and break through. Truly [they say of us], they laid a fine foundation, which is faith in Christ, but what good is just a beginning? Beginning, middle and the end, that is, something beginning, proceeding and completed, belongs together, but this is not from you. It is given us by God. So these upside down, devilish people know how to dress up their godless misleading frauds, and call it God's Word, so that they can do even more and greater harm under God's name. For the devil will not quickly be nasty or black in his servants but rather completely pure, clean and white. In this way he wants to be regarded as pure. So he moves in all his words and work as though it is God's own truth, word and work. By this, the German proverb comes to us: "In God's name begins every misfortune."

So let us note well that this is the devil's own characteristic and custom. When he cannot do harm with persecution and destruction, he does it rather by wanting to build and make someone else's work better; [work] which God himself has made and wants us to have [just] as he made it.

Altb. VI, 551: Commentary on Galatians, 1535, cf. AE, 26 & 27

Take not Thy saving Word away, Our souls' true comfort, staff and stay.
Abide with us and keep us free From errors, foll'wing only Thee. (*TLH* 125: 3)

Friday

Which yet is not another gospel; but there are some who have confounded you and want to overturn the gospel of Christ. Galatians 1:7

That is, they are not only desirous to have you by confounding you, but they also want to topple the gospel of Christ to the ground and completely wipe it out. For Satan commonly proceeds with two agendas. First, Satan does not allow people to be satisfied, so he misleads and confuses many people with his false prophets with the understanding that by this [dissatisfaction] the devil will completely topple and take away the gospel. He allows no peace until he brings this about. Thereafter, [secondly] at the same time, these topplers of the gospel can suffer or hear nothing so evil as when someone says to them that they are apostles of the devil. Yes, they can majestically and with self-satisfaction praise themselves, how they are the true apostles of Christ and the most pure evangelical preachers on earth.

Yet nothing else is possible while they mix the law with the gospel. They must be topplers of the gospel. For [with them] the two things must, of necessity, be one. Either Christ remains and the law falls, or the law remains and the gospel falls. For Christ and the law cannot reign and be the Lord in the conscience, one with another. When the righteousness of the law has taken its place, there the righteousness of grace cannot have its place; and again, when the righteousness of grace holds sway, there the righteousness of the law cannot. One must wipe out the other and have its place. Can you not believe that God would forgive your sins for the sake of Christ, who has paid so richly for it; namely that he died for it and shed his blood for it? How would you not evermore be able to believe that he will forgive you your sins for which you would not be able to withstand God's judgment? Will you stand in the judgment for the sake of the Lord or your own works, which you have never done as the law required your whole life, as you yourself must admit? Therefore, it is not possible that the preaching of grace and the preaching of the law could remain alike together and that they both alike should be able to make people right and saved. Therefore, one must curtly do away with one of them and let it fall and alone hold to the other.

But while the Jews doubted this doctrine, we do not want that to happen to us now. I would gladly have these two kinds of righteousness together; one that makes me right by grace, and the other, that makes me acceptable to God by works of the law. But when one wants to mix the law's righteousness with grace's righteousness, then such mixing is nothing else, says St. Paul, than overturning the gospel. So when it comes to a battle [of the two], when you take the matter up, the biggest bunch has the numerical advantage even if the smallest is right. For Christ with his bunch is too weak, and the preaching of the gospel is a foolish preaching, but the world and its prince, the devil, are strong. What he presents and teaches through his apostles has in every way a better splendor and appearance than what Christ does through his own. So these "topplers" let the righteousness of faith and grace go, and bring up the other righteousness of works and of the law instead, which they also defend. But we take comfort in this, that the devil with his members, as strong as he is, cannot bring about what he plans and has in mind. He can mislead a few poor stupid human consciences and make them err, but the gospel of Christ he must also let remain unharmed. For although it can often happen that the truth must needs suffer, yet it is not possible that it can be completely in every way buried, for the Word of the Lord remains forever.

Altb. VI, 553–554: Commentary on Galatians, 1535, cf. AE, 26 & 27

Our foes, O God, are in Thy hand, Thou knowest their endeavor;
But only give us strength to stand And let us waver never,
Though reason strives with faith, and still It fears to wholly trust Thy will
And sees not Thy salvation. (*ELHB* 284: 7)

Saturday

But even if we or an angel from heaven would preach a gospel that is different than what we have preached, let him be damned. Galatians 1:8

It is certainly for the sake of the people that St. Paul is highly agitated and very earnestly jealous, so much so that he could even have condemned the angels. For he says freely, "Even if it were we, me and my brothers, Timothy and Titus, who purely preached Christ, yes, even if it were an angel from heaven (not to mention those who have misled and troubled your conscience), etc., yet I would rather that I myself, my brothers, yes, even an angel from heaven be damned, than that my gospel be overturned." He is truly worked up to so audaciously curse not only himself and his brothers, but also an angel from heaven.

In Greek, *anathema*, in Hebrew, *herem*, means something that is damned, accursed, banned and immediately, completely, severed from anything in communion with God. So Joshua says of the city of

Jericho, that it should be an eternal *anathema*, that is, a cursed, banned thing which should nevermore be rebuilt. And in Leviticus 27 it also stands written, "When a man or even an animal, whatever it is, is banned, it will be put to death and in no way be allowed near the people." So Amalek and a few cities had to become banned through God's judgment and were demolished real estate.

So now this is St. Paul's meaning, "It would be better to me that I and the others and even that an angel in heaven would be eternally cursed and banned and cut off from God than that we should preach another gospel above that which we have previously preached." And St. Paul does not do this for nothing as he proved above. He wants first, before all, to be banned, if he found himself to have erred in this. For all of the extravagant works-people also sought to do this, namely that they at first battled for their own errors, so that they could then even more freely battle and denounce the so-called errors and defects of others.

So now St. Paul resolves that there is no other gospel than that which he previously preached, so that there will be no other preaching either from himself or from others, even if an angel from heaven should do it. He had preached a gospel which he didn't make up himself, but which God had promised from the beginning through his holy prophets and in the holy Scriptures, as he shows in Romans 1. He speaks this kind of judgment for this reason; that were he himself or another, and even if it were an angel from heaven, to preach another gospel than was previously preached, that same one would be cursed. So the Word of the gospel, which God once sent from heaven, neither will nor shall evermore be repealed until the last day.

Altb. VI, 554: Commentary on Galatians, 1535, cf. AE, 26 & 27

That Thou art with us, Lord, proclaim And put our enemies to shame;
Confound them in their haughtiness And help Thine own in their distress. (*TLH* 265: 4)

The Sixth Week after Epiphany

Sunday

*The Lord said to my Lord, "Sit at my right hand until I
give your enemies to you as your footstool." Psalm 110:1*

Sit (he says) upon a kingly throne. Reign and be Lord and king,
but where? "On the throne of the House of David," say the prophet
Isaiah and the angel Gabriel, Luke 2, as God promised David. But
here he goes much further and higher. He doesn't say the Lord has
said "sit on David's throne" or "be the heir to David's throne," but
rather "sit at my right hand." That means he is lifted high with a
word and selected as a splendid king, not over the poor city of
Jerusalem, nor the kingdom of Babylon, Rome, or Constantinople
nor the whole face of the earth which would certainly be a great
power; yes, not even over heaven, the stars and everything one can
see with his eyes, but rather, much higher and farther. He says "sit
next to me" on the high throne where I sit. Be the same as me. Not
at my feet but rather to my right side, in the same majesty and might
that are called "divine might."

That would be a true king; more lordly and greater than anyone
can comprehend or describe. Truly, with just a few words Christ is
lifted upward from the earth over all of heaven (as St. Paul says). If
it were not enough that he said (as the Jews always did and still do
evaluate and consider him) that he should sit on David's throne and
reign in his house and that his dominion would be mightier than any
who came before him, and finally that he would subject all other
kingdoms to fear before him, how, [in addition] does he ascend
above all heights that he is now seated at the right hand of the
majesty as high as God himself sits and reigns? I thought that he
should sit here below where the psalm was written and as it was
previously said of David. Certainly he should sit upon the earth as a
man and a king who reigns over man. As such he remains as he is
described in the other psalms. But for him it is too poor that he
would be a Lord and king over all kings of the earth. Rather he will
be praised, acknowledged and honored as the one who ascends and
is seated above, where God himself sits over all the angels. Such a
king as reigns there is not only over all men, but also over heaven,
the angels and everything that is under God. So all the angels must
call him their Lord as in Luke 2.

Now who could speak so of Christ and foretell so mightily about
his ascension to heaven and his kingdom? Yes, who could grasp this

well enough and believe it not only at the time when it was not yet seen but also at the time of this holy prophet who was so sure and declares this so clearly? It is because he was justly and rightly praising his Lord that he is right in saying that all kings and lords, yes, the whole world, (as also the Scriptures said) and every angel will petition him. So what are all kings and princes with all their might and rule compared to this one who is seated and reigns on the throne of divine majesty? They are poor beggars and miserable people who cannot even advise, help or save themselves even in the most trivial trouble that befalls this body and this temporal life.

Altb. VII, 330–331: Commentary on Psalm 110, 1539

O God of God, O Light of Light, Thou Prince of Peace, Thou King of kings!
To Thee where angels know no night The song of praise forever rings.
To Him who sits upon the throne, The Lamb once slain for sinful men,
Be honor, might, all by Him won, Glory and praise! Amen, Amen. (*TLH* 132: 1)

Monday

"My kingdom is not of this world." John 18:36

With these words he would also now describe his kingdom; what it is and how it is performed. Namely, it is not a mortal or worldly earthly rule as other lords and kings rule on earth. Rather, it is a spiritual heavenly administration that is not carried on by temporal goods, nor by what this mortal life encounters, as does one who rules and defends land and people, preserves justice and peace, parcels out goods, provides for wife and children, rules the house, farms the fields, drives the animals, etc. For those things are sufficiently established in the world by God's order, Genesis 1, and thereby he has given all of this world's goods, might, kingdom, glory, art and wisdom, etc. But rather his graces extend over hearts and consciences by which men should live before God, making them free of sin and death, having his righteousness and eternal life and overcoming every misfortune. In summary, it is not a temporal, mortal kingdom that must stop all the might and administration of kings and lords on earth. But rather his reign must also be in heavenly eternal ways and give only immortal, eternal goods.

That is why the king with his dominion and administration is completely immeasurably higher than all kaisers, kings and lords that have been or ever can be on earth. Yes, together with their power, crowns, splendor and glory those who are called kings and lords are not worthy to be compared to this Lord. For what is all worldly power, dominion, and administration, even at its best, other than a short temporal matter? Even when a lord is a king and reigns for a term of forty or fifty years (which is rare), his dominion seldom remains standing after his demise. Even if it stands for a long time, it must finally stop and receive an end both of land and people. Because of that, all earthly power and administration, even that which is established and is carried out in the best way, is yet a weak, yes, truly a poor miserable beggar's kingdom. It can never bring about anything that succeeds. Rather, disobedience, unrest and other misfortunes remain there, for the people are too wicked and disobedient. The programs are too dangerous and often out of human control, so that all reason and wisdom are too weak and poor. So it is nothing but an old tattered hide which one must always clean and repair with much trouble and toil. Yet all the effort avails nothing to get it to go as it should.

Now all this still happens in the programs where there are lords who have power and might and money and goods to help it along so far [as they are able]. But if that assistance should stop, their programs are powerless. So no one being devoured in death, no matter how lordly and mighty he is, can save himself for so much as an hour with all his goods, power and might in a mortal crises, sickness or danger of death. But rather he must despair of all human help and lay under the oppression of a pestilence or fever. But this king is not such a lord. Though he does not reign with money and goods or in evident ways, yet mightily he has all things in his hand. His power and might are such a power and might that he still rules and is mighty when all human power, might and wisdom ceases. He can save and help where no man, yes, no creature on earth or in heaven, can help; namely against sins. So they cannot damn us. So death doesn't endanger us, the devil must not stop us from coming to him.

So, you see why David boasts so highly of this Lord. He throws himself, with all his crown, kingdom, dominion and power, under him and will be ruled by him. He would not have done this if it were not another kingdom, power and dominion, nor would he have said it. If not another kingdom, then, according to this temporal and temporary administration, he was himself a mighty lord and had everything that belonged to it, given to him by God himself. Then he did not need to receive doctrine from anyone else on earth or be subject to anyone. But to this other king he justly gives glory so that he knows him beforehand and confesses him as his Lord (even though he is his son). For Christ has a throne and kingdom that neither he nor any king on earth could subjugate with any power. Namely, he is at the right hand of God where everything that is under God must be ruled under his authority and he so reigns to save all people from the devil, sins and death under which they all live. No creature can help him accomplish this. In their place he gives heavenly, imperishable goods, eternal life and eternal peace.

Altb. VII, 333: Commentary on Psalm 110, 1539

Deep in the prophets' sacred page, Grand in the poets' winged word,
Slowly in type, from age to age, Nations beheld their coming Lord,
Till through the deep Judean night Rang out the song "Good will to men!"
Hymned by the first-born sons of light, Reechoed now, "Good will!" Amen. (*TLH* 132: 2)

Tuesday

But now my kingdom is not from here. . . John 18:36

This is a wondrous kingdom. For this king sits above at the right hand of God where he is invisible; an eternal and eternally imperishable person. Yet his nation and people here under on earth in this miserable and perishable existence are thrown under death and every kind of trouble (as any man can encounter on earth). So we all must be delivered into the grave and become ashes. This king's might and power (which is here so richly praised that it is called eternal, mighty power) are almost never exhibited openly because the Christian on earth has it no better than the other people. They are tormented with all kinds of trouble and heartaches not only by external anxiety, sadness and affliction of sins and death (which the godless do not feel so much but rather can "safely" and freely scorn [the Lord and his own] until the little hour arrives when he comes into the Lord's house), that as St. Paul says in appraising this life, "We are yet the most miserable people on earth."

Because this Lord Christ surely sits above at the right hand of God, and he does not have or lead a kingdom of death or sadness, but a kingdom of life where there is peace, joy and deliverance from all trouble, then it must also follow that his own do not remain in death, anxiety, terror, trial and sorrow, but must be torn away from death or grave and all lamenting, with soul and body restored to life. So he lives without sins and evil just as Christ also in his own person became a man and had condescended to take on our poor miserable nature (as he still does). So he begins this kingdom in us and thereby also receives into himself all human infirmity and misfortune. For that reason he had need to die. But as he sits as a Lord and king at the right hand of God, so he could not remain in death and sorrow, but must be God's power to tear through death and grave and everything. He sits where he can fashion such a kingdom in us and bestow it.

See, that is the majesty of this king above everything. He is glorious and mighty both in heaven and on earth. For he is a Lord not as the others, being over land and people, cities and villages, silver and gold, body and goods. Rather he is a Lord and king over the eternal treasures, which are God's own unto peace and joy and all kingdoms to eternal righteousness and life. Although this temporality is also in his hands, namely all the world's might and power, with which he can do what he desires so that all princes and lords must be subjected to him and cannot grab for anything more or any further than he desires, especially death and sins have been laid under his feet as the following verse shows.

Additionally, [these goods] now belong to faith which receives this king. This faith learns to regard Christ in this way and to hold him as sure so that such faith possesses this Lord. The Lord did not need to seat himself above for his own sake or to command the angels for a little while. Rather, because of it, he mightily leads such an administration that he has all hearts in his hand. His Christendom is truly ruled and led, saved, defended and preserved. To all who believe in and call on him he truly gives such gifts as St. Paul says in Ephesians 4 and in the 68th Psalm. For he has gone up into the heights and is seated at the right hand of God to give divine gifts to man.

But whoever would be established and preserved by this faith must not see things according to outward appearances and nature, nor follow natural reason's thinking or his own heart's feelings. Rather as faith's manner and character is described in Hebrews 11, it will hold fast and not doubt that which it does not see. For to our seeing and feeling nothing appears (as said above) that indicates that Christ rules so mightily by us but rather we see and feel the contrary; that there is nothing but empty weakness and a lack of aptitude before our eyes in Christendom. It looks so miserable and forsaken, without help and rescue from the world. Christians are overwhelmed and tread under foot and also overcome and pressed by the devil, sins, death, hellish terror and fear. They also suffer especially the same kinds of misfortune, danger and need experienced by all kinds of people. Therefore, the art and masterpiece of faith is that it goes forth to war and attacks such feelings and thinking and so holds to the plain words. So it hears all things that this Christ (although invisible) proclaims and [hears] that this Christ is seated above at God's right hand and will always desire to remain and reign mightily over us. Yet to the world he is hidden and buried. So this "sit at my right hand," because it is God himself speaking, must surely be true and remain. No creature can overthrow it or make it false. For he cannot lie about himself even when it seems, feels and everything appears as it does [to the contrary].

Altb. VII, 334: Commentary on Psalm 110, 1539

That life of truth, those deeds of love, That death of pain mid hate and scorn,
These all are past, and now above He reigns our King, once crowned with thorn.
Lift up your heads, ye heav'nly gates; So sang His hosts, unheard by men;
Lift up your heads, for you He waits, We lift them up. Amen, Amen. (*TLH* 132: 3)

Wednesday

"And where I am, there shall my servants be also." John 12:26

But where are the people who are now able to praise and rejoice not because they have treasures of gold and silver, great favor and friends, upon which the world so highly rejoices and lifts high their hands, but rather because they have Christ as their Lord sitting at the right hand of God? Who say, "this is my boast and my praise, that I am baptized into this man and received into and live in his kingdom."? David here speaks of him who sits above in the divine majesty and is yet of his flesh and blood and is my brother (as he calls himself). What are the world's goods, glory, splendor and might but a miserable passing nature, yes, a stink and mire compared to this?

This joy would certainly follow if the faith within us were as David's. With such a faith would also come sure comfort and defiance against all tribulations of sins, death, devil and the world. So whoever believes this without doubting, that he has a Lord sitting above who is our flesh and blood, he could not despair or doubt on account of sins. For he did not take flesh and blood to condemn human nature, but that he would help the sinner out of God's wrath and all trouble (that they were in before). He has not gone up to be seated there that he would bang on the heads of those who are baptized into him and believing in him, but that he continually represent, intercede for and reconcile them as a true, right, eternal high priest as he is described thereafter.

So a Christian can be defiant against death. If I yet must be committed under the earth and become ashes, I also have a Lord up above who is my flesh and blood, who nevermore dies there and is only life. Also he has become my Lord, that I not remain under death or the devil's power, but live with him so that death can no longer throttle me much. Christ can and will give me yet more life, as St. Paul says in Romans 14, "whether we live or die, we are the Lord's, for that is why he has died and is risen, that he be Lord over heaven and earth." Therefore, though I should die, yet I will live for my Lord lives, who also is Lord in death. He will not leave me in death but as he lives, so I will live also as he himself says, "I live and you will also live. Where I am, my servants will be also." St. Bernard also had this joy and comfort in his heart that he could say, "How yet will I sorrow and despair? My flesh and blood still resides above in heaven who will be to me (I hope) no enemy." That is a true, spiritual, heavenly, divine thought of faith; which can apportion such praise to itself that it is also somewhat rich, noble, learned and holy enough, but that knows before God nothing to boast of or to trust other than this Lord.

Altb. VII, 335–336: Commentary on Psalm 110, 1539

Nations afar, in ignorance deep, Isles of the sea, where darkness lay,
These hear His voice, they wake from sleep, And throng with joy the upward way.
They cry with us, "Send forth Thy light, O Lamb, once slain for sinful man;
Burst Satan's bonds, O God of might; Set all men free!" Amen, Amen.
(*TLH* 132: 4)

Thursday

And they cry with a great voice and say, "Lord, holy and true, how long do you rule and not avenge our blood on those who live on earth?" Revelation 6:10

You would like to ask some questions here. Why does God peek through his fingers so long and allow so many enemies to become so strong and mighty and rant and rage against the Christian, so that there is no end? Could he not defeat them or make an end to all of them at once, that they cease to exist, or just suddenly make them vanish?

Answer: This shows only that we have a God who is for us and all of Christendom. For if he would have quickly thrown to the ground the Roman Empire or his other enemies in the beginning all at once and destroyed them into ashes, where would there have been room for us to remain for we were not yet born? Or if he were to do it now, where would the ones remain who should yet be baptized? But (says Hebrews 2), the saints before us would not be complete without us nor would they come to glory after us, although this work has already been established for a long time and the judgment has been rendered and has gone out in the presence of all the enemies.

Yet it cannot be executed so quickly or at once, but rather it will proceed mightily and slowly until his kingdom finally is spread through the whole world. More, who belong to heaven above, are always being brought in. When this is done, all at once the enemies of the kingdom become completely destroyed as St. Paul says in 1 Corinthians 15. This verse also says, "He must rule until all his enemies lie under his feet." In this he will always have enemies (as the following verse says further). They storm and do what they can against the Christians but no longer than he, when he breaks the seal, establishes the time and has brought together the little hour in which he will make a complete end.

Therefore, no one who is a Christian should think or hope that we would have peace on earth or be free of enemies but rather they will judge and discharge us joyfully. For Christianity must always be afflicted and persecuted by enemies and have one after another until the last day. But this is not for our sakes but for the sake of our dear brothers who shall be born after us and will also come to Christ. Had not our fathers before us needed to suffer for our sakes and trusted that we would also follow them so that Christianity would not be drawn under? And must they not also for that reason lie under the earth and wait for their final redemption until we also come to them? Why then do we want to have it better than them and not also desire to suffer for our brothers, yes for our own children and children's children? It is surely better that we suffer for a short time and that Turk, pope, tyrants and all the world practice their mischief upon us than that one of our brothers be lost or remain behind.

Therefore, we should gladly see these things and, while it is not promised, we should implore God that our enemies not be all exterminated at once and suffer all they give us with joy. With this we have the comfort that there are yet many who also follow us and the count will be fulfilled. As also in Revelation 6 it is said to the souls (who lie under that altar, beheaded for the sake of God's Word and who say to God, "Lord, how long do you reign and not avenge our blood on those who live on earth?"), that they will rest a little time until their fellow servants and brothers have finally come who should yet also suffer death as they. There we must also look forward to what he himself looks forward to; namely to the number which is not yet fulfilled and that daily must become fulfilled until we all can be gathered together. Under this we trust that we have this king seated as Lord who has already thrown many of these enemies under his feet and always overthrows one after another. But finally he will wipe them all out at once. If we lose our head, are overcome by them and are trampled under their feet (as it often seems) he has not forgotten us but rather, according to his timing, he will establish us again as before, whole and exalted so that the enemies lie eternally also under our feet.

So now it must also be in Christianity on earth as it also happened to the Lord himself. They, like him, must suffer by the devil and the world in such a way that they run and trample them under their feet. So the Christians also experience this and miserably complain as they describe it in Isaiah 54 and 62. They are miserable and desolate, as poor ships, over whom all storms pass and everyone treads on their head and runs over them. But (he says) I will act soon that you tread on those who tread on you so that you will not suffer long what you now suffer. But eternally they must be tread by you. So as this king's throne is eternally established and remains, so also the footstool for his feet will remain.

Altb. VII, 342–343: Commentary on Psalm 110, 1539

Sing to the Lord a glorious song, Sing to His name, His love forthtell;
Sing on, heaven's host, His praise prolong; Sing, ye who now on earth do dwell:
Worthy the Lamb for sinners slain; From angels praise and thanks from men;
Worthy the lamb, enthroned to reign, Glory and power! Amen, Amen. (*TLH* 132: 5)

Friday

Death, I will be poison to you; grave, I will be a pestilence to you. Hosea 13:14

But death encompasses everything that precedes death, i.e., both sins and the law. As sin irritates and drives the conscience, it is thus powerful to death as St. Paul also says, "The prick or sting of death is sin but the power of sins is the law."

So because this Christ is and shall be a Lord and king of righteousness, of life, freedom and comfort, it must also follow from this that he regards everything that is against these things or hinders us as sin, death, terror of the Lord, disturbance and sadness of the conscience as his enemies. For all those are also the armor and weapons of the arch-enemy, the devil. He is also called in Scripture a master of death and all of his might and splendor is nothing other than that he leads the people by sins into death of body and soul. For that, Christ must also reverse death completely to destroy the devil's power over the Christian, as he has already spiritually done. He [the Christian] subdues it through faith and grasps onto life in him to the last day when he will completely exterminate it so that he shall defy death and hell, "Death, where is your sting? Grave, where is your victory?" As he says through the prophet Hosea, "Death, I will be your death. Death I will be your poison."

Also note here this comfort. All of these enemies are not called our enemies nor enemies of Christianity, but enemies of the Lord Christ. "[They are] Your (God's) enemies" (he says), although they still really grab and confront the Christians so that they must be plagued and suffer by them, for Christ himself is sitting above at the right hand of God. They must now leave him unassailed and certainly cannot rumple a single hair of his head much less tear his throne from him. Yet they are called and truly are not our [enemies] but his enemies. So the world and the devil do not attack and plague us for the sake of worldly matters nor for our service nor because of guilt, but only because we believe in this Lord and confess his Word, else they would be one with us and we would remain before them unhindered. Therefore, he must mark these as his own enemies against his own person. So all that oppresses a true Christian, whether from the devil or the world, terror over sins, fear and sadness of the heart, martyrdom or death; he [Jesus] receives it all as if it happens to himself as he also says through the prophet Zechariah, Chapter 2, "Who pokes you pokes the apple of my eye." To Paul who was pressing to Damascus to bind and accuse Christians in Acts 9, Jesus says from heaven above, "Saul, Saul, why do you persecute me?" Or, "I am Jesus, whom you persecute."

Therefore, if we feel terror from sins, fear and sadness of the heart, martyrdom, and death, then we should know that those are not our enemies, but our Lord's (who is our flesh and blood). We look to him to be a foe to these our enemies and to comfort us and turn their attention to Christ. "Do you not know who the Lord is that sits at the right hand of God by whom you are already called and judged to be the footstool of God? Go there and seek what you want. You wish to shout and bite at me and it must be allowed you to grab and scratch at me while my Lord is above your head so that he can and will trample you with his feet." For he will overcome and subjugate all such enemies not only for himself, as they first and foremost have throttled and done away with his own body and soul when he wrestled and battled with them, that he shed his innocent blood; but he has also conquered us and with all his right and might he takes us. The devil, death, law and all hell have as little right to us, when we are in Christ, as they have to him.

Altb. VII, 343–344: Commentary on Psalm 110, 1539

In peace and joy I now depart at God's disposing;
For full of comfort is my heart, soft reposing.
So the Lord hath promised me, and death is but a slumber. (*TLH* 137: 1)

Saturday

The Lord will send the scepter of his kingdom out of Zion;
to subjugate your enemies. Psalm 110:2

This scepter has the praise and title in Psalm 45 that it is held as a straight and true scepter, as a beautiful little white staff, the strongest through and through, without any branches or knots. That is praise for the preaching of the gospel. For such a good, straight, constant and well ordered kingdom is not to be found on earth. No men, no matter how clever, wise and highly educated, are able to establish one that doesn't somewhat bend and branch, that is, have all kinds of flaws. For we even see that Moses' law, though given and established by God and proclaimed by Moses and the prophets, does not proceed as it should. Nor does it order the people as it was intended. We experience (I think) of lords and princes and those who are to rule, that their justice and order, even when they are best done and made, never go as they wish and need constant repairs and adjustment that they be made to work somewhat. So many failures happen (that one cannot repair or excise with more laws, nor can they be anticipated or previously experienced), so that justice must be allowed to bend and stretch according to the necessity of business and commerce, causing justice to suffer. So you can be sure that justice will be none too strong. Even when injustice or evil is done, where it should have held strong and true as it was established, it must become somewhat weakened or even soften.

So the builder, when he cuts off only the coarsest parts of the lumber or planks, doesn't let himself be bothered if it isn't altogether straight and true or if it still has a few splinters or knots from branches. He only judges it as a whole with the plumb line. Or also, the mason does not worry if a stone or two in the wall is too wide and sticks out, or if one of them curves a bit so long as the outer wall according to the measurement and plummet is true and remains in line. For one must not throw away a whole tree or leave behind a wall for the sake of a few knot holes or imperfect stones.

But such weaknesses and deficiencies are not to be found in this kingdom. Rather it is a completely straight, right line with no branches, bends or curves. All is made straight and right. For it is not called ours but God's true plummet or staff and scepter. The justice and righteousness that is in Christ does not depend on our works or wisdom. So even if we were Moses or David or one of the prophets, and should make law and righteousness and rule the people with it, yet nothing would come of it. For the people are such coarse and uncut trees, full of branches and knots, that even if we planed and cut for a long time and made such a good plumb line, it would not work. For we are coarse bent lumber and logs and as always happens in human life and ways, finally, the plane weakens the wood and many things happen that should not. It is ruined. But this administration and right measure is established on another person who has no deficiency, curve or flaw. His Word is the kind of truth and righteousness that needs no planing or correction but proceeds directly back to him and makes a straight line without bow or bend. So it is said, "He that believes and is baptized will be saved." In other words, "Whoever holds my Words will never see death." That is, in short, the whole of what is established by Christ; that no one is able of himself to seek anywhere else or proclaim anything else. For if anyone would proclaim something else or something "better" it would be too heavy for him or he would establish too much. Once established he could not support it or would need another's help.

In summary, all other righteousnesses depend on our life and works. Who does them (Moses writes) shall live by them. But it is a tree with huge branches. According to the measure of righteousness it cannot conform. As man makes of it what he will, it cannot go right as also Solomon complains in his preaching. Even when one has worked hard and long, yet the conscience is not helped nor the heart freed. But here it is God himself who takes and grabs the hands and allows us to preach not of our work but of what he would accomplish. He crafts his righteousness, which is grace or forgiveness of sins through Christ and the power of the Holy Ghost. There all is made straight that we become worthy and are given his kingdom. Such people serve him and are useful unto every good.

Altb. VII, 346-347: Commentary on Psalm 110, 1539

'Tis Christ that wrought this work for me, my faithful Savior,
Whom Thou hast made mine eyes to see by thy favor.
Now I know He is my Life, My Help in need and dying. (*TLH* 137: 2)

Septuagesima

Sunday

But many who are the first will become the last, and the last will become the first. Matthew 19:30

So now we must consider these two words, "last" and "first," as pulling in two directions; one in the way God considers it and the other as it is before people. So those that are first in the sight of people, that is, those who consider and deem themselves as first before their neighbors and before God, these are preposterous before God, for they are the last before God and farthest from him. On the other hand, those who are last before people, that is, who regard themselves and let themselves be considered as the furthest removed and last before God, also go forth as [appearing to man to be] preposterous, for they are nearest and first before God. Now whoever wants to be safe examines himself in light of this passage, "Who exalts himself will be abased." For that explains that the one who is first before man is last before God. The least before men is the first before God. Then again, the first before God is the last among people. But this gospel does not just speak about the simple ranking of first and last, as if the high ones in the world are nothing before God, like the heathen [also think] who know nothing about God. Rather, God treats all alike whether in the world they judge themselves to be first or last. This is dealing with high things and not everyone can handle it. This is alarming to 'great' believers because Christ first says this to the apostles themselves. For it never fails that even one who is poor before the world, weak, despised and yet suffers some things well for the sake of God, uses his appearance as "nothing" to fill his heart with hidden pride because he thinks himself first before God. Even so this one is last. On the other hand another will be so broken down and dimwitted so he thinks he is the last before God even if he has great honor and goods before the world. Even so this one is first.

One also observes how the most high saints had fear for themselves no matter how many high holy offices were given them. David cries in Psalm 131, "If my soul had not been established and stilled, then my soul would have been undone, as one who is abandoned by his mother." Also in another place, "Do not let the foot of pride come to me." So often he was also attacked by outrage, insolence, haughtiness, Psalm 119. Also, St. Paul says in 2 Corinthians 12, "So that I not be overcome by high revelations, a thorn of the flesh has been given me" etc. As we have heard in the epistle, what the common people encounter, which everyone without doubt suffers, can secretly become a trial as if they had [already] become safe [and immune to them] and thought, "we are now near and there is no need. We know God. We have done this or that." They have not [rightly] seen themselves for they have made themselves first before God. Do you see how Saul fell? How David let himself fall? How Peter must fall? How many disciples of Paul fell? Therefore, it is also now necessary that one preach this gospel to our times, to those who know the gospel, to me and my family, too. They could teach and master the world and firmly believe that they are the nearest [to God] and [that they] have eaten the Holy Ghost, bones, feathers and all. For why have so many sects now arisen, one considering this, another considering that to be the gospel? Without doubt, because none of them respected this passage to engage it and let it take root, the first are the last. Or if it took root in them they considered themselves safe and without fear as they esteemed themselves as the first. Therefore, a lot happens to them in accord with this passage so that they become last, to proceed [presumptuously] and toss such scandalous teaching and blasphemy against God and his Word.

Kirchenpost. 631–632: Sermon on the Gospel for Septuagesima

Before Thee, God, who knowest all, With grief and shame I prostrate fall.
I see my sins against Thee, Lord, The sins of thought, of deed, and word.
They press me sore; I cry to Thee: O God, be merciful to me! (*TLH* 318: 1)

Monday

And a winnowing fork is in his hand; he will sweep his threshing floor and gather the wheat in his barn. But the chaff he will burn with everlasting fire. Matthew 3:12

I say again that if you desire to obtain forgiveness of sins and become right and saved before God and so escape the coming wrath, that is such a horrible punishment and eternal damnation, then repent, let yourself be baptized from the one I bear witness of, who is the only one who forgives sins, baptizes with the Holy Ghost, and brings righteousness, life and salvation. From now on it doesn't help to be of Abraham's seed and to be circumcised and bear the name of God's people. Therefore, do not take long to consider if you are sinners but rather acknowledge with just earnestness that you are stuck over your ears in sins and are in need of help and desire and seek the same with your heart. By this you can be advised and helped. And such help, he says, is already at hand, for I am not sent to preach to you about a baptism that only washes the uncleanness of the flesh (as many kinds are commanded in the law of Moses), but rather of a baptism that will be called and actually be a baptism of repentance unto the forgiveness of sins. Therefore, if you desire to partake in this help, then repent, confess your sins and be baptized unto the forgiveness of sins. But if you remain standing upon your delusion that you are yourself good and holy for the sake of your circumcision, law and services rendered to God, then you are commanded to stop, for all advice and council are wasted on you.

So we also must say to our people: It does nothing, dear friend, that you think that you desire to zealously pursue becoming a strict monk or join some difficult religious order, and to do away with your body and life with vigils, prayers, fasts, etc., so that God would behold such hard repentance and bloodletting and forgive your sins for it and receive you into heaven. You are insane and you cheat yourself. What you and all people do is much too poor to remove even the most measly sin, no matter what you do and whatever you call it. For becoming free from sins and righteous must be accomplished another way, namely, that they become forgiven you from the great grace of God for the sake of Christ. Now should you escape God's wrath and eternal punishment that you have earned by your sins, then you must come to it by this way and through no other.

So now it is called repentance, that the man know and acknowledge from the heart that he, as the Scriptures say, is conceived and born in sins and therefore is by nature a child of wrath, of eternal death and guilty of damnation. All works are lost and they [the works] make evil only more annoying because one thinks he will be justified by them. This can only be established by Christ, who is the only mediator between God and men, who has himself done all things for us. Through him we have the forgiveness of sins. If you believe that, then you have it. If not, then you will always be lost even if you should be martyred to death. For it is called forgiveness, not bartering of sins; a gift, not a service; what God has given even to you out of pure grace for the sake of Christ; given as a gift, that you, poor maggot sack, cannot barter, purchase or redeem from him. That's what Luke means when he says that John was preaching the baptism of repentance unto the forgiveness of sins.

Altb. VII, 432–433: First Sermon on Infant Baptism of the Little Children of Anhalt. 1541

O Lord, my God, to Thee I pray: Oh, cast me not in wrath away!
Let Thy good Spirit ne'er depart, But let Him draw to Thee my heart
That truly penitent I be: O God, be merciful to me! (*TLH* 318: 2)

Tuesday

Repent for the kingdom of heaven is at hand. Matthew 3:2

So the preaching of repentance not only makes guilty and damns those in the world who are open sinners before God, but also much more those who want to be good and holy for the sake of their works and their own righteousness. It addresses every person, no one excepted, even if he is a pharisee, teacher of the law, priest, Levite, etc., pope, cardinal, bishop, monk, parson, spiritual layman, etc.; that they should repent and know that all their doing and life before God is useful for nothing and is only sinful and must be something else. From this it is easy to note that it cannot be repentance if I want to buy and make satisfaction for sins through my works (as the papists teach of their repentance). So because I am a sinner and child of wrath by nature, as the Scriptures say, I could not weaken sins with more sins, but rather only make more of them.

It is called repentance when I believe God's Word that shows me and declares to me that I am a sinner and damned before God, and my heart is in terror for it; that I by this or that have become disobedient to God, never rightly observing his commandments or considering them, much less having kept the greatest or the least of them, yet I do not doubt, but rather direct myself to Christ to seek grace and help from him and also firmly believe—I will find it. For he is the Lamb of God from eternity there to be seen. He bears all the sins of the world and through his death shall redeem them. So John reveals both. First, he shows us all our sins through his preaching and thereafter [secondly he] also [shows] where we will find help. This preaching does not return without fruit. It always finds students who are converted and made better through it. For the evangelist Matthew says that many people from all walks of life and lands were coming to John in the wilderness, were baptized by him in the Jordan and confessed their sins. St. Luke also portrays it in Chapter 7 and says, "All people that heard John and the publicans justified God," that is, they believed his Word which John preached to them, that they were sinners and damned. "But the pharisees and the scribes" (says St. Luke, further) "despised God's counsel against them and did not allow themselves to be baptized." For they stood apart. They were already good and godly enough, for John's preaching did not take root. Yes, they allowed themselves to think that they already knew much better than he could tell them. So they despised God's counsel, which he had certified. He had commanded [John] to proclaim that they should receive this preaching and

138

baptism from John and in this and by no other way were they to receive the forgiveness of sins and be saved, but that they repent and be baptized into faith in Christ (which John proclaimed) unto the forgiveness of sins.

Altb. VII, 434–435: First Sermon on Infant Baptism of the Little Children of Anhalt. 1541

O Jesus, let Thy precious blood Be to my soul a cleansing flood.
Turn not, O Lord, Thy guest away, But grant that justified I may
Go to my house at peace with Thee: O God, be merciful to me! (*TLH* 318: 3)

Wednesday

At that time Jesus came out of Galilee unto the Jordan to John, that he be baptized by him. Matthew 3:13

Now while John so preached and baptized (Matthew continues to say), Jesus came out of Galilee unto the Jordan to him and desired baptism. That is surely a marvelous turnabout. The pharisees and scribes, who are full of sins and damnation, desire to have no sins, know of no repentance and do not allow themselves to be baptized. Compare that with Christ, who is without any sins and alone deserves the good reputation of never having committed any sins, and all his Words and works are inoffensive and even holy and saving, so that he needed no repentance, baptism or forgiveness of sins. He comes and desires to be baptized by John, his servant. The others are all conceived in sin, born and live in sins, so that they should justly repent and be baptized. John is also there for the likes of them. Yet many of them, especially the pharisees and scribes (as said), do not want it [performed for them] and the one who is innocent and holy, he does want it.

But why does he come to baptism when no sin and uncleanness is on him which baptism will take away? That will become a saving baptism. John resists here a single sinner, who has no sin upon his person. Yet he is the greatest sinner, who has and bears all the sins of the world. Because of this, he also is baptized and confesses with this act that he is a sinner, but not for himself. Rather [he confesses this] for us. For he altogether bears you and me personally, and stands in our place because we are sinners. Since no one, especially the haughty saint, wants to be a sinner, then he must become one sinner for all, take on the form of sinful flesh, and cry out, as many psalms witness, on the cross in his suffering over the load of sins that he bears and says, Psalm 40: "My sins have encompassed me, that I cannot see; they are more then the hairs on my head," and Psalm

41, "Lord, be merciful to me, save my soul; for I have sinned against you." Psalm 69, "God, you know my folly, and my sins are not hidden from you." And Psalm 22, "My God, why have you forsaken me?"

In these and other psalms Christ speaks as a sinful person. How has he then sinned, or how does he arrive at this conclusion that he is a sinner? It comes to him as Isaiah says in Chapter 53 about him, "The Lord heaped our sins upon him." So then when we (says the prophet) all wandered in error like sheep, then God sent this counsel, who took all peoples' sins. He laid them upon his head (who alone is without any sin). So he becomes the greatest, yes, by far the greatest sinner upon earth, and besides him there are none, for the text says, the Lord has cast all our sins upon him.

Because now he has become a sinner, upon whom all of our sins have been laid, then he truly needed the baptism, and must allow himself the baptism unto the forgiveness of sins. Not for his person, which is guiltless and without blemish, but rather for our sakes, whose sins he bore. The same put himself in the baptism and washed them from himself, that is, from us, in whose person he is bearing them, that they must go under and drown in his baptism. That is why John is ordained, that he bring the people to the baptism of repentance, but foremost and chiefly his office is given that he witness of Christ and baptize him, so that he is also actually and truthfully called the baptizer of the Lord Christ. For if Christ is not with us in this, and not baptized for our sakes, then we are lost. Now because God the Lord has laid on him the sins of all mankind, that he must bear them and make satisfaction for them, so he comes to John, allows him to baptize him for the good of me, you and all the world, so that he purify us from sins and make us righteous and saved.

Altb. VII, 435: First Sermon on Infant Baptism of the Little Children of Anhalt. 1541

On Jordan's bank the Baptist's cry Announces that the Lord is nigh;
Come, then, and hearken, for he brings Glad tidings from the King of kings. (*TLH* 63: 1)

Thursday

Against you alone have I sinned and done evil before you,
so that you are proven true in your words and remain pure
when you judge. Psalm 51:4

That is, I am nothing before you but a sinner. What I do is evil and I can find nothing in me that can stand before you unpunishable. I say such things because you, Lord, remain true in your Words and you cannot be convicted when you judge. That is, would I not want to confess and say that I am nothing but a sinner before you, then I would be accusing your Word of lying and condemn you, as the hypocrites and works-righteous saints do. Therefore, I do not wish to be so impudent and say I am no sinner like they do. That would account you, Lord, to be a liar, and your judgment, through which all my actions and nature are damned, which you have spoken over me, would be accused as a lie. So I confess that I am a sinner and a condemned man, because you truly are right and your Word remains true and unaccusable, even when it is challenged and persecuted. For the hypocrites want to make themselves righteous by their own works. They take their case against God with vigor, cursing and accusing his Word of lying, but it is called: *Ut vincas, cum judicaris*, you will not thereafter remain before him. Finally they are rightly caught and forced to see it, and they are ruined in their sins.

The Jews that did not believe John's preaching, did not repent or allow themselves to be baptized, but rather despised God's counsel, said John must have a devil, and that what he preached of God must have been untrue and lies, therefore they [also] must be accused, go to the ground and the depths and be ruined in body and soul. But God remains right. So what his Word and judgment treats, there he shall and will alone be right. Now his Word says that all men are liars before him. So his judgment falls upon them that they are also guilty of death. Do not accuse him. Give him credit for doing right, not injustice. But if you wish to have rights, then seek it in other matters. Go into worldly governance, where you can exercise your rights against your enemies, who do you harm, that take what is yours, etc. There you can appeal to your rights, and seek and demand them. But when you deal with God and stand before his judgment, then think upon no rights, but rather account yourself wrong and him right if you would find his grace. Should you do so, then you with David and all the saints will say, "Dear Lord, I confess, feel and believe that I am a damned sinner, for which I pray you to absolve, wash and baptize me for the sake of Christ, for I know that you are gracious to me, I have forgiveness of sins and am pure and snow white."

Altb. VII, 436: First Sermon on Infant Baptism of the Little Children of Anhalt. 1541

Yet, though conscience voice appall me, Father, I will seek Thy face;
Tho' Thy child I dare not call me, Yet receive me to Thy grace.
Do not for my sins forsake me; Do not let Thy wrath o'ertake me. (*TLH* 326: 2)

Friday

I baptize you with the baptism of repentance. But the one who comes after me is mightier than I, whose shoes I am not worthy to carry. He will baptize you with the Holy Ghost and with fire. Matthew 3:11

He is saying, "I am not the man who forgives sins and gives the Holy Ghost. But yet I baptize because of the one who does this, who will soon come to you." Therefore, those whom John had baptized and had died before the baptism of Christ likewise were saved. For they believed that Christ with his baptism was coming and that they would be baptized with the Holy Ghost and fire; that is, that he, as the true Lamb of God, offered on the tree of the cross, would die for all the sins of the whole world and by that broadcast that all who believe on him have the forgiveness of sins and shall receive the Holy Ghost who would enlighten, sanctify, comfort and strengthen them, etc., just as the saintly fathers (David and others) also believed before them.

Therefore, there is no difference except this; that before, each one had believed on the coming Christ, but we believe on the one who has come. Both they and we have one Christ, who is yesterday, today and in eternity; Hebrews 13. Only the time frame is different. They were before but we are after. Now whoever would believe with us John's witness, that he is the Lamb of God who bears the sins of the world, and he baptizes with the Holy Ghost, will be saved with us, God grant it, whether he come before or after; it is a single faith. For what everyone who is baptized by John has believed about the coming Christ, that we also now believe identically of the one who has come. We receive the same grace. Yet a great power lies in the fact that we believe that now he has come, for the Jews and also we gentiles. We will always have one Christ, who yet will come. The Jews do not believe that this one who has come is Christ, but rather insist that he will yet come. They make a pure mockery out of our faith and baptism.

So also the pope with his gang surely says, Christ has come and died for our sins, etc. But at the core of their truth, they also act in their doctrine and life as if no salvation is ever worked through Christ's death and the shedding of his blood nor any baptism given by him, in summary, as if he had not yet come. For they teach that through their own works they repent and make satisfaction. That's why I say great power rests upon it, when one believes on the Christ who has appeared or is coming. So David or the fathers had believed in their time that Christ was to come. Else they would have become damned, as now the Jews who do not believe that he has come have become lost and damned.

Altb. VII, 436–437: First Sermon on Infant Baptism of the Little Children of Anhalt. 1541

For Thy Son did suffer for me, Gave Himself to rescue me,
Died to heal me and restore me, Reconciled me unto Thee.
'Tis alone His cross can vanquish These dark fears and soothe this anguish. (*TLH* 326: 3)

Saturday

Surely I need to be baptized by you, and do you come to me? Matthew 3:14

So he says, I am a sinner, therefore I justly should receive, Lord, the baptism from you to become cleansed and absolved from sins by you. For he had already understood that Christ had no sins. Yet Christ would be the one who would bear all the sins of the world and alone exercised the forgiveness of sins and would give the Holy Ghost. Therefore he says, "It is necessary that I be baptized by you." But Christ says, "Now let it be so. For so it is proper for us to fulfill all righteousness." In other words, "My baptism is just, for I will wash away and drown all the world's sins that by this all righteousness and salvation will be administered." So the baptism is also ordained by God primarily for the sake of Christ and thereafter for the sake of all people. For first he must through his own body sanctify the baptism and through that take away the sins and because of that also those who believe on him have forgiveness of sins. So the baptism is not a useless empty thing, as the sects blasphemously say, but rather it contains the administration of all righteousness.

So now repentance (as John preaches unto the forgiveness of sins) is chiefly established that you account God right and confess that your sentence is just where he says that we are all sinners and damned. When you do that from the heart, then the repentance has begun. What more can I do? Bend down and be baptized. For I (says Christ) have administered my baptism so that whoever believes and receives such a baptism would have forgiveness of sins. My Father with me and the Holy Ghost will dwell with him. Then you see, as we also said yesterday, that above Christ, after he was baptized, from that hour on (the same previously in John's baptism was never seen) the heavens opened (and hereafter the earth, graves, hell and everything stood open) and the Holy Ghost was seen in the form of a dove and the Father's voice was heard over this baptism and said he was well pleased with this. Then this son, who stood there and was baptized by John, was so well pleasing to him that if he bore the sins of a thousand worlds upon himself, they all would have to be drowned and weakened in his baptism. But because God was so well pleased with Jesus, then he is also pleased with those who believe on him and are baptized according to his mandate.

Also, in the baptism, not only are sins forgiven, but we become made safe and sure that God has great pleasure because of it. He with Christ and the Holy Ghost wants to be with us when it is administered and he himself is the baptizer, even if such a glorious revelation of divine majesty now is not visibly seen, as that time on the Jordan. Then it is enough that it is seen one time as a witness and sign of the truth. So we should readily be accustomed to see these matters with the eyes of faith. Such a glorious revelation and divine clarity and pomp is shown because of what Christ's baptism means for us. This all is not done or described for the sake of Christ (for he was not baptized for himself), but rather for the comfort and strengthening of our faith, for which he also has received baptism.

Altb. VII, 438–439: Second Sermon on Infant Baptism of the Little Children of Anhalt, 1541

Then on Him I cast my burden, Sink it in the depths below.
Let me know Thy gracious pardon, Wash me, make me white as snow.
Let Thy Spirit leave me never; Make me only Thine forever. (*TLH* 326: 4)

Sexagesima

Sunday

But those on the good soil hear and hold it in a fine, good heart and bring forth fruit in patience. Luke 8:15

Those who hear the Word and steadfastly hold onto it also risk and suffer everything for it. The devil himself does not take or seduce it away. Also, the heat of persecution does not snatch it away. Also, the thorns of lust and the avarice of temporal life do not hinder it but rather it brings forth fruit. So they also teach others the same and increase the kingdom of God. Thus they also do good in love to their neighbor. So he says, "With patience," for such people must suffer much for the sake of the Word; insults and disgrace from the fanatics and heretics; hate and insults with injury to body and goods from the persecutors, not to mention what the thorns and afflictions of their own flesh do. This is rightly called a Word that belongs to the cross. For whoever will hold it must bear and overcome cross and misfortune with patience.

He says, "In a fine good heart," like a field that stands tilled, ready and wide without thorns or grass, a purely beautiful plot. So is a heart also fine and pure, wide and roomy, which is without worry and avarice concerning temporal nourishment so that God's Word finds plenty of room there. But the field is good, not only when it lies fine and ready, but rather also when it is laden and fruitful. It has good soil and is rich with corn, not as the stony or gravelly field. A heart has good ground and is used by the Spirit when it is strong, laden and good. It retains the Word and brings forth fruit in patience. There we see why it is no wonder that so few are true Christians; for the seed falls not only in the good field, which is only a fourth, a small portion. Christians are not true who praise and honor the doctrine of the gospel, but who like Demas, St. Paul's disciple, finally forsakes him (2 Timothy 4), and also who are like the disciples of Christ (John 6), who shrink away from him so that he himself cries out and says here, "Whoever has ears, let him hear," as if he would say, "Oh, how few are the true Christians!" Yes, one is not allowed to believe all who call themselves Christians and hear the gospel. There is more to it than that.

This is all said to us to teach that we should not allow ourselves to be irritated because so many misuse the gospel and few hold it rightly, though it is annoying to preach to those who treat it so scandalously and even strive against the gospel. For it is a preaching that shall go out so generally that it also will be delivered to all creatures, as Christ says in the last chapter of Mark, "Preach the gospel to every creature," and Psalm 19, "Your cord goes out into every land and your counsel to the ends of the earth." Why should it matter so much to us that many despise it? It must be so, for many are called but few are chosen. For the sake of the good earth that brings fruit with patience, the seed must also fall on the path, on the rock and under the stone, since we also are sure that God's Word does not go out without fruit, but rather always also finds good soil, as he says here; that some of the seed of the sower also falls on good soil, not only on the path, under the thorns and on the rocks. For where the gospel goes, there are Christians, Isaiah 55, "My Word shall not return void, etc."

Now that some bring forth thirtyfold, some sixtyfold, some one hundredfold (Matthew 13), is to say that at a particular place more people will be converted than at another, and that one apostle or preacher preaches farther or more than the other. For there are not the same amount of people in every place and also not all Christians give [witness] alike and the preachers do not preach equally far and wide, but rather it is as God has supplied and ordered it. The Word of St. Paul, who had preached most widely and voluminously, could truly be described as the hundred-fold fruit.

Stuttg. I, 646–647: Sermon on Sexagesima, Luke 8: 5-15

Almighty God, Thy Word is cast Like seed into the ground;
Now let the dew of heav'n descend And righteous fruits abound. (*TLH* 49: 1)

Monday

To you is given to know the mystery of the kingdom of God; but to the others in parables, that they do not see it even if they see it and do not understand even if they hear it. Luke 8:10

But what is he saying, "To you it is given to know the mystery of the kingdom of God"? What mystery? If one will not know it, then why should one preach it? Mystery means a buried, secret thing, that one does not know, and "mysteries of the kingdom of God" are the things buried in the kingdom of God, where Christ is with all his grace, which he has revealed to us, when St. Paul names him. For whoever rightly knows Christ, knows what God's kingdom is and what is in it, and therefore he calls it a mystery because it is spiritual and hidden and yet remains where the Spirit is not apparent. So although there are many who saw and heard it, just as many today preach Christ and [many] hear how he is given for us, yet they do not receive it. But that is all still on the tongue and not in the heart, for they do not believe it themselves and also do not experience it, as St. Paul says in 1 Corinthians 2, "The natural man receives nothing from the Spirit of God." Therefore, he says here, "To you is given," that is, the Spirit gives it to you, so you not only hear and see it, but also know and believe it with your heart. So it is now no longer a mystery to you. But others, who hear it just as you do, but do not have faith in the heart; they see and do not understand, for it is a mystery and remains unknown to them. All that they hear is nothing but a parable or a dark passage. That is also observed among our fanatics, who know a lot to preach about Christ, but because they themselves do not experience it in their hearts, they go on from there and leave the true foundation of the mystery behind and proceed with questions and odd little discoveries. Also, when it comes to their assembling together, they know practically nothing about how they will trust God and find forgiveness of sins in Christ.

But St. Mark says (Mark 4), Christ had spoken to the people in parables for that reason, that they could perceive, each according to his ability. How does this fit with what St. Matthew says (Matthew 13), that he speaks with parables so that they would not perceive? They must easily go together, that St. Mark will say: The parables serve the purpose that the coarse people would grasp it externally even if they do not perceive, yet later they could be taught and informed. For the parables naturally attract the simple and they remember them easily, because they are taken from the common things that the people experience. But Matthew would say that no one is able to understand these parables no matter how well they hear and remember them, if the Spirit doesn't reveal and make it known. The parables are preached, therefore, that people not understand them, but rather that it naturally follows that where the Spirit does not reveal, no one understands them. But yet Christ has taken these words out of Isaiah 6, in which the high understanding of divine administration became active, that he hid and revealed those things he intends to do as he had planned from eternity.

Stuttg. I, 647-648: Sermon on Sexagesima, Luke 8: 5-15

God's Word a treasure is to me, Thro' sorrow's night my sun shall be,
The shield of faith in battle. The Father's hand hath written there
My title as His child and heir, "The kingdom's thine forever."
That promise faileth never. (*TLH* 48: 2)

Tuesday

The lesser wealth that a righteous one has is better than the wealth of the many godless. Psalm 37:16

For they have it with all disgrace and shame before God as robbers. Now I would surely rather have a penny as a pious man than many thousands of dollars as a scoundrel. But the godless do not question whether the money is his god that he is faithful to.

Oh, that we also could sing so well such praise as this verse! For we have yet such a definite Word of God and the other heap of people is so defiant against everything and so boastful, that they rely on the kaiser, kings, prince, that is, upon their wealth and might, and they have neither God nor his Word. They do not think of giving thanks for their wealth and might, as God's gifts, but rather they make their wealth and might into their god. They rob and steal. They are God's thieves and scoundrels, according to all they have, and they possess everything with disgrace and shame. It is their boast and blasphemy and shame to accuse God, their patron, of lying. They blaspheme him and persecute him with all of his servants and his whole kingdom (where God gives out salvation and little fortune, amen, which they can do well without).

But we could boast that God has given us his Word. Let them be rich and we be beggars. Let them be powerful but us weak. Let them be happy but us sad, them wonderful, but us despised, they lively, but us dead, they everything but us nothing. So what? Yet they have no God, but rather must themselves make a beggarly, lousy god from their pennies. Oh, what pitiful material for a god! Oh, pitiful god-making! But we have God, and praise the true God. They must let us keep this ruby. Next to him, all of their kingdoms are smelly dung and mire.

Now if we must suffer much, what is harmed? It means: If you would be a Christian, *sufficit tibi gratia mea*, give thanks that you have my Word and through the Word, myself. What is harmed by your need, hunger and pestilence? What does it hurt you by being beaten by the prince; or the wantonness of the knave; of the whole world's disgrace; all the devils wrath? You have God's Word, and they don't. You are in abiding grace, and they aren't. You are my child, they are my enemies. Beloved, take my Word as my self, also as a treasure, also as a kingdom, also as a heavenly kingdom in your distress, misery and trouble. My Word remains forever, and you also in the Word. Your misery and every pride passes away as quickly as a thought.

Altb. V, 946: Commentary on the 147th Psalm, 1532

The Word they still shall let remain, Nor any thanks have for it;
He's by our side upon the plain With His good gifts and Spirit.
And take they our life, Goods, fame, child and wife,
Let these all be gone, They yet have nothing won;
The Kingdom ours remaineth. (*TLH* 262: 4)

Wednesday

He sends his counsel upon the earth; his Word quickly
spreads. Psalm 147:15

He reveals the golden art through which God bestows and gives
such good deeds. He speaks. It costs God nothing more than a Word,
that is called *fiat*, Genesis 1. For he is in need of no food, hammer,
anvil or pliers in order to make fast the bolt [of the city gate]. He
needs no stone or mortar to fashion [a boarder of] peace. He also
needs no women nor commerce nor coins to make the children rich
and blissful. So he also does not need any plows or harrows to
satisfy us with wheat, but rather he speaks to the bolt: "Be fastened."
And it is fastened tight. And to the citizens: "Be rich and blissful."
So they are rich and blissful. And to the walls, "you bring peace"
and so there is peace there and to the earth: "Bear wheat," so she
bears wheat, as the 33rd Psalm also says, "When he speaks, it is
established." and Psalm 78,"He spoke, and there came [vermin ?]."

So also here, he sends his counsel to earth, (that is) he speaks
with the earth, and everything that is on it. The 107th Psalm speaks
in this way of those who are sick unto death and yet recover, "He
sends his Word and makes you well." That is, he says, "Be healthy,"
so one is healthy. Therefore, since he doesn't need any doctor, he
rather speaks them well with his Word. Also Psalm 148, "Fire, hail,
snow, mist and storm winds; these your Words bestow." That is,
they do as he counsels them. His talking or speaking is such a
creative thing as we read in Genesis 1:1, that he has made the world
through his speaking. And St. Paul in Romans 4, "He calls to that
which is not so that it is or must come into being. His Word (he
says) runs fast." That is, it accomplishes all that he wants easily and
quickly. And as soon as he speaks, it appears, as God spoke in
Genesis 1:1 and it was. It is not such a lazy, sick, dead Word, as is
human word and command. Even when such [human word]
proclaims and commands a lot of things, yet nothing happens, or
almost nothing, for the kings' and lords' word or command does
little and does it slowly. It doesn't run forth. It creeps and crawls
with leisure, as one says, "It is a command of the governor," that is,

it won't happen. Yes, when God's Word doesn't come after it and speak, when you, king or prince, say, "do this," nothing will come of it. My Word must come to it afterward and do it. When given by the command of the prince's might, and by the subject's fear and obedience to do it, apart from God's Word, it will yet be called and remain only the prince's command.

But if God speaks to the earth, "become green," then it easily becomes green in response. "Grow," and the stalk responds by growing. "Bear wheat," and it bears wheat and everything happens easily and soon. We see before our eyes that his Word does not crawl, but rather runs; yes it springs and is accomplished in a single leap and in an instant. So if he commands something to be in the border, then there is instantly peace, which no prince's command [apart from God's command] can create or preserve. When he blesses the people in the city and declares they should have good fortune, then pure good fortune quickly breaks out, when, apart [from his Word], no commerce or publicity was able to help. When he declares the bolt is to hold fast, then the city is well kept and defended where apart [from his Word] no wall or defense could defend and keep it.

Altb. V, 941–942: Commentary on the 147th Psalm, 1532

Now thank we all our God With hearts and hands and voices;
Who wondrous things hath done In whom His world rejoices;
Who from our mother's arms Hath led us on our ways,
With countless gifts of love That still is ours today. (*TLH* 36: 1)

Thursday

He satisfies you with the best wheat. Psalm 147:14

That is, he richly gives you the corn and fruits upon the field, and all kinds of necessary food and drink, to nourish the body. And he says, thereafter, that he gives not only corn, but rather *adipem*, select and sweet wheat, and not only gives it, but completely and richly satisfies us with it. With this he would reveal that he gives us enough to eat and to drink, as also St. Paul says in 1 Timothy 6, "Who richly gives us all things to enjoy." And that is also true. For all year, so much grows (where God is merciful and will not afflict with hunger), that the world cannot consume it, but rather remains used to it. So also avarice grows and never has enough. If the richness of earth were only corn and its water only wine, and the mountains were pure gold, yet they could not satisfy a greedy person, even if he had it all himself.

But who now believes that these are God's gifts when we have corn and wine and all kinds of fruits so richly? Where are they who thank and praise him for it? Yes, of course, one parties and lives in luxury, and then again one lends it out for profit and makes a killing and oppresses the poor and everyone and we go along with it as if we had made it ourselves, no thanks to God, as if God had not created it. Just as now the farmers and nobility press their wantonness with their situation. They have the land and the fruits in it and also now would have the money because other people have nothing and they alone have everything. Even so, if they would rightly consider it, in time they would find that they themselves have nothing. Let them go and produce!

We should learn here. God be praised and thanked, that he lets the corn grow. We should acknowledge that it is not our work, but it is rather his blessing and gift that corn and wine and all kinds of fruit grow. By that we eat and drink and have all necessities, as also the Lord's prayer informs us, that we say, "Give us our daily bread." Here we confess with the word "give," that it is God's gift and not our creation. And were he not to give, then not a stalk of corn would grow and our fields would be empty. Yes, it is such a strong gift that they must be wondrously preserved through God's power until we hunt for them and are satisfied. For how soon could all the corn in the world spoil, freeze, become moldy, be devoured by worms, or become spoiled by water? And even while it is yet growing, how soon it can be ruined by heat, weather, hail and be devoured by beetles and other creatures? And who can number all the dangers that corn and wine must withstand even when it comes off the field? It can even then be consumed by moths and fly away. The devil would not allow a single stalk or leaf to sprout and grow if God did not defend them.

Therefore, when we see a field or corn, we should not only acknowledge God's goodness but also his might and think thus: Oh, you dear corn, that God gives us so fully as out of abundant, gentle goodness, with great power he defends you from the time you are sown until you come unto my table. Through countless dangers and all troubles you have come to me. For how mightily he rips you through the fingers and hands of the devil, that grab, enclose and strike to ruin you and put us to death with hunger. Yes, surely that is how we should think! We have other ways of acting than to acknowledge such grace and power of God. We are the ones who have done the most for the corn. If we had not labored, then God had not been able to give us anything. So we depart hardened lumps and blocks and meanwhile keep on profiteering. With greed we use such mighty, gracious gifts of God and also use them to oppress both God and man.

Altb. V, 940–941: Commentary on the 147th Psalm, 1532

All the plenty summer pours; Autumn's rich, o'erflowing stores;
Flocks that whiten all the plain; Yellow sheaves of ripened grain
Lord, for these our souls shall raise Grateful vows and solemn praise. (*TLH* 572: 2)

Friday

Jerusalem praise the Lord, Zion honor your God. Psalm 147:12

He does not charge any great work, or costly gems, for these great treasures as many would like to say. He charges the very lightest work, namely praise and thanks, which are given with no trouble or cost. For what is easier to do, than say, "praised be you, merciful God, for I thank you for your kindness and gifts," or "you are a good, true God and kind Father," etc.? No one needs to run up to Rome or make any similar effort. In short, what kind of trouble and labor do you read or hear of in this psalm? Since we cannot do such an easy service to God, what will we do in great and difficult services to God; as those contained in the Ten Commandments, and suffering all evil of body and life for his sake, risking wealth and honor for him? Truly, whoever can or will not say *gratias* to God will never do or suffer anything for the sake of God.

It is a great scandal (where we can be ashamed), that one must bid us to thanksgiving like lazy people and be awakened to it like the sleeping. But we count the benefits, take and name and build upon them so that we daily receive them. We use them and live by them constantly. So we ourselves should rightly bid and exhort ourselves to thanksgiving, without psalms and external reminders. The blessings themselves should stir, draw and inflame us [to it]. But nothing will come out. One must request and intimidate and strike in the mouth, as this psalm does, yet our lazy nave [the old Adam] does not even do such an easy, lusty, happy little work and beautiful little service to God. "Phooie" to our scandal, that we do not become afraid or blush when we hear or read such a verse in the Psalms!

But it is much more scandalous that one must also call us beneficiaries and say to Jerusalem, "Friend, praise the Lord," and to Zion, "Friend, praise your God." Is Zion yet such a worthy and a just, good servant, etc.? For there are many who daily use all divine favor and see and truly feel that they have great gifts and all wealth; but they do not think once from whom they have it, or that it is God who gave it to them. They rather receive it as if it came naturally or as if they had earned them by their labor, flesh and wisdom. They also consider that God must give it to them and that they are not guilty for not giving thanks. No animal lives so shamefully, no sow, as the world lives. For a sow yet knows the woman or maid from whom she seeks to eat the grape husks, bran and leavings. She runs there and cries out. But the world does not know or regard God at all, who does good so richly and overwhelmingly. It keeps silent about it lest they should thank and praise him for it. From this one sees how this easy and light psalm is so cut to pieces and drowned out daily by all the spiritual people in the church who remain so uninformed and void of understanding; by these blind and thick people one must attribute this also to Jerusalem and Zion itself. What then will the wealth of Babylon and Sodom do? People almost never acknowledge God and his gifts and thank him.

Altb. V, 936: Commentary on the 147th Psalm, 1532

Lord 'tis not that I did choose Thee; That, I know, could never be;
For this heart would still refuse Thee Had Thy grace not chosen me.
Thou hast from the sin that stained me Washed and cleansed and set me free
And unto this end ordained me, That I ever live for Thee. (*TLH* 37: 1)

Saturday

You shall not add anything to what I have given you and shall also not take from it. Deuteronomy 4:2

So before Moses established or taught anything, he took care above all things that nothing be added or subtracted from it. This passage briefly condemns all human laws and also concludes that in matters belonging to the conscience, nothing is competent but the law and the Word of God. In that the will of God will be sufficient, which according to this passage also claims [precedence over] reason and necessities.

For ever since we were drowned in blindness through Adam's sins, so also we do not know God in all his will and advice. Is it not only foolish but rather impossible that we of ourselves prepare the light and way through which we come to God and grasp what he would have happen to us? As he says in the book of wisdom, "The thoughts of man are fearful and unsure, for what man will know what God desires?"

Therefore, since God revealed his law, by which he informs us of his will, so he retains our praise, Psalm 116, "Every man is a liar, every man is idolatrous." And Isaiah 55, "As the heaven is exalted over the earth, so my thoughts are exalted over your ways."

Because of this, it is a completely foolish argument and reasoning of the sophists, when they ply the free will and define it in this way: I have the free will and will to rule a cow, or to throw away money, therefore, I have also the freedom and power to do what God desires and to serve him. It is as much as saying: I want to tread the earth with my feet and go up from the earth, so that [by it] I also will go to heaven and walk on the clouds.

Man still has the knowledge and free will from the first creation to deal with the creatures who are smaller than he according to his pleasure. But it [such knowledge] does not conduct itself and do what pleases God, his head. That it doesn't know and desire. There free will ends, is completely blind, powerless, yes, dead and accursed. Therefore, it should not dare to choose or act, but rather should rely alone upon a single Word of God. It should add nothing to it and take nothing away. If it did, it would become unsure that it is God's Word. He should tread on no paths but where he is sure. Where God's Word is, he will not yield. What a necessary warning!

Now you bring contrary evidence: Why, then, are so many books of the prophets added to (these books of Moses)? And David had ordered that a temple be built, by doing away with the tent of Moses and he administered the Levites into orders and Joshua had done much and commanded the people many things. This could also be said of many others.

I answer: That is not called adding or subtracting when one teaches with other or more words the same as Moses did. In this manner the prophets have not taught and explained themselves, but rather Moses, and according to his law they judged and sentenced the king and the people.

Because of this Moses says here of the people and not of God: "You shall not add. . ." For why doubt about whether God according to the advance of time would like to add or subtract? For he, even if he adds or subtracts, yet remains true and his Word is always true and leads us and truly preserves us.

Altb. V, 1046-1047: Commentary on Deuteronomy, 1525

God's Word is our great heritage And shall be ours forever;
To spread its light from age to age Shall be our chief endeavor.
Through life it guides our way, In death it is our stay.
Lord, grant, while worlds endure, We keep its teachings pure
Throughout all generations. (*TLH* 283: 1)

Quinquagesima

Sunday

Behold, the hour is coming and is already here that you will be scattered, and each go his own way and leave me alone. But I am not alone, for my Father is with me. John 16:32

Here he reveals the one he always trusted. For he had a small group with him in these last hours. Death was imminent. He already sees the stripes and chains binding him. His captors were ready, all prepared and in armor. Also he would be forsaken by these few, his disciples, yet he was comforted in this: "Even if all the world is against me and also this little bunch abandons me, yet I will not be defeated, for I still have the Father with me." These are excellent, majestic words, that steady Christ securely. But who among the Christians could repeat [this assurance]? How can each [Christian] be so sure of this matter and also say, "It is fine even if everyone rejects me, so long as the Father still is by me." But where will such words be said without sobbing, sighing, and whining? I should marvel at this because Christ himself also went through this misery. He must be so completely abandoned by all the world, and also by his dearest friends.

So as a true man, he had to act in the natural way. He should also see his own all shrink away from him and flee. Practically no one stands by him or stays, as he complained much when he experienced it in the psalter, as in Psalm 31, "Who sees me on the street flees before me." And Psalm 38, "All my friends and acquaintances flee far from me." As in the 22nd Psalm, "Save my desolate soul, under vain cruel unicorns." So he has also experienced that kind of misery much deeper than we, whatever it is; to be so alone or forsaken. Without doubt heavy sighs and hot tyrants had oppressed him heavily, yes, as he stood so alone at trial, forsaken by all people, also by those who depended on him. He might know something of this. I say also of myself, as a poor example, that it [may someday] come my way that all will fall from me that are still with me. Even if they do not actually march against me, they might stand in such fear and doubt that I would not know if they were for me or against me. I might not anticipate anyone standing by me any longer.

I am often amazed at St. John Huss' being burned at the stake in Constance (we would call him holy and honor him, because he also did not deserve such measures, as we also experience). He had been able to stand so solidly against all the world, pope, kaiser and the whole council. Not a single man stood by him there. Instead he was cursed and persecuted by everyone. Do you think that jail was more confining than the restraints of death? Yet he had need to comfort himself and overcome such anxiety even with this passage by which Christ comforts himself, "I am alone and yet am not alone for the Father is by me." For it works woe and makes an awkward heart when a person instantly loses all his friends, for whom he had cared, along with all his wealth and livelihood. How should the apostles become courageous when Christ was an embarrassment to them so that they left him in his hour of need? When I myself (where God is for me) would begin to fall away at that thought, or to stand so alone by myself, so that I no longer stayed with him, what then would become my protection and deliverance?

Therefore, he commands this Word for a good purpose. Without doubt it comes out of a heavy heart, and the situation had become burdensome and distasteful to him, so here he protects himself by separating himself from all mankind and saying, "Even if I must for your own good stop and have pain, so that you leave me so completely alone, even my own friends, apostles and all the doomed world, then I am not [really alone]. For I have a Father, who does not leave me, for I suffer and die because of the Word and command which he has given me."

Altb. VII, 229–230: Sermons on the Gospel of St. John Chapters 14–16, 1537; cf. AE 24

Jesus, I will ponder now On Thy holy Passion;
With Thy Spirit me endow For such meditation.
Grant that I in love and faith May the image cherish
Of Thy suff'ring, pain, and death That I may not perish. (*TLH* 140: 1)

Monday

In the world you have trouble; but take comfort, I have overcome the world. John 16:33

These words should fortify a Christian and make him greater than heaven and earth. He says, "I have spoken these things to you, and I have overcome the world," as if to say, "Friend, write this (I) very large, so that you hold it well in your eyes and heart. For that 'you' and 'your' (as he says, 'spoken to you,' and 'you will have trouble') is just a little word, as small as a single little pebble on the sun, yes, it becomes much smaller than a pebble (which is called nothing). Even if you are ever so small, yet I can and will still make you great since I am the one who says these things." He does not say he is speaking of the Roman or Turkish kings, who seem so big and wondrous before the world. He also doesn't say this of all the saintly angels in heaven or of all the creatures, but rather, "I," "I say it, of those who are to come and shall be adorned immeasurably and unknowably greater than them. Therefore, only consider what I say, and hold onto that, not on what is outside of me and what afflicts you so. Then when you would compare yourself with our great enemies, pope, kaiser, kings, world, yes devil and death, you would become so strong and great that you must be defiant against them all."

"I have murdered and devoured so many of you," says death and the devil, "for almost six thousand years now! Yes often many thousands are carried off in a single day. What is one man to me? If I can all at once devour a whole animal (says the wolf) will I not also be able to gulp down a gnat?" The world and the devil consider us as gnats, that they do not notice in their throats when they swallow us. But we will neither consider ourselves so poor nor they so big and horrible as it seems. We are poor and small compared to the power of the devil and death, but we also hang onto the same one who said, "I," "I have overcome the world." So we will see if all the world, devil and death have such wide throats that they swallow us. They swallow us, but as if a bone becomes lodged in their throat. They must, then, choke. So as little as Christ has been devoured and consumed, so little will they also consume us.

Christ would still gladly speak into us this courage so we learn to trust in him and rely upon him. For he considers us and sees well that we are in ourselves very weak and (as we measure ourselves) are too shocked and terrified before the great giants, death, devil and the world. "This I know very well," he says. "Therefore, I will bind you to me and also me to you, so that you should place your confidence and trust on me. For I have already overcome the world. The great and small, rich and poor, come together and want to be the great, immense monster that will swallow and devour you as a little bitsy gnat. I will become a great camel in his throat and break through his stomach, that he burst and must give you back, without his thanks. For I am the one who said to you, 'only turn both of your eyes from you and them and see who I am!', so that you can say, 'Listen, death, devil, pope, kaiser and world, you truly make yourselves great, flash your long sharp claws, and open your throat wide, so that next to you I am a poor little worm, that is true. But what did you think about the one who says here, "I am the one who has overcome the world, and that such a one spoke to me and bid me rely on him confidently?" ' "

Altb. VII, 231: Sermons on the Gospel of St. John Chapters 14–16, 1537; cf. AE 24

Go, then, earthly fame and treasure! Come, disaster, scorn and pain!
In Thy service, pain is pleasure; With Thy favor, loss is gain.
I have called Thee Abba, Father! I have stayed my heart on Thee.
Storms may howl, and clouds may gather, All must work for good to me. (*TLH* 423: 3)

Tuesday

I yet have much to say to you, but now you cannot bear it. John 16:12

The dear Lord dearly wants to strengthen his disciples and prepare them for what they would encounter in the world after his departure. He comforts them with what the Holy Ghost would administer through them. But he saw that he could not speak this into their hearts now with his Words until the Holy Ghost himself come and place it in their office. Then they would be ready to learn and experience it. Therefore, now he breaks off and what he now cannot administer with Words he commends to the Holy Ghost who would deliver it richly. They would then gladly learn all that they now could not understand or bear. They would be preserved until the end in truth.

But this text has been stretched and martyred through the pope's great doctrinal might, to strengthen and justify his lying office. And although now they are beginning to be ashamed of themselves so as not to speak so loudly of it, yet we must also say something about it, so that we retain the text purely and the error remain in the light; that by our own teaching no one forget how scandalously it was previously perverted. They have these comforting Words that he speaks to his Christians of suffering and comfort, but they present their own man-made laws, filling Christianity with them that one must regard everything that they say as an article of faith and necessary for salvation, which yet do not belong to Christ's kingdom at all. The Holy Ghost has nothing to do with it. But so that we make such things clear, let us first see the Lord Christ's meaning.

There are two kinds of life among men on earth. One lived in fine, comfortable, quiet and peaceful ways and the other an unpleasant, hard and troubled life, full of sorrow and heartache. This difference is easy to understand and everyone already knows that a hungry and needy person is and lives a different existence than those who are full and have enough of everything. Whoever is rich and satisfied, speaks only of great things, but the one in hunger suffers, doesn't ask much about kingdoms and great wealth and is happy if he can hunt up a piece of bread. Now Christ speaks here only with those who suffer need and weakness, who become pressed, miserable, persecuted and plagued by the world. He says this to comfort them as the one who already knew and understood how it was with their mind and courage, and who must administer and care for his sayings and Words, after they were commissioned. He says, "I would have liked to have said to you much more because I must leave you behind, but there is no longer time and you are still too weak for it. If I should take the time to tell what needs yet to be said, how you will be persecuted, and what you will suffer because of your preaching, which the Holy Ghost will do through you, it would scare you too much. But rather, now my suffering begins and you will see and have your highest grief because of it. Therefore, I will now spare you of speaking any more of it until the Holy Ghost comes, who will strengthen you and give you such courage that you will be able to bear it all."

This is the true, simple understanding of this text, that he speaks of the suffering to come which they will have after his departure. He says, "I have much to say to you of this." What kind of "much"? Namely much suffering, grief, persecution, heartache from the devil and the world.

Altb. VII, 203: Sermons on the Gospel of St. John Chapters 14–16, 1537; cf. AE 24

Man may trouble and distress me, 'Twill but drive me to Thy breast;
Life with trials hard may press me, Heav'n will bring me sweeter rest.
Oh, 'tis not in grief to harm me While Thy love is left to me;
Oh, 'twere not in joy to charm me Were that joy unmixed with Thee. (*TLH* 423: 4)

Wednesday

But now I go up to him who sent me, and no one among you asks me, "Where do you go?" John 16:5

What does it mean that he says, "None of you asks me: 'Where are you going?' " Had he not told them above in the fourteenth chapter, "Where I am going, you know; and you also know the way."? And hadn't he said after the supper that through one of his disciples he would be betrayed and he would be given over to death so that Peter even said to him, "Lord, I would go with you into prison and death."? Also Saint Thomas had previously asked him where or by what way he would go from them. Why does he here say the opposite, that they did not know it and also wouldn't ask of it? If the sharp, clever masters (I mean our crude pope's asses) had heard it, they would have soon found it to be a contradiction, and they would make Christ himself disagreeable as if he didn't know or think about what he was saying. But the explanation and understanding of it are in the Words where he says, "Where I go." He says, "You are so completely beat up and terrified over this Word that you hear I will no longer be with you, that you do not think to ask more about where I am going, nor does it go into your heart. For if you knew you would not be so spent and terrified. But now, because you want to know nothing of it you do not ask any more about it though you rightly should ask and discover what it means that I go. If so, you could have comfort and not be troubled over my departure."

So above, they spoke superficially about his departure and asked superficially about the city and streets he would take. But here he speaks about it so that they would not speculate about how he would depart, but rather how very good it is that he goes. "Therefore you should not ask (he would say) which streets or paths that I will go but rather: Where and why I go away, that is, how it is of service to you. For such a departure is not for me, but for your sake. But I must now prepare you well because you cannot think about where I am going. Now you can neither be comforted nor rejoice over this. Rather you are so completely destroyed by it that when you hear that I will leave you, you cannot think or ask any further about it to find the comfort in it. It is now contrary and frightening to you. For you are so used to me and like to have me with you so much that you cannot stand for me to be apart from you as I will be taken from you."

So he would wake them up and lift them a little from their sadness in which they were drowning because they heard that he would leave. So he, of all people, is a kind man and he would have made his own [disciples] joyful and glad because of him, for they would not be robbed of such loving company and friendship in the usual way. But because they would be left alone and find no loving treasure or friendship to take his place, but rather hear the accusation [against him], they [also] would be cursed, pursued and plagued in the world and especially by their own people. For they would gladly also leave, if they were allowed, or flee before this grief and cry, "Shall we then also now be completely lost?" Therefore, he comes himself, before they even began to ask, with the answer because of their [troubled] thoughts: "On no, not so, dear disciples. Don't think as it naturally seems to you about my leaving you, but rather think how good it is for you. Let us yet talk a little about what I mean to do; here you should ask and be assured of the reason I go away and what good it does for you."

Altb. VII, 193–194: Sermons on the Gospel of St. John Chapters 14–16, 1537; cf. AE 24

And when my soul is lying Weak, trembling, and opprest,
He pleads with groans and sighing That cannot be exprest;
But God's quick eye discerns them, Although they give no sound,
And into language turns them E'en in the heart's deep ground. (*TLH* 528: 8)

Thursday

So that the Scripture is fulfilled, as written in your law:
They hated me without reason. John 15:25

From reading the Psalms you know that this is the boast and title
of the world. This is its sour little fruit; that it must persecute [me]
without any shame or reason, but for pure pleasure. They hate me
because I preach to them of God's grace and their salvation and you,
as you belong to me, are my disciples and confess me. In summary,
because of the Word all this is done. That creates this hate and scorn;
else the two of them, they and we, would not be so hostile and
dangerous. But now we preach his Word. We must not only be
despised but also hated. Yet they have no reason for this. Rather,
because of it, they have great and many simple reasons to love, to
serve and to thank us.

We must know this so we conduct ourselves appropriately when
this is added to us. It comes our way for the sake of our preaching
or confessing the Word. You yourself will experience this both from
the outside among the enemies and also internally among ourselves,
where the devil himself also wants to advise and educate you. He
would bring you into dreariness, impatience, heavy spirits, and lay
you in all plagues. Who does all this? Surely not Christ, nor his dear
Spirit, but rather the unpleasant, desperate devil, who spears such
thorns into the heart not because you are a sinner as others,
adulterers, thieves, etc., but rather he is your enemy because you are
a Christian. He will not suffer you to be called a Christian or that
you hang upon Christ, or that you should speak or think a good word
about him. But rather he would gladly embitter your heart with pure
dung and gall, that you should despair, "Why has he made me a
Christian? Why don't I just let him go? Then I would have peace."

Therefore, when you should fear and experience such things
encountered in your office or inside yourself, hurry to confront him
[the enemy] and say, "Now I see why the devil gives me such a hard
time. He wants to frighten and hunt and destroy my office,
preaching, confession and faith, so I expect from my Lord Christ
nothing good, nor praise, honor or call upon him. For the devil is
Christ's sworn and declared enemy. But you also have hell fire, you

unpleasant Satan, and to your spite I will all the more preach and praise this man, my heart comforted and trusting in his blood and death, even should you also explode [upon me] with all of hell." If you would stay by Christ, you must learn and practice this. For that is the devil's doing. He would rip us away from Christ and the way of our flesh is that it will not pay attention, but also hates him even when we still ought to give him all honor and lift up our hands and have our heart's comfort and joy in him.

That is the resolve of this text or picture of the world with which he comforts his own. That must be so. It is not done for the sake of us but for the sake of Christ. But they also serve to show that there is no counsel for their sins and they can have no pardon because they consciously and evilly do not desire to hear Christ or us. "Therefore, let them do" (he says) "what they want. It is written in the Scriptures and foreseen in the future. Only do not let your heart become dull or give way to doubt, if you see and feel such things, as all the world so defiantly curses and persecutes you as a heretic and as the devil's own, and boasts in opposition to your salvation and service to God. But rather know that it must go that way for me and my name, that they hate me with more anger than any devil or evil person upon the earth; but yet nothing will come of or prevail from their hatred and evil against me or against you."

Altb. VII, 175: Sermons on the Gospel of St. John Chapters 14–16, 1537; cf. AE 24

With Thee, Lord, Have I cast my lot; O Faithful God, forsake me not,
To Thee my soul commending. Lord, be my Stay, Lead Thou the way
Now and when life is ending. (*TLH* 524: 6)

Friday

The servant is not above his master. If they have pursued me they will also pursue you; if they have opposed my Word, they will also oppose your Word. John 15:20

That is the third passage by which he comforts them by a comparison or example. It would have to be a scandalous, insane servant who would lie there under the oven and snore or laugh and be in good spirits when his master comes into danger of body and life. The servant can be no nobler nor have it better than his master. And a good servant, who conducts his bodily affairs and life with and for the master says, "Where my master stays, there I also stay." Christ means for us by this comparison, that we should not allow ourselves to become soured or act lazy if we must suffer something for his sake and with him in the world. "I am your Lord," (he wants to say), "you are my ministers and servants. Why would you have it better than I have?" It just doesn't fit that the head wear a crown of thorns and the members sit upon a soft pillow. As he also says in Luke 6, "When it happens to the servant as to his master, then he will be perfect; that is, then things happen rightly as they should. He is a right, true servant who suffers good and evil with his master."

This is the comparison. Now he makes it certain, "They have persecuted me, so they will also persecute you." Who strikes the master on the mouth will not give the servant an easy vacation; who despises the madam will not be shy before the maid. So do not let yourself become strange and odd if someone despises you and will not take your Word and curses you. For it was also that way with me. Therefore, let it be rendered against me, as the one who encountered it the most and only be bold and confident against it. Do not let the devil and the world be sufficient to make you sigh or grow a single grey hair for the sake of their blows and defiance as I also, God be praised, never have done or will do. For the sake of my sins, when it comes to my life, the devil can surely make me afraid and anxious. But when I see that is done for the sake of Christ, then I ask nothing about his terror and scorn. If he wants to devour me, he must first devour the one above. In my Lord Christ's matters he will not make me sad, but only he will be made a fool and most pridefully despised. For I know that it drowns him and his scales in the depths and can make him the biggest fool. For they will want to be regarded but will be made to fear with all their power and scorn.

Altb. VII, 170: Sermons on the Gospel of St. John Chapters 14–16, 1537; cf. AE 24

Naught, naught, can now condemn me Nor set my hope aside;
Now hell no more can claim me, Its fury I deride.
No sentence e'er reproves me, No ill destroys my peace;
For Christ, my Savior, loves me And shields me with His grace. (*TLH* 528: 6)

Saturday

But they will do all this to you for the sake of my name.
For they do not know the one that sent me. John 15:21

As we have heard, this also is a comfort. The hate by which they hate you will increase not for the sake of evil deeds or sins as if you were a rogue or a thief, murderer or adulterer, but only because you would preach of me and say that I shed my blood and died for the world and that they can become holy by me and only by me. That is the reason for all the hatred and persecution in the world; a truly praiseworthy reason. The name of Christ from your mouth will be to them pure mire and death, and be called the teaching of the devil and heresy. So, if you desire to have peace in the world, then demure and be silent about me. Let them live and teach as they desire and deceive and seduce you, everyone with their monkery, indulgences, incense, masses,etc., and what is in their own name and action. Do this and they will let you alone. But if you would teach against such things and others, how they must be made blessed by Christ and their involvement adds nothing to help, then know that because of it you must be hated and persecuted to the fullest extent.

But because they do such things to you (he says), the consequence is that they do not know him who has sent me. You should not let yourself become angry because of it nor take revenge on them. They are already altogether avenged and already have their punishment waiting. You could not bring about or desire such a great suffering for them, or have them more mortally by the throat. They are struck with blindness and delusion, possessed by the devil. They are mad and crazy. What more would you place upon them? Only let them rant and rage all they want, they already have begun their judgment, damnation and hell. For what more terrible punishment and plague is there upon the earth than spiritual blindness or delusion, namely that they can no longer hear or tolerate a person who tells them how they should become saved? How should I have a greater revenge upon the pope, bishops and rulers than I see with my own eyes how they are plagued by God that they become blind and rant and rage? When God justly rages and allows his earnest punishment to go forth, first he shuts the peoples' eyes so they go off blind from one pit to another, just as was done to King Pharaoh in Egypt until he drowned in the Red Sea, and after that the Jews in Christ and his apostles time until Jerusalem was left with no stone upon another. Therefore, they do so (says he) both to me and you, for they do not know either me or the one who sent me.

Yes, (you say) shall we not know of the one we praise and confess; that he is our God, who has made heaven and earth, and gives us all wealth, land and people, wife and children, etc.? So all the world boasts of the earth even the Jews, Turks and the pope. Or shall we not all know the one almighty God whom we [everyone] serve[s] and honor[s]? Yes, but more, we also believe (says the pope's church) on Jesus Christ and the Holy Ghost and have Baptism and the Sacrament and the Holy Scriptures and are heirs of the throne of the holy apostles, etc. Will we then be [called by you] so blind that we do not acknowledge him? Certainly not, he [the pope] says. Then [says Christ and his followers] why do you persecute and murder me, whom God has sent? So if they would know the Father then they must also receive me as the one sent by him, with all honor and joy as their dear Lord and savior. But now that I have come, they lead me and beat me and put me on a cross to murder me. That is the honor they do me and the thanks they show to God.

Altb. VII, 170-171: Sermons on the Gospel of St. John Chapters 14-16, 1537; cf. AE 24

O God, forsake me not! Lord, I am Thine forever.
Grant me true faith in Thee; Grant that I leave Thee never.
Grant me a blessed end When my good fight is fought;
Help me in life and death O God, forsake me not! (*TLH* 402: 5)

Invocavit

Sunday

Man does not live by bread alone, but by every Word that proceeds from the mouth of God. Matthew 4:4

In this answer you can hear that the devil is set against the life, of first Christ and thereafter the Christian church. For this reason the disciples were not able to see how they could survive this present passing life, but rather [they saw] the devil and his household parade by. But the Lord is set against this tyrant and says, "This temporal life here on earth is not the only thing. But the Word of God is worth much more, which you should much rather preserve and not falsify it. For Moses says that man does not live only by having bread and corn, but there must be a greater provision than bread and corn so that a person could also remain after this life. Nothing else can bring this except that a person have God's Word so that he will remain in the true eternal life." By this he defends and comforts himself against the kind of bodily afflictions by which the devil would induce him to forsake the Word.

I say, that is the defense by which the holy martyrs have fended off the tyrants and said to them with joyful courage, "Even if you took gold and wealth, wife and child and also life, what would you have gained or I lost, since I have food for eternal life, which you cannot take? Even if you deprive me of food so that my body must languish away and die, nevertheless the eternal food will remain by me, the Word of God, which, as Peter says, is orally preached, but is an imperishable seed and the living Word, which remains forever." Therefore, whoever believes it has the food that brings him unto eternal life. So where the Word remains, there he will also remain since Paul calls it, "A power of God that makes all who believe in it holy." So also Christ speaks in John 4, "Whoever drinks of the water that I will give will never thirst, but the water that I have will be in him a fountain of water that springs in eternal life." There he calls his Word a living spring that springs in each hour of this life.

Even so in the beginning the black devil quickly beset Christianity. Those Christians journeyed in the true wilderness and thought they would be completely exterminated, not only with hunger and all kinds of paucity of bodily life, but also with being hunted, robbed, murdered, etc. By it they were made so very weary that they fell from faith. Yet the greater part remained steadfast, defended themselves confidently against the devil, and also overcame him through God's Word alone, that they had retained through faith. Also learn from the example of Christ, "Man does not live by bread alone, but rather by every Word that proceeds from the mouth of God." So because it is a living and eternal Word it can also eternally preserve those who believe in it even if they die.

Altb. VI, 1063-1064: First Sermon on the Afflictions of Christ and his Church, 1537

The Word they still shall let remain Nor any thanks have for it;
He's by our side upon the plain With His good gifts and Spirit.
And take they our life, Goods, fame, child, and wife,
Let these all be gone, They yet have nothing won;
The Kingdom ours remaineth. (*TLH* 262: 4)

Monday

You shall not tempt the Lord your God. Matthew 4:7

This is when the devil led him high in the air and set him on the pinnacle of the temple and said to him, "Say, cast yourself down, etc." That is, "If you are a highly enlightened man, with great spiritual gifts given of God, much better, more learned and holier that anyone else; as you consider God, then it must definitely be true. It cannot fail. Therefore, since God has manifested these things, you must not keep these things only for yourself but communicate it to others." This devilish pride makes you sure and impudent, that you spit out your own drivel without the fear and command of God and pour it out among the people, that is, some new doctrine without and against God's Word. That is then called tempting God and wanting to fly in the air without wings where nothing else has previously flown. Then in the devil's name plunge to ruin and break your neck.

This is what all heretics do whenever they rely on their own thoughts, or put a wax nose upon the Scriptures so that it must conform to their own lies. This is as if I or someone else wanted to cross over the Rhine without a bridge and say, "Oh, I will believe and trust in God that I have his Word that his angel will protect me that I not drown." No! You don't have a command of God to do that! So go by the way upon which the angels shall defend you, not through the water, but over the bridge. If you fall in and drown this will truly prove to you that you have tempted God.

This is a skill beyond the capability of flesh and blood. It is rather the skill of the Holy Ghost that one rightly and surely divide God's Word and see if it is used rightly or wrongly. For the devil can also work an art and demonstrates it even to the highest master of it, Christ, himself. Because of this, you should not let yourself become frightened too quickly if the charismatic and heretic boasts, "Here is Scripture, here is God's Word, etc." But rather than fear, hold Scripture against Scripture as Christ does here. Then even the heretics themselves who are the heartiest enemies against the Word, and persecute most of it, present themselves as if they help and administer it. Then if they would help you with the Scripture, and dress it up in their lies, you must answer, "No, I don't care that you say you have God's Word on your side. For you must also see that you don't tempt God. And even if it were God's Word by which you would help me, do you also actually want to take away or add to that Word? So let it first be seen whether this is the meaning the Holy Spirit gave it and if you use it properly. For our Lord God will not be angry if I do not receive his Word in the way that you use and explain it. For the devil and every heretic, even if he is adorned in God's Word, yet does not use it rightly. Therefore, my Lord Christ has warned me about this both with his example and elsewhere, etc."

But, as said, it is the art and gift of the Holy Ghost that one is defended from such false doctrine, as the holy bishops and other Christians have been defended from the devil and his apostles, the heretics, through the Holy Ghost. It is true that many will be deceived and seduced through their hypocrisy and lies as they brag of their holiness and truth. But against this, those who have acknowledged the hypocritical devil are always known. And their apostle doesn't let himself be moved from his high art and wisdom, but rather he is marked as an apparent hypocrite and fraud even when they have once clothed themselves with Scripture and God's name.

Altb. VI, 1066-1067: First Sermon on the Afflictions of Christ and his Church, 1537

The haughty spirits, Lord, restrain Who o'er Thy church with might would reign
And always set forth something new, Devised to change Thy doctrine true. (*TLH* 292: 6)

Tuesday

You shall worship the Lord your God, and serve him only. Matthew 4:10

Now what the black devil with his sword, and the angelic devil with the book, or Scripture could not do, the god of this world finally attempts when he says, "Kneel before me and worship me and I will give you all of this, for it is mine." That is the divine devil, who would be worshiped. But he will be worshiped when someone teaches and preaches lies, like monk's orders, human commands, decrees and statutes instead of the gospel, faith and the commands of God. That is what the papacy and his godlessness has done. And he presents all that he teaches and does as God's Word and says that only those who regard his doctrine and commands are right and divine and the only true church. Those who oppose him are heretics and accursed people.

So the pope has worshiped the devil and received the world, honor, wealth, money, kingdom and power over kaiser, kings, princes and lords for it and also the name and title of "most holy." Those whom he blesses and makes saints must accept this and nothing else. On the other hand, those whom he had cursed and damned must be regarded as such. Only what he has done must be called true and well done when he has curried favor with the kaisers, kings, etc. They are deposed, allowed to be assassinated, or one banished by another against all that is truth and justice. Yet no (ruler) has been allowed to punish if someone other than the pope has condemned him to be handed over to the devil. Yes, and there is more. This is all despite a few princes or kings who earned his scribblings by doing him harm.

He has such power, that he boasts he is the highest and holiest upon the earth because he has knelt at the feet of Satan and worshiped him. For is it not worshiping Satan when one holds the devil's doctrine higher and holier than the Word of God; and against right teaching God's Word is falsified, blasphemed, lied about and persecuted as the most vile heresy; and when those who teach it and honor it, etc., are held as children of the devil and accursed? I surely think it is called toppling God from his throne and setting the devil in his place and worshiping him as God. This is the basic soup and the last abomination by which Christianity will be plagued in the last days, from which no one can save her except the one man, Christ. The pious, God-fearing Caesar, Constantine, steered towards the black devil when he fashioned Christian peace and quiet before the tyrant, and provided for the servants of the church. After that, when the bright angelic devil had tortured and entrenched Christianity with his heresy for a long time, our Lord God again gave some pious, Christian kaisers like Theodosius, Arcadius, Honorius, who defended the church against the Arians. But here, no worldly power will protect or save it from the last and most vile devil. For as the Revelation of John says in chapter 13, the dragon has given his power, his throne and great might to the beast who has seven heads and ten crowns, which shows that when the pope had conquered Carous Magnum and through him all caesars that would come thereafter, they must seek his favor and acknowledge him as their overlord. Therefore, the church will now have no other Lord protector, who will protect her against the devil and antichrist and free her from the last tribulation, but the true Lord Protector, Christ, who says here, "Depart from me, Satan, for you are not the man that one should worship, the one of whom it is written and established, 'You shall worship God, your Lord, and serve him only.' "

Altb. VI, 1069–1070: Second Sermon on the Afflictions of Christ and his Church, 1537

Let me be Thine forever, Thou faithful God and Lord;
Let me forsake Thee never Nor wander from Thy word.
Lord, do not let me waver, But give me steadfastness,
And for such grace forever Thy holy name I'll bless. (*TLH* 334: 1)

Wednesday

Blessed is he whom you choose and whom you cause to approach you so that he dwells in your courts. He has rich comfort in your house, your holy temple. Psalm 65:4

This is a true work of David in which he leads all the other prophets in boasting because of everything that comes with God's Word and service and also of his kingdom, which God gave him. In the second part he is especially fluent as he is also in a few other psalms. So here he shows how great it is when God reveals his glory and grace so that he chooses a person and causes him to approach. That person dwells in his holy temple and to him will be apportioned every wealth, comfort and sweetness that is in his house or temple. He attends to these gifts and highly praises and boasts of them as St. Paul also boasts because of them and considers them his greatest treasure, having and confessing God's Word. For before the world it is a completely despiseable thing that leads one in a poor way and has the look of heresy. Or when it is not accursed and persecuted, they let it lay and do not pay any attention to it. Rather, they turn their backs to it and attend to their own affairs as those who do not ask much after God and his kingdom. But this holy prophet lifts those to whom grace is revealed and so can become good, high and nobly lifted above the crowd. He wants to come to God's house or church, or even to his churchyard. For he names all three: "in your house, court and your holy temple."

Now at the time (while King David lived) God had not yet built a house or temple, except the tent Moses established with the ark and the mercy seat. Also, there was no established place, even though he

[David] proposed to build a costly temple and also gathered great supplies for it, though its construction was prevented until his son's, Solomon's, reign. Yet he acted out of a true, great, full joy and thankfulness and called the place where God dwells a castle or temple or God's house and God's home though it was still a humble tent only 20 yards long and 10 yards wide, without a window and almost dark. It only had an open space, 100 yards long and 50 yards wide, like a churchyard. Yet he praises it so wonderfully for all of its wealth and grace, because a person is also called and chosen [by God himself] to come so near the ark and tabernacle. Now it was not yet wooden panels and crafted tapestries, but a churchyard without walls, encompassed by net. Why then does he boast of it so highly over all castles and royal palaces, yes, over all the world's wealth and treasures?

Answer: He was a man of God and full of the Spirit and he knew well that God had established this very same place so he would speak there and be present. Whoever would come did so in order to hear God himself, and whatever he prayed or whatever would be said to him there would be sure and certain. There I would also confidently run, if I knew of such a place or house (even if it were made of only leaves or cobwebs), where I could hear (as from God himself) what I need to be saved and should have all that I prayed for. I would not pay attention to how poor a place it always is. How many do you think there were and still are who would run to it from all over the country and would have adorned it gladly with all their wealth? For there they found a place where they could hear the comfort; that God is gracious to them and would hear their prayers! But as someone said, "They bear onions, they also bring garlic, they run in their ignorant delusion, in which they come again." But if we definitely knew such a place, where God would speak to us from heaven, who would not run there even from the ends of the earth, and trade no earthly treasure for it?

Altb. VI, 171: Sermon on the 65th Psalm Preached at Dessau for the Prince of Anhalt, 1534

Oh, grant that in Thy holy Word We here may live and die, dear Lord;
And when our journey endeth here, Receive us into glory there. (*TLH* 292: 9)

Thursday

You hear prayer, so all flesh comes to you. Psalm 65:2

Everyone who wants to pray and give thanks should come to you there. For there is no other God upon the earth. Where do you go? Or where would one find him? In previous times to Jerusalem, or in Zion (as he has said), but now nowhere except into the Lord Christ, in whom all the world and all places have been placed, who only comes here (apart from all others gods and services). Why is that? Because you are such a God who gladly allows prayer and also gladly hears. This is his true praise, for which he is also honored. One should learn to know this of him from this psalm and regard it as sure; that he gladly hears praying and will also heed it.

Why do we lack something when God does not give us what we desire and need? Surely it is because of our error, that we are so lazy and lax to pray, and not God's fault. For he will not lie to you when he says that he is the God who gladly hears prayer; not only one or a few peoples' prayers (like the great saints), but of all people upon the earth. For he says, "All flesh comes to me," that is all who can be called human. If now you are flesh and blood, then you are also called and encouraged in this. You stand under this verse the same as I do, and I as well as you, and together we are allured and whistled to the same as this or any other saint. For he is not only a God of the Jews or priests (as if they alone can pray), but rather the God of me and everyone whom we call flesh or human. For I am just as baptized into his name and believe in the same God as all the rest, so he will surely hear my prayer just as gladly as the others.

So it is truly our own failure that we do not do this. For he gladly would hear and act for the sake of his name and would be praised and extolled that he gladly hears praying and also will gladly give what you pray. But that doesn't happen. No one does it. For we ourselves don't want to do him the service of praying for comfort and do not pay any attention to his desire to gladly hear and to give as we would ask. But since we do not pray, then he cannot give. We ourselves see to it that the devil comes over us, plagues and hinders us in every kingdom. That is the first deficiency and harm by which we harm ourselves. We cast prayer away from us by which we could be rid of every misfortune. If we would only pray confidently his Word and promise in the true Zion, that is, in faith in Christ, who promised us that everything that we ask in his name, we would receive.

Altb. VI, 169: Sermon on the 65th Psalm Preached at Dessau for the Prince of Anhalt, 1534

If God Himself be for us, I may a host defy;
For when I pray, before me My foes, confounded, fly.
If Christ, my Head and Master, Befriend me from above,
What foe or what disaster Can drive me from His love? (*TLH* 528: 1)

Friday

God, man praises you in the silence of Zion and to you he will make his vow. Psalm 65:1

Oh what a fine, praise-worthy God you are (he would say), that you give and preserve each of the three-fold kingdoms in the world (as he would hereafter ordain), so we are also guilty. For that, we are also to praise and thank you and this is done in the silence of Zion, or in Jerusalem, where the spiritual kingdom and God's service operates. For in that time there was no other place or city where one should plead to God, but he had bound every human heart that desired to meet and implore the true God to this place, which, if they were not able bodily to go there, yet in their hearts they must turn to it and see and only call out to God, where he himself dwelt. They were to know and acknowledge no other God.

It was this way in the time before Christ, but now Zion has become so big and wide that it fills heaven and earth. For everyone [in the old Zion] now is crumbled and destroyed along with his temple, Divine Service, together with the whole church. But God has built a greater and more glorious one in its place in Christ, where this Christ is present with his Word and Sacrament. This is also the true Zion. Because of this, whoever now believes in Christ and confesses him, praising and calling out [to him], praises and thanks the true God in the true Zion or Jerusalem.

But he adds this little word to it: *in Silentio*, in silence. So this also is the characteristic of a Christian that wants to pray and praise, that he can be a little patient and passive, and not curse or grumble, or become displeased with God if it doesn't soon happen as he wants it to be, but it is called, as the 4th Psalm says, "Be angry, but do not sin, speak with your heart upon your bed and be quiet or be still." Or Isaiah 30:15: "*In silentio et in spirit fortitudo vestra.* If you were silent and hoped, you would be helped."

This is so that you learn to praise and thank God even if it doesn't come so quickly as we desire, but rather be accustomed to his manner and be patient when he misses something. For that is still a beggarly thing that you praise and thank him when he gives what you desire and as you desire, but true praise and thanks must be performed such that you remain still and secure and await his help with patience. For he is the kind of God that does not allow a person to determine time or place, what, when or how he should give, so that we learn to rightly confess him and be sure that he knows better than we ourselves how he should do what is necessary and good for us.

See, that is why he says praise God in silence, that you not become impatient but rather learn patience and hope and always remain in faith. For we see how the people are when they fall into impatience, how they rage and bluster and atrociously demand. You must tell them to be still (that is, patient). By such impatience they hinder themselves so that they cannot pray or praise. On the other hand, though, when you praise him in quietness, or patience, so that you hope and suffer a little while, as he desires, it pleases him. This is his dearest work and Divine Service (as He would now say), as when we pray on behalf of Christianity against the heretic and seducer, that his name be hallowed, his kingdom come and the fanatics and the scandals cease.

Altb. VI, 168: Sermon on the 65th Psalm Preached at Dessau for the Prince of Anhalt, 1534

Why restless, why cast down, my soul? Hope still; and thou shalt sing
The praise of Him who is thy God, Thy health's eternal Spring. (*TLH* 525: 3)

Saturday

Our iniquity presses us hard; you will forgive our sins. Psalm 65:3

That is the stone that weighs heavily upon the heart of everyone so that we are not able to pray. Oh, I would gladly pray (we say), if I knew that my prayer would be accepted by him. I will let others pray who are more pious and gifted than I am. For I am a poor sinful person and where there are sins prayer is not valid. God is angry with them and doesn't heed them. By such thoughts the devil strikes prayer down and destroys it so that nothing is prayed even if someone desires to. Now it is true that the pray-er is a sinner and that sin is no small matter since the psalmist himself reveals and acknowledges that it justly frightens and drives him back. He also feels the heavy stone (which he calls our sins), that lays there and presses so that he cannot lift up his heart. For who is able to lift up his heart and eyes to God, when he knows that he is angry towards him and he has earned every trouble? So seldom does anyone pray, but he leaves it for another and thinks, "I cannot pray now and will let those pray who are pious and wait until I also become pious." So neither I, nor you, nor anyone prays. How will you then find anyone, finally, who prays?

Now how would you advise him? We cannot argue, for it is established and true that we are altogether sinners and our sins oppress us heavily. But if you know no advice, then attend to what this verse teaches you if you feel such a trial that your heart says, "Oh, you are now not gifted to pray. Don't you feel your sins, how you have angered

God?", etc. When you encounter such things that hinder your prayer then do what you hear in this verse and see the prophet's speaking and doing. Our sins oppress us (he says), that is true, but if I should not pray because of that, and not soon begin, then when I do not feel my sins, I will never get back to doing it and the devil put me in a prison so that I would never be able to open my mouth.

No, not so (he says), but rather see at once how to get rid of this great weight. Do you say, "How? Should I go up to Rome, or run to St. James, or do penance so long until I no longer feel the sins and become worthy to pray?" No, that would accomplish nothing but when that was done you would only fall painfully before God with this need and would speak as is here stated, "Oh Lord, our sins oppress us." If we already know that we should pray and you gladly hear, we would not be able to come to you with this great burden, yet since you desire prayer and command all flesh to come to you, then I come with it and lay my great burden down before you and pray that you forgive my sins and desire to be merciful to me.

See to it that your prayer begins rightly! And even in the highest need, when you are oppressed and hindered or unskilled so that you cannot pray, and also the heavy stone abuses your heart see to it, that you proceed rightly in that situation. Otherwise you will also never pray a true prayer. For I have also encountered this and it can still easily happen to me when I begin to pray that the devil also leads me to such thoughts, "Oh, I am not skilled. I will wait a while and meanwhile do something else until I become more skilled." I become more and more distanced from it from one hour to another; from one day to another. So finally I must, with diminished might, go ahead and pray when I feel altogether the least gifted at it. For it is said, "Who is not skilled today, is even less skilled tomorrow and through delaying no one becomes skilled." If you do not learn to pray when you are unskilled and you feel your difficulties, you will never learn to pray. For when the sweet thought comes, "Say, now I am gifted, now I want to pray rightly," that will probably be the devil [speaking] to make your prayer sinful and shameful. Therefore, there is nothing better than to say, "When I feel unskilled and feel the burden of sins, then I will do as the prophet David and all the people of God have done that have become much holier than we have and yet lamented over their sins. They did not allow themselves to be hindered. So my sins will also not hinder me. But rather I will even more run to pray and bring to God this same necessity in all matters."

Altb. VI, 169–170: Sermon on the 65th Psalm Preached at Dessau for the Prince of Anhalt, 1534

With broken heart and contrite sigh, A trembling sinner, Lord, I cry.
Thy pard'ning grace is rich and free O God, be merciful to me. (*TLH* 323: 1)

Reminiscere

Sunday

Lord, vindicate me, for I am innocent. Psalm 26:1

Vindication is mentioned so often. As David says, "Pass judgment; be the judge in this matter." God will still hold a judgment and a verdict for the poor and orphaned who are terrified or oppressed; who become persecuted, plagued and tried but have no one who shields them or frees them from the powerful hand and tyranny.

But God must hold a judgment upon the earth. For there is a discord, hostility and disunity in the midst of the world, between the true and false prophets. There is no one who will or can quiet or throw off this discord except only by the divine Word. That alone must here judge and be the divider. Those whom the devil takes begin with false doctrine and sectarianism. He holds them fast. He possesses their hearts. He makes them deaf and blind so they can hear and see nothing. They can not allow or hear even the clear, bright and public witness of the Holy Scriptures. For they are so gripped between the claws [of these errors], that they cannot be freed from them. In previous times the councils didn't help even when great courage and effort had divided the pure teachers from the heretics, and when they wanted to judge and determine how one should rightly teach and believe. But they have judged a little and expelled the sectarian spirits with their false doctrine and errors. The pope has compelled his own with the ban, but he has hardly helped the matter at all.[5]

But bottom line, there is no other counsel or help in these matters than that you look up to heaven, sigh and pray that God would be judge in these matters and say, "You know dear God, that we have done rightly and they are not right. But we cannot report it to anyone for they will not let you speak and they continually burst forth with their false doctrine. Because of this, dear God, take your sword in your hand and strike them; put the game to an end." So it often happens when the sectarian spirits fail, they are brought to shame in their lies and the divine Word on the other hand, which was long regarded as shameful and dishonorable, will again be honored.

So God ordains that his own, who have God's Word, first will be defeated, oppressed and troubled. But everyone must fail who once

----

[5]That is, by the threat and compulsion of excommunication

oppresses them harshly. So also the pope's sect will also fail. Who does this? This psalm cries out, "Lord, vindicate me, for I am innocent."

We always pray for such a judgment against the false teachers, so we say, "Dear God, give a judgment for me, speak the judgment for me." And even as God hears the cry, the enthusiasts[6] and sectarian spirits must therefore in their time become a scandal and fail.

Erl. 39, 108–110: Sermon on the 26th Psalm, 1525

May God root out all heresy	Therefore saith God, "I must arise,
And of false teachers rid us	The poor My help are needing;
Who proudly say: "now, where is he	To Me ascend My peoples' cries,
That shall our speech forbid us?	And I have heard their pleading.
By right or might we shall prevail;	For them My saving Word shall fight
What we determine cannot fail;	And fearlessly and sharply smite,
We own no lord and master."	The poor with might defending." (*TLH* 260: 3–4)

Monday

Test me Lord and search me, try my heart and my mind. Psalm 26:2

He desires that God would try him just as a goldsmith makes the silver ore go through the fire, melts it and makes it shiny and pure. The human heart is also thoroughly contaminated so that it cannot itself feel it. Therefore, he says, "Lord, you test my heart. I do not see how it can be that I have become wooden and made into a barrel and should now become spit upon and despised." For if I were a failure and stupid and then were discouraged when people abandon me, then that would be evil. But if I laugh when someone despises me, then that is good.

Now I know many preachers who stand there and preach confidently. So many [hearers] retain their doctrine because they preach so confidently. But if their listeners depart from their doctrine, then they themselves would stop preaching and depart from their own doctrine. Their heart is not in it. Although they call on Christ with their mouths they are not serious about it. But a Christian says, "I hope in God whether people praise me or if they dishonor me, whether they go here or there. I do not preach for my sake. I don't need to preach. For my sake I would rather be silent. But I do

---

[6]Enthusiasts are those who believe they have the Holy Ghost in them so that they speak authoritatively in the Church though their teaching contradicts Scriptures.

it to your service. If now you accept the preaching, good for you, but if you depart from it, then you have a judge over you. And as I do not preach it for my own sake so you also should not accept it on my account." When you see the defection and falling away and that God sends persecution, then first you will see the heart of the preacher. If he can let favor, honor, fortune and followers go, then that is good, but it is born into us and stuck deep within us that we would rather see that the people favor us. But if they defect, then we are annoyed. This truly reveals that the heart is unclean. Such a heart would say, "sweep only what is good my way."

The "heart" means the way a person thinks. "Kidneys" is desire and lust of the flesh when I proceed with what I desire and what I think. Such thinking and desire is in Hebrew called "heart" [mind in English] and "kidneys" [heart in English]. The heart of a false preacher is directed unto itself, driving inward to his own heart. He desires to seek his own honor. So David would say, "This is the false way, when I must have what I desire and love. Therefore, I want to protect myself that I also not seek to be honored and celebrated for the sake of the preaching of the divine Word."

So it is a dangerous thing when a preacher that has rightly preached God's Word has a great following and fortune so that people praise him. And again if someone even spoke evil of him [it is a dangerous thing] that he [the preacher, that is] would curse, deride and despise that one. For honor and praise comforts one, but burdens and shame oppress and make him sad. There he stands between two dangers. If he stands in honor and the old Adam feels it, then it seems good to him. Just as the tongue quickly tastes and experiences what is herbal and bitter, like wormwood, or what is sweet, like sugar or honey; so it hurts if he hears someone saying shameful things or lies about him. But that preacher is a false one, whose kidneys are not protected from his desire to be comforted by praise for himself. He laughs himself to death if one exalts and praises him. When another blasphemes him, then he grieves himself to death. Anyone who directs and conducts the preaching office with the goal that he has comfort by it turns his eyes from the divine Word to his pleasure and does not say, "Only correct me well," as David says here. "Let me not have pleasure in myself, or in having my desire and honor," but only say this, "I want Your honor, and I seek the blessing for my neighbor."

Erl. 39, 115-117: Sermon on the 26th Psalm, 1525

As silver tried by fire is pure From all adulteration,
So thro' God's Word shall men endure Each trial and tribulation.
Its light beams brighter thro' the cross, And, purified from human dross,
It shines through every nation. (*TLH* 260: 5)

Tuesday

*I despise the congregation of the wicked, and I sit not
among the godless. Psalm 26:5*

I am their enemy. Also, I will have nothing to do with the
wicked. What I say is what I mean from the heart. I depart from
them with my heart. So you should have nothing to do with the
wicked and the godless as the psalm especially says: *Perfecto odio
oderam eos*, and also as the first psalm praises the blessed Christian
who excludes and closes out the wicked where David says, "Blessed
are they who do not walk in the counsel of the godless nor tread in
the way of the sinner, nor sit in the seat of the mocker." If you go
with them much anyway, then you make their false doctrine, lies and
errors your own and finally partake in them. Whoever embraces
pitch soils himself with it. So also says the eighteenth psalm, "With
the saints you are holy and with the pious you are good." Or "by
purity you are pure and by folly you are made foolish."

Now you all raise a question, "Did not the Lord Christ
command that we also should love our enemies?" How does David
brag of himself that he hates the assembly of the evil and does not sit
among the godless? Should we not do only good things and heap
burning coals upon the heads of the enemies? Yes, I should hate
them, but for no other reason than on account of their false doctrine.
Apart from that I should allow myself to serve them in the interest
of converting some of them. I must hate them for God's sake, who
has commanded and desires that you should cling only to his Word.
This is a holy hate and enmity that proceeds out of love. For love
proceeds under faith and faith is the master of love. A Christian says,
"I will not forsake God for the sake of men. What I cannot love
along with [loving] God, that thing I should hate. Now if you preach
something that is contrary to God, then all love and friendship sink;
because of that I hate you and will do you no good works." For faith
should lie above and there proceeds the hate. Love is off when it
spoils the Word of God. But when it involves my person, even my
goods or my honor and body, by these I will show them only honor
and service. For these same goods are God's and given by God so
that you help your neighbor with them. They are not God's Word.
One can risk them and yet remain. But God's Word is not placed in
risk because the same belongs to our Lord God. There say, "I will
gladly forsake what I have from God that has been given for the sake
of my serving. But what God himself is and what belongs to our
Lord God, that I will not forsake nor allow to depart. And if I were

to give you my temporal goods then God can surely give me others. But I will retain God for my sake. For we could gladly give away the temporal goods and gifts that we have received from God. Because of this, faith rules, measures and is master over love just as long as the Word of God remains pure and faith goes in the tradition [handed down].

So David wants to say now, "I hate them not because they do evil to me and make me sad or because they lead a wicked and evil life; but rather because they despise, shame, blaspheme, falsify and persecute God's Word." So look to how you shall be established. And also look to how you should act against the false teachers and sectarian spirits.

Erl. 39, 121-122: Sermon on the 26th Psalm, 1525

Lord, put to shame Thy foes who breathe defiance
And vainly make their might their sole reliance;
In mercy turn to us, the poor and stricken,
Our hope to quicken.

Be Thou our Helper and our strong defender;
Speak to our foes and cause them to surrender.
Yea, long before their plans have been completed,
They are defeated. (*TLH* 269: 2-3)

Wednesday

For the kingdom of God stays not in Words, but in power.
1 Corinthians 4:20

But the power is this: That you cannot only speak of the kingdom of God, but you also know by deeds that God is mighty and active in us through his Spirit. As he says above in the second chapter [of Galatians], verses eight and nine concerning himself, "Who has become mighty in Peter among the circumcised and who is also mighty with me among the gentiles," etc.

Therefore, when a preacher also teaches in that way, so that the Word is not without fruit, but rather is powerful in those who hear it, that is, when faith, hope, love, patience, etc. follow from the preaching; there God bestows the Spirit and works his deeds among those who hear the gospel. St. Paul also speaks in this manner here. Our Lord God bestowed the abundance of the Spirit and deeds have been done under him. He would like to say, "Our Lord God has bestowed and worked so much from my preaching that you have not only begun to believe, but have also led a holy life, produced good fruits of faith and suffered many kinds of misfortunes and adversities. Or, through the same power of the Spirit you have even become different people than you were before. Before you were idolaters, enemies of God, blasphemers, lustful, adulterers, wrathful, impatient, envious, etc. But now you are believing children of God, gentle, chaste, mild, patient, lovers of your neighbor, etc." He also witnesses of them in Galatians 4:14–16 that they received him (Paul) as an angel of God, yes, as Christ himself. They had so much love that they would have been glad to have given him the eyes from their heads.

That a person could have so much love for his neighbor that he brings him to his favorite things and is willing also to bestow his money, goods, eyes, life and everything, etc., and thereafter also is ready to suffer all kinds of adversities, are truly powers of the Spirit. "And such powers," he says, "you received and had prior to the false apostles coming to you. You have received them, though, not through the law, but rather from God, who bestowed the Spirit upon you and daily has increased him in you, so that the gospel has gone forth under you in the best way with doctrine, faith, deeds and suffering. While you had such a good report, and your own conscience was convinced of them, why is it that you no longer do those good deeds which you practiced before? What has so turned and changed you that you no longer have such love as you did before? For now you would not so freely receive Paul as if he were an angel sent of God, or, yes, as Christ Jesus himself. You would let things be as they are rather than pluck out your eyes and share them with me. How does it now happen that you no longer have ardor for me as before but rather now join yourself to the false apostles who are so friendly, yet lead you so evilly and terribly?"

This also happens to us. When we, through God's grace, first began to preach the gospel, there were many everywhere who gladly heard that kind of preaching and honored us well. Power and fruits of faith followed also from the preaching of the gospel. But what happened? Unexpectedly the charismatics, anabaptists and reformed thereafter wiped it out. They destroyed and tore up into a pile what we previously had built and enriched with so much great effort and labor over a long period of time. They acted at first as if they were our best friends and that they received our doctrine with great thanksgiving. But now they become our bitterest foes so that they cannot stand to hear our name spoken. Such misfortune is a sign of the devil who works such power and fruits in his members so that among them the powers of the Holy Ghost are instantly and completely forsaken.

So now the holy apostle says, "By your own experience you have learned, dear Galatians, that these great powers surely do not come from the works of the law. For just as before you heard the preaching of faith you did not have them, so you also do not have them now because the false apostles lead and rule you."

We would also say now to those who boast how they are free from the pope's tyranny and are now evangelical, "Dear friends, declare now, have you conquered the tyranny of the pope and obtained the Christian freedom through the teaching of the charismatics, or through us, when we first preached faith in Christ? If you would confess the truth then you must say, 'Truly we have obtained it through the preaching of faith.' "

Walch VIII, 2022–2025: Lectures on Galatians, 1523

Give to Thy Word impressive pow'r That in our hearts, from this good hour,
As fire it may be glowing; That we confess the Father, Son,
And Thee, the Spirit, Three in One, Thy glory ever showing,
Stay Thou, Guide now Our souls ever That we never May forsake Thee,
But by faith their Refuge make Thee. (*TLH* 235: 2)

Thursday

But the law is not faith. Rather the man who does it will live by it. Galatians 3:12

So now St. Paul compares the two types of righteousness in this passage as also in Romans 10: 4-5; namely that of the law and that of faith. He says, "The man who does it, will live by it", etc. It is as if he said, "It would be good that we did the law. But since no one does it, we must flee to Christ, who is the end of the law and makes all who believe on him right, the same as is done under the law." By this he frees us, who were under the law, Galatians 4:5. When we believe on that one, we receive the Holy Ghost and begin to do the law. But what is yet lacking will not be reckoned against us for the sake of faith in Christ. In this life, faith will cease, for we will see God no longer in a mirror and a dark Word as we do now, but rather face to face. That is, the eternal majesty will be altogether clear, in which we will see God just as he is. Then there will be a truly real and completed perception of God, a true complete love to God, along with right reason and a right and good will, not in the manner of the world, or even now as theology teaches concerning it, but rather with a heavenly, divine and eternal [perception]. But in the meantime, so long as we are in this life, we await in the spirit through faith the righteousness which we hope for. But those who would obtain forgiveness of sins through the law, will never receive it but rather are under and remain under the curse; they also hinder Christ.

So now St. Paul only calls those righteous who would become righteous through the promise, or through faith in the promise, without works of the law. Therefore, what is said concerning the works of the law without and outside of faith is a purely fictitious thing. On account of that they do none of the law when they want to obtain righteousness by doing the law. For St. Paul concludes the matter curtly and says in general, without any exception and distinction, that all who are under the curse, who would be right through the works of the law, would truly escape the curse, if they did the law rightly.

For it is true that the man who does it will live by it. But where is such a person? Nowhere. Yet the law, in a secondary way, is sufficient for a person's office. First, it defends against the wicked in the world, to prevent them from doing what they by nature want to do. Thereafter, it also stirs the conscience before God, etc. You could understand this passage as concerning those who desire to do it in worldly life, "The man who does them shall live by it." That is, those who would be obedient to worldly authority are secure against the gallows, stocks and other punishments. For worldly authority has neither right nor might against the obedient. They cannot punish him in body or possessions but must rather let him be free. For it is obvious that you must have laws and harsh appropriate punishments in the worldly kingdom so that the wild, uncivilized people will be held in check and that those who will not abide such a defense must always be prosecuted so that the others can have freedom.

But St. Paul does not at all speak concerning this handling of the law. Rather, he treats it as it is done before God and how it should be considered before God.

Walch VIII, 2155-2157: Lectures on Galatians, 1523

God these commandments gave therein	Help, Lord Jesus Christ, for we
To show thee, child of man, thy sin	A Mediator have in Thee,
And make thee also to perceive	Our works cannot salvation gain;
How man unto God should live.	They merit but endless pain.
Have mercy, Lord!	Have mercy, Lord! (*TLH* 287: 11-12)

Friday

By your victory, your people will bring willing sacrifices in the beauty of holiness. Psalm 110:3

Here it is shown what should be the use of the Word and preaching. It should have such power that the people will be drawn willingly to it. This cannot be done by any power or skill upon earth. Namely, it is not like the law, which drives us with requirements which we cannot meet. Nor does it plague us with compulsion, fear and cursing. Rather, this preaching shows us counsel, comfort and help. We do not remain under God's wrath and damnation (to which we are sentenced by the law). Rather, from both sins and death we obtain salvation by God's grace and receive power that we live in the new and true obedience towards God.

Now this is the beloved joyous preaching of the gospel of Christ. It proclaims what we have before this king. Namely, although we are sinners and are born and live under God's wrath, damned through the law to eternal death, yet God has had mercy on us and sent us his Son, Christ, in the flesh, born without sin of a virgin. He gives him to us so that we might also have the forgiveness of sins, be freed from death, have eternal righteousness and eternal life. All this is from pure grace and mercy, without our merit, merely for the sake of this same Christ. With his suffering and death he paid for our sins and reconciled us with the Father. Through his resurrection he conquered death and weakened it in himself so that he dedicates and gives everything to us.

Additionally, he calls us and also gives us his Holy Spirit, and through him works in our heart firm comfort, begins to work obedience and also gives power and strength against sins and the fear of death and protects and preserves against every power of the devil. For that reason he has gone up to heaven, that he reigns mightily in us so that we conquer sins, death and the devil. And if we yet are sinful and cannot act with such pure and complete obedience, yet it will not be counted against us, because he, as our mediator and High Priest, intercedes and approaches the Father for us.

Behold! Through such preaching we also come to this, so that we become his tribe and his people (as this text says), who come there wanting to be obedient to God. For where God ceases to be angry with us and will no longer damn us for the sake of our sins as we have merited, but rather gives and extends his grace and mercy to us; there the heart, which previously fled from God and was his enemy can cling to a child-like happy confidence towards him. When a person is so comforted and encouraged by faith, he receives new thoughts, courage and mind towards God. He begins to love him and to call upon him from the heart and wait on his help in every need. He receives zeal and love for his commands and is ready to go and suffer what he should for the sake of God. For he will be ruled by the Holy Ghost so that no one will be able to compel him or force him with the law and punishment as before. And if his obedience is yet weak, yes, impure and incomplete, and much disobedience yet reigns in him, then he comforts himself by grace and forgiveness through Christ and also he strives against and resists sinful desires through the help and strength of the Holy Ghost. He thus conquers them until both sins and death completely cease and are exterminated in this sinful and mortal body.

*Erl. 40, 117–119: Lecture on the 110th Psalm, **Dixit Dominus**, 1539*

Oh, rich the gifts Thou bringest, Thyself made poor and weak!
O Love beyond expression, That thus can sinners seek!
For this, O Lord, will we Our joyous tribute bring Thee
And glad hosannas sing Thee And ever grateful be. (*TLH* 69: 6)

Saturday

Your children will be born to you as the dew of the morning. Psalm 110:3

So will it happen (he would say) in this kingdom that children will be born to our Lord Christ; not in a natural way from flesh and blood, nor through the help of man or his works, nor as people can [by fallen nature] grasp and understand it. Rather, it is a spiritual, heavenly birth through the hidden, divine power of the Holy Ghost who works through the Word in people and makes new, believing hearts. For, as is said above, what belongs to this kingdom and belongs to Christ puts to an end the old nature and it becomes a new nature. To this end flesh and blood, mother or father, and what belongs to human ability, adds nothing. For one does not become a Christian by flesh and blood, but rather they give only a sinful birth. What is human (born in sin unto death) cannot make a child of God. As Christ says in John 3, "What is born of flesh is flesh." Or, "Unless a man is born again he cannot enter the kingdom of God."

Therefore, in these passages, everything that man could brag about from his own abilities and works is here powerfully canceled. But in contrast to this is all that both the prophets and Moses had always sown and laid as the high counsel and comfort for their people, the Jews. From this they had found that they were Abraham's seed and children and heirs of the holy Patriarchs and for this alone they were called God's people and children of the kingdom, as the true nobility of the world. They were promised the inheritance of all the nations. They also comforted and boasted of themselves proudly for this and held to all of it so rigidly that no one could take it from them. They would not hear or suffer it when the prophets would chastise them. Also, for that reason, the apostles and preachers of the gospel were persecuted so relentlessly until they were driven to the ground. For this was (as they thought) their sure ground and they resolved against any opposition, "We are surely children of the holy fathers. We have the law, given by God and also the promise of the Christ. Surely God would not reject his people, etc." Also in these days, they cannot entertain the thought that they should be told that they should have taught differently over the last fifteen hundred years, lest because of it they should so scandalously fail and be destroyed. For they so completely desire to alone be called the people of God and through their Messiah to become lords of the whole world.

Now this psalm clearly says the opposite. In God's kingdom nothing will be valued concerning birth, nor being descended or coming from Abraham, or his lineage and tribe, nor anything possible by the birth of flesh and blood. For if a person would be a Christian by them, then all or most of the Jews would also have received this Christ (who was also from their race and Abraham's seed). But rather there must be another birth from heaven above so that you become another person through divine power and through faith in Christ. As he should also say here: "You are truly children of Abraham and of the holy fathers, of the tribe and race which is promised Christ. But by that you are not yet God's children and such a natural birth and ancestry will not help you in any way if you do not forsake your appraisal of such a fleshly birth and all of your boasting but receive this Christ as did your fathers. For your father, Abraham, also did not become God's child through his birth (even though he also descended for the old holy ancestors). He himself received another birth and had to become a believer, so he would be God's friend and a father of many nations." So also, those who would be true children of Abraham, that is, whoever becomes a Christian (whether they are Jews or Gentiles) obtains this neither from themselves nor from their fathers. But they become born anew through faith in this Christ, as St. Paul richly details in Romans 4.

Erl. 40, 129–131: Lecture on the 110th Psalm, **Dixit Dominus,** *1539*

Hallelujah! Let praises ring! Unto our Triune God we sing;
Blest be His name forever! With angel hosts let us adore
And sing His praises more and more For all His grace and favor!
Singing, ringing: Holy, Holy, God is holy, Spread the story
Of our God, the Lord of Glory! (*TLH* 23: 4)

Oculi

Sunday

For those propelled by the Holy Ghost are children of God.
Romans 8:14

The devil also sows his seed among us even to those who are called Christians and boast of the gospel. So we are to look not to their mouth but rather to the works of those who call themselves Christians; not to what they say but what they do. For it is easy to boast of God, Christ and the Spirit but on top of that they give evidence whether this is rightly formed so that the Spirit also works in them and is powerful to extinguish and put sins to death. For where the Spirit is, there he is also definitely not idle nor without power. But rather he gives evidence that he rules and propels the person. The person hearkens to him and follows him. That kind of person has the comfort that he is a child of God. God rules and works within him so that he is not in death but rather has life.

Now it says that such a heart that is driven by the Spirit of God gladly receives the hearing of the Word of God and believes on Christ for he has grace and the forgiveness of sins in him (Christ). This faith confesses and gives proof of itself before the world. It seeks God's glory above all things so he lives without public offense. Faith serves other people, is obedient, patient, chaste, modest, gentle, kind, etc. And even if such a person is somewhat rash and has stumbled, yet he is quickly restored through penance and he stops the sinning. For the Holy Ghost teaches and informs him of all of this so he hears the Word and receives it and does not willfully oppose the Holy Ghost.

On the other hand the devil, which is also a spirit, also compels the hearts of the world. But he does it in a way that you can easily see that it is not a good spirit nor is it God's Spirit. For he drives his own to the opposite of what God's Spirit compels, that they have no desire to hear God's Word nor to follow it. They despise God, are stubborn, proud, greedy and unmerciful.

Therefore, let each one look to himself so that he does not deceive himself. For many want to be called Christians who yet are not. But one should note and see that they are not all driven by the Spirit of God. So they must have a spirit who compels them. It is not God's Spirit, which [always] compels contrary to the flesh, so it must be the other, evil spirit, which compels according to the flesh and it lusts against God's Spirit. Therefore, they must also be contrary to the things of God and his dear children, sons and daughters, who are called to eternal life and glory. On the contrary, they are cast away and separated from God. They are children of the devil and heirs with him of eternal fire.

Erl. 9, 177–178: Trinity 8 Sermon on Romans 8:12-17

O Holy Spirit, enter in And in our hearts Thy work begin,
Thy temple deign to make us; Sun of the soul, Thou Light divine,
Around and in is brightly shine, To joy and gladness wake us
That we, In Thee Truly living To Thee giving Prayer unceasing
May in love be still increasing. (*TLH* 235: 1)

Monday

For you have not received a timid spirit so that you always must fear; but rather you have received a child-like spirit through whom we call, "Abba, dear Father." Romans 8:15

Here the power of the kingdom of Christ, the actual work and the true high service performed by God, is described which the Holy Ghost works in the believer. Namely, the comfort through which the heart is freed from terror and fear of sins, becomes established in freedom and its deep prayer attentively waits in faith for help from God. This cannot happen through the law and your own holiness. For by that a person can never secure a true definite comfort of God's grace and love him, but always remains in sorrow and anxiety of wrath and the curse. Since the matter remains in such doubt, he flees before God and cannot call on him. But, on the other hand, where there is faith in Christ the Holy Ghost works in the heart both comfort and true childlike confidence that does not doubt God's gracious will and attention. For God has promised his grace and help, comfort and attention. This promise is not on the basis of our worthiness, but rather on that of Christ; on his Son's name and service.

The prophet Zechariah also spoke of both these works of the Holy Ghost, comfort and prayer, in Chapter 12:10. He says that God would bestow a new preaching and work in the kingdom of Christ. There he would pour out "the Spirit of grace and prayer" that is the same Spirit that assures us that we are the children of God and that compels our heart to cry out to him with zealous prayer.

The Hebrew word, "Abba," which means (as he himself defines it) dear Father, is the cry of a little child who is the heir and so stammers out of an unfailing child-like confidence in its father, "Ab,

188

Ab." For it is the easiest word that a child can learn to say. Or as those who spoke the old German language could say much easier, "Etha, Etha." Faith through the Holy Ghost also speaks such an unfailing, child-like word, but out of a deep heart and (as he says after this) with unspeakable sighs; especially when he is in battle and in need against the doubt of the flesh and the terror and trials of the devil so that he must defend himself against them and say, "Oh, dear Father! Yes, you are my dear Father. For yes, you have given your own dear Son for me so that you will not be angry with me or cast me away; for you see my need and weakness, therefore you will help and save me."

Erl. 9, 180–181: Trinity 8 Sermon on Romans 8:12-17

For He can plead for me with sighings That are unspeakable to lips like mine;
He bids me pray with earnest crying, Bears witness with my soul that I am Thine,
Joint heir with Christ, and thus may dare to say:
O heav'nly Father, hear me when I pray! (*TLH* 21: 4)

Tuesday

For we are children and so are also heirs, namely heirs of God and co-heirs of Christ, so as we also suffer with him, we also will be raised with him to glory. Romans 8:17

There you hear the high praise, honor and glory of the Christian. Let go of the world's praise, pride and honor, which is nothing but (as it is finally and ultimately considered) that they are the children of the devil. But consider for yourself what this means that a poor miserable sinner should be honored by God. For he is not called a slave or servant of God but rather God's son and heir. Yet a person or even all the world should wish, as it might, that they could be called God's cow or frog, by which they could only be praised for belonging to God and they were his own. For who would not much rather belong to this Lord and Creator? But now he says that we who believe on Christ will not be his servants and maids but his own sons, daughters and heirs. Who could praise this and proclaim it enough? Is it not yet too much to describe and grasp?

But here we see our great human weakness. For if we truly believed this without doubting, what would we fear and what would or could do us harm? For whoever can speak from the heart to God, "You are my dear Father, and I your child," could easily withstand all the devils and the spite of hell and freely despise all the world's burdens and blows. A believer has that kind of heart towards his

Father, before whom every creature must tremble and without whom nothing is possible. So he also has that kind of heritage and glory that by virtue of this fact no creature can do him harm or damage.

But he also adds this little line to it, "So we suffer also with him." By this we know that we must also live upon earth and prove ourselves as good obedient children who do not follow the flesh. And for the sake of this glory we suffer what we experience and we mortify the flesh. When we do that, then we will and can majestically comfort ourselves and with truth we can rejoice and boast as he has said, "Whom the Holy Ghost compels (that we do not follow the flesh), these are children of God."

Oh what a great thing it is for a person who does not follow his lusts but is rather established against them with strong faith and suffering. It is called great nobility, honor and glory upon earth to be the child of a mighty famous king or kaiser. How much higher would it be if someone could truly boast of being the son of the highest angel? But what is all this compared to those who are called and named by God himself and elected as a son and heir of the high divine majesty? For such a heritage and inheritance must surely bring a great unspeakable majesty and rule, power and honor, over all that is in heaven and earth.

Erl. 9, 183–184: Trinity 8 Sermon on Romans 8:12-17

When thus my heart in prayer ascendeth, Through Thine own Holy Spirit, unto Thee,
Thy heart, O Father, kindly bendeth Its fervent love and favor unto me,
Rejoicing my petition to fulfil Which I have made according to Thy will. (*TLH* 21: 5)

Wednesday

But we have such a confidence in God through Christ. Not that we are sufficient in ourselves to think in that way as deserving it; but rather our sufficiency is from God. 2 Corinthians 3:4,5

Every preacher should have this boast, that he is sure and his heart stands in this confidence and can say, "I have this confidence and courage to God from Christ, that my doctrine and preaching is truly God's Word." So also when he conducts other offices in the church, when he baptizes a child, absolves and comforts a sinner, that also must be done in the sure confidence that it is Christ's command.

Whoever cannot boast of this and would still teach and rule in the church, "to him it would be better," as Christ says in Matthew 18:6, "that he would be sunk in a deep sea with a millstone around

190

his neck," for he preaches and creates nothing else than the devil's lies and death. Until now our papists did this when they taught long and much, making it up as they went along. By these things they thought they would become holy so that their heart and thoughts were always doubtful. Who knows whether or not these things pleased God? Also, the doctrine and works of all the heretics and sectarian spirits were definitely not from a confidence in Christ but rather their doctrine only demanded people to praise them. They sought the praise and honor of the people.

(He says:) "Not that we are sufficient of ourselves to think anything as if it came from us." He says all of this, as said, against the false spirits, who regarded themselves so excellently capable and specially made and elected so that they should help the people. They thought what they said and did should put everyone in awe.

But we know that we also are of the same clay and glue out of which they are made. Yes, we also have a greater calling from God. By that we cannot brag that we are able to do anything in ourselves to advise or help the people or even think they would be helped by it (that is helped by something in us). For it is not our affair nor is it our confidence, nor did anything that concerns these matters of how one is established before God and comes to eternal life fly out of our head. In other things that concern temporal life and ways, you could brag and present what your reason teaches, and what thoughts your head can come up with, as how you should make clothes and shoes, or rule the house and home and animals. There practice your reason as well as you can, so that the cloth or leather is drawn and cut, as the taylor or shoemaker plans. But in these spiritual matters truly human thoughts give way, but other thoughts, skills and confidences prevail, which God himself gives and shows through his Word.

For who could think up or prove that three persons of the eternal Godhead are one God and that the second person, God's Son, had need to become a man, born of a virgin and that there can be no other way to life than that he be crucified for us? Surely that would never for eternity be heard or preached and also would never be experienced, learned or believed, had not God, himself, revealed it.

Therefore, those who would brag about themselves in this high action are great blind fools and are annoying people. They think that they can help people when they preach what they have thought or experienced.

Erl. 9, 230–231: Trinity 12 Sermon on 2 Cor. 3.4–11

God's Word is our great heritage And shall be ours forever;
To spread its light from age to age Shall be our chief endeavor.
Through life it guides our way, In death it is our stay
Lord, grant, while worlds endure, We keep its teachings pure
Throughout all generations. (*TLH* 283: 1)

Thursday

For the letter kills, but the Spirit makes alive. 2 Corinthians 3:6

Even if you could bring together every law, praised and exalted its preaching in the highest, as it should be praised, still that is no more than the "letter," the kind of thing that is taught and spoken, but will never happen. For "letter" names every kind of law, doctrine and preaching that only remains in the Word or lies on the paper or note and is not then done. Just as when a prince or counselor lets a law be unenforced. If it is not enforced then it remains nothing more than an official document upon which is written what should happen, but nothing comes of it. So also God's law, since it is not observed, even if it is the highest doctrine and God's eternal will, yet it must suffer to be made by people into a purely empty document or an empty husk. Without heart and fruit it brings neither life nor salvation. It could even be called a true lazy tablet. In it is written and revealed not what people do, but what people forsake and, as the world says, a ruler's law that remains undone and unheeded. St. Augustine also understood it in this way. He said, concerning the seventeenth psalm, "What is the law without grace, but letter without Spirit?" For the [human] nature cannot and does not desire to observe them when Christ is not there with his grace.

Again, St. Paul calls the gospel an "Office of the Spirit," for he acts to announce that same might because it is quite a different Word than the law in the human heart. Namely, it brings with it the Holy Ghost and makes a different heart. Then the person, when driven to terror and fear through the preaching of the law, hears this preaching which no longer says to him what God demands of him, but what God has done for him. This is done for him not by means of the sinner's works, but by Christ. This preaching bids him believe and to be sure that for the sake of his Son God will forgive him sins and receive him as his child.

Where the heart receives and believes such preaching, God soon lifts the heart and gives comfort so that it no longer flees before God, but now turns to him. Since it finds and feels such grace and mercy from him, it begins to be kindly disposed to him. Such a person now begins to call upon God from the heart and to retain and honor him as his dear God. Such faith and comfort is ever more strengthened. Desire and love ever increase towards his laws and obedience. Additionally, such a believer would have God compel him still more with the Word of the gospel by which the human heart is awakened so that it confesses that Word and he reminds himself of the great grace and mercy of God. The Holy Ghost thus becomes mightier and mightier. See that all this is not of the law or human power and works, but rather it is a new heavenly power of the Holy Ghost which Christ impresses with his works into the heart and makes a true little book out of it which is not letter and plain writing, but is truly alive and active.

Erl. 9, 239–240: Trinity 12 Sermon on 2 Cor. 3.4–11

The law reveals the guilt of sin And makes men conscience-stricken;
The gospel then doth enter in The sinful soul to quicken.
Come to the cross, trust Christ, and live; The law no peace can ever give,
No comfort and no blessing. (*TLH* 377: 8)

Friday

Do not wonder, my brothers, if the world hates you. 1 John 3:13

This will be the reason that should move Christians to remain in love. He compares this to the reason that the world hates us, which is their own evil. It is no wonder (he would say), that the world hates you. For there is a great difference between them and you. The world is already pleased in the devil's kingdom and eternal death with their own evil works, disbelief, pride, despising the Word of God and his grace, hating and persecuting the pious. They will not be told or helped so that they could come out of it. Rather, they stubbornly and impenitently are openly condemned by their own conscience and want to remain in it.

But we who are Christians are now much different people, God be praised. Namely, we come out of death and through death are established into life through the confession and faith of the Son of God who loved us and gave himself for us. Those who have received grace and mercy from God shall be moved (he says) so that they do not let themselves be enraged or overcome by the world's unthankfulness, hate and evil. They do not stop doing good works because of that lest they also would become evil, lest they also lose their treasure. For they do not have this because of themselves, but out of pure grace, that was also theirs previously, just as surely when they were yet lying in the kingdom and power of death, in evil works, without faith and love.

Therefore, remember and comfort yourself with your great wealth and promises that you have before everyone. What is it to you who have life that the world hates and persecutes you when it is in death and remains there? Whom do they hurt by their hate? They will not take the life from you that you have and they do not, nor can they bring you under death through which you have already come through Christ; even if they do a lot so that they would blaspheme you somewhat with evil words, or if they take your wealth or that foul stinking maggot sack [referring to our bodily life]. For this life has already been surrendered beforehand. It must rot and by that you will finally be helped into life out of this bodily death.

For there will be much more for you than you smell on yourself. You have joy because you are established from death unto life, but the rest must remain in eternal death. Because they plan to take both the heavenly kingdom and the earthly kingdom from you, they must lose body and soul. How could they be more horribly punished and become rank by hatred and envy? Should you yet rather show love both to the devil and the world? You would then give yourself much less sorrow that would ruin your salvation and comfort for their sakes and so lose such a treasure through impatience and lust for revenge. Yet, you should much more pity their misery and damnation, for you will not go that way. You must yet have pure favor but the world only [can have] harm. You must consider the little trouble which you suffer bodily and temporarily here and there as altogether dear.

Erl. 9, 46–48: Trinity 2 Sermon on 1 John 3:13–18

O little flock, fear not the Foe
Who madly seeks your overthrow;
Dread not his rage and pow'r.
What tho' your courage sometimes faints,
His seeming triumph o'er God's saints
Lasts but a little hour.

As true as God's own Word is true,
Not earth nor hell with all their crew
Against us shall prevail.
A jest and byword are they grown;
God is with us, we are His own;
Our vict'ry cannot fail.
(*TLH* 263: 1–3)

Saturday

For if we are children then we are also heirs, namely heirs of God and co-heirs with Christ. For we suffer with him so that we also will be raised to glory with him. Romans 8:17

In this passage he intentionally makes the connection that whoever wants to be a brother and co-heir with Christ should think that he is also a co-martyr and co-sufferer with Christ. He wants to say that there are probably many Christians who gladly desire to be co-heirs with Christ and sit in the same rule with the Lord Christ.

But they do not want to suffer with him. They separate themselves from him in this passage so that they will not be partakers of his suffering. But, he says, it cannot be that the inheritance will follow without suffering coming first. The reason is that Christ, our dear Lord and Savior, had need to previously suffer before he came to glory. So we must also be co-martyrs. Before we come into the inheritance, we must, with the Lord Christ, be mocked, reviled, despised, crowned with thorns and be put to death by the whole world. It can be no different.

For faith and doctrine brings with it the likeness of Christ. So whoever would be a brother and co-heir of Christ must also suffer with him. Who would live with him must first die with him, just as many brothers in a house must not only share good things but also bad things. As they say, "who would share food must also share the work."

With this St. Paul would earnestly exhort us not to be false Christians who only seek good and gentle things from the Lord Christ. Rather, "If we share his glory, which is eternal and surpasses everything, we also previously bear the trouble that is only temporal and light." 2 Corinthians 4:17.

Therefore, when he says, "For we suffer with him," he means that we not only should have co-suffering that will trouble us when evil occurs; although that kind of co-suffering will also come to the Christian and is a work of mercy and his Christian virtue; but we ourselves should also suffer, *non solum affectu, sed etiam effectu*; we are also stuck fast in the same kind of suffering. As our Lord Christ was persecuted, we also will be so persecuted. As the devil had tortured and tormented him, we also will be tortured and tormented by him day and night. As he treated Christ, indeed, he will let us have no peace if our Lord God does not prevent him.

That is called not only an inner, but an actual co-suffering as recorded in Hebrews 10:32f, "You have endured and greatly struggled with suffering as you were made a spectacle by both reproaches and tribulations," etc. St. Paul also speaks here of this kind of co-suffering, that even as our inheritance and joy as brothers and co-heirs with Christ does not only reside in the heart of hope but should rather be an active and actual inheritance, so our co-suffering will also be an active and actual co-suffering which is also a part of our co-inheritance.

Erl. 9, 96–98: Trinity 4 Sermon on Romans 8:18–22

Then let us follow Christ, our Lord, And take the cross appointed
And, firmly clinging to His Word, In suffering be undaunted.
For who bears not the battle's strain The crown of life shall not obtain. (*TLH* 421: 5)

Laetare

Sunday

Thus says the Lord of Sabbaoth, "Turn to me," says the Lord of Sabbaoth; "And I will turn to you," says the Lord of Sabbaoth. Zechariah 1:3

That is, show that you are my people; [that you] serve me alone, and are obedient to my commands: So I will turn to you again for I am your God, and I will again do everything good and defend you before all the world as I did before I moved away from you because your fathers were not good and you had turned from me. Turning changes things. When your fathers turned from me, so I also turned from them. So turn again to me and I will also turn again to you.

I say this because the scholastics and sophists use this passage in favor of free will, as if a person could turn himself, since God says here, "Turn to me." Yet this text does not say what a person is able to do, but what he is obligated to do. For when he says, "Turn to me," he shows that they should turn, that is, keep all the commandments and be good. Now whether or not a person of himself is able to do this, the Scripture does not say here. But it says this well enough in other places. What one can do and should do are quite far removed from each other. So one must not use the passage nor understand "can do" where it speaks of "should do." I have written more concerning this in my pamphlet, *"Servum arbitrium."* [7]

Let us see why the prophet, who should comfort the poor frightened people, further frightens them before anything else and begins with threats and shows the rod. It is the skill and manner of the Holy Ghost that he begins sharp and hard and thereafter becomes friendly and sweet. Then again, the devil goes in softly and goes out sour. So also a father at first looks hard and sharp at his child but thereafter he is his dear child and he gives only sweet love. So also here, since this prophet will give much comfort, he starts out hard and earnestly. This is not only the manner and skill of the Holy Ghost but it is what we need. For as has been said, these poor people had many obstacles, having more than forty years of hardship away from their neighbors and under the ruler of Persia. As Haggai said, this kind of great judgment (as is always raised against God's Word) had probably made the people weary, since they turned themselves

---

[7] Luther's *Bondage of the Will*

away from God as their fathers had done when some of them sided with the heathen, like the high priest's son, who was taken by Tobia, a daughter of the heathen, of whom Nehemiah writes. For this reason it was necessary to advise and terrify them with the rod first, so they would not let themselves take this judgment lightly and come like their fathers under sins and punishment.

In this a person tries to excuse himself, "What can I do? If I do not run with the crowd I must let go of wife, child, goods, honor and life. Then how will I support myself? Where will I stay?" For just this reason one feels he must let God's Word go, or as if God could not defend or provide for such a person, so it [God's Word] must be lost for that reason. This is like those in the gospel who also excused themselves; one had a field, the other bought oxen, the third took a wife. So Ahaz, the king of Judah wanted to be generous to the gods of Syria and for that lost his grace from God. Oh, this is a great, strong, high preaching that Zachariah does here, although the Words sound simple. But when one sees what was happening at the time, then it becomes an excellent, necessary preaching to preserve the people so they do not turn away from God and fall away from his Word. Even so a Christian must check, call and cry out when a persecution, revolt or heresy goes forth and rages, so that he preserves the people lest they change and turn themselves from God.

Erl. 42, 134–136: Commentary on the Prophet Zechariah, 1527; cf. AE 20

When all my deeds I am reviewing, The deeds that I admire the most,
I find in all my thought and doing That there is naught whereof to boast.
Yet this sweet comfort shall abide In mercy I can still confide. (*TLH* 385: 8)

Monday

Preach and say, "Thus says the Lord of Sabbaoth, 'I have a great zeal for Jerusalem and Zion.' " Zechariah 1:14

Here you see in every Word the tender, fatherly way they are spoken. They sound like no other words but those of a dear father, who after the rod again invites his child to himself and gives him the very best words. He stops and throws away the rod, yes, he rages against the rod, leers at it and treads it under his feet as if it were the rod and not he that had done it [the chastising]. This is the best interpretation of his distemper, since he has meant it for good and it is not wrath. It rather becomes pure love. He gives him thereafter a penny or apple as a sign of the truth so that the poor child forgets the rod and he establishes him again as his child. Even so God acts here with the Jews. First he begins to rage against the rod, as if he had not done it, but rather the heathen have done it and says, "I have been zealous for Jerusalem," etc. That is, I have not truly become angry so that I would discard or forsake my people. Rather as a father punishes his child, and a man his wife, and is angry with them, so it is with me.

He is not zealous with an evil wrath which enemies have with one another. Rather it is a wrath of love, a friendly, fatherly wrath, as those who have love for each other become angry. Such "love" additionally serves the purpose that the resulting love is even warmer and becomes completely new. For if such wrath did not occasionally come between those in love, then the love would become stagnant and rust would consume it like iron. But this zeal sweeps it off well, so that the love again becomes new so often as they rage with each other, since they are in love. Therefore, I try to call the wrathful love *zelum* or zeal. For where love rages, it does no harm.

But when hate and jealousy rage, they ruin and destroy as much as they can. For loving zeal searches and wants to distinguish the evil (which it hates) from the good (which he loves) so that his love may preserve what is good: as a father would preserve his dear child, but puts an end to its sins; and a man wants also to preserve his dear wife, but wants to confront her shamefulness or lack of virtue. Then again, wrathful hate wants to ruin and bring to nothing both the good with the evil.

So God also says here, that he has not become wrathful over Jerusalem because of hate and enmity, but rather he has been zealous as a father and was angry out of love so that he could withdraw his blessing from their lack of virtue and preserve them as his children. He defines himself as having this zeal and says, "I was a little wrathful;" as if he would say, "My zeal is a short, little wrath that doesn't last long." So he doesn't bite all the way through but rather he has a little temper so that he turn away the evil. So he excuses his wrath and invites the peoples' heart back in such a lovely way.

And for sure, when one sees who it is that speaks in this way, namely God himself, then they are truly sweet Words, yes Words of life, joy and all blessedness. Then, even if one were in death or hell, and heard such Words from God, he would have to be lively and joyous because of these Words. But we let them go, despise them, as spoken by just a man, and do not believe that God himself speaks. Why don't we also taste how sweet they are?

Erl. 42, 151-153: Commentary on the Prophet Zechariah, 1527; cf. AE 20

The will of God is always best And shall be done forever;
And they who trust in Him are blest, He will forsake them never.
He helps indeed In time of need, He chastens with forbearing;
They who depend on God, their Friend, Shall not be left despairing. (*TLH* 517: 1)

Tuesday

"And I will," says the Lord, "Be a fiery wall around her and will be in her and will reveal my glory within her." Zechariah 2:5

Here we see again that this will be a spiritual Jerusalem. It shall be without a wall, and yet it shall have a wall. Where God himself is now the wall and there shall be no physical wall, that must be a spiritual city. For God cannot be a physical wall.

But are these not overflowing, comforting, lovely Words? Where are the Christians who believe this? Give me one who truly believes and holds this as true that God is so around him as a fiery wall where he goes or strays. Before whom would such a Christian be afraid? There are some kings who have two or three thousand men around them; and a long time ago, the bad king, Attila, had five hundred thousand men with him, so that he not only frightened the Roman Empire, but also the whole world. And the Turk also has many people around him, and the king in Persia, Xerxes, had eleven hundred thousand men with him. Now, all of these in a heap, what are they compared to those who have God as a fiery wall around them? They are beggars and poor defenseless people. With all such great fare and heavy armor, where much can be broken up and stopped, yet they cannot do so much as make their life safe for a single second. Yet in his most joyous night Attila had to be choked in blood that tried to flow out of his nose; and the King of Persia fled with a skiff on the sea. But a Christian needs no paid soldiers as his entourage, neither armor nor rations, but goes free and has a fiery wall around him which defends his life in eternity.

So also it is well sung in the 125th Psalm, "Those who trust in the Lord will not fall, and remain eternally as Mount Zion. Surrounding Jerusalem are mountains, and the Lord surrounds his people from now unto eternity." Mountains are around Jerusalem and the Lord himself is around his people. Mountains are even better than walls. Who would attack a city over mountains? But here it is even firmer and safer, for the Lord himself will be a fiery wall. Who will or can strive against and through fire? With this God comforts us, as he will not only be to us a wall to shelter us, but he will also frighten our foes, and consume them like a fire. This is also what he had advised the children of Israel, Exodus 14, where the angel of God stood as a cloud of fire between the Egyptians and Israel so that they could not reach them the whole night until in the morning God plunged the children of Israel into the sea and broke their enemies down. 2 Kings 6 reads the same way where the prophet Elisha showed his servant fiery mountains and chariots around the city and said, "Those with us are many more than with them."

But this also belongs to faith, since God holds his fiery wall so hidden that not only can no person see it, but also he lets his own people be persecuted and slain as if he had not drawn even a straw mat or cobweb around them, not to speak of a fiery wall. The flesh is so weak that it can not grasp or believe such passages and comforting promises. But the Holy Ghost must give and teach it.

Erl. 42, 167–169: Commentary on the Prophet Zechariah, 1527; cf. AE 20

Thus God shall from all evil Forever make us free,
From sin, and from the devil, From all adversity,
From sickness, pain, and sadness, From troubles, cares, and fears,
And grant us heavenly gladness And wipe away our tears. (*TLH* 67: 7)

Wednesday

Whoever attacks you, attacks the apple of my eye. Zechariah 2:8

The Words mean something to us, "Whoever attacks you, attacks the apple of my eye." That should be the treasure and comfort in Christ's kingdom, which is truly unspeakable. He doesn't leave it at being a fiery wall around us. Rather he says here we are so dear, as the apple of his eye. Well, that is a lot! Yet how completely shameful our unbelief remains. It so often deprives us of these comforting promises so we should not honor and keep them. It is too far from our senses, for what we see happening is so different. He lets us be so horribly persecuted. John the Baptizer was beheaded for the sake of a whore. Do you call that, "Whoever attacks you, attacks the apple of my eye?" So also [it is with] every other martyr and saint.

The pope and his followers have used this passage well to their advantage, that whoever has not given them rents, or whoever had not donated goods for the orders, had attacked the apple of the Lord's eye. So the Scripture must help one [know], God grant it, whether or not we are Christians. But let go of the devil and his followers.

But where there is a Christian who believes that this is true, friend, what can he think if he sees something that does him harm? He must not quickly think of wrath and rod; he must not only be patient, but also be merciful and pity his foes and say, "Oh, you poor man, what are you doing now? You do nothing to me, but you poke the one in the eyes who, unfortunately, is too mighty for you and is called God." By this he is moved, not only to suffer patiently, but also to pray, yes, even to die for his foe, if [by this] he might be saved from the wrath of the one he pokes in the eye. Now there is nothing so unpleasant than to be poked many times in the eye. By this God reveals himself to us as a comfort to frighten the foes, how completely nasty and aggravating this is for him to bear when we are attacked, so that we have no need to get angry or to rage. He never lies, that we must be attacked, since he says, "Whoever attacks you. . ."; but those who attempt it will not be permitted for long.

So now he will say, "Dear Jews, until now you have been tried by the heathen surrounding you. Well, in the future not only these same heathen, but all heathen who have attacked you will attack me. They shall again be subjected and be under you, as you are Christians and belong to me."

Erl. 42, 179–180: Commentary on the Prophet Zechariah, 1527; cf. AE 20

For though the evil world revile me And prove herself my bitter foe
Or by her smile seek to beguile me, I trust her not; her wiles I know.
In Thee alone my soul rejoices, Thy praise alone it gladly voices,
For Thou art true when friendships flee. The world may hate but cannot fell me;
Would mighty waves of trial quell me, I anchor in Thy loyalty. (*TLH* 362: 2)

Thursday

But Jonah was in the hold of the ship reclining and sleeping. Jonah 1:5

That could well be called a stone-dead sleep, which would be his last. He soon must journey into death. But so it always goes with sinners, and God treats them even as he does Jonah. For Jonah had greatly sinned against God. But since God was silent and restrained the punishment, and didn't attack the sin, or strike so quickly, it is the nature and characteristic of sins that they delude and harden the sinner so that he becomes secure in them and does not fear. He rather lies in them and sleeps and does not see what a great storm and misfortune is at hand above him. It horribly awakens him.

So God sits back for a while as if he had forgotten the sins while he delays and tests what the children of men will do, if they also want to repent, as the 11th Psalm says, "The eyelids of the Lord test the children of man." But nothing happens. There is not repentance or regret. Jonah would sleep his whole life away. If God would forget about his sins, he wouldn't give them another thought.

In Jonah, this means that in the middle of the storm he sleeps deeply and soundly in the hold of the ship. He says, "He is completely blind, hardened, sunk, yes, dead, and lying at the bottom of an impenitent heart." He would also remain lying there eternally and be ruined. For sins do not allow any kind of power in man to do good, whether by free will or reason. There he lays and snores in his sins, does not hear and see or even feel what the wrath of God is doing or bringing about above him.

But the sailor wakes him up and commands him to pray to his God. Another raises him up for he is in danger as God is behind him with punishment and has not forgotten his sins. Then the conscience carries on. Then the sins come again and become active. There sin is the prick of death and it shows God's wrath. Then to him not only the ship, but the world becomes too small. Yes, surely he should cry out to God. He was more afraid [of God] than anyone on the ship. For he felt and noted, his conscience also informed him, that this storm was for him and God's wrath was coming over him. Oh, how humbled he is! He absolved everyone who was on the ship and didn't regard them as the sinners. He saw no others' sins there, but his own.

For this is what remorse does when it comes. It bites and terrifies the conscience so that all the world is good except he alone is a sinner. All the world is pleasing to God except him alone. There God's wrath comes for no one but for him alone. It [this remorse] also thinks that there is no other wrath than that which it feels and finds itself the most pitiful creature. This is what it also did with Adam and Eve when they had sinned. Had God not come in the cool of the day, they nevermore would have thought of their sin. But when he came they hid. So also Peter, after he had denied Christ did not feel any sins and was dead until Christ looked upon him. Then he felt them again and wept bitterly. Jonah also slept in the hold of the ship. So it happens now. Sins make people stubborn, insensible, practically completely dead, so that one senses neither himself nor God, and goes about safe without fear, until God himself comes and wakes him up. By this the glory of free will is laid completely aside.

Now Jonah does not call out to his God, but sits and trembles before God's wrath and it bites him with death, which will devour him at any moment. And even though the people pray uselessly to their gods and do what they can, yet Jonah sees and feels that this has happened for his sake. He is not so good that he can come out with it and confess his sin, but he lets the poor people suffer such terror and danger and misery for his sake, until God presses the sin to him so that he must confess. Because he betrayed God, he was betrayed by the casting of lots.

Erl. 41, 356–358: Lectures on Jonah, 1526; cf. AE 19

My Savior sinners doth receive Who find no rest and no salvation,
To whom no man can comfort give, So great their guilt and condemnation;
For whom the world is all too small, Their sins both them and God appall;
With whom the Law itself hath broken, On whom its judgment hath been spoken,
To them the Gospel hope doth give: My Savior sinners doth receive.
My Savior sinners doth receive. (*TLH* 386: 1)

Friday

*I am a Hebrew and fear the Lord God of heaven, who
made the sea and the dry land. Jonah 1:9*

Here comes the confession and it brings the sin into the light.
Then comes the true battle between Jonah and death. Yet this is the
greatest thing done. For though death and the wrath of God pressed
in and mightily seized Jonah, yet the heavy load of sins breaking his
heart and conscience becomes somewhat lighter through confession
of this sin. Faith begins to burn, although very weakly. For he
confesses the true God, maker of heaven and earth, which is not a
poor beginning of faith and salvation.

For a completely doubting and desparate conscience does not
open the mouth so wide but silences it or blasphemes God and cannot
think of God. It must grasp or speak otherwise of him as if he were
a horrible tyrant or the devil and it would only gladly flee far away
from him. Yes, it would rather that God did not exist so that it would
not have to suffer such things from him. It also forgets confession
and does not confess its sins. So it is so completely sunk and stuck
in fear that it can neither see nor feel anything more than fear and
only thinks of how it can make itself free. Yet it cannot make itself
free because the sins adhere to it. So it remains eternally stuck in sins
and death.

From this let us learn the true art and right exercise to come out
of all need and fear, namely, that one give attention to sin before all
things; and quickly and freely confess them so there will never be
this kind of great danger or need. For before all things the heart must
first be helped so that it becomes lighter and receives courage.
Thereafter the whole life is so much easier to talk about. So first the
conscience must receive salvation and courage from its load so that
every need will find good counsel. For in such a case, when God's
wrath comes, there are two parts at hand, the sins and the fear. Now
where there are uninformed hearts, they hurry into the matter
overturned and wrong, while they let the sins remain and only see
the fear and how they must make themselves free. That doesn't help

anything and so they must doubt. All reason works in this way when grace and the Spirit are not nearby. But where there are understanding hearts, they hurry to turn their thoughts from the fear and look mostly at their sins, that they acknowledge them and be free of them, even if the fear should always remain. They surrender to this, as Jonah does here.

But that is the characteristic and manner of the godless. They fear and regard the punishment, but they do not heed the sin. They would gladly always sin if not for the punishment. That doesn't do anything, but rather the punishment always adheres to the sin. Then again, the God-fearing skill is this, that they fear and regard the sins. They do not give so much attention to the punishment, but would rather be in the punishment without sins than remain in the sins without punishment.

But Jonah says that here. "I fear the God of heaven," is said in Hebrew; for they call God's service fearing God, as it is good to note from Isaiah chapter 29, where he says, "They fear me according to the commandments of men;" that is, they think that they honor and serve me by the commandments of men. For Jonah hangs them both together, "I am a Hebrew and fear God in heaven." So from that time on he became obedient to God and heeded him. But he would also say here, "I do not honor and serve strange gods, like you and the other heathen, but the one true God."

Erl. 41, 363-365: Lectures on Jonah, 1526; cf. AE 19

Oh, draw us ever unto Thee, Thou Friend of sinners, gracious Savior;
Help us that we may fervently Desire Thy pardon, peace, and favor.
When guilty conscience doth reprove, Reveal to us Thy heart of love.
May we, our wretchedness beholding, See then Thy pardoning grace unfolding
And say: "To God all glory be: My Savior, Christ, receiveth me." (*TLH* 386: 5)

Saturday

Jonah said to them, "Take me and cast me into the sea and the sea will be still for you. For I know that such a great storm is coming over you for my sake." Jonah 1:12

Let us see here from Jonah what faith can do from a pure heart and what it can accomplish. Here stands an important example of faith. As we have mentioned above, he is like an almighty person, and triumphs in all things that are against him.

In the first place, he takes the sins of the others upon himself and confesses that it is for his sake that this storm is coming. With this he is bound and pronounces all the rest free. He alone remains the sinner so that the others must all be good. Here he brings enough love and confesses what he has done to the people when he brought them into this danger and he lets it all fall on him. And against this love he finds here a fine thankful place. For these kind people do not demand such a high confession, and would gladly give him the sins, are satisfied by the public penance and confession, and try with all their might to help him back again to land. So love is repaid with love. But it will not be.

Next, he takes and bears this conscience full of sin upon himself before God that he is also sinful and scandalous before God, as the one whose heart is mightily drowned. He confesses that he has acted horribly both towards God and man. This shame is now a thousand times greater so that he must blush before God. For there is no corner or hole in all creation, even in hell, where he might slink. Rather he must let himself be seen by every creature and stand before them with all shame, as the evil conscience already feels when it is driven. So you must not consider Jonah here as if he would hereafter be freed and restored to honor; rather how he is stuck in shame and does not see where he should ever come out of it again. For thus a heart would wish or seek something that would make the shame and the conscience less troubling. But God works all glory and comfort out of eyesight and lets only shame be there. That is the misery.

In the third place, death naturally follows after sins as the punishment as St. Paul says in 1 Corinthians 15, "But the power of sins is the law, but the prick or cutting edge of death is sins." So Jonah sees here that nothing is at hand but bitter death. He gives himself to it and speaks judgment over his own life, "Throw me into the sea." He is saying, "I must die, otherwise there will be no peace." So you must not consider Jonah [in this situation] in light of the ending. Since we know the whole story, how he is delivered, we don't think much about it and it moves us but little. But you must see how Jonah is encouraged in this spot. He sees not a glimmer of life left, nor of salvation, but rather only death, death, death is there, so he must despair of life and submit to death. So when God treats us in the same way he lets us see life in death, or shows our soul a place and room, a way and manner, where it should tread and walk upon, where we also should cross over and remain. Then death would not be bitter, but would be a jump over a flat stream where one sees and feels a sure ground and bank on both sides. But now he shows us none of it and we must jump from the sure bank of this life into the chasm where there is no feeling, nor sight, nor feet nor standing, but rather rely upon God's advice and forbearance, just as here Jonah is thrown out of the ship so that he falls into the sea were he feels no ground and is forsaken of all creatures, and goes in only by God's forbearance.

In the fourth place, he also bears God's wrath in death. For he does not feel how death is coming over him out of grace, but out of wrath, earned by his sins.

Erl. 41, 366–368: Lectures on Jonah, 1526; cf. AE 19

In God, my faithful God, I trust when dark my road;
Tho' many woes o'ertake me, Yet He will not forsake me.
His love it is doth send them And, when 'tis best, will end them. (*TLH* 526: 1)

Judica

Sunday

*Now remain faith, hope and love, these three; but the
greatest of these is love. 1 Corinthians 13:13*

Here the apostle speaks of the enduring nature of love and the
temporary nature of the other gifts and not of their [relative] worth
or power. To speak of their worth, not only faith but also the Word
are greater than love. For this Word is God's power, that makes holy
all who believe, Romans 1:16. It must not cease. So love is the fruit
and work of the Word, yet both will remain. Faith enthrones God
himself. It enables and does all things. Yet it must cease. And love
gives and does good to the neighbor as a consequence of faith while
faith remains.

Now "love is greater than faith and hope" is a truth. It
remains longer and eternally, so that faith is much shorter and
smaller, as it only has a temporal duration. Just as I can say that
Christianity is greater on earth than Christ. By that I would not
say that Christianity is in itself better and worth more than Christ,
but that it has spread out longer and wider on earth than Christ
did, who was only three years in one small place. Christianity was
worldwide from its beginning. So also love is longer and wider
than faith and hope. For faith only has to do with God in the heart
in this life. But love has to do with God and all the world,
eternally. None the less, just as Christ is immeasurably better,
more noble and of greater value than Christianity, even if he is a
small, single person, so also faith is better, worthier and more
valuable than love even if it lasts a shorter time and concerns one
single person and God.

But St. Paul compels such praise for love to strike at the false
teachers. He makes nothing of their boast of faith and gifts without
love. He wants to say, "If you do not have love, which lasts forever,
then everything else that you brag about is passing and will be lost
by it." For though the Word of God and gifts of the Spirit are
eternal, yet the outward office and husk of eternal Words, and the
outward use and various gifts cease, so that your boast and pride
must go to ashes. So it remains that faith makes right through the
Word and brings love. But both Word and faith cease, and
righteousness and love, conceived through it, remain eternally. Just
as a building constructed with scaffolds remains, but the scaffolds
cease.

See now what a small word love is and how quickly it is said. But who would have sought so much generous virtue and skill in this single virtue which St. Paul ascribes to love against so much that is not virtuous? I think he calls love praiseworthy and portrays it as being much better than what the heathen blasphemously ascribe to virtue. There he has presented a pattern which must rightfully shame the false teachers that speak much of love and not one shred of it is found in them. For these words are truly only great stings and storms against such teachers so often as he speaks a virtue of love. So he praises love and reveals its character in such a way that he wants them all to compare them with those who do not have any, so that you could well write a little note next to each passage and say: "but you act much differently."

Erl. 8, 124–125: Sermon on Quinquagesima on 1 Cor. 13

All that for my soul is needful He with loving care provides,
Nor of that is He unheedful Which my body needs besides.
When my strength cannot avail me, When my powers can do no more,
Doth my God His strength outpour; In my need He doth not fail me.
All things else have but their day, God's great love abides for aye. (*TLH* 25: 3)

Monday

We are God's co-workers; you are God's field of labor and God's building. 1 Corinthians 3:9

That is, we preach. We work on you with the external Word through preaching and exhortation. But God gives the blessing and increase inwardly through the Spirit, that our outward Word not work in vain. So God is inwardly the true Master, who does the best work. We help and serve him outwardly through the preaching office.

He praises such co-helpers so that the outward Word should not be despised as if they were not in need of it or as if they could do it so well. So even though God surely could direct all things inwardly without the external Word, only through the Spirit, yet he will not do that, but rather has the preacher as co-helper and co-worker and he works through their Word, where and when he will. Since the preachers have the office, title and honor that they are God's co-workers, no one should be so learned or holy that he would despise or neglect the most beggarly preacher since he does not know when the moment will come in which God will do his work on him through the preacher.

On the other hand he shows the danger, "that one not neglect grace." By this he shows that the preaching of the gospel is not an eternal, lasting, resident teaching. Rather it is like a moving downpour, that runs its course; where it falls it falls and where it doesn't it doesn't. But it doesn't return, and also doesn't remain, but rather the sun and heat follow and dry it up. That is also what is experienced. In no place in the world has the gospel remained pure and clean over one man's thoughts. Rather, so long as those who bring it remain, it stands and has been received. But when these leave, the light also leaves, followed quickly by the fanatics and false teachers.

So Moses also proclaimed in Deuteronomy 31:29, that the children of Israel would soon be ruined after his death. The book of Judges goes on to say that it also happened. So as soon as a judge died, the Word of God ceased, so often they again fell away and it was worse for them. And King Joash did right so long as the high priest Jehoiadah lived. Afterwards it fell apart. And after the time of Christ and his apostles, the world was full of sectarian spirits and false teachers, as St. Paul also proclaimed in Acts 20:29 and said, "I know, that after my departure, horrible wolves will come from among you that will not help the flock." So it is also now. We have the gospel pure and fine, and it is the time of grace or salvation, and the acceptable day; but soon after it will be finished, should the world continue to stand.

But they receive the grace of God in vain. It can be no other way. If a person hears the pure Word of God, in which God's grace is presented and worshiped and nothing happens besides that, it is not received. They remain as they were.

Erl. 8, 126–127: Sermon on Quinquagesima on 1 Cor. 13

Oh, grant that in Thy holy Word We here may live and die, dear Lord;
And when our journey endeth here, Receive us into glory there. (*TLH* 292: 9)

Tuesday

Strive to enter through the narrow gate. For there are
many, I say to you, who seek how they can come in and
will not be able to. Luke 13:24

So why not? Because they do not know what the narrow gate is. It is faith, which is little to man. Yes, he makes it into practically nothing, for [by it] he must despair of all his works, and only hasten to God's grace and also on account of it let everything else go. But the non-Saints think that the narrow gates are their good works. Therefore they do not become small, do not despair of themselves, yes, they gather works with great sacks, hang them around themselves and would like to go forward. But even in this they go backwards, as a camel with his great load would go through the eye of a needle.

If one now tells them about faith, they mock and laugh and speak as if one were regarding them as Turks or heathen, that they first should learn about faith. Should there be so many monks, nuns, pastors and they don't know faith? Who doesn't know what it is to believe? Even open sinners know about it. Therefore, as if they had their fill of things pertaining to faith, they think that thereafter they must be concerned with works and they regard faith (as I have said) as practically nothing. For they do not [really] know about it and also do not know how it alone makes one righteous.

They talk about faith that they have received from Christ and hold that it is all true; as the devils also believe and do not become good thereafter through it. But that is not a Christian faith. It is more of a dream than a faith. As we have heard enought in previous Postils[8], it is not enough for a person if he wants to be a Christian, that he believes that all of what is said of Christ is true, which is the non-saint's faith. Rather, he must not doubt it or waver whether he is one of those who are given such grace and mercy, and have definitely received them through Baptism or the Sacrament. When he believes that, then he must freely say of himself that he is holy, good, righteous and a child of God, sure of salvation, and no longer doubt it; not because of himself, nor because of his services and works, but rather because of the pure mercy of God in Christ, poured out upon him. He considers this so great, and it is, that he does not doubt that it makes him holy and a child of God. For when he doubts this, he most highly dishonors his Baptism and Sacrament and belies God's Word and grace in the Sacraments.

There should not be fear or wavering here. For he is good and a child of God out of grace. But he only fears and worries how he remains established in this unto the end since he is still in all kinds of danger and sorrow. For every blessing is definitely there. But it is doubtful and a source of worry whether he will overcome and be kept by it so that one must wander in fear. So this kind of faith does not brag about works or itself but rather only on God and his grace. The same also would and could not leave him as long as this boast

---

[8]Published books of sermons for the year of liturgical readings appointed in the lectionary of the church.

210

endures. But as long as it endures he does not know if some trial might drive him from it. For when such a boast ceases, then grace also ceases.

Erl. 7, 242–243: Sermon on the Sunday after Christmas, Gal. 4:1–8

Tender Shepherd, never leave them, Never let them go astray;
By Thy warning love directed, May they walk the narrow way!
Thus direct them, thus defend them, Lest thy fall an easy prey. (*TLH* 627: 2)

Wednesday

But before faith came, we were guarded under the law and reserved until faith, which would be revealed. Galatians 3:23

See here how it is said, "No one will be right through the law and works." If we would want to become right through the law there would be no need of faith. It would also be false that St. Paul says here, "Through faith we are justified." Faith and works are mutually exclusive when it comes to justification. If you account justification to faith, you must take away works, law and nature. If you account it to works, then you must take away faith. One must be true and the other false. They can not both be true. Therefore, of the law there must be no other power or ability but to make sinners, or let sinners keep on sinning. What does not justify, that definitely makes sinners or lets sinners remain as such. Further, since the law certainly has to do with sins and sinners, there must be something more that it can do to them than to let poor sinners remain as they are. What kind of creature would it be that lets what it finds remain as it is?

So now, what can the law bring about if it doesn't justify or improve, and doesn't let remain [unchanged] what it finds? It would have to be a strange creation if it did not justify, nor let remain unchanged what is; so it necessarily follows that it must increase the sins, as St. Paul says in Romans 5:20, "The law was added so that sins might increase." It works in those that it captures and restrains their hand and for outwardly wicked people, it awakens only great hate and resistance in the heart against it, just as a boy becomes so resistant to his task master that the harder he punishes him, or his desires are prohibited, his hate and rebellion is nothing but multiplied as what he evilly desires is forbidden him. It would never have been increased if that desire were not opposed.

So before the law a person sins and the evil nature simply does not think of the law. But when the law comes and opposes and threatens, then first the nature becomes evil and resistant to the law.

It begins not only to love the sin but also to hate righteousness. So that is what the law creates in the sins and sinners. That is what St. Paul calls "sins being increased through the law." So he is silent about anyone being justified through the law. But blessed is he who understands and acknowledges this. For the works-saints do not understand it at all. They account to nature no such evil nor this hate for the law. They find much good in it. Therefore, they don't understand a single letter of St. Paul, who never says anything else of the law. And if we would speak rightly, we will also find it so in our hearts.

He also says: until Christ, the law was our task master. So no one ought undertake another faith than on Christ. The law was necessary until Abraham's seed, Christ, on whom every saint has believed since the beginning.

Erl. 7, 293-295: Sermon on the Sunday after Christmas, Gal. 4:1-8

It was a false, misleading dream That God His law had given
That sinners could themselves redeem And by their works gain heaven.
The law is but a mirror bright To bring the inbred sin to light
That lurks within our nature. (*TLH* 377: 3)

Thursday

And the Lord looked favorably upon Abel and his sacrifice; but he did not look favorably upon Cain and his offering. Cain was angry and his countenance fell. Genesis 4:4,5

First he regarded Abel, the person, and thereafter the offering. His person was previously good, right and acceptable. Thereafter, for the sake of the person, the offering was also. The person was not acceptable for the sake of the offering. Then again, he did not regard Cain and his offering. So also, first he did not regard Cain, the person, and thereafter he also did not regard his offering. From this text it is certain that it is not possible for a work to be good before God if the person is not previously good and acceptable. Then again, it is not possible that a work is evil before God unless the person is previously evil and unacceptable. That is now enough on this and certainly there are two kinds of good works, some before and some after being justified. Those that go before only appear so and are of no use, but the ones that follow are rightly made good.

See, this is the battle between God and the proud saints where [human] nature fights and rages against the Holy Ghost. But the whole of Scripture is concerned with this. God in the Scriptures concludes that all works before justification are evil and of no use and he desires them to be justified and made good first. Again, he concludes that every person, if they are still by nature in the first birth, are unjust and evil, as Psalm 116:11 says, "All men are liars." Genesis 6:5, "Every thought and desire of the human heart is always evil." Therefore he can do no good works. What he does instead are pure works of Cain.

Here Frau Hulda walks out with the wiped nose, the [fallen] nature, and she can bark against God and chastise his lies. She hangs around herself her old rag-fair, the straw armor, this natural light, reason, the free will, the natural powers, following which the heathen books and human teaching are exalted. She rallies with her fiddle and says, "Those that come before justification are also good works and are not works of Cain as God says. And they are so good that through them the person is justified." So also Aristotle had taught, "Whoever does many good works, he is good through them." Because of this they also hasten ardently so they overturn the Scriptures, thinking that God should first regard the works and then the person. Such devilish teachings now predominate in all the high schools, convents and cloisters and there are altogether only Cain-saints, that God does not regard.

On the other hand, since now they base everything only on works, and don't regard the person and justification as being so great, they go farther. They also give the works after justification all the credit. Their chief justification is in saying, "Faith without works is nothing," as James 2:26 says. By this passage, since they do not rightly understand it, they consider faith poorly and remain clinging to works. They want to flatter God with them so that for the sake of them [works] he should also let the person please him. They continuously strive after both against each other. God regards the person; so Cain regards his works. God will reward the works for the sake of the person. So Cain will have the person crowned for the sake of his works. God does not shy away from his thoughts, as just and right. So the boy Cain also does not let his errors be overruled from the beginning of the world to the end. One should not throw away his good works, nor regard his reason as nothing, nor regard his free will as lacking virtue, else he rages with God and slays his brother Abel to the ground, as every historian teaches abundantly.

Erl. 7, 238–240: Sermon on the Sunday after Christmas, Gal. 4:1–8

Since Christ hath full atonement made And brought to us salvation,
Each Christian therefore may be glad And build on this foundation.
Thy grace alone, dear Lord, I plead, Thy death is now my life indeed,
For Thou has paid my ransom. (*TLH* 377: 6)

Friday

*You should not dream that I have come to undo the law and the
prophets. I have not come to undo, but to fulfill them. Matthew 5:17*

We believe that only Christ has fulfilled the law, as he says in
Matthew 5:17, "I have not come to undo the law, but to fulfill it."
This also gives the meaning of the testament that says in Genesis
22:18 that all the world is accursed and shall be blessed in the Seed
of Abraham. Now everyone is accursed and separated from the
blessing, for people are not good and all are only like Cain. So their
works must also not be good, as said above, for God regards not the
works but first the person, Abel and Cain. The works of the law
make no one good, nor do they justify.

Since, then, Christ casts aside all works of the law and
demanded first personal benediction and goodness, it had the
appearance that he cast aside good works, and would undo the law,
though he rightly taught to do good works. So he speaks against such
dreams in Matthew 5:17, "You should not dream that I have come
to undo the law, because I cast away the works of the law. I will
accomplish more [for you] through faith in me, which first makes a
person good, and then good works follow."

So also, when St. Paul casts away all works of the law and
exalts only faith in Romans 3:31, he says, "How? Do we overthrow
the law through faith? Far from it. Rather we establish the law."
Even as now people say one would forbid good works if we
overthrew the convents and cloistered life in their works, yet we
would rather that they first believed rightly. Through that their
person would be made good and would receive salvation in Christ,
Abraham's Seed, and then do good works that serve for the discipline
of the body and the need of the neighbor which the cloister and
convent duties never do, as has sufficiently been said.

It should be noted, though, that no one can fulfill the law so that
he can be free of the law and be under it no longer. Therefore, we
must get used to Paul's speaking of being under the law, so that we
know who is under it and who is not. All who do good works that
are also commanded because of fear of punishment or the search for
reward are under the law because they must be good and do good
and yet do not do it gladly. Therefore, the law is their lord and
driver, but they are its servants and prisoners. All people outside of
Christ, the blessed Seed of Abraham, are this way, which experience
and one's own conscience must acknowledge. For if there were no
compelling law and punishment, or reward, but they rather were left

to their free desires so that they might do whatever they wanted to do unpunished and unrewarded, then they would do evil and leave what is good until the trial and judgment got their attention. But now the law with threats and promises lies in his way. It restrains the evil and does good; not out of love of what is good, and hatred of the evil, but rather out of fear of punishment or in view of reward. Therefore, they are under the law and driven by it as a servant. These are the Cain-saints.

But those who are not under the law do what is good and forsake the evil, not considering the law with its threats, promises, punishments and rewards. Rather it is from a free zealous desire for and love of good and hatred for what is evil, that God's law well pleases them. Even if it were not commanded, they would still have it no other way and would yet do good and forsake evil. Those are the true children. The [fallen] nature is unable to do this, but the Seed of Abraham, Christ, makes such people with his benediction through his grace and Holy Ghost. Therefore, not being under the law is not to say so much that one is free to do evil, what he wants, or to do no good works. Rather, it is to say that one does not do good and forsake evil out of fear, compulsion and the necessity of the law, but rather out of free love and a zealous desire.

Erl. 7, 265-2657: Sermon on the Sunday after Christmas, Gal. 4:1-8

From faith in Christ, whene'er 'tis right, Good works are surely flowing;
The faith is dead that shuns the light, No good works ever showing.
By faith alone the just shall live, Good works alone the proof can give
Of love, which true faith worketh. (*ELHB* 314: 10)

Saturday

And you know that to the righteous no law is given, but rather to the unrighteous, disobedient, the godless and sinners, the profane and the unspiritual, to the slayers of fathers and mothers, to the murderers. 1 Timothy 1:9

That is, he [the righteous] does every good thing, and lets the evil depart from himself, uncompelled, without fear of punishment and seeking reward. As in Romans 6:15, "You are not under the law, but rather under grace," that is, you are children, not servants. You do everything good without compulsion and being driven, out of a free desire. Or, Romans 8:15, "You have not received the spirit of servitude that you must be afraid, but rather you have received the spirit of sonship by which we cry: 'Abba, dear Father.' " The law gives a fearing, servant, Cainish spirit; but grace gives a free, childlike, Abelish spirit, through Christ, the Seed of Abraham, of whom Psalm 51:12 says, "Create in me, O God, a new spirit." Or after that, Psalm 110:3 calls Christ's people, "the ones glad to be in the holy place."

For Christ has fulfilled the law and done everything out of a free will, not from the necessity and compulsion of the law. And apart from him there is no one who has and no one that will also do this, unless he has it from and through Christ. Therefore, St. Paul says here, he was made under the law to save those who were under the law.

That is now the fifth thing, that we believe that he has done good for us so that he makes us children from slaves. Why does it say, "that he saves those who were under the law."? Without doubt, he saved us from the law. But how did he save us from the law? As it says, not by destroying and doing away with the law, but through the gift of a free willing spirit that does everything uncompelled, undriven, without consideration of the law with its threats and rewards, but just as if there were no law, done in an entirely natural way, as Adam and Eve did before the fall.

But how does he give us such a spirit and save us from the law? In no other way than through faith. For whoever believes that Christ has come and has done everything so that he saves us, is surely saved. As he believes, so it happens to him. This same faith brings with it this same spirit that makes him a child, as here the apostle presents it and says, Christ has saved us from the law, that we receive the adoption of sons. That all must happen through faith, as said.

Erl. 7, 267-268: Sermon on the Sunday after Christmas, Gal. 4:1-8

He's just 'for God, and he alone, Who by this faith is living;
This faith will by good works be known, To God the glory giving.
Faith gives thee peace with God above, But thou thy neighbor, too, wilt love
If thou art a new creature. (*ELHB* 314: 8)

Palmarum

Sunday

Behold, we go up to Jerusalem and everything will be fulfilled which is written through the prophets concerning the Son of man. Luke 18:31

By this we are informed that Scripture is only fulfilled through the suffering of Christ. Also, the Scriptures speak of nothing but Christ. They all have to do with Christ who must fulfill them by his death. But his death must accomplish what our death can add nothing to. For our death is a sinful accursed death. But if our death is sin and accursed, which is our gravest and most difficult suffering and misfortune, what will our suffering and martyrdom earn? And since our sufferings are nothing and lost, what should our good works do, since suffering is always more noble and better than works? Christ must here be unique, and that is what our faith must hold fast to.

But he says such words beforehand; before he achieved the suffering while he was on the way, traveling up to Jerusalem. Even so, at the Easter festival, when the disciples didn't consider his suffering as such a small thing, they did not consider being joyous on that festival. He did this so that they would thereafter become even stronger in faith when they remembered that he said these things beforehand and that he willingly had given himself over to suffer and he was not crucified through the might and wit of the Jews, his foes, just as Isaiah 53:7 long before had announced that he would willingly and gladly let himself be offered. Also the angel exhorted the women on Easter Day, Luke 24:6, that they should remember these Words that he says here so that they would know and even more steadfastly believe that he had desired to suffer for our good.

This is the true basis of rightly knowing Christ's suffering; when one not only knows and grasps his suffering, but also his heart and willingness to suffer. For whoever regards his suffering so that he doesn't see his inward willingness and heart must be much more terrified by it than joyful. But if one sees his heart and willingness in it, that makes it a true comfort, assurance and [creates] desire for Christ. Therefore the 40th Psalm, verses 7 & 8, praises such willingness of God and Christ in suffering where it says, "In the book it is written of me that I shall do your will, my God, and I do it gladly." The epistle to the Hebrews says of this in Chapter 10:10, "Through such desire we are all sanctified." It doesn't say, "through the suffering and blood of Christ," which is also true, but, "through the desire of God and Christ," that they both have become one desire to sanctify us through his blood. He shows such a willingness to suffer also here in the gospel where he previously proclaimed he would go up to Jerusalem and let himself be crucified. He wants to say, "Behold my heart, that I do it willingly, uncompelled and gladly, so that you are not frightened by it or upset when you see it, lest you think that I don't gladly do it, must do it, or that I am undone and the Jews do it with their might."

Erl. 11, 95–96: Sermon on Quinquagesima, Luke 18:31–43

Thy cross I'll place before me, Its saving power be o'er me,
Wherever I may be; Thine innocence revealing,
Thy love and mercy sealing, The pledge of truth and constancy. (*TLH* 171: 9)

Monday

Surely he bore our infirmity and took upon himself our sorrows. Isaiah 53:4

The prophet adds this; why Christ had need to suffer, and what he accomplished and won by it. He lays the foundation and builds the great and necessary article of our faith, of justification. Namely, we believe that Christ was martyred and put to death for our sake, as also St. Paul teaches, that Christ has become a malediction for us all. For it is not enough that one knows that Christ has suffered, but rather he must know the necessity of the same. That is, he must believe, as the prophet testifies here, that he has borne our infirmities; that he has suffered not for his sake, or for his sins, but for us; namely, that he bore all the plague and sin and all the sorrows that were laden and heaped upon him, which we poor sinners should have suffered and borne. So whoever rightly understands and knows this passage, has already learned the sum and substance of all of Christianity and our faith. For from this rich, full fountain the holy apostle Paul has fashioned so many epistles rich in grace and takes from this flood an abundance of many blessed passages and rich comforts.

From this one can now be assured and mightily acknowledge on sure grounds that all human industry and labor is accursed. Also all wisdom, righteousness, all good works and service are accursed, by which people would seek and earn salvation, without the dear Lord Christ. Since human ability fails and is overthrown through this single passage, all this establishes that Christ has suffered for us. Then, since this is true, that he has suffered for us, one must consider all our righteousness, good works and services, which we trusted, as nothing (as St. Paul says in Philippians 3, as mire). That must all walk away from us and fade and we forsake them with our whole hearts for an alien righteousness. We consider it as if we were suspended between heaven and earth. We grasp and hang on with faith to the righteousness that one can neither see nor feel, which is alone proclaimed and given us through the Word. And this is the reason that no one can learn or grasp this doctrine of the Christian's justification without the true master and teacher, the Holy Ghost. For this reason alone the Jews do not receive Christ, that they will not have their own righteousness and holy life taken or dropped, nor let the works of the law curse them. Yet Christ became flesh and a man for this reason; that we, who are children of wrath and were sentenced to damnation, are preserved and made blessed through his righteousness.

Altb. VI, 360–361: Commentary on Isaiah, 1534

Lord Jesus, we give thanks to Thee That Thou hast died to set us free;
Made righteous thro' Thy precious blood, We now are reconciled to God. (*TLH* 173: 1)

Tuesday

Father, the hour is here that you glorify your Son so that your Son also glorify you. John 17:1

These are such meager, simple Words that they do not appear to be worth much in the eyes of the world. But who can sufficiently fathom what great matters and excellent zeal lie behind them? In such brevity it is prayed, "Dear Father, glorify me," but not leaving it at that, "even so that I can glorify you." But glorify means nothing other than praising and lifting high, making majestic and apparent, so that all the world knows it and can sing and tell of it. He reveals with the Word what his situation is and what necessity drove him to such a prayer. He wants to say that after this he would suffer and die the most shameful death so that all his glory, light, name and honor becomes eclipsed and will be dimmed. Now he has accomplished, gloriously preached and worked a great thing, making known his great might and power. All the world justly might have praised, honored and worshiped him most gloriously. But the opposite befell him. Instead of the honor and praise that belonged to him, he was covered with pure shame and scandal and had to hang upon the cross between two murderers, and die as the most offensive, desperate villain that the earth has ever borne. Never was any murderer treated so shamefully and slanderously.

For the world is otherwise so good, when it deals with the most offensive evil doers. Everyone is patient with them, pities their misery, and the world lets itself show mercy. But only towards this Christ, who is savior of the world, everyone must be happy because of his death. The Jews gave him such a cold shoulder that they could not be satisfied. Everyone thought that it was the greatest service to God, and pleasing to the world, that this man was removed from the earth. For they thought of him as the most shameful worm that could come onto the earth. They would rather suffer and bear all kinds of plagues [than him].

That is called truly throwing a dear, excellent man into the darkness. So must the dear Christ, the whole world's light and salvation, be received and honored by the world so that people ban him and sweep him out of the world as the most terrible devil. So now the Jews still follow most of their fathers and would much rather be allowed to suffer every devil and misfortune than to hear the name of Christ and his mother, Mary. So it also happens to the dear gospel. To the papistic crowd with all of our foes, no devil or misfortune is such a foe as our doctrine. Our doctrine must be accursed, damned and banned for [to them] there is no more evil noise on earth than our gospel and his Word. Behold, now Christ says his hour is coming and at hand; for he prays with such thought and zeal as if he were already hanging on the cross. He wants to say, "Now I am stuck in the middle of shame and death, and lie in deeper darkness. Now it is the time that you have appointed, exalted and established honor for me, since my light is so completely dimmed, and the world tramples me under its feet. Everyone sees me and curses me, so there is no help or counsel, for this is what you yourself are also doing."

Altb. VI, 222: Sermon on John 17, 1534

O sacred Head, now wounded, With grief and shame weighed down,
Now scornfully surrounded With thorns, Thine only crown.
O sacred Head, what glory, What bliss, till now was thine!
Yet, tho' despised and gory, I joy to call Thee mine. (*TLH* 172: 1)

Wednesday

God has not spared his own Son, but has given him for us all. Romans 8:32

We Christians must distinguish in the same way the *idiomata* (properties) of both of the two natures in the person of Christ since

Christ is God and man in one person. So what is said of him as a man, one must also say of God, namely: Christ died and Christ is God. Therefore God is dead. Not the detached God, but rather the God that is united with the humanity. For of the God detached [from the human nature] both are false, namely, that Christ is God, and God is dead. Both are false. For there God is not man. But when Nestorius thought it is queer that God dies, he should think it is surely queer that God became man. For by that the God who cannot die is the one that dies, suffers and must have every human *idiomata*. Else what would this same man be, with whom God is personally united, if he should not have true human *idiomata*. He would have to be a ghost as the Manacheans had previously taught. Then again, what one says of God must also be allotted to the man. Namely: God has created the world and is almighty. But man, Christ, is God. So the man, Christ, has created the world and is almighty. The reason is that the one person is of God and man, therefore the person bears the *idiomata* of both natures.

Oh, Lord God, by such a blessed comforting article, one should always be joyous, peace loving and firm in true faith. He would sing, praise and thank God the Father for such inexpressible mercy. For us he has let his dear Son become a man and brother just like us. So the miserable devil brings such apathy through haughty, overambitious, despairing people that the dear and blessed joy must be prevented us and ruined. That is grievous to God! For we Christians must know: When God is not in the scales and it gives the weight, then we in our pan sink to the ground. [9] So think: If it should not be said that God has died for us, but rather only a man, then we are lost. But if God's death, and God's dying is in the pan of the scales, then he sinks down and we go up as a light, flimsy pan. But he can also easily go up again or jump out of his pan. He could not remain in the pan, but he must have become a man just like us, so that it could be said, "God died, God's torment, God's blood, God's death." For God in his nature cannot die, but now God and man are united in one person. So it is right to say, "God's death," when the man would die, who is one thing or one person with God.

Altb. VII, 268–269: Of Councils and the Church, 1539; cf. AE 41

O sorrow dread! God's Son is dead!
But by His expiation Of our guilt upon the cross
Gained for us salvation. (*TLH* 167: 2)

---

[9]Reffering to the pans on the scales or balance of justice.

Thursday

This is my body given for you, this do in my remembrance.
This is the cup of the New Testament in my blood that is
shed for you. Luke 22:19, 20

This is so cordially spoken, not venomous or angry, yes, much more cordial than a father can speak to his son. For this is all to be done, he says, that you should not forget him. He would gladly fashion this remembrance in our eyes, mouth and heart, so that his holy suffering would not be forgotten, as he was crucified, dead, resurrected again from death for our sake. He has commanded such a remembrance so we zealously use it in just this way so that it would ever increase to other and new people. That is needed not only so one is instructed by the Words that they learn to confess Christ as their savior and become saved, but rather that one connect them [these Words, that is] to such outward services of God so that they always then have reason to boast and have comfort of their savior and redeemer, Christ. For the Word effects this by the Lord's institution of his testament. Therefore we will not become tired of such a remembrance. Where good friends gather together, they can sit the whole night talking and forget to sleep. So then why should a person become so tired of being preached to and taught the costly price by which our dear Lord Christ has purchased us?

But now this Sacrament, or Lord's Supper, is not only instituted so that Christ should be praised. For he could easily say, "I don't need your praises at all, I can surely do without them and just as well remain God's Son, whether you praise me or not. I become neither better nor worse for your praise." But we need such a testament and Lord's Supper for our good. For see what the Words say. He distributes the bread and says, "Take and eat, this is my body, this is given for you." Thereafter he administers the cup and says, "Drink all of it, this is my blood of the New Testament, which is shed for you for the forgiveness of sins." That should, first of all, be the highest comfort that any Christian can hear, of the Lord Christ's body that is given for you, and his blood shed for your sins. For whoever believes this, it is impossible for him that his sins or anything else should be allowed to drive them to doubt. Reason: He knows that this treasure, by which his sins are taken away, is far wider and bigger than his sins. But with this comfort which openly proceeds in the Word, Christ does not leave it at that. With the bread he gives you his body to eat and with the wine his blood to drink, as the Words themselves plainly bring, even if they are grievous to the devil. Upon this you receive for your person such body and blood that benefits you and it shall be your own; even as you receive it for yourself by your mouth and not for someone else. Therefore, it is also done chiefly so that each one believe Christ has suffered for him and not only for St. Peter, St. Paul and the other saints. That is what Christ would make certain to every Christian in his testament since each one for himself uses and receives such a testament, that is, the body and blood. So it is not wrongly said that one has and receives forgiveness of sins in this Sacrament. These Words proclaim, "here is my body and blood." Whoever receives, eats and drinks, and believes this now, that the Lord Christ's body is given for him and his blood is shed for him for the forgiveness of sins, should he not have the forgiveness of sins?

Hauspost. 166: First Sermon on Maunday Thursday on 1 Cor. 11.23–26

O Lord, we praise Thee, bless Thee, and adore Thee,
In thanksgiving bow before Thee.
Thou with Thy body and Thy blood didst nourish
Our weak souls that they may flourish: O Lord, have mercy!
May Thy body, Lord, born of Mary, That our sins and sorrows did carry,
And Thy blood for us plead In all trial, fear and need:
O Lord, have mercy! (*TLH* 313: 1)

Friday

And at the ninth hour Jesus called out aloud and said, "Eli, Eli, lama sabachthani?" That is, "My God, My God, why have you forsaken me?" Matthew 27:46

I will say something of this so that we do not completely pass over this rich verse. First, one cannot understand what it means to be forsaken of God except when we previously know what God is. God is the life, light, wisdom, truth, righteousness, might, joy, honor, peace, salvation and everything good. But to be forsaken of God is to be in death, in darkness, in folly, in lies, in sins, in evil, in weakness, in sadness, in shame, in distress, in doubt, in damnation, in every evil. What follows from this? Would we want to make Christ as a fool, as a liar, as a sinner, as an evil knave, as a misleader, as someone who is damned? That is what I have referred to, that this passage is somewhat hidden and high, which not everyone can grasp.

But look for yourself at this. Everyone admits and no one denies that in Christ at the same time are the highest joy and the highest sadness, the highest weakness and the highest power, the highest honor, and the highest shame, the highest peace and the highest distress, the highest life and the highest death. This verse reveals that sufficiently where he, just as he speaks in this way about himself, cries out that he is forsaken of God. For no one speaks so to God: "My God!" who is completely forsaken from God. Now there are some times when Christians have been forsaken (which I could also say), so why could a person not also say that he has been forsaken completely and by the whole God? For nothing hinders this but only the usage and understanding of the common man. Yet what should be more against faith and more terrible to hear, even to the heathen faced with some great devastation, than if someone should say that a man could at the same time live that highest life and yet also die that highest death?

What would we say in addition to this? Should we say that Christ is both the most just and the most sinful? The biggest liar and the highest truth? The highest glory and the highest despair? The most blessed and the most damned? For if we do not say so, then I cannot understand how he is forsaken of God, since many saints like Jacob, Job, David, Ezekiel, are in a way forsaken. Therefore, Christ is much more forsaken, above all saints, who in himself has born all of our transgressions and afflictions.

Here my heart tells me: Christ is truly just and remained just, who had committed no sins, nor was any lie found in his mouth. For why should he be conceived and born of the virgin by the Holy Ghost in order to be without sins; how could he have been able to save us from our sins? But at this time, when he suffered, he had taken upon himself all our sins as if they had actually become his own. He has also suffered for them everything that we had need to suffer, and what the damned now suffer, as St. Paul says from the 69th Psalm in Romans 15, "The reproaches of those who reproached you fell upon me." And Isaiah 53 states, "Truly he bore our griefs, etc." But now the punishment of God, by which he would punish sins is not only the pain of death, but also a fear and terror of a troubled conscience, that experiences the eternal wrath and considers itself as if it should be eternally forsaken and be dispelled from the presence of God, as David confesses in the 31st Psalm, where he said, "But I said in my fear, I am cast from his presence." So it definitely follows from this that Christ has suffered fear and terror of a troubled conscience and that there he tasted eternal wrath.

Altb. II, 693: Lecture on the Ninth Psalm, 1524

Lamb of God, pure and holy, Who on the cross didst suffer,
Ever patient and lowly, Thyself to scorn didst offer.
All sins Thou borest for us, Else had despair reigned o'er us;
Have mercy on us, O Jesus! O Jesus! (*TLH* 146: 1)

Saturday

And Joseph took the body and wrapped him in linen. And
he laid him in his new tomb. Matthew 27:59, 60

The evangelist specifically reports how the tomb where they laid
the Lord in a garden was a new tomb where no one was laid before,
and Joseph himself had seen to it. This is not only done so that the
witness of the resurrection would be even surer, but also so that since
here a special body would be entombed, the likes of which had never
before come on earth, he must also have a special resting place or
tomb.

Our dear Lord Christ had flesh and blood as we do, except the
eternal Father had clothed his Son in holy flesh and blood. There this
flesh and blood would now have its rest. He had been buried in a
special new grave. Yet this grave is not his own, but Joseph's. For
just as Christ did not become a man and die for himself, but for our
sakes, so he also lay for our sakes in the tomb and his tomb is our
tomb. But as he therefore had no tomb of his own, for he would not
remain in death and in the tomb, so we also will be awakened out of
it on the last day through his resurrection and live with him eternally.

It is also good to take note of the example of Joseph, who had
allowed his tomb to be made alive. It is good to gather from this that
he has not forgotten [the nature of this life] for an instant, as all of
the children of the world do, consigning themselves to this temporal
world as if they would stay here forever. But on the other hand,
those who fear God consider their whole life here on earth as a
pilgrimage. For they know that they have no enduring city, and so
they turn to a better one, namely an eternal and heavenly fatherland.
Whoever travels the country, even if he finds a good lodging, does
not take it as his house. He knows that he is not home. The Christian
also does this, considering this life as he does a neighboring city. If
one considers it good, he receives it with thanks. But if it is, as is
common, a cold, evil, dishonest lodging, then he comforts himself
that it is only for an evil night, so it will be better. This is also what
the good Joseph had done. He is rich and a respected citizen of the
city of Jerusalem. But his thoughts were always, "You have no
enduring existence, you must also lie down." So he is left in his
garden, where he had a great desire to make a tomb, where he will
await the joyous resurrection through the Lord Christ, along with all
of the saints.

Hauspost. 259–260: Thirteenth Passion Sermon

So rest, my Rest,
Thou Ever-blest!
Thy grave with sinners making;
By Thy precious dearth from sin
My dead soul awadening.

Breath of all breath!
I know from death
Thou wilt my dust awaken;
Wherefore should I dread the grave
Or my faith be shaken! (*ELHB* 216: 1,3,4)

How cold art Thou,
My Savior, now!
Thy fervent love hath driven
Thee into the cold, dark grave
That I might gain heaven.

Easter Week

Sunday

*But if Christ is not risen, then our faith is in vain, for then
we are still in our sins and those who sleep in Christ are
lost. 1 Corinthians 15:17,18*

Our Lord, Jesus Christ, is "risen from the dead on the third
day." A strong, mighty faith is one that makes this article strong,
mighty and good for us. One should mark these words, "Christ is
risen from the dead," and write them with capital letters, with
lettering as great as a tower, even as big as heaven and earth, that we
neither see, hear, think nor know anything besides this article. So we
do not therefore speak and confess this article in the creed only as we
recite a fable, a little fairy tale or history, but rather that it be strong,
truthful and living in our hearts. We call that "faith," when we are
so impressed by it that we are completely and utterly bound in it,
even as if nothing were ever written besides this: Christ is arisen. In
this, St. Paul is a true master when he gives praise in Romans 4,
"Christ is given for the sake of our sins and raised for the sake of
our justification." Ephesians 2, "Though we were dead in sins, he
has made us alive with Christ, and has raised us with him, and set us
with him in the heavenly realm, in Christ Jesus." 1 Thessalonians 4,
"So we believe that Christ has died and is arisen, so God will also
bring with him all who are asleep in Christ."

So if we believed this, then we had lived and died well. For
Christ has not only conquered death and is raised from the dead for
himself, but rather you must keep them [Christ, death and
resurrection] together so that it is invested in us and so we also are
established and connected with his rising. By this and through this we
are also arisen and must live with him forever. Our resurrection and
life are rooted in Christ. They are as sure as though it already had
taken place, except that it is yet hidden and not evident. We will
watch this article so attentively that all others are nothing next to it,
as if we could see nothing else in heaven and earth. If you should see
a Christian dead and buried, and laying as nothing but a dead corpse
and before your eyes and ears are only the vain grave songs of
mourning and words of death, yes, only death, yet you should
remove such a fatal picture from your eyes and through faith behold
underneath it another picture. For every picture of death that you will
see is not a grave and dead corpse, but only life and a beautiful,
compelling garden and Paradise in which there are no dead, but

rather only new, living, joyful people. For because it is true that Christ is arisen from the dead, we already have the best benefit of the resurrection; that anything compared to the bodily resurrection of the flesh from the grave (that is yet to come) is too poor to consider. For what are we and all the world next to Christ, our head? Barely a little drop compared to the sea, or a little stone compared to a mountain. Now because Christ, the head of Christendom, through whom she lives and has everything, is so great, he fills heaven and earth, and next to him, the sun, moon and all creatures are nothing. He is arisen from the grave and by that has become a mighty Lord of all things, also of death and hell. So we also must, as his members, by his resurrection be affected and calmed and even become a partaker in it, for he has accomplished it completely for our sakes. For as he has received all things through his resurrection, that both heaven and earth, sun and moon and all creation must arise and become new, so he will also bring us with them.

Erl. 3, 288–290: Sermon for Easter Evening, 1532

Christ is arisen From the grave's dark prison,
We now rejoice with gladness; Christ will end all sadness,
Lord, have mercy.
All our hopes were ended Had Jesus not ascended
From the grave triumphantly. For this, Lord Christ, we worship Thee.
Lord, have mercy.
Hallelujah! Hallelujah! Hallelujah!
We now rejoice with gladness; Christ will end all sadness.
Lord have mercy.   (*TLH* 187)

Monday

I will preach your name to my brothers, I will praise you in the congregation. Psalm 22:23

Here you see what the dear saints would readily imply from this Word. They have already been moved by this great wonderful title, that we should be called Christ's brothers! No human heart can experience what a great thing this is, that he makes himself our brother and gives us, who did not ask for it, freedom.

If, now, a heart could believe such a thing ardently, before whom would it fear? Or what would break him? But our miserable unbelief is so great that we cannot get hold of the Words. So, dear Lord God, what is this, when he calls us brothers? Namely this, that he makes us into God's children and his coheirs, Romans 8:16,17.

So now this unites us. It relates us with the inheritance and the wealth that he has. [This is] where a poor, miserable beggar finds himself standing with the greatest and highest king, for we are surely full of sins, under the devil's might, and always have an evil conscience, terror and heartache. But Christ is the Son of God, full of righteousness, wisdom, life, joy and comfort. Who will relate such wealth to all those he has made heirs of God? Now he has passed out all this wealth to all who want to have it in the Word, where he calls us brothers. For he clearly says so in Matthew 12:50, "Who does the will of my Father is my mother, brother and sister." So now, this is the Father's will, as John reveals, that one believe on the Son. He would have his Son believed, that we hold it as certain and believe that everything is true that he has told us. Well then, since that is being done, as you hear in this passage, you are Christ's mother and brother and sister and all related to one another.

These are the kind of Words that no man or angel can complacently dismiss and cross out as if they were worthy of them. How could the dear Lord Christ speak in a kinder and more loving manner? These are the kindest names that could have people under them, mother, brother, sister, etc., that go through bone and marrow. "I am your brother," he says. "If I have a quarter, a dollar, you also have them; eternal righteousness, eternal life, wisdom, joy and comfort. Everything that I have will also be yours. If you have sins, guilt, shame, hell, death and devil, that shall be mine. I have enough tender to buy you back, and pay for you." Now whoever can believe this trustworthy saying, would already be in Paradise and heaven. What would such a heart that believes these words fear? Or why should it be sorrowful? It must say: I will regret nothing for I have this kind brother. Now if sins, an evil conscience, terror over death and hell, persecution from the world, and what ever other things should also come, then I can be comforted by these words and say, "I am a brother of Christ, established in the common wealth and single inheritance. Because of that I will not let all these things trouble me," and so forth.

Altb. V, 576–577: Second Sermon Concerning Mary Magdalene, John 20, 1531

Awake, my heart, with gladness, See what today is done;
Now, after gloom and sadness, Comes forth the glorious Sun.
My Savior there was laid Where our bed must be made
When to the realms of light Our spirit wings its flight. (TLH 192: 1)

Tuesday

Since they all come from one, both the one who is holy and the ones made holy, therefore he is not ashamed to call them brothers. Hebrews 2:11

These are great, deep words that cannot be learned or grasped at once. So consider yourself, dear friend. How shall I come to this and walk in such pride, while I am such a great sinner and have so scandalously misspent my life, that after that I shall be called and be Christ's brother? It will not stick in our hearts. Therefore, as long as we live, we would learn enough if only we could learn well that there is no worse guilt than our impenitent hardened disbelief. On account of this, we, who feel yet a nagging and evil conscience, have a definite sign, that we don't believe this comforting preaching, that he wants to be so gracious as he was to his dear apostles. Let us only beware for this reason; that we will not let ourselves think that it can be for us. We have enough to learn our whole life long about each individual teaching, as trifling or easy as they might seem.

Now behold, dear friends, that this is called a Christian brotherhood, next to which there is no other brotherhood to be joined, whatever it is called. I do not desire to share my good works with you, if you don't want to share them (says Christ). Such [brothers] are always hung on the gallows among the stinking thieves. For all such brotherhoods rip us away from this brotherhood of Christ, which shares and bestows upon us all that Christ is and has. Friends, these Words are not thrown into the wind as if they had been spoken to a person at his ease. They are truly Words upon which one can die, and even then [in death] one first experiences how strong and comforting this preaching is, when one is stuck in grave trouble. In this Christian brotherhood no saint has any more than another. St. Peter and St. Paul have no more in it than Mary Magdalene and I and you. In summary, take them all together in a heap, so that all the brothers are alike and there is no difference between people. Mary, the mother of the Lord and John the baptizer, and the thief on the cross have even the same wealth as you and I do and all who are baptized and do the will of the Father. Now what do all the saints have? They have this: that their sins are forgiven, and comfort and help are promised in all needs by Christ against sins, death and devil. That I have and you also, and all the believers.

But it is true that you and I do not hold such things and believe as strongly as John the Baptizer, St. Paul, etc. But nevertheless it is the one treasure. Even as when two could hold a cup of maltwater in their hands, the one holding with shaking hands and the other steadily. So also two could hold a bag full of gold, one with a weak hand and the other with a strong hand. The hand God gives is either strong or weak, but either way it makes no difference as they hold the bag. So also there is no difference between me and the apostles, even if they hold the treasure stronger. Nevertheless I shall and must know that I also have the same treasure as all the holy prophets, apostles and all the saints have had.

It is very strange and unjust that out of that crowd, the thief, who is a great sinner, as I am and you are, should be able to say, "I have the same as some sent of Christ, as St. Peter." "God protect us from such pride!" (the hypocrites say). And if you say that, then, it is a fool's humility and unthankfulness, more than true humility. For when they say this, they desire to earn it with their works, so that they might become like the saints. But we say this because we are like the dear saints, whatever their names are, and do not assign this to ourselves because of our works. But the hypocrites, who present themselves as being so humble, want to be received through their works, which always fall behind where the devil will surely find them and make them a burden. A Christian should and must say, "I know very well that I have, with St. Peter, deserved hell, but that I now am as rich and holy as St. Peter, only because I have earned it as much as he has. It is purely God's kindness and grace." But one cannot bring the crazy saints of the pope to this realization. Unfortunately, they want to bend it with works. That is then a truly devilish pride, when a man wants to come into this brotherhood by his own virtue.

Altb. V, 577-578: Second Sermon Concerning Mary Magdalene, John 20, 1531

Now I will cling forever To Christ, my Savior true;
My Lord will leave me never, Whate'er He passeth through.
He rends death's iron chain, He breaks through sin and pain,
He shatters hell's dark thrall, I follow Him through all. (*TLH* 192: 6)

Wednesday

I go to my Father and your Father, to my God and your God. John 20:17

With this he desires to reveal that we don't have a different Father and also he does not have a different one. Rather, we are not the Father's sons in the same way he is. He is the Father's natural born Son from eternity, and not an elected son whom he received from another family as a son, as one calls it *Filios adoptionis*, and he had this one before all the others. So now it is great and mighty that he says, "and to your Father," because this is a complete and true brotherhood, when God is not angry with us to judge us, or our tyrant and hangman, but rather our Father. So with this Word he opens heaven and makes everything certain in faith by fatherly grace and mercy.

Poor Peter, when he had denied Christ, sat in a closed room, John 20:19, for fear of the Jews. If he would only hear the name of Christ, his heart would be terrified. For he could not think otherwise, than that God is the enemy of the sinner, and had made hell to punish sinners, as we then also would have thought. Should St. Peter and everyone else, stuck in such fear and affliction, receive another perspective, then it must turn out otherwise. An evil conscience can be no different than what wicked people are, who also should find this [other perspective] at once. So now Christ, with the Words, "I go up to my Father and to your Father," completely washes and cleanses such a heart and says, "Friend, it is not as it seems to you. I am your brother, so my Father is your Father." Thus he removes from the heart the angry perception and establishes a kind and true one on the spot.

But think about him after the way a father's heart is fixed towards his sons and children. I speak now not of such fathers that you occasionally run across who are not worthy to be called a human being, who care nothing about their children. We even see in the wild animals, which are creatures of nature, that they are endowed by nature with love for their offspring. I am ashamed of [such hating parents] who are capable of better. So Christ now gives us with this Word, "and to your Father and God," everything that the Father has and desires, that we should have all of that as an inheritance. If one would believe that, what would follow from that? I would think: Well then! If he is my Father, then there can be no terrifying, angry picture of him. Before whom, then, will I fear or to whom shall I pay attention? For he is greater, mightier, more powerful than all the world and all creatures, so one sees nothing but fatherly goodness.

Now, when this is not believed, we are turned around and sins lie on the path, for we are not then given the heavenly heritage. My heart always says, "I would gladly believe everything if only I were like St. Peter or St. Paul." So we always want to proceed with works, we don't want to be given to, and we say, "I could believe that Mary, St. Peter, St. Paul, are the sister and brothers of Christ, but I have not earned it and am also not worthy of such a great inheritance." But that is purely an assertion made by a fool. Do you not hear that it is a shared gift? As St. Peter is, so is also a poor, needy sinner and so are you. For this Word says that same thing to you, as to Peter, that you are God's son, and God is your Father, that God no longer desires to be terrifying to you or to be your enemy. St. Peter now embraces this Word, "and to your father and God," and so is assured by the Words' sound, God is Father and he his son. If you now desire to be as Peter, then also do as he does and grasp the Word with such faith.

Dear Lord God, there is nothing more to do, than one grasp and only hold on and let him give. So believe only the Word and be proud, boastful and defiant because of it. For the treasure is well worth boastfulness and defiance. Christ wants to be your brother so God will be your Father. Now all the angels must be your friends, the universe must laugh with you and the sun, moon and all the stars must be joyful with you, hell must be completely closed to you and nothing else must be there but the fatherly and merciful will of God. See how beautifully and lovingly the dear Lord Christ can speak.

Altb. V, 579: Second Sermon Concerning Mary Magdalene, John 20, 1531

Thou, mighty Father, in Thy Son Didst love me 'ere Thou hadst begun
This ancient world's foundation. Thy Son hath made a friend of me,
And when in spirit Him I see, I joy in tribulation. What bliss is this!
He that liveth to me giveth Life forever;
Nothing me from Him can sever. (*TLH* 343: 5)

Thursday

But I did not proclaim myself. I knew nothing before you but Jesus Christ, the crucified. 1 Corinthians 2:2

What kind of boast is this that he writes that he knew nothing but the crucified Christ? It is the sort of matter that no human reason or wisdom can grasp, also that cannot be added to even if one has thoroughly studied the gospel and learned it. For it is a wisdom that is mighty, mysterious and hidden and nothing is apparent because it is clothed under weakness, as Christ on the cross, where he poured out all power and divine strength, hangs there as a miserable, forsaken man and appears as though God would not help him. St. Paul says that he knows and preaches nothing but of this. For the Christ, who works by doing miracles in public, proceeds and breaks in with power that everyone sees is easily learned and recognized. But to know the weak Christ, who hangs on the cross and lay in death, that belongs to a greater understanding. Who does not know it must push it away and be annoyed by it.

Surely one also finds true Christians who already know the gospel, and yet they are dissatisfied in their own lives and think that they would also like to become good. But they feel in themselves that it will never come forth, so they begin to despair and think that they are lost because they do not receive the strength that they should have, [which they] desire and also want; that if Christ were strong in them he would reveal himself in great deeds. But our Lord God does that so that he would humble us to the point that we see that we are such weak creatures, miserably cursed and forsaken men, that if Christ does not come with his righteousness to help us and by his might bear our weakness and help us, we would be lost. Behold, that is the high wisdom that we have and because of it the whole world is annoyed.

But by this we have not given up, [thinking] that one should retreat and always remain weak. For we do not preach that one should be weak, but rather that one should bear and acknowledge the weakness of the Christian. This is not done so that Christ should hang on the cross as a murderer or sorcerer but rather that one learn by it how deeply the strength lies buried under the weakness and how God's power is revealed in weakness. So it is not to praise the fact that we are weak, or that also we should be and remain that way, but rather one should learn that no one should consider one who is weak as no Christian for that reason, and so that when he himself feels weakness, he does not despair. So it is done that we acknowledge our weakness and always trust that we will be stronger. For Christ did not suffer or lay in the grave forever, but he came forth from it again and walked into life.

Therefore, no one should think that this is the essential manner and office of a Christian. It is first a beginning, in which one will take it a day at a time, only that one look to the future so as not to give up and become doubtful when he is so weak that all seems lost. But rather that he work with it for a time until he become stronger and stronger and endure and bear the weakness until God helps and puts it away. Therefore, if you also should see your neighbor in frailty, that he is all tripped up, do not think that he is lost. God will not put up with one condemning the other. That [judgment] is his office since we are all yet sinners. Because of that, you will not do that or let him lay fallen and you will throw yourself under him and lift him up in every way. He desires that we help each other and bear each others' weaknesses.

Erl. 11, 257–259: Second Sermon on the Gospel for Easter Monday

Jesus Christ, my sure Defense And my Savior, ever liveth;
Knowing this, my confidence Rests upon the hope it giveth
Though the night of death be fraught
Still with many an anxious thought. (*TLH* 206: 1)

Friday

We have believed and known that you are Christ, the Son of the living God. John 6:69

In the Words are three parts. First, he casts away and cuts off all other doctrines. Secondly, he says, there is no better doctrine then Jesus Christ's. Thirdly, what does he give? What kind of doctrine? In response to this he answers, that it deals with this: "You are the Christ, the Son of the living God." We should also stick with this and receive this doctrine, for it is the one doctrine which gives eternal life and calls the single man Christ the Son of the living God. What this Christ is now, or the one that is the Son of the living God, you hear daily. He is named CHRIST and is born true man in order that we would be saved as the prophets and Holy Scriptures foretold of him.

So here St. Peter baptizes him, gives him his true name, that he is truly man and the savior of the world. He describes him first according to his human nature as the one of whom all the prophets have preached. Thereafter he calls him a Son of the living God, not a Son of a dead God, or the Son of an idol as the heathen have had, but rather of the true living God. There now stands our article of the Christian faith because of which we believe that Christ is God and man. Additionally, that he should be Christ, that is, our intercessor, priest and pastor, who shall make the offering for us and atone for us, as also he brings with him his Office as Priest. Then also he is our king who can protect us mightily from the devil, sins and death.

He is a priest next to God and a king against death, devil and all trouble; for as the Holy Scriptures say, he is a high priest, who has offered himself on the cross, by which he has administered his office, taking all sins upon himself. And now it names Christ our Messiah, that he shall redeem us out of death's revenge on us, as a mightier Lord, that we not fear before our sins, and also overcome the devil and before God find grace and be his dear brothers. We have no need to be afraid of anything. And if the world pursues us so that we must suffer much, and death and the devil unleash their revenge upon us again, then they will still not triumph against us.

That is our doctrine. It is what his Words mean, that Christ is the Son of God. In these Words the whole preaching is established so we preach from the Christian faith or teach of the faith on Christ. Whoever has this Word, this chief part of the Christian doctrine, has everything, nothing excluded. Then one sees that this is Christ, God's Son, hidden from our eyes. One does not see him, but we will see him on the last day. Until then we have the Words of life, faith and also experience that Jesus is Christ, the Son of God, the Priest and king who shall be our Lord.

Altb. V, 701-702: Sermons on the Gospel of St. John Chapters 6-8; cf. AE 23

Jesus, my redeemer lives; I, too, unto life shall waken.
Endless joy my Savior gives; Shall my courage, then, be shaken?
Shall I fear, or could the Head Rise and leave His members dead? (*TLH* 206: 2)

Saturday

So it is written and so must Christ suffer and rise from the dead on the third day and repentance and the forgiveness of sins will be preached in his name unto all peoples beginning at Jerusalem. Luke 24:46,47

Here you see that the gospel is the kind of preaching that embraces repentance and the forgiveness of sins and that it should not be preached in a corner, but rather before everyone *en mass*, so that one holds on to it or does not. Then it goes to the next territory that people hear it so that it creates fruit. Therefore, one should not get annoyed when only a few hold onto it and not say that it has lost, but rather find satisfaction in that Christ has commanded and bid [men] to preach to all the world, so that whoever holds onto it holds onto it. But this is especially remarkable that he says, "So it is written and so must Christ suffer and rise, that repentance and forgiveness of sins be preached in his name."

First we would see these two parts: he calls repentance improvement; not what we have called repentance, where one whipped and castrated one's self in order to make satisfaction for sins and when the priest prescribed one or many acts of contrition. The Scriptures speak of none of this. But rather repentance is called actually a changing and improvement of the whole life. When a man acknowledges that he is a sinner and feels that his life is unrighteous, that he then stand up and walk in a better manner with all his life in words and works and do all that from his heart.

What then is repentance in his name? With this, he excludes repentance that is not done in his name. Therefore, the text clearly divides them so that we must regard two kinds of repentance.

First, repentance that is not in his name is when I proceed with my own works and through them dare to blot out sins as we have all previously learned [under the Roman penance system]. Therefore, that is not a repentance in God's name, but rather in the devil's name. For one establishes it so that he wishes to be restored to God by his own works and abilities. God cannot put up with that.

But the other, repentance in HIS name, works in this way: To those who believe in Christ, God gives improvement through the same faith, not for a moment or an hour, but rather through their whole life. So a Christian man will not swiftly become completely pure, but rather the improvement and change lasts as long as he lives, until he dies. Even when we do the best things, we will yet always find that we still have something to sweep away. So, even if all loads were already overcome, yet this is not overcome — that we are terrified of death. For few are ever encountered who desire death with joy. Therefore, we must from day to day become older yet better. This is what St. Paul means where he says in 2 Corinthians 4:16, "The outer man decays but the inner one is renewed from day to day." So we hear the gospel everyday, and Christ shows us his hands and feet that we always are better enlightened in our understanding and become better and better.

So Christ would say, do not receive anyone, who would improve your life with your own works and in his name. For no one [else] is the enemy of sins, no one [else] does repentance and intends to improve his life, for such improvement cannot be granted, except in my name. Only the name does it and it brings with itself the man's added desire for it and his gladly becoming different. But when one compels human teaching and works, then I go [that is, Jesus goes] to the back of the classroom and thinks: "Oh, so you have no desire to pray, have no need of confession or to go to the Sacrament! How does your repentance help you, which has no life or desire? You do these things [your good works] under compulsion, out of law or because of guilt, yet you would rather have that [your own works]? But what is the reason? It is because that is repentance in the devil's name, in your name, or the pope's name. Therefore, you also must go to the back of the classroom and make it [your life] only more annoying and since you would prefer that there were no Sacrament or confession if it meant that you didn't have to do it." That is called repentance in our name, that comes from our own skills.

Erl. 11, 263–265: Second Sermon on the Gospel for Easter Monday

The words which absolution give
Are His who died that we might live;
The minister whom Christ has sent
Is but His humble instrument.
5-6)

When ministers lay on their hands,
Absolved by Christ the sinner stands;
He who by grace the Word believes
The purchase of His blood receives. (*TLH* 331:

Week of Quasimodogeniti

Sunday

Whosesoever's sins you remit, they are remitted unto them; and whosesoever's sins you retain, they are retained. John 20:23

Here all Christians are given this power, while a few have appropriated it to themselves alone as the pope, the bishops, priests and monks. They say openly and unabashedly that this power is given to them alone, and not also to the laity. But Christ speaks here neither of the priests nor the monks, but says, "Receive the Holy Ghost." Whoever has the Holy Ghost is given this power, that is, whoever is a Christian. But who is a Christian? He who believes. Whoever believes has the Holy Ghost. So each Christian has the power to retain or remit sins, which the pope, bishops, priests and monks have.

Do I understand correctly, that I can hear confession, baptize, preach, administer the Sacrament? No. St. Paul says, "Let everything be done decently and in good order." If everyone would hear confession, baptize, distribute the Sacrament, how could it be done? Or if everyone would preach, who would listen? If we all alike were to preach what a continuous babble it would be like a bunch of frogs in a pond.

Therefore it should be carried out in the congregation that one who is fit be chosen, who administers the Sacrament, preaches, hears confession and baptizes. We all already have this power but no one should presume to use it publicly unless he is also chosen through the congregation. Privately, however, I may well use it. So when my neighbor comes and says, "Friend, I have trouble in my conscience, absolve me." Then I can freely do that. But I say it must occur privately. If I would sit in the back of the church, and also someone else, and we would all hear confessions, how would it look? Consider this example: When under a nobleman there are many heirs, by concession they elect one among them who alone rules for the sake of the others. For if each would want to rule over the property and people how could it work? Though they all still have this power that he has, he rules. So it is with this power to retain and remit sins.

But this Word, "To remit or retain sins," concerns more than those who receive confession and those who will give an absolution. It is service to our neighbor. For underlying all services it is greatest that I free him from sins and release him from the devil and hell. But how does that happen? Through the gospel, I preach to him and tell him how he should receive the works of Christ and firmly believe that Christ's righteousness is his, and his sins are Christ's. That, I say, is the greatest service that I can show my neighbor.

Accursed is the life that one lives to himself and not to his neighbor; and again, blessed is that life in which one lives towards and serves not himself but his neighbor with teaching, with chastizing, with help wherever and however it can happen. When my neighbor errs, I should chastize him. If he cannot follow me, then I should hope for him with patience, as Christ did with Judas, who had the bag of money and went to the dogs, ending badly. Christ knew it well, yet he had patience with him and warned him repeatedly, though it did not help, until he made himself a scandal.

Erl. 11, 318–320: Second Sermon on Easter I, John 20:19-31

The words which absolution give Are His who died that we might live;
The minister whom Christ has sent Is but His humble instrument. (*TLH* 331: 6)

Monday

So also, if I forgive someone something, I forgive it for your sake in place of Christ. 2 Corinthians 2:10

Yes, you say, you have certainly spoken the absolution to me, but who knows if it is sure and true before God that my sins are forgiven? Answer: If I have said and done it as a man, you could well say, "I do not know if your absolution helps and has power or not." But so that you may be sure of the matter, you must be directed by God's Word so you can say, "The Pastor has not called me to believe it, but rather God has spoken and done this through him. I am sure of this. For my Lord Christ has commanded this and said, 'As the Father has sent me, even so send I you.' " This is what he makes of those whom he has commanded to do this. Just as Christ was when they were sent, so all those who are sent by him should [in the same way] act and teach just that for which Christ is sent by the Father, namely to retain and remit sins. Hasten there. That does it; else, without such command the absolution would be nothing.

If now you are sad and troubled for the sake of your sins and terrified before death, by which God will eternally punish sins, you want to hear this from your pastor [*Seelsorger*], or if you cannot have him, then he comforts you by your Christian neighbor with these or similar words, "Dear brother or sister, I see that you are withdrawn and broken because of your sins which you feel and now it is terrible for you. But listen and let me tell you to be comforted and mended, for Christ, your Lord and savior, who has come for the sake of your sins to save you, has commanded, both through the public office of the called servants and in necessity each individual in common, that one comfort another for his sake and in his name speak freedom from sins." If you, I say, should hear such comfort, then receive it with joy and thanksgiving as if you heard it from Christ himself. So your heart will be established in peace, set right and comforted and it can then joyfully say, "I have heard a man speak with me and comfort me. For the sake of his person I would not believe a single word of it, but I believe in my Lord Christ who has given this wealth of grace and forgiveness and has given men such a command and power that they should retain and remit sins in his name."

Therefore, every Christian should become accustomed, when the devil attacks and suggests he is a great sinner, so he must be lost and damned, etc., that he doesn't chew on it long or remain alone, but rather that he go out or let his pastor [*Seelsorger*] be called for, or else a good friend. He should lament his need, and receive counsel and comfort from him. Let him be grounded on this; that Christ says here, "Whosoesoever's sins you remit," etc., and in another place, "Where two or three are together in my name, there I am in the midst of them." And what he says to him in Christ's name, from the Scripture, that he believe; as now he believes, so it shall be to him.

Erl. 11, 334–336: Second Sermon on Easter I, John 20:19–31

However great our sin may be,	When ministers lay on their hands,
The absolution sets us free,	Absolved by Christ the sinner stands;
Appointed by God's own dear Son	He who by grace the Word believes
To bring the pardon He has won.	The purchase of His blood receives. (*ELHB* 426: 7–8)

Tuesday

So the other disciples said to him, "We have seen the Lord." But he said to them, "Unless I see the nail marks in his hands and put my fingers in the nail holes and put my hand into his side, I will not believe it." John 20:25

It seems that this is a fine brave man who wants the matter figured out because he will not quickly believe the others. For he had seen that the Lord was put to death three days ago on the cross and the nails went through his hands and feet and the spear was thrust into his side. He had so firmly remembered him this way that he barely heeded what the others told him, that he was resurrected.

Therefore, he speaks so stubbornly, "Unless I see the nail marks in his hands and put my hand into his side, I will not believe it." He makes such a strong hyperbole that he will not only believe through his eyes, but with touching and groping with his hands. He wants to say: "No one can tell me so that I believe but I will stand fast on my 'no' if I do not see it, as you said that you have seen him. But should I believe it, then he must come so near to me that if it were possible, I would touch his soul and grasp him with my eyes."

That is called being stuck hard and fast in unbelief. And it is a wonder what he meant by presuming such an audacious proposal that he lay his hand and finger in the holes of the wounds. For if he should be so wise then he would consider: If Christ is living again, so death is overcome, all the wounds from the crown of thorns and whips would be gone, so that the five wounds also would have been healed and gone.

Now this happened as an example and comfort for us that the high apostles also must fail and stumble so we see how Christ reveals himself in his kingdom to the weak and puts an end to this. Also, we see how Christ is patient with those who are yet hard and stubborn and will not condemn and reject them for it so they remain his disciples and not defame him maliciously and become his foes. With this he teaches us that we should not become annoyed or disheartened over such people. Rather, following this example, we deal carefully with them, serving their weakness with our strength until they are straightened out and become strong. But further, it also proves (as I began to say) that the resurrection of the Lord is not only surely revealed since it is witnessed through this unbelieving and obstinant Thomas, who was stuck in such disbelief until the eighth day, and lay purely completely insensible, but also its power is made known and it becomes useful to us. [It tells us] how to observe Thomas being brought from disbelief to faith and out of doubt to sure knowledge and a glorious good confession.

This happens now, says the evangelist, first on the eighth day after his resurrection, when Thomas, against all the others' witness, strengthened himself in unbelief. Now he is completely dying away and no one hoped that Christ would make a special appearance to him. Christ comes there and shows him even the same stigmata and wounds so fresh, as he had shown the others eight days before. He tells him to put out his finger and hand and put them in the nail marks and his side. He allows him so much that he not only sees, as the others, but he also might grasp and feel as he had said, "Unless I see his hand," etc., and he also says, "Do not be unbelieving, but believing."

Erl. 11, 348–350: Second Sermon on Easter I, John 20:19–31

No longer Thomas then denied; He saw the feet, the hands, the side;
"Thou art my Lord and God," he cried: Alleluia! (*TLH* 208: 7)

Wednesday

Thereafter he said to Thomas, "Put out your finger and see my hands; and put out your hand and put it in my side; and do not be unbelieving, but believing." Thomas answered and said to him, "My Lord and my God." John 20:27, 28

There you see that Christ does not let it remain a story but rather it is up to him that Thomas become completely believing. He resurrects him from his stubborn unbelief and sins. So mightily and immediately St. Thomas begins to say to Christ, "My Lord and my God!" There he is already another man, not the old Thomas Didymus (which in German is "twin," not a "doubter," as one has determined from the text, but with miss-understanding), who just previously was so completely set in unbelief and was perishing, that he also would not believe unless he put his finger in his wounds. Rather, he suddenly makes a glorious confession and preaching concerning Christ, the likes of which no apostle to that time had yet preached, namely, that the person who was resurrected is true God and man. For it is an excellent Word when he says, "My Lord and my God!" He is not drunk and also does not speak cynically or in jest. So he also does not think of any false God because he surely is not lying. Also he is not chastized by Christ for this, but rather he affirms his faith which must be true and zealous.

Now that is the power of the resurrection of Christ, that St. Thomas, who was so deeply and rigidly stuck more than the others in unbelief, so suddenly changes and becomes a completely different man, who from now on freely confesses that he not only believes that Christ is resurrected, but he is so enlightened through the power of the resurrection of Christ that now he also definitely believes and confesses his Lord is true God and man. Through him, as he is now resurrected from unbelief, from all of sins' chief sources, he would also on the last day rise from death and with him live eternally in unspeakable glory and bliss. As Christ himself further says to him, "Thomas, since you have seen, you believe. Blessed are they that do not see, and yet believe."

Finally, I will not trouble if he put his finger into the wounds, if Christ also in the future after the resurrection has retained the wounds and the nail marks. Yet I would go so far as to say that these do not look horrible as before, but rather beautiful and comforting. And if they should still be fresh, open and red, as the painters portray it, I will leave for others to discuss. Yet it is very good that it is portrayed for the common man, that he has a remembrance and picture that reminds and admonishes him of the suffering and wounds of Christ. And it may well be that he has retained the same signs or marks, which on the last day will shine much more beautifully and gloriously than his whole body, and he will show them to all the world as the Scripture says, "They will see the one whom they have pierced," Zechariah 12:10. But I commend remembering this in every devotion.

But this is the chief part so we should learn and retain this gospel; that we believe that ours is the resurrection of Christ and it works in us that we should rise both from sin and death. As St. Paul speaks of it everywhere so richly and comfortingly and Christ himself here says, "Blessed are they that do not see yet believe." St. John teaches and exhorts at the close of his gospel about the use and necessity of the resurrection and says, "These things are written so that you believe that Jesus is the Christ, the Son of God and that through faith you have life in his name."

Erl. 11, 350–352: Third Sermon for the Sunday after Easter

I am content! My Jesus is my Lord, My Prince of life and Peace;
His heart is yearning for my future bliss And for my soul's release.
The home where He, my Master, liveth He also to His servant giveth.
I am content! I am content! (*TLH* 196: 3)

Thursday

As the Father sent me, so send I you. John 20:21

But how has God the Father sent Christ? [Answer:] To do nothing but the will of the Father, namely, to save the world. He has not sent him that he should earn heaven with good works. He did many good works, yes, all of his life was nothing else but good work. But for whom did he do it but for the people who needed it, as we read all over in the gospel? For everything that he did, he did in order to serve us by it. "As now my Father sent me," he says here, "so send I you. My Father has sent me to fulfill the law, to bear the sins of the world, to slay death, to conquer hell and the devil; not for my sake, for I didn't need it; but rather all of it for your sake and for your good, that I serve you by it. So you also should do for him."

Through faith, which will save you and make you good before God, you will accomplish everything, conquering death, sins, hell and devil. But you shall prove that faith with love, so that all of your works should be judged by it, not that you would earn something by it; for everything that is in heaven and earth is already yours. Rather, you serve your neighbor with them. For if you would not give these signs then it is sure that your faith is not rightly fashioned. Not that it is commanded that we do good works through this Word, for when faith is rightly fashioned in hearts, then one is not commanded much to do good works, they follow of themselves; rather, the works are only a sign of the love that is available to faith.

That is what St. Peter also says in 2 Peter 1:5, where he exhorts us to apply diligence that we should confirm our faith with good works and prove it. But those are good works that we do for our neighbor, by which we serve him. This alone will be required of a Christian, that he love. For through faith he is already good and saved, as St. Paul says in Romans 13:8, "Let no one be required anything, but that you love one another. For whoever loves another has fulfilled the law." Therefore, Christ says in John 13:34,35 to his disciples, "A new command I give you, that you love one another, as I have loved you; by this everyone will know that you are my disciples, that you have loved one another."

So we must now prove ourselves before the world, that everyone sees that we retain God's command, and yet not so that I become saved or good through it. For this reason I am obedient to authority. For I know Christ was obedient to authority and didn't have to be, but did it for our sake. Therefore, I will also do it for Christ's sake and for the good of my neighbor. And all this only because I prove my faith through love and so through every commandment. In this manner the apostles exhort us in their writings to good works. Not that we become good and saved through them, but only that we make sure and prove our faith by it both before us and other people.

Erl. 11, 317-318: Second Sermon on Easter Tuesday

Oh, may we ne'er with thankless heart
Forget from whom our blessings flow!
Still, Lord, Thy heav'nly grace impart;
Still teach us what to Thee we owe.
Lord, may our lives with fruit divine
Return Thy care and prove us Thine. (*TLH* 567: 2)

Friday

Behold this one will be placed for a falling and a rising of many in Israel as a sign which will be spoken against. Luke 2:34

But isn't it a misery that the savior and the Light of the world should be spoken against, judged and condemned? It would be right that he should be sought out and rallied to from one end of the world to another. But one learns from this what the world is and what nature does with your free will. Namely, it is of the devil's kingdom and God's foe, and acts not only against God's will, but rather madly and frantically persecutes and slays even the savior, who would help it to retain God's commandment. But one thing follows another. Those who reject him must also speak against him and cannot do anything else. Then again, those who rise up to him must confess him, speak well of him and preach. They can do nothing else. But the sword goes through his soul as he follows [the Lord].

Now note the Words. He does not say, "He will be spoken against." Rather, he is placed as a "sign that will always be spoken against." Just as one places a target or a mark for the marksmen so that all of the bows and rifles, arrows and bullets are directed and aimed at it, this one is placed for this; that the shots go nowhere but at this sign. So Christ is the target where everyone is directed. Every opponent targets on him completely. Even if the opponents are highly divided yet in this they become unanimous. They speak against Christ. That is proven in Luke 23:12 where Pilate and Herod were mortal enemies, yet they became one over and against Christ. The pharisees and sadducees were also for the most part divided, but against Christ they all became one. So David marveled and said of it in Psalm 2:1-2, "Why do the people rage? And why do the people seek such a vain thing? Why do the kings of the earth march together and the princes become one against God and against his Christ?"

So also every heretic, as many as they are and no matter how they oppose each other, yet they were all united against the Christian, united church. And now also, even though no bishop regards another, no convent, no order and cloister respects the others, and there are as many sects and divisions as there are clods of dirt; yet they are all of one mind against the gospel. Just as the Prophet Assaph wrote in Psalm 83:6-8, "All the peoples are gathered against the people of Israel: Edom, Ishmael, Moab, Hagar, Gebal, Ammon, Amalek, Philistia, Tyre, Assyria," who were never united with each other. The evil and lying are always divided. But against the truth and righteousness they must become one so that all strife, every opposition is placed on this sign and target. And it seems to them they have a ready reason for this. For each sect fights only against their partial opponents: Pilate against Herod, pharisees against sadducees, Arius against Sabellius, monks verses priests. But among their opposition each sect had their ties and friends, and it was only a partial opposition and partly peace.

But Christ is purely undesireable and totaly absurd. They all punished him. He meant as much to Pilate as to Herod, to the pharisees as much as the sadducees, and this *in toto*. So, as he is against them all; so again, they fall in all together against him. So the truth is against all lies and falsehood. Therefore all their lies hang together against the truth and they make one target for all opposition. It must always happen in this way. For no one finds Christ and the truth as good and taking his own part; as the Psalter says in Psalm 116:11, "All men are liars." So he must punish them all without division and discard their concerns so that they all together fall short of his grace and become needy. But not all can stand for this and desire his grace, yes, the smaller portion does.

Erl. 10, 262–264: Sermon on the Sunday after Christmas, Luke 2:33-40

Lord, put to shame Thy foes who breathe defiance
And vainly make their might their sole reliance;
In mercy turn to us, the poor and stricken,
Our hope to quicken. (*TLH* 269: 2)

Saturday

Do you think that the Lord desires sacrifice and burnt offering as he does obedience to the voice of the Lord? Behold, obedience is better than sacrifice and paying attention is better than the fat of a ram. 1 Samuel 15:22

A pious maid, who occuppies herself doing what is commanded her and according to her office sweeps the house, or carries out the chamber pot; or a servant, in the same way, plows and runs; these go up straight to heaven on the right road, while another who goes to St. James, or to church and totally ignores his office and work goes straight to hell.

So we must close our eyes and not behold the works, if they are big, small, glorious, despiseable, spiritual, physical, or what appearance and reputation they have upon the earth; but rather on the command and obedience that are in them; whether the same work is truly impressive and completely godly or if it is so poor as lifting a blade of straw. But if it is not of obedience and the command, then the work is not right and is condemnable, truly the devil's own, even if it were something so great as awakening the dead.

Then this is certain. God's eyes do not look at the works, but rather on the obedience of the works. So he also desires that we should look upon his command and calling, of which St. Paul says in 1 Corinthians 7:17, "Let each one remain in the calling in which he is called." And St. Peter in 1 Peter 4:10, "You will be as the true good steward, or people called in manifold grace; that each one serve and be available to the others by grace as he has received it." See, St. Peter says that the grace and gifts of God are not singular but manifold. And each should accept his own, use them and by them be useful to others.

What a fine thing it would be if it so happened that each remained with what was their own and served others with it so they would go together on the true road up to heaven. So writes St. Paul in Romans 12:4-6 and 1 Corinthians 12:12, that the body has many members, but not all members do the same works. So we also in the Christian congregation are many members, but not all have the same works. So no one should do the others' work, but rather each accept his own and all in one united obedience, in many types of commands and manifold works, move in unanimity.

Then you say: "So, should not one follow the dear Saints' lives and example? Why do we preach about them then?" Answer: One should preach them so that God is praised by it, and to motivate us and also to comfort us with God's goodness and grace so that not works, but rather obedience is illustrated by it. Not that one should leave [his own] obedience behind so we are led so deeply into works [of the great saints] that we would depart completely from [our own] obedience, so that we would gape our mouths at their works and despise our own command and calling. Therefore, there is no doubt that it is only the most miserable devil's work that one becomes anxious to serve God only in church, at the altar, at mass, singing, reading, offering and doing the like as if all other works were nothing or of no use. How could the devil better lead us from the true way than when he compels us to serve God so narrowly, only in the church and the works that are done therein?

Erl. 10, 236–238: Sermon on the Feast of St. Stephen, Matthew 23:34-39

Help me to mend my ways, O Lord,
And gladly to obey Thy Word.
While here I live, abide with me;
And when I die, take me to Thee. (*TLH* 328: 4)

Week of Misericordias Domini

Sunday

Be strong in the Lord, and in the might of his strength.
Ephesians 6:10

It is often said: Think, so that you hold fast and remain with the one who welcomed you. Let each bear his faith and his office well, and don't follow or allow the devil's prompting and that of your own flesh, or the world's charm. Defend yourself that you do not let yourself cause offense or be saddened and weak so that you become lazy and sluggish. For there it will weigh heavy and be a battle since we have such a foe (as we will hear) that always attacks and presses hard with all his might and skill and continuously covers us with evil thoughts and poisonous shameful tongues, turning both our ears and hearts completely blue so that we should not have good words or work zealously. So in our station or office we become negligent, careless, listless and impatient until he brings it about that you no longer stand fast, but wander loose and unstable and fall from one thing to another both in doctrine and life.

Being strong in the Lord means that one remains fast and immoveable and retains the doctrine, received of the Lord. Thus he teaches us how we should believe on Christ and thereafter live so that each one serves his neighbor in his station and calling and truly and willingly attends to them. So whoever would be a good preacher and pastor will have his hands full that he conducts his office rightly; that he preaches purely and clearly, warns, prays, and watches that the devil not rule over secret cliques [in the church] and hinder him in his office, or that he let himself act impatiently and be drowned by the unthankfulness of the world and evil mouths, not to mention the way he himself has to battle against the devil and flesh in his own person so that he remain in faith, etc.

So also in other stations each should first learn and not despise (as the worldly bunch does) God's Word and thereafter see what his station [work/vocation] requires. There you will find enough that hinders and battles you, both against your faith and against your office [work]. Therefore, you must arm yourself against this and think that it is proper and my duty to believe and live as a married man or woman, son, daughter, mayor, lord, servant, maid, etc. There I will remain and let nothing hinder me. Nor will I be tempted or afraid.

See, that is why St. Paul uses these very words, "Be strong in the Lord," etc. Else he could well have said it with plain words, as

248

he usually does and as we are accustomed to speaking when we present the doctrine, "Let each see to it that he rightly believe and do what is commanded him." But here he purposely gives the reason for such mighty words, "Strengthen yourself," or "be strong." Namely, as said, that whoever will remain with this doctrine and his office, must arm himself and additionally use strength. For it is not a matter that proceeds so easily and that you can do it yourself without hindrance and opposition. It doesn't get done without tribulation. Therefore, it is necessary that one wake up and be watchful and hear nothing else nor let himself err about what lies ahead on the road; that he briskly bursts ahead and constantly perseveres and goes forward.

For he doesn't want such bad Christians that bring nothing more from their Christianity than the knowledge and the washing and that would not consider how they can bring these things into their lives. Rather, they [Christians] consider that it must be lived and done. Therefore, strength also belongs to such a Christian and such strength which is God's. It is not of the world, nor of flesh and blood, namely, as I now have said, that each one (who is directed by God's Word, that he knows how he should be established before God and rightly live) think, "I will remain with this, and neither know nor hear and follow any other." By this he could be firm if any sectarian spirit should come and want to spoil the doctrine and understanding of Christ for him, or if a useless mouth wanted to draw and entice him away from his appointed office and work. For the devil leaves no one unassailed, if not through the world then inwardly in the heart through his prompting and false thoughts and through our own flesh. For he has nothing else to do but attack and hinder so that you do not remain in pure doctrine and so that you not fear that a small root [of false doctrine or dissatisfaction] will become a tree.

Altb. V, 986–987: Some Good Preaching on the Christian's Armor & Weapons, 1532

Therefore let us watch and pray, Knowing He will hear us
As we see from day to day Dangers ever near us,
And the end Doth impend Our redemption neareth
When the Lord appeareth. (*TLH* 446: 6)

Monday

The weak you have not tended, the sick you have not healed, the wounded you have not bound up, the erring you have not corrected and the lost you have not sought; but you have ruled them sternly and harshly. Ezekiel 34:4

To open he says, "One should strengthen the sheep who are weak." That is, the consciences that are weak in faith and have a timid spirit and are weak at heart, one should not drive and say, "You must do this, you must be strong; if you are so weak, then you are lost." That is not strengthening the weak. St. Paul says so in Romans 14:1, "Receive the weak in faith and do not trouble their conscience." And soon thereafter he says, Chapter 15:1, "But we who are strong should bear the frailty of the weak." Therefore, even if they are weak, one should not compel them with strength, but rather comfort them so that they do not despair. With time they will be stronger.

So also says Isaiah, the prophet, of Christ, Chapter 42:3, "He will not break the bruised reed and the glowing ember he will not extinguish." The bruised reeds are the poor, weak and bruised consciences that are easily shattered. They struggle and despair over God. There he does not go forth and trample it with his feet. That is not his way. Rather, he goes carefully that he doesn't break it. Or that glowing ember that yet burns a little and has more smoke than fire, are also these same people. They should not despair. He will not extinguish it completely but rather always kindle it and strengthen it more and more. That is surely a great comfort for all who know it. So whoever does not lead a weak conscience carefully is surely no good shepherd.

For another, the prophet says, "Those who were sick you should have helped." Who are the sick? Those who have outward infirmities in their visible works. The first concerns the conscience when it is weak. The other concerns the outward walk that sometimes purrs along and is wonderful, and here and there fails, overcome with anger and other foolish works, as also the apostles sometimes stumbled in coarse ways. Those are outwardly weak in works before the people, so that one is aggravated because of them, and says, "they are wondrous and strange." These he will also not throw away. For his kingdom is not ordered in such a way that only strong and healthy people are in it, for such things belong to this life; but rather Christ is established for this, that he receives and helps these people.

So even if we are so weak and sick, we should not despair or say, "We are not of the kingdom of Christ." Rather, the more we feel our weakness, the more and more we should return to him. He is there for this reason; that he help us and make us strong. If now you are sick and a sinner, and feel your need, then you have even more reason to say to him, "Dear Lord, I come even for this reason, that I am a sinner, that you help me and make me good." So the need compels you in. The greater your weakness, the greater is your necessity that you be healed. He also desires this and so he woos us that we gladly come to him. But all who are not shepherds like this think that they will make the people good if they yell and drive as a foe and they only make it worse, as one sees that it happens now when people act so foolishly. Everything is so miserably scattered even as the prophet says here.

In the third place: "What was broken you have not bound up." Being broken is as when one breaks a bone in two or is otherwise wounded, that is, a Christian is not only weak and has a break so that he sometimes stumbles; but rather he also comes into great trial so that he breaks a bone, as when he falls and denies the gospel, as St. Peter did when he denied Christ. Now, if one has already fallen like that, so that it drives him back or completely buries him, nevertheless you should not discard him as if he never belonged to this kingdom. Then you must let Christ have his way, that only pure rich grace and mercy dwells in his kingdom. So he only wants to help those who feel their trouble and misery and would gladly be out of them, so that it will be a completely comforting kingdom and he a comforting, friendly shepherd. For he woos everyone and charms them to come to him.

Erl. 12, 6–8: Sermon on the Second Sunday after Easter, John 10:12–16

Come as a shepherd; guard and keep This fold from hell and world and sin;
Nourish the lambs and feed the sheep; The wounded heal, the lost bring in.
(*TLH* 484: 2)

Tuesday

For we have not battled with flesh and blood, but with princes and powers, namely with the rulers of the world, that rule in the darkness of this world with the evil spirits under heaven. Ephesians 6:12

That you might stand against the cunning onslaught of the devil, etc., he here begins to illustrate and show what kind of foe we have and how he tries to battle and take us. He advises us of his plots and skills by which he pursues us. So we should guard ourselves before him and arm ourselves with the whole armor of God of which he has spoken and will yet say more of. But he calls his attack and battle skill a "cunning onslaught" to show that he is the kind of foe that is not only mightier than we (as he will soon say after this), but rather he is also an unsurpassed deceiver and an evil one. He directs all of his conflicts with cunning and deceit. He does not grab us openly in a way easy to see, as a foe before whom we could guard ourselves by seeing where he wants to break us. Rather, he slinks all around us and sees where he can secretly and treacherously rush in and captivate us when we least expect it.

So you should not worry that he will attack you where he sees that you are armed, where you have spotted him and have drawn your sword, but rather watch where you are in disrepair and unguarded. There he could find a breach, and sneak up on you so that suddenly and unforeseen he might catch and fall upon you. For he is so clever and well practiced that he knows that when we have the Word and are sure of it, he can do and win nothing, even if he seizes us with all his might. And even if he persecuted all of Christianity through tyranny with raging, madness, sword, fire, water, etc., still that is not his true hold, or his strongest and mightiest weapon. For by now he has already experienced that he cannot subdue God's kingdom or weaken Christianity even if he takes their life and limb. Rather, it only becomes stronger and grows more through it as if through their blood it [as a plant] is moistened and watered that it grows even more beautiful and hearty. As some of the ancient fathers have said, the church was planted by the dear apostles but sprinkled [watered] by the martyrs.

Therefore, he retreats and turns to the other side, as he approaches us with cunning and brings the Word to bear. He invents all kinds of deceptions and traps and comes adorned in such a beautiful appearance, not as a foe, but as a friend. He even presents the Word and Scriptures which we have and presents everything as an angel of light (as St. Paul says) and becomes a bright, snow white devil, who would blind us in this way so that we will not see or mark his deception, as the snake had deceived Eve. By this he does the first great remarkable harm.

So now it is frightening, hard and dangerous to battle and slay this foe who attacks us with pure malice and cunning and is such a clever deceptive spirit that all of the world's reason, wisdom and cleverness are nothing compared to him. We should be expectant and serious on all sides as he lays in wait there for us and seeks one chink [in our defense] after another where he would secretly devour us before we are ready. He also doesn't give up. If he is unsuccessful once or twice and is beaten back, he always comes again and brings other schemes by which he would enchant us and make a continual cry before our eyes with a beautiful pretence and appearance so that we should not see his malice and cunning.

So we would be completely lost and we could not stand an hour before his deception if we did not have this as comfort and were sure that we have God's armor, that is, his Word, pure and clean. This he can not take away, in as much as we hold it and we stand protected by it, ever more watchful, and are warned of his deception.

From this it follows that we are not secure or lazy or sleepy, but rather always give him attention and are on the lookout, and protected with God's Word. We wait on all sides since there is one who slinks all around us (as St. Paul says) and he seeks as a lion where he can devour us. That is why St. Paul portrays him so terribly, that we do not give him such poor attention, but rather are zealous. He portrays our danger right before our eyes, since our salvation and eternal life depend on this.

Altb. V, 990–991: Some Good Preaching on a Christian's Armor and Weapons, 1532

Come as a shepherd; guard and keep This fold from hell and world and sin;
Nourish the lambs and feed the sheep; The wounded heal, the lost bring in. (*TLH* 484: 2)

Wednesday

Now if our gospel is hidden, it is hidden to those that are lost in whom the god of this world has blinded the reason of the unbelievers so that they do not see the bright light of the gospel of the glory of Christ, who is the exact image of God. 2 Corinthians 4:3,4

Through this darkness he has enveloped the whole world and preserves his rule so that no knowledge of God and his will enlightens its heart. Through these hearts he speaks and works and directs all kinds of error, false doctrine and heresy, strife and bones of contention in faith and also hate and envy, war and revolts among people, that in short, his rule is nothing other than both pure lies and murder. So St. Paul and also Christ himself sets out to call the world a kingdom of darkness and its ways and works a rule of darkness since they do not know God's Word nor do they want to hear it. It [this world] does not see of itself that it is under the devil's might and rule. That is called a true inner darkness in the heart that is without faith. Such a heart is the devil's dwelling and home for he steals in and makes it so that one does not know God's Word (even if one sees and hears it), nor can it receive and suffer it, but rather it despises and persecutes the same. For his [the devil's] lies discard the truth and light. So the devil holds the world in constant obedience to him against God and his Word.

And since he calls him "lord of the world," and says that he lords over these, he sufficiently explains that human hearts are strongly committed so that they must think, speak and do what he desires. And here no one can brag of his free will and of the light of human reason, as if one could serve God well through them and do his will. Rather here it is established that everything proceeds and remains in darkness, according to the will of the devil even if fine, wise, learned, respectable and good people are under them. For the devil must have such people in his rule and not be sneaky and dark in all things through public evil and immorality, but rather he would also look beautiful and pretty white, else his rule on earth could not remain. So he also has a desire that he would rather be good and will have only the best and sweetest [people] on earth and the loveliest dwellings.

So even if a few living in the world appear to be the best, have high reasoning abilities, and many luxurious gifts of God, are apt to rule and advise other people, etc., yet in them is only darkness and they are the same as those under them; in subjection to the devil's service. So we see in all the world that the lords and princes, the smartest and most learned people must believe, speak and do what he wants. Even though God's Word is preached so brightly and clearly that it shines in their eyes, yet they must not understand it. Yes, even if they know it and without their thanks they acknowledge that it is the truth, yet they must not heed it or follow after it lest it weaken their darkness and the devil's lies. For this they persecute the Christians so that they complete the devil's obedience and will. They verify this and similar texts in the Scripture.

Altb. V, 997: Some Good Preaching on a Christian's Armor and Weapons, 1532

Word of the ever-living God,
Will of His glorious Son;
Without thee, how could earth be trod
Or heaven itself be won?

Lord, grant us all aright to learn
The wisdom it imparts
And to its heavenly teaching turn
With simple, childlike hearts. (*TLH* 291: 4-5)

Thursday

So now stand, gird your loins with truth. Ephesians 6:14

Now he begins to name our armor and weapons and shows how we should be forearmed in them and resign ourselves to this war so that we might in all places maintain the ability to subjugate and battle the devil where he attacks us. He sets forth six kinds of armor but it is all in the Pauline style and is not well said in German. First, their loins are to be girded with truth, that is, they lead a rightly fashioned life, in which there is no hypocrisy, but zeal. For the Scriptures call truth a rightly fashioned way of life that is not false or deceptive. Therefore he says, "first see to it that you are, as a person, a rightly fashioned Christian and you zealously receive those things pertaining to the Word and faith. For whoever would be in Christianity and does not accept the matter seriously, but rather only lets himself be numbered with the group, wants to enjoy it, and yet will not engage in the battle; that one will soon become part of the devil's group. For he did not gird himself. That is, he was not girded up and armored with the truth and the right zeal, as a soldier should be.

So girding the loins in the Scriptures refers to what we are saying; girding and arming ourselves so one is prepared and ready to run or to fight so that nothing may hinder him when he [Satan] should strike around him or he needs to escape the foe. Just as one tries to say it in German, "You must lift your legs high to run away from a rogue." So also Christ says to his disciples, Luke 12, "Let your loins be girded and your lights shine." That is, always be armed and ready, like the servants who await their master and should greet him if he comes home in the night. Or, in 2 Kings 4 the prophet Elisha says to his servant, "Gird your loins and take your staff." That is, gird yourself and get on your way. This shows that whoever is in a station of life where he has something to accomplish, is to run and to do it, that he be armed and diligently ready and attack it with desire.

So this should be first. It is appropriate in this battle to be girded and ready, that is, that we keep in mind that it must be battled and fought and that we give ourselves to it with zeal and be ready to do it rightly. For the other false Christians, that do not receive it with diligence and truth, go forth in false security and without care. They seek good days or their own honor and pleasure as if they should not fight. They do mortal shame to Christianity, as the devil always mixes in some of these who go along with good appearance and in name, but they have no heart or zeal. Through them the devil does more harm than through the others who are apart from us, as St. Paul laments everywhere about such false Christians and false workers. So the devil himself also fights against us through our flesh, if we are not rightly fashioned, that we become negligent and lazy so we do not receive and carry out our duties as diligently as we should. Therefore we must here be armed against this and fight and alertly awaken and preserve ourselves that we do not also speak in such laziness and security and finally in pure hypocrisy.

Altb. V, 1000: Some Good Preaching on a Christian's Armor and Weapons, 1532

Watch against the devil's snares Lest asleep he find thee;
For indeed no pains he spares To deceive and blind thee,
Satan's prey Oft are they Who secure are sleeping
And no watch are keeping. (*TLH* 446: 2)

Friday

And having put on the breastplate of righteousness. Ephesians 6:14

When the first part is there, that the office of Christian is borne without hypocrisy, then this must also follow thereafter, that one protect the breast with the breastplate of righteousness; which is a good conscience; that a Christian so live that he offend no one so that no man can complain against him, as the apostle always boasts, as he says in 2 Corinthians 1, "Our boast is this, namely, the witness of our conscience, that we have walked in the world in simplicity and godly purity." And Moses and the prophets were also defiant against everyone, that they had taken no donkey or anything else from anyone, nor had they come close to doing this or anything shameful.

This he calls the breastplate of righteousness, a guiltless right life and an outgoing attitude to all people, so that you do no one harm or sorrow, but rather are ready to serve and do good to everyone so that no one can shame our conscience nor can the devil himself complain or advance that we have not lived rightly. So when this comfort is absent, a person lives so crudely and ruinously, as does the great heap of the world, that there the devil has already defeated him so that he cannot stand. He gives him a stroke to the breast so that his heart and courage fail him and he makes his conscience terrified and broken. Then that hinders and weakens him very much; that one would stand against his own heart and conscience and at the same time battle the devil, who even attacks a rightly-fashioned life and work and gladly wants to make it sinful.

This is why the dear apostles always exhort that the believers should lead the kind of life that is unassailable before the world and everyone, which should also serve that our heart become even more joyful, hold faith ever faster and stronger, and be able to become sure, as St. Peter says of it in 2 Peter 1, "Dear brothers, act ever more diligently to make your calling and election sure," etc. For through my living an outwardly godly life before the world and being bold and boasting before everyman, I become sure of my faith, as a good tree does through true good fruits. For along with this it also becomes immoveable and strong.

Those who cannot do this, who publicly go in sins and with an evil life, bury and weaken the same, yes, they hinder faith so that their heart cannot grasp such sure comforting witness that he has a gracious God, and that his sins are forgiven him, since he is yet stuck in them [public sins] and does not depart from them. So John also says, 1 John 4, where he exhorts to love, "In this is love completed in us, that we have joy on the day of judgment." As if he should say, "That is a rightly fashioned, completed love, that can defiantly boast of such things even before God's judgment, against the devil and the world, that such love has done everyone good, and it knows that all the world must give this testimony and no one has a complaint against him. Thus the heart is not undone before God's judgment, nor must his faith sink for the sake of his evil life."

Altb. V, 1000–1001: Some Good Preaching on a Christian's Armor and Weapons, 1532

Help me as the morn is breaking, In the spirit to arise,
So from careless sloth awaking, That, when o'er the aged skies
Shall the Judgment Day appear, I may see it without fear. (*TLH* 549: 4)

Saturday

But above all things, take up the shield of faith, by which you can extinguish all the fiery darts of the evil one. Ephesians 6:16

The previous parts serve to establish one against people so that we cannot be attacked for the sake of this outward life, since we are armored; that no one can complain against us or take our boast and defiance. But the following three [weapons] are given that we should be dedicated to battle the devil when he attacks us so that we can stand before God against the evil spirit, who shoots (as he here says) at us with fiery darts and assaults our conscience with God's judgment. He so accuses it that nothing can please or help, even if we have stood well before the world, treated everyone with honesty and have lived in peace.

There he will surely turn it around and ruin all the best things you have done and terrify you with it to torture the conscience and make it so anxious and troubled that you do not know how to stand. He hunts and drives you into misbelief and doubt so that he makes your belt and girding, breastplate and armor useless, as those already know who used these things and have experienced the high spiritual trials, although there are few who have. The other common bunch doesn't understand about this, nor do they receive this.

So now he goes on that we must above all things (he says) also grasp a good strong shield for defense, when he [the devil] wants to tear at your conscience, trample your heart and make your life useless; that you are too loosely girded, or have not done enough with sufficient diligence, nor always done what you should towards every man. You must approach him and lift your shield, so that he cannot harm you or break through with his darts.

Faith is now such a shield as he himself proves, which holds to the Word of Christ and grasps him and answers the devil, "If I am a sinner and have not rightly lived, or done too little, there is a man, holy and pure, who has given himself and died for me and is given me of the Father so that he is my own with his holiness and righteousness, etc. There I am preserved. My life and doings remain where that is possible. I will gladly act and preserve as much as I can and am guiltless to the people. But where that fails and does not divert the blow (since if it is outside of Christ it cannot be preserved), then my Christ helps and preserves me, against whom you cannot complain. There I rely upon my shield, which is sure for me, and stands against every power and gate of hell."

For this reason he says, "By this shield you can extinguish the fiery darts of the evil one." He says this as a well experienced man who was often in this position, yes, as one attacked by the devil daily. And he experienced that nothing held or stood in such a battle, if the devil lays hold of one, and nothing is enough, having all kinds of belts, breastplates and shoes, and everything is armored and stands ready, if one does not have another, through whom one can dispel and divert the poisonous darts. For they go and push through every armor and what is ours, yes, even through the heart.

Altb. V, 1001–1002: Some Good Preaching on a Christian's Armor and Weapons, 1532

Abide with us, O Savior Tender, That bitter day when life shall end,
When to the grave we must surrender, And fear and pain our hearts shall rend.
The shield of faith do Thou bestow When trembling we must meet the foe.
(*TLH* 194: 4)

Week of Jubilate

Sunday

A little while and you will not see me; but in a little while you will see me, for I go to the Father. John 16:16

Here an example is brought forth that we should readily take a hold of and take to heart if, as in the days of the apostles, we are beset with sorrow, in fear, in need. We should also plan to be strong and rejoice because Christ is again resurrected. We now know that that happened. But the disciples did not know how he would be resurrected or what he meant by resurrection because they were so weary and troubled. They heard that they would see him again but they did not understand what it was or how it would happen. So they said to one another, "What is this that he is saying to us about a little while? We don't know what he is saying." They had so completely been overtaken by trouble and misery that they doubted completely and didn't know what he meant by this and how he would be seen again.

Therefore, we must also feel the "little while" in us, as the disciples felt it. For this is written for us as an example and as a teaching so that we are comforted through it and bettered by it. And we should use it as a wise saying, yes, we should feel and experience it so that we can always say, "God is at times near and at times he vanishes away." While waiting for him I will think how the world will not move or compel me at all; it goes over me. I do not see him [Christ] at all. But in this little time one must see and note that we are then altogether strong and stable. It will happen to us as it does the disciples here. We could not act any differently towards him than as it is written here. As they also were not able to do anything else.

The first "little time" that he speaks of when he says, "A little while and you will not see me," they have already understood when they saw that he was imprisoned and condemned. But the other "little time," where he says, "And after a little time you will see me." That they couldn't perceive. And we also cannot perceive it. Yes, he says there, "For I go to the Father," but much less could they understand that. It also happens that way to us. Though we know and hear that the tribulation, misfortune and trouble will last a little time, yet we now see that it always seems different than what we believe. Then we doubt and falter and no one is able to put up with it. We surely hear. We even know that it will not stay long, but how we will be relieved we cannot understand, as the disciples here [could not].

Since they now do not understand, why does Christ say it to them? Or why is this written? So we should not doubt but rather hold fast to the Word, as he says it. So the Word is sure and nothing else even though everything seems to be quite different [than what the Word says], as it will. And though we sometimes fall away from the Word, we should not for that reason remain completely away from it, but rather turn back to it. For he brings his Word yet again to correct. Even if the man cannot believe it, still God helps him with it. He does that without [human] reason, without free will and without the work of man. Yes, the evangelist says that the disciples did not perceive the Words that the Lord spoke to them. Much less would they receive the Word that would follow. So free will and human reason know nothing concerning the things that belong to the soul's salvation. What is here below, the free will can receive and know well, as when reason hears the cock crowing and understands it. But next to God's work and Word, they [human will and reason] must be condemned and reason doesn't know how to accommodate itself to it nor how to be rid of it, although they let themselves think they know a lot about it. But this sight is too bright for them. It makes them even more discouraged and blinder.

This is being illustrated for us in the disciples, who even were with the Lord for a long time. Yet they did not understand what he was saying to them. Now we also will not learn or understand this when we experience it. Then we will say, "That was against me so I felt I was lost, but when I was in trouble it didn't last long. I was stuck in tribulation, in adversity, but God soon helped me out.

Erl. 12, 58–60: Sermon on the Third Sunday after Easter, John 16:16–23

Other refuge have I none; Hangs my helpless soul on Thee;
Leave, ah, leave me not alone, Still support and comfort me!
All my trust on Thee is stayed, All my help from Thee I bring;
Cover my defenseless head With the shadow of Thy wing. (*TLH* 345: 2)

Monday

He struck me so that I should fall; but the Lord helped me.
Psalm 118:13

See here how great the need and how many kinds of foes there are. First he says all the heathen, who are many and are mighty, are against the poor little bunch [of believers]. But it also must be this way. They set themselves against God and his Word so that it is made abundantly plain how human resolve and comfort is completely nothing compared to God, as Psalm 2 also says, "The heathen rage and the kings set themselves against Christ," etc. All other teachings and gods can be tolerated, so that no people or country sets itself against them, except when God's Word comes. Then all the world is aroused and from end to end it piles on its ranting and raving so it is said, "They surround me." "Me, me," he says. "I am alone, whom they must surround." The Romans had all the gods of the world, a few hundred, which they could put up with. But the one Christ they could not stand. Just as now all the teachings of the monks and priests, as shameful as they are, even when they have been shameful before all the world even to the very edge and also plagued and tortured bodies and souls, yet all that is tolerated. But now the Word of God comes and teaches pure peace and grace, and also forgives their oppression. Then every one must break off from, slander and persecute it. Why? They have nothing to do (he says), but they must surround me, me, who has the Word. The devil must adhere himself to me, as Christ says in John 15, "If you were of the world, then the world would have loved you. But since I have chosen you from the world, so the world has a grudge against you."

For another thing, they are not only many, but they also use all of their might and act with all power, zeal, industry and labor and grab on. For he says two times in the eleventh verse: *circumdederunt me, circumdederunt me*, they surround me, they surround me. By this he shows they persist, press forth, do not quit, do not become tired, press and press continuously, do not stop, until you go to the ground, even if they often fail. They do not turn away, always one new plan of attack after another, one resolution after another. For the devil, their god, who so drives them does not let them vacation or rest so long as they are able. For such heathen rage against Christ and his Word by the devil's machination, else it would not be possible. If it were only a human work they would soon become tired and weary of it, especially when they would sense that they had been so often repelled and failed and were put to shame, as such persecutions always are.

Thirdly, they are also not only zealous, active and restless; but they are bitter, hateful and poisonous in the worst way, which also makes them so restless. And because of their lost restlessness and purposeless raging over their not getting much done, for they cannot do it so soon as they want, but often fail, they must bring and let fail so many kinds of plans and resolutions, it makes them even more grim and hateful. The more they fail, the more they are driven, the crazier they become so that through this they should be exhorted to penitence. So one slander prepares for another and one lie sharpens another. Restlessness makes them grim and grimness makes them restless and so they must run forth, storm and bluster in the devil's service, as he drives and hunts them. They can not cease or stop themselves. Therefore he says here, "They surround me like bees." A bee is such an angry, irritable little beast. When it is angry, it sticks its stinger in its foe and leaves it in unseen so that it loses its life in the process and can never again make honey. For when a bee loses his stinger and doesn't die, from then on he can make no more honey. So he has lost this noble and sweet handwork because of his wrath and thirst for revenge. He must from then on carry and bring water for the other bees so that it can eat. It must become the slave of the other bees of the hive.[10]

So the foes of Christ are so consumed with revenge and hate that they are conquered because of it before they can do any harm or can avenge themselves. So they eternally lose all grace to do good and to be true Christians. They scrape and flit with their wings and stick their stingers in the Christian from behind. So they satisfy their little desires with their eternal harm and ruin both here and there.

Altb. V, 179–180: Lecture on the 118th Psalm, 1530

Preserve Thy Word, O Savior,
To us this latter day
And let Thy kingdom flourish,
Enlarge Thy Church, we pray.
O, keep our faith from failing,
Keep hope's bright star aglow.
Let naught from Thy Word turn us
While wand'ring here below.

Preserve, O Lord, Thy Zion,
Bought dearly with Thy blood;
Protect what Thou hast chosen
Against the foes' dread brood.
Be Thou her great Defender
When dangers gather round;
E'en tho' the earth be crumbling,
Safe will Thy Church be found. (*TLH* 264: 1–3)

Tuesday

But to the godless God says, "What right do you have to proclaim what is mine and to take my testament in your mouth; for you hate instruction and cast my Word away." Psalm 50:16, 17

So my antinomians[11] also do now. They preach very well and (as I can not think otherwise) with true zeal for the grace of Christ, of

---

[10]Luther's bee illustration is not infallible. The current state of bee knowledge acknowledges that once a bee loses his stinger he has made the ultimate sacrifice for the hive and perishes.

[11]Refers to those who believed that after conversion the law has no applicability to a Christian's life, but only the Gospel.

forgiveness of sins and what more is to be said about the article of redemption. But they flee this *Consequens*, as the devil, that they should tell the people of the Third Article, of sanctification, that is, of the new life in Christ. For they think one should not terrify or trouble the people; but rather always preach comfortingly of grace and the forgiveness of sins in Christ and for their life they avoid these or similar words, "Hear this, if you would be a Christian and at the same time an adulterer, whoremonger, full of filth, prideful, greedy, a usurer, envious, vengeful, remaining in evil, etc." But they rather say, "Hear this. If you are an adulterer, a whoremonger, a greedy person or some other kind of sinner. If only you believe then you are holy and don't need to fear the law; Christ has fulfilled everything."

Friend, tell me, is that not called condemning the *Antecedens* and negating the *Consequens*? Yes, it is even called both taking away and making nothing out of Christ, even if he is preached in the highest way. It is purely yes and no in the same sentence. For such a Christ is nothing and he is not one that has died for the kind of sinners that do not depart from sins after the forgiveness of sins, and lead a new life. So they preach well upon the Christ of the Nestorian and Eutychean; a Christ that is Christ and yet is not. And they are fine Easter preachers, but shameful Pentecost preachers. For they preach nothing of *de sanctificatione et vivificatione Spiritus Sancti*, of the sanctification of the Holy Ghost, but only of the redemption of Christ. So Christ is Christ (as they rightly preach in a lofty way), but he has earned redemption from sins and death, so that the Holy Ghost should make us new men out of the Old Adam, so that we die to sins and live to righteousness, as St. Paul teaches (Romans 6:2f), beginning and receiving it here on earth and completing it thereafter. For Christ has not only earned *Gratium*, grace, but also *Donum*, the gift of the Holy Ghost, that we not only have forgiveness of sins, but also the end of sins (John 1:16,17). Now whoever does not refrain from sinning, but rather remains in the previous evil ways must have another Christ who is from the antinomians. The true Christ is not there even if every angel cries, "Pure Christ, Christ!" and he must be accursed with his new Christ.

Now see what evil *Dialectici* we are in high matters that are over our heads, or that we are not used to. In the same way that we affirm something we negate it. But in lower matters, there we are very sharp *Dialectici*. For a peasant, no matter how coarse he is easily understands and knows, "Whoever gives me a penny has not given me a dollar." For this is natural to him and he easily sees the difference. But our *Antinomi* do not see that they preach Christ without and against the Holy Ghost, since they want to let the people remain in their old ways and yet speak in a holy way. Yet the consequence is that a Christian should have the Holy Ghost and lead a new life or know that he has no Christ. So the asses want to be better *Dialectici* than Master Philip and Aristotle, of Luther I must be silent, since the pope is pleased alone with them. They are too high flying for me. Well then, the *Dialectica* of Nestorius and Eutyches is a common trouble, especially in Scriptural matters; but in lower matters they know enough to put an end to such things. As in subtle matters the jurists and regents also have enough to do when sometimes they must hear both a yes and a no and make a difficult decision.

Erl. 25, 323-325: On Councils and the Church, 1539; cf. AE 41

From faith in Christ, whene'er 'tis right, Good works are surely flowing;
The faith is dead that shuns the light, No good works ever showing.
By faith alone the just shall live, Good works alone the proof can give
Of love, which true faith worketh. (*ELHB* 314: 10)

Wednesday

One sings with joy of the battle in the tents of the righteous. The right hand of the Lord retains the victory. Psalm 118:15

Earlier, he related and sang out his experience of how God had helped him. Now he goes farther to a common example of all saints and says that it happens to all the righteous in this way. They will be persecuted for the sake of the Word and name of God. But since they trust God and do not build on a human [foundation], he helps them to sing this kind of song and praise God as Moses had sung with the children of Israel, Exodus 15. As Deborah sang, Judges 5. As Hannah sang, 1 Samuel 2, and so forth, one after another. It is one voice. That is, when I survey all the saints, especially in the New Testament, it happens to them in the same way. So I also hear in their tents this voice of joy, that is, a happy singing and a song of salvation and victory, as God helps them. So we are united with their voice in singing, praise and thanks, just as we also are unanimous in the faith and trust in a single God. We are also alike in suffering every thing. Even as St. Peter comforts us in 1 Peter 5, "And know that your brothers in the world have suffered even the same things."

If this were not such a special comfort, that one knows and sees that it happens to all saints as it does to us, St. Peter would not have revealed this. This psalm also would not speak so readily about it. Then it must rightfully comfort and strengthen me to see that as Saint

Paul and the apostles also had the Word, God, faith, the cross and all alike, so do I. As one says, *Gaudium est miseris, socios habere poenarum.* It comforts the miserable that they do not suffer alone. That is, above all, a fine true word when one uses it rightly and it is shared among Christians. For an unusual suffering terrifies a person very much that he should feel so singled out and suffer before all people so pecularly. Then again it is comforting when many suffer in one way. Then such terrible thoughts do not so readily occur as if he alone were culled out and rejected. But it is even more comforting when they all suffer alike and no one remains free, as it happens among Christians.

But the psalm does not speak here about the suffering of the righteous, but rather of victory and joy. This makes the comfort even stronger, so that we see the happiest illustrations before us as the redeemed. We are secure that we and all the righteous will also sing so joyously. But he just as well shows the suffering of the righteous with the little word "salvation" and thereafter more words are given by which he lets us understand that the righteous have honestly suffered and fought in the battle of faith. It wouldn't be called salvation or victory were there also not this joyous song. But now, as there is always much suffering (as St. Paul says, that among us there is much suffering of Christ), so there is also always much salvation and victory, singing and joy, praise and thanks, wherever the righteous are.

Altb. V, 183–184: Lecture on the 118th Psalm, 1530

O God, Thou faithful God,
Thou Fountain ever flowing,
Who good and perfect gifts
In mercy art bestowing,
Give me a healthy frame,
And may I have within
A conscience free from blame,
A soul unhurt by sin!

If dangers gather round,
Still keep me calm and fearless;
Help me to bear the cross
When life is dark and cheerless;
And let me win my foe
With words and actions kind.
When counsel I would know,
Good counsel let me find. (*TLH* 395: 1, 4)

Thursday

Just as the rain and snow fall from heaven and do not return again; rather it moistens the earth and makes it fruitful and grow, that it gives seeds to the sower and bread to eat. So shall the Word also be, which goes out of my mouth. It shall not return to me empty, but rather it shall do what pleases me and shall accomplish that for which I send it. Isaiah 55:10, 11

So a child's faith teaches us (as said), that there is a holy Christian people on earth and it must remain until the end of the earth. For it is an article of faith that cannot cease until what they believe occurs that, as Christ promised (Matthew 28:20), "I am with you until the end of the world." By what will or can a poor erring man yet note where in the world such holy Christian people are? Such a people shall surely be in this life and on earth, for it is still believed, that a heavenly existance and eternal life is to come. They have it but not yet. Therefore, this people must still be here and remain in this life and in this world until the end of the world. For they say, "I believe in another life." By this they acknowledge that it is not yet in this life, but rather they believe, hope and long for a true fatherland and life. Presently they must remain and wait in misery, as one sings in songs of the Holy Ghost, "When we go home from this misery. Kyrie Eleison." It is speaking of this.

First, this holy Christian people is recognized when it has the Holy Word of God. But such recognition goes on unevenly, as St. Paul says (1 Corinthians 3:12, 13). A few have it completely pure, a few not completely pure. Those who have it pure are called those building on the foundation with gold, silver, and jewels. Those who have it impure are called building on the foundation with hay, straw, and wood. Yet through fire they become pure. Of this more than enough is said above. This is the chief part and the great cornerstone, by which the Christian people are called holy. For God's Word is holy and makes all holy whom it stirs. Yes, it is the holiness of God himself, Romans 1:16, "It is the power of God that makes holy all who believe"; and 1 Timothy 4:5, "All become holy through Word and prayer." For the Holy Ghost himself compels it and salves or makes holy the Church, that is, the holy Christian people; with this and not with the annointing of the pope, by which he salves or makes holy fingers, clothing, robes, cup and stein. For these same people do not ever learn about loving God, believing, praising, becoming pure. They want to adorn the maggot sack [body] and thereafter destroy and pollute it with annointing and holiness, that is, such a holiness as the maggot sack [that is, this sinful body] can have.

But this sanctuary is the true salvation, the true salve, which salves to eternity, even if you can have no pope's crown or bishop's miter, but live a plain simple life and need to die; just as the little baby (and all of us), naked and without any adornment must be baptized. But we speak of the external Word, orally preached through men, as through you and me. For this is what Christ has left behind as an external sign by which one should acknowledge his church, or his holy Christian people in the world. We also speak of the oral Word that is believed earnestly and publicly confessed before the world, as he says (Matthew 10:32,33; Mark 8:9), "Whoever confesses me before people, him will I confess before my Father and his angels." There are many who know it well in secret but do not want to confess it. Many have it, but they do not believe on it or act in accordance with it. For there are few who believe and act according to it. As the parable of the seed says in Matthew 13:4, three parts of the field received it well and had it, but only the fourth part, the fine, good field, brought forth fruit with patience.

Now where you hear or see this Word taught, believed, confessed and acted upon, there have no doubt that there must surely be a true *Ecclesia sancta catholica*, a holy Christian people (1 Peter 2:9), even if there are only a few. For God's Word does not go up unsuccessfully, Isaiah 55:11, but must have a little fourth or part of the field. Even if there were no signs [of response to it], then this alone would be sufficient to know that the same must be a holy Christian people. For God's Word cannot be without God's people. Then again, God's people cannot be without God's Word. Else why would one want to preach or hear preaching, if God's people were not there? And what could or would God's people believe if God's Word were not there?

Erl. 25, 358–360: On Councils and the Church, 1539; cf. AE 41

Precious Jesus, I beseech Thee, May Thy words take root in me;
May this gift from heav'n enrich me So that I bear fruit for Thee!
Take them never from my heart Till I see Thee as Thou art,
When in heav'nly bliss and glory I shall greet Thee and adore Thee. (*TLH* 296: 4)

Friday

You are all children of God through faith in Christ Jesus. For as many of you as are baptized have put on Christ. Galatians 3:26, 27

For another, one recognizes God's people, or the holy Christian Church, by the Holy Sacrament of Baptism, where it is rightly taught, believed and used according to Christ's mandate. For that is also a public sign and an abundant salvation through which God's people become holy. For it is a holy washing of the new birth through the Holy Ghost (Titus 3:5), in which we bathe and are washed by the Holy Ghost from sins and death as in the innocent, holy blood of the Lamb of God. Where you see such signs, there know that definitely the Church or the holy Christian people must be, regardless of their appearance, even if the pope did not baptize or you do not know their holiness and power, as when the little children know nothing of it except when they grow. They unfortunately may become seduced from their baptism as St. Peter laments in 2 Peter 2:18. They are being torn away through unchastity who had truly escaped and now wander in error. Yes, you should not also err as to whose baptism it is. For it is not the property of the baptizer, nor is it given by him, but rather it belongs to the little ones baptized for whom it is established and given by God, just as the Word of God is not the possession of the preacher (he will himself also hear and believe it), but it is the disciples who would hear and believe it. It is given for them.

In the third place one knows God's people or a holy Christian people, by the holy Sacrament of the Altar, where it is given out, believed and received according to the institution of Christ. For it is also a public sign and true salvation left by Christ through which his people become holy. By this his people practice and publicly acknowledge that they are Christians, as it is with the Word and with Baptism. Here also, never mind if the pope does not hold the mass, if he has ordained you, confirmed or anointed you, or prescribed the gowns worn in the mass, you can receive it well without any clothes (as one does sick in bed), except that you are compelled by outward modesty to be clothed chastely and honorably. You also should not ask if you have a tonsure or if you are anointed. Also, do not dispute if you are male or female, young or old, so little as you inquire about them in baptism and preaching. It is enough that you are consecrated and anointed with the holy anointing of God, of the Word of God and Baptism and this Sacrament. In that way you are anointed high and glorious enough and dressed as a priest.

Also, do not be confused by how holy the man giving it out is, or if he has two wives. For the Sacrament does not belong to the one administering it, but rather to the one it is given to, except that he also receives it. But he is one of those that receives it and for that reason it is also given him. Now wherever you see this Sacrament administered in its right usage, know for sure that God's people are there. For as said above about the Word, wherever God's Word is, there the church must be and also where Baptism and the Sacrament are, God's people must be. For no one has, gives, practices, uses, and confesses such morsels of saving acts except God's people, even if some false and unbelieving Christians are secretly under them. But these are not a part of the people of God, especially since they are hidden. For the church, or God's people, would not publicly put up with them, but rather battles them and would make them holy, too. Or, if they would not want that, it expels them from the holy things through the ban [of excommunication] and regards them as heathen, Matthew 18:17.

Erl. 25, 361–363: On Councils and the Church, 1539; cf. AE 41

And when they leave their childhood home, When Satan comes alluring,
May their baptismal grace become A refuge reassuring!
Blest he who then can say: "God's cov'nant stands for aye."
He ne'er shall be undone Who trusts in God alone
God is his mighty Father. (*TLH* 337: 4)

Saturday

*For the Lord chastised me sorely, but did not give me
death. Psalm 118:18*

What is this? He has boasted that he would not die but live. To
this end the flesh, world, men and princes have accused him to make
him weak and faint. Is it not called dying when you are burned,
beheaded, drowned, throttled, cursed and hunted? I think that you
should truly say if you can call that a life. "Where is your God? Let
him help you. Let's see if Elijah will come and save you." Upon this
he answers, "Remain fast and be comforted. Oh, friend it is nothing.
This death is only a fatherly rod. It is not wrath. It is the fox tail. It
is not serious. He chastises me as a dear father does his dear child.
It surely causes some sorrow, and is not pure sweetness, but it is a
rod. It does not kill. Rather, it helps ever more towards life." Then
again, it is a good interpreter and a strong *Confutatio*, that can make
a holy rod out of the word death. This is a skill which the Holy
Ghost and the right hand of God must teach. For it does harm to
most people when one blasphemes and mocks, wags his head and
misinterprets it as the Jews did to Christ on the cross. Flesh and
blood act in the opposite way. It makes a salutary rod into death and
hell, for it soon wants to doubt and despair. Where bread fails, we
do not interpret things as going well.

But whoever can sing this verse has a much greater skill when
the devil compels such misguided prayers when death is there, as he
did to the beloved Job and many other saints. He can portray death
to the heart so mightily, not poorly as a person speaks of it, if you
are burned, drowned, etc. Rather, he can expound on what a
terrifying, horrible thing death is and by that the devil compels
thoughts of God's wrath and buries and strikes the heart with mighty
thoughts so unbearable and insufferable.

On this bases a true interpreter [is recognized], who can outcry
and out wind the devil with this verse and say, "Yet it is not death
or wrath. It is a gracious chastising and fatherly punishment, yet I
know that he has not given me over to death and I will still not
believe that it is wrath. And if all the devils of hell say it in unison,

yes, even if an angel of heaven said it, then let him be damned. Even if God himself said it, then I would still not believe he forsook me. He presented himself to Abraham so angrily yet he would not press it so far, for he does not revoke his Word. It should be said that he chastises me, but he will not put me to death. I remain with what he says and I do not accept what others think or interpret or explain."

He mightily feels death, but he will not [die]. And it shall not be called death, but rather he regards it as the right hand of God. And it is also true that God sends such a death, but he understands it by God that it will not be called death, nor shall it [death] be permitted, but rather it shall be the father's rod and child's punishment. Well, those are all high Words that are not in the hearts of the people or princes, nor can they enter such hearts, as Saint Paul says, 1 Corinthians 2, "We speak of the hidden, covered wisdom of God, which no prince of this world knows." This time it is said of this beautiful song of the dear saints.

Altb. V, 188: Lecture on the 118th Psalm, 1530

God is my Comfort and my Trust, My Hope and Life abiding;
And to His counsel, wise and just, I yield, in Him confiding.
The very hairs, His Word declares, Upon my head He numbers.
By night and day God is my Stay, He never sleeps nor slumbers. (*TLH* 517: 2)

Week of Cantate

Sunday

You child of man, how is the wood of a vine better than other wood? Or a vine before other wood in the forests? Can one also make something of it? Or can you make a peg of it upon which one could hang something? Ezekiel 15:2,3

Yet the vine is the most noble wood so long as it stays on the plant; for it has the most noble sap and fruit, yet that honor departs as soon as it becomes severed from the plant. Then it has no use, the prophet says, so that one cannot even make a peg or handle upon which to hang something. Rather, it is of no use to anyone but that one throw it into the fire so that it is burned and destroyed to ashes. So also here, Christ says, whatever branch does not remain in me (as on the true vine) can bear no more fruit nor do anything good that pleases God. It must be cut off from the vine, so that it does not hinder the other branches. Then, as it is removed and thrown from the vineyard, it must dry out. It is of no use to anyone but that one tie it in a bundle and throw it into fire and let it burn there until it burns completely to ashes.

All this is said against all who are not rightly fashioned, believing Christians and are still impudent spirits. For they dream that they alone are sufficient. They think they can do so much outside of Christ that they remain rooted and green. They want to be trusted as the best foremost branches. They [believe they] should not be disregarded but rather think they should be sought out and honored because Christianity could not stand or remain without them. This is how the pope, bishops, along with other sects boast. But against this he warns us that we guard ourselves and make sure that we remain in him and not in such false, dark prattling. For this reason it is well established. He says that it would happen to all who do not remain in him. First they must be cleared away as he also says in the first Psalm, "The godless will not remain standing in the judgment nor in the congregation of the righteous." When they first exalt themselves they become differentiated from the bunch of those who rightly preach and believe, which is the true office of righteousness of Christianity and the assembly or congregation of God. You see for yourself that rightly-fashioned preachers and false preachers cannot suffer to be with each other and rightly-fashioned Christians and false Christians separate themselves from each other, for the Word or the doctrine divides their hearts. So we could not remain with the popish bunch any more than we could with the anabaptists and the other sects and on the other hand they could also not stay with us. Rather, we are divided like winter and summer. In summary, they could not remain with the true bunch nor remain by the Word, but rather must be thrown away so that it is apparent to everyone that they have become false and useless branches.

Now, they don't see a problem but only maintain that they are not separated from us because they are cut off or are cast away, but they want to be the nearest to God and be the truly greatest branches. But we regard them as cut off, thrown away, useless branches because they openly chide and condemn us, which we must suffer. Yet it is as Christ said, that they must be pruned and cut away. In the same way as on the threshing floor when the farmer throws the grain; the grain goes in one place, but the husks are separated and cannot remain with the grain. So when God's Word does this, he has the winnowing fork in his hand so the husks, that is, the false Christians, go where they will be destroyed but the grain remains on the threshing floor. Now whoever remains in the pure doctrine and faith in Christ has this comfort, that he is a true honorable branch and what he does are only good fruits. Then again, all the others no matter how great, mighty, learned, clever and holy they are called, yet they are only lazy, useless branches that one prunes off and throws away.

This is frightening enough if it is believed that for this [that is, rejection of true doctrine] a person should know that he must be cut off from Christ and Christianity and robbed of the Word, Baptism and Sacrament, the intercession of Christ, his blood and Spirit and everything that is in Christ and Christianity. That is already an all too horrible harm, which thereafter brings even greater ones. But they do not heed it for they are counseled in false doctrine and by it are bewitched and blinded so that they can do nothing else.

Altb. VII, 150: Sermons on the Gospel of St. John Chapters 14–16, 1538; cf. AE 24

O Thou Lord of my salvation, Grant my soul Thy blood-bo't peace.
By Thy tears of lamentation Bid my faith and love increase.
Grant me grace to love Thy Word, Grace to keep the message heard,
Grace to own Thee as my Treasure, Grace to love Thee without measure. (*TLH* 419: 3)

Monday

Whoever does not remain in me will be cast away and dried up as a branch that one collects and throws into the fire to be burned. John 15:6

That is, the longer it goes on, the more wicked they become until they become hardened and calloused, as the branch which has lost its sap and is completely dried out so that it can no longer bend, but rather only breaks. So also, when a person falls from me and is ripped out of the vine, this has already happened to him. For one will find no other vine without and outside of this one. So they fall ever longer and deeper in impenitence until it is complete.

For these are the two terrible falls by which a person is ruined to the bottom of hell. The first, that he falls from Christ, the other, that he becomes impenitent in disbelief and sins. The first fall can be yet repented of, if one returns again to the vine in time (that is, to the doctrine and faith of Christ). But if one remains dried out and impenitent in error, he is like Pharaoh, Judas and the others who will not or cannot turn again to penitence. As now also in the popish bunch, they well know that they have not done right and are of no use, and yet at the same time they raise their head, so that they also are persistent and impenitent, wantonly desiring not to come to Christ. They are already so deep in hell, as they should be, for one cannot sin higher nor harder than one who falls in this way from faith and will not turn again. That is the sin unto death for which there is nothing that will help. But they dream that it will not harm them at all and the wine tastes so good to them as if they are yet rich and satisfied, sitting in honor and might. But look what follows this.

Thirdly, one gathers them and throws them into fire and burns them. They are so entrenched in the previous two parts and could not become worse. For now there is nothing left but waiting for punishment. Since they do not remain in Christ and will not come back, then he will act accordingly. He allows this opposition [for a while] until they are gathered up, bound and thrown into the fire so that they burn. That is finally the judgment; that they should be removed. So guard yourself that you not be counseled into such a terrible fall. For [good things] will not be given to those who so desire to remain without Christ but set themselves against him in impenitence and yet go on securely as if they will do well by this. But rather the sure and the irrevocable sentence is spoken that they will be gathered away and be put together into a bundle to everlasting fire.

For this gathering is nothing other than what is so often said: No one thinks that they are the kind of person who will turn away, especially if he is a Cartusian or Einsiedler, running and making pilgrimages up to Rome or Jerusalem, making and doing what they always do. In this way, they will not come out of the cords and bands nor escape the punishment. Rather, with the impenitent pharaoh, Judas, Caiaphas, Herod, Mohammed, pope and all other sects, they are gathered together and bound so they will all together be punished. This already happens now before the last day when he continually gathers them, one after another, so that they are in the grave and already judged and all that is left is to throw them into the fire. Then, one impenitent person after another will be lined up until they all come together. None of them remains or escapes no matter how mighty, learned, clever and secure he might be. Then the fire will be kindled and they will be thrown in. That is the end and the reward they have waited for since they fell from Christ and desire counsel and help outside of him.

Sure, the world says, what's the harm of it? It is done at an evil time. Yes, he sets an evil verdict in addition to it and says: They will be burned. It will not be a fire that only roasts and singes them a little and thereafter stops, like the fire and suffering Christians must go through on earth, that certainly causes them harm but yet must soon give them back. Even if they also become ashes for it, yet they are not consumed by it but rather are only saved and purified. But with these it will not happen in such a way that they might hope to come again out of it. Nothing will help those outside of Christ. They will not be a little singed or roasted, but eternally remain in it and completely pulverized. For it will be a fire that is never quenched as Christ says in Mark 9.

Altb. VII, 151: Sermons on the Gospel of St. John Chapters 14–16, 1538; cf. AE 24

While the wicked are confounded,
Doomed to flames of woe unbounded,
Call me, with Thy saints surrounded.

Low I kneel with heart-submission,
See, like ashes, my contrition;
Help me in my last condition! (*TLH* 607: 16–17)

Tuesday

If you so remain in me and my Words remain in you then you will ask what you want and it will be given to you. John 15:7

See how highly this man praises a Christian life. No one had understood it rightly or would have liked to ask, "Friend how does one remain in Christ? How am I [attached] or how do I remain a

274

branch in this vine?" So he sets forth this explanation in addition and says, "Only give attention to my Word, for everything depends upon it. If my Word remains in you, that is, that you believe and confess the Article that the child's faith teaches: 'I believe in Jesus Christ, our Lord, crucified, dead, resurrected, sitting at the right hand of the Father for me,' and what goes along with that, and you remain with it and are ready to risk and leave everything over it, before you would receive other doctrines and works, if you remain so in the Words, then I remain in you, and also you in me. And both are so rooted and incarnate in each other that my Word and your heart become one thing and you can no longer ask how I am stuck into you or you into me for you will see it in all of life. But now you cannot grasp or understand anything except that you have my Word and through faith you are washed in my blood and through my Spirit you are anointed and conquer. So everything you live and do is therefore well done and pure good fruit."

And you should not only have that but also whatever you ask for after that. By those things you shall be preserved and you definitely will receive them. What more do you want? Everything that you do shall be good and acceptable and you will be a dear child. Your works cannot be ruined even if you are yet sometimes fragile and like a child or sick person which makes you unclean. Yet he will not so quickly cast you away but will ever more purify and improve you. So you shall also have the power, glory and majesty, that what you merely ask for will be given you. If you now have a deficiency or need that weighs upon you, then only call to him and open your mouth in trust, as a child calls to his father who is pleased with everything his child does so long as he clings to his father, especially when he stammers to him and asks for something from him. He gladly does and gives what the child should have and not only that, but he cares for the child and thinks only about how he might give everything that he needs. "In this way," says Christ, "you should count on this from my Father and me so that you remain in the stem and a branch on the vine."

Altb. VII, 151–152: Sermons on the Gospel of St. John Chapters 14–16, 1538; cf. AE 24

Since He returned to claim His throne,
Great gifts for men obtaining,
My heart shall rest in Him alone,
No other rest remaining;
For where my Treasure went before,
There all my tho'ts shall ever soar
To still their deepest yearning.

Oh, grant, dear Lord, this grace to me,
Recalling Thine ascension,
That I may ever walk with Thee,
Adoring Thy redemption;
And then, when all my days shall cease,
Let me depart in joy and peace
In answer to my pleading. (*TLH* 216: 2–3)

Wednesday

Whoever loves me will cling to my Word. John 14:23

Dear Jude (he would say) this thing is done so that one must not ask if king, kaiser, Caiphas or Herod is learned or not, but rather if I am. That is the answer to this question. In this preaching and administration, that I will initiate, it will apply [equally] to me the same as it does to what is in the world, to one as to another. I will not visualize or pick anyone out in particular. In the world there surely must be a differentiation of persons and callings. A servant cannot be lord. The lord must not be a servant. The student cannot be the master and so forth. But I have nothing to do with that and it doesn't effect me.

But I will administer an order in which we all will be the same. A king and a lord who is born today is over many lands and people; even so, he should receive my Baptism and surrender to me as a poor beggar. Again, this person should hear the gospel, receive preaching or the Sacrament and become holy in the same way as everyone else. So he [Christ] will make everyone alike and make one cake out of all of them. That is a different way than the world runs, which must have and retain its own and lets Christ go and remain alone. But he has not come so that he would administer a worldly kingdom, but rather a heavenly one.

Therefore, he answers the apostle Jude, "It doesn't depend upon what the world is, but rather it stands upon my having said to you that I desire to reveal myself to you and to those that have loved me, not to the one that wears a three tiered crown or scarlet robe[12], not to those who are called noble, mighty, strong, rich, learned, wise, clever and holy, but rather to those who have loved me, God grant it, whether he is called king, prince, pope, bishop, priest, doctor, layman, lord or servant, small or great. In my kingdom all such differences come to an end."

That is the reason that I will not reveal myself to the world. For she is so crazy and foolish that she would teach me how to rule and would be my master. Why (you ask) did he not reveal himself to the high priests in Jerusalem, so that they could give witness to him and establish his teaching? As they said in John 7, "Do the leaders or pharisees believe in him?" As one now also says, "Where do some of the great kings, princes and lords receive the gospel? If Rome,

---

[12]Refers to the office of the pope.

through the pope, cardinals and bishops, or the highly learned men of Paris taught it and it were received by way of the kaiser and kings, then we would also believe in it, etc."

But now Christ says, "I will not do it. I will be untaught and unmastered and they should be my students and they will be happy to say, '*Audiam, quid loquatur Dominus*, I will be glad to hear and learn what he says to me.' So I cannot reveal myself to the world or remain one with her. They should hear and learn from me. They want to be wiser than me and tell me how I should do things." There the egg teaches the chicken and (as Christ says) wisdom must go to school and let the children fashion her rightly as when the pope always wants to teach him [Christ] with his gangs of monks, how he [Christ] should regard their orders and special works and make them holy because of them. But he will also remain unaffected and untaught by them or anyone.

Altb. VII, 114–115: Sermons on the Gospel of St. John Chapters 14–16, 1538; cf. AE 24

I pray Thee, dear Lord Jesus, My heart to keep and train
That I Thy holy temple From youth to age remain.
Turn Thou my tho'ts forever From worldly wisdom's lore;
If I but learn to know Thee, I shall not want for more. Amen. (*TLH* 655: 1)

Thursday

And my Father will love him. John 14:23

That is what we have often heard, that Christ always and with great diligence draws us to the Father against the miserable thoughts that divide Christ from the Father and that hearts imagine, "Even if I already believe in Christ, who knows if the Father is pleased with me?" Therefore, he wants to always lead us to the Father's heart so that we should not worry or fear; so that we have only love for him and that we throw and tear out of our hearts all wrath and terror. For the devil has no other dart by which he can conquer us than that he portrays God as unmerciful and wrathful. Where he can trample a heart with this, no person is can joyfully bear it. So Christ always fights against this and gives us this defense against it, that we should be sure. He, himself, is our surety so that believing in him and being in his love, there is no more wrath in heaven and earth, but rather nothing put pure fatherly love and every goodness; that God smiles at us with all the angels and has us in his eyes as on his dear children. You should desire nothing more than that you bring such a gaze from there. He purely pours it out from heaven without any wrath and terror and it fills you with pure security and joy so that your heart remains only on Christ and regards itself as his.

That is a fine loving preaching. It costs us no harsh labor and no one needs to go on a distant pilgrimage for it, or to run or torment himself with tough works. It costs nothing more, than that we have it already with us, namely, that our heart holds surely upon it with faith, and outwardly we confess it with our mouth, and show this faith and give witness to it through love to our neighbor. Even if you also must suffer the devil's and the world's hate and enmity for it, yet you have here the comfort that you can surely bear these things, and, yes, also ignore it. For what can harm you, even if all the world becomes your great foe, attacks and pursues you? For you know that you have the Lord Christ against it as your friend, and not only him, but also the Father. Through his Son's mouth he has promised and witnessed to you that he should love you and value you for the sake of faith and the confession of Christ. Since you now have this Lord on your side, along with all the angels and saints, what can trouble or scare you in the face of the wrath of the world? And what do they accomplish with their hate and rage against you except that they load themselves with God's unbearable wrath and curse? For they will not be able to bear it, but must eternally be ruined by it when that little hour will come upon them.

Altb. VII, 115: Sermons on the Gospel of St. John Chapters 14–16, 1538; cf. AE 24

Hallelujah! Let praises ring! Unto the Lamb of God we sing,
In whom we are elected. He bo't His Church with His own blood,
He cleansed her in that blessed flood, And as His Bride selected.
Holy, holy Is our union And communion. His befriending
Gives us joy and peace unending. (*TLH* 23: 2)

Friday

And we will come to him and make our dwelling with him.
John 14:23

He would not remain in the same way that "I and the Father have loved him who loved me" up to this time. Rather, "We will come to him and make our dwelling with him." He [who so loved God] would not only be safe before the coming wrath, devil, death, hell and all misfortune, but he should also here on earth have us as a dwelling with him and we would daily be his guests, yes, fellow tenants and comrades at table. You shall experience that but the world will not. For the world is not worthy of this honor and majesty since they will not hear or receive my Word. Yes, they also hate and persecute it. But you, who remain in me and hold my Words, do not be afraid and do not turn because of it, as the world sets itself against me and you, but rather let the Father and me worry about you, for you already have a sure dwelling that is prepared for you by us in heaven. So then if you must suffer in the world (for it will suffer neither you nor me), then you shall also on earth be our castle and dwelling with whom we will remain until the end.

That is called a true rich comfort and a high honor above the peoples. For what can be called a greater honor and majesty than that we poor, miserable people on earth should be the dwelling, pleasure garden or Paradise of the divine majesty, yes, his heavenly kingdom? And what you say and do shall please him and be called spoken and done through him. And whoever does evil or harm to you will have done it to him. Also, he will defend you well in body and soul so that no one will devour you for he has previously devoured him. Comfort is given them so that if a single hair of theirs is crumpled it is then his will and it was done to him before. In short, he will have your actions right and go forth against all devils and the world's ranting and raging. Then both the Father and Christ are no longer God so that we will only be safe in the next life of grace, love and friendship, but also here. What we teach as Christians should be right and what we live is pleasing to God and acceptable. This shall go forth and remain unstoppable. Yes (you say), it seems and looks to me far differently; that the world has the advantage and their actions go forth against the Christians and that God is not with me, but he rather holds with them and dwells with them, as they then could defiantly boast against us, "God dwells here. Here is the church, etc." Yes, you must not look only here on this single part of the present situation, as it now goes and stands before your eyes. Rather, grasp the whole thing and the administration of Christianity before you. For they have previously also hunted Christianity and (as the historians say) murdered seventy thousand Christians in one day so that they thought they would completely exterminate Christianity, but what did they accomplish? It went on anyway and it was attacked even more so that the more they made martyrs and murdered, the greater Christianity became. For we are here at home (says Christ), I and the Father, and we will dwell here, that you should not be attacked nor by being attacked go down to ruin as it happened to Jerusalem and Rome.

Altb. VII, 115–116: Sermons on the Gospel of St. John Chapters 14–16, 1538; cf. AE 24

Then cleansed be every Christian breast And furnished for so great a Guest.
Yea, let us each our hearts prepare For Christ to come and enter there. (*TLH* 63: 2)

Saturday

Do you not know that you are God's temple and the Spirit of God dwells in you? 1 Corinthians 3:16

He wants to say, "One who has life from God, a keeper of the divine Words, a holder of divine commandments shall be our house, castle and dwelling. We are his daily guests and table companions and will dwell with him and stay forever." The world thinks that Christians are already stuck. It lays upon them every martyrdom and persecution, but God the Father, Son and Holy Ghost always stays there and says, "Dear sir, act gently. Let us also have yet a little house or two upon the earth. Do not drive us away so completely. Let us be accepted, since we have created the depths of the earth and all that is upon it. Let those who are worthy also have a little right to their home. If not, then you should flee and take yourself out of the saddle."

But now Moses says something quite different about this. He turns it around and says God is our house, fortress and dwelling, but we are the ones that dwell in him, his guests. For the little word *Moan* means in German a dwelling, as also in Psalm 76, "God is acknowledged in Judah, in Israel his name is glorious, in Salem is his tabernacle and his dwelling in Zion." But he is also careful to say that he would reveal that all of our hope should rest in God and that those saved by God in the world, even if they are persecuted, martyred and harassed and many are murdered, yet not all will be lost and trampled. Rather, they have the divine majesty as a dwelling place and shall be at peace forever.

St. Paul speaks in this way also in Colossians 3, "You are dead and your life is hidden with Christ in God." As if he would say: where Christ hung upon the cross, no one could judge otherwise than that he was finished, especially when he cried, "My God, my God, why have you forsaken me?" Yet his life was hidden in God. For even as he died on the cross and went into hell, yet death could not slay him and hell could not hold him. Rather, he slew death and broke hell asunder and rose again in power from the dead and lives eternally.

Now as Christ's life was hidden in God when he died on the cross, so also is every Christian's life hidden in God. For when Christians are persecuted, bear the cross and die before the eyes of the world, there God yet regards their death as a life and it truly is also a life, Psalm 116, "How precious in God's sight is the death of a Christian!" Now it is valued as nothing but suffering and death.

But when Christ will appear on the last day in his glory, then we will also appear with him in glory. We should not and will not have it better than our dear Lord and master Jesus Christ. We also will not have it any worse. That is our comfort. God the Father will stand by us in all our concerns, having his divine eyes upon us. And when we lie under the cross, he will so clearly and quickly look upon us as he looked upon his own dear Son. In summary, he will be our refuge and asylum, our sanctuary, house, fortress and dwelling.

Altb. VIII, 169–170: Lecture on Psalm 90, 1541

Soul, adorn thyself with gladness, Leave behind all gloom and sadness;
Come into the daylight's splendor, There with joy thy praises render
Unto Him whose grace unbounded Hath this wondrous Supper founded.
High o'er all the heav'ns He reigneth, Yet to dwell with thee He deigneth. (*TLH* 305: 1)

Week of Rogate

Sunday

But turn to the prayer of your servant and to his supplication, Lord, my God, so that you hear the praise and prayer that your servant makes to you today. 1 Kings 8:28

When I should pray and speak with God for myself there are so quickly a hundred thousand hindrances before I get to it. There the devil can throw all kinds of excuses in the way and they block and hinder it on every side so that I retreat and never think of it. Just try it if you haven't experienced it and resolve to earnestly pray and you will surely see how many kinds of thoughts will flood you and draw you away from it so that you cannot rightly begin.

So that we speak only of the greatest and most occupying hindrances that delay and stop us, this is the first; that we think through the devil's insight: "Oh, now you are not yet very gifted to pray. Wait for another half hour or day until you become more gifted or until you have accomplished this or that." Meanwhile the devil is there and leads you away during that half hour so that you don't think any more of it for the whole day. So from one day to another he rushes and hinders you with other thoughts. That is the most common hindrance and a true evil trick and wickedness of the devil (as he often advises me and others). In addition, he finds an advantage in our flesh and blood that even without this [counsel] it is also foul and cold so that we cannot pray in the way we would like to. And even if we begin something, yet soon we flutter off with foreign useless thoughts and because of it lose the prayer.

For another, thoughts like these also naturally surface, "How can you pray to God and speak the 'Our Father?' You are too unworthy and live daily in sins. If you were better, and had gone to confession and to the Sacrament then you would not only desire to pray and be gifted to do so, but you would also be zealous to pray. Then you could hold a steadfast confidence towards God and say from the heart the 'Our Father.' " That is the true difficult hindrance with which the heart must wrestle and reel until it castes the great hindrance away and can begin to walk and call against such feelings of its unworthiness before God. Ask anyone and tell me, how easily a person can dispel such thoughts and say from the heart, "My dear Father in heaven."

In the congregation and among the people it is somewhat easier where we all walk together and say with each other "Father." But going from there it is not so easy when we are alone and each should pray for himself. There our heart speaks against it and the devil drives and fills us with such thoughts, like a live coal, "You are a shameful person and a waste of space. How can you come before God and call him Father?" Therefore, rightly praying is a terrifically difficult matter and an art above all arts, not for the sake of the words or the work of the mouth, but rather, that the heart could be convinced and with complete confidence walk before God and say, "Our Father." For whoever can grasp such confidence in faith even a little is already over the great mountain and has laid the first stone to pray and it follows then as it ought.

In the third place, the still devil comes kicking so that he makes your prayer fruitless through these thoughts, "Friend, what are you praying? Don't you see how quiet it is around you? Do you dare think that God pays attention and hears your prayer?" He leads you into doubt so that you despise your prayer and should beat at the wind so you never experience what prayer is and can do. I have experienced what is at stake and seen it in others, especially in St. Bernard. He exhorted his family very fervently not to go to the church to pray with that kind of doubt and as if it were an adventure to see whether or not God would regard and hear your prayer. For truly it does not please God that you would come before him and say, "Dear Father in heaven," when you do not believe it.

Altb. VII, 217–218: Sermons on the Gospel of St. John, Chapters 14–16, 1538; cf. AE 24

From depths of woe I cry to Thee, Lord, hear me, I implore Thee.
Bend down Thy gracious ear to me, My prayer let come before Thee.
If Thou rememb'rest each misdeed, If each should have its rightful meed,
Who may abide Thy presence? (*TLH* 329: 1)

Monday

The prayer of the pitiful breaks through the clouds and does not let up until it comes through and does not cease until it is beheld in the highest. Sirach 35:21

This also is proper to a battle, that one withstands all devilish ideas and our own thoughts and here you must mightily brace your heart and say, "You miserable devil, if you want that then follow a fool or a witch. If I am not gifted, desirous or devotional enough this hour or day, then in a half hour or eight days I will be much less gifted, therefore lying under such lack of skill, I will meanwhile pray an "Our Father" while I am still so ungifted." So accustom yourself every night to go to bed and fall asleep with the "Our Father" and tomorrow get up out of bed with the same. And this will give you reason, time and place [to pray] before you do something else. Then you come to do this first without considering or thinking how gifted you are or are not, before the devil rushes you and gets you to wait. For it is better prayed now in a state of half-giftedness than later in fullness, and it is only difficult and annoying when you begin to pray, even if you find yourself completely ungifted and resistant to praying.

Also do this when he attacks you and lifts up your unworthiness and tells you to wait until you become better and purer or you will never get around to beginning. For if you were worthy, you would nevermore have to pray. So only quickly begin in the midst of those feelings and get to it smartly and just skip [thinking about] worthiness and unworthiness even if you are stuck in the middle of sins. Yes, what if you even wanted to come out of that sin in that hour, what should you do? Would you for that reason always remain without prayer until you come for absolution? Not on your life. Rather, much better in the middle of sins kneel down and pray from the heart, "Oh dear Father, forgive me and help me out of this." By that you could throw down the devil deeper and hold him eternally there. So must you also in the midst of death and in all misfortune pray and the deeper you are buried, the stronger. And what would it mean if you would not begin until you felt redemption and help? So must the prophet Jonah in the midst of the great fish pray and call out under the hard unbearable consciousness of his sins and in the midst of feeling death and hell as he himself confessed, Jonah 2. And David, even in the true feeling and terror of his sins and unworthiness had prayed his psalms, as the 6th, 51st and 130th.

In the same way also against the third trial, where the devil would make you doubt if your prayer will be heard and he shows you that he [God] is too high and too great for you to boast to the high majesty, that he is your Father and you are his dear child and that your prayer is well pleasing to him, etc., there you must all the more defend your comfort and throw your prayer into God's Word and promise, yes, in his own order and command and say, "Dear Sir, you know that I do not come of myself and of my own presumption before you, for were I to consider these, I could not lift up my eyes before you and would not know how I should begin to pray. But upon this I come, that you yourself have commanded and earnestly summoned me that we should call to you and you have also made a promise. And in addition, you sent your own Son, who taught us what we should pray and he has spoken the Words before me. Therefore, I know that this prayer pleases you. As great as my presumption to call myself your child may seem, yet I must be obedient to you, who would have it so. By this I will not accuse you of lying and because of more sins become even more hardened against you both through despising your command and through not believing in your promise."

Altb. VII, 218: Sermons on the Gospel of St. John, Chapters 14-16, 1538; cf. AE 24

Amen I say, not fearing That God rejects my prayer;
I doubt not he is hearing And granting me His care.
Thus I go on my way And do not look behind me,
But ply the task assigned me; God's help shall be my stay. (TLH 548: 6)

Tuesday

Truly, truly I say to you, when you ask the Father anything in my name he will give it unto you. John 16:23

Seize and hold these Words in your heart. For here you hear that he not only gives the promise but also empowers and enacts it with a two-fold oath and swears it upon the highest. "Believe me. As God lives, I will not lie to you." Now whoever wants to be a Christian should, at this point, already turn a little red in the face and be ashamed of himself before him [Jesus] because he has heard these Words and still his heart has not prayed. Is it not an eternal shame before God and the world, that Christ must swear to us so richly and highly and yet we do not believe it or let ourselves be moved so that because of it we at once began to pray? Yet what would we say before God's judgment and against our own conscience? When we are asked, "Have you also sometimes earnestly and with an undoubting heart prayed to the heavenly Father that his name be hallowed? Didn't you know how earnestly I have commanded it and how richly I have sworn of it also, if you would only pray from your heart?" It is only right (I say) that we ourselves should be shamefaced and yet fear God's terrifying judgment since we so poorly regard both his command and his rich promise and we let it be said to us for nothing. Then it will not help you that you want to be excused by the excuse, "Sure, but I didn't know if I was worthy, or, I didn't feel the desire or gifted enough, or I had to do other business."

Here you say, "How is this promise always true when often he doesn't give what I request? He doesn't even let David be an exception [to this], praying for his son's life, 2 Samuel 12." Answer: I have often said how one should order and present a prayer, so that one not specify in our prayer the measure, the result, the manner, the place or person, but rather leave such things to his command as he knows that he will give it and what is needed by us. For this reason he has also established this order and established three ends in the "Our Father" which must always take precedence, namely that his name be hallowed, his kingdom and his will, and thereafter our daily bread, deliverance from evil and every need, etc. The best part must be called: Thy name, Thy kingdom, etc. When that proceeds, then whatever is included in our needs will surely follow. Therefore, St. John says in 1 John 5, "That is the joy that we have towards him, that as we pray for anything according to his will, he hears us." And St. Paul in Romans 8, "We do not know what we should pray for as is proper, but rather the Spirit himself pleads for us what pleases God."

Now that is certainly his will, as his Word (as the Ten Commandments and the "Our Father") says that he will save you from all evil and not leave you in tribulation. Or he will give you your daily bread, etc. If it were not his will he would not have commanded you to pray, so that the last four petitions (which treat our temporal needs in this life) are surely also his will. Since the three take precedence, they are actually called his. So you have his will complete and clear. He definitely wants us to consider nothing besides what the "Our Father" shows us so you might pray that everything happens according to his will so that it is surely heard. But you must pray according to this pattern so that you not break or overturn this order, or skip the most important parts.

Altb. VII, 219–220: Sermons on the Gospel of St. John, Chapters 14–16, 1538; cf. AE 24

And what Thy Spirit thus hath taught me
To seek from Thee must needs be such a prayer
As Thou wilt grant, through Him who bought me
And raised me up to be Thy child and heir.
In Jesus' name I boldly seek Thy face
And take from Thee, my Father, grace for grace. (*TLH* 21: 6)

Wednesday

And I do not say to you that I will pray the Father for you. For the Father, himself, has loved you because you love me and believe in me because I have come forth from him. John 16:26, 27

This is after the farewell and the good night (about which he had said many Words), as good friends try to comfort each other, nearing a strong new beginning. He cannot leave them because of the great love that he has for the disciples. He must also tack this on in addition, "I do not say (he says) that I will pray for you, but rather you yourself will pray. For he, the Father, himself has loved you, etc." How does this come about? Have we not already, here and previously, always heard that we could not come before God and make any prayer without this mediator who is also sent from the Father and that our prayers must go only through his person and in his name so that it will please God? How then does he say here that he will not pray for them? Surely, as they can do nothing without him and it only would be giving ourselves this honor, right and power just as previously the Turks, Jews, priests and monks both teach and believe [about prayer]. They take this as an affirmation of their own prayers and good works that have been sold to the people. They want to make a command out of this and say, "Has Christ himself not established this when he says it is not necessary that he pray for you, but they themselves should pray?"

Answer: Yes, but one thing stands with it that you also must take with that and keep these two together and not narrow and patch the text, omitting the one and letting the other one stand. For he says, "The Father himself has loved you because you believed me." For he will not so let himself be taken out of the middle so that they should pray without or outside of him. But when we have this mediator in our hearts and believe that he comes from God and does the will of his Father to take away our sins and death, etc., then we can also pray ourselves. Such is an acceptable prayer before God for the sake of this man who stands in the middle between the Father and us. For we already have his prayer, through which he has implored the Father for us, which he has one time made but which yet remains and works in eternity, so that our prayer will also be pleasing to him and heard.

With this faith such a thought is correct, so that I can say, "I know that my heavenly Father heartily wants to hear what I pray. Yes, so far as I have this savior, Christ, in my heart, who has prayed for me, so my prayer is acceptable through his." We so intertwine our prayer in his that eternally he is with every man as the mediator through whom we come to God. Our prayer that we make lives in him and is dressed in him, as St. Paul says that we put on Christ, and everything shall be done in him so that it will be acceptable before God.

No differentiation is possible at all except that it comes forth from him and must go through him so that our prayer is acceptable and he brings us to the inheritance and glory. He makes us like himself in all things and he and our prayer must be one cake just as his life is our life and our members are his members as Paul says in Ephesians 5, "We are members of his body, of his flesh and his bone." He must remind them of this glory to increase their comfort so much even in these last Words that they believe that he is sent also from God's counsel and will. Then they pray being comforted in him and do everything that a Christian should. For this part must not be left out and forgotten else it would be made into nothing but a Turkish or a heathen prayer and worship.

Altb. VII, 226–227: Sermons on the Gospel of St. John, Chapters 14–16, 1538; cf. AE 24

Amen, that is, So shall it be. Confirm our faith and hope in Thee
That we may doubt not, but believe What here we ask we shall receive.
Thus in Thy name and at Thy word We say: Amen. Oh, hear us, Lord! (*TLH* 458: 9)

Thursday

Feast of the Ascension

And the Lord, after he had spoken to them, was taken up into heaven and seated at the right hand of God. Mark 16:19

On this day of the Festival of the Ascension we celebrate. We take care to preach of the article of our Christian faith: "Ascended into heaven", which, as a high article, is completely incomprehensible to human understanding. The more reason dwells on this and thinks of it, the more it seems that it is not true. For human reason cannot grasp it; that a man of flesh and blood has gone up to heaven and become a Lord over all creatures and has equal power with God. Many barely believe such things of God, not to mention of a human being.

Therefore, in matters of faith, which treat the divine nature and will and our salvation, close your eyes and ears and all your senses and only hear and diligently pay attention to what and how the Scriptures speak of it. They plainly wrap us in God's Word. Judge according to it [God's Word] and do not desire to judge and fall upon it with your reason. Else it will definitely happen to us as it does to a person who directly looks upon the sun with open eyes. The more and longer he looks at it, the greater harm he does to his eyes. So it also happens here. The more one wants to ground and judge this and other articles of our faith with reason and investigate it by human wisdom, the more he will be in error and the blinder he becomes.

This we observe in our time among the sects, both sacramentarians and anabaptists and others. Therefore, among them there is neither counsel nor help.

Now whoever wants to know the necessity and power of this article: "Ascended into heaven," regards along with it this passage of the Holy Scripture in which is bound this Article as the Holy Ghost long before established and grounded in Psalm 68:18 with clear and meaningful words: "You have gone into heaven and have taken the prisoners captive and have given gifts to men."

The dear patriarchs and prophets have spoken so surely and confidently of this and other articles of our Christian faith that without any doubt they have believed the same [as we do] even if these were only fulfilled and would be brought into action many years later. Then again, we who know these things and daily confess our faith, that everything is accomplished and completed, and also hear the prophets, apostles and the gospel of Scripture presented daily, also act as though we held it as a lie and hear it in no other way than as if it were just a story and tale. We let it go into one ear and out the other. But the apostles and the believers in the beginning of Christianity have beheld this with great zeal and noted the passages of the holy prophets of the articles of faith with sharp eyes, brought forth and completely explained [in Christ]. See that St. Paul presents this passage from the 68th Psalm in Ephesians 4:8, "You are ascended into heaven," and he describes in great measure the comforting fruit and power of the ascension of Christ.

Erl. 18, 169–170: Sermon on the Fruit and Power of the Ascension, 1527

Since He returned to claim His throne, Great gifts for men obtaining,
My heart shall rest in Him alone, No other rest remaining;
For where my Treasure went before, There all my tho'ts shall ever soar
To still their deepest yearning. (*TLH* 216: 2)

Friday

Therefore he said, "He has ascended on high and has led captivity captive and has given gifts to man." Ephesians 4:8

Since then he has gone up, what is he doing? What is his office? Is he sitting up there on a golden throne? Does he let the angels play before him and court him, or is he idle? No! Listen to what the prophet and Saint Paul say further in verse 8, "He has not only ascended but has also led captivity captive and has given men gifts." There you hear what his office is. He accomplishes two kinds of things. He has captivated captivity and does not stop doing it, but holds it constantly captive; that is one. The other: He has given gifts to man. He still gives them without ceasing until the end of the world and distributes them among his Christians.

But now this is very lovingly and comfortingly spoken, where he says he has captured captivity. The Scriptures often speak in other places in the same way, as in Galatians 2:19, "By the law I have died to the law." And Romans 8:2, "The law of the Spirit that now brings life in Christ Jesus has made me free from the law of sins and death." Or, verse 3, "God sent his Son in the form of sinful flesh and cursed the sins in the flesh through sins." And 2 Corinthians 5:21, "God has made him sin who knew no sin so that we in him would be righteousness that holds before God." So also in Hosea 13:14, "I will free them from sins and save them from death. Death, I will be your death and hell I will be your poison." Or, Luke 11:22, "The stronger one (Christ) overcame the strong one (the devil)." So also here: He has led captivity captive. It doesn't say: He has done away with captivity so that it might after some years come again. He has taken it captive so that it is no longer able to take anyone captive.

What then is the captivity that Christ has taken captive? Some have pressed for the interpretation that Christ has freed the holy patriarchs out of the outer prisons of hell when he went up to heaven. But that is not the thought revealed here by the words themselves which portray to us another kind of captivity that took me and you and all men captive; namely, a spiritual one through which the soul is captivated and is held captive unto eternal death so that were they not saved by the one who went up into heaven, they would be like a thief or murderer sentenced to physical death.

So now this is the captivity that took and held us captivated, the law, sins, death, devil and hell. For there stands the law, pleading and compelling us so that we should be good and "Love God with our whole heart and our neighbors as ourselves." We don't do that and it is impossible for us to do. But since we do not do it, it takes us captive. That is, it accuses us and a judgment falls over us so that we are guilty of eternal death and damnation. For his judgment sounds in Deuteronomy 27:26, "Cursed is everyone who does not fulfill all the Words of this law that he acts according to them." Or, as St. Paul repeats and clarifies in this passage, Galatians 3:10, "Cursed is everyone who does not remain in all that is written in the book of the law, that he do it."

Erl. 18, 173–175: Sermon on the Fruit and Power of the Ascension, 1527

We therefore heartily rejoice And sing His praise with cheerful voice;
He captive led captivity, From bitter death He set us free.
Hallelujah! (*TLH* 223: 4)

Saturday

So says the Lord, the King of Israel and his savior, the Lord of hosts, "I am the first and I am the last, and apart from me there is no God." Isaiah 44:6

Now this verse mightily establishes and powerfully concludes what we teach and believe both of the person of the Lord Christ and also of his kingdom. Namely, first of all that he is at the same time both truly and naturally man and also truly God. He must be a true man, as said above, since the prophet calls him his Lord as he should be born (as it was prophesied of him) of his blood and flesh and upon his throne or house and among his people be a ruler or royal Lord over his people, as he himself would later reveal that he should rule in a physical location and even among the people at Zion. But that he would be truly God will be powerfully made known. Through these words he establishes him as God in all things alike; namely, as the right hand, in the same majesty and might which is above every created thing.

Indeed, it is easy to believe that he is truly a man and if this would be the only thing said of Christ would this be opposed or be regarded as a lie? But that he is not only man, but also at the same time he should be believed as true, eternal, almighty God, there it gets stuck and is different than any other belief on earth. For this is the article of faith that is too high for reason and human wisdom. This article always needs to be preserved and stands to battle against the wise lofty spirits. It is blasphemed and mocked by the Turks, Jews and other high flying masters over God's Word. The Arians and others have masterfully twisted this matter and want to bore a hole in this article with their glosses and explanations. But God's Word will not let itself be shoved aside so with twisting and explaining. It is too clear and too mighty and stands against all that is brought against it by people.

So it stands here upon solid ground. It is powerfully decided: since he speaks in this way, this Lord (the promised Christ, David's Son) sits at God's right hand at the place where no mere man, yes, also no angel dares to sit, namely on God's own throne or seat. So this text doesn't suffer it to be said or to be believed that he is merely a man, or another creature (as in the Arian dream they liked him to be called) under God. For it is firmly forbidden in Scripture, that one should make any creature like God. Also, one should set no other God beside him, as he says in Isaiah 44, "I am the first and the last and apart from or next to me is no God. Whom would you make the same as me?" And the First Commandment suffers no other God next to him, but rather he will alone remain God and Lord over all that is. So since he here and elsewhere places this Christ next to himself, where no one should or can set any one but God, then he must be even the same divine nature and be alike in might, eternal power and majesty. And since he sits at the right hand of God, then he must also be called Lord and prayed to as Lord not only by David and all the kings of earth, but also by all the angels in heaven, Psalm 72. This is what they said to the shepherds in Luke 2. They were not ashamed to call this child in the manger their Lord.

Altb. VII, 331: Lecture on the 110th Psalm, 1539

Ascended to His throne on high, Hid from our sight, yet always nigh,
He rules and reigns at God's right hand And has all pow'r at his command.
Hallelujah! (*TLH* 223: 2)

Week of Exaudi

Sunday

And you will also give witness, for you were with me from the beginning. John 15:27

So first, when you become sure through the Holy Ghost, who will witness to you, then you will also have need to witness of me. For that reason I have chosen you to apostleship. You have heard my Words and doctrine and seen my works and ways and all things that you will preach. But the Holy Ghost must be there first, else you do nothing. For the conscience is too weak because of sins. Yes, there is no sin so small that the conscience could prevail against it even if it were such a small thing as laughing in church. When death approaches, then the conscience is much too weak.

So another must come first and make the exposed, troubled conscience calm so that it bears up [the conscience] as if all the sins lay on the other. It must be just as almighty as the one who promises this so that what was fearing like a smoking leaf is now unafraid before every devil; the conscience that previously couldn't even withstand a laugh is now preserved against every sin. For that is the use and fruit of the Holy Ghost that sins be turned around for the highest and best use.

So Paul boasts to Timothy about his conversion. He had lived in such evil and now held his sins so rejectable that he makes a hymn and sings of them so, "I thank the one that has worked powerfully towards me through Jesus Christ, our Lord, that he has accounted me as righteous and placed me in this office when I previously was a blasphemer and persecutor and a reviler. But his mercy restored me for I have done it without knowing, in unbelief. But the rich grace of our Lord Jesus Christ has come to me even more through faith and love in Christ Jesus. For it is definitely true and a rich saying that Christ Jesus has come into the world to save sinners, among whom I am the greatest. But for this reason his mercy has come to me; as an example to those who will believe in him unto eternal life. But to God, the eternal King, the unsurpassable and invisible, the all-wise, be glory and praise from eternity to eternity. Amen." 1 Timothy 1:12-17. I think that is called singing a little tune which the Holy Ghost accomplishes when he comes into the heart.

Erl. 12, 227–228: Sermon on the Sunday after the Ascension, John 15:26-16:4

They have come from tribulation
And have washed their robes in blood,
Washed them in the blood of Jesus;
Tried they were, and firm they stood.
Mocked, imprisoned, stoned, tormented,
Sawn asunder, slain with sword,
They have conquered death and Satan
By the might of Christ the Lord.

God of God, the One-begotten
Light of Light, Emmanuel,
In whose body, joined together,
All the saints forever dwell,
Pour upon us of Thy fullness
That we may forevermore
God the Father, God the Spirit,
One with Thee on high adore. (*TLH* 471: 3,6)

Monday

They will place you under the ban. But the time is coming when whoever puts you to death will think he is doing God a service. John 16:2

This is truly a wonder. The church reigns over and against all human understanding. Whoever heard of such a thing that this should be the manner through which God wants to submit all the world under Christ, broadcast his Word to all places and bring his church together; especially when so much opposition appears and it goes on so miserably that the dear apostles must lose their heads in shame and that not they with their little bunch but their opponents have the title and are called God's people and church? That should be strong enough to take the erring dream of the disciples out of their hearts of a physical kingdom of Christ. They are not to teach a hope of worldly or temporal wealth, glory, might, peace, but rather think that he must have something else in mind to give them since here he allows them to suffer such shame and death.

This is why he announces these things beforehand so that his Christians are armed against this and know what kind of comfort they will have so that the Holy Ghost then would witness of him against such misery. That is also very necessary. For surely it must be the revelation and working of the Holy Ghost that these things are perceived and understood. Else who could believe that this crucified, cursed and banned Jesus [who is] in his disciples and students should be the true Son of God, the Lord of life and eternal glory?

So now in this text the picture of the kingdom of Christ is presented. In the opposing kingdom of the world he is treated as predicted in the first promise of the gospel where the church had her first beginning. God said to the snake: "I will put enmity between you and the woman and between your seed and her seed. He shall trample your head but you will strike him in the heel." Genesis 3:15. This enmity must always go on in the world and remain in the eternal enmity and eternal strife. So wherever Christ comes with his

294

preaching, he tramples the snake. It then soon begins to rage against him. It strikes and bites him with its poisonous tongue and teeth. This frightens you. But it has won nothing by it. It nevertheless lays under the feet of this seed of the woman who steps on his head and goes forth so long as its poison and wrath is wreaked upon him. Its might becomes nothing so that it can do no more harm.

That is our comfort and victory which we have in Christ. He will preserve his church in spite of and against the devil's wrath and might. But in this we must suffer the kind of strikes and mortal bites of the devil that harm our flesh and blood. It is the most difficult matter that those who want to be and are also called God's children and the Christian Church must see and suffer such things. But we must learn this and get used to it. For Christ himself and all the saints did not have it any better.

This also became hard and sour for our first father, Adam, that he had to learn this passage, "I will put enmity between you, etc." of his own children when his first born son, given him by God, struck his brother to death for the sake of his offering and service to God. Thereafter, the dear fathers Abraham, Isaac, etc., had need to experience it in their own households (in which there was the true church), that one brother persecuted the other (who yet from one father saw, learned and had received one kind of faith, God's Word and God's service). Therefore, it should not make us wonder or feel strange if we also must experience the same thing, not only from the papists from whom we now have been condemned and we should already know what they have in mind against us and we should expect it of them, but also from those who are now among us and also are called "evangelicals" and yet are not rightly formed.

Erl. 12, 239–241: Sermon on the Sunday after the Ascension, John 15:26–16:4

As silver tried by fire is pure From all adulteration,
So thro' God's Word shall men endure Each trial and temptation.
Its light beams brighter thro' the cross, And, purified from human dross,
It shines through every nation. (*TLH* 260: 5)

Tuesday

I praise you, Father, and Lord of heaven and earth that you have hidden this from the wise and the clever and have revealed it to the little ones. Matthew 11:25

See if we must not also do as Christ does here and take the Words from his mouth to pray and thank God that now also his Word is withdrawn from the clever and wise, the pious and holy ones in this world, and he reveals it to the little ones and the sinners. We preach and scream that Christ alone is our blessedness, salvation and satisfaction and that faith alone makes us holy. The wise and holy people counterattack this. The more we give these people the reasons for our preaching and bring the truth into the daylight, the angrier they become. If one confronts them with the judgment of God they ignore it. Their heart is harder than an anvil that doesn't ask about any blows no matter how hard one strikes it.

So this is also what the wisest, most learned and holiest people do. When one of them has grasped a single thought within his heart, he will not let himself be driven from it no matter how one goes about it. So they stay in their heads. But what does Christ do with them here? He lets them go and turns himself from the hardened people to God, his heavenly Father, thanks and praises him and finds enough joy for his revealing it to the little ones. He will not grieve that we should depart from the people. He also doesn't build upon us [who receive it]. Rather, we should look only upon God and trust in him alone. When our God laughs, what fear do we have of man? Why should we ask about the peoples' rage? Do what Christ does. Praise the Father and always preach forth. Who receives it will receive it. It is God's Word. To whom he gives it has it. Those to whom he doesn't give it will have to reckon with him, for he [Christ] is obligated to and guilty of no one.

God will not rush to forsake his ways for the sake of the wise. It is his skill to make something out of nothing, life out of death, righteousness out of sin, honor out of shame, riches out of poverty. And in summary, what is great there before God he will make little.

Since now we know that our God will help those that need it, what will we allow to upset us? Why are we not comforted and happy? For since he wants to have wise men, angels, saints and good ones where will we poor fools and miserable sinners remain? Then God is also there for the proclamation to the heathen. Where fear and disaster are at hand, who can help in such needs? So now God's attribute is that he helps. So it must follow that he helps where there is no help. The wise and clever in this world know nothing of that.

But here the wise and those who understand are those who have his gift. They call upon the Lord. These know that everyone else rules here in order to inherit wealth and goods. Those in faith abandon their own wisdom altogether. They would not depart a hair's girth in divine matters and spiritual concerns. They would not have their affairs cursed and will not be held as unwise before God. These leave behind any thoughts that are counseled out of their own wisdom and in the final evaluation will not be found to be fools, but wise.

Altb. III, 680: Sermon on the Gospel for the 5th Sunday after Epiphany, 1527

All are alike before the Highest; 'Tis easy for our God, we know,
To raise thee up, though low thou liest, To make the rich man poor and low.
True wonders still by Him are wrought Who setteth up and brings to naught. (*TLH* 518: 6)

Wednesday

Yes, Father, for it has become well pleasing before you.
Matthew 11:26

As the Lord would say, "Oh Father, that is the single reason that it pleases you." But what kind of God is so pleased that the people are blinded? Is he still a God who does not desire the death of the sinner? Yes, it is true. But Scripture says in Exodus 33 and Romans 9, "To whom I am gracious, I am gracious and to whom I have mercy, I have mercy." God is not guilty of anything to anyone. Therefore he acts unjustly to no one. He also does good to those who remain hardened. God has the skill to help the poor and does not inquire much after the great and wise [no matter] how much they also rage about this. He lets them remain in their obstinacy. For this reason when you see them raging, ranting and raving, then God has commanded it and say: This also is well pleasing to God, who of pure grace and without any service and without any works has revealed the hidden to the poor, despised little bunch, as Christ also says to his disciples in Luke 12, "Fear not, little flock, for it is our Father's good pleasure to give you the kingdom."

But these are not the little ones who are needy and poor outwardly in their life and walk, or those who are unlearned in the Scriptures. For those people want to remain gross blockheads, learn nothing, and want to present themselves as the unlearned who are the little, poor and silent; as those who were experienced in the Scripture also want to ignore it as if nothing were said in it. Yes, these same prideful haughty louts are the true "wise" ones who inwardly inflate themselves and think much of themselves. They despise others and think they alone know everything. Therefore, God also hides it [His Word] from them and will not reveal this hiddeness to such proud bunglers. So it can also happen that a beggar in a grey gown and long beard can have a more prideful spirit that ten princes in golden gowns.

God sees the true inner humble heart that sees itself as accursed and only turns to God's help out of grace. To these God also reveals his will. But those who want to be clever before God and will not let their matters be accursed, he discards and shows a great might against them so that his small poor little bunch need not fear them.

As he hardens the wise heart, much more can he hinder their fists and all their assaults, for God will not praise their works and their wisdom. He will let them have absolutely no boast. There has never been any saint who could have done a miracle for the sake of some human work that he could accomplish. Rather, in every situation it is written: He has called out to God. He has believed.

Altb. III, 681: Sermon on the Gospel for the 5th Sunday after Epiphany, 1527

My own good works availed me naught,
No merit they attaining;
Free will against God's judgment fought,
Dead to all good remaining.
My fears increased till sheer despair
Left naught but death to be my share;
The pangs of hell I suffered.

But God beheld my wretched state
Before the world's foundation,
And, mindful of His mercies great,
He planned my soul's salvation.
A father's heart He turned to me,
Sought my redemption fervently:
He gave His dearest Treasure. (*TLH* 387: 3,4)

Thursday

All things are given me by the Father. Matthew 11:27

That is a true great boast which Christ makes here. He boasts that he is truly God and a Son of God when he says, "To me all things are given." Here he excludes nothing but, in short, what is now God is under him [that is, subject to him]. Our Father also teaches this. Nothing is excepted here, neither angel nor devil, neither sins nor righteousness, neither death nor life, neither shame nor honor. Everything that one can name is under Christ and must submit to him. So now Christ is seated over everything. All things are his so he must be somewhat higher than a creature or a created thing, else not every creature could be his and lay under his feet.

That is the glory that is the same as God's glory that he gives to this Christ. Therefore, he is the true God and a natural Son of God. For God says so in the prophet Isaiah, chapter 42, "My glory will I not give to another." So now God's glory is nothing other than being over all creatures, giving life, overcoming the devil, treading death and sins under his feet. Those are true divine works that belong to God alone. He has the glory which he alone will retain and no one can share. But the one who shares it must also truly be God. The devil is already a lord of death and sins in the godless and the unbelievers but he cannot make anything alive.

Now Christ has had all things altogether under him from eternity. Yet he has not been a man from eternity. But, at the appointed time, he became a man as promised in the prophets and as revealed through the Holy Ghost for our sakes so that all things are placed under him. For that Word to do me any good then I must know a place where I can find God and all things. So now Christ says to me, "If you want to have all things, then seek it in me," for in Christ are all things and all things are placed under him. Also everything good is placed in him and in him the Godhead physically dwells. Apart from him, you will find nothing good. In the single Christ all believers must become complete and saved and receive everything connected with him.

Altb. III, 682: Sermon on the Gospel for the 5th Sunday after Epiphany, 1527

'Tis the name that whoso preacheth Speaks like music to the ear;
Who in prayer this name beseecheth Sweetest comfort findeth near;
Who its perfect wisdom reacheth Heavenly joy possesseth here. (*TLH* 116: 4)

Friday

No one knows the Son but only the Father; and no one knows the Father but only the Son and those to whom the Son has revealed him. Matthew 11:27

Lord, who would have thought that this despised Christ should be the Son of God? For with these little words, "no one" he excludes all things that are not Christ.

Reason cannot understand that all things should lay under this Christ, and he should yet die on the cross so shamefully and ignominiously. What kind of Lord of life and death is this? It doesn't matter how it appears; as if he could not retain life for himself since he died so shamefully. He snuck into the throat of death so that all the world thought he had been slain and he was done for. Yet he is God's Son. He alone knows the Father and there is no other creature that will reveal him except this Son. To whom the Son does not reveal it to their hearts, no work, service or preparation can help him in eternity. It is only God's attribute and work that he has pity on those in misery and teaches those who do not understand.

The Christian faith and the Christian life remain in the single Word: revealed from God. For where that is not at hand, no heart will ever rightly acknowledge this mystery that has been hidden from the world. But now God has revealed this from eternity to his chosen saints. For he will have it found, else it would still be hidden before everyone and remain a true mystery. What here will the freemen, yes, even the imprisoned servant say or do in addition for his good? Who will come to this light and mystery by his reason or his will?

When it is hidden from him by the almighty, strong, God, then no preparation or good work will do him any good. No creature can come to this confession unless only Christ reveals it to your heart. There all reason, every skill and desire of reason, or the free will of dreams, goes to the bottom and is good for nothing before God. Christ alone must do it and give it.

Altb. III, 682: Sermon on the Gospel for the 5th Sunday after Epiphany, 1527

That life of truth, those deeds of love That death of pain mid hate and scorn
These all are past, and now above He reigns our King, once crowned with thorn.
Lift up your heads, ye heav'nly gates; So sang His hosts, unheard by men;
Lift up your heads, for you He waits. We lift them up. Amen, Amen. (*TLH* 132: 3)

Saturday

Come unto me all who are weary and heavy laden and I will give you life. Matthew 11:28

Oh, what a strange summons that is! Why doesn't he call the strong, the rich, the healthy, the learned, kings, princes and lords? For no other reason than that it pleases him. Are you now battling your disbelief, hunger, poverty, shame or other afflictions? Where else will you run? Christ has already said he has all things in his hand. Now he calls you miserable people to himself. He promises here that since he can do it, so also he gladly does it. Phooey to your great sins. It is still shameful and sin that they should shine on us where he lifts above us sweet, fatherly, comforting Words. Yet we gape elsewhere, where there is nothing permanent or good. Everything good is only looked for in Christ, for in him God has invested to overflowing and hidden every treasure of wisdom and every good thing. We should run as on pins and needles after such a kind helper who wants to enliven us and calls to himself only the weak, troubled, poor, sad and ladened people.

But what is the reason that we let these Words die in the wind and do not seek his help and do not run only to him who has all things in his hand and wants to give plenty of every good thing? This is the reason: The person of Christ is too poor. No one believes, no one trusts in him that he desires to and will give. Our accursed unbelief does not give him this honor that it believe that he can do it. Therefore, we also receive nothing and it serves us right that we remain poor bunglers both in body and soul. God has bodily placed everything good, also the very Godhead, in this Christ, as said. So whoever needs something be it for body or soul, whoever comes to him finds it much richer by him than we could ask or think. Whoever despises this Christ and wants to seek the forgiveness of sins or a good conscience, eternal life, health, righteousness, salvation or this thing or that in the cloister, at Rome, in the holy sepulcher or anywhere else in his works, such a person calls Christ a liar as a useless savior and blasphemes his blood, death and resurrection. For such a person it is also right that there is no help here or there. For he sets Christ out of the way through whom alone we can and should come to the Father and to everything good.

So for this unthankfulness it would be right that God lets us scratch and claw day and night in the sweat of our face and yet for nothing. So the earthly kingdom brings nothing but pure thorns and thistles. God will definitely do this not only in bodily food, but also concerning the Word. Let everyone only look to themselves. We remain so wild and failing when we should give a few dollars for the sake of God into the general offering or else bring a needy person to the house. It isn't done from the heart, much less from the treasure chest. What is the reason? This is it: Money is our idol because the heart constantly is set upon it. Were the eternal, true, natural God in us through faith, oh, how he would be a bake oven for us of Christian love burning within us! If only we believed that the gentle, kind, rich, mighty Christ not only can help us in all our concerns from which we call to him, as he said above: "All things are given to me by my Father," but that he would also gladly give and share with us gently and richly, it would soon be better for us.

Altb. III, 681: Sermon on the Gospel for the 5th Sunday after Epiphany, 1527

Be of good cheer; your cause belongs To Him who can avenge your wrongs;
Leave it to Him, our Lord. Tho' hidden yet from mortal eyes,
His Gideon shall for you arise,   Uphold you and His Word. (*TLH* 263: 2)

Week of the Feast of Pentecost

Sunday

And he lit upon each of them and they were all full of the Holy Ghost. Acts 2:3,4

So you hear: He (the Holy Ghost) comes here and fills the disciples who previously sat in sorrow and fear. He makes their tongues fiery and cloven. He inflames them so that they become bold and free by Christ to preach and to fear nothing. There you see clearly that it is not his office to write books or to make laws. Rather, he is the kind of Spirit that writes in the heart and creates a new courage that the person becomes joyful before God. Love has overcome him. Thereafter he serves the people with a joyful heart.

But how does he [the Holy Ghost] do it and what is the tool that he uses to change the heart and make it new? He does it by proclaiming and preaching of the Lord Jesus Christ, as Christ himself says in John 15:26, "When the Comforter comes, which I will send you from the Father, he will witness of me." Now we have often heard that the gospel as God allows it to be preached in the world and announced to everyone is that since no one can become good through the law, but only becomes worse, therefore he has sent down his dear Son that he die and shed his blood for our sins which we could not be rid of through our powers and works.

But those who receive such preaching now have heard it so that it also is believed. Therefore, God also gives the Holy Ghost who impresses such preaching into the heart so that they would have it therein and live according to it. For it is so definitely sure. Christ has done it all. He has taken away sins and overcome everything so that through him we should be lords over all things. There the treasure lies in one heap. But he is not shared and applied over all by that. Therefore, if we should have him, then the Holy Ghost must come, who would give it into our hearts so that we believe and speak, "I am also one who shall have such favor." So then through the gospel this grace is offered and also declared to everyone who hears it, as he says in Matthew 11:28, "Come to me all who are heavy laden . . ."

Now when we believe that God has helped us and given us such a great treasure, then it never fails that the human heart must become desirous towards God and be encouraged and say, "Dear Father, if it is your will that you reveal to me this great love and faithfulness which is too great to measure, then I will also gladly have you from the heart and happily and gladly do what pleases you."

Then the heart never looks at God with envious eyes and doesn't imagine that God will throw him into hell as previously, before the Holy Ghost came, when it experienced no goodness, no love or faithfulness but only the wrath and displeasure of God. But now the Holy Ghost impresses these things upon the heart, that God is so kind and gracious to him that it will be joyous and unafraid. Then it does and suffers what it has to and suffers for the sake of God.

So you should learn to know the Holy Ghost so that you know where he is given and what his office is. Namely, that he gives us the treasure, Christ, and everything that he has and is through the gospel he proclaims. He applies it to us and gives it into your heart so that he is your own. Now when he hands it out and you experience such things in your heart it follows that one must say: "Is this what it means that my previous works have added nothing to help me, but the Holy Ghost must do it; what will I do with my works and rules?" So every human work and law becomes useless, and even the law of Moses. For the Holy Ghost teaches better than him, than every book, for he understands the Scriptures better than all of them. They only get stuck in circles teaching the law.

Erl. 8, 308–309: Sermon on the First Day of Pentecost, Acts 2:1–13

Thou didst come that fire to kindle; Fain would we Thy torches prove,
Far and wide Thy beacons lighting With th' undying spark of love.
Only feed our flame, we pray Thee, With Thy breathings from above. (*TLH* 641: 5)

Monday

God has so loved the world that he gave his only begotten Son so that all who believe in him will not perish, but have eternal life. John 3:16

Here let us see what rich comforting Words these are that will offer and give us this great excellent work of God and his unspeakable treasure, presented to those who are in every circumstance and manner of life. First, the person of that gift is not a man, kaiser or king and also not an angel. Rather he is the high majesty, God himself, next to whom all people, no matter how rich, mighty and great, are nothing but straw and ashes. And you can say more of him. He is unassailable, immeasurable and uncreated.

He is no longer one who drives us, who only demands things from us and, as Moses calls him in Deuteronomy 4:24, "a consuming and devouring fire." Rather he is a rich, gushing eternally born source of grace and gifts. He could rightly be called the true die-hard giver. Compared to him what are all the kaisers and kings with their gifts, gods, silver, land and people? Here the heart should swell and grow with desire, dreams and anticipation of what this Lord and God will still give. For his giving must easily be somewhat greater and more excellent as is appropriate for this high majesty and kind Lord. Easily, everything that is in heaven and on earth must become small and poor compared to such a giver and his gifts.

Another thing: What is the reason for his giving and what moves him to do it? That is nothing but pure inexpressible love. For he does not give out of guilt or duty or because someone had asked and begged him. Rather, his own goodness moved him as a Lord who gladly gives. It is his desire and joy to give, purely for that [reason] without our seeking it. And as there is no greater giver than God, so there is also no greater virtue in God or man than love. For whatever one has love for, there he places and spends everything, also life and limb. So compared to this, patience, humility and other virtues are nothing, or else all of them complete this [love] and are included [in it]. For the one I love, I will not easily be angry with, nor treat him unjustly nor mock him nor be insufferable. Rather I am ready to serve, counsel and help him where ever I see that he needs me. In summary, he has me completely with body, goods and in every need.

Therefore, the heart should evermore grow and become great against every sorrow, since such a wealth of unfounded love of God is placed before us. That love flows from a fatherly heart and springs here from the highest virtue, that is the spring of all good. This also makes the gift precious and valuable. As it is praised in the old saying, one considers even a poor gift as precious and says, "It comes from a beloved hand." So where there is love and friendship one doesn't consider the gift as much as the heart, even if it brings a great burden as a gift. If God were to give me only one eye, hand or foot and I knew that he did it out of fatherly love, then it should be to me much dearer than many a thousand worlds. As when he gives us the dear Baptism, his Word, Absolution, Sacrament; that should be to us our daily paradise and heavenly kingdom; not for the sake of the appearance of these gifts, which is not much before the world, but rather for the sake of the great love from which he gives them.

Erl. 12, 325-326: Second Sermon on Pentecost Monday, John 3:16-21

Thou, mighty Father, in Thy Son Didst love me ere Thou hadst begun
This ancient world's foundation. Thy Son hath made a friend of me,
And when in spirit Him I see, I joy in tribulation.
What bliss Is this! He that liveth To me giveth Life forever;
Nothing me from Him can sever. (*TLH* 343: 5)

Tuesday

*God has so loved the world that he gave his only begotten
Son so that all who believe in him will not perish, but have
eternal life. John 3:16*

Thirdly, consider the gift itself, for doubtless it must be
something precious and unspeakably great that this rich giver gives
to us from his hearty, great love. Now what does he give? Not a
great king's wealth, not one or more worlds full of gold or silver,
not heaven and earth with all that is in them, not all of creation, but
rather his Son, who is as great as he himself. That is, an eternal
ungraspable present, just as the giver and his love are ungraspable.
That is the fount and source of all grace, goodness and mercy, yes,
the seat and source of eternal wealth and the treasure of God. That
is a love not in word but with deed and made known in the highest
measure with the most precious goods and work that God himself has
and is capable of.

What more will or can he give and do? For since he gives the
Son what did he retain that he did not give? Yes, he gives himself by
it, whole and complete, as Paul says in Romans 8:32, "So if he has
not spared his only born Son how should he not have given
everything with him?" It is easy to see that everything must be given
with this one who is his beloved, only begotten Son, the heir and
Lord of all creation. And all of creation is put under us, angels,
devils, death, life, heaven and earth, sins, righteousness, past and
future, as St. Paul says in 1 Corinthians 3:22,23, "Everything is
yours. But you are Christ's. But Christ is God's." For in this Son it
is all and all.

Fourthly, how and in what manner is the Son given? There look
at what he does and suffers. For our sakes he became a man, under
the law, that is, under God's wrath (for the sake of our sins) and put
under death, and the most shameful of deaths, lifted on the wood and
hung in the air, damned, as Christ said shortly before. He took upon
himself the whole ranting and raging of hell and had to fight it. That
is called giving in the highest way. Yet in that way he trampled the
same devil, sins, death and hell under his feet and ruled through his
resurrection and ascension. He gives all this to us for our own so that
we should have both him and everything that he has done. But all
that is not so he should reckon that gift to be a loan or wages. He
will not loan, lend and be repaid. Rather, it should be called freely
given and a gift of pure gentle grace. For here the receiver neither
can nor should do anything more than open his hand and receive it;

as it is given him from God and as he already needs it, he receives it with love and thanks.

In the fifth place, the one that receives this is also portrayed. It is named in one word: the world. That is first a wondrous strange love and giving. For here is a completely foreign counterpart. That which is loved is contrary to the one who is loving. How does this love of God harmonize with the world and what does he find here that he should pour himself out so completely to her? If it would be said that he had loved the angels that would still be a glorious noble creature that is worth loving. But what is here in the world is something else; a great heap of the kind of people who do not fear, trust, or love God. They do not thank or praise him. They misuse all of creation, blaspheme his name, despise his Word. They are also disobedient, murderers, adulterers, thieves and knaves, liars, gossipers, full of lies and every evil virtue. In short, they trample every command and in every matter they are contrary and obstinate. They cling to God's enemy, the miserable devil.

See this tender sweet fruit of the beautiful beloved bride and daughter [that is, the church] that he gives his dear Son along with everything. He would have more than enough reason, when he hears the world call, to demolish it in a second with his thunder and lightening into a heap of powder, and throw it to the bottom of hell. For the word "world" sounds immeasurably shameful before God and it is wonderfully strange to have them placed together in a sentence. God loves the world—two such highly contrary things. Just as one might say, "God has loved death and hell, and he is a friend of his bitter eternal foe, the damned devil."

Erl. 12, 326–328: Second Sermon on Pentecost Monday, John 3:16-21

But God beheld my wretched state Before the world's foundation,
And, mindful of His mercies great, He planned my soul's salvation.
A father's heart He turned to me, Sought my redemption fervently:
He gave His dearest Treasure. (*TLH* 387: 4)

Wednesday

So that all who believe in him will not perish, but have eternal life. John 3:16

Now what is the way by which one grasps this treasure and gift? What is the bag or the purse in which one should lay it? It is only faith, as Christ says here, "So that all who believe in him will not perish . . ." Faith holds out open hands and opens the sack and lets him do only good. For as God, the giver, bestows such things through his love, so we are the receivers through faith which does nothing but receives the gift. So it is not our doing and cannot be earned through our works. It is already bestowed and given there. Only, "that you open your mouth, or better your heart, and hold still and let yourself be filled." Psalm 81:10. That cannot happen through anything apart from your believing these Words. As you hear, so he here calls forth faith and this treasure becomes completely your own.

And here you also see what faith is and what it is called. Namely, a plain, empty thought of Christ, that he is born of the virgin, suffered, crucified, resurrected, gone up to heaven. But such a heart is resolved and grasps the Son of God, as the Words say, and holds it as sure that God gave his only begotten Son for us and has so loved us that we will not be lost for his sake, but will have eternal life.

Therefore, he also says specifically, "All who believe in him." So it is the kind of believer that does not look according to his own works and also not according to the strength or worthiness of his faith, what kind of *qualitas*, or that it is implanted or some poured-in virtue laying in his heart as the blind sophists dream and fantasize about it. Rather, he clings to Christ outside of himself and is certain of him as given for his own good; that he is loved by God for his sake and not for the sake of his own work, worthiness or service. For all that is not yet the treasure given from God. One should believe on Christ, God's Son.

Faith itself would have no use apart from the present or gift. Then it would be nothing but a poor empty vessel. Yet look upon [that vessel of faith] and find comfort in what it grasps and holds. Only for the sake of that, one's faith is a valuable thing because one can say, "Faith might be a poor little monstrance or tabernacle[13] but in it lies such a noble gem, pearl or emerald that heaven and earth cannot behold it."

So here we learn from Scripture of faith that we only become righteous and please God through faith, since faith is the only thing that grasps and beholds this treasure, the Son of God.

Erl. 12, 332–334: Second Sermon on Pentecost Monday, John 3:16-21

We now implore God the Holy Ghost For the true faith, which we need the most, That in our last moments He may befriend us And, as homeward we journey, attend us. Lord, have mercy! (*TLH* 231: 1)

---

[13]Both "monstrance" and "tabernacle" refer to the container on the altar which houses sacramental bread and is reverenced for that which it contains in Catholic piety.

Thursday

For God has not sent his Son into the world to judge the world but that the world through him be saved. John 3:17

You hear loud and clear what God's will and thought is about the world, that is, his will concerning even those who have sin and for that reason are already under the judgment and verdict of damnation. With this he takes out of the way everything that would terrify us for the sake of sins. For he says sharply and clearly that Christ was sent and established his kingdom not so that he should judge and condemn. For such judgment and verdict is there already through the law, over all people, since they all are born in sin, so that they are already sentenced to death and to the hangman on a rope and they never fail to be punished by the sword. There comes Christ in the middle of it by God's command. He tells the judge and bailiff to stop and makes those who are judged redeemed and alive. That is the reason that he comes, to help the world, which he has already condemned. These words also show this when he says, "that the world might be saved." For with this he clearly explains that the world must be condemned, otherwise why would they need to be saved?

But that was in the time of the Jews and it is still an unheeded preaching. For in no way could they accept that they were in the position that necessitated Christ's coming to save them, who were lost and condemned. Rather, they hoped for the kind of Christ who would praise, value and honor them for the sake of their laws and holiness, just as they also opposed him in John 8:33 where he says how the Son of God must make them free: "We are Abraham's children and have never been servants of anyone." As if they would say, "How can you say you were sent to bring us salvation? We certainly are not condemned people as the heathen are."

But now we hear that Christ was sent to make these same people saved who are judged and condemned. By this we should know that he has come for our sakes, who acknowledge and experience these things. He wants to save us. For there must still be a few who become saved so that he has not come for nothing. That could be no one else but those who are oppressed and terrified by their misery and condemnation. To them this kind Word is said: "For God so loved the world . . ." That is, even those who feel no love but rather pure wrath and damnation. God has sent his Son not to judge but to save those that are already judged. For it is preached unheeded to the others. Whoever does

not believe that he is a sinner and condemned will believe much
less that he is saved through Christ.

Erl. 12, 338–339: Second Sermon on Pentecost Monday, John 3:16-21

He blotted out with His own blood The judgment that against us stood;
He full atonement for us made, And all our debt He fully paid. (*TLH* 163: 2)

Friday

*I am the gate. Anyone who enters by me shall be saved and
will come in and go out and find pasture. John 10:9*

When the gate is opened by the shepherd and he enters it, the
sheep have their comfort and help. As Christ says at the end of this
gospel; "I have come that you have life and have it abundantly." So
as Christ himself rules, leads, goes, pastures and preserves, works
in them through his Word and the power of the Holy Ghost so that
they daily increase, are richer in understanding, stronger in faith,
comfort, patience, victory in suffering, etc., also they are given good
fruits from him, more teaching, service and help. So in Christianity,
the office or the work of the shepherd continuously carries on where
Christ gathers them to himself, and does everything with them; yet
still through his voice, that is, the external Word and preaching.

Therefore, he also calls himself the gate through which the sheep go
in and go out. So just as he himself is the shepherd, so also the preaching
through which he comes and through which he is known and also the
faith in our hearts through which his power and work is experienced is
nothing else but Christ. And so he dwells and works in us and we are
completely found in him, in our life and works. So everyone goes to him
out of and through faith. We are pleasing to God only for his sake and
we are comforted by and rely on nothing but that.

As he has said of his office, which he conducts through his
Word, so he also says of his lambs, who remain in his kingdom, that
when the gate is opened by him, they immediately hear his voice and
learn to know it. For this is the comforting joyful voice through
which they are saved from terror and fear. They come into freedom
for they can expect of God in Christ every grace and comfort. And
once they have grasped the shepherd, they hold only to him with all
of their confidence and listen to no other doctrine. For they have, as
is characteristic of a lamb, very sensitive ears and they quickly learn
to recognize the voice of their shepherd and to distinguish it from
every other voice so that they remain unmoved by all the others that
claim to be shepherds.

For they have the experience of their own conscience and the witness of the Holy Ghost in their hearts so that no other doctrine or Word can bring comfort or bring true confidence as the calling of God to his people, than this shepherd, Christ. Therefore, be moved by this voice without wavering and doubt. Do not gape and look at what others teach and do, what the world receives or the Councils decide. Rather, even if there were nobody on earth that held onto him with you, yet nevertheless you would be sure of the true voice of your shepherd.

Erl. 12, 360–362: Second Sermon on Pentecost Monday, John 3:16-21

He leads me to the place
Where heav'nly pasture grows,
Where living waters gently pass
And full salvation flows.

If e'er I go astray,
He doth my soul reclaim
And guides me in His own right way
For His most holy name. (*TLH* 426: 2–3)

Saturday

And when he has released his sheep he goes ahead of them and the sheep follow after him, for they know his voice. John 10:4

This going out, as I have touched on above, is Christian freedom. Christians are now free and no longer confined and imprisoned as before under the terrible compulsion and fear of the law and divine judgment. Rather, under Christ's sweet kingdom of grace they are happily pastured and fed, as St. Paul says of it in Romans 6:14, "You are no longer under the law, but under grace," or in Galatians 3:25, "Now that faith has come, we are no longer under the taskmaster."

This is not the kind of freedom where the sheep now can run from their shepherd without protection or protector into error as they would do of themselves. Nor can a Christian do everything that his flesh desires. Rather, now they are protected from the terror and fear of the wolf, the thief and the murderer. They go under their dear shepherd and follow with desire and love as he leads and drives them since they know that he goes ahead of them and rules kindly so that they can no longer become guilty or condemned by the law even if they also have not completely fulfilled the law due to the weakness of their flesh.

So since the Lord and God's Son, the Shepherd, is there, who has called his sheep under his grace, shelter and protection, then whoever would accuse or condemn his lamb must first do it to Christ himself; as St. Paul says wonderfully and defiantly in Romans 8:1,

"There is no condemnation for those who are in Christ Jesus." Or in verses 33 and 34, "Who will accuse the elect of God? God is here, who makes you just. Who will condemn you? Christ is here, who has died and is arisen, who sits at the right hand of God and goes ahead of us."

I say that is the freedom of the conscience from the condemnation of the law, which has no claim on us since we are in Christ. For the outward bodily life does not belong here [under such freedom], but it has its external rule and law that doesn't spoil the spiritual nature [of freedom] in Christ.

Erl. 12, 363-364: Second Sermon for Pentecost Tuesday, John 10:1-11

Lord, Thou Fount of joy forever, Thou art mine, I am Thine,
No one can us sever. I am Thine, because Thou gavest
Life and blood For my good, By thy death me savest. (*ELHB* 510: 11)

Week of Holy Trinity

Sunday

For from him and through him and in him are all things.
To him be glory forever! Romans 11:36

What we wish to highly praise (he wants to say) is that everything that has being and, of course, also all of our wisdom and abilities do not come from ourselves. These have their source in him [God], are preserved by him and must persist in him, as he says in Acts 17:28, "In him we live and have our being," and also in Psalm 100:3, "He has made us and not we ourselves." That is why we are and why we can act. Thus we live, have peace and safety, and in short, we encounter good and evil. That doesn't happen by chance and accident, but everything is through his divine counsel and pleasure. For he is concerned for us and reigns. He gives good things. He helps and protects us in our needs as his people and his sheep.

But when he says "everything is from him, through him, and in him," it is most simply saying this: Beginning, middle and end are all God's. All creatures have their source from him and also their increase; how big, long, high and wide they will grow. It is (when we speak most crudely of it) just as it is in the beginning of every little kernel of corn. Out of the dead seed in the earth a root grows, after which the plant grows out of the seed and becomes a blade and a little leaf, ear and kernel. Finally it is established and stands. It has its three parts [beginning, middle and end], which it should have. So all creatures have their beginning, middle and end so long as they are and remain. When all is done, every creature is nothing more [than this]. If it already has begun and grows, yet hasn't reached its end so that it is complete, that doesn't mean the end won't come. In summary: It must all belong to God. So where he doesn't begin, nothing can be or become. When he stops, then nothing can stand. For he has not made the world in the way a carpenter builds a house, who afterwards leaves it and lets it stand as it may. Rather God remains with it and preserves everything as he has made it. Otherwise it could neither stand nor remain.

But St. Paul does not say this crudely (as other places): "From him are all things," but he adds yet two things to it. He makes a trio, and yet brings all three parts together again and resolves them into one, when he says: "To him be glory," etc. By this, without doubt, he wishes to show this article of the three distinct persons of the divine being, even if he does not express it with names, as here he has no need to. The old teachers also considered this passage a witness of the Holy Trinity. Namely, that all things were made by God the Father through the Son and are preserved in the Holy Ghost through God's favor; as also Saint Paul says carefully in 1 Corinthians 8:6, "We have only one God, the Father, from whom are all things; and one Lord, Jesus Christ, through whom are all things," etc. And of the Holy Ghost in Genesis 1:31, "God saw all of his work, that it was very good."

So Scripture teaches us that already the work of the creation of all creatures belongs to the one God or the whole Godhead that was yet a single nature just as also there were three distinct persons. So one rightly says that everything comes to us, stands and remains from the Father, as from the first person, through the Son, who is from the Father, and in the Holy Ghost, who proceeds from the Father and the Son. Yet all three remain in one indivisible Godhead.

But how and in what sort of manner such distinction of the Persons in the Divine Nature occurred from eternity, that we must and will leave without [proposing] a reason [for it]. Just as we cannot find a reason in our coarse understanding of God's creation. No creature is so clever that he could understand in himself his own three parts: beginning, middle and end. From these he can differentiate himself, yet these are so dependent on each other that one cannot divide them from one another as an observer. Who has been able to observe or say how it happens that little leaves grow from a tree, or a little kernel of corn becomes a root, and a cherry from out of a blossom grows through wood and pit, or else how the human body and members grow and come to be; or what is the sight of the eye; how it happens that the tongue makes so many kinds of different sounds and words, which go indivisibly into so many ears and hearts? Much less, [do we observe] the inward powers of the soul with its thoughts, reasoning and meditations, etc. So what is it, if we dare to dissect and grasp God's eternal invisible nature with understanding?

Erl. 9, 18–20: Sermon on Holy Trinity, Romans 11:33–36

Holy God, we praise Thy name; Lord of all, we bow before Thee.
All on earth Thy scepter claim, All in heav'n above adore Thee.
Infinite Thy vast domain, Everlasting is Thy reign. (*TLH* 250: 1)

Monday

Jesus said to him, "Am I with you so long, and you do not know me? Philip, whoever sees me sees the Father. Why do you then say to me, 'Show us the Father.'?" John 14:9

Here some people get concerned. Do they call on the person of the Father, or the divine being when they pray: "Our Father?" It is no wonder that a person might take on wondering thoughts and not grasp this article so that sometimes some might think they will err or use the wrong words. But when the basis of faith remains intact, such a splinter, chip, or blade of straw causes no harm. But the ground of faith (as you've heard) is that you believe that there are three persons in the single Godhead and each individual person is itself alone completely God; that the persons are not confused, the nature not divided, but that the persons be distinguished and the unity of the nature remain. For that is what the angels in eternity cannot see and marvel over enough to satisfy them (as St. Paul says), and they are eternally saved by that. If they would bring their seeing it to an end, then their blessedness would also run out and end. So also we want to see this and through it be eternally blessed, as the Lord says in John 17, "This is eternal life, that they know you, the only true God, and Jesus Christ, whom you have sent." In this, faith must throw itself onto the Word. Reason can do nothing here but say that it is impossible and contradictory that three persons are each completely God, and yet there can be no more than a single God and that only the Son is a man. But whoever has the Father and the Son, to him the Holy Ghost will also be acknowledged from the Father and the Son.

So you have heard above that the Father is our complete God and Father, the Son is our complete God and Father, the Holy Ghost is our complete God and Father; and yet there is no more than one God, our Father. So the nature is undivided. Therefore, whichever person you call, you have called upon the true and only God in three persons, since each individual person himself is completely God. Here you can not err or fail. For Jesus Christ is no other God, or Father, or Creator than is the Father and the Holy Ghost, even if he is another person. Even so is also the Father and Holy Ghost.

Therefore, is it not only false but also impossible and futile if you want to call "Father" the person of the Father as a distinct being, and not at the same time call on the Son and the Holy Ghost with the Father? For that is called dividing the divine nature and cutting off the Son and Holy Ghost. That cannot be. Then following such a manner of the personal Fatherhood, the Father no longer would have the one Son, and the Son no longer would have the one Father. Such a Father he is not to the Son, and his Son is not so [treated]. Rather, the one Son is from his Father in eternity as Psalm 2 says, "The Lord said to me: You are my Son, today I have begotten you." Though you are thirty, forty, fifty years behind your parent, as long ago as you are made and baptized, you are a temporal son of all three persons of God: *quia opera trinitatis ad extra sunt indivisa; sic cultus trinitatis ad extra est indivisus*; what God works towards his creatures is done by all three persons without division.

So there is a single divine nature of all three persons, and what we, or creation, does to a single person, we do that towards the single God and all three persons without division. For he is to us a single God, and in himself three distinct persons; as the Lord Christ himself says in John 14, "Philip, whoever sees me sees the Father. How do you say then, 'Show us the Father.'? Do you not believe that I am in the Father and the Father in me?"

Erl. 37, 53–55: On the Last Words of David, 2 Samuel 23:1–7, 1545

Holy Father, holy Son, Holy Spirit, three we name Thee;
Though in essence only one, Undivided God we claim Thee,
And, adoring bend the knee While we own the mystery. (*TLH* 250: 4)

Tuesday

Jesus answered and said to him, "Verily, verily, I say to you that unless a person is born again, he cannot see the kingdom of God." John 3:3

What else is said in these words but this: You do many good works and think that you are good and innocent so that you must please God. But I say to you that before God all of that is lost and cursed, whatever you have done or lived, or what you can yet live and do; and not only your work, but also your heart and whole nature, that is, everything that you are and desire, it must all be given up. The tree with its root, along with the fruits, must all be thrown away and utterly burned, and a new tree made.

So this first passage of this preaching of Christ to Nicodemus is nothing else but a true sharp preaching of repentance in which Christ as a true preacher warns him that he misunderstands and is far from the kingdom of God. So the doors of heaven are shut against him and Christ refuses him, yes, he curses him and gives him over to the devil. For he, as he now lives and can live, could never come to the kingdom of God, but must be lost in the things of the devil, [and must] remain under death and the hellish power. Through this [curse] Christ would bring him to knowledge, to a true understanding and life before God. So this kind of preaching of repentance is also especially necessary to people who are like Nicodemus, so that those who go about in their works righteousness and are blameless before the world can also become holy and righteous before God.

So Christ always begins his preaching of the gospel with this part. He reveals and teaches first what they cannot understand or know from the law; that all people, as they are and live by nature, are cursed and under sins, as also St. Paul advised and rightly showed in the beginning of the Epistle to the Romans. This is also first established with finality in this passage. Man by his nature and according to all his abilities cannot fulfill the law, even if he understands himself to have done so. And it is not called keeping the law when he outwardly does works according to human might. For the law cannot help people to become good before God, nor save from sins and eternal wrath.

For if such abilities were in mankind and in his nature through the law, these matters would be moot. Then he [Christ] would not be able to say, as he says here in general of all mankind, "Unless a person is born again, he cannot see the kingdom of God." This says so well that in this old nature, which mankind has, no matter how exalted it may rise, having wonderful understanding, wisdom, and virtue, it is not able to come out of sins' and death's power, nor please God. Yes, it cannot even see or know how it can come to God's kingdom. Therefore, he must just become a completely different person, that is, the whole person must become another person with a new understanding, thoughts, reasoning and heart.

By this you see, as with a mighty thunderclap, that all doctrine and everyone's bragging which teaches or attempts to become righteous through any powers or works of the human nature, or even any of these same things that sit next to faith and say that they also must do something in addition [to faith] are all put away. For in this passage you hear clearly that the man must be born or become something different before he sees God's kingdom and does something that pleases God. Now no works can accomplish a human birth. Should a person do anything, he must previously have been born. But here a new birth is made such that the old birth's works and deeds will not avail or help, since that is already completely thrown away and cursed.

Erl. 12, 399–401: Second Sermon on Trinity Sunday, John 3:1-15

Chief of sinners though I be, Christ is All in all to me;
All my wants to Him are known, All my sorrows are His own.
Safe with Him from earthly strife, He sustains the hidden life. (*TLH* 342: 4)

Wednesday

Jesus answered, "Verily, verily, I say to you, unless one is born of water and the Spirit he cannot come into the kingdom of God." John 3:6

He speaks here of the office which John the Baptizer had begun as the forerunner and servant of Christ which the pharisees and Nicodemus had previously known and seen. He would advise him concerning this office and thereby have the preaching and Baptism of John established so that this kind of office should go on and prosper as God also had ordained. For through it [John's office], one may be born again and no one will come to heaven who does not receive or despises it.

He wants to say: Even that office and Baptism which John performed and that you pharisees did not desire to receive, nor [did you] want [to] be troubled with him, but rather raged against it [his office] as a new unusual preaching against your holiness according to the law—you must all receive this if you would see God's kingdom. And your Moses and your ritual washings, purifications, offerings, service to God and holiness here do not help, nor are they necessary. Only this office, which proclaims me and baptizes in connection with me, as John did, will help. You will not be able to come into God's kingdom and become holy in any other way.

And with this he praises this office so it is clear that it is the Holy Ghost's office and work through which a man becomes born again. It is not just a crude Baptism of water, but the Holy Ghost is also there with it. Whoever is so baptized is not only baptized by the water but of the Holy Ghost. It could not be said of other water baths or baptisms or in the Jewish baths and washings with all their ceremonies, that the Spirit would be there, else there wouldn't be a need for a new baptism and it could not be said that without considering Moses' law and service to God, there must be another way through which a man becomes born anew of the Spirit. It follows that the Spirit is neither given nor does he work through any of them.

So he reveals that there is no other work or means through which a man is born anew and comes to God's kingdom except by this office of preaching and Baptism. The Holy Ghost is bound to this, who works through this kind of office in the hearts of people. So he does not speak of the kind of Spirit who is buried and cannot be recognized as he is—as a person in his divine Nature, himself naked and without means. Rather, he makes himself visible in the external office where one hears and sees him, namely in the preaching office of the gospel and the Sacraments. For God also will not act and deal with the Spirit secretly and buried, or make each person an exception, else who could come to learn of it or be sure where or how he might seek or experience the Holy Ghost? Rather, he has ordained that the Holy Ghost should be visible before the eyes of man by the Word and Sacrament and work through such an outward [that is, public] office, so that you might know what is happening there is truly done by the Holy Ghost.

That is why these words, "Unless a person is born of water and the Spirit," say so much. He is saying: A person must become born anew through this preaching of the gospel and the office of Baptism, in which the Holy Ghost works, etc. For through the Word he enlightens the heart and reveals God's wrath over sins and again God's grace, promised for the sake of his Son, Christ, through which the heart is inflamed, begins to believe and now turns to God, trusting his grace, calling on him. The Baptism wakens and strengthens your faith as a true sign next to the Word that he washes away and effaces our sins. It speaks to us such sure, steadfast promises of grace to grasp, and to give us the Holy Ghost, etc.

Erl. 12, 405–407: Second Sermon on Trinity Sunday, John 3:1–15

With one accord, O God, we pray: Grant us Thy Holy Spirit;
Look Thou on our infirmity Thro' Jesus' blood and merit.
Grant us to grow in grace each day That by this Sacrament we may
Eternal life inherit. (*TLH* 301: 2)

Thursday

The wind blows where it will and you can hear its voice.
But you know not from where it comes and where it goes.
So is each one who is born of the Spirit. John 3:8

Dear Nicodemus, he says, I will tell you how it happens. It is not the kind of thing that must happen and stand before eyes, thoughts and reason, as if you could think and understand these things, so that you could hold and grasp it. Rather, it is the type of matter and work that is bestowed above human reason and thoughts, through the Holy Ghost, in people.

It happens in the human heart just as it does outside with the wind that wanders and blows when and where it will and goes through everything that grows, moves and lives. It is no more than a little wind that lays still for a long time but suddenly raises itself and begins to blow and sound so you do not know where it comes from. It weaves here, now there. Suddenly it makes all kinds of changes in weather and yet you cannot see or grasp what it is. But you only hear that it whispers and lets itself be felt that it is there. It rises and weaves as you see it go on the water or on the field of corn. But you cannot say if it will blow, if, where or how far it will stay ahead or behind you, nor its duration, size and mass nor if and how it will come or go.

In short: It is completely out of human hand and might to grasp or rule the wind and tell it how it should rain or be calm. Rather, it goes on its own, free. It directs its own work how, when, where it will; unhindered and unstoppable. Thus in this no person is able to do anything and also [no one] can predict how it will go and where it will be. Rather, as Psalm 135:7 says, "God brings it here and lets it go out of his chests and heavenly places, from there to where you cannot know or ever predict."

"So," he says, "is everyone who is born of the Spirit." There you must not look and gape at the great wonderful works of the apparent saints, so that the eyes fill and so these spiritual things would rule in your understanding and cling to the law and outward being; how "the saint" does great works, how he lives and tries, and [for those reasons he] should be called newly born and an heir of the heavenly kingdom. It is not allowed here to hold and grasp [this Spirit's work in this way], or paint and portray it so that you could say, "Behold, there you see the man who is a good Jew and also a pharisee, who keeps the law with great zeal and ardor. So he is a living saint and God's child," etc.

This new birth that makes God's children is different. In other words, the righteousness that is before God is another that performs in the hearts of men not through a person's own work and intention. For all that is "flesh" and that cannot see God's kingdom. It is rather through the Word of the gospel which reveals and makes visible to the heart both God's wrath over man unto repentance, and his grace through the mediator, Christ, to the comfort and peace of the conscience before God.

In such high great work, nothing special or glorious is seen outwardly. For it comes in nothing more than water and the Word, so you hear and experience it. Yet that is the power and work of the Holy Ghost, who inflames the heart and awakens it to true fear of God, to right trust and comfort of grace, and also, to true prayer. And so the heart is renewed so that a person who clings to that work with the heart, conquers God's wrath, sins, death, flesh and the world, turns to God heartily, desires and loves battle for all that is good.

Those are the true living works of the Holy Ghost, much greater and glorious than the other works-holiness which has a great good appearance and puffs itself up before the eyes of men and yet is nothing but death. By this [works-righteousness] the heart will in no way be changed. [Such a heart] follows no trust, sure comfort or improvement, but rather remains in the old fleshly thoughts and ways without repentance in doubt and disbelief, in hidden despising, disobedience, hate and enmity against God just as it previously made itself known in true war and terror of the conscience, which is nothing but simply fleeing and doubting and finally guilt and blasphemy against God.

Erl. 12, 410–412: Second Sermon on Trinity Sunday, John 3:1–15

Before Thee, God, who knowest all, With grief and shame I prostrate fall.
I see my sins against Thee, Lord, The sins of thought, of deed, and word.
They press me sore; I cry to Thee: O God, be merciful to me! (*TLH* 318: 1)

Friday

No one goes up to heaven but the one who has come down from heaven, namely, the Son of Man, who is in heaven. John 3:13

By this he testifies concerning himself what he had previously spoken concerning the new birth and God's kingdom so you also know that no one can come to it except only through him and for his sake, else it wouldn't even help if someone gladly desired to be made clean and new from his first birth through the Spirit. For even then, no one could come if he were not brought to the way and had received it. So there would not even be the power and Spirit in Baptism if it were not given through him [Christ] and for his sake. Therefore, this is now the chief thing by which we can also come through it up to heaven, as he will directly prove.

But he portrays himself as the promised savior come from heaven, that is, the true Son of God from eternity. Since he comes from heaven, he must always be begotten of God. But he has journeyed from heaven or come not as an angel journeys from there and appears and thereafter vanishes and departs. Rather, he took upon himself the human nature and as John says in John 1:14, "dwelt among us," etc. Therefore, he calls himself here the Son of Man, that is, truly man, so he also has flesh and blood like us.

But this actual descent of the Son of God means that he has been cast down into our misery and need, that is, God's eternal wrath, earned by our sins. He has taken them upon him, and he became an offering for them. As he himself says, he must be lifted up. But because this man has come from heaven, he must be in his own person without any sins, guiltless and in divine purity, so that he is not called born of the flesh as we are, but born of the Holy Ghost. His flesh is not sinful but pure, holy flesh and blood. Because of that he could also make our sinful flesh and blood pure and holy through his holiness and his holy unblemished offering.

But what does it mean that he says, "The Son of Man, who is in heaven"? How can he have come from heaven and yet be in heaven? Didn't he first return on the fortieth day after his resurrection into the clouds? Even as he has ascended, he is also in our flesh and blood and had humbled himself under all people unto death and cross as he was forsaken and cursed by God. But yet, [even] in that he was never separated from God, but always remained with God and was also always in heaven and always is; since he is always actually beholding the Father and reigns and works with him in the same power and might, except that such [power and might] were too deeply buried to see it because he was descended, that is, when he emptied himself of his divine appearance, as St. Paul says in Philippians 2:7. [He says] he went about in the form of a servant through suffering and death until he was freed from them. He was raised up again and sat at the right hand of God. There he is revealed as the Lord over death and hell and all creatures also according to his human nature, when he was lifted into the clouds before the eyes of the disciples. So also he will visibly come again and will be revealed to all people.

So this is what it means that the Son of Man comes down and again goes up to heaven and yet also remains in heaven in the divine nature, might and eternal unity with the Father. So he is not speaking here of the bodily changing of location, but rather of the spiritual journey of his descent and ascent, that is, of his suffering and death and resurrection and of the heavenly fellowship with the Father, which is not bound to the bodily practices, place or location. He had this from eternity and also in the human nature, as soon as he received it, in such a heavenly manner that it always was and still remains.

Erl. 12, 421–423: Second Sermon on Trinity Sunday, John 3:1–15

The mighty Son of God, His majesty concealing,
Dwells with our fallen race To give us balm and healing.
The everlasting God Descends from realms above,
Becomes a winsome Child, Reveals His father's love. (*TLH* 93: 2)

Saturday

That all who believe in him will not perish, but have eternal life. John 3:15

Now Christ shows: "That all who believe in him will not perish, but have eternal life." That is just what was said about the snake [in the wilderness]: "Whoever looks upon it shall recover." So Christ is seen upon the cross; believe on him. By this sins are effaced, that they cannot make us suffer, or even if they have made us suffer, they shall not harm us. So it all depends on this sight and on no work. But as every sight is done bodily, so this is accomplished spiritually in the heart, in order that we believe that Christ has blotted out our sins with his innocence.

Now that would also not yet help us, even if he were put to death on the cross a thousand times, as little as it would have helped anyone if they had themselves commanded a thousand snakes [be raised], if the Word were not there, namely as it is written here: "Everyone who believes on him shall not perish, etc." These Words personalize or apply it to us and make us sure that we also come up to heaven, that is, that we shall have God's grace, victory over sins, death and the power of the devil, for the sake of this lifted and crucified Christ. So we believe this and so we become dependent and hang upon him.

Behold, this is the figure in which is portrayed and illustrated supremely both the misery and need of the whole human race and the office and salvation of the Lord Christ and the manner by which they are received; how all people are fatally wounded by the fiery, hellish poison of the devil, and there was no skill or help possible to remove them if God's Son were not also given and revealed in order to remove such works of the devil, as 1 John 3:8 says, not through great, visible power, might, craft and strength of his divine majesty, but rather through the highest weakness and powerlessness, that is, through his suffering and death, where he hung on the cross as a cursed evil worm. Yet this deadly form of a snake is only a saving death and a living medicine. Those poisoned and ruined by the bite of sins are eternally well and pure through it.

It is quite wondrous to say and believe that such salvation and help takes place so utterly without any human aid, just as every poor person had to submit to the fiery serpents. Even if they sought all kinds of medicine that they might find, yet it would not have helped, but they would become even more vexed the longer and the more they had to deal with the snakes and were bitten, to defend

322

themselves from the snakes. Finally when all help was lost and there was no more hope or comfort, nothing else was placed before them than that they should let a likeness of a brass snake be erected. They would have preferred something better fastened to it and displayed. They only needed to behold this power with uplifted eyes. And yet so it must happen—that whoever followed this Word of God was even so quickly made whole and stayed well.

So also here, whoever wants to have sure help and salvation against sins and eternal death must also hear and follow this wonderful counsel of God and let go of all other comfort, wisdom and work but only lift his heart unto this Christ. For he was raised up for us, bearing our sins and death on his body. So it is proven, "that there is no other name under heaven that will help by which we might be saved than this crucified Christ." Acts 4:12.

So now he has presented the whole preaching of the new birth or righteousness of people before God, through every passage. It is also necessary to learn in this way. He tells from where and through what means they come and how they will be received—it is from the Word, Baptism and the Spirit who works through them by the service and sacrifice of Christ, for whose sake God's grace and eternal life are given us. He speaks of the faith through which these things are applied to us. Therefore, this whole preaching is now brought together so that the end agrees with the beginning. So you ask: How does the new birth happen, that the Spirit through the water and the Word makes people children of God? Just as Christ says here, that you grasp the comfort against the terror that comes because of your sins, and steadfastly believe that Christ, God's Son, for your sake has come down from heaven and was lifted for you on the cross so that you might not be lost, but might have eternal life. This faith is the treasure chest and the shrine, which clings to the forgiveness of sins and the heritage of eternal life. Man is saved by it, as Christ says, "Your faith has saved you."

Erl. 12, 427–429: Second Sermon on Trinity Sunday, John 3:1–15

The Son obeyed His Father's will, Was born of virgin mother,
And God's good pleasure to fulfill, He came to be my Brother.
No Garb of pomp or power He wore, A servant's form, like mine, He bore,
To lead the devil captive. (*TLH* 387: 6)

Week of Trinity I

Sunday

God is love and who remains in love remains in God and God in him. 1 John 4:16

This is truly begun in excellence. Love is excellently praised and lifted up and strongly admonished and made charming by its highest and fullest example. It is so simply spoken (as is St. John's way), that I cannot attain it and must marvel how he can speak of such exalted things with such utter simplicity and with such common plain words. When nothing else could move us or compel us to love, yet this will accomplish it, when we behold the example of the high majesty. For God (he says) is himself love. If that is true, then it must follow that whoever remains in love remains in God and, then again, God in him. Therefore, this matter of love is no paltry thing. So if you desire to know what kind of thing it may be, then I cannot tell you anything better than that it is God himself. Now how can you praise it higher than that? For what is higher and greater than God? So is this not marvelously and powerfully spoken? For with this single Word, he says and grasps more than a man can explain.

The apostle, St. Paul, also has written gloriously about it. He praises it with sheer might and many words in 1 Corinthians 13 through the whole chapter where he numbers all of its benefits and virtues: "Love is patient, kind, is not jealous, does not parade itself, is not stubborn, does not inflate itself, does not seek after its own, is not provoked." And again: "It bears everything, hopes everything, believes everything, etc." But yet with all this not so much is given or spoken so mightily as with these few words: Love is God himself, or God is love. With this he formulates the sweetest and kindest [words] and charms us in the highest and most appealing way so that we pursue it and think what a precious thing it is when a person arrives at the point that he loves God and his neighbor from the heart. For who does this has the kind of wealth which is called and is God himself.

If he says: Love is a greater richer treasure than many hundred-thousand dollars, or a great kingdom, who would not have great desire for it and pursue it as far as he ever could run and set his blood and sweat upon it to where he hoped or wished to receive it? Surely even when it is only something smaller, a good house, or a sack of money, wouldn't they strive after them? But what are all these? What are all the wealth and goods of the world, power, might, wisdom, justice? What are the sun and moon, heaven and all created things, all angels and saints compared to this? Love is nothing but the one, eternal, undescribable wealth and highest treasure, which is called God himself. Out of him everything flows and has its being. [Everything] is established in and through this same love and whoever remains in love, since he remains in God and God in him, he and God will be one cake.

Such words would impel not only the popes, but also we ourselves to say that faith alone does not make us righteous, but rather also love, because it gives us so much. For who remains in love, remains in God and God in him, but whoever has God, has everything. But he [the pope] has not first taught how we become righteous before God and come to grace, or grasp the love with which he has loved us through Christ, which can be done in no other way but through faith, as God himself says in the previous verse, "Whoever confesses that Jesus is the Son of God, in him God dwells and he in God. And we have known and believed the love that God has for us." But he wants us to draw near here to this example to compel us even more to love. For he certainly gladly desires to awaken and ignite his Christians so that they burn in love towards one another. Therefore, he lifts and values it so highly, even as it should be.

So how could you describe this more fully? If you said more it might be a high, noble quality of the soul and the most precious and complete virtue, as the philosophers and works righteous people say of it. But all of that kind of talk is against this, for with his whole mouth he shuts that all out and says: God is himself love, and his being is nothing but pure love. Because of that, if someone wanted to picture and capsulize God, then he must capsulize a kind of description that is pure love—as if the divine nature is nothing but an oven aflame and burning with such a love that fills heaven and earth. And again, if you could picture and describe love, you would have to make a description that is not a creation or human, yes, not familiar or heavenly, but rather as if it were God himself.

Altb. VI, 47: Some Good Preaching from the First Epistle of John on Love, 1533

Thou sacred Love, grace on us bestow, Set our hearts with heav'nly fire aglow
That with hearts united we love each other, Of one mind, in peace with ev'ry brother.
Lord, have mercy! (*TLH* 231: 3)

Monday

And who remains in love remains in God and God in him.
1 John 4:16

St. John also wants to say: Whoever desires to serve and do good for the world truly must not think that by that he will earn thanks or honor and wealth. For whoever acts for that reason and wants to see how men thank him has already lost and ruined his good deed and will not long remain in love. Now the whole world is so constructed that they neither will nor can suffer unthankfulness and being despised for their good deeds. Rather, as soon as anyone once for any reason enrages him [the good deed doer], or doesn't thank him so well as he would like, then the world seems enraged against him and he raises such a hue and cry: I've done him so much good and I would gladly have shared the heart of my body with him! See how he repays me. See what thanks I have for it, etc.! That is called a heathen good deed (which even the whores and idiots can do), because they serve someone so that he thanks them for it and they must be celebrated as if they were God, and yet they are prisoners. For no heathen is so crazy when he does you good and you do not thank him that he does not rage and withdraw his support. Yes, a cow would certainly rage if she should long give milk and you would not give her grass.

But among Christians you do not find this revenge and withdrawing help, but rather they persevere and remain in love. For it is a divine, free, uninflated, yes, also a forlorn [that is, lost or wasted] love in the people and so the good deeds are poured out in that way. For he [the Christian] does not speak as the world does. I have done and given so much for you and you repaid me like a scoundrel and a rascal. So from now on I will give you nothing good nor help you, even if I could lift a single finger to save you from death. But rather he turns the page and says: I have served you and done you good and you repaid me with evil, so I have received nothing for my kind heart and good deed but pure unthankfulness. But it doesn't matter that you should be so evil and unthankful and my love should be much too good for your evil. That is as far as one punishes what there is to punish. But after that, his hand and heart are not shut away from him when he needs love.

So you see what is there when love remains, both crudely among the people, but much more in a spiritual manner which Saint John chiefly exhorts. Namely, that in the doctrine and Christianity one should bear and be patient with each other, help and counsel, even when one is unthankful and does evil for good. But this doesn't come from the human heart, for such love is not a natural attribute, nor is it grown in our garden. Rather it is a gift of the Holy Ghost, that a person could give love for sorrow and all kinds of good for all mischief and evil. For this reason he says, "Who remains in love remains in God, etc." That is, where there is love, there is God and he lives there. It is not a natural nor human, much less devilish love, but rather it is heavenly and divine.

For God alone is the one who does not stop doing pure good for the world in spite of the world's unthankfulness and despising. Rather every vice and evil is devoured and consumed by the fire of his love. A Christian should also have such a heart so he does not let himself be drained of favor and kindness and not become so wrathful and bitter that his heart does not remain sweet by such divine love.

In order that we might be able to make it even lighter, he gives a great comfort and wants to say: If you remain so in love that you trust and have good courage, it is sure that you have a divine life. Yes, God himself is in and with you so that you remain in God and God in you. This is not so that you get a gracious God through this love, for previously this must be done through faith. No one (as said) has or is capable of such divine love except those who are made righteous through faith in Christ and have received the forgiveness of sins. And the love of God is known and felt in the heart through which he [the Christian] must be inflamed so that he also fashions such love towards God and his neighbor. For no one has loved God before (as St. John himself says previously and following in this epistle) but rather God has loved us and sent his Son to reconcile our sins and through this makes us his children. When one has already grasped such love through faith, then these fruits follow. We also make known such love and have a sure sign and witness. For true Christians remain in love and remain in God and he remains in us.

How could he give us stronger comfort or value love any higher but that it makes a divine person which is one cake with him (God) and can boast when he loves his neighbor and keeps doing good to his unthankfulness and annoying works, even if he makes him ashamed and pursues him for his good deeds, for he has acted as God? Not as if he had founded a great church like at Rome or Cologne, but something more and greater than heaven and earth, namely, the kind of work that is called a divine work and the best that the high majesty himself does. Now to us it is nothing if he has established a church or a hospital so that he could swell up his heart and inflate himself and so everyone would think: Oh, that is a precious and costly work! That's something not everyone can do, which God must especially regard and reward, etc.

Altb. VI, 51–52: Some Good Preaching from the First Epistle of John on Love, 1533

Lord, through my faith dwell Thou in me, Let faith grow ever stronger,
That it is fruitful more and more In works to God and neighbor,
That it be active through such love With joy and patience from above,
My neighbor ever serving. (Original Tranlation of verse quoted in Link)

Tuesday

But there was a beggar named Lazarus who lay before his gates covered with sores. Luke 16:20

If we want to be Christians we must get used to the fact that the devil pursues us everywhere so we have grief and he especially grabs us when and where we are weakest. He also used such a coward's art in Paradise. For he did not try Adam, but first the weak Eve and thereafter always reigns where there seems to be vulnerability. That is how you also must think when he comes. Such thoughts are not yours, nor did they grow in your heart, but they are thoughts that the devil places in you and you must suffer them. He also speaks into your heart so that you think: I call on our Lord God, but he doesn't hear. Therefore he will not pay attention to me. He is my enemy and not my friend, else he would help me.

So it is important that you are well built upon God's Word. For Christ has promised that he will surely listen to us. But we should certainly keep ourselves from wanting to prescribe for him the time, place and person through whom and by whom he will heed and help us. For time, place and person are *Accidentia* that remain in God's hand and we should not know them. The *Substantia* is God's grace and promise which is doubtless and sure. So you should hang on to this prophecy and not let these things concern you even if you don't know the time, place, person and details of how things will work out.

So you pray and it seems that nothing will come of your prayer. Then turn around and make a distinction between your malady and your faith. For surely you acknowledge that you are a Christian and are baptized into the death of Christ. Pay careful attention to such a call and let Christ be your best comfort. For if you have come this far and confess that God gave you his Son and has given him into death for your sins, then against such gifts and grace all bodily pain and illness are practically nothing. If it were possible you would wish to have even a thousand-fold more illnesses before you should do without such great treasures.

Therefore, learn here this difference and practice the *dialecticam* and say, "God's plan and will is that I should believe on his Son, Jesus Christ, and God has additionally granted me his Holy Ghost. For without the Holy Ghost I could not have such thoughts of Christ, that I believe he is given me by God and has died for me. But to testify to such faith I have been baptized and through that Baptism I became a member of his spiritual body."

Now if the devil's plan comes against this, then make this differentiation and say, "I am baptized and believe on Christ. Therefore, it must also follow that I pray in the name of Christ and that God will hear me, as Christ says, 'I do not say that I will pray to the Father for you, for he himself, the Father, has loved you.' But God has not with that released me so that I should not suffer from anything. He has loved me for the sake of his Son, Jesus Christ, as a Father has loved his child. But he intends for a time to hide his love so that it seems as though he were angry with me and will not hear me."

That is his manner of treating us. It is a true divine manner, as the 97th Psalm says. "Clouds and darkness surround me," and the 18th, "His form is surrounded in darkness and black thick clouds, in which he is hidden." And Paul in 1 Corinthians 13, "Now we see through a mirror in a dark word, but then face to face." We could not look him in the eye, but rather must see his back.

Therefore, my dear brother, learn. Now you are in a kind of school where you should learn the doctrine of faith, not speculatively out of books, as previously, but practically and in action. It may well seem to you that God doesn't want you. That is, by nature, in every human being. Now you fall into sins or suffer illness and disaster so that this vexation is always there that you think that God is angry. The devil also helps this along. If you begin to encounter such need and want to pray, he always blasts the heart: Oh! It doesn't help. It will become better in some other way.

Altb. VI, 338: Comforting Advice for the Afflicted, 1534

Though I be by sin o'ertaken, Though I lie in helplessness,
Though I be by friends forsaken And must suffer sore distress,
Though I be despised, contemned, And by all the world condemned,
Though the dark grave yawn before me, Yet the light of hope shines o'er me. (*TLH* 207: 3)

Wednesday

And do you think that I have come to this land without the Lord to destroy it? The Lord surely spoke to me: "Go up to this land to destroy it." Isaiah 36:10

How is it when the devil throws out and advances such sins against you that are truly sins and that you also have committed and cannot deny? How does one handle this matter, as when the devil troubled David for the sake of his committing adultery; St. Peter because he had denied the Lord Christ? All these come together between two witnesses that conquer us, namely, God's law and our conscience. It is also not possible to deny the sins. So now I acknowledge the sins so the punishment is at the door and eternal death added to it, where God's law drowns me. With this he [the devil] drives us to despair as he had done to Cain and Judas, the betrayer. Now when it comes to such a great need, then you must have God's help. For this reason, one must have a Christian with him who can comfort him with God's Word and dismiss the despair through God's Word, or the Holy Ghost must speak and give one of God's promises in his heart. The devil has pressed you so hard that you have confessed and not denied that you acknowledge the sins and have earned eternal death, like Judas. But you should not follow after Judas, but warm and comfort yourself and behold Christ, as St. Paul did, and see and remember what Christ has suffered for you. For Christ, our dear Lord, has your penitence and confession, and he has erased your miserable handwriting with his dear precious blood and made it nothing, so that your sins can nevermore be so great. Since you are exterminated and made clean through his blood, then they cannot harm you when you believe this with a strong faith.

For, if you were apart from Christ, then you would have nothing to defend you against sins and the devil. But since you are in Christ, call upon him, and are sealed and marked by his Baptism, then your confession of sins that you have committed is changed into a disavowal so that you are able to resist the devil. Yes, you should even defy him and say, "Even if I am a poor sinner, yet I am no longer a sinner. I am a sinner for the sake of myself and apart from Christ, but in my Lord Jesus Christ and not because of me, I am no sinner. For with his precious blood he has wiped away all my sins, as I firmly believe. For this reason I am also Baptized as a sure sign. Also through God's Word I am absolved and free of my sins, cleared and declared unbound. And I have been fed and have drunk of the Sacrament of the true body and blood of my dear Lord Jesus Christ, as through sure signs of grace, and that I have received forgiveness of sins, which my dear Lord Jesus Christ has purchased, earned and secured by his blood."

For this reason a man must comfort and strengthen himself. Even if you have sinned, as your own conscience then accuses you, nevertheless you should not despair. But when this happens it is also necessary in the conscience's accusation, when the conscience remains *paroxysmus* and the battle at its height so that it is so great that a person in such a battle, which flesh and blood and human understanding cannot endure, that such a person stand and not fall. In such a battle one should stick with it and it is his duty to acknowledge that it is God the Holy Ghost's gift that he comforts our heart and with his gifts he exhorts us and bestows it [this comfort] upon us so that we do not desire the conscience's accusation unto despair, as when the devil afflicts us for the sake of doctrine, but that we determine among us that our doctrine and preaching, which we insist upon, hear and have, are rightly fashioned and true. And even if we, in addition, have sins on us, then we place them in the love of the Father and so we pray: "Forgive us our trespasses," etc. In this way you overcome the devil so that he must give way.

Altb. VI, 345–346: Lectures on Isaiah 36 & 37, 1534

Oh, draw me, Savior, e'er to Thee; So shall I run and never tire.
With gracious words still comfort me; Be Thou my Hope, my sole Desire.
Free me from every guilt and fear; No sin can harm if Thou art near. (*TLH* 349: 5)

Thursday

Then the affliction will only teach you to attend to the Word. Isaiah 28:19

There is no stronger or better remedy in the midst of an affliction, because of the vexing thoughts that usually leap out of your thoughts and heart, which trap you, than that you quickly read or hear God's Word and thus extinguish the devil's fiery darts in the best way. But whoever doesn't want to follow this counsel rather hangs onto those harsh and vexing thoughts and can do nothing but add more wood and straw to the fire until he is spent and driven to the ground and despair by the devil, who is like a thousand artists. He is overcome. For the devil drives us most heavily to this single strife that he establishes, with the thought that God is angry with us to strike our faith and trust to the ground. If you should try to defend yourself in this spiritual battle with human help, apart from God's Word, you would do nothing more than to give battle against the mighty spirit, the devil, naked and unarmed. So if it happens to you, you do not want to hold your power against the devil's might. Then you would readily find what a completely different battle and affliction it is if you do not have God's Word in your hand already (which, as St. Paul writes in Romans 1, alone is the power of God). For without God's Word, that man will strive and war by human powers and weapons against the devil who had often broadly held the field since the beginning of the world and is such an experienced and practiced warrior.

So let go of that idea, by which the devil would capture your heart. Beware lest you dispute with him. For he can disguise himself as an angel of light, appearing to be the glorious person of Christ, and because he also knows the Holy Scripture, as you see in Matthew 4, he can even use the most wonderful words of Christ himself against a Christian and his faith. When you are in that kind of an affliction let your courage and thought not wander and say, "I know and am sure of no other Christ than the one given by the Father, who has died for me and my sins. I know that he is not angry with me, but that he is kind and gracious to me." For he [Christ] has no other way to bring it into your heart, but that he will be good to me and he died for me. If you do not reproach the devil with these and similar words and cast yourself quickly upon the Holy Scriptures to read them as the truth, then you must be driven to the ground and despair. For the devil can easily bring it about that he extinguishes the weak little spark of faith if we do not always increase, strengthen and bring it further with God's Word.

Beyond this, this poor but yet important and necessary advice follows. If a person is troubled and is melancholy he should not be alone but quickly see to it that he speak with good friends about something, whatever he desires. For when you speak with someone your heart is brought by this from troubling thoughts because for most people in trials, lonely places are frightening and dangerous. For this reason King Solomon rightly said in Ecclesiastes 4, "Whoever is alone will have trouble! If he falls there is no one there to help him." For the word of another Christian has great power over and above the crowd. Therefore all who are stuck in affliction should know this and remember that they hear and believe that the voice and discussion of the brother Christian neighbor is none other that the Word and voice of God himself and as if God himself is speaking. And if a person had no such preacher, or another to comfort him with God's Word, it is then better that he hear other people speak than the devil's blasphemous work and fiery darts speaking and piercing his heart.

I have previously presented and laid out this common law, rule and doctrine of how one should conduct himself in a spiritual affliction. It is based on this; that each one rightly oppose the devil with his courage and heart since he finds that he will have help in these good thoughts, advice and considerations. Let no one remove it from your mind, that whoever had been given Christian faith will always have afflictions. For the passage from Paul to Timothy is true: "that all who would have a godly life in Christ will suffer persecution."

Now one can easily overcome bodily afflictions, like sadness, avarice, boasting, scandal and the like. But there is sadness and labor when the devil sets before us God's wrath and then also our own conscience helps and convicts us with its testimony. Then the devil disturbs and mightily frightens that conscience with many examples of God's wrath which are revealed in divine Scriptures and happen everyday. That is, then, the mightiest and most disturbing punishment in which the devil and all his powers and attributes attack and present you with the most wrathful and unmerciful picture of God.

Altb. VI, 347: Lectures on Isaiah 36 & 37, 1534

Who clings with resolution
To Him whom Satan hates
Must look for persecution;
For him the burden waits
Of mockery, shame, and losses,
Heaped on his blameless head;
A thousand plagues and crosses
Will be his daily bread.

From me this is not hidden,
Yet I am not afraid;
I leave my cares, as bidden,
To whom my vows were paid.
Though life and limb it cost me
and everything I own,
Unshaken shall I trust Thee
And cleave to Thee alone. (*TLH* 528: 11–12)

Friday

But he said to him, "You have rightly answered. Do this and you shall live." Luke 10:28

This is surely right and true if you also understand it properly. You should tell me the right understanding for I already know that I should be good and keep the law, but how do I accomplish that? Or what does it mean to be good? You say: It means having a good conscience, a clean heart and doing everything that God has commanded. That's right. But give me one of those people or show me a person who could say that. You will not bring me a heart or conscience at length that God could not punish or curse. Now the law requires such a heart (as is said enough) that has a truly good conscience before God. Where can a person get this? That is the question and the matter we consider—surely not here where you preach the judgment seat. But there, that you have a pure unblemished faith which grasps Christ and receives and has from him everything that the law demands. There everything is pure and there is a good conscience. Such a person is called good and righteous before God. Then even if I have already failed, he stands in my place and has so much righteousness that he can fulfill my, and all human deficiency.

So we show how one also receives this so he becomes good before God. But they only perform good things before people where something else makes them good. They want to act as if these [good things before man] should also count something before God. They mix them into one stew because they know nothing of this nor have they experienced what they say or what they [truly] are. For what is it that you cry out: whoever wants to go to heaven must keep the law. You won't bring it about that way. So look at yourself and search in your penance and you will find that you were born and live in sin and are unable to give what the law demands. What are you spewing from your mouth to the people with such words, "You should be good. You should be pure." Nothing comes of that. No one shows that he can do it. I hear the words well enough, what the law demands, but how do I bring it about that I do it? So you advise me back to myself and say, "You must do good works." But how do I stand before God when I have done good works and am good before the people for a long time as you teach me? Can I be sure that God also regards me as good for that? For my own heart and conscience are against me and say "no" to that.

But you ought to teach me as does St. Paul here and always; that it must gush from the plain unassailable faith that we receive at the mercy seat before all things and there get and lose what is lacking in us, as in the passage: keep the law, rightly understood. For that is the desire of the law, that you be completely good before God, just as before people. If you have that, then go out among the people and practice love and do good works. Then you come rightly to the matter and all such passages are fulfilled, for by that a person gives and does what the law demands. First before God, yet not through yourself but through Christ, without whom we could do nothing before God. Thereafter through yourself before other people; now through faith or Christ which is completely good inwardly, thereafter outwards through your doing; yet along side of that the forgiveness of sins goes along with it. So the righteousness of a Christian consists much more in this [faith] than anything else, for in his own actions, which any old laundryman can return [to God], and without forgiveness these works he bears are only his own actions.

See how St. Paul battles the error and lack of understanding that the law boasts and compels, and yet in itself the law does not teach or show how one can also do it or how it can be brought about. It can do no more than blab the words "Commandment, keep the law, be good, do good works," etc. Just as now all the books ooze and all the churches vomit with such useless twaddle that they themselves do not understand. But they never say a word about what St. Paul teaches here as the chief part; how love should proceed from a pure heart, good conscience and unblemished faith. So ever more say: "Keep the law," but don't compel that old meaning again.

Altb. VI, 43–44: Essence of the Christian Life from 1 Timothy 1, 1533

Here our souls, by Jesus sated, More and more shall be translated
Earth's temptations far above; Freed from sin's abhorred dominion,
Soaring on angelic pinion, They shall reach the Source of love. (*TLH* 282: 3)

Saturday

In this love is completely with us because we have joy on the day of judgment; for just as he is, so are we in this world. 1 John 4:17

This is also a great provocation to love and very useful, that we should have joy on the day of judgment. But he speaks always, as I have said, against the false brothers and hypocritical Christians that only have the gospel in their mouth and on their tongues and retain only the foam. They let themselves think that they have the gospel and faith that stays only in Words in which there are a lot one could ignore. And when they have heard it one time, they alone are the masters of the art and no one is so capable of it as they are to know how to judge everyone else and to reprove all the world. And no one is so evangelical as they. But it is only purely a husk. You see they do not deem thereafter to live and make known love that you should see they are serious. They have brought forth none of these things except they have heard that one who receives forgiveness of sins becomes holy only through faith and cannot receive them through works. They always then proceed under the name of faith and become more annoyed than before and live so that the world must also battle them so that they should stand before God.

Now the apostle also says: "No that doesn't do anything even if it is true that we have and receive everything through faith. But when we do not let faith show through love, then it will definitely be nothing but a pure false dream of faith in which you deceive yourself. So look upon your fruits and where they are not rightly fashioned, don't comfort yourself by your false dreams of faith and grace." Because of this he warns in this passage that you should not think that the gospel and faith remain only in Words and thoughts that we have from it, but that it must be the kind of thing that is planted in the heart and breaks forth and lets itself be known through love and the kind of love that is whole and rightly fashioned to either friend or foe.

So that is (he says) a fine well rounded love that lacks nothing. This also makes one confident and can give comfort on the day of judgment. With these words it brings one before judgment. He can see that this is serious and not beating at the wind as if nothing were at stake or that nothing so hard and strong is commanded. But he refers to my understanding the final judgment of God and it could also be understood, as some also think, of the judgment or sentence through which the Christian will be martyred or cursed, which is also not far off. For it also must follow that the conscience must give an answer as before God. Whoever conquers that [the conscience] will also conquer in the final judgment.

Now whatever or whenever it may be, the judgment that faith will assure itself with comes when this is encountered; when you must hold out your head,[14] or then be in the stocks or when the last day comes, that you can have a comfort and conquer. Then there will surely be no lying and deceiving, but one will be there who will judge and lay your faith upon the trial and test if it is rightly fashioned. There the poor empty faith will not help, for it will find of itself that it did nothing nor was it advised by love, but rather was envious, hateful, greedy and hard and only carried the right name. It had to be showy before everyone and would not allow itself to be buried. Rather, when he was challenged, the great proud spirit presented such a great evident holiness that everyone should say that he alone was a true Christian. Such appearance lasted a long time and let itself sparkle and shine but when the hour of trial comes, all such prattle falls behind and you will find in a fine way if you believed rightly and have done true works of faith.

Therefore, see to it (he wants to say) that you do not have the poor sufferable husk of love floating on the tongue. For that is called a cold, foul, incompetent love. But rather that it is a completely full love, which is the kernel and core that can make your heart glad so you do not have to be afraid or shrink but go happily before God and the world and say, "God be praised! I have lived so that my neighbor cannot accuse me, that I have not stolen from, hated, robed, defamed anyone, but have done good to everyone, as much as I could." But when there is complaint: "I have boasted for myself about the gospel and done no good for my neighbor. Everything was for me greedy and scraping, prideful and disobedient, hateful and envious," so my heart must say, "Woe is me! What kind of Christian have I become. Look how I have informed my faith!" Then you would become so worried and sad that both the gospel and faith would collapse (if God does not otherwise interpose and preserve you). Then the devil will be behind you and observe your record and say, "What can you brag concerning faith and Christ when you did not acknowledge him your whole life?"

Altb. VI, 53-54: Some Good Preaching from the First Epistle of St. John on Love, 1533

Now richly to my waiting heart, O Thou, my God, deign to impart
The grace of love undying. In Thy blest body let me be,
E'en as the branch is in the tree, Thy life my life supplying.
Sighing, Crying, For the savor Of Thy favor; Resting never
Till I rest in Thee forever. (*TLH* 343: 3)

---

[14]That is, placing one's head upon the chopping block.

Week of Trinity II

Sunday

You prepare a table before me in the presence of my enemies. You anoint my head with oil and your gifts overflow. Psalm 23:5

The prophet wants to show with these words, "you prepare a table before me in the presence of my enemies," the great, glorious, marvelous power of the dear Word. As if he would say: You have captivated me so well, Lord, and you feed me so wonderfully at your table. For you have prepared for me, that is you cover me, with so much unsurpassing mercy by your dear Word that I not only have a rich comfort through your Word inwardly in my heart against my evil conscience, sins, fear and terror of death, God's wrath and justice, but also externally I become a hearty and unconquerable hero through the same. All my enemies can accomplish nothing against me. Yes, the more they rage and are mad and foolish against me, yes, all the more I am safe, happy and also have good things. Such happiness and bold courage comes from nowhere but that I, Lord, have your Word. That gives me such power and comfort against my enemies that even if they rage and rant as strenuously as they can, my mind is even more peaceful than when I sit at a table where I have everything my heart desires to eat, drink, enjoy, and crave, along with the playing of stringed instruments, etc.

There you hear once again how highly David exalts and praises the dear Word. Namely, that the faithful win and are victorious through it against the devil, world, flesh, sins, conscience and death. For when a person has the Word, and holds fast to it with faith, these enemies (that would otherwise be overwhelming) must all shrink back and surrender. And it is also a wondrous victory and power and also a truly proud, haughty boast of those in faith that they oppose and overcome all these terrible and apparently almighty enemies, but not with raging, biting, striving against them, hitting them back, revenge, and with counsel and help they seek here and there [apart from the Word]. Rather [they overcome] by food, drink, good living, sitting, being happy and at peace, all of which happens, as said, through the Word. For eating and drinking in the Scripture is called believing, holding fast to the Word. From this follows: peace, joy of spirit, comfort, strength, victory over all misfortune.

Reason cannot judge [rightly] in this wonderful victory of those in faith, for it here goes contrary to all thoughts. The world always persecutes and throttles the Christian out-of-hand as the most noxious people on earth. When human reason observes this, it can think nothing but that the Christians are defeated people and their enemies are on top and are victorious. So the Jews treated Jesus, the apostles and the believers. They always put them to death. When they throttled them or at least had expelled them a little, they cried out: "We won!" When they have done us some harm, they do not bother with us any more. Now, after all that, we will take pleasure in this. When they were in the most safety, the Lord God sent the Romans over them who treated them so horribly that it is terrifying to hear about it. Then after a few hundred years, he also rewarded the Romans who put to death many thousand martyrs through the whole Roman empire. He let the city of Rome be subjected by the Goths and Wends four times in a few years. Finally the kingdom was razed and flattened to the ground, etc. So who won? The Jews and Romans, who shed the blood of the saints as if it were water, or the poor Christians who were condemned like sheep to the slaughter and had no other defense or weapon than the dear Word?

So with these words David shows how the Holy Christian Church is established (for he speaks here not only concerning himself). He gives her her color and finely portrays her, that she is before God a lush green pasture, upon which grass and fresh waters are flowing, that is, that she is God's Paradise and heavenly garden, adorned with his gifts and having his unspeakable treasure, the dear Word and the holy Sacraments, by which she instructs, rules, quickens and comforts his flock.

Altb. VI, 903–904: Explanation at Table of the 23rd Psalm, 1536

Thou spreadst a table in my sight,   Thy unction grace bestoweth;
And, oh! the transport of delight   With which my cup o'erfloweth. (*TLH* 431: 5)

Monday

You anoint my head with oil, and your gifts overflow. Psalm 23:5

With these abounding words (you anoint my head with oil and your gifts overflow), the prophet now wants to show the great rich comfort which the faithful have through the Word. Their consciences are safe, happy and already at peace in the midst of all kinds of afflictions and troubles, even in death. He wants to say, "The Lord, in truth, makes of me a strange warrior and wondrously equips me against my foes. I would think that he should dress me in armor, set a helm upon my head, give a sword into my hand and warn me that if I am careful and watch myself, I will not be overcome by my enemies. Yet [instead] he sets me before a table and prepares me a glorious meal. He anoints my head with costly oil, or (according to our customs) he presents me with a wreath as if I should go to joy and dancing and not battle with my foes. And there is no lack. He pours it out to me full so that I quickly drink of joyful, good things and am satisfied. So now the prepared table IS my armor, the costly oil is my helm, my full cup is the sword given me by which I defeat all my enemies." But isn't that a wonderful armament and yet a wondrous victory?

But he wants to say this, "Lord, your guests that sit at your table, are the believers. They will not only be strong and bold giants against all your enemies, but they will also be joyous and satisfied. When you deliver them to such accomplishments, it makes your guests pursue acts that are of great worth. You feed them so wonderfully. You make them zealous and happy. You give to them with such abundance that they become drunk." All of that happens through the Word of grace. For through that, the Lord, our Shepherd, feeds and strengthens his believers' hearts, that they all can present comfort in the presence of all their enemies and can say with the prophets, "I am not afraid before many hundredthousands that lie against me." And above in the fourth verse: "I fear no evil, for you, Lord, are with me," etc. So he gives them the Holy Ghost with, and also through this same Word, who not only makes them courageous and bold, but also [makes them] so safe and happy that they become drunk in the presence of great and overpowering joy.

So he speaks here of the spiritual strengthening, joy and drunkenness that is a divine power, Romans 1. And also the joy as St. Paul calls it in the Holy Ghost, Romans 14; a holy drunkenness in which the people are not full of wine out of which disorderly behavior follows, but rather being full of the Holy Ghost, Ephesians 5. And this is the armor and the weapon by which our Lord God prepares his believers against the devil and the world: Namely, he gives the Word of God into their mouth and the courage, that is, the Holy Ghost, into their hearts. With such equipment you attack all your enemies unafraid and joyfully and strike and overcome them with all their might, wisdom and holiness. The apostles were such warriors on Pentecost. They marched in Jerusalem against the rulers and chief priest's command and stood there as if they were purely gods and all the others only grasshoppers. They were going about with all power and joy as if they were drunk so that a few who were there mocked them and said, "They are full of sweet wine," etc. But St. Peter reveals from the prophet Joel that they were not full of wine, but were rather full of the Holy Ghost. And after that he struck forth with his sword, that is, he opened his mouth and preached and struck the devil, adding three thousand souls at once, etc.

And in the believers such power, joy and holy drunkenness, not only gives evidence of itself when they stand and have peace, but also when they suffer and die. When the council in Jerusalem let the apostles go with a warning, they were happy because they had become worthy to suffer insult for the sake of Christ's name, Acts 15. Many martyrs, both male and female went to death with happy hearts and laughing mouths as if they were going to a good life or a dance; the kind of people you see in St. Agnes, St. Agatha, the virgins who were 13 or 14 years old, and many others. They have not only conquered the world, the devil and death through Christ boldly and confidently, but their hearts also received such good things over and above them, just as if they were drunk with great joy which drowns the devil so much by their abundance when someone despises them by their great might and cunning.

Altb. VI, 905–906: Explanation at Table of the 23rd Psalm, 1536

Amid surrounding foes   Thou dost my table spread;
My cup with blessing overflows,   And joy exalts my head. (*TLH* 426: 5)

Tuesday

Lord, I call upon you; for the fire has consumed the meadows in the wilderness and the flames have kindled all the trees of the field. Joel 1:19

But it is good that this and many more similar prayers are in the prophets and also in other parts of Scripture. They are presented here and there to shun the unnecessary twaddle and heathen thoughts, which they themselves prescribe and make, in which they [the heathen] are so unaccustomed and unpracticed in spiritual matters. For they are stuck in pure error because they think that it is enough if they only think about their need and misfortune. But they consider praying or telling God their situation with sure words as unnecessary and without purpose, since God observes the heart and already knows and understands our thoughts without it.

But if this is true, why then has the Lord Christ taught the "Our Father"? Why did he repeat the prayer three times with the same words when he sweat bloody sweat in the garden for us and was subjected to death? Why had he made such a long prayer for us and the church in the last supper as John desired to describe it?

On account of this we must be resolved and say that the supplication or prayer that is made by the mouth is true prayer and is not done without sure result and application because it is commanded and is used and kept by the Son of God himself.

Then again, there are some that think that because long idle talk is forbidden, [such praying people] are sinful if they use and employ many words in their prayers. But these people do not understand the reason why Christ condemns useless prattle and mumbling. For if you consider and think rightly about it, he does not condemn long prayer but rather unbelief that doubts God's promise. For those who make such long prayers act as if God did not understand the matter, like an unlearned, undiscerning judge for whom you finally must direct and clarify the issue with many words, or as if he does not want to hear us or want to heed it. [They act] as if he could be awakened and compelled through some long prayer. That is done sinfully and wrongly.

So we should believe both without any doubt. First, as Christ also says, that our heavenly Father already knows what we need and should have. Second, that he heartily wants to heed it with all his gracious will, Luke 11, "So as you, who are evil, can give your children good gifts much more will your Father in heaven give the Holy Ghost to those who pray to him."

A careless, harsh or severe judge must have a long account through which he becomes informed of a matter in order to take it in well and rightly understand it. He is not soon moved and turned with a few words, much less do they make him understand. But the heavenly Father, says Jesus, is not of that kind of mind. Therefore, it is enough when you show with a few words what you would like to have because he already knows it before you ever ask, as it is written, "Before you ask, I will answer." And because he is kind and merciful he will gladly give what you ask. Just as when a father already knows what his children need and what the child wants to have, it gives him pleasure when his child humbles himself and asks him for it. The father also wants that to happen.

Those who do not give God this praise and honor, that he knows and understands, is gracious and good, might make good words when they pray, but they do not pray rightly. Now these are the attributes of the prayer of the monks and papists, in which what is encouraged and noticed is not God's promise (which is necessary), but rather the Lord Christ's martyrs and suffering on the cross, the Saints' intercession, our service and the like.

This prophet makes his prayer in this place long and completely full, but not because he would teach God and also not because he thought to move God with these words, but because his heart's oppressing need compelled him. He could not make such need a brief matter. And when he was quickly compelled by the present need and misfortune, he awakened himself so that the prayer became even stronger, heartier and desirous.

Daniel did the same in the long prayer for the salvation of his people; also in Psalm 79, he says with hearty pure words: "They have shed blood in Jerusalem like water and there was no one to bury them," etc. This is not said as if God did not know it, nor that he had to be moved and awakened by it to bring help, nor that he himself did not gladly want to help these poor down-trodden people. No, rather the misfortune that one feels is so deep and built so strong in the heart of the dear Christian that they let themselves think that one could not get at such trouble and need with words or a single prayer, much less ever bring it to an end.

Altb. VI, 930–931: Lectures on Joel, 1536; cf. AE 18

Thou, Holy Spirit, teachest The soul to pray aright;
Thy songs have sweetest music, Thy prayers have wondrous might.
Unheard they cannot fall, They pierce the highest heaven
'Til He His help hath given Who surely helpeth all. (*TLH* 228: 4)

Wednesday

So the Lord now says, "Turn to me with your whole heart, with fasting, with weeping, with lamentation." Joel 2:12

This is a beautiful, glorious exhortation to true penitence and it would be well worth it for you now, in the time of the church, to be quickly driven to it. A sinful human life is nothing but a continual turning away from God, who himself is gracious and turns us through his Word. But we turn our backs to him (as evil, disobedient, stubborn children against their father, who, when he calls them, reveal their contrariness) and go wherever we want and not to where he calls us through his Word.

Where such an opposing manner, the disobedience and stubbornness, grows more numerous and strong, a person's highest desire and joy is only to have many reasons and provocations to sin. Yes, the godless strive by the flesh and so despise and are without God's commands with no shame. The Lord Christ actually pictures such a life in the likeness of a straying sheep who strays far from the flock and wanders in error with ever greater danger until the wolf comes and it is caught and devoured.

Even in this way, the people of Israel turned from God. He spoke with them. And through the prophets they willfully opposed him against the right road. They turned their backs, left the true service of God and wandered to find counsel, Psalm 81, as in the time when King Manasseh ruled when, it seems, Joel had lived. He was clearly exiled because he could not foresee the punishment or avoid it. King Manasseh was taken away up to Babylon, as described in the second book of Chronicles, chapter 33. So the land was troubled and ravaged in so many ways by enemies, dangerous animals and vermin.

But just as it is with those who depart from a path, so it is with those who stray and then don't know the way to the right path. The further they go the farther they go from the right road. So also the Jews, when they had turned from God with their godless ways, sought help to be saved from their common punishment and misfortune and so increased them and made them only greater and harder with their false services to God who was only so much more enraged.

It is just as the papists heap up their danger, anxiety and need and hold one mass after another, call on the dead saints, prepare for daily prayer, employ fasts. With these and similar self-chosen works and false thoughts, they do not lessen God's wrath but rather make it only greater and harsher for that is not the right way to appease God's wrath.

That is why God says here, "Turn to me;" that is, "do not turn your back to me when I speak to you. Listen to me and heed me and do this with your whole heart so that the turning or penitence is not false or artificial." For God summons the whole heart, He will not and cannot suffer that one should fear another god and trust in him. As Christ also says, "No one can serve two masters."

But it is also the practice among us and it is almost universal, that when we hear in the Words what we should do, and then also observe the old services of God, the common customs; we do not dispose of them, drop them and condemn them. For he says, "With your whole heart turn to me." Because of that, we have the highest eager concern for the Word of God, look only upon it and take nothing away from it. That is the first and foremost, that we shall have respect for the Word.

But what does this Word teach? What does it show us as the way to reconcile God? With fasting, crying and lamentation turn to me, and do not tear your clothes but your heart, says the prophet. That is the first part of repentance as the prophet teaches. But the Jews had a well known practice and custom, that they tore their clothing in trials and tribulations. So Annanias the high priest ripped his cloak when he wanted to show how blasphemy (As this is what the Word of our dear Lord Christ meant to the godless chief hypocrite when Jesus said: "From now on you will see the Son of

Man sitting on the right hand of power," Matthew 16.) against God made him mad. There are many similar examples in the Old Testament.

Altb. VI, 937–938: Lectures on Joel, 1536; cf. AE 18

And wilt Thou pardon, Lord
A sinner such as I,
Although Thy book his crimes record
Of such a crimson dye?

So deep are they engraved,
So terrible their fear.
The righteous scarcely shall be saved,
And where shall I appear? (*TLH* 322: 1–2)

Thursday

Tear your hearts and not your clothes and turn to the Lord your God. For he is gracious, merciful, patient and of great kindness, and he repents of punishing. Joel 2:13

The prophet says distinctly in clear plain terms, "Do not tear your clothing but your hearts." With this he wants to show that it should be a true earnest pain and suffering, not manufactured. Then when the people are weary in trouble and need and bear sorrow, yet that same sorrow is no more intense than is proper. For the true pain and fervent sorrow to which the prophet exhorts is not that one cries out terribly and laments over his misfortune as we suffer and that it oppresses us and tries us, as it commonly happens.

Rather, that one rightly behold and consider the reason for such misfortune and punishment, namely sins through which we have transgressed. Because of this, he lets suffering be the reason that he desists [from sin], does it no more and improves himself. That is true pain and heartache and the right beginning of true repentance.

An unfaithful wife and adulterer knows and feels the curse and also her misery over her outward disgrace and scandal for which she then is frightened and sad. That is nothing new. Yes, it is the attribute and the nature of the old Adam that he has love for himself, is troubled and speaks up and laments when it goes evil for him. But he does not acknowledge or consider also the reason for the punishment. The [adultery] is also not an enemy or repugnant to him.

But the pain, remorse and sorrow of which the Holy Ghost here preaches, is that man not only feel the punishment, but rather the sins, that you terribly offended and enraged God, your creator and Lord, with your adultery or other such sins. And you have also been thrown into eternal wrath, disgrace and condemnation. Now when the heart rightly compels and stirs up such feelings, there follows, as one says, a good resolution and that heart will no longer seek a reason for forbidden indecency, fleshly desires and evil works. Yes, the heart terrifies and shocks itself when it thinks of the committed sins and has a terror and shame because of such filth.

Such pain and sorrow is a work of the Holy Ghost which terrifies the heart through the Word of the law. It is not as the papists teach, a human work that we could do, so often as it pleases us. Rather, the heart must be stirred and awakened in this manner through the Word by the Holy Ghost. Apart from this and without this the old man remains. According to his skill and as he was long ago, he has desire and pleasure over sins and seeks reason, time, place and opportunity for sins. And when at last he brings it about, he is happy and rewards himself as if he had planned well.

So it is common, when pestilence or evil times occur, that one is sorrowful and laments. But how many do you find, even among us, who consider rightly and with seriousness from where such trial and punishment come and through it are reminded so they desist from sinning, improve their life, and decrease and abstain from greed, usury, persecuting, devouring and drunkeness, pride and procrastination and similar misdeeds in their calling and station?

The Jews were also saddened in the captivity when their enemy and vermin afflicted them, hurt them and injured them sorely. But they did not trouble themselves much and did not have sorrow that they offended and enraged God through idolatry, had despised God's Word, his prophets and preachers. These sins had brought this punishment and misfortune and were the reason for it.

That's why God calls and commands by the prophets that they tear their hearts and not their clothes. That is, he wants them to have true earnest remorse and sorrow because of the sins they have committed. When that happens, there follows a true improvement of life. For the heart hears and receives God's Word with zeal, follows his desires and his heart is dark no more. So he lays aside idolatry, false services to God, trust in his own works and the whole swarm of other sins that a godless way of life brings, compels and drags along with it.

God would have such a grief and sorrow from us. But concerning fasts he considers not only that it is done because of the command, but rather also that it is a sign of a true troubled and afflicted heart in which there is a zeal to which this [fasting] also bears witness. The sinners in Luke 7, who lay at the feet of the Lord Christ, didn't speak a single word, but Christ understood their tears well, told them to be at peace and happy, for their sins were already forgiven.

The prophet commends such crying here also. For in repentance, this is the first measure, namely, the sins are truly known and acknowledged, and because of this there is earnest sorrow and affliction with true sadness and remorse that one has offended and enraged God.

Altb. VI, 938-939: Lectures on Joel, 1536; cf. AE 18

When all my deeds I am reviewing, The deeds that I admire the most,
I find in all my thought and doing That there is naught whereof to boast.
Yet this sweet comfort shall abide In mercy I can still confide. (*TLH* 385: 8)

Friday

Tear your hearts and not your clothes and turn to the Lord your God. For he is gracious, merciful, patient and of great kindness, and he repents of punishing. Joel 2:13

This is a thoroughly beautiful, glorious passage by which the prophet would again set aright, comfort and rightly strengthen hearts that are terrified by their sins by painting God in his true colors, portraying and impressing [him] upon them, that they might firmly believe they have a gracious God who has pardoned and forgiven their sins for the sake of his dear Son. This repentance or turning to God is rightly perfected when, in addition, a sure hope and trust in God's goodness and mercy may come.

So when we use this passage rightly, first we establish this and similar kind, sweet, lovely names of God and are comforted against disbelief and doubt. Then we also use it as an example which we follow, changing and improving our life in whatever is evil and against God in us.

The first name, which the prophet gives God is said in Hebrew "*chanun.*" The common translation is mercy, but actually it is grace, friendship, kindness. But how and what it may be one can understand well by the opposite. We are by skill and nature unmerciful and unfriendly when we become upset and angry. Then one cannot easily reconcile with us. We cannot be easily brought to peace. We are not quick to pardon and forgive. As Homer, the heathen poet, describes Achilles, that he was a harsh man who was not easily reconciled; so we have that in common [with Achilles] all too often.

On the contrary, God is of such a mind by manner and nature that he lets himself easily bend and be moved. He quickly is reconciled and called upon. As soon as one is raised up to pray, if only one word is said, then he will soften and gladly pardons everything that he has done against him and that he has sinned.

This title or name of God is set, above all, against your thoughts which picture God as an unkind, hard, wrathful tyrant, master of the stocks and hangman, whose wrath cannot ever be appeased. We agree with this when our conscience is peaceful and not overcome by any sins. But on the other hand, when punishment is at hand and drowns us, we flee before God as did Adam in Paradise. We hide.

But we should consider that we have transgressed against the kind, merciful, mighty God. Then even if he punishes, yet he doesn't act that way according to his manner and nature. He always has a soft and friendly heart so he soon lets himself be moved and turned, even when it seems to us that he is angry. For his punishment serves the purpose of us not falling deeper into sins, but that we turn [from them] and live.

Why then do you flee before the kind, gracious and hearty love of the Father? He pursues you not that he slay you to death but rather much more that he bring you to the right way. Therefore, hold still. Turn to him with your whole heart so he will be merciful to you and pardon your sins. Fall before his feet so that he will be merciful to you, so that he will receive you gladly to grace.

But those who are in heavy affliction rightly feel God's wrath against their sins. They cannot be advised of this so that they believe it for they have completely different thoughts about God. Then one should turn his eyes and behold the comforting, sure, public sign of grace, that God has not even spared his own Son, but has given him up for the sake of all.

Place this work before your eyes and think on it quickly. For God has done this for the poor sinners to better and comfort them. So now he receives sinners in a friendly way. He has revealed and made known by the death of his own Son that he is not bearing a grudge to them but rather desires that they should be holy and freed from eternal death. Why then would you want to doubt how God thinks about you after you have been reconciled to him through his Son?

But here you say: I am a great sinner, have enraged and offended God terribly, have become disobedient to him and not done his will, which I justly should have done. Well, even if it is just so, since it is the pure truth (for we don't want to lie about our vice and sins) that you have not turned from them, have not become good, but now have become an evil fool and a disobedient child yet do you want to conclude and say on that account that God has also turned and has become different? Yes, depart from evil and become better. Have you become a sinner? Stop and do it no more. Ask after grace and forgiveness, place hope on Christ and believe that God is reconciled to you through him and that this reconciliation is eternal, not for one or two days, one or two years, but rather this remains to eternity. So you will hold the opinion inside that the prophet is not lying, that he is called (*chanun*) kind, gracious, friendly and is reconciled easily and gladly.

Altb. VI, 939–940: Lectures on Joel, 1536; cf. AE 18

If my sins give me alarm And my conscience grieve me,
Let Thy cross my fear disarm, Peace of conscience give me.
Grant that I may trust in Thee And Thy holy Passion.
If His Son so loveth me, God must have compassion. (*TLH* 140: 5)

Saturday

Who knows, he may repent and leave a blessing after you, to offer food offering and drink offering to the Lord, your God. Joel 2:14

In our passage this way of speaking (who knows?) sounds *dubitative*, as if one doubts if something can come of it. But it is a truly fine, skillful word of a repentant heart. For it clings to both things, namely: In the first place, we feel our sins which make it so that we must think and hold it as sure that God is justly angry and punishes us. On the other hand, at the same time, we hope and believe God will help us to receive grace because by nature he is kind and gracious. He readily and gladly lets himself be reconciled. As also when the outcast in the gospel says: "If you want to, you can make me clean," he first fell with these words at Christ's feet and freely acknowledged that he had justly received this punishment. On the other hand he reveals his faith and hope which laughed in such feelings of sins because if he wanted to, Christ could and would help.

But our form and manner of praying should constantly be and remain this way: First, that we are saddened in our heart on account of sins. On the other hand we arise and hope that God hears us for the sake of his mercy which is done in Christ and yet prevails. This faith and hope makes penitence, as said above, perfected. It gives God his rightful honor. Therefore it is also the most welcome service of God and the dearest offering, of which the hypocrite knows nothing. Much less is he able to do it.

But that which he says about blessing is rightly understood concerning bodily blessing. When the people would repent and become better, then the Lord would richly bless with all kinds of gracious benefices, also saving them from the Babylonian enemies. Yet the prophet also includes in it the promise of Christ which is fulfilled in the latter days. Then in addition, the Lord has graciously blessed his people so that true eat and drink offerings (doing away with the invented and self-chosen ones done by the hypocrites) again were instituted, that is, rightly fashioned services of God, as believing, confessing, calling on God in need, calling out to and praising God's goodness and mercy, etc. But we will also always remember this, that God adorned and gilded us with his blessing so that we serve him by it and not that we should misuse it with unnecessary pomp or revelry as is commonly done.

So now this is a beautiful and holy exhortation to true penance which is opposed to the pope's teaching and [under the papacy] was most scandalously tossed aside and fought against. Yes, it is completely and thoroughly annulled and changed. The prophet teaches: That one should turn to the Lord with his whole heart, that is, quickly hear God's Word, keep hold of it, flee from sin and gladly become sin's enemy. Upon God's goodness and mercy in Christ thereafter he builds and trusts. In these two parts he hangs the whole doctrine of repentance.

But hear the pope about this. First he teaches much about *contritio* or sorrow, and says that it is a work of our free will, remains in our arbitrariness, as if we have that ability whenever we want, and earn forgiveness of sins, etc., which is false and incorrect.

Secondly, he lays this burden on those whose sins oppress them; they must confess and reveal them and enumerate them word for word to the priest or servant of the church without omission. And he says further that such oral confession is necessary and merits holiness.

Thirdly, he would have the works of satisfaction by which one should make satisfaction for their sins with human works, say a few "Our Fathers," say the rosary, fast a few days, do this work or that. These same works, since they are always done with mistakes or insufficiently and are never able to give peace to the conscience, are justly called a sea and an abyss out of which, if he once enters into it, a person can nevermore come to a port and shore.

This filth and child of ruin teaches neither of the terror nor the fear which the law makes and delivers in the heart when it shows us God's wrath and makes us guilty and lamenting before God's judgment. He teaches nothing about faith, nothing of the promise which, when they grasp it with faith, since it alone brings us the forgiveness of sins, alone delivers and comforts the heart that is sorrowful, frightened and dismayed by fear of God's wrath.

But if one has immediately sought after the works of satisfaction, there he sees the devil's poison and roguery. One fasts on a few appointed days, another says a few little prayers that he doesn't understand. A few think that they will receive the forgiveness of sins through pilgrimages up to Rome, to St. James, through the intercession of silent idols and dead people, with idolatry and other similar lies and foolish works.

Altb. VI, 943–944: Lectures on Joel, 1536; cf. AE 18

To me He spake: Hold fast to Me, I am thy Rock and Castle;
Thy Ransom I Myself will be, For thee I strive and wrestle;
For I am with thee, I am thine, And evermore thou shalt be Mine:
The foe shall not divide us. (*TLH* 387: 7)

Week of Trinity III

Sunday

Come unto me, all who are tired and heavy laden, and I will refresh you. Matthew 11:28

He would say, "Run and seek where you want, hear and learn everything that one can preach, yet you will not find peace or joy of the heart. [You will find it] only by accompanying me." We would rather allow the preaching of a good life, the Ten Commandments and all kinds of doctrine; but to preach to the conscience stuck in anxiety and terror over sins, there is no other Word that will attach life [to such a conscience] but that of Christ. For that is the poor lost little lamb, which can neither have nor suffer any master except this fine single shepherd. For he does not use the driving or demands of the law, but rather treats him in the sweetest and gentlest manner, and takes upon himself the lamb with all its need, sins and fear, and he himself does what the lamb should do; as we will hear further.

So here one does well to distinguish, as I have previously said, between the two kinds of preaching, or the voice of Moses and that of Christic so that one not let any nourishment come to the lost lamb from Moses, even if he preaches as best he can. For it is when one wants to boil another that he so "comforts" an afflicted conscience with the law saying things like: be courageous, you have certainly not committed murder, or committed adultery, or done the great sins, or you meant well, etc. That is also a comfort, but it doesn't last long, and cannot withstand the pangs. For in that is no greater or higher comfort than what rests upon you yourself. With that the poor little lamb is not helped at all. He remains just as bothered and lost and cannot help himself, or come to his shepherd.

But if he should be helped, one must show him the true shepherd, who comes and seeks him there, that he might again hold the lamb and let his voice sound, so that it can experience a true comfort; that the lamb might answer Moses and say, "I no longer pay attention to either your comfort or your terror, and make it ever so bad as you can, let me be a murderer and a mass murderer and one who has hung my father and my mother, but now, since I am in fear and terror before God's wrath and eternal damnation, yet I will not hear or follow you. For I myself feel and confess that I am a poor lost sheep. But this is my salvation and comfort upon which I rely, that I have the shepherd who himself sought me, his lost little sheep, and he bears me upon his shoulders. So let us not dispute how good or evil I am, but rather how I come to Christ."

Therefore one must always preach to where the people are. For I have said that this doctrine does not serve for a coarse, hard person. Just as it is not useful to give a coarse, hard person a great piece of candy and a costly desert that belong to a sick person. Rather, one should give him a good piece of hard bread and cheese and a drink of water. But other weak and sweet foods are reserved for the sick or for young children who are not able to digest anything coarse. So you must also take care here that you divide it rightly and give each his portion as a wise householder, so that you withhold Moses and the law preaching until you find hard, reckless people who live in security and without fear. Let them eat only coarse food, that is, the wrathful Moses who lightninged and thundered from Mount Sinai. The children of Israel struggled and were slain in the wilderness; King Pharaoh was drowned in the Red Sea.

But where there are beleaguered, weak hearts and consciences that have now become lost little sheep, there only be silent about Moses and all works to God that are done by the law and speak only of the works of the time of grace done through Christ, and portray him for the good of the poor conscience as he reveals himself near the lost lamb. Namely, that he is the dear, good Shepherd who is so anxious and troubled for the sake of the sheep that he forsakes all so that he might only restore the lamb again and does not give up until he brings it home. For it is his sorrow when a person is stuck in sins, beset and oppressed, and he cannot stand that he remain there and be ruined. Rather he draws near on the feet of the gospel in the most friendly way, only that you come to him and let him take and carry you upon his shoulders and be called his dearest lamb.

Erl. 13, 50–52: Second Sermon on Trinity 3, Luke 15:1–10

The Lord's my Shepherd, I'll not want; He makes me down to lie
In pastures green; He leadeth me The quiet waters by. (*TLH* 436: 1)

Monday

And when he has found it, he lays it upon his shoulder with joy. Luke 15:5

Compared to the others, see how kindly he is as soon as he has found the little lamb. He bestows his joy and unspeakable signs and gifts. For he does not give him a single law or compulsion and thus let him walk on his own. He would have a right to drive him forward as the other shepherds. But rather, he draws near and lays it upon his shoulders and himself carries it the whole way through the wilderness. He takes all the work and worry upon himself so that the lamb has only peace and ease and desires this from the heart. Yes, he is only filled with joy that he has it back. Also behold how good it is for the dear lamb. He lies completely in peace and safety upon his shepherd's shoulders. Also, the lamb desires to lie softly and does not want to leave. He is safe and without worry despite the dogs and the wolves, that is, despite all errors and lies, danger and ruin. That is surely a kind picture, and is excellent, lovely and comforting to behold.

For our Lord Christ does this when he redeems us as he lovingly did once and for all in his suffering and death; but now he always uses this power spiritually through his Word. With it he lays us upon his shoulder, carries and defends us, that we are safe before all danger of sins, of devils and death, even if they still terrify us and rear their ugly heads as if they would rip us away and devour us. So this carrying delivers our satisfaction and preserves us before all misfortune and does not let us fear; just as the lamb, laying upon the shepherd's shoulders, lets nothing afflict it even if the hounds are fiendishly yelping and the wolf creeps near. Rather it hangs its head behind without worry and sleeps soundly anyway.

So also with us, when we remain in the faith of this article: "I believe in Jesus Christ, our Lord, who suffered, died and arose for us, etc." So we need not worry that we will be lost, or that the devil might devour us, if he has already hoisted us upon his shoulder. Then we are not on our own legs, and don't go forth on our feet, but rather we are hanging on the neck of our dear Shepherd and lay upon his back, where we are already safe. For sins, death and hell, even if they present themselves, evil and terrifying, must leave him unassailable, else we poor lambs would be quickly lost and ruined.

So the sheep cannot defend itself or watch out for itself, to keep things from going wrong, if ever the shepherd does not always direct and attend it. If it errs and is lost, it cannot find itself or come to the shepherd, but rather the shepherd himself must go out to him and search as long as it takes to find it. When he has found it, he places it upon his back and carries it, that it not be terrified, hunted or become seized by the wolf when he is near.

So we also could neither help nor advise ourselves to find peace and quiet in our conscience and run away from the devil, death and hell, if Christ himself had not again fetched and called us to himself with his Word. It is by this that we come to him and are in faith. We are not able of ourselves to hold on or to remain if he himself did not always lift and carry us through that same Word and power. For the devil always stalks us and prowls after us as a roaring lion (as St.

Peter says in his first letter, chapter 5:8), that he might devour us. But here it is of no value if we brag about something of our free will or powers, neither to start nor to proceed nor to be preserved. Rather Christ, our Shepherd, alone must do everything.

But in this we are now safe, so long as we lay on Christ's back, that we would yet remain there before all terror and misfortune. For he would surely not allow us to be ripped from his neck, nor would he cast us from him. He is so happy and has such good courage only because he again has the little lamb and shall bring him to the other house. In short, there is no terror, driving or demand, but rather only a friendly carrying and pure life of grace, by which he cares for his lambs in the gentlest way.

Erl. 13, 53–57: Second Sermon on Trinity 3, Luke 15:1–10

My soul He doth restore again And me to walk doth make
Within the paths of righteousness, E'en for His own name's sake. (*TLH* 436: 2)

Tuesday

But this is the will of the one who sent me; that who sees the Son and believes on him has eternal life and I will raise him up on the last day. John 6:40

There you must discern (whether you like it or not), that the Ten Commandments are not the Son of God. Then all the holiness and righteousness of the Jews, which they have done, are also not the Son of God. Rather, the Son is something other than all the holiness and the compelling life of Saint Hieronymous, Ambrose and Augustine, or of the whole papacy's good works and the merits of all the saints. It is a bit higher than all the holiness of the saints. The Lord testifies to our heart that he is outside of and over everything that is called good works and the Ten Commandments, for they are not the Son of God. Even if the works were also just as prescribed in the commandments, that one should love God with his whole heart, soul and all his might, which is commanded from God himself, yet they would not be the Son of God. And even if you also understood and undertook to do the law—to love God and your neighbor, then, you see, you are not yet the Son of God. Rather, this is the will and plan of the Father. He wants us to see the Son and believe in him and have eternal life. God desires that it penetrate the heart, as it is plainly and clearly enough said if one would only heed him, that whoever has the Son shall also have eternal life and the forgiveness of sins and be free of death. But why? Only because you hear and see the Son and believe in him.

This is nobly and powerfully spoken against all good works, but one always prods us as to whether, then, one should do good works. Yes, they will follow faith, for faith must have good works, but the life is not preserved through works, for it is impossible that one could keep the law. No saint can ever be found on earth who has loved God and his neighbor with all his heart as he has loved himself. Rather the law has become an unbearable, undesirable load and burden, as also St. Peter says in the fifteenth chapter of the Acts of the Apostles; that "the law is a yoke or burden that neither you nor your fathers have been able to bear." That says that all saints are disposed of for they were not able to do the law. But what must we then do, that we be saved? We shall behold Christ and hang upon him and cling to him, love him and believe in the Son. He shall be the one through whom we shall be saved and preserved, whom we will not lose. God has decided this, and through him I have righteousness and eternal life, so I hang upon him. But should you not hang on him, though you should lead a holier life than St. Heironymus, you are yet lost.

But when I say, "Lord Christ, I remain by you and hang on you, or believe on you, so you are the only one." Then I will go on and take the Ten Commandments and practice myself in good works. But my main concern will be that I will hold onto Christ, and that through him will be given life. After the chief article I will then begin to love God and my neighbor as much as I can and do all good things and then stand safe because my good works do not help me. My life and work are too small and poor to use them to drown death, close hell, take away sins and open heaven. God has not told me that I should be the person that could give life or be able to preserve myself, for we cannot keep the law. The papists previously told us that the commandments of God will preserve us. But it is impossible for us to keep them. So God gives us a man, of whom it is said, "He will not leave us, he shall preserve us that we not be ruined, and under him we shall not be ruined nor die."

But this makes this doctrine despicable. Everyone thinks that it is a poor terrible thing that one should hear that he does nothing but see and believe. It stays (separated) in two parts, in the seeing and believing. Yes, it is easily said, but no one knows what true faith is. He that does is a high doctor and teacher, as no saint has been able to complete his training or become completely established. For in every case saints have been stuck in doubt, in death's compulsion and outward dangers. Then one sees the power and working of faith above all in afflictions, as faith overcomes sins, death devil and hell, which are not the deadly enemies (they had seemed). They drive a sweat out of one and break one's legs and make heaven and earth too poor. In faith there is no one who could help when the devil and death come but only this person who speaks, "I will be the one who will not forsake you." That is what the Father desires. Then you learn what faith is.

Altb. V, 646: Sermons on the Gospel of St. John, Chapters 6–8, 1530-2; cf. AE 23

Yea, tho' I walk in death's dark vale, Yet will I fear no ill;
For Thou art with me, and Thy rod And staff me comfort still. (*TLH* 436: 3)

Wednesday

Do not grumble one to another. No one can come to me unless the Father, who has sent me, draw him. John 6:43,44

What does "no one" mean? Do you think it only means a cow or donkey or other beast? Rather, no one in the whole world is an exception who, with everyone else, is called the human race, even the mightiest, the holiest, smartest and most learned. That is easily said but this is such a mighty passage, that it precipitates and buries all human wisdom, understanding, reason, righteousness and holiness and also all that is called religion and service to God. For to come to this article and salvation in Christ, no wisdom, intelligence, blood sacrifice or giving alms helps, nor even what the whole human race undertakes with wisdom, with piety or holiness, for it says, "No one can come to me except the Father draw him." One should learn that.

But it is a completely comforting and sweet preaching to the Christian heart, although it also sounds annoying and is a frightening and insufferable preaching to the fanatics and others who grumble because no one should come elsewhere but to Christ and that there must be nothing else besides Christ who saves us, namely the bread which comes from heaven. When it does not grow in the heart, then the godless cannot hear that their own part is nothing and they say, "Then what does my life in the cloister do? My alms? My holy disciplined life? And good works?" You account everything besides this as nothing, for [when you don't] you bring hell fire upon your head. So, should all then be lost? Yes, it is always purely lost, for Christ says consistently that one cannot come to Christ by them, even if you want to do them and would climb into heaven by them.

Therefore, this is the kind of preaching that they must grumble about and they cannot receive. It is unbearable to them when I say to the Turk, Jew and pope: "All your work and laws are lost and you are damned with all your righteousness." By this what have I served? A grumbling anger and wrath. For the Jews do not desire their costly wisdom and the law in Moses to be nothing, nor the Turks to let their religion be attacked, so also the monks and papists cannot let their acts, heresies and life also be damned. And the Lord would as much as say, "So then why am I here? Am I not the way? You do not do it, so your power and works also do not help or make you clean, for no one can so resign himself to me or in me, or believe in me except one whom the Father brings."

This word: Father—sits as an antithesis against all human works, holy life, reason and righteousness, which do not draw one to God, but rather drive you away and make a grumbler and quarreler out of you or cause you yet to doubt. For Christ says clearly, "He only comes to me, and otherwise no one experiences faith except those whom the Father draws to me."

This drawing is not as the hangman draws a thief upon the scaffold and gallows, but rather it is a friendly alluring and engaging [drawing], whereby as an amiable person draws people to himself because he is friendly and likeable, and everyone gladly goes to him, so God also properly allures and brings people to himself. Thus they are willingly and gladly near him and will show by this that no one could think he came to him because he was wise, for if you would use your wisdom he would anger you. But rather, the Father presents to you his great mercy and gives you discernment, that he has sent the Christ into the world of Fatherly love, as John 3 states, "For whosoever believes in him will not perish but have eternal life," and you hear that God is not your enemy but is your gracious merciful Father, and he gives his Son for you and lets him die for you and raises him again from the dead, and reveals to you his Son, and he has him preach to you. Now when that is rightly taught, then one comes to him, that is, he is drawn.

Otherwise, one runs from our Lord God, as if the devil or a tyrant were chasing him, when one preaches that God is angry and one must appease him with good works and have the intercession of the saints unless one wants to be damned. That is not drawing, but terrorizing. The conscience cannot be established in peace by this, but rather stays in fear, restlessness and care, becomes God's hidden enemy, does not confess Christ and also does not come to him. It does not fail to follow that they do not believe in Christ, but rather they have a God such as the Turks, Jews and papists have a God, namely, one who sits in heaven as a judge and demands of us good works for our sins.

Altb. V, 652–653: Sermons on the Gospel of St. John, Chapters 6–8, 1530-2; cf. AE 23

My table Thou hast furnished In presence of my foes;
My head thou dost with oil anoint, And my cup overflows. (*TLH* 436: 4)

Thursday

Not that anyone has seen the Father, but only the one who is from the Father has seen the Father. John 6:46

He would also like us to understand by these words, that he would show things pertaining to the Father from himself. But that is not the meaning as he then himself presents and clarifies it, contradicting what might be commonly understood. For he would say, "One must not so isolate me [from the Father] and complain about me being from the Father, so that God would grant (such knowledge of himself) into that person's own heart [apart from Christ], and therefore allow me [Christ] to go and depart and always preach (unheeded)." The enthusiasts and fanatics also despise and cast away the external Word or the preaching office and say, "this has nothing to do with the preaching office and the external Word. If it did, the people would become ever more pious and better from it. Many hear it now and thereafter remain just as wicked as before, and among those that hear the Word of God, not all of them come quickly to Christ." But don't you speak as they do, i.e., "Yes, the oral Word does not help, so I will go into the closet, speculate and meditate until the Father shows me and calms my heart." Out, out with your thoughts, with those nothings, for there is the nasty devil, and even if all your thoughts were as sweet as candy, yet they are of the nasty devil. For the Lord Christ says here, "Not that anyone has seen the Father, except the one who is from the Father, who has seen the Father." Therefore, do not think (he would say), that I believe that you can see the Father without me. No! No! See that without Christ you will not come to the Father and without the Father you cannot be brought to the Son. No one will see the Father without Christ. If you would then come up to the Father, then do not leave Christ behind you, for apart from him you will not.

So he joins and binds them (Christ and the Father) so tightly so as to warn and direct that one does not mediate to the Father outside of Christ, which he so earnestly forbids. For one should not think that he can come to the Father apart from the person of Christ. No one hears or knows anything of the Father but the one who has come from the Father. Therefore, he will not suffer or allow that one seek after God outside of Christ. Because of this, we cast down the enthusiasts for he says, "Through me and in me you will see the Father. Apart from me is no other way to know the Father."

Do not run off with the idea that one could come to the Father without the person of the Son. Therefore, he binds our ears and heart to the Word of this man. For I must have it through this single man who has seen the Father if I should also know, see and hear the Father, for he witnesses to you of the Father. Why does he [God] bring him [Jesus] to me? So that he [Jesus] gives him [the Father] in the Word, and through my mouth he speaks with you, and witnesses in this way to your heart. If you receive the Word, that Christ speaks to you as the Father's Word, that Word takes you no further than to the person, to the Father.

Because the Lord Christ speaks this way from the Father, no flattering spirit will battle there, and you will not depart from him nor seek God in heaven and thus allow this man Christ to be called a liar. For I shall neither seek nor find any God outside of this man Christ. But I find ONE, so I will not correct or judge him, else I will encounter a wrathful God. So the Father leads us and witnesses to us of the Son, through his mouth, doctrine and Word. For the doctrine goes from the Father through the Son, and by this he witnesses to us to the Son. If you have him, then you grasp and see the true Son of God, or you have and grasp, then, also God the Father himself. The whole Holy Trinity is known in the person of Christ. So when we come to the Son, then we are also with the Father. Who sees the person born of the virgin Mary sees also the Son of God, for the Father provides you the Son's Word and person. On this everything is pegged, that everything will remain in the person of Christ, so one thinks of nothing else nor has in his mind anything else from God. Then when this person speaks, you hear the Father's Word and voice. For it is God the Father's voice which the Son preaches and speaks, that he is sent into the world, suffered and died, etc., for you. And by this he gives your heart confidence and leads you only to Christ and brings you no farther. He also informs you in no other way than the voice of the Father when he speaks through the Son.

He did not act this way in other saints, from whom I also hear God's Word, or through whom God spoke with me, as by the prophets Isaiah, Moses, Jeremiah, St. John the Baptist or St. Paul. He does not lead me to them, for he does not say, "When you hear Jeremiah or Isaiah, then you have enough." For their Words are not enough. The Father does not do that when he speaks so through the prophets, but rather he says this regarding his Son. For it says, "The Father witnesses to you of me." Remain by the person of Christ. For only the Lord Christ's Word is the Father's Word. Do not be fickle in your learning and do not let your thoughts go to and fro. Do not become irritated by this. For when the Son is in his humanity and flesh, and he preaches, then you also truly hear the Father himself preaching.

Altb. V, 653–654: Sermons on the Gospel of St. John, Chapters 6–8, 1530-2; cf. AE 23

Goodness and mercy, all my life, Shall surely follow me;
And in God's house forevermore My dwelling place shall be. (*TLH* 436: 5)

Friday

It is written in the prophets, You will all be taught of God.
Whoever now hears it from the Father and learns it, he
comes to me. John 6.45

So he says, "Who wants to be a Christian and be called a member
or disciple of the Lord Christ shall immediately hear God himself."
How, then, do I hear him? How shall I be taught by him? A fanatic runs
to a corner, shuts his mouth, must neither read nor learn, but rather
waits until our Lord God speaks with him and waits for the Holy Ghost
and says, "Oh, this is being taught by God." Yes, that is the devil's idea
of what it is to be taught of God. If one hears the Word of the Lord
Christ and learns from him and is then sure that it is God's Word—that
is what is called hearing God himself. And even if it were a donkey who
says it, as it happened with Balaam, yet it would be God's Word. So if
you hear the preaching of St. Paul or of me, then you would hear God
the Father, himself. You would not be my student, but rather the
Father's student for I do not speak it, but he does. I am also not your
master, but we both, you and I alike, have one master and teacher, the
Father, who taught it to us. We are, both as preachers and listeners, only
students. The only difference is that God speaks through me to you.

Moses and the prophets have preached. But there we do not hear
God himself. For Moses has mediated the law from angels and he
also had a different inferior mandate. For with the preaching of the
law one only compels the people to good works. Just as when I hear
the king, I do not thereby hear God, even if it is God's will that I
should be obedient to the king and do what he commands, and honor
my elders. When I now hear Moses, who compels good works, I
hear him just as one who declares the king's or the prince's
commands and words. But that is not hearing God himself. For when
God himself speaks with mankind, they cannot hear anything but
pure grace, mercy and everything good. It is fatherly, kind speech,
as he is by nature gracious, good and kind. You hear such things
spoken from God the Father and not through a knight or through
another mediator, as previously through the angels, or through Moses
or even a ruler, which is always a law preachment. Rather, from
now on, he himself speaks to us through his Son and the Holy Ghost,
and so one hears a Fatherly voice where is only unbounded and

unspeakable love and grace. He speaks only mercy, goodness, sweetness and love. For that is also what God means.

Reason will not come up with this doctrine, for it judges this doctrine as unfair. So it is called a divine teaching that one will be taught by God himself. We hear only his Word and regard that it is God's Word. I cannot originate that Word, but I hear it through the mouth of Christ, and I can not understand, hear, learn or believe if he does not give it into my heart. If we were not drawn by the Father, then we would not consider it in this way as the Father's Word. So this is called being taught by God and coming to Christ. If you can, be sure that it is God's Word. The evil also hear it just as well as the good through the mouth of Christ, but they do not learn it. But when you regard it as God's Word and receive it, then you have learned it from God. If the other "wise people" try to improve it, then they make a great law and commandment out of Baptism, Faith, the Lord's Supper and the gospel as do the anabaptists and sacramentarians [Baptists and the Reformed]. That does not rightly belong to God's Word and so does not name God but rather you hear the angel, prophet, elder or the king. But one must hear God himself, namely through his Son, through the mouth of Christ and believe his Word, for it is in your ears and he gives it into you that it is his Word. And if you believe that he has spoken his Word, then you have learned it from him and you are a true student of Christ and drawn by God. That is a pure sweet doctrine.

Altb. V, 657–658: Sermons on the Gospel of St. John, Chapters 6–8, 1530-2; cf. AE 23

O God, our Lord, Thy holy Word	For this today our thanks we say
Was long a hidden treasure	And gladly glorify Thee.
Till to its place I was by grace	Thy mercy show and grace bestow
Restored in fullest measure.	On all who still deny Thee. (*TLH* 266: 1)

Saturday

Truly, truly, I say to you, whoever believes on me has eternal life. John 6:47

Now one could preach on these Words for a hundred thousand years and underline it again and again. Yes, one cannot speak of it enough. For Christ directly says to those who believe in him that they should have eternal life and does not say: "Who believes on me WILL have eternal life," but rather (he says) "as soon as you believe you have it ALREADY." He speaks not of a future gift but rather of a present gift, namely: if you can believe on me, then you are saved and eternal life is already your gift.

From this text one can judge everything over which we now dispute and fight, for Christ is the foundation of our justification. For we say that our good works do not lead us up to heaven or help us in any way before God, but rather only our faith. The works should be done well and they will be performed in obedience to God and in practiced goodness, but they will not accomplish the achievement of salvation. I already have eternal life. I do not battle here on earth. I can no longer accomplish it but rather here in this life it must be obtained and gotten. But how does one get it? God begins it and becomes your master, preaches to you, begins the eternal life. He preaches to you the oral and external Word, and by this enriches the heart so that one receives the Word and believes him. So lift yourself up and never leave this same Word behind, which you hear and believe in, so that you come no farther than the person of Christ, born of the virgin Mary. Thus you can believe in him and hang yourself upon him so that you are not unstuck with him by bodily and spiritual death. You already have eternal life.

This is a clear, bright text if you have Christ, whom I have presented to you to believe. Thus you have eternal life and should be free of eternal death. But if we are free of eternal death then we are also freed from temporal death. And all of the slavery and the list of trespasses that bring temporal death are taken away as are sins. With sins taken away, so also the law is taken away. Now as the law is fulfilled and taken away, so also is God's wrath and sentence taken away, as is the devil, death and hell locked out, and everything is laid aside and defeated, else it would not be called eternal life. If you believe on Christ, everything is taken away from you. Hell is already drowned, sins removed, death overcome and you have eternal righteousness, salvation and life. Who will measure such a treasure? There you will truly be found. I have not misled you with faith.

There are, however, impudent, crude and unholy spirits who do not know what faith is and say, "Oh, faith is a poor thing. Who does not believe?" You surely see it. But that is an unholy spirit belonging to impudent people who never have experienced what is called faith. And it is of the Father when a person arises and considers what he is so that he entrusts himself to these Words with his whole heart and zeal in all afflictions. If you did that and earnestly believed then you will speak otherwise and not speak so disgracefully about faith. Yes, you say, even if I believe on Christ, yet I will feel death even as I and everyone else must die. I am afraid of death and of sins, as also the saints like St. Peter and St. Paul and others likewise complained, and as the Lord's Prayer also petitions about this when it also says: "Forgive us our trespasses."

None of the saints in Christianity says that he is without death, without fear, without sins and afflictions. So how does Christ boast, "Whoever believes on me has eternal life?" I may now pray against sins, because there are two contrary things: we have eternal life and at the same time we pray against sins, death, devil and hell.

Now this is definitely true, that who believes in Christ has eternal life but the following is still lacking—I still feel sins. Death and hell smother me because I have eternal life and Christ in faith and not yet in deed. But if faith should be established then an outward feeling of death, of hell, of the devil, of sins and the law must yet remain. If you feel that, then it is only a battle that desires to hinder you so that you should not have eternal life and that would take Christ away from you. But these sins will not retain you and in that situation one should say, "I believe in Christ Jesus, who is mine, and so far as I have him and believe on him, so far I am pious and have eternal life for he is Lord over all."

Therefore, if I have him, so I have everything surely, for he is himself nothing else but pure righteousness, life, and eternal salvation and a Lord over death. Christ is without any lacking or failure. The eternal life, joy, righteousness and salvation; the treasure is completely at hand. This I have in Christ, for he is everything. There is no infirmity. Nothing can cause him a defficiency even if it is yet a defficient in me since I yet cannot completely cling and believe. As much as I now grasp and believe it, so much I have and I remain with that. So I always receive it and learn yet always more and more to believe until it will come in the next life where I then will completely grasp and know it. What is lacking will also not stop us and we will no longer feel the sins or be terrified by death, or fear the devil. Flesh and blood is yet the wall between me and Christ, which will than also be taken away, and there will be Christ with only righteousness and salvation.

Altb. V, 661–662: Sermons on the Gospel of St. John, Chapters 6–8, 1530-2; cf. AE 23

Salvation free by faith in Thee, That is Thy gospel's preaching,
The heart and core of Bible lore In all its sacred teaching.
In Christ we must put all our trust, Not in our deeds or labor;
With conscience pure and heart secure Love thee, Lord, and our neighbor. (*TLH* 266: 2)

Week of Trinity IV

Sunday

For I am sure that the sufferings of this time are not worthy to be compared to the glory that will be revealed to us. Romans 8:18

Only see how he turns his back against the world as if he overlooks any misfortune or tragedy on earth and sees only pure joy. Certainly, evil strikes, he says, yet what is our sorrow now compared to the unspeakable joy and glory which shall be revealed to us? It is not even worth comparing or calling it sorrow. But what is yet missing is our seeing the great and excellent glory which we await with bodily eyes. We fumble around, not taking to heart that we shall never die and that we shall receive over this body one that cannot suffer or become sick, etc. Whoever could have that held in his heart must also say that even if he would be burned and drowned ten times, if it were possible, that would yet be nothing compared to the coming glorious life. For what is temporal suffering, no matter how long it lasts, compared to everlasting life? It is not even worth one boasting about how much he's suffered, or calling it a service.

That's how I consider it, says St. Paul, and you Christians should also learn to consider it so. You also will find that it is impossible to compare the eternal with that which ends. For what is a single penny compared to a world full of thousand dollar bills? But even such a comparison does not apply, since both are still corruptible. Therefore, all the world's suffering is nothing compared to the glory of the eternal existence, which we shall see and possess. Because of this I beg you, dear brothers, do not shy away from any suffering, even if you become strangled. This is your rightful co-inheritance. So this will also happen to you, for this also is a part of your inheritance, that is your co-inheritance. But what is this suffering when one compares it to the eternal glory, which is prepared for you and is already acquired for you through your savior, Jesus Christ? Is it not noble to encourage each other in this way! St. Paul makes a little drop and a small spark out of every sorrow on earth; but out of every glory for which we hope he makes an endless sea and a great fire.

But why do we fail to regard such suffering as so trifling and not regard the glory as so great as St. Paul does here? By this failure it is easy to see our natural disposition. If someone says but a harsh word to most people then they will swiftly turn over mountains and rip out trees. Those who are that insufferable do not understand a word of this glorious comfort of St. Paul. A Christian should not present himself in that way when evil confronts him that he scream and cry out against injustice. Be that as it may. But how is it that you exalt your suffering as being so great and do not think at once of heaven and what is awaiting you there? Why do you also exalt yourself so highly? If you want to be a Christian, then you must certainly not conduct yourself in that way. If you would bear the affairs of your life, you want to conduct them in a right and orderly way.

But here it must be otherwise. For if you desire to be a co-heir of the Lord Jesus Christ and yet not be like your brother and not suffer as he did, then he will likewise not acknowledge you on the last day as his brother or co-heir. Rather, he will say to you, "Where do you have your crown of thorns, cross, nails and scourge, (which belong to you) since you want to become an abomination to the whole world," just as he and all his members have been from the beginning of the world until now? But if you cannot acknowledge such things then he will also not be able to regard you as his brother. In summary, it must be co-suffered, and all must be conformed to the Son of God, as said before, or we will not be exalted to the glory.

Erl. 9, 98–100: Sermon on Trinity 4, Romans 8:18–22, 1535

Thy ways, O Lord, with wise design Are framed upon Thy throne above,
And every dark and bending line Meets in the center of Thy love. (*TLH* 530: 1)

Monday

For our afflictions, which are temporal and light, fashion for us an eternal and surpassing mighty glory, that we do not see as visible but it is invisible. For what is visible is temporal, but what is invisible is eternal. 2 Cor. 4:17,18

When he calls it glory, which should be visible, he shows why it is a mistake that one suffers with so little desire to do so. Namely, it is because his faith is yet weak and he will not see into the hidden glory which should be already revealed to us. For if it were a glory which one could see with his eyes, say, what fine patient martyrs we would be! If someone would stand in the Elbe sometime with a box full of money and say, "Whoever will dare and swim over here shall have the box and its money," wouldn't everyone get up for a swim for the sake of the money which they saw before their eyes?

What does an adventurer or a mercenary do? He receives four guldens a month and sets himself down before food and tins, in the knowledge that death follows. Also a trader walks and runs here, there and everywhere in the world for the sake of money and goods, risking body and life for it, whether or not God lets the goods he deals for be worth it. What must one suffer for the sake of a hope before he makes it, whether he gets it right away or he is hindered? So in the world people do and suffer everything for the sake of honor, goods and power; for it is visible before their eyes.

But here, because it is not apparent, it is very difficult for the Old Adam to believe that God will give such a beautiful body, joyful courage and clean soul on the last day; and that I shall become a greater lord than any king on earth. I easily see the evidence against it. Because of this, faith is condemned as heresy. Everyone is now burned or else undone for [true faith], which remains contrary to [evidence of] glory, wealth and honor. That is why it strikes us as so unpleasant, as we are given into suffering while the hidden redemption and glory await. On the other hand, the world exalts in its courage and great work. It does and suffers whatever comes for the sake of shameful mammon which the moth and rust consume and the thief steals.

Therefore, St. Paul says: "I know for sure that a great glory awaits us, compared to which all suffering on earth is a great nothing. But it is yet to be revealed to you." Therefore, if only a rough wind blows under our eyes or a little misfortune overshadows us, we rise to cry and scream, swelling it so high up that the heavens are filled with our cries. But if faith were there, this would be a paltry matter, even if such sorrow lasted thirty, forty or even more years. Yes, we would consider it trifling to even think about it. This is true only because our Lord God also has considered it with his own judgment, in which he has dealt with our sins. Oh! How much can one say about great suffering or about a reward for suffering, how we yet come completely unworthily to such great grace and unspeakable glory? For we become as children and heirs of God through Christ; brothers and coheirs with Christ.

So we might well say: I would gladly be silent in my sufferings and not boast or cry out much in them but rather patiently bear all that my dear God has given and set out for me. I will even thank him with all my heart that he has called me to great overwhelming goodness and grace. But as I have said, it will not happen because of our pitiful, weak flesh, which lets us be moved more by the present than by the future. Therefore, the Holy Ghost must be the schoolmaster that this comfort sinks into our hearts.

But it is especially good to note here that he speaks with so many words of this glory that shall be revealed to us. By this he shows that not only St. Peter and St. Paul, etc., will be partakers of this glory, as we may think, but we and all Christians also belong. Yes, even the slightest little child that is baptized and dies receives this glory through his death, as his shared suffering, and has inherited and been given this unspeakable glory which is his through the Lord Jesus Christ, into whose death he is baptized.

Erl. 9, 101–103: Sermon on Trinity 4, Romans 8:18–22, 1535

With feeble light and half obscure Poor mortals Thine arrangements view,
Not knowing that the least are sure And the mysterious just and true. (*TLH* 530: 2)

Tuesday

Then Jesus spoke again to him, "I go away, and you will seek me and you will die in your sins. Where I go you cannot follow." John 8:21

That one should seek him and not find him is amazing. Is he not yet so merciful and gracious as he declared, "He who seeks me will find me and who knocks, it will be opened to them." How shall one not find him and enter if he seeks him? It is completely contradictory that he says, "You will seek me and not find me." It is a miserable business and a pitiful thing if he goes away so that if one seek and has a longing for him and would like to have him yet he can no longer find him or receive him. In the holy Scriptures one can preach nothing more horrible. He says, "Now, while I am here and offer my services to you, you have the fair before your door, so if you do not want to have me, crucify me, and throw me out of the city. But then when I go, you will want me a hundred times more to be exhumed from the earth but you will not find a hair of me."

Now seeking Christ is seeking help, grace, life, comfort, salvation, holiness, redemption from death, sins, devil and hell. You desire Christ as a redeemer. Yes, you seek all that is Christ and the reason he has come into the world. And do the Jews seek him now? How they fast, pray, read, preach, give and work! And they take pains more than anyone and seek how they might become holy. But such exertion will be in vain and forlorn. It is frightening that these great efforts before God, with all their services to God, should be completely empty. He does not say, "I go away and you will seek the devil, do evil works, lead a promiscuous and foolish life. No, rather you will arise with excellent works, to attain what I am, but it will all be effort and work that avails nothing."

We have seen this in the Jews and also in the papacy. I became a monk and watched through the night, fasted, prayed and sequestered and tortured my body so that I kept obedience and lived purely; that's what you still find among priests, nuns and monks. I speak of the pious and rightly fashioned monks in the world for whom it has become an earnest zeal and not of the whoremongers and fools who are stuck in the obscene loose life. I speak of those who have let it be unpleasant for them, like me, and sought and tortured themselves because they desired to attain what Christ is so that they would be saved. What have they accomplished by it? Have they found him? Christ says, "You will remain and die in your sins." That is what they have achieved.

That is a frightening judgment, to cast away such great labor and work and that he says, "I go away, so run, give, build, make whatever you want, even fast to the point of death, but know that it is all in vain." We also see it in the anabaptists. We could not bring about such an obedient group in our circles, nor have such devotion, nor allow so much giving and confession, or be so faithful to our preachers as the anabaptists are and to have their devotion. They forsake wife and child, money, goods, house and home; they let it all go and act just as if they were foolish and crazy. Also these sacramental enthusiasts do everything so stubbornly and thus so firmly, for it says, "You seek me. But nothing will come of it," for it says, "You will not find me." The pope also works and seeks what I, Christ, am, but he will not find me.

Hereafter, God has given his grace that every town and city has the gospel and its own preacher and they have it for free. One need not give the preacher much. But now-a-days if one could let the preacher die of hunger, he would do it. Thereafter they help the citizens, farmers and those who are faithful to the rulers, but people will no longer have the gospel. Now Christ says, "I go away. If you do not want me, then I will make for you other preachers and pastors that shall serve before you." So also, if we should be dead, then you will want at once to fetch a good preacher from Rome and find none. Yes, people will desire that the preachers which they now do not tolerate or give a piece of bread to be exhumed ten times over from the earth and they would carry them on their backs. Where a nobleman, citizen and farmer use their good efforts, people run to them, seek them, gladly want to give, work for them above all others, but no one finds (Christ).

I have often said this and will also say it again so that you do not forget it. This city, Wittenberg, used to give the monks more than a thousand guldens a year besides what was given the priests. It is not a town so poor that now it gives to the monks and priests it once paid so much barely five, six, eight or ten guldens. For instance what had the private mass cost and a pilgrimage of one running to St.

James? This was all a seeking of Christ, even though he was not there.

Now Christ is available, but the nobleman says, "What more can I ask about? What difference would it make if there were no preacher any more? For I know well that one becomes saved and right through Christ. I need no preacher. I know how I become saved and should call on Christ." Well then, you will surely see how necessary and important a preacher will be. He does not say, "I go away, and you will have peace and be made joyful," but rather he affirms thereafter that when he is gone, then first we will seek him. That is the greatest aggravation when the gospel has departed. Then the seeking follows and when the present dear teacher and world is departed, then pastors will appear who are a hundred times more burdensome, whom one must follow and obey with great works and charges. But that will all be worthless.

Altb. V, 773–774: Sermons on the Gospel of St. John, Chapters 6–8, 1530–2; cf. AE 23

Thy flock, Thine own peculiar care, Tho' now they seem to roam uneyed,
Are led or driven only where The best and safest may abide. (*TLH* 530: 3)

Wednesday

And you will die in your sins. John 8:21

You shall and must die in your sins. It is terrible that many seek and discover ways to life and still must die, for here this searching is nullified because he says, "You will remain and die in your sins and not find me." If Christ's Word does not remain, but is taken away, then great "holiness" will still go on and such works will be done which appear holy and as a precious life. But that precious life will not extinguish a single sin, or bring you out of death, but you are stuck deeper in death. You think you already believe and are sure that that is the truth.

The Jews and Turks say, "Do you think that God is such a terrible tyrant that he should put away from himself such a great bunch of people and let them die?" No, we seek Christ, want to be holy, are baptized, are unwavering as to our outward conduct, that that conduct should loose us from sins, make us holy and lead us to heaven. But the text says, "No," and the man Christ does not lie, who is the only man that regarded this Word as so great that he opposed so many people for the sake of retaining one morsel of it. He does not mind making himself despised against so many hundred thousand Turks, Jews, popes and fanatics, who speak against him with poor words. He says, "You are as the chaff, but my Word is as a rock." So he makes himself great against the powerful people so they do not acknowledge him; for the Word is mighty and powerful. Whoever will not believe it wants to let it pass by even if what I say is the truth.

Whoever does not wish to recognize Christ lets him go. He will also say to such a one, "You also are of the opinion of the world and the fanatics that want to be greater than my Word, but I say no to that." That is pridefully preached when he says, "I go away, and you will seek me, but not find me and you will die in your sins." They are simple words, but they color the past, present and coming world. Everything is in the Word, "You will seek me and not find me and die in your sins." There are many and great, important people from the beginning of the world already struck; it is simply declared, that they are regarded just as a spark compared to great fire, and as a drop compared to the ocean, or a pebble compared to the sun or to a great mountain.

But the world turns it around and thinks, who are you, Christ? You are the spark and a pebble but we Jews are a great people; the whole clan of the heathen, of the Turks and Jews, should this great bunch of people be valued less than the Christians? Should we not be so much as you, Christ, of whom you preach: Who believes, he has it. Who does not believe, will he be told? So who believes on Christ will have eternal life. If their way is apart from Christ, it is certain that there is only pure judgment. Now, apart from faith on Christ, great services to God, great donations and great works are done. Many important, learned people become monks and greater things happen among those that have fallen away from and are oriented away from Christ, than what the Christians themselves do. For they seek the man Christ by doing these things, but apart from faith they do not find him. They remain in judgment and neither the smallness of their sins nor a vain word can deliver them.

That is what Christ says here. "They shall not atone for one sin, either theirs or that of another, but rather they shall die in their sins and not escape eternal death and ruin." Who was able to preach that in the papacy and say that a Carthusian monk could not atone for sins with his great works? Yes, they have not only sold their works, but also in the long run acted so that their customary works mitigated something else. But Christ here overthrows all of these brotherhoods and says that they can and shall atone for not one sin, neither theirs nor those of another. Nor do they redeem from death for a moment, but shall all be damned.

That is a two-fold punishment and it happens justly. For one here on earth is martyred and pursued with a harsher and yet vain holiness. So the devil's martyrs thereby martyr themselves and thereafter must remain the devil's eternally. They will not receive the Lord Christ with thanksgiving and happy hearts so they might live freely, be holy and blessed, because now a believer has tribulation with their holy life. They are martyred to death and cannot go on with a pure peace so that he accomplishes what has been appointed him in his vocation. But it does not help and is a poorly sung song, but they must have their bodily (self devised) suffering and eternal hell fire. A monk has done himself harm in the cloister, but when he dies, then he is damned both here and there.

Altb. V, 775: Sermons on the Gospel of St. John, Chapters 6–8, 1530–2; cf. AE 23

They neither know nor trace the way; But while they trust Thy guardian eye,
Their feet shall ne'er to ruin stray, Nor shall the weakest fall or die. (*TLH* 530: 4)

Thursday

Where I go, you cannot follow. John 8:21

You will seek me and try to follow where I go but you cannot follow for the door is shut. Everything that you substitute for me is cast away. Your mighty works add nothing. Your desire to live a holy life shall help at all. That is a frightening and horrible preaching, but the world is very artful. By establishing such an adamant attitude and an iron and stony heart, it is deluded and stuck and hears nothing of this, saying: Where has Christ gone? Now he is out of this temporal and mortal life, freed from death and all misfortune and concern, and brought from all evil to all good and only sits at the right hand of his heavenly Father. The Jews also would try to follow and go in to seek Christ, but they will not be able to come therein. That is too harshly said, so the pope should ban this gospel of John for he cannot stand one saying to him that it is impossible for man to reach eternal life with his good works and enter heaven. But they do not believe it. Rather they brag about their good works. They not only want to become saved by them, but they also want to have super–abundant works by which they purchase the world that it also might be saved by this.

Against this Christ says that it is not only difficult but also impossible that one do that to protect himself from flesh and blood, from disbelief and fanatics, and quickly learn to know the true Christ, to hear the preaching of the gospel and receive Christ. But he sees that you can do so little. For this reason he must have such thunderbolts by which he strikes hearts, and, yes, the whole world and all people. The Jews had had the temple and the great service of God which God himself instituted. That was no pleasure, as was witnessed through Scriptures. So also when you compare that (with this Word of Christ), that the striving and work, by which they served God day and night, and also add to that their intense study and work not only had to be forgiven, but also was incapable of making one holy. Whom will this not frighten? And those in the papacy who are in earnest, as we had been, think the same way. All our great works should be forgiven where we have also run, donated and given. They all shall be called vain and an impossible thing.

But it is true. It is all surely in vain, if God in the end has not come to help and if one departs from faith in Christ. I am sure that many people in the cloisters and outside of them have believed and have grasped Christ despite what they have said and cried out: Oh, my dear Lord Jesus Christ, you are my savior. And they have doubted their holy life and good works by which many of them wanted to be preserved. And it has become a good practice that one who is dying be given a wood crucifix to behold or given into their hand by which they have remembered and trusted in the suffering and death of the Lord Christ. But the others, who have bragged about their good works and have become hardened, are taken to such a heaven where it hisses and burns, for they have become separated from Christ and have not built upon his death and suffering, that they should live by them. There this text becomes true. It is not possible that they could follow where he is.

Altb. V, 775-776: Sermons on the Gospel of St. John, Chapters 6–8, 1530-2; cf. AE 23

My favored soul shall meekly learn To lay her reason at Thy throne;
Too weak They secrets to discern, I'll trust Thee for my Guide alone. (*TLH* 530: 5)

Friday

And he said to them, "You are from below, and I am from up above; you are from this world, I am not from this world." John 8:23

He comforts himself and wants to say, "It doesn't matter if I am sweet or sour, if I preach sharp or bitter, yet it will not help you when you do not follow my preaching and implore me for more of it. It does not strike you as harmonious because you are from below and I come from God above and tell you the truth, but you despise it. Now it is this way because you are born in the ways of evil and are polluted enough by it that you are prideful and fat. You whore and act the fool, rob and steal, and you shall find this out as soon as you come into the judgment. There you and I will be together. You are fools that want to stay that way."

Only Christ says these Words, and whoever is a Christian also says this, "I am from above." Who shall preach in the world and make others good and becomes persecuted must say, "Where shall I go?" He says, "This alone is my comfort and courage, that I am sent of God, for my office is also from God." But you speak and do nothing but what you were born to do from the earth, where you do not want to separate the people in an unfriendly manner, and you also will not tolerate Christ and his own to be here. It might be better and also sound better if Christ portrays himself as being friendly and says, "I am only a preacher, you are my students," they would say, "We want to hear you." But rather he says, "We will separate ourselves from one another, for you always want to have your own thoughts direct your life and reasoning."

So the pope, the monks and bishops also want to follow their own thoughts and say, "Oh, the gospel does nothing." But the Lord Christ says here, "Now you don't want to have what I give and you desire to remain upon the earth, so you are now not able to plunge into what I preach. I would gladly remain before you. You should allow Christ and the gospel to remain. It will be shown who brags about something else. You are from below and I am not from the world, but from God and above. These Words divide us as summer and winter and exclude one from the other." He builds you heaven and eternal life. If you now do not desire to have him, he expels you. He allows you to do it and will give you death, sins and the fires of hell. But they reply to him so derisively and bitingly.

They give him such a dirty and venomous answer that I myself would likewise say, "Get out! It doesn't matter to me. Let it be seen who is sorry and who deceives whom. You are from the world and I am not. It is not a small matter that we will soon see [what I say is true] and if you also witness it, then you will also find out." So also the Lord Christ separated himself from his supposed disciples and from the people, which is frightening, and said, "You are there and I am here and after a time as I have said, 'You will die in your sins.' " That is the close of this preaching.

Now a new preaching proceeds as the Lord says, "If you will not believe that I am from above, then you will die in your sins." And John the Evangelist says that they have not understood this Word, that he had touched the Father in the sermon. He sets here such a mighty defiant Word, that he cannot speak out this Word enough, for he says, "You must believe that I am from the Father or you will die." It is pridefully spoken when he says, "I am the man. On me rides everything. Where I am not, there is nothing. And those whom you have answered and treated with mockery and sarcasm shall know, I will not die or be killed much, but will be immortal." The pointed Words annoy them, and the Lord Christ is speaking in hidden anger, "Do you want to know who I am? I am God and you can do what you want with me. If you do not believe it is all me, then you are nothing and you must die in your sins." No prophet, apostle or evangelist may preach in this way and say, "Believe in God and also believe on me, that I am God, or if you do not then everything about you is worthless." The Jews could say, "Do you think that there is no one else who could save from death and sin besides you that we should believe on you? You think that we must die if we do not believe in you as if outside of you there were no God? Who has the authority that the people be saved by him from sins, death and hell, but God?" And you say, "You see the same God, etc. (i.e., in Christ) . . ."

To this the Lord Christ says, "Who I am, that I am. If you do not believe that I am that one, then you will die in your sins. Seek God elsewhere yet in that there is no life, for only in me is there life. Because you do not remain here, so you are in death."

Altb. V, 777–778: Sermons on the Gospel of St. John, Chapters 6–8, 1530–2; cf. AE 23

The Savior calls: let ev'ry ear Attend the heav'nly sound.
Ye doubting souls, dismiss your fear; Hope smiles reviving round. (*TLH* 281: 1)

Saturday

I have much to say and set right among you, but the one who sent me is true and what I have heard from him, that I speak before the world. John 8:26

He comforts himself and speaks about this great evil, "I have much to say, to preach and to straighten out for you, and must make many kinds of great sermons, teach and straighten out great matters." This is a hidden answer, which he gives the rogues, in which he comforts himself by his office, as when I say, "Christ is sent and should a preacher come under a great people, he has a great advantage, for he has God, who is extolled in Holy Scriptures, and a divine service, which is instituted through Moses and the prophets, but is established through miracles, and he will (as Jesus did) put all of them aside." As he said, "As I will rage at you, I will destroy and annul everything. I will uproot many things, prepare a doubt, and not only do away with the doves and moneychangers before the church, but also the temple, sacrifice, sanctuary, priests, kings, princes and even Moses himself and straighten out and condemn what you have and do."

So that makes Christ even angrier with their mockery, because they become even more wanton and defiant. He says, "I will preach that neither Jerusalem nor a single wall, yes, not a stone upon another or a single stick, in short NOTHING will remain. Also I will now condemn you with your mocking ways, so that my sermon shall be known for doing many great things." And yet I also think that he did this, that he should preach through his apostles that not a stone, yes, not a hair's breadth, not even a little pile of dust is remaining of the city of Jerusalem, of the priesthood, of the kings, of the kingdom, of the services of God, temple and people, even though these services of God were gloriously established and God also gave great people such as Elijah, Jeremiah, Isaiah and other great prophets. They delivered the nation with great miracles so that this people had a very great advantage that they had also highly praised [God]. The Jews also boasted about these things. All this is taken away just as it was given. For the Lord Christ says, "I will preach so that not a single crumb of this shall remain."

I also speak so to the pope, "Oh, what I have yet to preach and say in order to deal with the pope, with his three-fold crown, and the cardinals and the bishops, priests and monks, that follow him with the Princes, Meinz, Heinz, Duke George; all shall go down to the devil and the lowest parts of hell. I will not only preach and remain by the Word, but I will also judge. What do I care about your despising and mockery? You shall not stop my mouth by that. It also shall not remain as you plan. Rather you shall be wrecked and go to the depths." The Lord Christ thinks, "I will not turn to them because the temple, or prophets and the kingdom belongs to Jerusalem and because they have a beautiful kingdom. If you do not believe, then I will preach, judge and straighten you out, so your boast, honor and service of God shall all be thrown away in a heap."

They could not believe this was true for it was undesirable to them. It still is. Only Christ has judgment and speaks, "I am the one." We do not speak as he speaks, but rather we only say, "We are your preachers, therefore your mass, indulgence, votives, and other works of delusion of the papacy are cast to the ground. We also speak and judge it in that way." But they mock what we have. Very well, but only in freedom can one [finally] laugh!

Altb. V, 780: Sermons on the Gospel of St. John, Chapters 6–8, 1530–2; cf. AE 23

Dear Savior, draw reluctant hearts; To thee let sinners fly
And take the bliss Thy love imparts And drink and never die. (*TLH* 281: 5)

Week of Trinity V

Sunday

Blessed are the poor in spirit for theirs is the kingdom of heaven. Matthew 5:3

Being spiritually poor, or poor before God, is not to be judged outwardly by money and goods nor by poverty or wealth. For there you see that the poorest and most miserable, foolish, beggars are the most fraudulent desperate rogues that commit all kinds of foolishness and vice which fine, honorable, people and rich citizens or lords and princes do not commit. Then again, many holy people have had enough money and goods, honor, land and people and never-the-less have been poor even with so many goods. You must rather consider the heart, so that you do not let wealth and possessions be the measure of whether they have something or nothing, much or little. External blessings should always be set aside as if a person had nothing. As time passes the heart must always be set upon the heavenly kingdom.

Then again, Scriptures call those "rich" who snatch and scratch after wealth and can never have enough whether or not they have money or goods. Those are truly ones, whom the law calls "rich bellies," who have the least in valuable goods and never let themselves be satisfied because God gives to them. So it is obvious that their heart is stuffed full of money and goods and by that you can consider them as if they have empty bags and chests. Again, also judge the poor man (who has faith) according to the heart as though he has a full chest, house and home. So the Christian faith is pre-eminent. Do not behold either poverty or wealth, but rather how the heart is set. Where there is godly desire, then he is spiritually rich. Then again, he is spiritually poor who does not hang upon this faith and can allow it to forsake his heart. As Christ says in another place, "Who forsakes house, field, child and wife, etc., he shall have back a hundred fold and also inherit eternal life." By this he would tear goods from the heart that it not hold these things as its treasure. He comforts his own so they must admit that they will receive much more and better also in this life than they could possibly lose.

Not that a person ought run from goods, house, home, wife and children and madly go into the countryside as the anabaptists, teach and burden their people. These want us to feel guilty for not preaching the law correctly because we possess house and home and remain with our wives and children. No, such crazy saints Christ will not have. But rather he says, "One can allow his heart to remain in house, home, wife and child even as if his heart is set on them and remains with them; and he supports them and serves them out of love, as God has commanded. Yet his heart is set such that when there is a need, he utterly lets them all go for the sake of God." If you are so gifted, then you have [already] forsaken all. Then the heart is not captured, but remains pure from avarice, attractions, comfort and is confident of all things. And if a rich person would be called spiritually poor, he may not, because of this, throw away his wealth. If he needs to, he will let them go, so he lets it go in God's name, but not because he is gladly free of wife, children, house and home. He much rather keeps them so long as God gives them and he serves God with them. Yet he is also ready when God would again take them back. So you see what it is to be poor spiritually and before God, or what is called having nothing spiritually and to lose everything.

So also consider the promise which Christ adds to this saying: ". . . for such is the kingdom of heaven." That is surely a great, important, glorious promise that we shall have a beautiful, majestic, tremendous, eternal wealth in heaven, because we here are gladly poor and do not heed temporal wealth. Here you experience a little bit of it, which is useful as long and as much as you know that hereafter you shall receive a crown, that you are a citizen and lord in heaven. This should surely induce us, if we want to be Christians, to be certain that his Words are true. But no one pays attention to who it is that says this, much less what he says. They let it pass by their ears, so that no one concerns himself further with it or takes them to heart.

But he shows even with these Words, which no one keeps, that he is therefore a true Christ. For both this passage and all the others that follow are only fruits of faith which the Holy Ghost himself must form in the heart. Where there is no faith, the heavenly kingdom will also remain outside. Then neither spiritual poverty, gentleness, etc. follow, but rather pure scratching, avarice, discord and clamoring for the sake of temporal wealth remain.

Erl. 43, 15–18: Commentary on the Sermon on the Mount, 1532; cf. AE 21

O God, forsake me not! Thy gracious presence lend me;
Lead Thou Thy helpless child; Thy Holy Spirit send me
That I my course may run. Be Thou my Light, my Lot,
My Staff, my Rock, my Shield O God, forsake me not! (*TLH* 402: 1)

Monday

Blessed are the sorrowful for they shall be comforted.
Matthew 5:4

You must not think that sadness only means crying and complaining, or wailing like children and women. This is not the true deep suffering that comes over the heart and spills out through the eyes. But such sorrow happens when the truly immense blows trample and storm against the heart so that one cannot even cry or complain.

Therefore, sorrowing and bearing suffering is not a strange kraut for the Christian, even if it doesn't always show, even as the Christian would gladly be joyous in Christ and show it outwardly as much as he can. For daily when they see so much evil, maliciousness, despising and blasphemy of God and his Word in the world, and in addition so much tragedy and misfortune which the devil administers in both the spiritual and worldly realms, they must see and feel in their hearts that they cannot have many happy thoughts, and their spiritual joy is very weak. And should they have to see it constantly and not occasionally turn their eyes away, then they could not be happy for an instant. It is enough that it occurs and tramples them more than they would like. They do not have to search very far to find it.

Therefore, only turn away from it and become a Christian, so that you learn what it means to sorrow and bear suffering. You need go no further than to take a wife and determine that you will nourish yourself by faith, that you have a desire for God's Word and do what is commanded in your husbandly vocation. Then you will soon experience, both from your neighbor and in your own house, that it will not happen as you would like it. And they will hinder and stop you so you have plenty to bear and must have heartaches. But the dear preacher especially must learn this well, and daily be used to it. For all kinds of envy, hate, scorn and mockery, unthankfulness, despising and blasphemy come to them that must consume them. By this their heart and soul are pierced through and they are tortured constantly.

But the world will not have such sorrow or patience in suffering. It seeks vocations and life that will only give them good days and in which they do not have to suffer anything from anyone; as the monk's and priestly office have become. For they cannot bear to serve other people in divine offices with pure suffering, effort and work and then get from it nothing but unthankfulness, despising and other evil malice as payment. Therefore, when things do not go as they wish, and they see each other with such a grim attitude, they cannot give anything but curses and thunder. Yes, also by shaking their fists, they want to obtain immediate wealth and honor, land and people. But God makes it so they cannot pursue these things so easily that they don't see suffering or suffer themselves. As reward he gives this to them. They do not serve and thus suffer willingly, so this makes their suffering doubly intense and difficult, adding wrath and impatience to their lack of comfort and a good conscience. But the Christians have an advantage that even if they bear suffering, yet in these sufferings they will be comforted and blessed both here and hereafter.

Therefore, whoever doesn't want to be a child of this world, and wants a part of Christ, lets himself also be found on the record that he helps sigh and bear suffering so that he also is comforted, as this promise says. One reads an example in the prophet, Ezekiel, chapter 9, how God sends out six men with a deadly attack against the city of Jerusalem. But he sent one of them with a writing pen. That one went through the midst of the city and wrote a mark on the forehead of all who would sigh and bear suffering there. For things had gone so scandalously in the city that they had to see what would pierce their heart. And who would be so marked would remain alive. But the others were slain. See, that is the Christian advantage, that even if they must also have only suffering and trouble in the world, that if the world is most secure and proceeds in pure joy, what goes around comes around. Suddenly misfortune comes over it when it must stand still and be ruined. But they (the Christians) are taken out and saved; as the beloved Lot was saved from Sodom where he had long been tortured in his heart and martyred (as St. Paul says) with their scandalous ways. Therefore, let the world now laugh and live in comfort according to their lust and pride. If you must sorrow and bear suffering and daily see what troubles your heart, then in sorrow hold firmly to this passage, that you let yourself be agreeable despite it and comfort yourself and make yourself externally lively and joyful as much as you can.

Erl. 4322-25: Commentary on the Sermon on the Mount, 1532; cf. AE 21

O God, forsake me not! Take not Thy Spirit from me
And suffer not the might Of sin to overcome me.
Increase my feeble faith, Which Thou Thyself hast wrought.
Be Thou my Strength and Pow'r O God, forsake me not! (*TLH* 402: 2)

Tuesday

Blessed are the meek for they will possess the earth. Matthew 5:5

Christ here indicts such crazy saints who think that everyone in the whole world is a lord and has the right to suffer nothing. They only bluster and rumble and drive with force to defend what belongs to them. Christ teaches us that whoever would rule and possess what is his, goods, house and home, etc, with joy, must be meek. By this he could administer and keep his head and bear what he must always suffer. For it happens without fail that your neighbor will occasionally ask you to do a lot [for him]. He may either ask you because of your duty or even out of malice. If it is duty, then you do not do well on his behalf if you will not or cannot bear his request. But if it is maliciousness, then you only make him angrier [if your refuse] because he comes and knocks on your door as an enemy. Then he also laughs and repents of his desire for your help. Then he will be enraged and do you harm so that you can have no joy or use what is his with peace.

Therefore, select one of the two as you wish: That you either live under people with meekness and patience and retain what you have with joy and a good conscience, or lose what is yours with grumbling and rumbling and then also have no peace. For it is established: "The meek shall possess the earth." See for yourself the strange heads that are always quarreling and striving over wealth and other things and none of them relents but rather they want everything to happen according to their plan. If they would no longer quarrel and battle then they would always win. Finally, they lose their land and family, house and home with discord along with an evil conscience thrown in. So God also speaks his blessing that says, "Be not meek, then you lose your land. Neither will you enjoy a morsel of food with joy. But if you would act rightly and have peace, then do not let malice and outrage to your neighbor dampen and extinguish you." Nothing else can be more beloved by the devil, nor can you do yourself more harm, than when you fiendishly rage and rumble. If you have an authority over you, then acknowledge it and act accordingly, for authority is established that the innocent do not suffer to be completely drawn under. In that way God also prevails so that his Word and order remain and you retain this promise about the land. So you have joy and blessing from God, but your neighbor unrest, especially God's displeasure and curse.

But this preaching is received by no one except those who are Christians and who believe and know that they have their treasure in heaven which is surely theirs and cannot be taken. So they also must have enough here even if they do not have a chest or pocket full of money. Since you know that, then, why do you wish to disrupt your peace and let it be taken? Surely you make yourself disturbed and rob yourself of such an important blessing.

Behold now how you have three passages with three rich promises, that whoever is a Christian must have enough both in time and eternity, even if he must suffer much both inwardly in the heart and outwardly. Again, the children of the world, because they will not suffer any poverty or sorrow or authority, retain and receive neither the heavenly kingdom nor temporal wealth with joy and peace. Of this you might read further in Psalm 37, which is the true commentary on this passage and richly describes how the meek possess the land and the godless will be expelled.

Erl. 4329–30: Commentary on the Sermon on the Mount, 1532; cf. AE 21

O God, forsake me not! Lord, hear my supplication!
In ev'ry evil hour Help me o'ercome temptation;
And when the Prince of hell, My conscience seeks to blot,
Be Thou not far from me O God, forsake me not! (*TLH* 402: 3)

Wednesday

Blessed are they who hunger and thirst after righteousness for they shall be satisfied. Matthew 5:6

In this place righteousness must not mean the chief righteousness of the Christian through which the person becomes good and acceptable before God. For I have previously said that these eight verses are nothing other than the teaching of the fruits and good works of a Christian, before which faith must previously exist as the tree trunk and chief part. In summary, his righteousness and salvation come without any work or service and out of this such verses all must grow and follow. So understand this as the external righteousness before the world, as we conduct ourselves towards each other. This, briefly and simply, is the meaning of these words: This is a rightly fashioned holy man, who always is supportive and strives with all his might to make things go well and that does the right thing unto everyone. With words and works, with advice and deeds, he helps to preserve and protect.

Now this is a precious verse which covers many good works. But it is also completely crazy. As when, for example, a preacher will find in this passage that he must be resigned to help and instruct each person in his vocation so that he conducts them in the right way and does what is necessary to the task. And when he sees that something is lacking and not going well, he is to be there, to warn, punish and correct however and whenever he can. But also I, as a preacher, am not to let myself be deficient in my office nor the others in theirs; that they follow my teaching and preaching. So I must act rightly on both counts. Now where there are the kind of people that accept themselves in this way and let themselves be earnest, gladly wanting to do what is right or to be found in a righteous attitude and works, these people will be hungry and thirsty for righteousness. And if that were the case, there would be no foolishness or wrong, but pure righteousness and blessed ways on the earth. For what is worldly righteousness other than that everyone does in his vocation what he is responsible for; which means the rights/responsibilities of each office; as a husband's rights and wife's rights, children's rights, knights and maid's rights in the house, citizen's rights in the city or the country? In these offices each is placed so they administer their office with readiness, care and faithfulness so other people should be helped and ruled; and that they also receive service and are truly obedient and act willingly.

But he does not establish anything that is worthless in such words: Hunger and thirst after righteousness. By this he would reveal that a great zeal, craving and desire, also an unceasing diligence belongs to such hunger. Where there is not such hunger and thirst then nothing will come from it. The reason is this: There are such great and numerous hindrances, both from the devil, who always lies and blocks the way, and from the world, and from her children, which are so evil that they cannot stand good people who gladly do right or would even help other people. But rather, they lay upon you every plague so that in the long run some become fatigued and discouraged by it. For it is too bad that one should see it going so scandalously and that for pure good deeds nothing is returned but unthankfulness, despising, hate and persecution as reward. Also, because of this, many people, who do not want to see such annoying things, finally completely despair over it and run from the people into the wilderness and become monks because of it so that this saying by and by becomes true: "Doubt makes a monk." Either one does not trust that he can nourish others and for the sake of his belly he runs into the cloister, as the great majority have done; or one despairs in the world and does not trust that he can remain good there, or help the people.

Erl. 4331-32: Commentary on the Sermon on the Mount, 1532; cf. AE 21

O God, forsake me not! Thy mercy I'm addressing;
O Father, God of Love, Grant me Thy heavenly blessing
To do when duty calls Whate'er Thou didst allot,
To do what pleaseth Thee O God, forsake me not! (*TLH* 402: 4)

Thursday

Blessed are the merciful for they shall receive mercy.
Matthew 5:7

Now this is a verse of mercy, that one gladly forgive sins and trespasses. Also, that one be gracious to those who suffer external need or need help. These graces are called works of mercy in Matthew 25. The prideful Jewish saints are incapable of this verse. For theirs is nothing but ice and frost, yes sticks and stony hearts with not a single drop of blood of desire or love to do good for the neighbor, just as they have no mercy to forgive sins. They care and seek only after their own paunch even while someone else is dying of hunger. So a public sinner has more mercy than such a saint. As the inevitable result, since they regard themselves alone as worthy and good, despising everyone and considering them nothing, they think that all the world should serve them alone and give them plenty while they are not responsible to give anything to anyone or to serve them.

That is why such preaching and exhortation is despised and futile among such saints and finds no students other than those who already cling to Christ and believe in him, who know in themselves no righteousness of their own. Rather, according to the previous verse, they are poor, pitiful and meek and are truly hungry and thirsty and do not despise anyone but rather receive everyone's needs and can suffer with them. This is adorned with a wonderful promise, "It is good for you that you are merciful. For you will find mercy, both here and there, and such mercy that unspeakably overshadows all human goodness and mercy." For there is no comparing our mercy with God's mercy nor our goodness with the eternal goodness in the heavenly kingdom. Nor does he let our mercy to the neighbor be so pleasant that it is but a penny compared to a million dollars, for when we are in need, he promises a drink of water, the heavenly kingdom.

But whoever will not allow himself to be moved by this excellent and comforting promise can turn the page and hear another reason, "Lost and condemned are the unmerciful, for they also will not experience mercy." How the world is now full of such people, from the nobility to the citizens and farmers. They sin so excellently against the gospel that not only do they give nothing to help the poor pastors and preachers, but rather also take and plague them where they can and set themselves against them as if they wanted to starve them and hunt them out of the world. Yet they act in complete safety, thinking that God should be silent about it and call everything they do good. But it will come upon them suddenly, I fear. All will encounter it, which will make me a true prophet. He will deal with them with all their lack of mercy and take their honor and wealth, body and life. In this God's Word remains true. Those who neither show nor want to have mercy are overcome by pure rage and eternal displeasure, as also St. James says, "An unmerciful judgment will consume whomever has not shown mercy."

So also Christ on the last day will draw such lack of mercy to the highest point when everything that they have done out of a lack of mercy is done against God himself. He himself speaks the curse over them, "I was hungry and thirsty and you did not give me food and drink (etc.) Therefore go, you cursed, into the eternal fire (etc.)." He truly warns and exhorts us out of pure grace and mercy. Whoever won't have it is entitled to the curse and eternal damnation.

Erl. 4337-38: Commentary on the Sermon on the Mount, 1532; cf. AE 21

O God, forsake me not! Lord, I am Thine forever.
Grant me true faith in Thee; Grant that I leave Thee never.
Grant me a blessed end When my good fight is fought;
Help me in life and death O God, forsake me not! (*TLH* 402: 5)

Friday

Blessed are the pure in heart for they shall see God. Matthew 5:8

Now what is a pure heart? Or where is it? Answer: It should first be said that you cannot climb up to heaven or run into a cloister after it and provide it with your own thoughts. But rather be on guard against all such efforts, as against pure muck and mire and know that a monk in the cloister, when he sits in his highest meditation and thinks on his Lord God, as he himself portrays God and dreams of what God is like, and would throw the world completely out of his heart, sits in the filth not up to his knees, but above his ears. For he turns to his own thoughts without God's Word, which are only lies and fraudulent as the Scriptures show throughout. But that is a pure heart, which beholds and thinks only upon what God said. By this everything that hangs upon that Word and proceeds into that heart becomes and is declared pure, as when a common, plain, manual laborer, a shoemaker or smith sits at home, even if he is dirty and sooty, or smells bad from polish and pitch and thinks, "My God has made me as a man and given me my house, wife and child, and commanded me to have life, and to provide with

my labor, etc." See, he goes with God's Word in his heart and even
if he stinks on the outside, yet inside he is only perfume before God.
But if he also comes into the high holiness, that he also grasps the
law and believes in Christ (without whom there can be no purity),
then he is pure through and through both inwardly in the heart to
God and outwardly to all who are under him upon earth; that all that
he lives and does, compells, establishes, eats and drinks, etc., is pure
to him and cannot make him unclean, as when he beholds his
honorable wife, or even jokes with her. Consider the Patriarch,
Isaac, in Genesis 26 where he was disguised like a monk [in
hypocrisy] and he was made unclean, for he had God's Word and
knew that God had given him the situation. But when he left his wife
and gave her allegiance to another, or delayed the work of his hands
or his office, and did what concerned another (as a brother instead
of a husband), etc., then he was no longer pure, for that was against
God's Word.

But so long as he remained in the twin parts of faith, namely in
the Word of faith towards God, by which his heart would be pure,
and in the Word of understanding that taught him what he should do
in his vocation towards his neighbor, then everything was clean to
him, even if he went on working with his hands and worked his
whole life with shoe polish. A poor servant girl, if she does what she
should do and also is a Christian, is a beautiful, pure, sacrifice
before God in heaven so that all the angels in heaven are gladdened
by her and have a desire to see her. Again the greatest Carthusian
monk, if he fasted to the point of death and wept tears over great
devotions and never thought of the world, and is still without faith in
Christ and love towards the neighbor, then he is pure stink and filth
both inwardly and outwardly that both God and the angels have pure
horror and disgust at him.

So you see how everything depends on God's Word, that what
is attached to it and proceeds from it must be all clean, pure and
snow white towards God and man. Paul says of this in Titus 1, "To
the pure everything is pure." and again, "To the unclean and
disbelieving nothing is pure." Why is this? What is impure is both
their mind and their conscience. How does this happen? They surely
say they know God, but with their works they lie; since they are the
ones over whom God is horrified. See the apostle portrays them so
horribly, and leers at the great judaizing saints. So consider a
Carthusian monk who thinks if he lives a strenuous order, obedience,
poverty and without a wife, cut off from the world, that thus he is
pure in all things. What is this but his own mind and conscience
without the Word of God and faith, growing from his own heart?
Through this they alone are holy and they despise the other unclean

people. St. Paul calls that an unclean mind, refering to all that they compose and think.

Erl. 4341–43: Commentary on the Sermon on the Mount, 1532; cf. AE 21

O Word of God Incarnate, O Wisdom from on high,
O Truth unchanged, unchanging, O Light of our dark sky
We praise Thee for the radiance That from the hallowed page,
A lantern to our footsteps, Shines on from age to age. (*TLH* 294: 1)

Saturday

Blessed are the peacemakers for they will be called the children of God. Matthew 5:9

Those called "peacemakers" are, first of all, those who help the country and people to have peace, as a good prince, counselor or lawyer, or an authority, who sits in his office and administration for the sake of peace. Thereafter also, good citizens and neighbors, who by means of their holy, good mouths, set right, conciliate and remove the discord and quarrelling (worked through evil, poisonous tongues) under husband and wife or a neighbor. St. Augustine boasted of his mother, Monica, when she would see two parties contesting each other she would always speak the best of both sides, and what she heard that was good, she would bring that to the other. But what she heard that was evil, she would be silent about or would soften as much as she could and thus reconcile one with the other. Among the women where the most scandalous charge, slander, especially rules, misfortune is often handed out by an evil tongue. There they serve as the bitter and poisonous bride of the devil. When they hear a word from someone, they point it, sharpen it, and use it to embitter others in the most wrathful way so that sometimes misery and death come of it.

Everyone does this, for the most scandalous things stick to us. Everyone gladly hears and speaks the most annoying things, devilish filth about the neighbor. They climb higher because they see another fall. If a wife were as beautiful as the sun and only had a mole or little spot on her face, then people would forget everything else and see only the little spot and speak of it. So if one were the most praiseworthy because of honor and virtue, yet when a poisonous tongue comes, it sees all of that immediately as a joke and makes of it such a scandal that all his praise and honor must be overshadowed. That is called a true poisonous spider that can suck out of a beautiful, lovely, rose nothing but poison, and ruin both the flower and the nectar out of which a little bee sucks only sweet honey and leaves the rose intact.

This is what those do who also can see nothing in other people but where they are frail and are unclean so that they can tell it. On the other hand, they cannot see their virtues. So there are many virtues among men that the devil cannot ruin, and yet he takes them from the eyes or disguises them so that you will not see them. As a wife, even if she were weak in every way and had no other virtue, she is still God's creature, and can carry a little water or wash windows. And there is no man upon earth so evil that he doesn't have something about him that one must praise. What is this, then, that one places the good away from his eyes and fashions and beholds what is impure as if one had a desire to see others only from their backside? But has not God himself clothed the dishonorable parts of the body and given them the most honor (as St. Paul says in 1 Corinthians 12)? And we are such dirty creatures that we only seek what is filthy and stinks and wallow in it like pigs.

See, these are also true children of the devil, who also, therefore, have the name that the devil is called when he is called *diabolus*, that is, a profaner and accuser, as those who have the devil's desire that he desecrate us unto rage and embitter us against each other so that he prescribes only murder and misery and allows no joy or harmony to remain between brother and neighbor, husband and wife.

Once I heard an example of two married people who lived with each other in such great love and harmony that people in the whole city spoke of it. And because he could not hinder such people, the devil sent an old windbag to the wife and brought it to her ears that her husband had found another and planned to get rid of her. So her heart was embittered against her husband. She (the gossip) gave her the advice that she should secretly take a carving knife with her, that she could withstand her husband. After that, the old gossip came to her husband and told him the same thing about his wife; how she wanted to murder him. As proof (she said) he would find a carving knife with her in bed that night. So he found it and cut her throat with it. Whether that is true or made up, it illustrates what evil, poisonous mouths can set up even between those who love each other from the heart. That is why they may rightly be called "devil's mouths" or "little devils", as he, the devil, *diabolus*, is called nothing else than a bitter, poisonous, evil mouth.

Erl. 4349-51: Commentary on the Sermon on the Mount, 1532; cf. AE 21

Oh, make Thy Church, dear Savior, A lamp of burnished gold
To bear before the nations Thy true light as of old!
Oh, teach Thy wand'ring pilgrims By this their path to trace
Till, clouds and darkness ended, They see Thee face to face! (*TLH* 294: 4)

Week of Trinity VI

Sunday

Behold, the time is coming, says the Lord, that I will raise up for David a righteous branch. Jeremiah 23:5

He says he will provide David a righteous branch. So also Zechariah said that he would truly come, Chapter 9, "Behold," he says, "your King comes to you, for he is a justifier and helper." The prophets have foreseen Christ in these ways just as we also consider him, namely, as a king who makes the world good. For the world is nothing but a barn full of fools. The world is the devil's kingdom, and flesh and blood are its high servants. All saints have complained about the misfortunes that trouble us and also all saints must complain as Paul reveals in Romans 7. Because of this, the dear fathers and prophets desired and called after the righteous branch—after this Christ, that he would make them good and right. He would take away sins and death. All pious, good hearts also crave this, and yes, even the evil do. For who would not rather have life than death and have righteousness rather than sins? Therefore St. Paul cries, "I am a miserable man. Who will free me from the body of death?" But all people do not cry out in this way, for it is not felt by all. The devil possesses many hearts and muddles them so that they cannot think about it.

So now this is the summary and chief verse of this epistle or prophecy. This king is pious and righteous, that is, without any sins. By this he is separated and differentiated from all other people that are all unrighteous, evil and sinful. If he were not righteous, he would not be born in this manner but as other children of man are born. So it follows that his mother must be a virgin. For it is said through the prophet David concerning all other men, "Behold, I am conceived of sinful seed, and my mother has conceived me in sin." Psalm 51. So this king must be born and conceived in a different manner, namely, without sins. So he will be righteous and not subject to death. So he must not be born of a wife through the action of a man but must be conceived of the Holy Ghost and be born from the holy, pure, virgin Mary.

But how does this happen that he is pure and not subject to death? Here, I say, does this come to him because he is descended from David? Is David's family yet also included in the malediction? Correct, but further, only this single virgin will be used of the stem of David. The rest was performed by the Holy Ghost, who made this birth pure, as the angel said to the virgin Mary in Luke 1, "The Holy Ghost is come over you and the power of the Most High will overshadow you. Therefore, the holy one who is born of you will also be called the Son of God." For this reason we have this kind of king who has a name above all other kings, that he is righteous and true in all things. So he also saves others and makes them right. Also these words demand that he must be true God and man. Although these words do not say it so openly and clearly, yet they include so much when we consider them in depth.

But the reason that he calls him a "branch" is that he speaks in the manner of the Hebrew language which calls children "branches," just as the cabbages, shrubs and trees grow. This does not sound so pleasant to our ears as it does in the ears of the Jews. God also says this of the kingdom of Babylon, Isaiah 14, "I will exterminate the name of Babel with its seed, branches and offspring."

Altb. III, 797: On a Passage from Jeremiah 23 Concerning Christ's Kingdom & Christian Freedom, 1527

O measureless Might, Ineffable Love,
While angels delight   To hymn Thee above,
Thy humbler creation, Though feeble their lays,
With true adoration Shall sing to Thy praise. (*TLH* 17: 6)

Monday

And he shall be a king who will reign well, and justice and righteousness will be delivered upon the earth. Jeremiah 23:5

These Words reveal that there is no righteousness on earth. I say this not only regarding the righteousness that is able to shine before God but also concerning the apparent righteousness which we can observe, which is only a gaudy beggar's cloak. For the world is a true school of fools under the devil. God established and ordered the sword and earthly government so that a bit of righteousness might yet be on earth. For there is no one who has righteousness that holds a candle to God. On the earth, also in the worldly kingdom, there is pure unrighteousness. In the spiritual kingdom also there is pure blasphemy as Psalm 14 says, "The Lord sees from heaven the children of man to see if any might understand or inquire of God. But they all stray and are incompetent together. There is no one who seeks God. No not one."

This proves that if man wants to see earth from heaven's view, then he sees pure blindness, foolishness, unrighteousness and wandering. It is nothing but a barn full of evil fools, not much better than what one found in the days of Noah. That was when God, through the flood, let everyone perish except for eight. But those [who are] so blind and unrighteous don't feel this much. Rather, they accept it as they learn the law, and continue to accept it until their quiet heart feels the actual burden placed on them by God's law. But the typical lump flits about like a happy bird.

Now, the child born of David would be righteous and pious, holy and without sin, so that he would be a king that would remain and reign eternally. Therefore he is a branch and shoot from David's stem since he must be mortal, born alive into a mortal life. On the other hand, he must die. But at the same time, he should remain always and reign eternally, so he must be immortal. How can this be? For this he must rise from the dead. This is what St. Peter says when he quotes David in the book of Acts, "it was impossible that he should be held by death." Psalm 16. Why? So that he should be king and reign forever. So you should remain in the Words that reveal the risen Christ; that he should be born and die and always reign, for he must rise from death.

The prophet further states that this king would proceed wisely—that is, with understanding and reason as David. 1 Kings 18, "He was wise in all his deeds." That is, he was the quickest and straightest of all of Saul's army. So Jeremiah also says of the coming king, "He will rule wisely." That is, "He will prudently reign."

So far we have heard of the person of the king. He would be born of the tree of David, should be a true man born of a virgin and should be a righteous king. This all goes with his person. It follows further, that what the king has, he shouldn't keep for himself but should go out and give it to mankind. This is what the prophet means here that he would proceed wisely. That is, he will reign with pure wisdom. He would say that he will lay aside the multitude of weapons, armor, provisions, swords and would supply and display a unique wisdom to make people good. This would be done not by the rack and gallows but by the gospel. Namely, he would grab their hearts and not their throats so they willingly come and follow him with joy. He is king because he helps the people. He works without sword and blows but only through the gospel. Therefore he also stands apart from death and lets his gospel be preached through the Holy Ghost throughout the world.

The prophet further states, "This king will administer justice and righteousness on earth." These two little words, "justice" and "righteousness" often stand together in the Bible. As in Isaiah 9, "On the throne of David and his kingdom, he judges with justice and righteousness to eternity." There he also speaks of the reign of Christ. We Germans say, "Right reign." The Jews describe it in two words and mean to say no more than we say in one word: "righteousness." Since there is no more to it than these two parts, Scripture uses these two words. Through justice or "right" God judges, that is, he discards what is evil. Through righteousness he acts that the people become pious, taken and protected for innocence.

Altb. III, 798–799: On a Passage from Jeremiah 23 Concerning Christ's Kingdom & Christian Freedom, 1527

Oh, Worship the King
All glorious above;
Oh, gratefully sing
His pow'r and His love,
Our Shield and Defender,
The Ancient of Days,
Pavilioned in splendor
And girded with praise!

Frail children of dust
And feeble as frail,
In Thee do we trust
Nor find Thee to fail.
Thy mercies, how tender,
How firm to the end,
Our Maker, Defender
Redeemer and Friend. (*TLH* 17: 1,5)

Tuesday

But to God be thanks, who has given us victory through Jesus Christ, our Lord. 1 Corinthians 15:57

Here is the big question: We have said that all people, even the holiest, are sinners and with Paul must implore God because of sins. "I am a miserable man. Who will rescue me from this body of death?" (Romans 7) We also observe that Christians die. Yes, even great Christians may suffer terrible deaths. What does this mean for me? Is it not true that redemption is FROM sin and death? That is what I have said. It is a spiritual kingdom for faith. That is, it is established in faith. Therefore, one must also see it then with the eyes of faith or else it will never ever be understood. So it still happens that death swallows us up. The kaiser, kings and tyrants have cut off the heads of holy apostles and martyrs. St. Paul had to suffer beheading. So also the lusts and inclinations to sin are still borne. Also, there are many clubs and sects that all set themselves against Christ. So where, then, is this life? Where, then, is the victory and subjection of death that is preached in this kingdom? To this I answer: We have the Lord and the might over sin and death. We have not yet overcome them. They are not yet finally gone. That's why Jeremiah says in chapter 23:5 that the king still persists in his work. For he yet rules over all times and still works for piety and righteousness. Just as a tailor who is making a coat is said to be "in his work" while he is yet making the coat. No one would say because of this that it is finished and already completed.

This is how it is in the on-going kingdom of Christ on earth that is "in the works." He still works and rules every day and continues from the first day until the last day until all is completed. While this is going on the Christians are still constantly falling into sins, although not willingly. But the Christian's advantage is that he has Christ. Whenever he feels sins, this one is already his Lord who brings him nothing that will cause him to be lost until the "old man" is completely dead and buried.

Therefore, if the Christian falls, Christ is also there, who reigns through his Spirit and overcomes sin and commands him to get up again and again. He says, "Stand up, brother. Be confident. You have no need." Just so, Christ is always in the battle and "in the work." He battles faithfully against the enemy. They set themselves against him, but finally he wins and they must be defeated. So it also goes in your life. God triumphs and has victory through Christ! St. Paul also speaks of this, "But to God be thanks who has given us the victory through our Lord Jesus Christ." And in 2 Corinthians 2, "To God be thanks, who holds the field for us always in Christ." So if ever a time comes that you are overcome, Christ is also there and he commands you to get up again and says, "Up, brother, up. You have no need." Again and again it happens. Each fall must be put behind you. Without falling there is no progress. Only see to it you don't remain down. There are falls and risings again and again as long as we live.

As Christ has now overcome sin, he has also therefore conquered death. If old man death comes and hangs on fast to you and wants to strangle you, Christ is also there and says, "Be lively, he cannot harm you." And if Christ is also there to hold you, then look you to no other! As you go to sleep, only boldly go through! It is appointed to be just a small thing. After a short time it will be better. One could even feel good because death is sharp and bitter since one need not submit to it, but overcomes it. For Christ has made death weak. Death's prod or spear is blunted, for death had run it up against Christ who overcame him and trod him under his foot.

Altb. III, 799–800: On a Passage from Jeremiah 23 Concerning Christ's Kingdom & Christian Freedom, 1527

O, may this bounteous God
Thro' all our life be near us,
With ever joyful hearts
And blessed peace to cheer us
And keep us in His grace
And guide us when perplexed
And free us from all ills
In this world and the next!

All praise and thanks to God
The Father now be given,
The Son, and Him who reigns
With them in highest heaven:
The one eternal God,
Whom earth and heaven adore!
For thus is was, is now,
And shall be evermore. (*TLH* 36: 2–3)

Wednesday

In an acceptable time, Judah will be helped and Israel will dwell safely. Jeremiah 23:6

Christ's kingdom is subject to the holy cross. It will always be that way where Christ's kingdom is planted by means of the gospel. Cross and persecution follow immediately. "If a strong man guard his palace, then his own dwell in peace. But when one stronger than he comes and beats him, then he captures his armor, and plunders the house, which he must abandon." How does this happen? When the gospel does not proceed, the devil is like this strong man in the world. He reigns mightily with great peace and courage so that all mankind sleeps and goes to hell. As we have seen until now in the papacy, there was always outstanding peace, but a dangerous and perverse peace. But in the gospel true peace is preached, which falls upon the empty, pretend peace of the powers and sects. Therefore, as the gospel now goes forth, it attacks the devil's kingdom and announces what fakes the devil is selling and how dark he is, and that is the nature of his kingdom. No matter how holy and pious it always seems to be, it only leads to hell and damnation which lay wide open, waiting to receive all the world. What is truly great and holy hangs itself on the gospel and does the devil harm by putting him and his kingdom to shame. Against this true peace he instigates trouble all the more in every area and uses whatever he can muster. He says, "I slept and have sat in peace a good long time, but you want to destroy my fortress. Just wait! I am going to break your sleep and make all the trials that you need! Sure, go ahead and have a breather until the battle where you'll get what's coming to you!" He does this everywhere as we can also see. As soon as the gospel is named we have peace as well as unrest. The gospel preaches peace that is still so far away that just around us we can see only the greatest lack of peace.

Where Christ reigns now through his gospel and Word there will be help. For just this purpose he gives us preaching and exhortation. Thus I can awaken the devil and powers and sects so that the whole world is leveled by the gospel. But let those be that rage and fuss. It is sure that they will not be able to do anything against the gospel of themselves. The Scriptures are full of promises to that effect, as in Psalm 33. "The Lord brings to nothing the council of the heathen, and turns around the thoughts of the peoples." And in Psalm 2 David says, "Why do the heathen rage and the people speak in vain? The kings of the lands depend on themselves and their lords plot with one another against the Lord and his anointed." But he assigned them to the little word "vain" or "nothing" and says, "But he who dwells in heaven laughs and the Lord mocks them." Why? If he is so strong and mighty then he can appoint a little wrath for you. Yet even if a thousand times as many enemies were against him, they could never rob from him any of those that he rules in peace. Rather, their raging means only a stronger faith and a sharper ability to discern things for those that have this insight.

The prophet gives an excellent word concerning this, "Judah will be helped and Israel will dwell in safety." So if you do not stand in faith, then in disbelief you will find definite proofs that this promise is not true. But can it be faith when one, refusing his faith, hangs Christ again on the cross? If someone cuts the heads off the apostles, if the Christian is driven from house and home and hunted from one town to another; even if Christ sends the apostles and preachers "as sheep among wolves," as he himself says in Matthew 10, what a great peace that is! These adversaries should be pursued with clubs and spears or dobermans! But Christ means his kingdom is peaceful and he will send help. The enemy would like to make it a kingdom of unrest with choke holds and murder. Yes, that's the way it looks. As I have said, God's kingdom is something else than what you see with your eyes. From a distance it shines as if it were forsaken and beyond hope. But what is near is only empty peace and useless help. But there you can overcome with victory through faith. Everything seems fine to the eye of the world as they fall upon Christ and bowl him over. In this way they want to kill and choke you like a slaughtered bird. The godless overwhelm you with confusion. The groups and sects want to claim their rights and triumph. But what is that? It won't last long. So don't turn back to them. The godless go down to perdition and the teachers of the spirit of the sects will be forgotten one day. Then you will see clearly how Christ did help his own and that we have been made lords over death, sin and the devil, which is not yet fully apparent.

Altb. III, 801–802: On a Passage from Jeremiah 23 Concerning Christ's Kingdom & Christian Freedom, 1527

And when within that lovely Paradise
At last I safely dwell,
What songs of bliss shall from my lips arise,
What joy my tongue shall tell.
While all the saints are singing
Hosannah o'er and o'er,
Pure Hallelujahs ringing
Around me evermore! (*TLH* 619: 7)

Thursday

And this shall be his name. He shall be called the LORD our Righteousness. Jeremiah 23:6

The first name that he is called, "the LORD," is proper to Jesus' nature as God. By this he administers nothing to us. The other name, our "Righteousness" is proper to his office, by which he serves us. So this name includes his entire office and is the fruit and the [meat of the] nut of this king. We have that kind of king, which is true but not only true God. He also approaches us in order to be our redeemer. This is our great trust, that this great and kind God is ours. But he has become ours. He has taken our flesh as his own. We should spell out such a name as this with letters of gold. Yes, not only letters of gold but also in drops of blood written at the foundations of our heart. Therefore, stand upon this, that Christ, the king, is not only God, but also our justifier, our righteousness, who would make us good and righteous. St. Paul also presents him in this way in many verses and especially in 1 Corinthians 1, where he says, "God has made Christ our wisdom, righteousness, holiness and freedom."

I have often said that the Christian life has two parts. First, that our sins that we commit are all completely forgiven and accounted for through Christ as we believe. And after that, our sins are not only forgiven us and so we are righteous, but we also are made altogether holy from the sins that follow, so those sins do not harm us. Then Christ is, in all, our total righteousness. He is this total righteousness and purity and thoroughly purifies us all from the sins that cling to our flesh. So this righteousness is ours by means of Christ and will be reckoned unto us. We are, then, without sin not by what we possess, but rather by way of the righteousness worked by Christ. When I believe in Christ, then Christ walks with his righteousness before God's sight in heaven and he answers for me. Therefore, we should and must also grasp his righteousness as our own and in that way be made bold as if that were our eternal birthright. Then these words, that he is named "our righteousness," are no joke.

You can see by this what kind of treasure we have in Christ, who can never die again, when we have Christ, himself, by faith. What hold will any death or sin have over a Christian in the hour of death? None! Death will be a cause for laughter. Sin does not accuse. Neither death nor sin, devil nor hell, can bring anything against the Christian for a faithful Christ abides with him. Now when death comes upon him, a believing Christian speaks of Christ. "Good wishes, dear death! What goodness do you bring? What are you looking for here? Don't you know who I have with me? Christ is my righteousness. Friend, go and take me along with you. If you take me, then I will follow you. You will bring me nothing but good." So the Christian defies death and says with St. Paul in 1 Corinthians 15, "Death where is your sting? Grave where is your victory?" And as he says in Philippians 1, "Christ is my life and to die is gain." I die, so I have gain because I come through it to life. See how a Christian deals with death! It is only his gain. You lose nothing to it, though its jaws cling to you until you die.

So go ahead to death also with your sins that lie ahead of you and that cling to you. That cannot hurt us or damn us. For Christ is with us who sweeps us off and purifies us. By this he prolongs your life from day to day and makes you holy even as your sins are yet increasing and adding to your evil. Then desire to die and press towards bliss and eternal life. This is what our being made holy means. Because Christ is our righteousness, do not fear. But he sweeps us off and purifies us as long as we live so we also become pure and holy just as Christ is holy. But that all comes from him.

Altb. III, 804–805: On a Passage from Jeremiah 23 Concerning Christ's Kingdom & Christian Freedom, 1527

From God shall naught divide me, For He is true for aye
And on my path will guide me, Who else should often stray.
His right hand holdeth me; For me He truly careth,
My burdens ever beareth Wherever I may be. (*TLH* 393: 1)

Friday

It is true. My Words are kind to the pious. Micah 2:7

This begins to take root in the heart of those who are pious and search out God's will. Then no need or grief will happen to them that is so great that the Lord by his Spirit does not abolish it to save his own. When, however, a person is not good and will not change according to God's will, then God truly punishes him and heaps up one misfortune upon another. This saying of the prophet is just like the clear teachings of all the promises in the law. These promises are given for you with conditions, like the promise of David's kingdom in the 132nd Psalm shows. The fruit of his body was promised David. He was given the assurances of the priesthood, peace, life, food and all kinds of good things and kindnesses. But still there was a stipulation, "When your offspring keep my covenant and my testimony which I taught you." The godless Jews scorned these conditions. They decided on "certain" services to God that they chose to do without and apart from God's commands. They depended too much upon their own desires and cravings and inquired nothing of God's Word.

Now the prophet responds with punishment of such sins. He stirs up frightening devastation, declaring that ungodly people are against the promises of God that God entrusted to them because he wanted to be their God. It is right, says the prophet. The promises are rightly made and will not fail. But only to those who are pious. Thus to the wicked, God promises nothing but wrath and eternal ruin. When the papists praise the promises which Christ has given his Christian Church, I do not say that the promises aren't true. But I say "no" to the proposition that you, the papists, are the Christian church; that your head is our Lord Jesus Christ when I see your plans and striving to shed innocent blood, and the idolatry and your false teaching which you stubbornly defend and want to make law. From this it follows that God speaks all good things to his church, but then he speaks every malice and harm to those who are not his church and his people, as the prophet expounds further.

We have already taught freely and frequently elsewhere about the difference between the promises of the law of the gospel. The prophet distributes promises here as is proper to the law, that God is gracious and promises every good, but to whom? To the good and so to those who keep the testimony and are obedient to the Word of God. That is what right behavior means. But our Lord Jesus Christ speaks differently. "I am not come to call the righteous, but the sinners." For the forgiveness of sins and eternal life will not be promised us on the basis of our worthiness or works, but by the Son of God, our Lord Jesus Christ, when we acknowledge our sins and believe that they are atoned and paid for through Christ.

Therefore, when the idiots preach to frighten consciences the things such as are here in the prophet Micah, you also want to hear the promise of the gospel presented as the final Word so that God will deal with sin and forgive. When we want to be good, we must remember that we can bring nothing to the promise of the gospel but faith by which we believe what Christ has done, what he has done for us. Thus, hoping in Christ's desire, we have forgiveness of sins and eternal life.

Altb. III, 88–90: Against the Heavenly Prophets in Matters of Images and Sacraments, 1525; cf. AE, 40

Lord of Glory, who hast bought us With Thy life-blood as the price,
Never grudging for the lost ones That tremendous sacrifice,
Give us faith to trust thee boldly, Hope, to stay our souls on Thee:
But, Oh! Best of all Thy graces, Give us Thine own charity. (*TLH* 442: 5)

Saturday

The Lord said to Satan, "Behold, he is in your hands except you cannot take his life." Job 2:6

We must resign ourselves to all this. For we are Christians and desire to be clean. In Christianity there is no peace and no end of cults, false brothers and all kinds of the devil's rage. Satan wants to be and must be with the children of God (Job 1). But where Satan comes to those children by God's permission and imposition, he does this in order to test the pious children of God. So it comes to pass that dear Job has his sheep taken, the thunder pounds his servants to death, the wind comes at midnight and rips apart his house and destroys all his children. But that is not enough. After all this, his body and soul suffer all kinds of plagues until even his own friends plague him and his own wife mocks him.

One reads the very same thing in the history of the Christian church. If one looks carefully, one finds from the beginning of Christianity such a tangled affair of sects, errors and all kinds of garbage, which is also found among the pagans. Where the devil rules with vigor, his reign is apparently better and quieter and surer than among those under Christ. In this manner the great emperors in the Roman Empire could say with great pomp and gentleness, "See how you fools consume one another and you still want to subject the world to your beliefs." Job's friends also, with the same attitude, pressured him and left him in complete darkness during his great misfortune. For Job was, to their eyes, the most hopeless villain on earth, who must surely be an enemy of God to be so painfully punished. If God does not always act to punish the wicked of the worldly powers so that they fight with one another and have every misfortune and grief, then a person judges that those worldly evils are not so displeasing to God as someone like Job, who suffers under Christ. For surely, a person under Christ should have piety, quietness, harmony and peace according to their own teachings and the predictions of all the prophets. In this matter there is "no counsel to help." But whoever is able to take hold of a Word of God can find an end by that and then obtain help. For God's Word is the great power. It rumbles like an earthquake under the devil, death, sins and exerts its mighty power. Will not his Word also rumble away against the sects, human wisdom and holiness, which the Word cannot stand? But it rumbles with a most blessed freedom so that it lets itself be received as the Word of God, even when no one can tell who is the cook (origin) and who is the waiter (who delivers it), who is God or the devil: where the church is or where antichrist is.

God always acts in this way so that he will not be seen in the things of man or by human wisdom, but only by his Word. God is praised and received by the Word that is over, under and outside of all things. When a person lies in death or in other need, then he must forget heaven and earth, sun and moon, father and mother, money and goods, and simply hold onto God's Word and by this travel through. Though this Word dwells in heaven and earth is behind him and in front if him, heaven and earth cannot advise him, let alone help. They cannot escort him through death, much less save him.

One must keep this in mind also in all unpleasantness that occurs in the church. We are not to obey what people allow or do. We are not to consider whether a person is great or not; if they are a Turk or a pope. Rather, we are to consider where and by whom the Word of God is being delivered. By that deliverance one can stop himself and be sure. This is the way you know you've found Job's house and the children of God, the holy Church. Let it be that way with you! And if you will not, then you can be vexed by the devil's works who must also rumble in Job's house so there it looks like the devil's house and all other houses look like God's. But Job's house stands to the end, when all others are damned and have vanished. Then that house is called "God's Word Stands Forever." "Heaven and earth may pass away, but my Word does not depart." Amen. That is true!

Altb. VII, 32: Advice to a Good Friend, 1538

Lord, Thy mercy will not leave me, Truth doth evermore abide.
Then in Thee I will confide. Since Thy Word cannot deceive me,
My salvation is to me Well assured eternally. (*TLH* 384: 4)

Week of Trinity VII

Sunday

Christ has given himself for our sins. Galatians 1:4

Aren't these Words like great thunderbolts against mankind, against all kinds of righteousness and against disciplined and holy lives that have the appearance of being great and wonderful? Such thunderclaps peal throughout the Word against all human holiness and wisdom, as it does in John 1, "Behold the Lamb of God, who bears the sins of the world." So you should very carefully consider this passage and all of them like it and not be fickle about what they mean by not heeding them or despising them. For it is of utmost importance what a poor, frightened, unsettled spirit finds as a dependable source of trust which it grasps by faith.

Do you want to be troubled by your sins? Would you rather be lost than to have a merciful God in heaven? Then surrender this passage and others like it that are such treasures to reach for. But rather than doing that, listen to what St. Paul says about the divine way as he says, "There is a man named Jesus Christ, who gave himself for our sins." These Words are truly rich, important, majestic and trustworthy. This salvation and payment for our sins was foreseen by Moses in the law and the prophets. They searched for the coming of the Christ of God's salvation. Because they had the knowledge and faith in this they could not be blessed by way of works that the law demanded but only through Christ who was promised to Abraham.

This is the most noble and trustworthy passage written by Paul. It is a true banner, a saving hope and a foundational teaching which the unholy papacy topples utterly with all its supposed religion, holiness and self-created holy orders and services to God. For if our sins could be worked out through our own deeds, services and satisfactions, then what, friend, was the great need that Christ give himself? Since he has given himself we should admit that our sins cannot be erased by our own works.

Further, we should also learn by these Words, "Who gave himself for our sins," that our sins are so great and countless and overwhelming that if all the world should be heaped together it would be doubtful that such a heap could make satisfaction for a single person. Since God has spent such a costly, unspeakable treasure, namely his dear Son, for this very purpose it is good to grasp that we can neither atone nor overcome our sins with our goodness and righteousness, even if we rendered every holy service. So these words, "who gave himself for us" truly prove the great strength and might of sin.

The great heap of humanity on earth are good companions. They go their merry way and throw their sin to the wind as if it were only a bad but trivial thing that is not very dangerous to them. If their sins begin to bite their conscience, they don't notice it much. They think, "There is no problem. I will think a bit on the matter and do this or that to make it right and God will be satisfied with that." But we should consider the greatness of the effective treasure given us so that we may also rightly know that sin's load on us is so great and heavy that all the world could not lift it off us. How can you remit them through your might and works? How can you make satisfaction with your works? Friends, grab this Word with your heart and consider it seriously and with diligence. Then you can learn to understand that in the word "sinners" inheres the eternal wrath of God along with all the power and might of hell-bent Satan. For this reason he ordains such misery, sorrow and heartache on earth that we can't find him for a moment of our lives and we must expect all kinds of misfortune with failure. And that is all the fault of sin.

Altb. VII, 23: On Galatians 1:4, Christ gave himself . . ., 1538

O Jesus Christ, do hear my prayer Keep and protect me e'er in Thee.
Enclose me in Thy sacred wounds, Protect me from my enemy.
(Original translation of verse in Link)

Monday

Who has given himself a ransom for all, so that this be preached in due time. 1 Timothy 2:6

All power lies in this: That we should at all times read in the Holy Scriptures in such Words as "for me," "for us," "for our sins," that they are said of US. And we should maintain this truth, that they actually point to us so that we hold them in strong faith and live and die by this. Then there will always be something great and excellent hidden under these Words that will never fail you. Because of this one can have a special longing for God's Word and to know what it says. But you can easily think Christ intends such Words only for St. Peter, Paul and other holy saints who alone were worthy of them. It is supremely difficult for most to think, on the contrary, that this concerns you, yourself, a poor, unworthy, damned sinner and that you should say to yourself, "Christ, God's Son, is given for YOUR sins, which are many, great and heavy and because of which you are not worthy of grace." That is a hard work and a great pain.

So it is a tragic affair when Christ's kindness and good work is praised and commended so he is said to have given himself for sinners and bought them with his holy life, but only those sinners who are worthy. But if a person were to purposely say, "He is for all of us; for he died for my sins, your sins and the whole world's sins," then he might stop short and think again so that God should not come so near him. For God cannot convince his heart to believe such a treasure comes to him as a gift by grace through Christ, without any service or worthiness of his own. For he wants to make a resolution of his will by which he would make everything clean and sinless and that apart from God. So if he says things like "Christ, God's Son, has given himself for our sins" or he hears similar words, yet he doesn't understand the "our" as applying to himself. Rather, it applies to someone else who is holy and worthy of such grace. He continues to believe that he could not partake of such grace until he has already paid for it by his works. These foolish and terrible thoughts are nonsense. That person neither understands nor perceives the immensity and power both of sin and of God's mercy. That is why he would prefer that sins not be so great and frightening as the Scriptures say they are. He would prefer to read that they are just an annoying, trivial, pity that one can easily correct without Christ's help. Thus these people will surely not give their sins another thought. It naturally follows that he live and persist in performing the most dreadful sins without any fear and timidity. When their overly patient conscience finally wakes up, they throw the pangs to the wind not thinking that there is any great problem. They do not know and feel what a great unbearable weight sin causes. It is not likely that they will understand what it means, "Christ has given himself for our sins." If they read something like this, it is no big deal but more like a big joke. If they want to look better they take on a false humility with hypocrisy. With this he outwardly allows himself to hear the words as though he were a sinner in need of Christ's help. But underneath, blind reason gladly presents itself before God as a sinner who says with his mouth, "I am a poor sinner," but at the same time thinks of himself in his heart as if he were pious and righteous. That kind of person feels no sin unto the terror of death, but finds himself healthy, clean and lively, needing nothing at all. When he thinks of himself in this way, then, he wants to believe that Christ, God's Son, is given for our sins but thinks of his own goodness. All people think this way according to their fallen nature, especially those who want to look best and holiest in the world.

Altb. VII, 24–25: On Galatians 1:4, Christ gave himself . . ., 1538

'Tis I who should be smitten, My doom should here be written:
Bound hand and foot in hell. The fetters and the scourging,
The floods around Him surge, 'Tis I who have deserved them well. (*TLH* 171: 5)

Tuesday

And the snake was more cunning that any of the animals of the field, that God the Lord had made and he spoke to the woman. "Yes now, should God have said to you, 'You should not eat of all the kinds of trees in the Garden?'" Genesis 3:1

The philosophers argue over the chief issue in this temptation when they ate this forbidden apple, whether Adam and Eve sinned by idolatry or by pride or by overconfidence or by wickedness. When we carefully consider the matter as it deserves, we find that this is a supreme and very devastating temptation and trial, for the snake attacked the good intentions of God and dared to prove by God's prohibition of the tree that God's intentions towards mankind were not good. He therefore even assaulted the image of God and the highest abilities that had been fully theirs. But that was no longer present after their human nature was ruined. By the image of God they applied themselves, turning to God and lifting themselves to the highest and best service to God, as God himself had appointed. That's why we dispute so futilely that it was this sin or that. The devil charmed Eve into the guilt of all sins. He incited her to act against the Word and will of God.

Moses writes carefully for that reason and says the snake "spoke." By the word he opposed the Word. But the Word, as the Lord had spoken it to Adam was this, "From the tree of the perception of good and evil, you may not eat." The Word was Adam's law and gospel, God's service and obedience, by which he could perform service to God in his innocence. So Satan set himself to turn Adam away from this. Satan would not only make him wise by the tree and take them home with him when they plucked the fruit, as the foolish and unexperienced think, and Satan surely did that, but by this plan he also made a new and different word than God's Word, as he still always desires to do in the church.

If the gospel is taught purely and cleary, the people will be sure of their faith and guard against idols. Wherever that happens, though, the devil does not rest. He applies himself and seeks by many ways to lead the people away from the Word or to make the Word seem false. In the Greek church, even during the times of the apostles, you find vigorous and well entrenched heretics of many kinds. One of them taught that Christ was not God's Son. Another said he was not Mary's Son. The anabaptists today also shamelessly and godlessly say that Christ did not receive flesh from Mary. In St. Basil's time, several others had attempted to renounce the Holy Ghost as God. We experience the same thing in our own time. After the pure teaching of the gospel comes forth daily, we find various people trying to detract from the work and Word of God. Now in addition to these, we also hear of other temptations by which the devil stirs the people to whoring, adultery and other shame and vice. But these are small compared to the temptations where Satan takes hold of God's Word and marches against the church and saints. This is much worse and more dangerous.

By this Satan made Adam and Eve his own. He gave them his own word and they were led to take that word and despair because of God. They believed Satan's lie. And when such a person is seen after Satan has so abused him, it is no wonder that he becomes haughty and a despiser of God and of man and becomes an adulterer, murderer, etc. Therefore, this is the sum and chief source of all the temptation which goes on after the fall unto the transgression of all God's laws. For faithlessness is the first matter and source of all sins. When the devil sows into the heart a contrary word, or one that is false, and has broken one to faithlessness, he easily brings him at last to the end that he has in mind.

So after Eve had taken hold of the word of the lie, it was easy for her to go to the forbidden tree and to pick an apple from it. Therefore, it is a foolish thought of the philosophers and monks that after Eve beheld the fruit she had an increasing desire to pick the apple until she finally was convinced and overcome to eat it. It was not the desire that created the temptation but the fact that they heard another word and tossed away what God had already said, when he said that if they ate of the tree they would die. So we should rather heed the Words that Moses wrote than any others.

Altb. IX 69–70: Lectures on Genesis, 1535; cf. AE 1

All mankind fell in Adams' fall	Thro' all man's pow'rs corruption creeps
One common sin infects us all;	And him in dreadful bondage keeps;
From sire to son the bane descends,	In guilt he draws his infant breath
And over all the curse impends.	And reaps its fruits of woe and death. (*TLH* 369: 1–2)

Wednesday

And should God have said, "You should not eat of all the kinds of trees in the garden?'" Genesis 3:1

First Satan acts as if he were God. Just as God had first preached to Adam so Satan preaches here to Eve. What it says in the proverb is true, "In God's name every calamity arises." So as God's

404

Word brings salvation if it is honestly brought, it also brings ruin when it is falsified. But I not only mean falsification when it is orally proclaimed but also in the inner thoughts, imaginations and intentions when they depart from the Word and cling to something else.

This is exactly what Moses shows when he says here "he spoke." This indicates that the devil was trying to separate Eve from what God had said when God spoke. So after Satan had gotten the Word out of the way, he immediately spoiled the best desire that man had and set man with himself against God. Satan had also destroyed and ruined their understanding so they doubted God's intentions. A disobedient hand, contrary to God, stretched itself out against God's Word to pick the apple and after that a disobedient lying mouth and teeth all followed that first doubt. To summarize, all wickedness follows faithlessness or doubt of God and his Word. Therefore what can evil be, but disobedience to God and attentiveness to the devil?

This kind of Satanic trick and evil follows every heretic. Under the guise of goodness and fear of God and his Word in the eyes of the people, he [the heretic] portrays another God, who is nowhere to be found. So consider their word carefully! Even if they look to you as if no one were holier or more devoted, that they witness to God, that they seek with all their hearts the church's advantage and blessing, and that no one is in greater need of God's mercy than they, and then they preach, teach and proclaim false doctrine which they commit by great effort to God's name and honor in order that it becomes widely known, you find that what a Christian should say much about, they do not wish to consider nor will they hold onto it because they are heretics or teachers of the devil. So they bury sound teaching and darken the knowledge of God.

Soon after the fall, we see that people let themselves be led unwarily from the Word into dangerous arguments. After they become dissatisfied with the Word, they ask "How?" and "Why?" this or that can be. Like Eve when she listened to the devil's word, they cling to doubt and are lost. Also when we doubt if God has desired to make us poor damned sinners good through Christ, it is easy to see that we become fooled and wear the dunce cap, persuaded that we must be made good through our own work.

The devil can make a new god in an instant or even sooner. He trips us up and makes us think upon that new god when he adds his own words to the old ones, but not the sort of Words that are given by God, namely, that we should preach atonement and the forgiveness of sins in the name of Christ. He rather gives the sort of words that tell us we should become a monk, etc., and pray a lot and fast and be cloistered, etc. If God's Word is then changed or falsified, then a new god arises, as Moses says in his song (Deuteronomy 32) "whom the fathers did not worship."

You should watch out for these traps of the devil. It would be fine if Satan would teach that one should murder, be sexually immoral, be disrespectful to parents. Then anyone could see that the devil is there advising what God had forbidden. Then we could easily guard against him. But where he presents a new word, disputing God's will, and turning the church, the people of God, away from God's name, it is not as easy for one to keep watch. This must be handled by sharp judgment and the testing of the spirit. But in such a test we can tell the difference between the right God and the new one in the same way Christ marks the difference when the devil wanted to tell him to turn the stone into bread and throw himself off the pinnacle of the temple. The devil wanted to advise him that he should go ahead and chance something without God's Word. But Christ did not let himself be deceived as Eve did. For Christ held the Word and kept himself by God's truth from being led off by what was not true, but false wisdom. So faithlessness and doubt in which one walks apart from the Word, is really a torture and the source of all sins. Because the world is full of this, the world dwells in idolatry, denies the truth and makes herself a new god.

Altb. IX 70-71: Lectures on Genesis, 1535; cf. AE 1

Lord, keep us steadfast in Thy Word; Curb those who fain by craft and sword
Would wrest' the kingdom from Thy Son And set at naught all He hath done. (*TLH* 261: 1)

Thursday

Then the snake spoke to the woman, "You will not suffer death. Rather, God knows that on the day you eat of it, your eyes will be opened and you will be as God and know what is good and evil." Genesis 3:4,5

We can see that when the devil sets out to tempt a person it is a frightening thing. One fall follows another and one sin causes a great and mighty fall. It was a great sin when Eve strayed from God and his Word and listened to the devil. It is an even greater one, as shown here, when Eve approved of the devil, whose lies God punishes and whom he will not let stand. So now she is no longer wandering from God alone as in the first matter, but now she has thrown in her lot with the devil to disobey God, to lie about God's Word and to believe the father of lies instead of God's Word.

This should warn us to learn what mankind has become. This illustrates it in a way that is wonderfully crafted by the wisdom of God. What does it show us? It shows us what we see with our own eyes. For the errorists of our own time also treasured the gospel in the beginning of its revelation and thanked God for it. For God gave us his Word once more in this time to restore those who have fallen from it and now they oppose us.

For example, the Arians began to fall from faith in the deity of God's Son. Soon they were foolishly saying that they were founding the true church. They pursued that goal with great cruelty.

We have also seen the same example among the anabaptists. For they make the Word doubtful in the same way as all those who first followed the devil. They make the sure Word a "perhaps." Then they change it from a "perhaps" to a "no." So they become apostate from God and persecutors of God. They follow their father, the devil, who, after he fell from heaven, desired sinners who would be the greatest enemies of Christ and his church.

This example is seen more and more. For we have no greater enemies than those who have fallen from our doctrine. This frightening word pursues these sinners: "The fools say in their heart: there is no God." It is not enough that they have strayed from God, but they also must persecute God and his Word.

One must, then, hold to this rule: one will see and feel conflict his whole life, but if we are sure that that which we have and teach is God's Word, we must let that be settled with innocent faith and not dispute over it out of idle debate. For all such inquisitive disputing will drag you to a plain fall.

We clearly have the Lord's Words of the Holy Supper, that he says of the bread, "This is my body, which is given for you," and of the cup, "this is the cup of the New Testament in my blood." When the sacramental "know it alls" depart from the faith of these Words and dispute what they also COULD mean, they teach in various degrees in a way that belies and contests Christ's Words, trying to make them less, as Eve did.

Also, when the Arian thinks of God, he first grabs hold of the proposition that God is the most simple unity. Perhaps then, Christ is not God. From there he runs with no scruples and without gathering any proof to a position completely and purely advocating and purely gushing forth with the teaching that Christ is not God. Because of this, he will not change his mind when John says, "The Word was God" or when Jesus' baptism is in the name of the Father and of the Son and of the Holy Ghost or when God has commanded that we believe in Christ, pray to him and call upon him. How could they set out so recklessly and presumptuously to judge God and his Word, which will judge us? So you should stand away from such trouble and persevere. If we hear that God's Word says something, we believe it and do not dispute over it and we heed Christ. Otherwise, our reason will take much more away from us.

Listen to the passage in Isaiah 7, "If you do not believe, you will not remain." If we also separate from one another as they want to have us splintered, then we will nevermore understand why their eyes see what they see, what the ears hear or even what the soul is. We will, then, bear such terrible requirements of works upon us every moment of the day. How will we understand these things, which are above all our five senses that can observe only what is in the world? How then, but only in God's Word which establishes that in the Holy Supper the bread is the body and the wine is the blood of Christ? Therefore, we should believe even though we don't understand and cannot understand.

So this third chapter of Moses deals with this whole tragedy and the simple words, "From the tree in the middle of Paradise you should not eat." But the simple minded do not understand the reason for these Words and why God would be this way. For as soon as they go off in their curiosity and are not satisfied that God had commanded and said it, they are lost. Their efforts [to explain it] follow the example of all similar attempts by which the devil contests the Word and faith. So dear Eve had already lost the Word, which God had spoken to Adam, when she desired to eat the apple. But if she had kept this Word it would have remained with her in worship before God and in faith. But here she goes ahead after she lost the Word. She finds herself in the company of God's wrath and in disobedience with the devil.

Its good for us to know this so we learn about temptation. As Peter says, stand fast and oppose the devil so that we hold fast to the Word and to ears that hear and do. By this we do not allow what is not in accordance with the Word. Then Eve's sorrow and trouble is a lesson for us that we not allow ourselves to depart from the Lord and to suffer that sorrowful end.

Altb. IX 75-76: Lectures on Genesis, 1535; cf. AE 1

O God, when evil comes,
On earth there is no peace.
The lot of sects and heretics
Allow us not our ease.
(Original translation of verse in Link)

When haughty spirits yet
Exalt themselves with might.
They always bring us something new
To take Your teachings true.

Friday

And the woman saw the tree was good to eat and lovely to look at and that it was a desirable tree, for it would make one wise. And she took of the fruit and ate and gave her husband also of it and he ate. Genesis 3:6

The word *"hiskil"* is Hebrew for "wise" and here it is called *"miskil,"* a greater than conventional wisdom and knowledge, as Psalm 14 says, "God looks from heaven upon the sons of man to see if anyone is wise and inquires of God," and Isaiah 52, "My servant shall deal wisely." All these refer to knowledge that reveals God. Eve originally had this light, or knowledge, in her heart as a bright sun because she had God's Word. Therefore, she also had knowledge concerning all creatures. But she wanted to climb higher and know God in another way than God had publicly given in his Word because she would not be satisfied with this wisdom. This terrifying fall by which she forsook the right knowledge and acted in a deep fog and blindness was the result.

But the devil acts now just as he did at that time! God bids us believe the gospel of his Son and be saved by it. This is the true knowledge as Christ says in John 17, "This is eternal life, that they know you, the only true God, and Jesus Christ, whom you have sent." A monk scorns this knowledge and in doing so, he pursues the service of God with religion and turns to something besides God. He puts on a cowl, girds himself with a cloak of repentance, is celibate, etc. He shows he wants to please God and be saved by that. This "high knowledge," by which he pursues serving God and religion, is something planted in his miserable human nature by the devil and original sin. So people depart from the Word, which God has given to save them, and they speak their own thoughts, as did Eve, who was previously formed in the right knowledge but had a desire for another knowledge, which was outside of and against God's Word. Under the influence of this knowledge, all plans, sight, thoughts, desires and works were dominated by sin.

You should not listen to anyone who has been taught so strangely and horribly that they argue that the apple caused such miserable ruin and concealed such death and sadness. When you hear such an explanation, you must laugh off the whole incident as a fable. But whoever reads this text in a straightforward way and thinks about it will easily see that the bite of the apple is not the big thing. Rather, the sin that Eve committed against both tables of the law, against God's Word and God himself is of greatest importance. For she placed herself completely under the instruction of the devil when she hurled God's Word far from her.

You cannot and should not diminish or explain away this chief teaching of this passage quoted above. The great and important lesson is that this is a miserable sin and a departure from God. We should see this and concentrate upon this rather than going off and speculating about the apple that was picked and eaten. If you only consider the physical act of eating and not the sin that preceded the act, you won't be able to follow what is said. God would then seem to be one who goes around with a frown on his face, striking all of humanity with such a terribly great punishment for such a trifling sin. Thinking that, you would become God's enemy and deny the truth of this Word or you would have to dismiss it as Epicurean wisdom, that is, as a fable.

So we should consider the Word. But it is God's Word. The sin must be as great as the Word is. The sin entices and subjects the whole human nature. That is how greatly the sin exerts itself to overcome God's Word which is so great and gushing that it cannot suffer being judged! For that Word belongs to the one who brings with him gushing righteousness, namely, God's Son, to conquer the sin.

This also shows us the devil's cunning. For he did not bring Eve to commit sin by means of her desire for the apple, but he rather snatched away the highest virtue of man, namely faith in the Word. Therefore, doubt and departure from God is the root and primal fountain of all sins, just as, on the opposite side, the first cause and root of righteousness is faith.

Altb. IX 77–78: Lectures on Genesis, 1535; cf. AE 1

The Savior calls; let every ear	Here springs of sacred pleasures rise
Attend the heav'nly sound.	To ease your ev'ry pain;
Ye doubting souls, dismiss your fear;	Immortal fountain, full supplies!
Hope smiles reviving round.	Nor shall you thirst in vain. (*TLH* 281: 1,3)

Saturday

And the Lord God called to Adam and spoke to him, "Where are you?" And he replied, "I heard your voice in the Garden and was afraid for I am naked. So I hid myself." Genesis 3:6

"Where are you?" are Words of law that proclaimed judgment conforming to God's knowledge. For everything is revealed and known before God, Hebrews 4. Even our thoughts are known in which we want to avoid him, to not see his face and to run from him. So when he says, "Where are you?" it is as if he would say, "So you think I don't see you?" He wanted Adam to see and experience that even when he was hidden, he was not concealed from God and that whoever runs from God has still not fled from God. This applies to our nature in its every sin. We muse in our foolish reason that we can flee before the wrath of God, from whom we cannot escape. That is the grossest foolishness, when we think more about how to escape from God then we do about turning again to him. But the sinful nature cannot return. What does that mean? How did Adam try to encourage himself when he'd heard God's voice? See where he stands! He is before the judgment seat of God who summoned him for punishment because he had such a foolish hope of hiding and concealing himself.

And he said, "I heard your voice in the Garden and was afraid, for I am naked. So I hid myself."

Just as Adam's running had been foolish, he also gives a foolish answer. After he sinned nearly all of his wisdom and counsel abandoned him. He wants to teach God, who created him that way, that he is naked. Adam makes himself an offense and bespeaks himself as a damned person by his own mouth. He also says that when he heard God's voice, in the same way he had heard it say that he was forbidden to eat of the tree, he was afraid. Why wasn't Adam afraid and why didn't he try to run away when he first heard God speak? Why did he stand there looking happy and straight that first time when he saw and heard God before him? But here he is disintegrating like a burning leaf! He is no longer Adam as he had been. He is completely changed and has become another man. Now he wants to protect himself with a lying pretense and wants to answer God with it. For how can it be that before he hadn't feared God, but had belonged to God by his fervent affection for him?

Let us learn that such perversions of virtue always follow sin. Such "virtue" consists of sinners themselves making accusations to excuse themselves and speaking differently than God speaks in order to defend themselves. So here Adam hides his sin and wants to protect himself by saying that he fled not because he sinned but because he heard God's voice and was afraid and because he was ashamed of his nakedness.

It didn't occur to the stupid bungler that he wasn't afraid before. He also hadn't been ashamed to be naked before. He was naked because God had made him so. Why should he not show himself in the simple way God had made him? Before, he had been naked in Paradise before God and all the animals. He had known that God loved him and he set his own desire on God. But now he was ashamed of himself because he was naked and he fled from God and hid himself. These are the sure arguments and attitudes by which Adam condemns himself, his sin exposed in the light of day.

This is how Adam and Eve became godless by the first law and how they cursed themselves. The darkness and all that is hidden in the human heart will be brought into the open. All human sin and evil deeds will be read as open books. God already knew that Adam had sinned and was guilty of death. But he asks Adam to give his own witness why he should be rejected, why after he once sinned he fled from God, which is also a sin, how it could be virtue and obedience to flee from God. Adam witnessed concerning himself that he hoped to perhaps hide the sin by saying the main reason for his running was God's voice and that he was naked. By this we learn sin's method and nature. Where God does not help quickly and does not again speak to the sinner, the sinner will flee from God every time. Since he wants to pardon his sin with lies, he piles one sin upon another until he finally slanders God and accuses him. So one sin slips into another and produces an eternal fall until at last God, in addition, gives the sinner much more guilt and accuses him so that the sinner knows his sin. Adam should have said, "Lord I have sinned." But he didn't do that. Rather, he showed how God had sinned and said nothing else than, "Lord, you sinned, so I would like to stay holy and stay in Paradise after the bite of apple, if you please." So these words show that Adam's heart and mind are set in sin. That is why he says, "I would not have run if your voice didn't frighten me."

Altb. IX 83–84: Lectures on Genesis, 1535; cf. AE 1

The Law of God is good and wise
And sets His will before our eyes,
Shows us the way of righteousness
And dooms to death when we transgress.

Its light of holiness imparts
The knowledge of our sinful hearts
That we may see our lost estate
And seek deliv'rance ere too late. (*TLH* 295: 1–2)

Week of Trinity VIII

Sunday

Adam said, "The woman that you have given me gave me of the tree and I ate." Genesis 3:12

Notice! Here a sinner's wickedness and mode of operation are illustrated. Adam does not allow himself any memory of his sin but he lies and excuses himself as long as he has a glimmer of hope of avoiding it. It is no wonder that he hoped first to hide the sin. Now, in addition to this, he complains to God when he is made aware that he has sinned. Further, it is a wonder that he keeps on making excuses even after his conscience convicted him and God himself told him that he had sinned. He did not say, "Lord, I have sinned. Forgive me my trespass. Be merciful." (Sin's strategy is to not allow the heart, finally, to flee TO God. Rather, it drives him to flee FROM God much more.) and Adam gives the guilt to his wife.

As even the scholastics still teach in their schools, man will always lie when he is reproached for an evil deed. Or else he will defend himself that he might appear to be in the right. Adam also does both. First he lies about the sin and says that it was God's voice that frightened him and not his sin. Then he switches over to defend himself by making a case that his deed was reasonable. He says, if you had not given me the woman then I wouldn't have eaten from the tree. Thus, he ascribes most of the error to God. He charges God with half of his own sin. So there is no end to sin when God's Word is weakened.

First this man sinned with disobedience and unfaithfulness. Now he makes his sins greater with feeble excuses and blasphemy against God. For he says, "I have not listened to the snake, have not desired the tree when I looked at it, have not stretched out my hand to pick the forbidden fruit. Rather, the wife you gave me did all that." In short, Adam will not admit that he sinned. Rather he wants to be pure and blameless.

This characteristic belongs in the description of sin and its nature. Where there is no promise of the forgiveness of sins, a sinner can do nothing but what Adam did. If God had said, "Adam, you have sinned, but I will remit your sin," then Adam would have cursed his sin vehemently and done so with humility, acknowledging it without lies. But since there was no promise of the forgiveness of sins at that time, he could feel and see nothing but death for transgressing the law. But because his fallen nature ran from that and displayed its nature in this way, Adam could not be brought to acknowledge his sin. So every sinner is also an enemy of his punishment. He regards God's righteousness and God himself in the same way. He makes every effort to inform God and all men that he suffers innocently [as a victim].

So Adam does away with his sin because he did not overhear the snake, much less pick the apple. "The woman," he says, "whom you have made for me has given me [the fruit] of the tree." Most people feel the same way about their sins. They fall into such despair that when the realization of their sins comes, they either hang themselves or blaspheme God. We know this from Job. He said, "Cursed be the day I was born, that I was not dead from my mother's body." They pass the guilt to God for [they say] he has erred. They become impatient and grumble against God because he has fashioned them unto death and damnation. A man is capable of doing nothing else if there is no hope of forgiveness and the promise of grace. Since the dead human nature is not sorry, it causes despair and blasphemy against God.

So these words, "The woman you gave me . . ." are full of rebellion and rage against God. He wants to say, "YOU brought this calamity upon me. If you had given the woman her own garden and not troubled me with living with her then I would still be living rightly without sin. It is your fault that I have now sinned. You are the one who made the woman for me." So Adam is presented here as a model of all who sin and then sinfully deny it. They can do nothing but accuse God and excuse themselves 'til they see that God is almighty and that they had had the ability to guard against their sin. It is terrifying for the sinner when his heart is not informed of the promise of the forgiveness of sins and does not trust in it. The law, when it is unaccompanied by the gospel and the realization of grace, will then orient such a person. He is, then, always oriented to despair and to an end with no remission.

Altb. IX 84–85: Lectures on Genesis, 1535; cf. AE 1

Thou alone, my God and Lord,
Art my Glory and Reward.
Thou hast bled for me and died;
In Thy wounds I safely hide.

Come, then, Lamb for sinners slain,
Come and ease me of my pain.
Evermore I cry to Thee:
Jesus, Jesus, come to me! (*TLH* 356: 5-6)

Monday

I will put enmity between you and the woman and between your seed and her Seed. Genesis 3:15

God does not say this for the sake of the devil. God doesn't consider him worth the effort of proclaiming his damnation. On the contrary, it would be enough that God damned him in his own will. But this is said for the sake of Adam and Eve. They hear Satan's judgment and are comforted, because they see that God is his enemy by nature and against him because he had inflicted on mankind such trouble and harm. So they view God's grace and mercy even here commencing in the midst of God's wrath awakened by sin and disobedience. Under the supreme threats of the Father, his heart breaks open. He is not so angry that he would cast away his son for the sake of sins, but he would reveal help. He foretells of victory against the enemy who had deceived and conquered human nature.

So there is not a unified judgment against Satan and mankind though man fell into sin through Satan. God did not place them together in their punishments. He is not able to act as if they had done good, which would contradict justice, but he separates them far from each other. He would yet be angry with man. But man had not listened to Satan because he wanted to. So the greater anger is against Satan. So he damns [Satan] harshly and punishes him so Adam and Eve could see and hear it. By this they can be encouraged and trust that it won't go so harshly in their case. Their first consolation was that the snake, and with him Satan, was accused and cursed for the sake of Adam and Eve.

In these words is also THE comfort. Before them, the ominous clouds were darkened. Then the bright sun lifted itself above the clouds. With loving splendor, God lights up their frightened hearts. Adam and Eve would not hear the kind of judgment against them as made against the snake. Rather, they would stand against the damned foe as on a mountain top in time of war. They would stand in the hope that help would come, the Son of God, the Seed of the woman. So the forgiveness of sins is shown here to Adam and Eve. They were taken completely in grace as they were declared free from sin and death, from hell and this terror and fear, which had strangled them right to death before the face of God. Then this comfort comes. God did not curse Adam and Eve as he did the snake. They would be left together in war with the snake. In this war they would be useless but it would turn out for the greatest good of man. This is the main comfort. Although this enemy converts them and disputes with them by cunning and deceit, yet there would be born a Seed who would crush the snake's head. Here the eternal destruction of the tyranny of Satan is revealed, even though they are unable to begin this battle without the mighty war this man must wage and fight.

But see how the war changes their fortune! The man's heel is placed in danger, but his head is safe and remains unforsaken and undefeated. On the other hand, through the Seed of the woman, not the tail or the belly but the head of the snake, would be trampled and humbled. As Christ clearly says, this victory would be given us. After the strong man is conquered, that which he robbed would be freed. So Christ would conquer sin and death through faith. The gates of hell would not prevail against him.

Altb. IX 90–91: Lectures on Genesis, 1535; cf. AE 1

Thou art the Life; the rending tomb
Proclaims Thy conqu'ring arm;
And those who put their trust in Thee
Nor death nor hell shall harm.

Thou art the Way, the Truth, the Life
Grant us that Way to know.
That Truth to keep, that Life to win,
Whose joys eternal flow. (*TLH* 355: 3–4)

Tuesday

That one will trample your head and you will prick his heel. Genesis 3:15

The promise is simultaneously clear and veiled. God says in general, "the woman's seed." By this he would make the devil suspicious of all that come from the woman. God plagues him with eternal sorrow and affliction. So this is a wonderful synecdoche [where the whole and a significant part are named simultaneously]. He says "the woman's Seed." It sounds as though God is speaking generally about the seed of every woman. But God is only addressing one, that is, the Seed of Mary, who is a mother without union with a man. As the first part, "I will put enmity between you and the woman," sounds as if it speaks of all women in general (for God wanted to make Satan suspicious of all, and also wanted to reveal hope for the pious, that they would be expecting their holiness and salvation from all who were born until the birth of the one who would come.), so also this passage "Between your seed . . ." is an individual among the seeds, the stem of Judah and the one placed in Joseph's care, who is born only from Mary.

So this text, which enlivened Adam and Eve, bringing the dead to the life that they had lost because of sin, also gave them more to hope for than what they previously possessed. As St. Paul also often describes this, "I die daily." Even if we don't want to call our temporal life a "death," it is yet truly nothing but a path to death. Just like someone infected by the plague succumbs quickly to death after he is infected, so also this life, once infected by sin, can no longer be called a life. Because of willing sin and the punishment of sin, it is called death.

But through Baptism we are brought again the life of hope or, much more, the hope of life. Above all this is true life, that we live before God. Before we received this, we were in the midst of death. We die and decay on the earth like other carrion as if there were no life left anywhere. Yet, believing in Christ, we have this hope. In the new day we will be awakened again unto eternal life. So Adam is also awakened by this preaching of the Lord not as if this life had fully come (the life which he had lost he had not yet again won), but he receives the hope of that life when he hears that Satan's tyranny would be stopped and destroyed.

This passage also delivers you salvation from the law, sin and death. It reveals a clear and sure hope of resurrection and renewal to another life after this one. As he will stomp the head of the snake, so he must also take care of death and weaken it. Now death is ineffective. So also, sin, by which death is earned, must also be taken care of. Sin is also put in its place. So the law, which shows who is lost, must also cease. But yet the law is also established at the same time by steadfast obedience. Now, while all of this will belong to them through and in the Seed, it is also clear and obvious that human nature cannot deal with sin or punishment nor endure death after the fall by its own desires or skills until the lost obedience would return. Those tasks belong to greater skill and greater strength than belong to mankind.

God's Son has become the needed sacrifice. He rectifies this situation so that he takes sins away, vanquishes death and again brings the lost obedience. In Christ we are mighty and established in such treasures, but in hope. Through hope, Adam, Eve, and all in faith live and overcome until the new day. The fear of death and the dark tyranny, which is everything, is made nothing by God's skill and power. Even if you make something of them again, that, too, is nothing. Look at Adam and Eve that are so full of sin and death. Yet as they hear the promise of the Seed of the woman who will crush the head of the serpent, they have hope and so do you. Namely, you hope that death is lifted, sin is made powerless, and righteousness, life, peace, etc., are restored. Our first parents lived and died in that hope. We also desire true holiness and righteousness by this hope.

We also live in the same hope. When we die, for the sake of Christ, we set our hope on life as the Word informs us. This trust and faith in the Lord Christ's service and good work are ours. By this completed salvation, by which we are all in all righteous, we can love God completely and our neighbor as ourselves. We wait for this free life. We come to it a little. But sin, which reigns mightily in all our members and inheres throughout us, either ruins or hinders this obedience.

Altb. IX 94: Lectures on Genesis, 1535; cf. AE 1

Tho' devils all the world should fill, All eager to devour us,
We tremble not, we fear no ill, They shall not overpower us.
This world's prince may still Scowl fierce as he will,
He can harm us none, He's judged; the deed is done.
One little Word can fell him. (*TLH* 262: 3)

Wednesday

By the sweat of your brow you shall eat your bread until you return to the ground from which you came. For you are of the earth and shall [go] to the earth. Genesis 3:19

We want to differentiate "sweat" according to the right amounts. The amount of sweat and work of one who remains in the home is great. In the political and worldly realm it is greater. In the office of the church it is greatest of all. Just look at Paul and you can easily grasp how he sweat in his office. How could we say that in the church there is no trouble, no sweat, where there is and always has been trouble because of devils and heretics, scandals, sins, injustice and the pressure of tyranny, and on top of that, plagues caused by all kinds of troubles? Would we want to say, in light of this, that those who take care of the church are not worth their bread?

We could say that the whole godless heap of pope, cardinals, etc., don't work. They serve only their bellies. They only dress on good days and eat up great delicacies. They are the kind referred to by St. Paul when he says, "Who will not work should not eat." In the church, preaching and teaching, administering the Sacrament, battling heretics and "know it alls," dispensing of scandals, improving and building the pious, etc., are called "work." Christ says that those who do this are workers worthy of their hire.

We would rightly consider Adam's work after the fall as far more difficult than ours. Among us, each works and sweats in his own occupation. But so long as Adam lived, he was obligated to hold all vocations together, namely, in the house, as well as in the worldly and spiritual realms. He needed to support and govern his household and bring all of them up in the fear of God. He was also simultaneously the king and priest. Whatever is troublesome, toil and dangerous in each of these vocations, was his task.

We must hold trust against troubles [in our vocations] and apply patience to our hearts. We see that our chosen wives also face such misery. But we still have the hope of the resurrection and of eternal life. Because every poor miserable person also has this hope, we should all trust in this hope and overcome all misfortune. No one who might wander for some time into an evil harbor should trust that it will be an evil night because of it since he might suffer hunger or a hard bed. But in the middle of such troubles we must think, "what are two or three years that bring us little sleep compared to eternity?"

Let misfortune and opposition come near us, as God sends them. Whether it be in house, politics or church office, we should not give way to impatience or cast away our concern for house, politics or the church because of opposition. In a warrior no one wants such a weak and cowardly heart that he throws away his weapon and wants to run at the first sound of thunder. We are not formed and appointed to wealth and to good lazy days, but to work and to sweat. You should not yield to misfortune but be ever bolder and engage it undauntedly, as one [popular] poet has said.

We can do that if we hold the hope of the resurrection and of eternal life against these temporal troubles and misfortunes. But these days no one wants to suffer these things. They would rather have some other burden that they will never bear. They would like to forsake their callings and vocations in which God has placed them. Whoever is called to teach in the church should do it boldly and faithfully and not ask about the danger and odious manner of the pope and bishops. For they should preach the gospel, rule the church, oversee spiritual matters, decide and order disputes by teaching and serve the church. But they do not do those things. Instead, they push great offices and high works onto talentless monks who only go out for the purpose of collecting money and to serve great banquets. Since they avoid and run away from the "sweat" they also lack consolation and refreshment. Since they will not regret that this is true, they also are unable to lead.

On the contrary, we, who must wear our sweat, must think in our own vocations that even if we bite into much that is sour and must have adversity, yet all of the troubles, worries and work will have their end. Moses includes this consolation as if it were very necessary to say it.

Altb. IX 102-103: Lectures on Genesis, 1535; cf. AE 1

Brief life is here our portion; Brief sorrow, short-lived care.
The life that knows no ending, The tearless life is there.
O happy retribution: Short toil eternal rest;
For mortals and for sinners A mansion with the blest. (*TLH* 448: 1)

Thursday

As we live by the Spirit, so let us also walk by the spirit.
Let us not be greedy and conceited to one another; to
indignation and hatred. Galatians 5:25, 26

As St. Augustine says, arrogant, personal opinion is the mother
of all heretics. That is a source and fountain of all kinds of sin and
calamity as historians in and outside of Scriptures report. These days
vain glory is a common trouble in the whole world and in every
station of life. Even heathen poets and writers of history vehemently
agree on this. No village, even if it is only one or two buildings, is
so trifling and small that its citizens do not want to be regarded as
better and more clever than citizens of other villages. These like-
minded clans, because of this epidemic called "vain glory," contend
that their heads are filled with better understanding and greater gifts
than others. They want to do things first and let those who are like
them in art, wisdom, etc., take a back seat to them. In short, they
yield nothing to others and do not let them be good or right. It is
said, "in all the world you cannot find anyone who doesn't want to
be better than the other." For this reason one feels weak [and
jealous] if anyone points a finger at someone in the crowd and says,
"There is a man that can do anything." Among the Greeks long ago,
one was an identifiable failure if he became vainly ambitious. In our
own day this problem is not only common among the citizens but
even among the princes and lords who rule the land and the people.
This is even a greater shame when it occurs among those who
oversee and serve the church in the spiritual offices.

Yes, it's true. If rulers, especially the great high heads, are
overcome by these epidemics, it is certain that not only the common
government and our rulers will become disorganized, destroyed and
changed in every way but also the great mighty kingdoms and
empires. You readily see this in history in and outside of Scriptures.
If these scandalous epidemics enter the spiritual government of the
church, then no one could compose sufficient words to describe the
resulting shame. Here we are not squabbling and scratching about
art, understanding, beauty, governance, politics, empire, etc. Rather,
it is about eternal life and salvation or eternal death and damnation.

Because of this, St. Paul warns everyone in the Office of the Ministry. He seriously urges that they guard against such trouble and says, "So we live by the Spirit . . ." He is saying, "It is true that we live in the Spirit. So let us remain in the order and the right path. Where the Spirit is, he renews people so they become different. That is, he turns ambitious, hot-tempered, jealous people into humble, soft, patient people. They do not, then, seek their own, but God's glory. They do not hate and become indignant with each other but approach each other with respect. Those that are ambitious and hate and become indignant with each other want to praise and present themselves rather than the Spirit. They wander from the Spirit. Since they would rather follow their flesh, they cheat themselves, fulfill their desires and have their judgment already. They do not inherit the kingdom."

There is no trouble more harmful than ambition and there is none more common. When our Lord God in his zeal sends out workers, Satan quickly activates HIS servants, who do not want to become lowlier or lesser in any way than those who preach rightly and have a right divine call. So disputes quickly arise. These are self-made masters who want to quickly change others and improve them. Their own teaching must be considered the best. What someone learned before they came along doesn't matter, etc. This is also the way their thoughts are presented. They are presented with a great show of virtuosity, understanding and with a spirit far greater than others that came before. Then those who are called by God should not keep silent, much less yield to them or allow them rights unless he can prove that his is the pure doctrine.

Altb. IX 866–867: Lectures on Genesis, 1535; cf. AE 1

Watch against thyself, my soul, Lest with grace thou trifle;
Let not self thy tho'ts control Nor God's mercy stifle.
Pride and sin lurk within All thy hopes to scatter;
Heed not when they flatter. (*TLH* 446: 4)

Friday

It will come to pass, whoever shall call upon the name of the Lord will be saved. Joel 2:32

When a heart is attached to the mercy of God, it arises, opens its mouth and breaks forth with a lively voice and earnestly implores God for salvation with fervent desire and hope. This is the correct method, form and wisdom in God-pleasing prayer. Rightly considered, this shows that no service of God is more unique than true prayer calling upon God. One cannot find this anywhere but in the true Christian church. It is true that God's name is used by almost everyone. But some, like the Turks, have neither Word nor Sacrament. Some, like the papists, are enemies of God's Word and persecute it. But the sacramentarians [reformed] use them without faith as if they were only useful as works, if they are even necessary at all. The pure call upon the name of the Lord, but many more handle it uselessly. They misuse, scandalize and abuse it, as Psalm 109 says of the Jews and others who crucified Christ. "Their prayers must be sin." Just as those who rightly call upon the name of the Lord in truth become blessed and feel an eternal benefit and fruit of prayer, so also those who pray and implore without faith, pile up and increase their sins. They, then, call for and hasten their own ruin and damnation.

But why didn't the prophet keep it simple and just say, "Who calls on the Lord . . ."? Why does he add "Whoever calls on the NAME of the Lord . . ." to this? Or, as the Hebrews say, "In the name of the Lord?" We should not think that he does this without a reason but that this is revealed based on well-considered advice. "The name" was used and understood as a common confession (of faith), by which we are informed of much. You are informed by the name of this one [distinct] from others, but you are also informed of all things concerning the God who is named. When you hear the name "St. Paul," you understand one who is distinct from other teachers, such as St. Augustine, Heironimous, etc. Moreover, since God has revealed himself through his Word, and since we begin to know God through his Word, we could never know of him if it weren't told us in his Word, as St. John says, "No one has ever seen God, but the Son who is in his Father's bosom. He has informed us of him." So when one prays in the name of the Lord, or calls on the name of the Lord, this is nothing but calling to God in faith and in trust in the promise that the Son of God, who is called the "Word," has brought this name from heaven. This Word is how God is disposed towards us and what is in his heart for us. He is not our enemy as described in the law. Rather, he has loved us and will save us as we have been freed from sin by his Son. That is why he sent his Son.

Altb. VI, 976: Lectures on Joel, 1536; cf. AE 18

In all the strife of mortal life Our feet shall stand securely;
Temptation's hour shall lose its pow'r, For Thou shalt guard us surely.
O God, renew with heav'nly dew Our body, soul and spirit
Until we stand at Thy right hand Through Jesus' saving merit. (*TLH* 437: 3)

Saturday

The Word that you hear is not mine but the Father's who has sent me. John 14:24

You notice that he is talking about the oral, preached Word they hear from him. He makes so much of it that whoever despises and dispenses of it must not despise the one who speaks it but rather the divine majesty. On the other hand, whoever trusts and retains this Word has a sure Word that establishes the Father's will and thoughts. Jesus will not let himself be silenced regarding himself. But, as he said, through the Word he shows us the Father, as he does throughout the gospel of John. He opposes the great attacks masterminded by the devil. Usually the devil operates through a[n apparently] pious God-fearing heart through which he would divide and sever God and Christ from each other. Under Satan, one can hear Christ's Words well enough, but yet other thoughts are added to the Words since he [that is, one under Satan] thinks he should look for God's thoughts and heart apart from Christ.

The devil can still cause this harm when someone clings only to the human nature of Christ and nothing more. The Words are allowed to be read and say that Christ is truly God. But then he struggles against it. For his heart cannot allow Christ and the Father to be so close and to be inseparable so it is sure that Jesus and his Father's Word are, from first to last, one united Word, heart and desire. This is how the ignorant hearts think, "Yes, I hear it well enough that Christ speaks to the troubled conscience to befriend and console it but who could know how things are between me and God in heaven?" That means that there is, then, no united God and Christ but one individual who is Christ and another who is God, who made him and is absent from him. Then people are prevented from violating or affecting God when they reject Christ. But Christ says more concerning this to Philip in John 14:9, "Who sees me, sees also the Father."

Also, he says in John 7:16, "My teaching is not mine, but of the one who sent me." This is just what he says here. "What you hear from me is surely my Father's Word and will. Do not inquire further, but be sorry that you think God is angry with you or thinks evil of you. You should rather be sure that he is gracious and kindly disposed towards you. He sent me from heaven for this purpose. He announces this to you."

So protect yourself from other thoughts and suggestions which cause you to be uncertain. Protect yourself from other "obvious" wills of God which you seek apart from Christ. If you seek in that way, you will undoubtedly fail. You will run on with your own prejudices and perversions that lead you to seek the naked majesty or you will be driven to the devil who wants to present his own ghost or splendor to you. For this devil also has the ability to present himself as if he were the majesty of God, as he did with Christ. He wants people to pray to him and listen to him. When he can't do that any more, he makes people confused with popular ideas and images that he offers so that he can rend their hearts away from Christ. A Christian must be ready and wise in his opposition to this. He must learn so his heart and thoughts are only fixed and bound on Christ's Word here. Apart from Christ, he will know or hear of no God as I have said often and fully in other places.

Erl. XII, 297–298: Third Sermon on Pentecost, John 14:23–31, 1522

How precious is the Book Divine,
By inspiration given!
Bright as a lamp its doctrines shine
To guide our souls to heaven.

It shows to man his wand'ring ways
And where his feet have trod.
And brings to view the matchless grace
Of a forgiving God. (*TLH* 285: 1,3)

Week of Trinity IX

Sunday

Make yourself friends with unrighteous mammon, so that when you are in want, they receive you in everlasting dwellings. Luke 16:9

We first learn why the Lord here gives the name "unrighteous" to mammon. Dishonest gains should be returned and never used in any other way. They ought not even be given as a gift to charity. As Isaiah writes in the 61st chapter, "I," says the Lord, "am he that loves what is right and hates stealing and robbery." It is popularly said, "Whoever wants to give service to God with offerings and alms should give what is his own or be satisfied not to give." For he has acquired what he has from God and that with a good conscience. You should not do anything with other peoples' goods except give back what was unjustly taken. Why does the Lord say "Make friends with unrighteous mammon."? To give it as alms to help the poor? Answer: The Lord doesn't call mammon or goods unrighteousness because it is unjustly taken (then, as above, one should give back the unrighteous goods), but because no one brings righteous mammon except a righteous, pious Christian, who acts in the fear of God and according to God's laws. Others use mammon according to the common saying, "Possessions give you courage, visibility, a plenteous life." By this mamon they easily and unjustly pass the poor people by whom they could well help. So goods and wealth must bear this scandalous name, "unrighteous."

The kind of pleasure God takes in such misused goods can be gathered from the passage in Ezekiel where he says, "Behold, your sister Sodom had the same error, pride and all abundance and peace as you and your daughters have. But you have refused to extend your hand to the poor and needy. You were haughty and are an abomination before me." So peace and having more than enough go together. You don't know how much mischief is worked by this and the fact that you don't help poor people. This is the common lament, yes, the misery, in all the world. So this scandalous name comes to possessions. This name is rightly and honestly won. It is always used in that way. So it is called unrighteous mammon, damned money and stolen goods, not for its own sake by its own attribute and nature (for what else can the poor penny, quarter, greenback, bread, meat, fish, wine and so forth do?), but because of man's role when he doesn't use them rightly.

That's why the teaching of today's gospel runs specifically in this direction. One ought not be stingy but rather use goods in a right way and make friends with them. God has approved of this. After this, when we die and are in need, that is, when we must leave everything behind us, we find friends there that receive us in eternal homes. So the good we do on behalf of the poor, showing them friendship and good works, will not only be a witness on the last day that we have behaved as brothers and Christians, but they will be repaid and rewarded. Then some will come and boast, "Lord, that one gave me a coat, some money, a piece of bread, a drink of water, when I was in need." Yes, as Christ says in Matthew 25, he, the Lord himself, will step forward and say before his heavenly Father, all the angels and saints, what good we did for him whenever we demonstrated our faith in that way. These friends will do this and help us in heaven if we have need when we must leave everything behind here below.

Whoever follows this teaching and uses money and goods that God has provided for the administration and aid of the poor, who cannot earn their own bread, makes righteous mammon out of unrighteous mammon. He changes misuse into proper use. So among Christians, they will never use money and goods for themselves, for their own splendor, glory, desires and haughtiness. This is what you see in the cities and towns as is commonly said, "I have corn and bread for me. Do you want to have it, too? Then buy your own." That is called unrighteous corn and bread that you use to sin and to your own ruin. You could use it for good and to serve and please God next time.

Erl. 4, 407–410: Sermon on Trinity 9, Mark 8:1–9, 1533

Take my life and let it be	Take my silver and my gold,
Consecrated Lord to Thee.	Not a mite would I withhold.
Take my moments and my days,	Take my intellect and use
Let them flow in ceaseless praise.	Every pow'r as Thou shalt choose. (*TLH* 400: 1,4)

Monday

Who has given himself for our sins, that he save us from this contrary, wicked world, according to the will of God, our Father. Galatians 1:4

With these words, "that he save us from this contrary, wicked world," St. Paul shows in a beautiful way the entire content and primary teaching of his epistle. Namely, that although we should be lost by way of sins, death and the devil's power yet through faith in Christ Jesus, God's Son, who has given himself for our sins to rescue us from the devil's kingdom which is here called the contrary wicked world, it must be apparent that apart from him no creature, no man, be he ever so holy and righteous as he could be, no angel, etc., could rescue us out of such a world. No creature, man or angel, has authority to dispel sins and save from the devil's tyranny and kingdom but only the high Divine Word of majesty. That is, Christ alone bears this title, expiates sin, saves from the devil's power, etc. He didn't do it for his own sake, nor was he under any obligation to do it. Because of this, we pay close attention to these little words, "For our sins," that he saved us. Whoever believes it has it and will ever praise and honor God in Jesus Christ.

But whoever calls this world we described above (as a contrary, evil, wicked world of the devil) a dear, faithful, willing and obedient knight and servant of God is of the devil. His good children and dear obedient little sons, the world, do everything that this murderer and father of lies does and says, for his sake in a masterful way. This world reckons itself as the very best. In the method of the world it hears lies, anger, false worship of God, hypocrisy, etc. and loves nothing better than them. On the other hand, the world is an enemy of truth. She persecutes and strangles it so they [that] teach [the truth are treated] as heretics and evil doers. The world wants to silence this truth to give you something else. For this reason, the world is also drowned in sins of the flesh, in murder, adultery, etc. For she acts as her father, the devil, who was a liar and a murderer from the beginning. People are so much wiser, more righteous and holy without Christ. Yes, they are enemies against the gospel and can only serve evil. In summary, the world is a double rogue because they are the best of all and the most pious. We were doubly godless rogues before the dear gospel came upon us from God's grace. Under the papacy we were also such rogues, especially we who were in religious orders, who carried both the title and name as if we were holy and spiritual people with higher vocation and service than the ordinary people.

Dear reader, also receive these Words that St. Paul speaks earnestly as true. Do not regard them as a fictitious fraud or dream when he says this world is "wicked." It cannot be seen, since many people in the world regard themselves as containing lordly virtues. Nor according to their outward glitter and appearance, can you tell if there is much holiness and deep wisdom inside. Don't let yourself be confused by all that. Rather, hear and mark what the Holy Ghost says through St. Paul. From this Word you can easily and truly come to know and judge the whole world. Namely, with all their wisdom, righteousness and power, they are in the unpleasant kingdom of the devil. From this it is clear that no one can be right to us, except only the Lord God who saves us by his only begotten Son.

Therefore, we should rightly honor and thank God, our dear Father, for his unspeakable compassion. For through his dear Son, he would loose us from the devil's kingdom in which we all began together and from which we were not able by our own ability to become free. We should freely and boldly confess with St. Paul that all our work and righteousness that we do to atone for our sins and by which we would flee from the devil's power are a great filth and excrement. Were we to pile them all together in a heap, they could not so much as bend a single little hair on the devil's head. This is also true of all the powers of free will, of all hypocritical righteousness, all monkery, masses, worship, vows, tonsures, along with all other abominations of the kingdom of antichrist in which pure teaching is suppressed. Such things should be freely tread upon and spat at as the venomous pestilence of the devil. Against all this, you raise high and exalt the lordship and the unsurpassable good deeds of our dear Lord, Jesus Christ, who rescued us through his death not from a few silly things, some good and some bad, but rather from the malicious and damned world.

So when St. Paul calls the world "wicked," by this title he announces that it is a kingdom of unrighteousness, blindness, error, sins, death, blasphemy against God, despair, and eternal damnation. In summary, the world is the devil's kingdom. Against it Christ's kingdom is one of righteousness, light, grace, the forgiveness of sins, peace, trust, eternal life and salvation. In his kingdom we are established apart from this wicked world through our dear Lord Jesus Christ, to whom together with the Father and the Holy Ghost will be honor and glory forever. Amen.

Altb. VII, 29–30: On Galatians 1:4, Christ gave himself . . ., 1538

Whence come these sorrows,
Whence this mortal anguish?
It is my sins for which
Thou, Lord, must languish;
Yea, all the wrath, the woe
Thou dost inherit,
This I do merit.

The sinless Son of God
Must die in sadness;
The sinful child of man
May live in gladness;
Man forfeited his life
and is acquitted,-
God is committed. (*TLH* 143: 3, 5)

Tuesday

*Let your heart not be troubled. Believe in God and so
believe in Me. John 14:1*

Jesus comes before the disciples as a good true Lord with this
comfort and exhortation because of their future trouble and fear so
that they are able to remain and not deny him. He enables them,
[telling them] that they should and must encounter them [that is,
troubles] so when they are revealed they should remember that Jesus
had previously said this and warned them against it. First of all he
says, "Let your heart not fear," as if to say, "I know well, my dear
child, how it will be for you when I go and leave you alone. You
will be overwhelmed with futile fear and terror and will see things
happen to me that will give you great reason to tremble so that your
heart would like to melt away. You will not know where you should
stay. I tell you this ahead of time, and even during it, so you do not
take it to heart so readily, but that you might be vigorous and
summon yourself to the war. When it happens, then think about my
warning so that you do not deny me or doubt so quickly," etc.

He wanted to strengthen and preserve their hearts with good
things for he knew full well what lay ahead. If they should feel the
same fear and anxiety, then they could hold on and be more readily
set against it. For if misfortune and fear followed what was coming,
then the heart should be prepared so that it could know a desirable
resting place or know someone who could tell it or remind it of a
word of consolation, making it easier to bear. This is the reason he
gives this preaching ahead of time. It is to reveal the coming fear so
that afterward, as a promise, they would remember these words and
by them persevere, even though this comfort did not help in this brief
hour before he came before the powers, until the Holy Spirit came.
For after this time, he was taken away and their hearts were emptied
of courage so they could not even stand up to a weak maid. All his
Words and work, and this comfort, were completely forgotten. So he
warned and comforted his beloved apostles because they were in
great need of it.

This is not written for their sakes, but for ours. We are to learn
to use this comfort in present and future troubles. Every Christian
should thus know that when he is baptized and joined to Christ he is
also joined unto fear and anxiety that would make his heart dull and
despondent because of one or many kinds of enmity and opposition.
The Christian has many enemies among the masses, should he want
to remain with his Lord. The world stands together with the devil

against him, daily opposing body and life so that his own flesh, reason and conscience constantly plague him, his fear and flinching readily oppose him as well as his own heart.

But one does not pay attention to these reasons for fear and flinching when they are not seen. Likewise, the Jews were not concerned or troubled that Christ cried over them and prophesied that the city of Jerusalem would be razed and destroyed and not one stone would remain upon another. So, when trouble is not yet near and the devil is not pursuing us and the hour does not bite, we also think that we are in no danger. We are hearty and courageous. We don't think we need comforting. But then we should be taught to consider that surely a fear will soon follow, either from the world through its displeasure, persecution, etc., or from the devil himself with his terrible poisonous darts and spears shot into your heart as fear, doubt or slander, etc.

So you also want to be a Christian like the apostles and all the saints. Rally yourselves and wait. Surely another little hour of trial will come and will hit your heart to make you fear and flinch. This manner of life is promised to all Christians so they learn to accustom themselves to it and quickly judge their affairs. If you are now secure, you should assume and take into account that it will soon be different. Think: I will be happy and of good courage so long as it is as God desires; tomorrow sadness; today life, tomorrow death; today fortune and security, tomorrow nothing but trouble. Then you will not so completely snore through everything as if you will have no troubles.

For the world is so crazy and foolish, so blind and impenitent, that it cannot help but think that if a little fortune comes and stays it will stay forever. The worldly people become drowned in themselves so they cannot foresee any chance of falling. They rather live as if both the devil and misfortune are no more. On the other hand, when suddenly trouble and fear follow, it overwhelms them. There is no way to make it back. Their heart is no longer courageous but shrinks and doubts badly as if this also will be eternal and there is no more comfort or hope. In summary, in times of peace, they don't plan a way of setting themselves against the possibility that fortunes might change once and for all. But rather they expect it will never be different. But contrary to this, if the weather changes for you and disease begins after having a healthy body, war and misfortune follow peace, hunger follows fullness, so there is no end to sadnesses, trembling and doubts, the worldly way of handling this should not be pursued by a Christian. But always think: Now there is peace and quiet, but it will be different tomorrow. The devil can shoot a spear into your heart or bring you some other tribulation. So see to it that for this reason you are aroused [to spot] where it comes from, so that you might stop and stand and draw comfort from God's Word.

Altb. VII, 47–48: Sermons on the Gospel of St. John, Chapters 14–16, 1538; cf. AE 24

Our God, our Help in ages past,
Our Hope for years to come,
Our Shelter from the stormy blast,
And our eternal Home! (*TLH* 123: 1)

Wednesday

I will not leave you as orphans. I will come to you. John 14:18

In both the world's opinion and our own feelings, it does seem that this little bunch of disciples are poor orphans, lost from both God and Christ. He seems to us to have forgotten. He suffers them to be burdened and scandalized, cursed, persecuted and murdered as if they were everyone's doormat. The devil would constantly terrify their hearts, grieve, and plague them so that they would want to be truly and rightly called orphans over and above all orphans and beyond all the forsaken people in the world. Scripture says that God himself must gather these, as those forsaken by every man, and call himself their Father.

But (says Christ) I will not leave you that way as it seems and feels to you. Rather, I give you this comfort to encourage you and make you certain that you are my true Christians and right church. I, myself, will also be with you and remain with my defense and advantage. I will now leave you bodily and visibly. You must, then, be alone to be thrown to the evil and might of the devil and the world. But the world will not be so mighty nor the devil make so much trouble. All their teaching and wisdom will not be so clever. For my Baptism and preaching will yet not be taken from me. My Holy Ghost will reign and work in you, even if it will always be resisted there, and he himself also will softly shine by you.

So if the Office of the Ministry and the reign of the Holy Spirit in Christendom would not always go on, it would be doubtful that Baptism, Sacrament and the remembrance of Christ would remain. Where would it be received, where it is not impelled [upon the hearer] by the public office? If it were offered through secret study and prayer, then others could not learn it and come to it. But God has given preachers in all times and he has spread his Word. It goes from the mouth to your own ears, though it is also sent very softly so that in many places it will fade, or even change and yet among a few it might be rightly considered. By most crowds it is dismissed.

In any event, God still remains with his own. In all times, he has given some who have preached against the false teaching of the papists and the crowds even if they are also persecuted by others and become buried for some brief times. Christendom is still preserved even in times of the highest and most difficult errors and heresies, as in the time of the Arians and thereafter and under horrid persecutions, as in the time of the martyrs. Christendom is most wonderfully defended, so she has remained and kept battling against the world and the devil and is established by the Holy Ghost and has spread herself yet further and further.

All Christendom together has this trustworthy promise. It shall not be forsaken and be without assistance and help. If it must be robbed of all human comfort, hope and assistance, yet Christ will not leave it alone and without defence. On the contrary, when it seems that Christ has left for a while without leaving comfort and defense and the devil together with the world (and also yourself, because of the weakness of your flesh) go insane, it will seem to you that you are by yourself and all things are buried and drowned. Then you must let yourself think about and experience the three days that Christ was taken from the disciples and laid in the grave by the most disgraceful injustice. Then should you not take the comfort he gives in these Words rather than letting yourself bring doubt? But against all that you feel and see hold onto this promise he speaks, for he speaks it to all, "I will not stay away from you. If I must bodily depart from you for a short time, I will not stay away long. But I will soon come back to you and be with you forever so you will be protected against all devils, the world, sin and death. You will live and be victorious with me."

Altb. VII, 103: Sermons on the Gospel of St. John, Chapters 14–16, 1538; cf. AE 24

Bear the cross, bear the cross. Zion, till thy latest breath
Bear the cross of scorn and jeering And be faithful unto death;
See the crown of life appearing. Zion, count all other things as loss.
Bear the cross, bear the cross! (*TLH* 479: 2)

Thursday

Who has and keeps my commandment is the one who loves me. Whoever loves me is beloved of my Father and I will love Him and reveal myself to him. John 14:21

What does this say? Hasn't Jesus already said they should be in him and that he wants to be in them, which they already have by faith? Why now does he say he will love them and reveal himself to them? Hadn't he already done these things? He has, indeed, already begun and laid the first stone. He has suffered for me and let the gospel be preached to me and let me be baptized. Because of that I already pray and have learned of him, as St. Paul says in Ephesians 1 and 1 John 4, "He had previously loved us . . ." So why does he say here that he wants to love them, who love him already, as if he didn't love them? Why does he want to reveal himself, as he said above, so they should preach about him whom they could not see, as if they did not have the revelation or believe in him?

Answer: It goes this way. . . . When a Christian has begun to be in Christ, he believes and lives in him and has love for him now. He begins to teach, confess and do what a Christian should do according to his Lord's will. Then the devil latches onto him. He overwhelms him with such cloud bursts inwardly through anxiety and fear and outwardly through all kinds of danger and misfortune. Then he feels no comfort and lets himself think and feel that God is in his heaven and not with him; that God has forgotten him. God conceals himself so well that we seem to be lost and to have no more help from him. So when he doesn't reveal himself and let his love be traced, we are sunk in despair.

God does a two-fold work in the Christian (as I have said more fully in earlier commentaries regarding his saying, "I will not die, but live"), namely, "comfort" and "help." He gives the comfort inwardly in the heart so the heart grasps his grace and by that holds itself up and is firm in trouble and sorrow. But if the heart has only comfort, then no one could persevere, for the devil attacks hearts so severely, especially the hearts of the apostles and their like, and makes them severe and bitter. Though up to that time he had begun to believe and is in Christ, he imagines that only the devil is in him and that Christ is not in him, but far away; that Christ has left him down here in hell for the devil is at the bottom. For he feels absolutely nothing but the vain terror and sorrow of heart. Outwardly there is hatred, envy, insult and persecution from the world and even from his best friends. It looks unmistakably as if he is utterly forsaken. He would like to say, "What will I do now? If I were not baptized and had not received and confessed the gospel, then I would not have such heartache. Before I still had good peace and luxury. Now I have no quiet night and day in the devil's sight or mine."

Also, because they come to Christ and have life and comfort in him they must be martyred and plagued and consider themselves pierced by the devil's revenge and experience a senseless death and heartache. One cannot stay in that condition forever. No one could bear that. So the second part must also follow from the outside, namely, help and redemption, as St. Paul says in 1 Corinthians 10, "God is faithful. He will not forsake you in your temptations, but will make the temptation win an ending, that you may bear it."

By this Christ comforts his suffering Christians. He will show them his life and reveal himself. He would say, "Go forth with your love and stand fast. If you thought I was cut off from you as far as heaven is from the earth then you have not survived the evil little hour. You do not feel me in you and the dark clouds block the sun, so you think only of terror and anxiety." As the 116th Psalm complains, "The stripes of death are upon me and hell's grief had befallen me." And Psalm 142, "I wanted to flee and yet cannot escape." That is no Christian at all. That one knows nothing of him [Christ] since he must doubt (He is still truly in Christ and Christ in him when he is baptized and believing). Neither Baptism nor the gospel, where no higher comfort can be found, could hold him.

[Christ would say:] But don't let this kind of thinking take your heart. For it is not as you feel or as it seems to you. For I have still other help and more help for you the first time, the next and even in the third instance of temptation. I will halt the onslaught that makes it seem to you that you have lost me in your trouble. You won't sink. But I will take the tribulation, fear and trouble that are now yours into me and I will again be in you! You will not feel the hour when the devil rages so readily. He will not devour you. Rather, you shall have a promise. If you rightly believe and love, yes, I will come and reveal myself so that in your tribulation you may trace the wonderful love that you have which belongs to both my Father and me.

Altb. VII, 111-112: Sermons on the Gospel of St. John, Chapters 14–16, 1538; cf. AE 24

In the hour of trial,
Jesus, plead for me
Lest by base denial
I depart from Thee.
When thou see'st me waver,
With a look recall
Nor for fear or favor
Suffer me to fall.

Should Thy mercy send me
Sorrow, toil and woe,
Or should pain attend me
On my path below,
Grant that I may never
Fail Thy hand to see;
Grant that I may ever
Cast my care on Thee. (*TLH* 516: 1,3)

Friday

You shall beat your swords into ploughs and your spears into sickles. No nation will take up arms against another and they will no longer learn to war. Micah 4:3

This is the true message of this passage. The prophet speaks with veiled Words about the fruit that follows the gospel, as it is spread out before the heathen. After the people are reminded of their sins and of the wrath and severe righteousness of God (the prophet says of the peoples, that they should be judged and of the heathen, that they should be punished), then they should be taught of the medicine by which you can counter that misfortune, namely, the forgiveness of sins through the Son of God, Jesus Christ, our Lord. They receive the one who has given himself as an offering or as St. Paul says so skillfully, as the ransom for our sin.

This comforting promise of the gospel sets aside such cruel terrors over sins and the Lord. It makes peaceful hearts. We see that God, the heavenly Father, will no longer be angry with us because of his dear Son's death. We again have one who loves us from his heart and we trust in his goodness and mercy. We thank him earnestly that he has saved Christians from death and sins through his Son, as St. Paul says plainly what this prophet has described with veiled words, Romans 5, "Now we are justified by faith and have peace with God." He wants to say that after hearts are persuaded that our sins are taken away by God's Son and that God would expiate us by his dear Son (which St. Paul says is the content of faith) then people perform all good works towards God when they come to know that God is stilled and satisfied. They comfort themselves with his compassion and are happy and charitable even in their cross and many dangers. The prophet speaks here of the kind of peace that ransoms the heart from the fear of death and the law of God through the holy gospel of the Son of God who has been given because of our sinful will.

Because all people have become alike through the gospel, both Jews and heathen (for God had subjected all to sin and also wants to show mercy to all), there follows a uniting or settlement between the people and external peace among the members of the church. The believers do not stay in bitter hatred which separated the Jew and the heathen when the wall of the law yet stood, Ephesians 2. For why should a Jew think himself better than a heathen or a heathen think himself better than a Jew when Jesus Christ, God's Son, is the same to all men and for their common good? For we are all baptized into Christ's death and live in the hope of eternal life that we secure through Christ.

It is the same with everyone. Before confessing the gospel, all were used by this hatred and animosity which were sharp swords and poisonous arrows. Now, after that, all live peacefully with one another. All are used only by the holy precious unity. Then they are like plows and sickles, formed together in this costly fruit of rightly-shaped faith to work for the harvest. Namely, they teach other people how they should become righteous and saved and they attract them through a god-pleasing life and unwavering walk. By these good things and with good works, they confess and hold to the things revealed by the gospel, the things revealed to us through God's Son.

So the prophet goes on, "No nation will lift a sword against another and they will no longer learn warfare." He would say: There is no greater unity among hearts after the people confess our Lord Christ. Their hearts are set free through the forgiveness of sins. They no longer desire to war when they become true Christians. They will not only desire to keep from doing others harm by hatred and jealousy, by profiteering and stinginess, but they want to give each other all kinds of service and charity with money and helpfulness because they are fellows and brothers. They gladly lend and borrow without profit. They especially want to reveal to others striking charity so that those who don't understand will learn, so the unwary are warned, the rotten are punished, the dull and terrified comforted, that those in peril are kept afloat, to encourage and strengthen the weak, etc. These offices should, by necessity, be in and remain in the Christian church.

Altb. VIII, 112–113: Lectures on Micah, 1542; cf. AE 18

Help us to serve Thee evermore
With hearts both pure and lowly;
And may Thy Word, that light divine,
Shine on in splendor holy
That we repentance show
In faith ever grow
The pow'r of sin destroy
And all that doth annoy.
Oh, make us faithful Christians.

And for Thy gospel let us dare
To sacrifice all treasure;
Teach us to bear Thy blessed cross,
To find in Thee all pleasure.
Oh, grant us steadfastness
In joy and distress,
That we Thee ne'er forsake.
Let us by grace partake
of endless joy and glory. (*TLH* 477: 3,4)

Saturday

And everyone will dwell without fear under his own grape vine and fig tree as the mouth of Jehovah Sabbaoth has spoken. Micah 4:4

These Words describe the great peace that hearts will taste. Such hearts hear, grasp and remain in this peace from the preaching of the good news. Yet, let's consider this first—that the prophet has not used only a single kind of tree in this peculiar teaching. He wants to speak of these trees because they bear fruit. They are useful only for the sake of the fruit. For the sake of the fruit, they are planted and grown, not for the sake of their beauty. So in the Christian church there are also many kinds of service and offices. Every Christian is a fruitful vine or fig tree in his own way.

There are two different offices, teaching and ruling. So there are also two kinds of plants, the grapevine and the fig tree. Yet both bear the most wonderful fruit.

A preacher or teacher shows God's gracious will and how people can be saved through the diligence which he puts in service of his office. But the worldly governments keep peace, protect the good and punish the evil. What greater difference can there be between fathers of these households? But if they are Christians, each has his noble fruits by which he helps and speaks to others. They also, then, have a care in their own special ways that they spread the confession of God, that in great troubles they comfort themselves and others through confidence in God's help, that they implore God that they overcome any present misfortune with the hope of immortality and eternal life, that they be patient and not vengeful, etc. So everyone in his own station in life has a grape vine and fig tree full of all the best fruit.

Such folk do this fearlessly, whether they are opposed by the world or the devil or any kind of danger that would rule them. Rather they hold this confidence that God's compassion has its rightful fruit, namely eternal life, as of primary importance. After that, no matter how mighty the tribulation they encounter, so much better than that trouble is the reason they have to exercise their faith through prayer. That reason is the promise that they will be redeemed and safe as the prophet says. It will be peaceful and each will eat his bread with joy.

But the prophet adds, "For the mouth of the Lord has spoken." He confirms this marvelous promise of the kingdom of Christ. We need this promise because of the scandalous thought that the kingdom of Judah is being devastated and pushed aside. Think about this kingdom of Christ not only as bumping up against the errors of the whole world and its religions, but rather, even one who is pure will doubt the comforting promise of the kingdom of Christ. So the prophet comforts the pious Christians so that they will be fearless in this misfortune that they share with the world and take comfort by hope in the coming kingdom of Christ in which there are both forgiveness of sins and eternal life. That means the greatest peace and best safety is secured for all who believe in Jesus Christ. Why? Because the mouth of the Lord has said so. What God says, no man can change or set aside.

Altb. VIII, 113–114: Lectures on Micah, 1542; cf. AE 18

Mid toil and tribulation and tumult of her war
She waits the consummation of peace forevermore,
Till with the vision glorious Her longing eyes are blest
And the great church victorious shall be the Church at rest. (*TLH* 473: 5)

Week of Trinity X

Sunday

And when He came near, he beheld the city and wept over it and said, "If you had wanted it, you would have recognized what makes for your peace. But now it is hidden from your eyes." Luke 19:41, 42

Learn from this diligently. Take note of what God regards as the greatest sin which he least tolerates. Namely, that his own people do not observe the time of his visitation. For the Lord is silent about all other sins and points only to this one so that his people might be safe. They not only turned away from the admonition and direction of their prophets but they also hastened to shed innocent blood. This had been overlooked until the Scripture says that Jerusalem would be altogether full of blood (in the same way that today's Germany dreadfully sins because she also wants to persecute the Word and God's servants in many ways). Following these sins, people divorce, go whoring, profiteering, are greedy, steal, party, get drunk and do more of the same boldly.

"I wanted to straighten out these deceived people," Christ says here, "by the Word and teach that you should be made good to improve you. For that reason, in the past I sent the prophets and John and the apostles. Yes, I, myself, have appeared, have preached, done miracles and administered everything by which I wanted to serve and make you better."

All other sins, no matter how great or small they may be, will not harm you. They are forgiven. You need no longer worry about them for eternity. Jerusalem should be well established and remain unassailed by her enemies if she would only acknowledge the time of her visitation. For I come to you not with a sword or clubs. I come gently as a savior. I preach and implore, "Repent, be better and be pious. Hear me and follow until the wrath comes with power. I seek to take you home."

But that means nothing to you now. All your sins, then, once again make themselves mighty, for you will not perceive that God himself is visiting you. Because you do not perceive it, you will regret it. As the proverb says, "Who is unwilling to be told cannot be helped." Isn't the one who puts his life in the devil's hands like a man that sits in the chair

438

of a sick barber[15]? Who would take the shears from the hand of the master and place them in the hands of the devil? But the Jews do exactly this with the Lord God. He permits us to call on him by the forgiveness of sins. He wants to be our gracious God. God gladly forgives and forgets but only so that you stop sinning and cling to his Word. But instead [Christ says] you trouble me. You say I have a devil. You call my preaching heresy and want to kill me on a cross. You don't want to be at peace. You have accomplished what you want. But all this is of the devil if God is the one who forgives sins and is gracious to you but not also the one who will send you great high gifts. But Satan turns you over to works to satisfy God. His version of grace is a terrible burden. If grace comes in the devil's way, then I couldn't bear it any longer and punishment is on its way. So if someone cannot stand the forgiveness of sins and God's grace then there are no longer any counsel and aid for him.

That is the main reason that the wrath of God is so very great and fearful. As the Jews wanted neither to see nor to hear his Word, God has also then neither heard nor seen their cries, prayers, and services to him. He would not withhold his wrath until Jerusalem was torn down to the ground so that one stone didn't remain upon another. So much so that one would like to say, "That is where his house stood but now it is flat and all is fallen to the ground." That is the way they wanted it! This is the frightening example that the evangelist has recorded for our learning. We can learn not to despise God's Word or let the time of our visitation pass by without its benefit.

We are to take special note that he says, "But now it is hidden from your eyes." It is common that one does not think that God will punish. On the contrary, God is pointing out his punishment out of his goodness and awaits improvement. The world thinks he will always remain silent and quiet. "Beware," says Christ, "if you don't want to see punishment." So consider it sure that where you do not improve, you will not avoid punishment. God warns for a while. Yet, he has also retained the right to lay all sorts of nets and cords. He will set up many unpleasant mousetraps because of evil fools, so that they might eventually flee to him.

Erl. 5, 5–7: First Sermon on Trinity 10, Luke 19:41–48, 1532

When men the offered help disdain	To Jesus we for refuge flee,
And wilfully in sin remain,	Who from the curse has set us free,
Its terror in their ear resounds	And humbly worship at His throne,
And keeps their wickedness in bounds.	Saved by His grace through faith alone. (*TLH* 295: 4,6)

---

[15]That is, a barber with shakey, unsteady hands.

Monday

*Israel spoke to Joseph, "Go and see if all is well with your brothers
and the flock and report to me how they are doing." And he sent him
to the Hebron valley to approach his kin. Genesis 37:14*

Joseph is sent. He rushes off to his brothers with a willing and
honest heart. For a little while he was lost in a field where he met a
man that showed him the way. Little did he suspect what great
danger he would meet and how near he was to his own ruin and
death. No one told him about it or warned him. God himself
delivered Joseph into the hands of his brothers, who, as a group,
were very cruel. For God (inasmuch as he allows himself here to be
observed) did not think much of father Jacob and his son, Joseph. He
acts as though he doesn't know what Joseph's brothers have already
planned which they had already made known. So God lets it happen.
The boy is sent from his father to be pushed out of the way to his
ruin. Where is the holy angel, Mahanaim, now, who rumbles up
above and who battled for Jacob against Esau? Will no one appear to
warn Jacob now and say, "Beware, do not send your son to the other
sons. They will kill him. You will be robbed of your heart's desire."
Every angel and God are quiet and still. This is truly wondrous,
completely unheard of. I cannot explain or understand it
with thoughts or words. God inflicts all this. Both Jacob, the father,
and Joseph, his son, are advised [through this silence] to go into
great ruin and, yes, even death.

But this is a great and marvelous comfort to us. We see that
God acts and rules among the holy patriarchs in the same way he
does among us. He leads this patriarch, Jacob, not only with empty
miracles and high spiritual exercises but also by common dangers
according to what he can bear. He acts in the same way as when we
encounter him. Joseph is a good, pious, innocent lad of about 17
years. He has the Holy Ghost by whom God is also merciful. The
Holy Ghost has fallen upon him. He also has the congregation of
Jacob, his father. He has led a holy Christian life. Yes, although it
seldom occurs to us, he is so severely beset with this miserable fall
that he has become worthless.

This example is written so that all of us are comforted. We are
reminded that we are poor people and that we should consider
ourselves subject to all that befalls man. So, if this trial can come to
the holy patriarch, who is full of the Holy Spirit, why should we
wonder and be angry or impatient if we also must experience the
same things? Shouldn't we much rather rejoice and thank God when

we feel that we are exercised and trampled under the same dangers in which God sought the most holy people from the beginning?

So when we are in such trouble and danger and feel the silence of God and the angels, then we should also notice that Joseph has to go through this miserable affliction and death repeatedly. Notice that the father grieves over his son and wants to fast in lamentation, even though Joseph is innocent of any harm against his treacherous brothers. So we should exhort each other to patience by these examples, for by the cross we bear, it will be the same for us. This example comes even closer and is personally applicable to us even more when we consider the example of the Son of God, himself. Though he is higher and above any comparisons, yet he says in Matthew 26, "The Son of Man indeed goes forth as it is written of him." It is as if neither his heavenly Father nor even his angels paid any attention while the fearsome Jews gave him over and he was reproached. They beat, wounded and crucified him miserably. Consider what happens at the time of his death where God is quiet and still and the angels are also silent. Yet because of this, they rejoice. For God doesn't say that Jacob and Joseph would be ruined by their calamity. Rather, through this comes God's help though this declaration of God is hidden and buried. He means it for good and to help. So through this visitation and punishment, God would avert starvation for Jacob and his children and would also create a situation by which the Egyptians might repent and come to the true knowledge of God so that many people would be won and saved.

Altb. IX, 1148-1149: Lectures on Genesis, 1535

I walk in danger all the way.
The thought shall never leave me
That Satan, who has marked his prey,
Is plotting to deceive me.
This Foe with hidden snares
May seize me unawares
If e'er I fail to watch and pray,
I walk in danger all the way.

I walk with Jesus all the way,
His guidance never fails me;
Within His wounds I find a stay
When Satan's power assails me;
And by His footsteps led,
My path I safely tread,
In spite of ills that threaten may,
I walk with Jesus all the way. (*TLH* 413: 1,5)

Tuesday

But shall God not also save his chosen who call upon him both day and night and have patience because of it? I say to you, he will rescue them quickly. Luke 18:7,8

Oh, that we could believe and cling to these Words of Christ, the Son of God. We could, then, have the spirit to say, "Well now, it seems my body and life are being taken and all my goods are gone. But I am sure of this; God, himself, is doing it and he is hidden above me and intends everything that is good for me." If we could talk like that, we would be true and pious Christians who have conquered the whole world. This also means that you regard God as right by your obedience and desires, as St. Paul exhorts in Romans 12, "Change through the renewing of your mind." But why? It naturally follows that when good things come that give pleasure, they must come purely by the will of God. By the renewing of your mind, you will learn that the same is also true in sorrows, lamentations and sighs that God has in store for you. But God wants to make an end of these.

By these words we know that neither the tremendous sins in our hearts nor the many godless hosts of the pope and the Turks and their fearsome blasphemies, that we must hear to the great pain of our hearts (so that we sigh and cry out "come, dear Lord!"), nor even, I say, such crying and sighing, will bring so many to loss that the redemption of the children of God will not come near and quickly. Whatever wants to rip the world to shreds will not be borne in God's patience for long, as Christ says in Luke 18. But he will soon save his chosen ones. He will come and not stay away. When he comes to judge, then he will find a way to confront the enemy and the blasphemer so that he is completely leveled to the ground while his church is upheld. So also there he had leveled all mankind by the flood. Then the people were all secure and had surely thought that no punishment or calamity could be nearby. Though there were still a few pious, holy and wise people, as all of them had thought themselves to be, they all came under God's visitation. This is true also of the Babylonian Empire. Also Sodom, Jerusalem and Rome were self-exalted and so were destroyed. Who leveled and destroyed them? It was by the sighs and tears in the hearts of Christ's believers. Moses had also cried out to the Lord at the Red Sea. What happened there? The sea separated itself and Pharaoh followed and had to be drowned. But the nation of Israel was saved in a wonderful way.

Such matters would be as useful as gold if we would learn this and become accustomed to it. In our misery and misfortune we can be comforted by such examples. From them we could fix firmly in our minds the fact that in our misery and misfortune, God, the Lord, wants to fashion and bring many good things. He also can do that. Let us, then, always and only follow what he says. Let us not murmur or despise God as the Jews did in the wilderness, of which the 106th Psalm speaks, "But they soon forgot his works and did not observe what he said." He favored them and wanted to help them, but they could not wait. They wanted to see what was promised in their hands. Therefore, they remained in the desert and did not enter Canaan. They despised the promised land, did not believe the Word of the Lord and murmured in their hearts.

In this way the holy patriarch, Jacob, was also in great trouble and anxiety. He would not have been able to lift himself out of it if he had not heard encouragement from his old father Isaac and those of his household, reminding him of the promise of God. By that he was restored again until his son, Joseph, returned when he received greater honor and authority. So this is truly great and magnificant that Joseph received authority over all of Egypt. If God, himself, had foretold this and said, "I will make sure that the loss of your son is because of great need and kindness," then he would have surely let his son go with good will and with joy. But God had kept this back from him and hid all of it from him. So first God put to death the "old man" and after that the "new man" rejoices and wants to be filled with countless new good deeds.

Meanwhile, though you have been buried, the heart can wake to faith, hope and patience, waiting upon divine help according to the teaching in Psalm 27, "Wait on the Lord. Take comfort and do not dismay. Wait on the Lord." God already knows the ending and the way out that this trial is winning which you yourself cannot see. Hold fast. For he will so mix it with sugar that even when you must die you shall yet in the resurrection of the dead again be crowned with eternal joy.

Altb. IX, 1150: Lectures on Genesis, 1535

Leave all to His direction; In wisdom He doth reign,
And in a way most wondrous His course He will maintain.
Soon He, His promise keeping, With wonder-working skill
Shall put away the sorrows That now thy spirit fill. (*TLH* 520: 8)

Wednesday

He sent a man before him, Joseph, who was sold as a slave. Psalm 105:17

What kind of sending is this? What kind of plan is spoken of here? A helper, or savior, is sent to Egypt to help Jacob and his whole household. How is he sent? He is thrown into the pit, sold and reported as dead to his father. Is that what you call sending a savior? Yes, that's what it is called, but only according to the way in which our Lord God is used to speaking. Joseph would be established as a great king but only as God sees to it. Jacob and Joseph do not see it. They are rather in a state of great anxiety and bear grief. That is why this is a special heavenly passage. He sends a helper or a savior and establishes him as a king while at the same time he is thrown into the pit and hell. We must get our hearts used to this passage so that we learn to understand what David says in another place, "The godless drown the righteous and grind their teeth over them. But the Lord laughs, for he sees that his time is coming when he will cause ruin and level them, etc." We cannot do that. We cannot see that far and hold onto faith when we only feel our greater weakness. But God holds fast with his promises. If you are not alone then you are not forgotten. But look further down the road and laugh about the adversaries for the reason that the psalmist writes in Psalm 2, "He who dwells in heaven laughs over them and the Lord mocks them."

But I still don't see it, you say. That is also true. And that's why we consider this example. We should also think on this in our tribulations. Our adversaries, even now, are being laughed over and punishment is closing over them. Though we are beset and plagued yet we are loved of God, for he bears a true concern for us and pays great attention to us, though in an utterly hidden way. As Isaiah says in chapter 45, "Truly, you are a hidden God, you the God of Israel, the savior."

We are yet satisfied that we have the Word and the Sacraments by which God is revealed to us. The fruit and the end of these means of grace will also follow you in time. Meanwhile, we shall trust and hold fast by these thoughts, "I have the means of grace and the Word with them. To these I will hold fast." No matter how vehemently the world and Satan rant and rage against me and assault me with all kinds of misery and misfortune, yet, oh, that we only are careful and diligent to suffer all this with a good conscience. In this there is no doubt that we are surely with God, by his great mercy, and that he holds us dear and precious. But the enemies are laughed over and mocked by God and held for endless suffering and even harsher punishment. So the laughter of our Lord God is hellish fire as follows in the 2nd Psalm, "He will first speak to them in wrath, and with his rage he will terrify them." Yes, guard yourself from such laughter!

Jacob and Joseph are children of God's grace. But his sellers are children of mockery, of wrath and damnation. Would to God that we could also learn this and keep both of these teachings. The flesh always gets in our way. But it is sure that a life in which one must suffer so much is the best and most precious life. That kind of life has no need for the forgiveness of that suffering, for it is suffered in innocence. I say this about good, saved, children, that is, those who suffer for the faith in Jesus Christ. They are not sinning but they bear these things and suffer because of the sins others want to do. This is discussed well by Socrates. "It is better to suffer unjustly than to do injustice." So whoever suffers in this way does not sin, but others do him injustice and he is afflicted. They sin. He knows that he is innocent. He understands that he is plagued and bears unfair behavior and can hold to his innocence and also see, even then, the promise of rescue. Such a sufferer is not afraid and doesn't despair in his heart, for he knows that he has not oppressed anyone. Rather, he alone bears the injustice and sins of others. When the conscience stands as a stone, then it cannot despair even if the likes of Caiaphas or Judas come and rage. We have already won. A good conscience is like a hard bedrock upon which you are divinely blessed children and you forsake misfortune and despise your enemies with a great, high, courage, as it is written in 1 Peter 3, "And who can accuse you, when you do good? And if they want you to suffer for the sake of righteousness, you are yet saved. Fear not over their spite and do not be terrified."

Altb. IX, 1175–1176: Lectures on Genesis, 1535

But if thou perseverest, Thou shalt deliverance find.
Behold, all unexpected He will thy soul unbind
And from the heavy burden Thy heart will soon set free;
And thou wilt see the blessing He had in mind for thee. (*TLH* 520: 10)

Thursday

But Jacob refused to be comforted and spoke: "I will go to my grave in grief for my son." And their father wept. Genesis 37:35

God help us that people become so rash and frightful that they can watch their own old father in such a desperate state of mind, suffering sorrow over such a long period of time! Woe to such people so full of the devil!

I barely believe that anyone could commit such sin that they intentionally and openly watch this old father pining to his grave. They have a total lack of compassion for their father, no human friendship at all. These people have no natural affection for life (which God has implanted in all creatures) or sensitivity for this father or grandfather. Do not the father and mother deserve honor? The old father must have seen this in his own sons. Now, after Joseph has been sold, this pain and lamentation comes to him. For twelve years he had felt constant sorrow because he lost his son and thought him dead. This excellent man, who should have been called the prize of the world, now cries and grieves himself to death.

There is truly nothing more amazing, that these brothers heard the Word of divine promise and blessing for so many years and were no better for it. They were exhorted often by the serious teaching and godliness of their father and grandfather. Yet they would not be moved by this pitiful tragedy to compassion for the pitiful, old, godly, gentleman who was so miserable because of them. They were hardened fellows as people become when they serve the devil. But now they have done all these harmful things not against their father and grandfather but against themselves. Simeon and Levi are driven through hope and desire for the birthright. Simeon becomes the pope and Levi the cardinal. Judah is somewhat more pious and faithful but yet he feared the might and power of the two brothers. Reuben was not respectable but became totally desperate because of the on-going scandal. Because of this, he had to be quiet as were Judas and Caiaphas. It was no wonder that our Lord God left Sodom and Gomorrah to fire that fell from heaven and leveled it. These boys were also, no doubt, left and ruined in the same way. Only a few pious, godly, little people were left to bear this tragedy (Namely, Isaac, the grandfather, Jacob the father, and Joseph, his son). At this time, they are like three true Atlantises. The three men bear the great weight to the point that God should have bombed it with pitch and sulfur.

As often as it is needed one must regard his sins as great and so heavy that he needs relief. For as long as you endlessly long for forgiveness of such sins, you should, then, also not doubt on account of your sinful intentions that God seeks after you. For Judas, when he despaired, laid the rope across his own neck and so died in that despair. So see to it that you yourself do not flee to misfortune and ruin. But when this kind of fall comes to you and you are overcome by some wrong, as St. Paul says, Galatians 6:1, then this example is good to note. You should consider that the holy patriarchs also became poor sinners and fell frightfully. I do not do such sins intentionally yet I know that I served the antichrist 15 years during which I held the sacrifice of the mass. But when my conscience cries out, I hold to these kinds of examples and the promise of the gospel. I am comforted by that. There is no blood guilt that could be so heavy and unjust as this evil deed of these brothers. By it, they tortured and murdered their father and brother and grandfather with anguish and heartache. They must definitely have felt in their conscience a great gruesome fear when they would see their brother as the king of Egypt. Because of this, all the misfortune that their descendants endured under Pharaoh was the true punishment by which God accounted and afflicted them for their sins. In summary, in Egypt they will have felt it all very well.

Altb. IX, 1179: Lectures on Genesis, 1535

Before Thee, God who knowest all, With grief and shame I prostrate fall.
I see my sins against Thee, Lord, The sins of thought, of deed, and word.
They press me sore; I cry to Thee: O God be merciful to me! (*TLH* 318: 1)

Friday

But the Midianites sold Joseph in Egypt to Potiphar, Pharaoh's officer and chief of the armed forces. Genesis 37:36.

God lets it happen. He seems quietly still, sleeping, deaf and completely hardened. He has no compassion at all and acts as if he also didn't know this dear son. All the angels are also silent as this treasure is snatched away to Egypt and sold for a little money (namely, 20 pieces of silver). But this fellow would yet become a great patriarch, prophet and regent. What is God doing here with his chosen ones? What kind of wondrous kingdom is it when the chosen children of God are led away and subjugated? What is this, that he forsakes and plagues them so miserably?

Poor, pitiful Joseph is taken by his owners and must travel past Hebron where the thought must have come to him, "See, my dear father lives there, who doesn't know what's happening to me. I cannot call out to him or see him or even do the slightest good for him tonight. This is a true, pitiful misery." I don't even want to speak of the old father. When he came to know this business, he cried out with tears and said, "I will go to the grave grieving for my son and I will go to him. Since I have lost my son, I will no longer love this life or accept it." The traders also would have liked to know about this costly treasure that they are transporting past Hebron to Egypt. They would have liked to know he would be lord of the whole kingdom to help the people in body and soul. Joseph, himself, would bestow a church and the right teaching of God and also bestow great things upon Egypt so that kingdom would become useful and good. For this purpose he needed first to be crucified and become dead until the day his resurrection and lordship came. Then he would not become proud but think on what he was before and how he was raised up to such a great lordship.

This is our Lord God and this is written for our comfort. In the Father and the Son's frightening cross it is as if God were deaf and dumb and ignorant. It appears he doesn't know these things are happening. But faith is still there. God speaks inwardly to this faith and says, "Dear Joseph, wait. Only believe and do not despair. Hold on to the promise that you heard from your father." God promised his forefathers and grandfather and then his father a Seed. He was to think of this same promise and remain hopeful and firm in that promise. But God delivers these Words to him with a wondrous silence in which Joseph sees and hears nothing. For God is the same. It is as if he were completely blind and dead. Joseph lives and holds only onto this common promise. "God had promised Abraham a Seed, etc. I believe in God on whom my fathers also believed." After this, God would speak with him majestically and with action when he would establish Joseph as ruler and savior of all Egypt. For the present, Joseph is dead and buried. He has his Good Friday and Sabbath. His father also dies but they are both raised again by the power of God who can even make the dead alive. The heart of the believer must yet live and rise again even if ten worlds bury him.

This example will sustain us so we employ patience in tragedy and so we do not become impatient and grumble against God no matter how great the tragedy, anxiety and trouble, that afflicts us. It is truly too bad that it is so terrible for this young heart of Joseph. It is not something that a human heart can bear or overcome without feeling pain and smarting. Joseph, also, undoubtedly, had great pain and became very troubled. He felt that he was torn from his dear father by great injustice and he was delivered from the hands of enemies into eternal servanthood. He would nevermore have anything of his own or hope to return to freedom and rest but must become the servant of a servant. The servanthood itself is hard and pitiful enough, if that were the only problem, but this good young man was further perplexed since he was robbed of his parents and all the friends of his life while yet in the flower of his youth. That is how God allows it to be for his children. So let us not murmur even if this also happens to us. Rather, there are many more signs of grace and proofs for our faith.

Altb. IX, 1179–1180: Lectures on Genesis, 1535

Should Thy mercy send me
Sorrow, toil and woe,
Or should pain attend me
On my path below,
Grant that I may never
Fail they hand to see;
Grant that I may ever
Cast my care on Thee.

When my last hour cometh,
Fraught with strife and pain,
When my dust returneth
To the dust again,
On Thy truth relying,
Through that mortal strife,
Jesus, take me, dying,
To eternal life. (*TLH* 516: 3-4)

Saturday

The Lord spake, "The people will no longer strive against my Spirit. For they are flesh." Genesis 6:3

The greatest punishment God threatens in the mouth of the holy patriarch is that he would no longer rule the people by his Word. That is, since everyone forsook his teaching he would not give His Word to the people from then on.

Germany, in our time, will also bring such a punishment upon herself. We see how the devil restlessly rushes on to seek every means to hinder God's Word. See how extensively he has already served up heretics and sects in our generation so that we must still be diligently concerned that people might have pure teaching. What will happen if now we are put to death! Then the devil will bring a whole heap of sacramental know-it-alls, anabaptists, antinomians, followers of Cervitas and Campagnias and other heretics. These cannot yet prevail against pure doctrine. By pious teachers and steady and diligent watchfulness, they are kept silent, but they imagine all kinds of opportunities to introduce and defend their teaching.

Whoever has kept the Word pure learns to accept it, to thank God for it and to seek the Lord while he is yet to be found. But if the Spirit of the teaching is passed over, then the Spirit of prayer, as Zacharias calls him, is also gone. For the Spirit of prayer adheres to the Spirit of grace. But this is the Spirit of grace which punishes sin and teaches the forgiveness of sins; who chastens and condemns idolatry and teaches about the right service of God; who punishes avarice, fornication, tyranny and teaches chastity, patience and doing right. Now the Lord here threatens that this Spirit will no longer order things. Then the Spirit of prayer will also be lifted so that it is impossible for one to pray when he doesn't have the Word.

So the office of a priest is two-fold. First, in his office he turns to God and prays for himself and his countrymen. Secondly, he turns himself from God to the people by the doctrine and the Word. So Samuel says in 1 Samuel 12, "Far be it from me to sin against the Lord, that I should stop praying for you and teaching you the good and right way." So he confesses that this [intercession and teaching] is one office.

For this reason the preaching office is justly praised and held as the highest treasure. If this is ever given up or ruined, then not only could no one pray but there could be only harm by the power of the devil. Nothing else could happen then but the people would grieve the Holy Spirit with all their works and they would fall into sins unto death for which one may not even pray. Other falls and sins are minor compared to this. For by this (the suspension or ruin of the preaching office) one turns himself away and forsakes hope that these falls and sins will be removed. When the Holy Spirit is grieved and the people will not be ordered and chastised by the Holy Ghost then there is a plague in which there is no hope of either counsel or help.

But how common these sins are in every vocation in our time! For neither prince, nor noble, nor city dweller, nor farmer wants to be chastised. But rather they, themselves, chastise and order the Holy Spirit when they do so to his servants and preachers. For they order the office around according to the person (filling it) and think this way: This preacher is poor and despised (i.e., easily ignored). So why should he have the power to correct me! For I am a prince, a nobleman, a magistrate. Rather, they suffer for this because they trample on the preaching and the Word. Who would say now that we don't have reason to fear God, too? Among us it is also as this verse describes the first world.

That is why these Words were handed down from father to son or from serious schoolmasters who zealously instructed some students for a period of 120 years before the flood came. He wanted to see if they would want to be better in this way. Where they did not, he threatened that his Spirit would no longer quarrel with them or chastise them.

This word, either quarreling with people or ordering them, actually belongs to the preaching office, which also presents it to the various congregations of people. So a preacher, or a servant of the Word, is a quarreling and judging man and must chastise what is not right by holding his office without regard to whom the person is, or what office they fill. Jeremiah did that diligently. So he also received hatred and enmity with great physical danger. Then he was afraid, wishing he had never been born!

Sometimes I say that of myself. Had I not been strengthened against it by God, this restless world of stubbornness and evil would have worn me out and put me to shame. The godless grieve the Holy Ghost to such a degree that on their account we, with Jeremiah, often wish we had not begun all this. I often ask God that he would allow this trouble to die along with us, so that when we are out of the way, the most dangerous end times will follow.

Elijah was also called the "troubler of Israel" for this reason by godless king Ahab because he chastised idolatry, tyranny and fornication which were in fashion in his time.

You will be thought of in the same way today if you grieve Germany and make her uneasy. But it is a good sign if the people scold us and call us quarrelsome men. For God's Spirit is the kind of Spirit that quarrels with and chastises the people and chides them.

Altb. IX, 178–179: Lectures on Genesis, 1535

The servant Thou has called And to Thy Church art giving
Preserve in doctrine pure And holiness of living.
Thy Spirit fill their hearts, Endue their tongues with power;
What they should boldly speak, Oh, give them in that hour! (*TLH* 485: 5)

Week of Trinity XI

Sunday

Two men had come to the temple to pray, one a pharisee, the other a tax collector. Luke 18:10

How nobly this gospel proceeds as our dear Lord Christ portrays true righteousness for us and shows how one may recognize it and discriminate between it and the righteousness of pride. It's as if he says, "You will probably find this man to be a living saint. He fasts, he gives alms, he honors his marriage, does wrong to no one and gladly hears preaching." Who could interpret this to mean that he is anything but a pious man?

But I say to you, "If you really want to know him you must not look at these things, which even a rogue can imitate. But you must look upon what is right as God sees it. You could wish that all the world were just like this fellow in their outer conduct. But that is not enough. Be careful that you do not trust in that kind of outward behavior, lest you be lost. See here that under such a holy life the very arrogance of the devil is buried. The devil could not stay in heaven with that kind of willful arrogance. Adam and Eve could not stay in paradise. How then will this fellow stay in the church?"

Fasting is good. Praying is good. Tithing is good. Faithfulness in marriage is good. Refraining from stealing or doing wrong are all good and right in themselves. But the pharisee spoils them all with his pride. By this pride all those acts become merely a cloak for the devil. So in the world, when someone does a good thing for another he begins to use his good work to make someone else his own [by obligation]. It does him more harm than good. As the proverb says, *nihil carius emitor quam quod donatur*, good gifts come at the highest price. How can God take pleasure in a holiness by which one would boast to him and swagger against him? Double treachery comes out of such holiness.

The prideful fellow also says here, "Oh God, do you also see that you have made me so good?" The world contains nothing but robbers, unrighteous and immoral people, but I am good, etc.! In such arrogance he does what he wants to but even if he sweat blood and gave himself to be burned with fire, before God it would be an abomination and the greatest sin. So Jesus says here, "I will be good and righteous in this way now. Beware that you don't have this prideful holiness. For if you soon trip, or completely fall into filth after a while, that would not discourage me so much as it would if you had every holiness and were prideful because of it."

The Lord closes the gospel with, "Whoever exalts himself will be humiliated; whoever humbles himself will be exalted." By this, everyone should learn to be humble and no one despise another. Humility means that I consider myself to be nothing but others to be much. But whoever considers and is preoccupied with himself because he is learned, good, rich, pious; that is called pride. The pharisee does this. He sees his fasting, tithing and the rest as something that elevates him. That's what the Lord would prohibit.

On the other hand, you observe no pride in the tax collector but true humility. He doesn't raise his voice and he prays only that God would be merciful to him. "You also learn," says the Lord, "that you say, I cannot boast about myself." I might want to do that because I am learned, rich and powerful. Then our Lord could say, "Dear sir, where did you get that? Did you get it from yourself? No? Where then? Is it not my gift?" "Yes, Lord, it is." "Why then do you boast? Should some one boast about himself, it is I that should do it, for I gave it all to you. You should not do that. Rather, you should say, 'If I am now rich then I still know that in an hour you can also make me poor. If I am wise and learned, then you can make me a fool with but one word.' " That's what it means to be humble and not boast about yourself and despise others because you are more attractive, nicer and richer than they.

It would be all right if we used such arrogance against the devil and said, "I have God's Word by which so many good things are given me. By that we can instruct and encourage and exhort each other. I have also helped by giving alms and I know from the Word that it is a good work. And I know, devil, that out of spite you would spite me for it!" Against the devil, I say, it is permitted to boast. But before God, to whom we owe everything you should not boast, but rather humble yourself.

Erl. 5, 22–24: First Sermon on Trinity 11, Luke 18:9–14, 1533

Love Divine, all love excelling,
Joy of heav'n, to earth come down,
Fix in us Thy humble dwelling,
All Thy faithful mercies crown.
Jesus, Thou art all compassion,
Pure, unbounded love Thou art;
Visit us with Thy salvation,
Enter ev'ry trembling heart.

Breathe, oh, breathe Thy loving Spirit
Into ev'ry troubled breast;
Let us all in Thee inherit,
Let us find the promised rest.
Take away the love of sinning;
Alpha and Omega be;
End of faith as its beginning,
Set our hearts at liberty. (*TLH* 351: 1–2)

Monday

The imagination of the human heart is evil from his youth.
Genesis 8:21

This bright, clear text concerns original sin. When this is little respected or dealt with gently, you become confused as when blind people cannot see in the light of day what they do everyday and what they do concerning themselves. Look at the youth, how they act completely according to their mortal ways and commit sins already early in their adulthood. You need a rod to bring them into order and so they can be instructed.

When a few years are added to them, they find themselves even more stubborn. It is an epidemic on us. Original sin tries to steer you and attack you with fierce indecency and the desires of the flesh. You take a wife now but soon you grow weary of her and want a different one. You want to command an office or to rule so that soon a great mountain of blasphemies like envy, divorce, pride, greed, avarice, rage, contrary spirit, etc., covers everything.

As one German saying goes, sin grows with the years and man becomes ever taller, more wicked, older, stingier; which are all such coarse, fat, sins that you will easily acknowledge this and grasp its truth. What will we say, then, about inward sins that grow in our hearts such as disbelief, security, the despising of God's Word, false and godless imaginations and thoughts, etc.?

Despite this, some want to consider a philosophical, soft, approach to original sin and call it good theology. But one cannot speak truthfully and be lenient about so many and great sins and blasphemies. It is no small epidemic or defect. Rather, it is the highest disorder and ill breeding that no other creature, save the devil, has.

But don't these same detractors have the witness of Scriptures to aid them to alter their opinions? Let's look at Moses. He does not say in this passage (as I also have shown above regarding the 6th chapter) that indecency, tyranny or other sins are evil. Rather, he says that the imagination of man's heart is evil. That means that all aptitude, wisdom, human reason with all their abilities which are used by reason, even when they are the best and deal with the best things are evil. Even if we do not condemn good works in the household or civil realms, yet the human heart pollutes those same good works when it uses them for its own glory, self-interest or for tyrannically opposing their neighbor or God.

One cannot so shade this text to make it say that this condition prevailed only among people before the flood. Rather, God speaks of it as the common condition into which man's heart is made. So in those times there was no other type of person, even those in the ark. God says this of all. The imagination of their hearts is evil.

No one is excluded, even the saints. This verdict applies to the three sons, to Ham, and the other two brothers by their nature. They are made the same. But this is what makes them different. They did not get stuck in the evil verdict of their heart because of faith in the promised Seed, the hope of forgiveness of sins. They were restored through the Holy Ghost who was given them to oppose and overcome this evil and ill-bred nature. Now, since Ham follows this nature later, he is completely and totally evil and should be completely and utterly lost. But because Shem and Japheth fight against it by the Spirit, they are not so completely evil, though they are still evil. But these have the Holy Ghost, by whom they strive against their human heritage and are made holy by him.

One might further want to complain here that God is unfair. The reason for God's counsel and victory seems to be that he wants to punish them. But he says that the imagination of man's heart is evil so that he might proclaim grace to them and that he might not employ such rage against them. He reveals that this is his good reason. Some clever people foolishly darken this doctrine to show that they completely disagree with the wisdom of God.

I just let such high flying reasoning fly over my head and let those useless spirits be concerned with it. I am gladly satisfied that this doctrine be presented so that we are convicted by it and understand it; namely, that God wants to reveal here that he will be reconciled and angry no more. Parents also do this when they punish their disobedient child for his action. After that, he gives the child kind words again and is reconciled to him. So this inconsistency is not only for the sake of punishing but also in service to the love that is finally bestowed. So the children, while they fear the correction, do not become enemies of their parents. I am well satisfied with this solution. Anyone who has better thoughts about it tears us from our faith which is exactly what they intend to do!

For this reason, you should gladly mark this text. It clearly reveals that human nature is ruined. Such a confession concerning fallen nature is especially useful and cannot be rightly understood without God's grace and mercy.

Altb. IX, 225–226: Lectures on Genesis, 1535

All mankind fell in Adam's fall,
One common sin infects us all;
From sire to son the bane descends,
And over all the curse impends.

Thro' all man's pow'rs corruption creeps
And him in dreadful bondage keeps;
In guilt he draws his infant breath
And reaps its fruits of woe and death. (*TLH* 369: 1–2)

Tuesday

Noah said, "Praised be God, the Lord of Shem, and Canaan will be a slave." Genesis 9:26

One should pay attention to these two great, excellent prophecies. They also apply to our own time, despite the fact that they are masterfully falsified by the Jews. You see that Ham is three times cursed. Yet this pulls him and points him to his glory and he is promised a living dynasty and a worldly kingdom.

The curse is repeated on many occasions because God does not forget such disobedience and the despising of elders. Nor can he leave them unpunished. He wants you to honor your elders and authorities and wants parents to be shown due honor and reverence as he says in Leviticus 19. You should give heed to a grey headed person and to the servants of the church. "Who despises you despises me," Matthew 10.

If children are determined to be disobedient to their elders, it is a sure sign that a curse and misfortune are not far away, just as the despising of the preaching office and authorities is also the same kind of forerunner. People in the first world [that is, before the flood] began to laugh at the patriarchs and despise their power. The flood followed that. In the tribe of Judah the youth began to lie in ambush against their parents and became haughty as Isaiah 3 says, so that many in Judah and Jerusalem were abased. When those ruined manners become the norm, you can safely bet and boldly say that misfortune and tragedy are not far off. Because of that, I have a just concern and fear that Germany is entering evil times. In it all culture and decency is ruined and evil.

But also take note of a rule here which Scripture not only states but can be experienced. Namely, that while God holds back the punishment and delays it, he is mocked by the world and is assaulted with lies. We should highlight this rule as we read all prophecy in Scriptures and carry it with us as a seal. Even here Ham hears the curse well. But since he cannot feel the curse he despises it and laughs in security.

Even so the first world laughed at Noah when he preached before the flood. Had they been able to believe, would they have kept erring so severely or would many more have improved and repented? Also, if Ham had heard the curse from his father and held it as true, he would have fallen at his father's feet and prayed for grace and pardon for the sins he committed.

But what is the reason for this security? It is nothing but this: that the God-sent prophecy can only be believed and not experienced as if it would take place so soon. So the prophecy exhibits two parts, namely, the promises of the prophecy and then the curses. That is why the flesh and our reason are constantly in opposition to them and they consider only themselves to be true.

So Ham became truly cursed by his father though he received the largest part of the world in his inheritance and ruled a great kingdom compared to the kingdoms of Shem and Japheth. If you compare them with Ham, they would actually be beggars next to him even with all his immorality.

So how can this prophecy be true? Answer: This and all other prophecies, whether they promise or curse, are not grasped by reason and they don't let themselves be felt. Rather, they are understood only by faith. Therefore, we also are valued as aliens are in this world. But who perseveres as such to the end will be saved as Christ says in Matthew 24.

So never let go of the fact that the pious remain by faith and in hope their whole lives. When your own understanding and your good works want to become entrapped by the examples of the world, then you will recognize the natural resistance to God in all of you. So Ham is cursed, yet he alone remains a great ruler. Shem and Japheth are saved though they alone bear the malediction and become plagued in many ways. Because of the hold of God's promises and curses upon the believer, he knows they will all be fulfilled in the long run but that he must now wait for it in faith. So although, as Habakkuk says, the prophecy will linger, it will surely come to pass and not remain foreign to us.

So here we have the presentation of the complete wrath of the Holy Spirit when he tells Ham that he will be servant of all servants, that is, the least of all despised and lowliest servants.

But when you observe history you see that Ham is a lord in the land of Canaan while Abraham, Isaac and Jacob and all their descendants that have the blessing live under the Canaanites as servants. Since the Egyptians are Ham's descendants, we see further what a miserable slavery Israel had to endure under them.

So in what sense is it true that Ham is cursed and Shem is blessed? It is true in the sense that one is waiting for what God prophecied and judged. But this passage reveals, then, first, that the godless cannot feel the measure [of their sin and its consequence] and secondly that God could not punish or give sin its immediate due, else man would have no room or time to repent.

Altb. IX, 252-253: Lectures on Genesis, 1535

Lord, as Thou wilt, deal Thou with me; No other wish I cherish.
In life and death I cling to Thee; Oh, do not let me perish!
Let not Thy grace from me depart And grant an ever patient heart
To bear what Thou dost send me. (*TLH* 406: 1)

Wednesday

And in you will all the families of the earth be blessed.
Genesis 12:3

Now we have THE true promise that should be written with golden letters and shouted and praised throughout the land. For this promise brings the eternal treasure and builds upon it. It can impart understanding by the loveliest wisdom that is found, like the previous promises that dwelt only among this race of people. But this promise should be administered and parcelled out to all peoples and families of the earth as the Words clearly say. So we will learn about this blessing God set before all people from no one else but from the Son of God, our Lord and savior, Jesus Christ.

This is the unfailing, true and unwavering meaning: Listen, Abraham, I have made a wonderful prophecy to you and your family. But that is still not enough. I will honor and adorn you with such a blessing that it will overflow and run out unto all families of the earth, and so forth. If Abraham has understood this promise completely and clearly, then he thinks this to himself and is assured: All families shall be blessed through me. So this blessing cannot be established because of me as a person. I won't live so long. I am not so blessed in and of myself that I could bless them. But the blessing of God's mercy is given to me to pass along, so that all the peoples will not become blessed by my personal will or my power, but it will come to them by one being born of my family who will be blessed in himself. He will bring the blessing with him. It will be showered upon all the families of the earth, far and wide. Therefore, he must be God and not only man, although he is also man. And he will take our flesh upon himself, so that he will be fashioned from my seed.

Without a doubt, Christ was invisioned in such thoughts of the Holy Patriarchs as Christ says in John 8, "Abraham, your father, was glad that he saw my day. He saw it and rejoiced." By all the families of the earth you should understand not the breadth of families at one particular time, but the length of time during which all families have ever lived upon the earth. This passage completely agrees with the command of Christ, "Go and preach the gospel to all creatures. He that believes and is baptized shall be saved. But who believes not will be damned." This blessing is already established after 1000 years and will stand and remain yet further unto the end of the world. The gates of hell, thrones, and the godless test and war against it in futility.

It is important that he doesn't say that all peoples would be incorporated by the Jews. He rather says that the promise that this nation holds should come from them to the heathen, in other words, to those not circumcised and who do not know of Moses and the law.

This is why we hold this blessing above all, against the curse under which all people are placed because of their sinfulness. This blessing is received through Christ. All who cling to him and believe in his name are turned to this blessing. This is a wonderful kindness of God. We are redeemed from sins, from death and the power of the devil; we come into the company of the angels of God and will be made partakers of eternal life.

The preaching of all the prophets comes flowing forth out of this promise with Christ and his kingdom, about the forgiveness of sins and the sending of the Holy Ghost, about the preservation and ordering of the church and about the punishment of unbelievers and so forth. So you see that these are necessarily dependent each upon the other, that a seed of Abraham should do this. So he must be a natural and true man. Then again, in order to be another [distinct from them], and that he should save all the families of the earth, he must then also be something higher and greater than a seed. This Seed of Abraham will be sent for the necessity caused by sin.

So, in short and terse words, the Holy Ghost clothes the mystery of the incarnation of Christ which later the holy prophets and patriarchs clarify further. Namely, through the Son of God the whole world would be saved, hell and death destroyed, the law fulfilled; sins forgiven, and eternal life and salvation given to all who would believe and should be given these gifts. Therefore, on the day of Christ of which John speaks, Abraham did not see the Christ with his living eyes, but by the Spirit, and he rejoiced. So while these things are unsure and impossible according to the flesh, they are [by the flesh] also unbelievable.

Altb. IX, 304: Lectures on Genesis, 1535

Let children hear the mighty deeds	To learn that in our God alone
Which God performed of old,	Their hope securely stands,
Which in our younger years we saw,	That they may ne'er forget His works,
And which our fathers told.	But walk in His commands. (*TLH* 629: 1,5)

Thursday

So Abraham set out as the Lord commanded him. Genesis 12:4

Faith is a lively and mighty thing. It is not a sleepy and lazy thought held suspended over the heart yet never swimming in it like a goose hovering over the water. It is rather like water that is heated and warmed by a fire so that if it still remains water, yet it is no longer cold but warm and a completely different kind of water. So faith, which is the work of the Holy Ghost, makes a different heart, mind and soul. It makes the whole person new.

That is the reason that faith is a high, weighty, mighty thing. If we would speak rightly about it we would say it is much more a living thing than a working thing. It changes the heart and soul. By it, reason stops plaguing itself by what it sees. Faith rather perceives what does not appear to the eyes. Faith regards these things against all reason and what reason sees. For this reason the faith of one may not be the same as another. What is heard [of God] contains little that is believable. The great heap of humanity holds onto actual things that one can feel and grasp more that it does the Word.

So this is now the mark and sign of true godly promises. They remain against human reason. Reason will not accept them. However, Satan's promises will easily take hold of reason without raising a doubt because they are in agreement with the voice of reason.

Mohammed taught that those who held his laws would have temporal honor, goodness and power in this life and after this life sensuality and joy. Reason accepts such teaching easily and believes in security. Because of this, Mohammed gets to stay at home and will not depart from his friends, house and home with Abraham. He rather held to what was present, stayed and had peace in that. But Abraham stuck strictly onto the Word that God spoke to him. He struck out and despised all danger that would come to him by going. He believed God would be his protector.

Before human reason Mohammed's teaching has a great appearance. So the papacy also is clothed with such a great appearance, with the service and intercession of the saints, the ability and power of good works, all of which is accepted by reason and is agreeable. For the papacy is vain and has a desire to lie for that reason. To the praise and glory of their own virtues, people would rather hear it said to them that they could purchase salvation with their works, fulfill the law and win righteousness. That means that reason is not put to death but rather made alive. That is why flesh and blood are so happy with this teaching and accept and believe such promises without doubting. But if reason heard what Abraham heard, "Set out from your fatherland, from your friends, and from your father's house to an unknown place. I will be your God," then soon it would retreat and regard this trip taken without seeing the destination as foolishness. Reason frightens itself and flees before danger and seeks and strives after security.

To sum it up, though the devil's promises are lies, yet the flesh agrees with them because they immediately bring ease. But God's promises, which are right and true, soon become a cross and the promise of salvation after the cross. So reason is annoyed on both counts. What is unsafe and out of the way, reason holds as bad and nothing. But before the cross, reason is abhorred and flees before it as before a misfortune that is eternal and endless. That is the reason that there are few who believe even though God is right in giving his promises. Those few, then, are those whose hearts are ruled by the Holy Ghost. These can follow Abraham setting off after the journey, despising sorrow, holding fast and clinging to the Word declared by God.

That is the reason that this text presented by Moses is a terrific example of faith in every way. With so few Words he grasps the history or saga of the most holy patriarch. "Abraham set out as the Lord had said to him."

But for where did he set out? [He set out] from Ur of the Chaldeans where he had his house, home, fields, a well established household, belongings, friends and relatives. He left there with no delay and followed what was unknown. The Lord had not yet shown him the land he would have. He only had this one hope, that the Lord had promised him a blessing. But when, where and how he would give it, Abraham had not seen.

So the Words are few, but they remarkably show that reason does not see truly good Words and right obedience. Reason doesn't think it necessary to act to please God. Rather, it has a desire to falsify Words and then act with an empty glitter of rich colors.

Altb. IX, 307–308: Lectures on Genesis, 1535

Oh, guide and lead me, Lord, While here below I wander
That I may follow Thee Till I shall see Thee yonder.
For if I led myself, I soon would go astray;
But if Thou leadest me, I keep the narrow way. (*TLH* 417: 6)

Friday

Abraham believed the Lord and he accounted it to him as righteousness. Genesis 15:6

No one ever treated this text so richly, clearly and powerfully as St. Paul in his letter to the Romans. He treats it in the third verse of the fourth Chapter. There he shows that one must not understand that this promise of the Seed or descendent applies to the mortal or fleshly seeds but rather to the spiritual and eternal inheritance.

Moses is not using a comparison from earthly or temporary things but from the heavenly. For the promise is heavenly and not according to the children of the flesh. Rather, he speaks of those of the spirit, as St. Paul calls them, children of the promise, as St. Paul clearly explains.

So Moses states here that Abraham has believed God. This is the first text in Scripture that mentions faith. Previously there has been faith. The earlier texts that Moses presented promote nothing but faith without extolling, praising or honoring faith itself. Since the Seed of the woman, the command to Noah (that he should make the ark and the threats of the flood), the command to Abraham (that he should leave his land, etc.), and the others are all great promises of God's Word; they all require faith. But these do not praise faith as this text does. So this text is one of the most prominent texts in the whole of Scripture.

Paul not only presents this faith diligently but he also diligently commends it to the church. He wants to talk about it endlessly. So this text is not just written for Abraham's sake, who has long since died. It is also for our sakes, so that we are also taught and strengthened. That's what you call right apostolic use of the Scriptures. Paul uses this sentence to surround the church. For all the gates of hell must be terrified before it because all who believe God's Word are justified.

Upon this I hold that I will not darken or obscure the very best teachers and expositors of the Bible with my commentaries and disputes. I will give the passage its meaning sharply by leaving it to Paul. Let him use all his industry and you will discover that the most prominent article of our faith, which the world and the devil cannot suffer, is grounded and built upon this text. Namely, that only by faith is one justified and saved. But faith is nothing other than approving the promises of God and holding a sure conviction that they are true. Upon this ground, the master of the letter to the Hebrews determined wonderfully that everything the saints have done was under faith. He says that they did all in faith. Without faith, then, no one can encounter God. What God predicts, he will have it so, so that we should believe. That is, we should hold it as true and sure and not doubt. It will come to pass just as the promise says.

If anyone would ask if Abraham was made righteous before this time, I would answer, yes. He had been made righteous for he had believed God. Who believes God has the Holy Ghost. The Holy Ghost clearly shows such a believer that because the promise is for a spiritual Seed you should surely, then, bring to your heart along with the Seed also what is the consequence of that Seed and what follows it. Whoever receives this Seed, or believes in Christ, is righteous. It happened to Abraham that when upon God's command he left his homeland, he also got into trouble. He had an outstanding faith. We are not all commanded to do such things. If it were also commanded us, it would not have said: Abraham believed God and it was accounted to him as righteousness. But here the Holy Ghost, speaking of the spiritual Seed, establishes the teaching by which he would make the church sure for all time; namely, that all who BELIEVE the promise with Abraham are truly justified.

The Holy Ghost wanted to establish in this passage, which actually belongs to him, that there is no other righteousness than believing in God's promise.

But from here springs a great debate between the law and faith. Namely, whether the law makes righteous and if faith displaces the law, and so forth. Paul rules on all of this when he brings to bear the aspect of timing in a masterful way. In this chapter, Moses speaks of the righteousness by which Abraham will be made righteous. This takes place before the law was given and the works of the law. Yes, even before the people of the Lord and before Moses, the lawgiver, was even born. So righteousness is not only not from the law, but also BEFORE the law. For this reason, the law and the works of the law do absolutely nothing.

How's that? Is the law unto righteousness completely unnecessary and incompetent? The answer is yes. And does faith alone make one saved without works? Yes. Or you will not believe and call Moses a liar when he says that Abraham was made righteous before the law was even given and before the works of the law; not because he had offered his son, who was not yet born, or because he had done this or that work, but, rather, when God gave him the promise and he believed.

Here is no preparation for grace, no faith formed and given through works, or from any previous attribute in man. But this says that Abraham in the middle of sins, doubt, fear and the highest affliction and consternation of his heart, is made righteous.

Altb. IX, 381–382: Lectures on Genesis, 1535

By grace I'm saved, grace free and boundless; My soul believe and doubt it not.
Why stagger at this word of promise? Hath Scripture ever falsehood taught?
Nay; then this word must true remain:
By grace thou, too, shalt heav'n obtain. (*TLH* 373: 1)

Saturday

*For no flesh will be righteous before Him by the works of
the law, for by the law comes the recognition of sins.
Romans 3:20*

Now we know that the works of the law are the highest and best
virtues. Should they not be done for righteousness? Not at all, says
Paul. Rather the only thing that counts is the mercy of God and [with
that] we will despise all our own works.

If God surely calls for our works and virtues and wants us not
to follow the lusts of the flesh but commands us to compel the flesh
and keep it in line and completely put it to death and then also tells
us that they could not be useful or helpful to us before God's justice,
then our works and virtues must be soiled and marked up with sinful
lust. If God had not determined that he would divert his eyes from
our sins, indeed, from our works and virtues, and that he considers
us righteous only for the sake of faith which is held in his Son, then
it is apparent to us that we are considered and made blessed only by
grace and God's mercy. Our righteousness is attributed to us. This
is also the very ground of our teaching. We become righteous before
God only by the mercy of God which declares us all righteous.

St. Paul also uses this text to form his further arguments. By
this, in his epistles to the Romans and Galatians, righteousness stems
from and is ascribed to faith and not to the works of the law. But
think how careless, blind and inattentive the teachers were that came
before. For example, Lyra, whom we regarded [at one time] as best,
has falsified this text in his commentary. For he said that faith is
rightly finished in the heart by being formed and made perfect
through love. Thereby, he holds that faith is barren and weak if it is
not made perfect with love. He rejects such imperfect faith. But he
is not saying anything else but that God does not esteem faith at all
but only regards love and works.

How does this compare to what Moses and Paul say? For if faith
is formed and completed by love, then it follows that the works are,
indeed, preeminent, that is, as God sees it. So as the works are,
[according to Lyra], that's how we ourselves are. So the love or the
works must be the living color, but the faith is a big zero, a
powerless nothing, an unliving thing.

Such unprofitable thoughts only come from a great and deep
blindness and ignorance of the Scripture, by a confounding of law
and gospel, of faith and works. These should be distinguished and
divided very far from each other. For the promise is the chief part

and preeminent in the teaching to which faith submits, or, to say it clearer, of which faith grasps hold. But such a faith is called faith and makes righteous when it is without doubt and is certain. It is that kind of faith when it is not a work that is ours, but rather God's work. Then the promise is a present, a gift or disposition of God by which God adds something to us. It is not our work if God does it or gives something. We only receive from him according to his grace and mercy.

Whoever believes in God in this way, as God has promised, and hopes that God is truthful as such a God, also wants to cling to what God has said to him. Then he IS righteous or will be accounted and made righteous.

After that is also the law. God not only made promises but he also orders and commands. But now that belongs to the law that you rule your will according to IT and GOD, who commands you to be obedient.

Now wouldn't someone say that the law is also a very important thing and then determine that the promise and the law are but one thing? But they are separated from each other. Faith alone grasps the promises of God but the works serve the law. How can it not be a great foolishness that man replaces this [with the idea that] faith is a plain and incomplete thing and then says rather that faith does not make one righteous unless it is formed and completed with love? Why don't we allow them both, faith and works, that each have their own place and dignity so far as each of them extends?

Faith is truly nothing else and desires nothing more than that it approves of God's promise or believes on it. So now such approval or faith is considered as righteousness. So why, foolish philosophers, do you teach love, hope and other virtues in place of what will be considered by God to be righteousness?

Altb. IX, 283-284: Lectures on Genesis, 1535

My soul, no more attempt to draw Thy life and comfort from the law.
Fly to the hope the gospel gives; The man that trusts the promise lives. (*TLH* 373: 1)

Week of Trinity XII

Sunday

Jesus gazed into heaven, sighed and said to him, "Ephphatha," that is "be opened." Mark 7:34

The Lord Jesus Christ is portrayed here as the one person that takes upon himself not only the problems of a city or a country but those of the whole world. John christens him as such in John 1:29. "Behold, that is the lamb of God who bears the sins of the world." Since he bears the sins, it follows that he also must have borne everything that belongs to sin and all that is a consequence of sin like the devil, death and hell.

This is why he also groans here as one who ought to groan. The prophets proclaimed long ago that he was the one who would suffer misery in his heart as a result of the calamity of all mankind. He did not do this for the sake of this single tongue and the ears of this poor man but it is a general groan over all tongues and ears, yes, over all hearts, bodies and souls and all people from Adam unto the last one to be born. Also, he does not sigh primarily because the man would still commit many sins in the future. But this is foremost—that Christ had seen the condition of all human flesh and blood which the devil brought to mortal injury in Paradise, making mankind deaf and dumb and subject to death and hellfire.

This struck Christ's eyes when he looked around and saw what great harm the devil had reeked out of one man's fall in Paradise. He considered not only the two ears but the whole bunch that followed Adam.

The gospel of Christ portrays him as the man who takes you and me and all of us, as we know ourselves to be, to himself when he is stuck in the midst of sins and injuries as we are. He groans over the terrible devil who has brought this infirmity.

This is surely the reason why he receives this man so seriously and acts by such a peculiar way and motion. It is as if he would say, "Your misery is mine. The fact that you are so captured in sins and death is now especially in my heart. So I must moan and act peculiarly because of this great thought." For he stood there so adventurously. If you compare this with his other works, this one is just as wonderful. He often had made others healthy or driven the devil out by one Word. He had also helped several individuals without even approaching them, like the centurion's servant in Matthew 8:13. But here he acts on behalf of two members, the tongue and ears, with special actions, as if he were especially concerned. By this he wants to show us that he had a peculiar insight about the man's condition.

One must also, then, allow this of our Lord and God. This is also the way of all human skill, even that which is seized by sin. It does not always act in the same way. But such skill has various ways of acting. That is also true of all the saints. So, while his heart and thoughts now seem to be somewhere else, he also acts here with gestures so that one must see that he is truly human in body and soul, which does not seem the same in every service, just as he was not always equally hungry or tired. As it happens with all people, things changed with him as St. Paul says in Philippians 2:7, "He took the form of a servant and was just as other men and in form was found as other men and so forth." One should not understand this only outwardly but also in the soul and thoughts of Jesus' heart, which is now highly desirous and yet at another time even more zealous, etc.

Now this is one [reason] why Christ acts this way, namely, that he is a true man also in his person so that he has stood in the place of all people and receives this one just as he does the whole human race. The other [reason] is also true and right. He was concerned within himself with the fact that if he made the man healthy, he yet would sin much. But it is drawn too narrow to only make note of the sins the man would commit.

For Christ, our Lord God, was not concerned and sorrowing only for one man's sins, but, as established in the Revelation Chapter 13:8, Christ had suffered for all sins from the beginning of the world, from the beginning unto all of us who would appear until the last person born upon the last day. That is why it is much too narrow to point only to the future sins this man would commit as the reason for the Lord's groan. Although he also revealed elsewhere how he has looked to the future life of a few people as he says to the infirm man in John 5:14, "You are now well. Sin no more lest you fall again into something worse."

So the dear Lord Christ had such a friendly heart that it caused him sorrow that a person should commit sin. For he knows well that sins cannot remain without punishment. Because of this, he weeps over the city of Jerusalem for he sees that their sins must be punished. So this is a friendly, loving heart that has no desire for this to happen where evil is going on.

Erl. 13, 305–308: First Sermon on Trinity 11, Luke 18:9–14, 1533

Though earthly trials should oppress me And cares from day to day increase;
Though earth's vain things should sore distress me And rob me of my Savior's peace;
Though I will be brought down to the dust
Still in His mercy I will trust. (*TLH* 385: 7)

Monday

I live, yet not I, but Christ lives in me. Galatians 2:20

When St. Paul says here "I live," it almost sounds as if he speaks of his person. But then he makes himself clear and says, "yet not I," that is, I live now and not myself in my person but rather Christ lives in me. The person lives, indeed, already but not by itself. Who is the "I" of which he says, "yet not I"? He is the one who is still under the law and has to act with the works of the law but is in all respects a much different person than Christ. St. Paul means to remove this same "I" from himself. So as a person different and cut off from Christ, he belongs to death and to hell, so he says "Yet not I, but Christ lives in me." By this Paul means that "my faith" gives the right color and clothes him just as color or the sunshine adorns and clothes a wall or a table. You must give this matter much weight. Christ is so near to us and dwells and remains so in us in a spiritual manner that we cannot know or understand [but must believe] that he does so as a light or paint covers a wall. So Paul says, "Christ, who is so near to me and with me, he has completely become one in me and remains with me. That same one lives in me, yes, even the life I have is Christ himself. So Christ and I are altogether one thing in this matter."

But Christ lives in me, so he cancels out the law freely, damns the sins and strangles death so it can never be the way it used to be. Where he is, he himself must weaken all this. So Christ is the true eternal peace, comfort, righteousness and life. Before him the law and its terror, tortures of conscience, sins, hell and death must give way. So Christ himself, who is in me and lives, swallows them up and takes them despite every misfortune that plagues and tortures me. Because Christ is the one thing that matters to me I will be free and clear of all fear of the law and death. I lay aside my old hide and all my being and am engrafted into Christ and established in his kingdom. This is a kingdom of grace, righteousness, peace, joy, life, eternal salvation and majesty. But while I am in him, no kind of misfortune can hurt me.

Despite all this, outwardly the old man in me is still under the law. But this matter explains a lot. Namely, so that I would be righteous before God, Christ and I must be bound to each other ever anew so that he lives in me and I in turn to him. This is very strange and wonderful to say. But while Christ lives in me so does all that is his. So I have good in me, grace, righteousness, life, peace and salvation and all the rest, which Christ so binds to me and which make me one with him, that we are spiritually, thoroughly, one body. But because Christ lives in me, then along with him grace, righteousness, eternal life and salvation are in me. Next to this, law, sins and death give way. Yes, one law through another law, one sinner through another Sinner, one death through another Death, one devil through another devil must be crucified, devoured and completely exterminated. So St. Paul would completely tear us from ourselves, from law and works, and plant us in Christ by faith so that in this matter of becoming righteous before God we will neither look to nor give attention to anything but grace alone. We should differentiate grace from law and works so far as the heaven is from the earth. So by this, there is absolutely nothing that has to be done.

St. Paul has, in addition to the above, declared his particular understanding, which is not mortal, but rather divine and heavenly. Other evangelists and apostles, as a whole, have not pursued this except only for St. John, who is also difficult to explain. If St. Paul had not explained this first, before all the others, and had not written this to us then none of the other saintly fathers would have written in this way. For this wisdom is completely unnatural and is difficult to listen to when you explain things like: I live, I live not; I am dead, but I am not dead; I am a sinner, I am no sinner; I have a law, I have no law, and so forth. And yet this is also, all the same, a very lively knowledge to explain especially to those who believe in Christ. So inasmuch as you consider yourself, then you are yet under the law and sin. But where you look to Christ, there you are dead to the law and have absolutely no sin, etc.

Based on this, if you consider this matter (of how one must become righteous before God) and you divide your own person from Christ's person, then you are already under the law and you must remain there. You live in yourself and not in Christ. That can only mean that you must be damned by the law and are truly dead before God. This is because you have only *fidem informatam caritate*, that is, you are left with the kind of faith by which only love [that is, your works of love as opposed to the merits of Christ] will help to make you righteous.

Altb. VI, 624–625: Lectures on Galatians, 1535; cf. AE 26,27

Hence, all fear and sadness! For the Lord of gladness,
Jesus enters in! Those who love the Father,
Though the storms may gather, Still have peace within.
Yea, whate'er I here must bear, Thou art still my purest Pleasure,
Jesus, priceless Treasure! (*TLH* 347: 6)

Tuesday

The life I now live in the flesh I live by faith in the Son of God who loved me and gave himself for me. Galatians 2:20

It is certainly true that I now live in the flesh. But it is the kind of life that I consider as no life at all, whatever sort of life it is in me. If you want to think rightly about it, it is no life. It is more like a mask under which another lives, namely Christ, who is truly my life which others cannot see. You can only hear it, as when you hear the whisper of the wind but don't know from where it comes or where it goes (John 3), so also you see me speak, eat, work, sleep. But you see nothing of my life. During this time of life, while I live, I surely live in the flesh, but my life is not from the flesh or according to the flesh. Rather, it is lived in faith, from out of faith and according to faith.

St. Paul doesn't lie that he yet lives in the flesh. For he does the same work as any natural man. He also uses all his bodily means that belong to this natural life to provide for his necessities, such as food, drink, clothing, and so forth, which is nothing other than living in the flesh. But he says that that kind of life is not life and that he doesn't live according to these means by which this bodily life seems to be supported. He surely uses these but he does not live because of them or for their sake, as the world lives out of these things and receives life from them. They know nothing more than this bodily life. They find hope and comfort in nothing else.

So he speaks of this temporal life that I now live. Therefore, I don't live by anything else but by faith in God's Son, that is, the Word which sounds from my mouth and is an enlivening sound, a noise that is not flesh but rather the Word of the Holy Ghost and Christ. My eye sees no fleshly face. By that I mean that it is not bestowed by the flesh, but from the Holy Ghost. So what I hear, though I hear it in the flesh, yet is not from the flesh, but rather from the Holy Ghost. The one Christ explains nothing else than what is chaste, reasonable, holy and godly, that is, what is necessary and in service to God's glory and future blessedness. All of this comes not from the flesh, nor is it supplied by the flesh and yet all the same, it is in the flesh. So I cannot teach, preach, write, pray, thank God, unless I apply my body's members to do it. By this such works become manifest and are distributed. These works, although they don't come from the flesh and also do not grow in the flesh, are rather given and manifested there from God in heaven. For example, I see a woman with my eyes, but chastely, so that I do not lust after her. For the eyes are a bodily part by which one sees. But the purity and chastity of this sight actually come from nowhere but heaven.

Of all creatures in this world, only the one Christ employs this method, so there appears to be no difference between him and all the godless men who eat, drink, dress themselves, listen, see, talk, act and conduct themselves alike. St. Paul says of Christ that he was found in the form of other men. Yet, at the same time, he is no less the one who is surpassingly different than the great crowd of people. So though I still live in the flesh, yet I do not live from out of myself. Rather, as I live, I live in faith of the Son of God. What I say to you flows from another well-spring. What you heard me tell you before was out of my own holiness. So after Paul was converted, he still spoke with his tongue and voice by which he had previously spoken. But his tongue and voice spoke blasphemy and abominable things against Christ and his church. But after he was converted, he still had the flesh, even his tongue and voice were completely unchanged as they had been before. But that tongue and voice spoke no more blasphemy but rather only spiritual speech, namely, of God's grace and goodness, love and praise, etc. These are not works of the flesh but are rather of faith and the Holy Ghost. So I indeed live in the flesh but not from the flesh according to the will of the flesh but in the faith of the Son of God.

By this it is good to understand where this new, alien, spiritual life comes from. The natural man can never understand this. For he neither knows nor understands the sort of life this is. He hears the wind blow, but where it comes from and where it goes he doesn't know. That is, as he hears the voice of a spiritual man, knows his face, his manner and actions, he knows not where the Words come from or why they are no longer blasphemous as before but rather they are holy and godly. It is also invisible to him where the new sense and will that bring these new works come from. So this same life is hidden and buried in the heart through faith, so that all flesh is completely put to death and dead and Christ alone reigns there with the Holy Ghost. This life now sees, hears, speaks, works and suffers all things in him though the flesh struggles against it. So this life is a fleshly life since it is still in the flesh and dwells there but it is especially a life in Christ, the Son of God, which has Christ dwelling through faith in every believer.

Altb. VI, 626–627: Lectures on Galatians, 1535; cf. AE 26,27

Oh, keep me watchful, then and humble And suffer me no more to stray;
Uphold me when my feet would stumble Nor let me loiter by the way.
Fill all my nature with Thy light, O radiance strong and bright! (*TLH* 399: 4)

Wednesday

Who loved me and gave himself for me . . . Galatians 2:20

I have often spoken at length of the fact that there is no better or surer advice by which you can fend off the sectarians than to rightly and thoroughly learn this lone article of justification that you have in Christ. When you lose that, it is already impossible to withstand or defend against a single error or sect. You see in our day among the fanatics, anabaptists, and despisers of the Sacrament, that when they have once fallen from this article they continue to fall for more and more errors. They cannot stop themselves or their people from falling from one error into another.

Friend, have you considered who the Son of God is and what sort of person he is and how great he is? What is heaven and earth compared to him? We would rather sink to the devil in the pit of hell and let all the fanatics and papists go off *en mass* with their righteousnesses, works and service, and even if they add the whole world; we would rather suffer than to have the truth of the gospel be darkened by them and the honor and majesty of Christ drawn under. Why is it that you brag so much about your work and service? If it were possible that I, a lost and condemned sinner, could have been ransomed by another treasure what need could there have been for the Son of God to be given? But because in heaven and on earth no other treasure was good enough to make sufficient satisfaction for my sins, then this great need compelled the Son of God to present himself for me. He did that gladly, willingly and with great love, as St. Paul says, "Who loved me and gave himself for me."

So these words, "Who loved me . . ." are full of great and powerful comfort. All these Words are powerful enough to awaken us to faith. Whoever can say the single little word "me" with such faith and mean himself, as St. Paul was able, would undoubtedly also know enough to dispute and fend against the righteousness that belongs to the law which would be done to commend us before God. For Christ has not given a sheep or an ox or gold or silver, but he gave himself for me. For me, I say, who was the most profane and condemned sinner. So now because God's Son has given himself for me in death, my heart is strengthened and comforted against God's wrath and misfortune. Paul declares these Words not only for himself but for all Christendom. He does not desire to say that he is exceptional. This is for all, so that each accepts and applies it to himself without doubt as the true power of faith. A works-righteous person could not say "Christ has loved me . . ."

These Words that preach clearly the grace and righteousness in Christ preserved Paul against the law's works and righteousness. He would say that although the law is also divine teaching and has God's honor and majesty, yet I did not live according to it. Nor did it give itself for me but it only frowned at me, accused and frightened me. But now I have another who saved me from the law so it can never frighten me any more; nor can sin or death. He has helped me to freedom, to the righteousness of God and to eternal life. And the one who has done this is named God's Son who loves me and has given himself for me, to whom be glory and honor to eternity. Amen.

Now faith grasps and holds Christ, the Son of God, who has given himself for us as St. Paul teaches here. Whoever grasps this one by faith also has righteousness and eternal life. Christ, God's Son, has given himself for us with pure love by which he not only saved us from sin and death but also acquired eternal righteousness and life for us. By these Words, St. Paul described the loveliest and most comforting aspects of Christ's office and priesthood. This office is that he makes us children of God, prays for sinners, offers himself the sacrifice for your sins, redeems you, teaches and comforts and so forth. So you must learn to rightly picture who Christ is in this way and not as the philosophers and fanatics do. They make him into a new law giver who did away with the old law and gave a new one in order to rule his city. But by that he is made a pusher and a tyrant. But you should picture him as God's Son, whom the Father offered not to gain our service and righteousness, but because of his pure love and mercy, as a sweet offering for us sinners, by which he would make us eternally holy.

Altb. VI, 630–631: Lectures on Galatians, 1535; cf. AE 26,27

When all my deeds I am reviewing, The deeds that I admire the most,
I find in all my thought and doing That there is naught whereof to boast.
Yet this sweet comfort shall abide In mercy I can still confide. (*TLH* 385: 8)

Thursday

Who gave himself for us, that he save us from all unrighteousness and purify a people unto himself, diligent unto good works. Titus 2:14

Christ is no Moses. That means he is no driver or lawgiver. He is rather a giver of grace and a merciful savior. In short, he is nothing but pure and immeasurable, overwhelming mercy. He not only sees to it that this is presented to us but also gives us himself by it. That is how you rightly picture Christ. However, when you allow him to be offered in another way, you could easily and quickly be destroyed in time of trial. But when one portrays Christ with the right hew and line, this is the greatest and highest work of Christ. It is also the most difficult task for it is distasteful for me to build onto Christ, as Paul also suffered to present him. Even if I have studied very long and diligently on this task [of presenting Christ] and have also been enriched by the fact that the gospel has been given pure and clear through God's grace, yet the poisonous teaching and the harmful opinion about Christ, that sees him as a lawgiver, has been so deeply rooted in me that it has oozed into my most inner bones like a subtle oil.

So you young people are much better off and more blessed than us older people. You are not so troubled with this poisonous teaching. As a child, I was so used to that teaching that I grew pale and frightened if only I heard the name of Christ used. I was told that I should consider him as nothing but a severe, wrathful judge. That's why now, when I rightly consider and confess Christ to others, it must be with some effort. First, I desire that my heart and conscience be free of that harmful old teaching about Christ as if he were only a law-giver and judge. I fight against this teaching and reject it. But it is a plague that will not surrender. It keeps coming back again and again. It afflicts me and will not turn away from me.

After that, I also have enough to do to hold onto the saving divine teaching that informs me of Christ, who loved me and gave himself for me, as definite and firm. I also hold it as sure that Christ alone is the true, reliable, only savior and maker of righteousness. You young people can come to know Christ much more easily than you could in the pope's steam-bath prepared by his dreadful human teaching, but in which he refused to sweat.

But since the office of Christ is to restore us to God, etc., we should say this if we feel melancholy or sad in heart. That sort of Christ would not give guilt as we, who have come under his name, might let it seem. The devil is the one who gives guilt. He is such an evil villain that he afflicts us under the name of Christ and plagues us by presenting himself as an angel of light.

That is why we must really learn this and learn it well. Not only can we speak about the work of Christ, but we also experience it in our life and thus hold it as sure because Christ is in no way a lawgiver. So if the devil comes under the appearance and mask of Christ and plagues us in Christ's name, we can definitely know and mark that it is not Christ, but the right nasty devil.

For Christ frightens and pushes no one. But his office is used to comfort a fearful, frightened and dull conscience. He presents himself as its greatest friend. St. Paul illustrates this especially well in this passage. He gives Christ this lovely and comforting title—that he has loved me and gave himself for me. By this it is sure that Christ loved those who are in terror and buried under sins and death's load, so that he gave himself for them, became our High Priest. That means he placed himself as the mediator between God and us poor sinners. What could be said that is lovelier or more readily heard? It is true. It must be actually and definitely true or the whole gospel must be a lie and false. We cannot be readily made just through the righteousness of the law, much less by our own righteousness.

This is why you should read these little words "me" and "for me" so that you immediately apply them and hold fast that these words have everything to do with you. Make it a habit to desire to apply this little word "me" to yourself with sure faith and not doubt that you among the many are also one to whom this little word applies. Note this and be sure that Christ did not only love Peter and Paul and the other apostles, but that the same measure of grace is offered to us and will surely come to us as to each one. For we are also meant by the word "me."

So, just as we cannot lie about our being altogether sinners and must acknowledge that Adam by his sin also ruined us and made us guilty, enemies of God, who belong to the wrath and justice of God and eternal death (as our poor frightened conscience feels and knows more and heavier than is helpful), so, on the other hand, we cannot lie that Christ died for our sins so that through his death he has made us right. For he did not freely die to make people righteous who were already righteous. But he died to help poor sinners to make them just, friends of God and dear children and heirs of all that is in heaven. So if I experience and acknowledge that I am a sinner for the sake of Adam's fall, why should I not also say that I am righteous and good for the sake of Christ's righteousness, especially when I hear that he loved me and has given himself for me?

Altb. VI, 631–632: Lectures on Galatians, 1535; cf. AE 26,27

Strive, man, to win that glory; Toil, man, to gain that light;
Send hope before to grasp it Till hope be lost in sight.
Exult, O dust and ashes, The Lord shall be thy part;
His only, His forever, Thou shalt be and thou art. (*TLH* 605: 4)

Friday

*Who now grants you the Spirit and does such deeds under
you, does he do this by works of the law or through the
preaching of faith? Galatians 3:5*

"Who gives you the Spirit . . ." That says you have not only
received the Spirit through the preaching of faith but you have
obtained everything, both knowledge and deed, by the preaching of
faith. He wants to say, "Our Lord God has revealed himself to you
so that he does not let the Spirit remain by you as if you received
him only once. But he increases and promotes his Spirit's power and
strength from day to day in you. So after you once received him, he
increases in you daily and becomes even greater and more active in
you."

By announcing the Words, "Who now gives you the Spirit," the
message is well received that the wonders worked in Galatia, or even
the smallest of the deeds worked, are all fruits of faith that true
children of the gospel take care to do. As the apostle says in another
place, "the kingdom of God does not remain in words, but in
power." But the power is not only that one can speak of the kingdom
of God but it also means that God is mighty and active in us through
his Spirit with deeds as he says of himself above in the second
Chapter, "Who is mighty with Peter unto the Jews and is also mighty
with me unto the heathen," and so forth.

So when a preacher teaches the Word, it is not without fruit
but it is powerful in fruits. So give your attention when faith,
hope, love, patience, etc., follow preaching. There God is
bestowing his Holy Spirit and he is working his deeds under those
who listen to the gospel. This is the way St. Paul is also speaking
here. Our Lord God bestowed the Holy Ghost to the Galatians
and did deeds under them. He wants to say, "Our Lord God has
given my preaching and worked so much through it that you have
not only become believers but also have led a holy life, brought
forth many good fruits of faith, and borne many misfortunes and
troubles. Through this same power of the Spirit, you even became
different people than you were before. Before, you were
idolaters, enemies of God, blasphemers, selfish, adulterers,
wrathful, impatient, jealous and so forth. But now you have
received the Word, are children of God, mild, chaste, gentle,
patient, and loving to your neighbor, etc." He illustrates that this
is true of them in chapter 4. They received him as an angel of
God, as Christ Jesus, himself. They held him so dearly that they

would have been willing to even give him the eyes from their heads [when they saw his bodily affliction].

Such a person has so much regard for his neighbor that he would be inclined to give the neighbor his best and to willingly bestow his money, goods, eyes, life and all, and so forth on him. More than that, he is willing to suffer all kinds of adversity. These are the unrestrained powers of the Spirit. You received these powers and held them before the false apostles had come to you. But you didn't receive them through the law, but from God, who gave you his Spirit and daily fortified it so the gospel would be under you with all its finest results; with teaching, faith, action and suffering. But while you had such a good attitude and your own conscience was convinced by him, how did it happen that you no longer do these deeds that concerned you before? Why do you no longer teach, believe, live a right life, do good, patiently bear adversity, as you did before? Now you no longer want to receive Paul as if he were an angel sent from God, or even as Jesus Christ, himself. You would not desire me, much less rip out your eyes and lose them [for my sake]. Evermore you depart from your zeal you had for me. Now you are friendly to the false apostles that burden you miserably and evilly.

This also now happens to us. When we first preached the gospel by God's grace, there were many everywhere who gladly heard this preaching and held us in honor and with a good opinion. Out of the preaching of the gospel, power and fruits of faith followed. But what happened? Unforeseen, the fanatic spirits, anabaptists and sacramentarians, broke in and destroyed that, wiping away what we had previously built; what we had given with great care and worked for over a long period of time. At first, they made out as if they were our best friends and that they received our teaching with great thanksgiving. But presently, they become our greatest enemies so they cannot even stand to hear our name. This misfortune from the devil has but one purpose. This is the reason the devil works such powers and works, such fruits that disguise him as with a cloak; so that the powers of the Holy Ghost are wholly and completely and immediately set aside.

Altb. VI, 658-659: Lectures on Galatians, 1535; cf. AE 26,27

Speak, O Lord, Thy servant heareth, To Thy Word I now give heed;
Life and Spirit Thy Word beareth, All Thy Word is true indeed.
Death's dread pow'r in me is rife; Jesus, may Thy Word of Life
Fill my soul with love's strong fervor That I cling to Thee forever. (*TLH* 296: 1)

Saturday

*But we preach the crucified Christ; to the Jews a scandal
and to the Greeks foolishness. 1 Corinthians 1:23*

All the articles of our Christian faith which reveal God through
his Word are blatantly impossible, absurd, lying, etc., before human
reason. How could the wise fools think that these are impossible,
absurd, etc.; that Christ should give us his body and blood to eat and
drink in communion, that Baptism should be the second birth and
renewing of the Holy Ghost, that the dead shall again rise on the last
day, that Christ, the Son of God, was conceived in the body of the
virgin Mary, born, became a man, suffered an ignominious death on
the cross, rose again, and sits on the right hand of the Father and
shall have power on heaven and on earth? What about the Jewish
unbelievers, who heard for themselves both the prophets and Christ
and that all Jerusalem together with the temple and the whole land
should be laid waste and destroyed? So how could these have been
heretical and devilish sounds in the pharisees' ears when Christ said
to them that tax collectors and whores would go to heaven before
them? Here St. Paul calls the gospel of the crucified Christ a Word
from the cross and a foolish preaching which the Jews hold as a
scandal and the Greeks as foolishness. It is impossible that reason
could understand and hold it as true, that man should hear and
believe God's Word as the highest and greatest service of God. It
always sounds so foolish, absurd, impossible, heretical, etc. So in all
times, heretics and godless men judge and make opinions about our
Lord God's Word.

But faith is given to throttle the neck of reason and to
strangle the brute. This faith deals with what the whole world
and all its creatures cannot strangle. How? You cling to God's
Word. You allow its truth and surety even if it still sounds so
foolish, impossible, etc. So Abraham had to capture it [reason]
and put it to death. He believed God's Word revealed to him
that God would give him a seed from his fruitless wife, Sarah,
who was dying away. Such a Word and promise did not make
Abraham's reason fall too quickly but that reason strived
against his faith and held the promise as foolish, absurd and an
impossible thing for Sarah to bear a son. She had not only
reached ninety years of age, making child birth impossible, but
also was naturally infertile all her life. Surely, in Abraham's
heart, faith and reason struggled over these matters and
competed with each other. Yet faith endlessly applied itself and

held the struggle and overcame and strangled God's most deadly and dangerous enemy, reason.

All believing people who enter with Abraham into the dark and buried obscurity of faith do this and strangle reason, saying, "Do you hear that, reason? You are a crazy, blind fool. You don't understand one little word about the things of God. So don't do your great trick of barking back. Hold your tongue, rather, and be still. You don't understand enough to be judge over God's Word. Rather, sit, listen to what he says to you and believe him." So faith chokes the beast which the whole world is unable to strangle. Our Lord God does that with faith. This is the most welcome act and service that he could ever reveal.

Compared to these activities of God's service, all acts and services that come from all the heathen along with all the works of all the monks and works-righteous people on earth are simply nothing to God. By this work, reason, which is easily the most powerful and undefeatable enemy of God, will be put to death. Reason despises God. It inquires neither of his might, majesty, wrath, righteousness, nor of his goodness, mercy, truth, etc. By faith's activity our Lord is given his honor. By it you believe that he is right, good, true and truthful, etc.; that all things are possible, that the Word is always holy, sure and truthful, etc. Yes, this is the most desirable service that God can reveal and do for a person. In all the world no service to God or worshipful praise will ever be found that is more pleasantly received or more pleasing to God than faith.

On the other hand, faithless works-righteous people become sour with their many kinds of works, fasts, prayers, cross and sufferings. But because they mean to still God's anger and buy his grace by them, they do not give God honor. That is, they do not hold that he is merciful, truthful and that his assurance or promise does enough. They regard him as a wrathful judge whom one must reconcile and quiet with works. By this they even despise God. They accuse him of lying in all his promises. They displace Christ and all his good works [with their own]. In short, they push God off of his throne and majesty to set themselves in his place.

Altb. VI, 664–665: Lectures on Galatians, 1535; cf. AE 26,27

Though reason cannot understand Yet faith this truth embraces;
Thy body, Lord, is everywhere At once in many places.
How this can be I leave to Thee, Thy Word alone sufficeth me,
I trust its truth unfailing. (*TLH* 306: 5)

Week of Trinity XIII

Sunday

Blessed are the eyes that see what you see. For I say to you, many prophets and kings wanted to see what you see and have not seen and to hear what you hear and have not heard it. Luke 10:23, 24

The evangelist reports that Jesus says this to his disciples just at a time when he was especially moved with joy in the spirit, or spiritual joy. For he thanked and praised his heavenly Father from his heart for the revelation of the gospel. You can see that this is his special gift, that he can declare among the disciples that their salvation depends on this. This passage is nothing but a praise of the gospel and that they lived in the time (and now saw and heard) of the revelation itself which brings the world redemption and salvation from sin and all misery. The dear prophets had previously and wonderfully foretold this time or revelation and zealously sought after it and proclaimed it among the crowds. This will be especially noticed in the Psalms and the prophet Isaiah. "So you are," he says, "blessed and more than blessed. For you have the truly golden year and the time of pure grace-filled blessing now. Therefore, just be sure to keep it and use it well!"

This is a great praise, a true exhortation, and yes, also an earnest complaint. He exhorts them to thankfulness for this grace but complains about the great unthankfulness of the world. There are so few people that confess and accept it while so many despise it. "So," the evangelist says, "Christ has made the disciples special and he praises them as if to say: 'Yes, yours are blessed eyes and ears by which you hear and see. It is such a pity that there are also so many eyes and ears that do not wish to see or hear it, though they have the same sort of eyes and ears.' " He shows this is a great and gushing treasure preached to bring comfort. Yet the great crowd must only despise and persecute it.

The wheel of time has been turned. The dear fathers and prophets would gladly have given their body and life to see their desire in their time. If it would have happened to them, their hearts would have been joyfully refreshed in life. It would have seemed to them that they were walking on rose petals. That's how it was for the pious old Simeon, Luke 2:28ff, when he had the savior in his arms even when the savior, being a baby, could not even speak or act. Simeon gave his life over joyfully so that his life and everything in it were no longer a concern. Good mother Eve, Genesis 4:1, already prayed for and anticipated him when God gave her first son to her. She thought it would be him. But after that, she implored even more anxiously when her hope in Cain failed. And after that, all the fathers' hearts likewise had clung and sighed for the same thing until he would come and let himself be seen and heard. The whole world should receive him with great joy. They should have called him blessed just as he himself praised this grace.

How happily good David thanked God when he first heard God's promise from the prophet Nathan in 2 Samuel 7:12f with a totally ardent heart. God would not only build him a house and establish a kingdom upon earth, but Christ would also be born of his body and an eternal kingdom would be pinned to [his person] by God's grace and mercy. Out of his great joy, David had no idea what he should say before God and how he should thank him. So David wrote many beautiful psalms, especially the 89th and later in his last will and testament he praises this great mercy and says, "that is all my salvation and desire," and so forth, 2 Samuel 23.

But now the desired holy time has come. I say, never mind that you experience the kind of people who don't want to hear and see or know and allow this unique gift of rich grace and the highest mercy of God. Surely even now you see and understand those who want to be considered church and called Christians, the pope, bishops and all their crowd, who ought to lift up their hands to heaven and thank God that they might be saved from their darkness and blindness by receiving the bright light of the gospel. But instead they carry fire and water, sharpen their swords and weapons, and hunt those that teach and publish the gospel to rid the world of them.

Even so, in our midst there are many who are unthankful, false Christians, who despise [the gospel] in great security.

Erl. 14, 18-20: Second Sermon for Trinity 13, Luke 10:23-37

Oh, come, Desire of nations, bind In one the hearts of all mankind;
O, bid our sad divisions cease, And be yourself our King of Peace. (*LW* 31: 7)

Monday

And Jacob was greatly frightened and worried. He divided the people with him and the sheep and the children and the camels into two bands and said, "If Esau comes to the first band and slays it, the rest will escape." Genesis 32:7, 8

St. Paul says in 2 Corinthians 1, "We were beaten by the crowds and the powers so that we despaired for our lives. We had

decided we must be headed to death. But that showed," he said, "that
we don't place our trust upon ourselves but rather on God who raises
the dead." What is this, dear Paul? Why are you not happy and
comfortable? Why do you also not make others happy? Will Paul,
such a great apostle, become so completely down-hearted so he
would rather die than live? Does the one who was full of the Holy
Ghost now let himself appear abandoned by God?

Yes. The first and foremost picture of this same battle is Christ
who had sweat blood in the garden. I say it is presented to us there.
It is also laid bare completely in the lives of the saints whose
examples are presented for a lesson so we learn to place our trust in
God rather than ourselves. This is the attribute of those saved of
God. They do not trust in themselves but only in God. That is, the
sort of God that raises the dead and calls those who are not into
being. For that is God's work. If you want to be saved of God and
confess and honor God as your Father, then consider that you must
dispute with the devil, the world and the flesh, with sins and the law.
Of these the world is the slightest enemy, even though the raging
wrath of the devil comes to us through the world's constantly
pursuing us. The devil helps the world and frightens the saved of
God. We also do not suffer this most feeble attack in such a way that
we can avoid the devil.

We should consider this as our most prominent presupposition
and truly learn it. In all our needs and trials, we trust God whose
own work it is to raise the dead. He establishes those who are afraid
of it [death] in comfort unto peace. So He takes a needy person and
saves him. He takes those who can do nothing but doubt and makes
them joyful. That is why Moses does not waste many words here nor
does he attempt to make this scene read as if the situation were easy
or safe as he describes this trial. He wants us to identify with this
example in our own hearts.

But what does Jacob do when his faith is under attack and
becomes weak, when his flesh rules this situation, when he doubts,
despairs and is burdened? Answer: First, he does whatever is
available for him to do as the papists also take care to say often, but
for a different reason. For they do not understand or speak rightly of
this matter. They don't know how to use it. As we have said above,
though we have the promise and law of God, you should not, for that
reason tempt God. That is to say, one should not neglect or despise
any means God gives to help but should use them when he can. God
did not give reason and also the counsel and help of reason to despise
them. Those who work against these are imprudent or doubting, as
if they would say, "I do just what I want. I cannot stop what is
inevitable and what should and must happen in a particular

situation." These are the words of those who doubt. But they are mistaken. They want to say with those words, whether I eat or not doesn't make any difference. But we should already observe that even if we have God's promise we do not seek God presumptuously and do not sin with doubt. If you have a lamp there is no need to fall out of a window and there is no need to wade through the middle of the Elbe [River] when you have a good bridge. Rather, each should do what reason teaches and advises and whatever else God ordains. He will readily give what will provide a way out.

So this is a very good example. Jacob did not leave one thing undone that he could do. He divided the people with him in order to send his brother a gift. He applied himself and did everything he possibly could. Someone else in that situation might have said, "You shouldn't do anything. It's obvious that you will be destroyed so it will do you no good to defend yourself." Someone else in that situation might have tried to argue, saying, "If I am being watched over then I cannot be lost, so I can do whatever I want." These are devilish words that you should guard against. It is true that whatever is foreseen will take place. But one must add that those things are not known to you. Even so, you cannot know if you will live or die tomorrow and God has not desired you to know it. But mindful of that, it is foolish for you to seek what God's counsel has hidden from you. But because you do not know it, as long as you live you should use the means that are necessary for life. If it is also expected that you may die within a month (as in a dire disease), even then you should not tempt God since you cannot be sure of it. You should rather use the means that are appropriate that make it possible to hold onto this life.

Altb. IX, 1008–1009: Lectures on Genesis, 1535

Arise, my soul, and banish Thy anguish and thy care.
Away with thoughts that sadden And heart and mind ensnare!
Thou art not lord and master Of thine own destiny;
Enthroned in highest heaven, God rules in equity. (*TLH* 520: 7)

Tuesday

God of my father, Abraham, and God of my father, Isaac;
Lord, you have said to me, "Return to your land and to
your friends and I will give you mercy." Genesis 32:9

This is an excellent example of a wonderful prayer. It has all the elements heard in a good prayer. Oh, who can pray so excellently!

In the New Testament the teaching and promise of prayer are very generously presented but who is able so to pray! Also, Jacob had not been able to pray this way before. But now he is so frightened. Everything happens and is ordered so that because of this fright he approaches prayer so that this kind of prayer should follow. Have mercy, my Lord God, and so forth. But the flesh which impels us sinfully to the law wants to return us to the law. That is a defect also in Jacob. He waits longer than is reasonable to pray. This is a weakness of the flesh. Instead of prayer, he first turned to his reason.

But he establishes his prayer well when he says, "God of my father, Abraham, etc." It is a bright prayer after a little darkness of faith which has strongly quarrelled [with reason]. This is also the prayer of Moses standing by the Red Sea. But first, Jacob grasps the God of Abraham and Isaac and calls to him because he is therefore also HIS Lord. So he admonishes God by using his promises that were revealed to Abraham and Isaac, especially what God himself had given and performed for him. This makes such a prayer very bright and great. He awakens to the faith that had previously quarreled and adheres to that faith's glowing daughter [prayer]. He says, "You declared the promise to Abraham and Isaac and also to me. You would not lie to us and you also still fight." This is truly a wonderful thing, a great and mighty comfort, a rich promise, upon which you can surely cling and yet at the same time tremble.

But his prayer goes further, "You said to me, return to your land," and all the rest. This is as much as saying, "You have brought me into this need, this trial and danger of my life." But it is a great comfort if one can say, "Lord God, I am not here because of any wise or foolish counsel, but rather YOU have said it and called me so that I did the right thing when I left Laban. So that makes this YOUR situation because it is your promise and assurance that is being attacked. You must rescue your truth and faith since this faith, and all its ways, did not come from me." This is the work of faith and the groan of which it is said, "The groan that moves heaven and earth" and is a very acceptable prayer. "You have said 'go' and I go in your obedience. I will return to my fatherland upon your command and as you have told me, dear Lord. But look what great road blocks have arisen. I have come into pure anxiety and am burdened. I don't know how to save myself by my own might and advice. So I am in need of your help." The others [with him] actually wouldn't pray, but rather attacked him, "If we had remained with Laban, we probably would be safe." But Jacob doesn't question that. He offers a very strong prayer.

But what more does he say now? "I will do good unto you." As if he would say, "This is surely your Word. You will not ruin me and will not ordain trouble for me. But you want to act in kindness to me in my fatherland where you have called me to return." You can see from this that he is not only attacked and plagued because of the charges that his brother had against him but because of his wives, children and clan who plagued him. "Dear father, dear husband, dear lord, what have you done? Why have you brought us into such great danger?" The complaints would have brought forth mighty words from him so he says, "Dear Lord God, listen how even the people tremble and my own heart is also tortured even though I know that you have promised me help and comfort."

So faith is revealed in this and lets itself be heard, though it is weak. Surely that faith would have told him, "Why are you so completely afraid? Will you completely ignore faith? Truly, we must not let hope fail as if we couldn't be saved. I will not ignore it, even if you might." In that manner faith helped itself and resisted the crying and impatience of his family. "God has not called me to return again into my land because he wants to do ill to me. It must turn out well. God will help us. Let us only use the help that is at hand and cry out to God!"

This kind of prayer is very acceptable to God. It appears in the most extreme need and when the danger is greatest, when all is lost. That is the unspeakable and powerful groan. With this the godly are aroused against doubt so they take courage and say, "Now it must no longer be. We will not be ruined. I will not die, but live," and so forth, as stated in the 118th Psalm. I have the promise that the Lord has said he will be merciful. Don't cry and wail and tremble so. God has called us from Mesopotamia and has returned us again to the fatherland.

Altb. IX, 1010–1011: Lectures on Genesis, 1535

And when my soul is lying
Weak, trembling and opprest,
He pleads with groans and sighing
That cannot be exprest;

But God's quick eye discerns them,
Although they give no sound,
And into language turns them
E'en in the heart's deep ground. (*TLH* 528: 8)

Wednesday

I am not worthy of all the mercy and truth you have given your servant, for I had no more than this staff when I passed over the Jordan and now I have become two bands. Genesis 32:10

One must not pray in this way, "Dear Lord God, regard me for I am a holy monk, I am a chaste virgin, I am a worthy bishop." Just as the pharisee says in Luke 18, "I fast twice a week and tithe, and so forth, and give many alms." One should put this hideous monster [of pride], the abomination, away from prayer and sweep it away. Otherwise prayer is ruined and becomes both an act of death and unthankfulness. It is made a total scandal by such stink and filth.

So one should say no more than Jacob who says, "I am not worthy of your mercy." He wants to say, "I'm also not worth your mercy or truth that you have always shown me and now show me, nor am I even able to render you any service. So I do not rely at all on my worthiness but on your mercy and promise." That is a right heart and a truthful prayer. In truth, this is our Lord God's opinion of us that St. Paul has expressed in I Corinthians 4, "What do you have that you have not received? So if you have received it, why do you boast?" So one should pray, "Dear Lord God, you have given me your promise and mercy. There is no worthiness in me. Up till now you have given me everything and acted towards me in a way I have not deserved, so you will also listen to me, the unworthy one, and graciously help me." Otherwise (should you pray in another way), God would punish you and say, "Why do you boast? You, who are dust and ashes! You are still earth and will return to the earth. Did I not shape you from dirt? Who bestowed life upon you? Everything you have turned into evil is altogether mine!"

So this is now the dual quality of a good prayer that God readily receives as a sweet aroma before him. That kind of prayer must be heard. The first quality is that you have grasped the promise and then that you put to death your anxiety. Thirdly, you thank God and confess that you are not even worth a single mercy but you pray and hope that he might help only out of grace and mercy. These virtues are completely praiseworthy and are also commanded by God: namely, chastity, temperance that you be gentle and help the poor. But you should not depend upon these. Our trust should not dwell on the law and the works of the law even though those works ought to be there. Rather, the trust should remain upon God's mercy and truth. Then prayer and the groan become a golden sacrifice.

Now the petition follows. Now what do you ask for, Jacob? You confess you are unworthy of my mercy. You confess that I am the one who made you a promise. You know that you have received everything out of great grace. What, then, do you ask for? What do you lack? Should God baptize, the child must have a name. Does God not know what we need? He truly knows it already. So Christ says so in Matthew 6, "Your Father knows what you need before you ask." Why then does he want me to groan, cry out and knock and then acknowledge that I am not worthy of his help?

Answer: That by this he would also have us think about what we need and lack. Otherwise we would be secure and snore and let ourselves dream that we are completely blessed people when we are yet most pitiful and poor in salvation. But we don't know that. We also do not learn it except in the time of pure tribulation. Jacob had life by God's grace. He had two camps. But in the blink of an eye he lost both and was made completely destitute. He didn't know that before while he even boasted and exalted. But now he was taken to school and taught what and how much he is able to do. In this we learn that our trust is not based on ourselves, but on God. So we rejoice in our gifts but we don't boast in them. This is very difficult to bring about because of our ruined nature that is completely spoiled by original sin. For we can easily fall into doubt if we are attacked and afflicted. If everything is fortunate and going well, then we are secure and proud. This is why the saints sometimes became disheartened and discouraged and then for a time encouraged again. By this they retained the teaching that one be careful and say: *Medio tutissimus ibis*. When one remains in between, it is best. But that is apparent only through tribulation. Therefore, we should not be impudent and take hold of our power or worthiness but we should place our trust only in God's grace and truth. These are firmly established, are eternally truthful and do not fade. Our faith can never fail when placed upon them.

Altb. IX, 1013–1014: Lectures on Genesis, 1535

The Gospel shows the Father's grace,
Who sent His Son to save our race,
Proclaims how Jesus lived and died
That man might thus be justified.
(*TLH* 297: 1,6)

May we in faith its tidings learn
Nor thanklessly its blessings spurn;
May we in faith its truth confess
And praise the Lord our Righteousness!

Thursday

Deliver me from the hand of my brother, from the hand of Esau. For I fear that he will come and slay me, the mothers and the children. Genesis 32:11

What does Jacob need now? Everything! He says, "My brother will kill me, my wives and my bands of people." So he was afraid. But where is the promise of God that he has grasped hold of by faith? Don't you know that God can change your brother's heart? God had declared and revealed mercy and truth to Jacob yet at the same time his flesh trembles and groans and runs from danger. This reveals the way original sin acts. It only regards the danger. He says, "I have already divided into two bands. But I also plainly see that soon I will lose everything and that I myself can hardly escape the danger of death." So he speaks in this way, "I fear that he is coming and will slay the mothers and their children." Faith is sometimes assaulted and becomes weak and doubts but yet at the same time it doesn't. Faith is careful to act when tribulation is near. Faith battles with the flesh and the thoughts [of both faith and doubt] run together resulting sometimes in despair and sometimes in good hope. "He wants to slay the mothers with their children," he says. By this you see his anxiety and fear. Soon he would lose all that he had instantly. When the report that his brother was approaching came, his goodness and hope soon sunk within him. But he yet remained pegged to the promise. Lord, you have said, "I want to give you kindness and make your seed as the sands of the sea, that one cannot count or number." This he holds against all doubt. So here he allows himself to ponder completely being sunk. That is the reason he says, "That he not come," and so forth. Those are words of the flesh that disputes there with a very weak faith. But he retained the Word. "Your truth," he says, "by which you have declared that you would do kindness and bless me and my seed, will preserve me, direct and comfort me. You will not bless me and my seed if Esau wipes me out and exterminates me."

Now God would be able to raise the seed and fulfill the blessing even if Jacob would have been exterminated. Just as the promise of the seed and the inheritance was hung upon Isaac but God commanded that he be offered [as a sacrifice] and Abraham also retained the faith that God could bring forth Isaac's seed from the ashes, as said above. Truly that became a very great trial. But Jacob, in his fear, had almost forgotten that God had said he wanted to be his God. So he began his prayer as said above, "Lord, you have said to me," and so forth. He not only had prayed this but also occasionally preached and exhorted his family about what this meant. He would have said many times to Rachel, "My dear Rachel, be comforted. Hope in God and his Word." They would have replied, "But he will slay us!" And Jacob would answer, "He will do nothing. I have prayed the Lord and he will defend and save us. Remember, God spoke with me and has promised me help." With such exhortation, preaching and prayer, he directed and comforted himself and his household.

These are very excellent words and a remarkable example in the history of the patriarchs. It teaches us that we grasp God's Word above all things and should hold fast to it so that we don't lose it or let go of it even if we are already losing everything else, even if Esau is already killing our sheep.

No matter how horribly the enemies press us, we should yet insist on faith in the promise and remain fixed on the Word and live in it, just as the patriarchs Abraham, Isaac and Jacob lived in it. So if you are weak as they were, you should still not reject the Word or allow it to be taken from your eyes and heart. Then the devil would triumph and drive you to despair.

Altb. IX, 1014–1015: Lectures on Genesis, 1535

If the way be drear, If the foe be near,
Let not faithless fears o'ertake us; Let not faith and hope forsake us;
For through many a woe To our home we go. (*TLH* 410: 2)

Friday

And Jacob called the place Peniel, "for I have seen the face of God and my soul is renewed." Genesis 32:30

Now this is a very happy ending and follows on the heels of battle. For Jacob now comes out of hell unto heaven, from death to life. It had truly become a hard and difficult battle that had been engaged. So he now thanks God and confesses his anxiety and need and doesn't want this place to keep its old name. He calls it Peniel as if to say, "This place should not be called a battle or the face of hell but a face of God." So he says, "I have seen God face to face. Now I clearly see that the wrestler who chased me is God himself. Why am I so perplexed? Why have I trembled so? I didn't know that this was the Lord my God."

And now we should say without contradiction that this was no angel but it was Jesus Christ, our Lord, who is the eternal God and has become a man who would be crucified by the Jews, who is familiar to the holy patriarchs and appeared often to them and spoke to them. Therefore, he revealed himself to the patriarchs in such a form that he would show that he would dwell in flesh and in human form with us on earth at some time.

This is the correct interpretation which we have not received or found in others. This man revealed himself when he gave Jacob the name "Israel." And Jacob himself says in this place, "I have seen God face to face." Our very same Lord, Jesus Christ, has thus pursued Jacob not to ruin him but to strengthen him and give him might and that he learn better the power of the promise by the fight. Surely he gave Jacob this power and strength that he triumphed and joyfully praised this face of the Lord.

488

He had not said this in the trouble and fight even as others did not try to speak such a joyful word under the cross. But even in this way, those saved of God and godly people must finally overcome in the battle and come to the point that they also see the sight of God. The same is said of the woman of Canaan who had seen and heard Christ, the Lord, when he entered a house to be concealed from her. But she followed him and kept holding on until she won his heart. He let it seem that he was too hard and he put the poor woman away from him. In short, he completely rejected her. But when the battle is over, we can also rejoice and give praise with the patriarch Jacob that we "Peniel," that is, that we have seen the face of God. Jacob also witnessed this very difficult war and experienced his joy. He would say, "Dear Lord God, how I was in great anxiety and under a burden and in great terror. But to God be praise and thanks! Now I am out of it and restored! My soul is freed and redeemed from all that anxiety. Now I thank the Lord, my God."

Altb. IX, 1029–1030: Lectures on Genesis, 1535

Jesus, lead Thou on till our rest is won; Heav'nly Leader, still direct us,
Still support, control, protect us,
Till we safely stand in our Fatherland. (*TLH* 410: 4)

Saturday

Jacob answered, "No, please! If I have found favor before you receive my gift from my hands. For I beheld your face as if it were the face of God. And you received me with pleasure." Genesis 33:10

Augustine asks if Jacob in this passage might be an idol server or if he had been hypocritical to his brother by saying he saw his [brother's] face as the face of God. He lets himself become very sour that Jacob had sinned. But it is a special gift to be able to speak of Scriptures so that someone can rightly understand it. So above, the wrestler said, "You have overcome God and man, that is, you have been pictured as being between the backs of God and your brother, which is a sign of wrath or an unfriendly heart." This figure of speech is the same in every language. If I am someone's enemy then I turn my face and eyes away from him and turn my back to him. That is a sign of wrath and unkindness. When it is said of God that he turns his face from someone and turns his back on them, it shows that he has lost grace, or the perception of grace, favor and mercy from God. Instead, everything comes as fear, sadness and doubt of God's intentions. In short, a troubled conscience then says, "I don't know how it is between God and me, and so forth."

So the face is not called the revelation of divine actions, but rather as it is stated in Psalm 67, "He lets his face enlighten us and is gracious to us." That is, he speaks to us as a friend. For instance in Psalm 4, "Lord, you raise the light of your face above us. You make my heart glad." As I say to those who are troubled, "Be comforted, my son, your sins are forgiven." Or, "Oh woman, your faith is great," and so forth. When he speaks to us in such a friendly way, it is as if his face enlightens us and he shows by his Words and deeds that his heart is favorable to us. I say that he reveals his face to us and shows these same things to us only in the Word and Sacraments. On the other hand, when he says, "You have committed adultery, have stolen, you will suffer death; the adulterers, whores, etc., will not inherit the kingdom of God"; as in 1 Thessalonians 4, "No one cheat his brother, for the Lord is the avenger over all," and Matthew 25, "These will go into eternal torment;" all such passages and Words terrorize and shake the heart. So these are because God turns his face from us.

Just as Jacob says above about God's face, which had turned to him, "My soul is relieved" because the Lord had spoken kindly to him and given him rich comfort in the promise and the blessing, even so also his brother is like the sun to him. His word gave evidence of his good intentions. This is the meaning and understanding of his words. He would like to say, "My dear brother, I have seen that your face has turned to me. Now that I see your face, it seems to me that I truly see the face of God." This is no hypocrisy or flattery but is earnestly spoken from the heart. For he wants to say by this, "I have rejoiced completely to see your face as if I had seen that God were meeting me."

However, you must recognize the friendly face of God in his promises in the Sacrament, though also, as a gracious prince in his external kindnesses and gifts. If, for example, a neighbor, or father or mother is reconciled with us, if I see that my parent's face is friendly, then I also see that God's face is friendly to me. This is like Jacob saying before that he had seen the Lord face to face. He sees the same face of God now also in the face of his brother. For he sees the mercy of God's will in the kindness and favor of his brother. In this manner, the face of God appears in all his creatures for it is God's work and evidence of God's will and presence. By this he shows that he is kind to us. By such external appearances he shows us his friendly and gracious face and his inner heart by his Word and promise.

Altb. IX, 1043-1044: Lectures on Genesis, 1535

Here the Redeemer's welcome voice Spreads heav'nly peace around,
And life and everlasting joys Attend the blissful sound. (*TLH* 284: 4)

Week of Trinity XIV

Sunday

But Jesus answered and said, "Were there not ten made clean? Where are the other nine? Are there none who returned and gave thanks besides this foreigner?" Luke 17:17-18

This is a very frightening example where ten [people] have such fine faith and are made healthy, yet nine lapse again and say no "thanks" to the Lord Christ for his kindness. But such an example should be of service to us from now on so we are thankful and defend ourselves against the scandalous burden of unthankfulness. Our Lord God would have this honor and it is only right that we should thank him for all his kindnesses. We also freely and willingly do this. That doesn't cost much effort or work. What harm is there in turning to God and saying, "Oh Lord, you have given me healthy eyes, healthy feet and hands and more. I thank you from my heart for them, for this is your gift." Also, what could it hurt to thank your father and mother, your master and mistress, your neighbor, when a kindness is returned to you from them. It doesn't break your arm. It is only right to do it so that it is evident whether the kindness was received as a kindness and so that everyone would be more inclined to do more good. That's what the Samaritan does here. He returns to the Lord and thanks him. It didn't cost him a penny but only a few words. It was received by the Lord so well that it is a wonder! Thankfulness is also received by people well. It makes them gentle. They are charmed by it so they might help again even more.

The heathen have said, "Unthankfulness is the greatest vice." Therefore if one scolds an unthankful person it is scolding at the highest level! We also experience that this fault is very common. Most people we encounter deserve thanks from us. Those who are mothers or fathers dare to give body and life, honor and goodness to their children. And how do the children regard them? What do they put them through? It is seldom reported that a child is thankful. The nasty devil does this. It is also true in other stations of life. So learn to guard against this great shameful vice. By it the fountainhead which gushes forth with all truth and kindness that is done by me should be all dried up! When one finds a thankless heart, then desire and love by which people would be helped to do some further good fade away. Whoever wants to help other people but receives no thanks for it throws up his hands because of it [unthankfulness] and it is a very annoying thing if he is not a Christian. That is the first word said. Everything is useless for a person without salvation. [He would say,] "Let him go on. I don't want to think of him or help him with one red cent." So the people become unwilling. That is the penalty for unthankfulness. It is still in the world and a very common vice.

So if you want to be a pious Christian then learn to be thankful first to God, our gracious Father in heaven, who gives and preserves body and life and also gives everything that belongs to eternal life. Also be thankful towards your parents, friends and neighbors who have become God [i.e., God's instrument] to you and by which he makes himself known as good. Because of this, when your neighbor is unable to repay you in kind with works he will show his thankfulness and friendliness to you with words. This establishes you well and God will also have [words of thanks] from you. It is the smallest matter. And since you cannot get even this smallest thing from the world, that it show thankfulness with words, it is no wonder that you cannot bring people to repay kindness (with kindness).

Hauspost., 424–425: Sermon on Trinity 14, Luke 17:11–19

We praise Thee, O God, Our Redeemer, Creator,
In grateful devotion our tribute we bring;
We lay it before Thee, we kneel and adore Thee,
We bless Thy holy name, glad praises we sing. (*TLH* 568: 1)

Monday

For his grace and truth rule over us eternally. Hallelujah!
Psalm 117:2

Because of these very fine words this verse does not deserve to be run over coldly or crudely. First he says, "His kindness," or grace. That is not our work, holiness and wisdom but rather his grace and mercy. So what is God's grace? It is that out of great mercy and for the sake of Christ, our dear bishop and mediator, he forgives all our sins, levels all wrath, leads from idolatry and error to the truth, cleanses, enlightens, sanctifies and makes our hearts righteous by faith and the Holy Ghost. He chooses us as children and heirs. He adorns and embellishes us with his gifts. He saves and protects us from the devil's rule and thereafter bestows eternal life and salvation. He also provides, gives and preserves this mortal life in all its troubles and needs. He does this through the service and the cooperation of all creatures in heaven and earth. None of this, even the smallest part of it, can ever be deserved. You ought not even speak of the great things. For through your idolatry, unthankfulness and despising, without exception, all these sorts of sins earn wrath, death and hell.

But because this is true (as it must be true), it naturally follows that our work, wisdom and holiness are nothing before God. So it is God's goodness and not our service. If it is our merit, then it is not God's goodness or grace, Romans 11.6. So it is not possible for the Jews with their law and works to persist, much less the heathen with their idolatry and also so little the sophists with the horror of their masses, convents, cloisters, pilgrimages and countless similar human institutions and works.

Why do they completely pursecute this teaching of God's grace and call it heresy? Because they do not want to despise their teaching and work which have been rejected. They will allow that God's grace has given us so much. But [they deny] that their own affairs should be so completely nothing and that before God they should only value [God's] naked pure grace. That must be called heresy. They want to also have their hand in their bosom and do so much with their free will that they would work off and buy his grace from God as well as all the benefits mentioned above. So it is not God's grace but our service that achieves grace. So we are the journeymen who lay the first cornerstone upon which God builds his grace and goodness and because of this he must thank, honor and adore us and we become him. But not (as this psalm says) that we must again thank, praise and worship him and that he is our God who has already begun goodness towards us and built a basis for our service by his grace.

There people chatter the psalm with their mouth but with their hearts they think and read it this way, "All the world should honor US and every people praise us. Our works rule them and our teaching should remain forever." They read it that way in their hearts. They cannot deny all their causes, letters, brotherhood charters. They are all convinced that by their vigils, masses for the dead and all their good works, they seal, confirm, promise and sell a permanent eternal purchase rightly and honestly. These are divided among their institutions that have been and are yet to come. By these they are saved from sins and eternal fire and saved. It is as if they were never baptized or were no longer Christians.

But where is God's previous grace which he does apart from [our] works? If it must be previously purchased through some foreign work [of Christ], then is it not blasphemous and horrid that works are set above God's grace? Is this not taking his deity from God and calling Christ a liar? Yet these do not repent and become better. They want to become hardened to it and still salvage and sweeten the same things. But their seals and letters, bulls and books, are too numerous in our day. These witness against them too strongly and they deserve no covering or sweetening.

Choose now as you wish. This verse has three interpretations. The first is like this: Our works rule over us over and above God's grace. The second: Our works rule without Christ but yet next to God's grace over us. The third: God's grace rules over and before any works, [which are both] through Christ. The first two are from the Jews, Turks, sophists and all false Christians. They are invented from their own heads. The third is of the Holy Ghost and all Christians.

Altb. V, 260–261: Lecture on Psalm 117, 1530

By Grace I'm saved, grace free and boundless: My soul, believe and doubt it not.
Why stagger at this Word of promise? Hath Scripture ever falsehood taught?
Nay: then this Word must true remain;
By grace thou, too, shalt heav'n obtain. (*TLH* 373: 1)

Tuesday

For his grace and truth rule over us eternally. Hallelujah.
Psalm 117:2

He says elsewhere: "Reigns," that is they reign over us, "*imperat et regnet gratia.*" This kingdom of grace is mightier than all wrath, sins and all evil in and over us. No sophist or works–righteous person has understood this word. They will not understand so it is impossible [for them] to know the meaning of the kingdom of grace or the heavenly kingdom or the kingdom of Christ. Their hearts are rather made up (as also my heart stood when I was a sophist) that when they are doing good they have grace. When they sin or fall or feel sins, then grace also fails and is lost so they must again seek and find it with their own works. They cannot think in any other way.

But that is not called the kingdom of grace, that reigns over works. Rather it is a kingdom of works that rules over grace. But reign, "*Gabar*" [in Hebrew], means here "to be responsible for" as to have the upper hand. This word is powerful. You must grasp the kingdom of grace in a child-like manner. In it God has a new great heaven over us through the gospel which we believe in and rely on. It is called grace/heaven and is much greater and more beautiful than this visible heaven and is also eternal, sure and immortal.

Whoever is under this heaven cannot sin or be sinful. So it is a grace/heaven, unending and eternal. If someone should sin or fall, he doesn't fall by that from this kingdom. He does not want to stay there [fallen] to go with the devil to hell, as the unbelievers do. Although they feel their sins, or death shows its teeth and the devil frightens, there is then much more grace that reigns over all sins and much more life that reigns over death and much more God who reigns over the devil.

In this kingdom such sins, death and devil are nothing but dark clouds under the living heaven which presently cover the heavens for a time. But they are not able to lord over it. They must remain under it. The heavens remain over it to rule and be Lord. But at last they must be put aside. So although sins bite, death frightens and the devil lets himself be felt in tribulation, they are yet but clouds. Grace and heaven rules and lies above. They must be under it and finally must give way. These cannot be put aside by works but rather only by faith that is sure that grace/heaven is over him apart from his works. He knows this as often as he sins or feels sins and takes comfort in it without any of his service and work.

However, those who want to deal with sins and death by works must also do them by necessity and must doubt because it is impossible to be aware of every sin, Psalm 19. The lesser part of the sins you can know. But if the devil of God's judgment would be revealed, which no one can be acquainted with or know, then the conscience would needs be frightened and say, "Oh Lord God, for these sins I have done nothing." For having become used to making satisfaction for sins with its works, it [the conscience] would be panicked with so many and great sins that it had never been aware of, much less made satisfaction. So it must, then, doubt.

So the devil imputes and makes all that person's good works into sin. Where does this lead? It leads to not knowing about the kingdom of grace, that God's goodness rules over us. It leads to not being accustomed to trusting his grace. So the works and the teaching of good works go to the ground and disappear like smoke. Sure, it's good to speak of works and of making satisfaction and earning money, that is, until the hour of testing comes when the devil and God's judgment stir the conscience. Then it [the conscience] finds how dangerous, poisonous, scandalous and cursed such teaching is. But that chastening is long waited for if God does not do special signs and wonders.

But who has the kingdom of grace has their heart set. Whether or not it feels sins, whether or not the devil invents sins, it does not value good works nor let God's judgment turn or frighten it. It says, "They are surely unpleasant dark clouds. But God's grace rules and governs above us. The grace/heaven is mightier than sin's clouds. Grace/heaven remains forever and the sinful clouds are set aside." So this verse does not lie. He makes it known that those believing God's judgment are frightened by sins, death and devil and flee them. But he says that you have a defense and grace lies above. He retains the upper hand and lordship so that you can sing, "Praised be God that his grace is over us and is mightier than our sins, etc."

See, that happens without works and must happen without works, else both grace and heaven would be lost in a blink of an eye as David also was tried and lamented in Psalm 119, "Were your law not my desire I would have faded away in my misery." But whoever does not have trials knows nothing of this and must handle his own sins to make satisfaction and drown them with his works. So this is nothing but putting out fire with blades of straw or measuring the wind with a bushel basket. It is the same forlorn and harmful sort of work.

Altb. V, 261–262: Lecture on Psalm 117, 1530

Here stands the font before our eyes Telling how God did receive us:
The altar recalls Christ's sacrifice And what His table doth give us;
Here sounds the Word that doth proclaim Christ yesterday, today, the same,
Yea, and for aye our Redeemer. *(TLH* 467: 6)

Wednesday

For his grace and truth reign over us eternally. Hallelujah.
Psalm 117:2

Thirdly, he says: "over us." Where? He separates himself from all others with these Words. He alone is over all sinners that confess and feel that they are set in sin, death and all misfortune. So the works–righteous people do not permit grace. They also do not feel sins or death or devil near them but by vain holiness they feel life and the heavenly kingdom and that they are beloved children.

So this verse seems false and lying on two counts. First, to our nature that resists our teaching and faith, so we must then forfeit God's grace and have only pure devil's teaching and God's wrath. Secondly, that our external nature won't allow itself to consider anything but that God is our enemy and has given us over to the devil. So both (1) teaching and (2) life seem to be nothing but the devil ruling over us and not God's grace. Again, here let yourself consider them our enemies and that God is our friend and that he rules over both teaching and life. For these Words are spiritual and understood only by faith in the Spirit and not according to the external life that informs our opinions, which will only become vain scandal and lies according to the psalm. Else other things would be found that could define the situation like this: "All the gentiles howl and blaspheme, so God's wrath and rage rules over us unceasingly."

But here I perceive something about the holy prophets and King David. In this psalm he becomes an unfaithful Jew who falls among the gentiles (see v.1). He lets go of Moses and all Judaism and becomes a gentile. So he speaks among the gentiles and not among the Jews and says they praise the Lord. This is clear and definite. He doesn't say this: "So God's goodness over you gentiles," but "over us" as if he were under the gentiles and were also a gentile. So with "us" he makes himself as a gentile and not the gentiles into Jews under one God without all the laws and without Moses but only through honor and praise.

By this he casts off the old law thoroughly and completely. He witnesses and shows that it is not necessary to hold it and that none of it was held. These laws were performed as signs of this glory and not as a work or service or a particular service to God as the Jews, Turks, sophists and human reason think. But now the glory itself has come among the gentiles in all the world so we should not so highly respect the signs of that glory (the law of Moses), which have become empty praise, but rather urge the glory itself which remains as neither distinctively Jewish nor gentile.

Further he says, "and his faithfulness," that is, his truth. By this Word he has promised and bound himself to be our God and will not turn his grace from us. By this we will be safe. This is how he has begun to make you as you should always remain and continue. It is done so that we should not doubt about his promise even if outward appearances seem completely different and only wrath appears and no mercy. He will hold true and faithful to his promise as we also hold fast to it with faith and not fall through disbelief and impatience. The only thing to do is to have a little hope so we bear the cross and do not become either faint or tired. For hope does not let itself become dishonored (according to St. Paul, Romans 5) and God cannot lie (Romans 3 & Titus 1). Therefore we must learn that goodness and grace is not safety, as mentioned above, but rather cross and trouble is seen, which we experience. Our adversaries have external goodness and grace though they are not aware of, much less do they respect, heavenly wrath as God describes it in his Word.

So this kingdom of grace is a hidden, buried kingdom in this world and remains so. It is obtained by the Word and faith until the time of its revelation. That is also why the godless do not want it and cannot be in it. But as it says in Psalm 2, "Let us rend his bonds and throw off his ropes from us." That is, "We do not want to suffer such a kingdom to reign over us." Luke 19:14: "We do not desire that these should be lord over us."

Why? Because this kingdom condemns and dismisses all of their own external works and ways in which they trust. It promotes only trust in God's grace which is hidden and buried. This is only promised through his Word and becomes attached through faith. So they compel vain blasphemy, curses and persecution against the dear kingdom of grace instead of praise and thanks. As mad people they dispute and rage against their own salvation and blessedness until they fall to the ground and attain that for which they wrestle. As Psalm 109 says, "He wants to have the flood which will also come upon him. He does not want the blessing so he will also live far from him." *Volenti non fit injuria.* One cannot give to anyone without receiving in return what is due.

As it is with grace, so it also occurs to the faithfulness and truth of God. Grace outwardly appears to be only empty wrath. It is buried deeply and covered with thick coats or hides. For grace curses and excludes our sinful nature and the world as a plague and the wrath of God. And we ourselves also feel nothing else in us as St. Peter says well in 2 Peter 1:19, "Only the Word enlightens us as in a darkened place." Yes, certainly in the darkest place.

So God's faithfulness and truth also incessantly seem as great lies before they become the truth. They are called heresy before the world. So it also always seems to us that God would allow us [to go] and not keep his Word. It begins to become a lie in our hearts.

Altb. V, 262–263: Lecture on Psalm 117, 1530

They have come from tribulation And have washed their robes in blood,
Washed them in the blood of Jesus; Tried they were, and firm they stood.
Mocked, imprisoned, stoned, tormented, Sawn asunder, slain with sword,
They have conquered death and Satan By the might of Christ the Lord. (*TLH* 471: 3)

Thursday

But you, speak as is proper according to saving doctrine.
Titus 2:1

The chief article of our Christian teaching in the Scripture is that we must become pious, alive and holy through God's pure grace. This is given us in Christ apart from any service. There is no other way or path, no other manner or work able to help us. So I see and encounter all too easily every day how much opposition the terrible devil has to this chief article that he might extinguish it.

If there were saints that esteemed it as an unimportant thing to completely and consistently bear [this article], it would be because they had convinced themselves that they knew it pretty well already and have at last finished learning it. I know all too well already how widely that kind of darkness prevails. Those who hold that opinion, for the most part, don't know how much depends on this article. If this article remains pure upon the blueprint, then Christianity also remains pure and is harmonious, without any gangs [cliques]. That is because this article alone makes and preserves Christianity and none other. Every other article would also be accepted by false Christians and hypocrites. But where it [this article] does not remain, it is impossible to defend against a single error or party spirit. I know that is true and have experienced as much. Without this article I could not displace the faith of the Turks or the Jews.

Where factions arrive or appear, have no doubt that they have definitely fallen from this chief article, irrespective [of the fact] that they blab a lot about Christ and dress and adorn themselves in such talk. This article prevents factions from forming. The Holy Ghost must also be there, who will not allow factions to go on but rather gives and preserves harmony. You especially find this in an inopportune and immature saint who brags on himself and already knows everything. He knows that we must be made holy by God's grace but positions himself as if this is to him an unimportant matter. Then do not doubt at all that this fellow doesn't know a thing about which he talks. Actually, you should resolve never to experience or taste his teachings again.

This is an art that you never finish learning or brag that you could. It is an art which will keep us in school. "Masters" also stay there. All who can rightly know it or understand it do not brag that they can know it all. Rather, they take some comfort from it as a lively savor and an aroma which they seek after and pursue. This makes them wonder. They cannot nail it down. They do not grasp it as they desire it. They permit it, hunger for it and long after it more and more. They have not attained it so that blessed are those who hunger and thirst after righteousness, as Christ spoke (Matthew 5).

When lust comes, then my thoughts run as in this example as I will explain. The devil had caught me when I did not think of this chief article. He plagued me with verses from Scripture that he knew would make earth become too narrow for me. Then human works and the law were all just. So in the whole papacy there seemed no error. In short, no one had erred except for Luther alone! All my best work, teaching, preaching and books seemed accursed. I seemed nearly like the terrible Mohammed to the prophets and as a Jew and a Turk. I had become an empty holiness.

So, dear brother, do not become proud or too secure and sure that you know Christ so well. As I now have confessed and made known to you, you heard what the devil wanted to do to Luther, who should be a pure doctor in this art by now. I had already preached, judged, wrote, spoken, sung and read a lot about it. Yet I must remain a schoolboy in it. Sometimes I am neither a schoolboy nor a master. So let me advise you not to say "Phooie." You stand? Take heed lest you fall. You know it all? Then watch that the art doesn't fail you. Have some fear. Be humble and pray that you grow in this art. Be on guard for the crafty devil, who is called "cleverness" or "wisdom," can always be there and he teaches everything in cleverness!

When you want to or must handle passages that concern the law and works or advice and examples of the fathers, then before all things take this chief article. Place it in front of you and find nothing else [in that passage] besides this article, by which the dear sun, Christ, shines so in our hearts that you can be free and secure him through and over all law, example, advice and work. Say "good." There is something good and right here. I know well, though, that they are good and right no further than in this life. Into the next life and grace, only Christ alone is good and right.

When you don't do this, then you have this for sure: That the law, advice, example and works, with their beautiful appearance will make you confused by their great appearance before man. Then you won't know where you live. I have seen it also in St. Bernard when this man begins to speak of Christ. Then what is humanly desired goes away. But when he speaks outside of this article and speaks of regulations and works, then it is no longer St. Bernard. So also with Augustine, Gregory and also all the others. When it is not Christ, they teach idle, worldly teaching as do philosophers and lawyers.

That is why Christ is called in Scriptures the cornerstone upon which all is built and anchored that should be established before God. But what is not upon him and not built and anchored on him must come to nothing. It cannot stand.

Altb. V, 265-266: Lecture on Psalm 117, 1530

Jesus, Jesus, only Jesus, Can my heartfelt longing still.
Lo, I pledge myself to Jesus What He wills alone to will.
For my heart, which He hath filled, Ever cries, Lord, as Thou wilt. (*TLH* 348: 1)

Friday

You are the salt of the earth. If the salt becomes unsalty how will one make it salty again? It is useful for nothing but that you pour it out and let the people trample it. Matthew 5:13

Salt that has lost its teeth and sharpness and is no longer spicy and bitey is called "unsalty." That happens when the Office of the Christian is ruined so that one ceases to chastise the people and show their need and inability. Nor is it self-preserved by repentance and confession if their office lets them do it as if they could be pious and righteous by such indulgences and by their own resource, their own holiness and self-elevated service. If the Christian allows this breach until the pure teachings and faith are completely ruined and Christ is lost and thus becomes completely ruined, then nothing is left that will help or give counsel.

By these Words he has seen this happen and prophecies of the year in the future when Christianity would be harmed and ruined in which this salt, or chastising office, would be left to lie. In its place would come so many swarms or parties and sects that would want to place their own actions as right teaching and service to God. Yet they are nothing but worldly, fleshly things that popped out of their own head and reason, by which they completely pollute [the world], as with wild, stinking, ruined flesh. The salt and chastising is then lost.

You see how much depends on this. Christianity above all establishes Christ and nothing else. This is easily attacked. But without this, Christianity cannot be established and Christ doesn't remain, nor does right understanding or life that runs in the tradition. Plainly there is no greater evil and ruin of Christianity than when the salt with which one flavors and salts all other things becomes unsalty. This is quickly done. The feet are swift and the Old Adam easily takes in this poison. For the Old Adam does not allow himself to remain in danger or venture life and limb or suffer persecution, insult and slander. So our bishops and the spiritual estate are the cleverest people on earth (though they are not so good that we would call them unsalty salt, for they are totally of the devil when they lead as if they were not bishops, but are themselves the greatest persecutors). For they preach so that they can stay out of danger and have money and goods and then also honor and might.

Whoever would part ways with all the world, kaiser, kings, princes, wisdom, teaching; and say that their ways are cursed before God, might as well place his head on the chopping block. But if I act as a hypocrite to them and let their stuff stand, then I remain unassailed and am accorded favor and honor, etc. So to keep my self-esteem I might also nevertheless preach the gospel along with all that. Yet I would all the same have become unsalty salt. For there I allow the people to be stuck in their own delusions and fleshly minds. Then they go to the devil and I in front of them.

So this office always possesses a lot of tribulation and hindrance, on the right and the left. One might like to clam up and be afraid to meet trouble and danger or persecution in fear because he wants to keep honor, goods and food. So we are weakened by this. We are foul and sulky thereafter. We readily let ourselves by driven to this and become weary as soon as we see that things will not turn out as we'd like it. We rationalize that our silence will be forgiven and that if we spoke, the people would only despise it and become more annoyed, the more we chastise them, anyway.

So we must be prepared against this and consider only Christ's command, who established this office and desires that we open our mouth briskly and chastise what is to be chastised, not considering our danger, hardship or need of food, or other people, evil and persecution. This comforts us. He has made us his salt and will still preserve us. He calls us comforted salt, not that we let ourselves turn away from that and let ourselves be frightened if the world will not suffer it and persecutes us for it. Nor do we despair if we likewise produce nothing as we desire. For what he calls us to, we should let that happen and be satisfied and let it be according to his command. It is up to him what and how much he accomplishes through us. If the people do not wish to hear or accept it, then we are no less salt and we have accomplished our office. We can, then, with all honor and happiness stand before God's judgment and answer on account of it that we have truly spoken to everyone and hidden nothing under the chair. They then have no excuse as if they didn't know better and were not told.

But those who let themselves be silent and quiet for the sake of favor, honor, goods and so forth; they will also have to hear it said of them, "There is our preacher and he didn't tell us." And you will not be excused if you would say, "Lord, they didn't want to hear." Then the Lord will reply, "Don't you know that I commanded you that you should be salty and freely warn? Shouldn't you have feared my Word more than them?"

Altb. V, 831–832: Commentary on the Sermon on the Mount, 1532; cf. AE 21

When all their labors seem in vain, Revive their sinking hopes again;
And when success crowns what they do, Oh, keep them humble, Lord, and true
They lay their trophies at Thy feet. (*TLH* 482: 3)

Saturday

You should not imagine that I have come to undo the law or the prophets. I have not come to undo but to fulfill them.
Matthew 5:17

The Lord Christ had established the office of the apostles and had earnestly commanded them. Now he goes further and gives them examples of both salt and light so they know what they should preach. He endeavors to chastise and improve both Jewish teaching and life, false delusions and works. Though, as said, he does not exercise the high chief teaching of faith at this time, he rather first undertakes clarifying and straightening out the law rightly which was completely darkened and turned around by the pharisees and teachers of the law. So that is a necessary article. The teaching of God's commands must be pure and rightly presented.

But that is purely a biting and intolerable salt that attacks and curses these people. For they neither taught nor lived rightly and so they did not allow others to do anything that is good and right. Yet these were the best and most holy. They taught God's commands daily and exercised themselves in the holy service of God, etc. But they were not able to chastise anyone. By this he gives them reason to boldly shout him down and accuse him of undoing the law and making a nothing of what God had nevertheless commanded, etc. Just as the pope and his bunch shout about us and scold us as heretics who forbid good works. He had already predicted that he would be accused of this fault and his teaching would be interpreted in that way. So he confronts this accusation by this forward and preface that it is not his intention to do away with the law. He came to teach and present it rightly against those who weaken the law.

This preface was good and necessary because of the high boasting they [the scribes and pharisees] did over the excellent appearance that they put on. Such appearances greatly encouraged them to believe that they alone were God's people, recipients of the prophets and the patriarchs. Anyone who understood them and chastised them must hear from that hour on, "Who are you that you alone are wise and criticize everyone as if we and our fathers have all gone astray, since we have and preach God's law?" That is what all the world cries against us. It says that we condemn the Holy Fathers and the whole church which cannot stray because they are led by the Holy Ghost, etc. But because you now criticize our teaching and life it is a sign that you condemn both the law and prophets, the fathers and the whole church.

Christ now answers this: "No, I truly do not wish to undo either the law or the prophets, but rather to stop and penetrate it harder and better than you do; so rigidly, in fact, that heaven and earth would sooner pass away before I would let one dot of the smallest letter of it pass away and thus take away its purpose or effect. Whoever despises the least law or teaches differently should become the least in the heavenly kingdom, even if he keep all the rest of it. So we are one in this article [he says]. One should teach Moses and the prophets exactly and keep it. But while we both want to do and to teach the law (as also now both the papacy and all the other parties and we boast that we all call upon one and the same Scripture, one gospel, God's Word), the reason that this is done, is to become sure how that part of the Scripture of God's law rightly leads, what it means and what it doesn't. Over this we quarrel. Here I must be salty and chastise. The Jews with their additions have twisted and ruined the law. I have come to set it straight. That's also why we have to assail the pope's teachings, who had ruined Scripture for us with their stink and filth.

But he doesn't lie that they are God's people, who have the law, the fathers and prophets. And we, likewise, do not lie or condemn Christians, Baptism, the gospel and so forth. But we duel over whether we should accept what they have anointed and allow the way they define and twist and have sullied the pure teaching with their nastiness and maggots, yes, with the devilish additions of their hoods, tonsures, indulgences, votives, sacrifice of the mass, etc., to be right. There we must also chastize and work lest we bless such stink and make it seem pure. So it is found that they are still the ones who undo the law and Scripture and make it a nothing. They adorn themselves with the beautiful names of Scripture, gospel, Christian Church and so on. Under this appearance their maggots have carried on and ruined things, for they are useless. After that, they cry out against us as if we attack the Christian Church, holy fathers, good works, etc.

Thus he says now, "I have not come to undo the law, but to fulfill it." That is, "I will not bring another or a new law, but the Scripture itself, which you have, use and sully. I handle it so that you know how one should use it." So the gospel of the preaching of Christ does not bring a new teaching that lays aside or changes the law. As St. Paul also says, this was previously promised in the Scripture and through the prophets. So we take what we have also from the Scripture, Baptism, Sacrament, and so forth, which they also have. We want to bring nothing new or better. We only do this so what is preached and handled is done rightly. We remove what does not agree with it.

Altb. V, 836: Commentary on the Sermon on the Mount, 1532; cf. AE 21

The Law commands and makes us know What duties to our God we owe:
But 'tis the Gospel must reveal Where lies our strength to do His will. (*TLH* 289: 2)

Week of Trinity XV

Sunday

*No one can serve two masters. Either he will hate the one
and love the other or he will cling to one and despise the
other. You cannot serve God and mammon. Matthew 6:24*

If you want to be God's servant, he's saying, then you cannot
serve money. It is called having "two masters" when those two are
against each other and not when they reign jointly. There are not two
opposing masters when I serve the prince or kaiser and also serve
God. For they are ordered in harmony with each other. When I obey
the lower one I also then obey the higher one. It is just as when a
father sends a servant to his wife or children and he commands the
servant what to do through them. There are not many lords but only
one lord of all. Everything is from that one. But it is called two lords
when they are against one another and they give contrary commands,
as, for example, God and the devil do. God says, "You shall not
covet money or have another god." But the devil says to the
contrary, "You surely may love money and serve mammon." This
is taught by human reason itself. One cannot bear to serve two lords
that are not in agreement with equal dedication. The world can do it
masterfully, as it's called in German, "hitting the tree with both sides
of the axe" or "one mouth blowing hot and cold," as when a
nobleman serves a prince and takes gold from him but then betrays
him and sells him out to another. Then he also takes gold from him
[his new master] and looks around to go where the fairest wind
blows, seeing where it is raining or where the sun shines. Then he
sells them both out and betrays them. But after that there is no
service. Reason dictates that that person is a traitor and a scoundrel.
How would you feel if you had a servant who took goods and wages
from you and considered another lord out of one eye and did nothing
to look out for your needs, but if evil fortune would come today or
tomorrow, he would jump aside and let you sit there?

So it is said rightly that whoever is a good servant with faithful
service must not cling to two masters but should rather say, "I live on
the master's bread whom I will serve as long as I am with him. I will act
in his best interests and turn to no other." But when the servant wants to
carry out some plan and steal something, then he belongs to the
hangman. For you should slaughter the hens who do nothing but eat, not
those who lay eggs. This is what the Jews did, thinking God should
regard them as great saints. They were satisfied with themselves when

they slaughtered and sacrificed their calves and cows in the temple even as they, at the same time, also coveted money where they even set up their shops in the temple and set up money exchange stations so that one had to quickly agree [to their deals] or else no one would leave there with an animal to sacrifice. Against such as these, Christ now establishes this passage so that no one think he can serve both God and mammon. It is impossible to remain his servant as he establishes [service] if you also want to covet money. So God's service is that one cling only to his Word and establish everything by that. Now whoever wants to live according to that and remain with it must repeat [this passage] immediately to mammon. For it is sure that as soon as a teacher or pastor becomes greedy, there is no use for him any longer and he also preaches, then, nothing good. Then he must become timid and cannot chastise anyone. He lets their donations stop his mouth. He lets the people do what they want. He won't do anything that will make anyone angry, especially anyone that is great and powerful. So he lets his service and office lapse which requires him to chastise the wicked. So also when a mayor or judge or anyone who has an office should remain in his position he should see that he does his duty. He should not think how rich he can become and that he gets his meals from it. But if he is mammon's servant then he lets himself be bribed with presents so that he is blinded and no longer sees how the people live. So he thinks, "Shall I punish these or those?" The ones he punishes are his enemies. He wants to leave his friends alone, etc. If he already had a lucrative service and sits in the office that God had ordained and given, and he cannot carry it out and enforce it, mammon has overcome his heart.

This is the condition of all the world. It (thinks it) is a paltry danger [to pursue] mammon. It makes it a beautiful sweet thought that you can also serve God. This is a scandalous plague by which the devil would blind man so that he no longer takes his Office and service honestly and is completely paralyzed by greed. It only happens because he regrets that people don't honor him and give him gifts.

This is why Christ established this strong reason not to entertain such thoughts and thus beat at the wind so weakly. But rather know that whoever bears his Office for the sake of money or food, honor or favor as he might wish to, God will not acknowledge him as his servant, but as his enemy.

Erl. 43, 231-232: Commentary on the Sermon on the Mount, 1532; cf. AE 21

Thou art mine; I love and own Thee. Light of Joy, Ne'er shall I
From my heart dethrone Thee. Savior, let me soon behold Thee
Face to face, — May Thy grace Evermore enfold me! (*TLH* 523: 8)

Monday

*All born of God overcome the world: And our faith is the
victor which has overcome the world. 1 John 5:4*

This is the sure sign of a true Christian. By this he knows that
he is born of God and is different from the false children who only
retain the froth (or foam) of the Word of God, but never experience
the power of it. Such a one is only a "moon child [16]" where there is
no true godly life and power. There is no one who is called "born of
God" who yet remains in the old dead worldly ways and follows the
devil's favor, lying and living in sins, as you once did. Rather, the
Christian resists the devil and his whole kingdom. Since they do not
overcome the world but let the world overcome them, they may want
to boast about faith and Christ but their own deeds witness against
them that they are not God's child. Considering the most basic and
greatest example, if you brag about being God's child and yet live in
hypocrisy, immorality and so forth, you are already overcome by the
devil and torn out of God's kingdom. If you are a greedy person and
want to do your neighbor evil by profiteering, exchanging money,
false goods and by unrighteous mammon, then you are surely the
devil's servant and prisoner. Even among the noble and high-minded
folk who should understand the devil's roguery and malice, even
there, he compels people with false teaching and forces them to
idolatry, false faith, presumption, doubt, blasphemy before God, etc.
You, who have given way to the devil and let yourself be seduced,
what will it help you to brag about the gospel and faith when you
have not yet rightly seized hold of God's Word and have not rightly
confessed God in Christ, but rather have proceeded in error and false
conceit begun and conceived by the devil?

Since this is not possible for poor human wisdom and will, nor
[do they have] the power or might to overcome and conquer such an
excellent enemy, a Christian must be prepared, as I have said, to
know how to be on guard for the devil's knavery and fraud and to
also withstand him. That is why he calls such a person "born of
God." He must be different than a heathen or a clever worldly
person so that he comes to rightly know God's Word and seizes hold
of it through faith and he practices and uses that faith in those battles
as his armor and defense. In that way, he can be firm against the

---

[16]Refers to a child born malformed or sickly with poor chances of
living.

devil and the world and retain the victory, for he has the necessary power and might by it. That [power and might] is God's Word and faith. These motivate him from then on and he cannot be overcome because he remains in them.

So John also says, following this text, "Since we are God's children, we keep his commands and his commands are not difficult. So whoever is born of God has overcome the world," and so forth. This birth is so strong that the devil, the world and everything is overcome. It's like a child born into the world without defect and whole, who is surely able to overcome a small, contagious illness. But if it is born amiss and sickly, or a "moon child," he perishes and is ruined by himself. For example, if I have faith and am born of God, then I will not afflict myself with lewdness and whoring nor shame someone else's child or spouse. The new birth already teaches me that I should not so shamefully throw away and willingly forsake my treasure which I have in Christ and the Holy Ghost who lives in me. That faith that he is and remains with me will not allow me to act against my conscience and God's Word and will. So when avarice tempts me to cheat and overcharge my neighbor or to close my hand to him when I should help him and give to him, then, if I am a Christian and have begun anew, my faith arouses itself unto him and reminds me, "Should I do my brother evil or let him suffer need and not mediate when I know that Christ has given his body and blood to me?" How can such [thoughts] come to a Christian heart that he believe that he has received an unspeakable eternal treasure through God's Son, and then leave its neighbor in weak need when he could just as well help him? Much less will he do him harm or injustice for the sake of some paltry scandalous gain. Rather he would much more think, "If I have become God's child and an heir of heaven, then all the world's goods should be much too little [compared to that] for me. Why should I cheat someone for the sake of a little money?"

Erl. 8, 219-221: Sermon on the Sunday after Easter, 1 John 5:4-10

Why should cross and trial grieve me? Christ is near with His cheer;
Never will He leave me. Who can rob me of the heaven
That God's Son for my own To my faith hath given. (*TLH* 523: 1)

Tuesday

The Lord said to my Lord, sit at my right hand till I lay your enemies at your feet as a footstool. Psalm 110:1

The Scripture teaches us that God's right hand is not in a particular place as where a body must or should be located as on a golden throne. Rather, it is the almighty power of God which can both be no place and yet must be in all places at the same time. For if it were in various places then it must be ascertainably and conclusively there just as everyone else who occupies a place must be discretely and conclusively there. But the divine might cannot and would not be so conclusive and measurable. For it is undetectable and immeasurable, outside and over everything that is or could be.

So it [the right hand] in actuality and by its nature must be in all places, even in the smallest leaf. The reason is that it is God who makes, works and contains all things through his almighty power and right hand as our faith informs us. For he doesn't send officials or angels when he wants to make or preserve something. All of that is his own work by his divine power. But if he makes and preserves, then he himself must be the one who makes and preserves both the inward and the most outward parts.

So God must be in each creature; in their outsides, in their insides, round and round, through and through, under and over, front and back. So nothing outside or inside of all creatures can exist that doesn't have God himself with his power. For he is the one who makes the skin. He is also the one who makes the bones. He is the one who makes the hair on the head. He is also the one who makes the marrow in the bone. He is the one who makes every little part of the hair. He is the one who makes every little part of the marrow. He must make everything both part and whole. His hand, which makes them must also be there. It cannot be absent.

The Scriptures mightily run this way in Isaiah 66:2 from Genesis 1:1, "Hath my hand not made all this?" Psalm 139:7-8, "Where can I hide before your Spirit? Where will I flee from your face? If I go heavenward, you are there. If I make my bed in hell you are also around me. If I took wings to the sunrise and sat at the ocean's end then your hand would still hold me."

What more shall I say? The Scriptures attribute all God's wonders and works to his right hand, as in Acts 4:10, "Christ is raised to the right hand of God." Psalm 118:15, 16, "Thy right hand, oh God, works wonders. The right hand of God raised me" and so forth. Paul says in Acts 17:27-28, "God is not far from any of us. For in him we live and move and have our being." And Romans 11:36, "From him and through him and upon him are all things." And Jeremiah 23:23-24, "Am I a God who is near and not a God who is far off? Do I not fill heaven and earth?" Isaiah 66:1, "Heaven is my throne and earth is my footstool." He does not say, "A piece of heaven is my throne. A piece or place on earth is my footstool."

But rather "my throne is where and what heaven is." Is heaven over, under or next to the earth? What or where earth is, whether it is the bottom of the sea, in death's grave or in the middle of the earth, there is my footstool. Now tell me, where is his head, arm, breast, body, that he fills the earth with his feet and fills heaven with his legs? Far, far he rules over and outside the world, over heaven and earth.

What does Isaiah want to say with this verse? Is he saying, as St. Hillary also commented on this, that God is by nature present at all extremes in and through all creatures in all their parts and places, and that the world is full of God who fills it without being perceived or measurable but also at the same time outside and over all creatures? These are all thoroughly imperceptible things to everyone. But it is yet an article of our faith, revealed brightly and mightily in all the Scriptures.

Erl. 30, 58–60: That the Words of Christ "This is my Body" Still Stand Fast Against the Enthusiasts, 1527 cf. AE 37

Blind unbelief is sure to err And scan His work in vain;
God is His own Interpreter, And He will make it plain. (*TLH* 514: 6)

Wednesday

And no one goes up to heaven, but he who came down from heaven, namely, the Son of Man, who is in heaven. John 3:13

It is our faith that our Lord Jesus Christ is substantially, naturally, truly God as the Scripture teaches us. The Godhead dwells bodily in him, completely and throughout, as St. Paul says in Colossians 2:9. Apart from Christ there is no God or Godhead as he says himself in John 14:9, "Philip, whoever sees me sees the Father. Do you not believe that the Father is in me and I in him?" Well then! Christ goes to earth and the whole Godhead is personally and substantially in him on earth.

Now I weigh this point: How can it be true both that God is in Christ upon the earth personally, actually, substantially in his mother's body, also in the crib, in the temple, in the dessert, in cities, in houses, garden, field, on the cross, in the grave and so forth, and yet also at the same time he is in heaven and with the Father? Is it not true and irrefutable, according to our faith that the Godhead is itself in Christ substantially, personally and actually in various places and yet in heaven with the Father at the same time?

It follows from that, that he is in the same way possessing heaven and earth substantially and personally and filling all things with his own nature and majesty according to the Scripture, Jeremiah 23:23, 24, "I fill heaven and earth and I am a God who is near." and Psalm 139:7, "Where will I flee before your face?"

Even so, Christ, God's Son, would be received in his mother's body and become a man. By his freedom, he must be there already, substantially and personally in the virgin's body. He drew the human nature to himself. For the Godhead is immoveable in itself and does not travel from one place to another as do creatures. So he did not climb down to there from heaven as with a ladder nor has he need to climb up to it as with a rope. Rather, he was already there in the virgin's body, substantially and personally, just as he was also at all the boundaries of the universe according to his divine nature, attribute and power. If he were now in one place, as in the virgin's body, and at the same time with the Father, as our faith compels, then he is also surely at all the ends of the universe. There can be no possible reason why he should be in the virgin's body and that it were not possible also to be at all the ends of the universe.

Yet Christ is somewhat different, higher and greater than all the other creatures. In him God is not only actually and substantially present, as in all the others, but he also dwells bodily in him. So that one person IS God and man. Again, I can say of all creatures that there is God or God is [present] in him. But Christ is also God himself. If someone were to slay a man he could well be called the murderer of a thing that is God's and in which God is. But whoever slays Christ, who is God's Son, has slain God and the Lord of glory himself. For God is not only in him but also dwells in him so that God and man become one person. That is the high work and wonder of God that makes a fool of all human reason and which faith alone must hold, else all is lost.

Therefore, we speak now only of the primary thing: how God is himself, personally, in all things. Without that, God would not even have desired man and would not have become a person comprised of deity and humanity. So he had need to be (as said) there previously in his mother's body, even as he is himself in the Godhead. Oh Lord God, where are those who believe all this? What will happen when reason comes here with it's own heretical thoughts? The Sacraments of the enthusiasts will then become a costly thing against this [right teaching]. So be it! God yet remains and also, then, what belongs to him.

Erl. 30, 62–64: That the Words of Christ "This is my Body" Still Stand Fast Against the Enthusiasts, 1527, cf. AE 37

The Word becomes incarnate And yet remains on high.
And cherubim sing anthems To shepherds from the sky.
Repeat the hymn again, "To God on high be glory
And peace on earth to men." *(TLH* 76: 2)

Thursday

Your Word is nothing but truth. Also the judgments of your
righteousness endure eternally. Psalm 119:160

The church must teach merely God's Word, or truth, and no
error or lies. How could it be otherwise? Since God's mouth is the
mouth of the church and again, God cannot lie, so also the church
cannot lie.

While it is surely true when speaking of life, that the holy
church is not without sins as she acknowledges in the Lord's Prayer,
"Forgive us our trespasses," and 1 John 1:8, "If we say that we have
no sin, we lie and make God a liar," since God sees us as altogether
sinners, Romans 3:23; Psalm 14:4; Psalm 57:7. But the teaching
must neither be sinful nor accusable. That does not belong in the
Lord's Prayer where we say, "Forgive us our trespasses." For the
teaching is not our doing but rather God's own Word, which cannot
sin or do wrong. So a preacher must not pray the Lord's Prayer nor
seek forgiveness of sins when he has preached, if he is a true
preacher, but must rather say and give praise with Jeremiah.
Jeremiah 17:16, "Lord, you know that what has proceeded from my
mouth is right and acceptable to you." Yes, with St. Paul, all the
apostles and prophets confidently say, *"Haec Dixit Dominus,"* this
God himself has said. And again, "I have become an apostle and
prophet of Jesus Christ in this preaching." Here it is not needed, yes,
it is not good to petition for forgiveness of sins as if it were not
rightly taught. For it is God's Word and not mine. So God neither
should nor can forgive me, but rather confirm, praise, crown and
say, "You have rightly taught, so I have spoken through you and the
Word is mine." Who cannot so boast of his preaching should forgo
preaching. For he surely lies and blasphemes God.

If the Word should be sinful or wrong how will or can the life
that follows it be set right? There the blind would definitely be
leading the blind and both would fall into a ditch (Matthew 15:14).
If the rule and square are false or bent, how will or can even a
master carpenter work with them? Also here, the life can be and
surely is sinful and unrighteous, yes, it is unfortunately sinful without
exception. But the teaching must be straight as a plumb line and

surely without sin. Therefore, nothing must be preached in the church except only that which is definite, pure and at one with God's Word. Where that fails there is no more church but the devil's school, just as a good wife (as the prophets always use as example) must not listen to others rather than her husband's words and requests in the house. If she hears another's voice which does not belong to her husband then she is surely a whore.

Now this is all that has been said: That the church must only teach God's Word and be sure of it. For through that Word the ground and pillar of truth is given and upon this rock the church is built and is called holy and innocent. That is, as they say rightly so well: The church cannot err, for God's Word which she teaches cannot err. But what else is taught or when it is doubtful that what is taught is indeed God's Word, that cannot be teaching of the church but rather must be teaching of the devil, lies and blasphemy. For the devil cannot say, "Thus says the Lord," (For he is a liar and the father of lies). But rather, as Christ says in John 8:44, "*ex propriis,*" from out of himself the devil must teach what is a lie. So must all of the devil's children, without God's Word, speak from out of themselves, that is, lie.

Erl. 26, 34–36: Against Hanswurst, 1541; cf. AE 41

God's Word is our great heritage And shall be ours forever;
To spread its light from age to age Shall be our chief endeavor.
Through life it guides our way, In death it is our stay.
Lord, grant, while worlds endure, We keep its teachings pure
Throughout all generations. (*TLH* 283: 1)

Friday

You are now clean for the sake of the Word that I have spoken to you. John 15:3

Now, friend, behold what a wondrous thing this is. We, who teach God's Word securely are also weak and dull because of great humility. We don't like to brag that we are God's church, his witnesses, servants, preachers and that God surely speaks through us. Yet we are surely all those things for we definitely have and teach his Word. Such humility follows from our earnest belief that God's Word is such a glorious, majestic thing that we acknowledge we are altogether unworthy that such a great matter should be spoken and performed through us, who still live in the flesh and blood. Yet our opponents, the devil, papists, sects and all the world, who are happy and unfearing, are boldly allowed to say out of their great holiness, "Here is God. We are God's church, prophets and apostles," even though they have made altogether false prophecies so that even Hanswurst[17] is allowed to brag that he is a Christian prince. But humility and fear in God's Word is always the true sign of the church's presence. Thirst and outrage in human devotion are the true signs of the devil. One must also mark this as steadfast in the pope's filthy affairs.

This [passage] is said about the doctrine, which must be pure and clear. It is dear, blessed, holy and one with God's Word, without addition. But the life that should daily be ordered, purified and sanctified according to the doctrine is not yet completely pure or holy as long as this maggot-sack, flesh and blood, lives. Yet while that life is under the work of purification, or sanctification, it always receives a savior through the [good] Samaritan [Jesus], and does not ruin itself further evermore with uncleanness. By grace that life is preserved unto good. It is gifted and forgiven and must be called pure for the sake of the Words by which it receives holiness and purity. So by this the Holy Christian Church does not become a whore, or unholy, as long as she is steadfast and remains upon the pure Word (that makes her holy). You are pure (says Christ in John 15:3) not because of you but rather because of the Word that I have spoken to you.

So the holiness of the Word and purity of the doctrine are so powerful and true that even if also Judas, Caiphas, Pilate, the Pope, Hanswurst or even the devil himself should preach the same or rightly baptize (without addition, pure and true), then the true pure Word, the true Holy Baptism would be received. For there must always be hypocrites and false Christians in the church and a Judas under the apostleship. But if the doctrine is impure so that it is not or is without God's Word then you have forgotten the evil fact that even if St. Peter or an angel of light were to preach it everything would be accursed (Galatians 1:8). So false teachers and baptizers or masters of the sacrament cannot be or remain in the church, as Psalm 1:5 says. For these same people do not only act against the Christian life, with which the church must put up, especially when that life is hidden, but they also act against the doctrine, which must publicly illuminate and shine, so that life is set right by it.

Erl. 26, 36–38: Against Hanswurst, 1541; cf. AE 41

---

[17]The name given by Luther to Duke Henry who opposed the Reformation through the assumption that the church's action must be right because it is the church. Such question begging is rewarded with the name *Hanswurst*, a carnival character of the time who went about with a large sausage around the neck in clown attire.

Elect from every nation, Yet one o'er all the earth. Her charter of salvation one Lord, one faith, one birth. One holy name she blesses Partakes one holy food, And to one hope she presses, With every grace endued.	The Church shall never perish! Her dear Lord, to defend, To guide, sustain, and cherish, Is with her to the end. Tho' there be those that hate her, False sons within her pale, Against both foe and traitor She ever shall prevail. (*TLH* 473: 2–3)

Saturday

In truth I say to you, what you would bind on earth will also be bound in heaven and what you would loose on earth shall also be loosed in heaven. Matthew 18:18

Mark this well. Hold it firm that the key is not only given to St. Peter, much less to the pope following St. Peter. For although the Lord speaks only with Peter, yet Peter stands there not as a person but in the place and person of all the disciples with whom Christ began to speak and to catechize. This is how all the teachers before the papacy of Kaiser Phocas established, understood, taught and held it in the whole of Christianity. In our day it is still held in the Eastern Church. So! What need is there for many Words? Light cannot be darkness. In Matthew 18:18, Christ does not speak only with St. Peter but with all the disciples: "In truth I say to you, what you would bind on earth will also be bound in heaven and what you would loose on earth shall also be loosed in heaven." Those are the Words of binding and loosing that he spoke above with St. Peter. If no announcement of the keys appears here, yet it is the office of the keys which is mightily expressed above in Matthew 16:19. Thereafter he spoke harshly of sinners that do not want to hear. He says, "Such you should consider as a heathen and a publican," and later, "In truth I say to you, what you would bind . . .", Matthew 18:17.

Yet it is truly more, as he says through 19:20, "Where two of you agree for what you would pray, that shall proceed to you from my Father in heaven. For where two or three are gathered in my name, there I am in the midst of them." Here we discover that even two or three gathered in Christ's name have all the power of St. Peter and the apostles. So the Lord is there, himself, as he says also in John 14:23, "Who loves me will keep my Words and my Father will love him and we will come to him and make our dwelling with him." Thereafter a person who has believed in Christ encounters a great deal of resistance as with Paphonitus at the council of Nicea and as Israel's kings, priests and people resisted the prophets. God will shortly loose himself from the multitude, [along with] the greatness, the height, the might and what belongs personally to him but is claimed by these people. He will only be by those who love and hold his Word, should they be as ordinary as stable boys. What does God say of high, great, mighty lords? That he alone is the greatest, highest and mightiest Lord.

If now the pope can stand firmly and proudly, which he cannot, upon Matthew 16, so we stand opposing him much more proudly and firmly upon Matthew 18. For it is not a different Christ who speaks with Peter in Matthew 16 and with other disciples in Matthew 18, speaking and giving the same Words and power to bind and loose sins. So the pope leads with his St. Peter binding and loosing what he can. We would regard the other apostles' power to bind and loose the same as St. Peter, even if there were a hundred thousand St. Peters or only one Peter and if all the world were popes so that an angel of heaven stood by them. For here we have the Lord himself who is over all angels and creatures. He says, "You all have the same power, keys and offices; even two poor Christians alone gathered in Christ's name." The pope and every devil should not make the Lord a fool, liar or a drunkard to us. Rather we would tread the pope under foot and say that he is a desperate liar, blasphemer and an idolatrous devil. He has absconded with the keys alone to himself under the name of St. Peter, though Christ has given them in common to all alike. He would make the Lord a liar with Matthew 16. Surely we must praise that!

But in John 20:21-23 the Lord doesn't just speak to St. Peter, but to all the apostles or disciples, "Just as the Father sent me, so I send you." Then he breathed on them (not St. Peter alone) and said to them, "Receive the Holy Ghost. Whose sins you forgive, they are forgiven and whosesoever's you retain, they are retained." I would like to hear what the pope's donkey says against that. Even if he had a thousand supremely foolish tongues, they must here be altogether put to shame. For the Words of the Lord are clear, "As my Father sent me, so I send you." You all. You all. Not just Peter alone. That is, what I preached by my Father's command and that he has built from me as a rock, even the same preaching, and no other should you preach and build. You shall all have the same might and have the keys to forgive and retain sins. So these are even the same Words of binding and loosing that he speaks concerning the keys to Peter. This is the Lord himself who speaks these things. Therefore, we ask nothing after what the pope's donkey in opposition rages in his filth.

Erl. 26, 165-167: Against the Roman Papacy Established by the Devil, 1545

We are God's house of living stones, Builded for His habitation;
He through baptismal grace us owns Heirs of His wondrous salvation.
Were we but two His name to tell, Yet He would deign with us to dwell,
With all His grace and His favor. (*TLH* 467: 3)

Week of Trinity XVI

Sunday

Jesus came and touched the coffin and the bearers stopped. And he said, "Son, I say to you, arise." And the dead man sat up and began to speak. And he gave him to his mother. Luke 7:14,15

From today's gospel about this widow, we shall learn the great power that God will work towards us through Christ on the last day when he will with one Word draw all people out of death and make the believers eternally holy. This will happen in the blinking of an eye so that we do not doubt at all that he has both the power and ability to do it, as he here shows, and he [also] gladly desires to do it. For here the example is presented. The widow's son is dead and has lost his hearing and all senses. But as soon as Christ speaks to him, he hears. That is surely a strange wonderful story. The one who doesn't hear, hears! The one who doesn't live, he lives. And nothing more happened but Christ opened his mouth and told him to arise. That single Word is so mighty that death must give way and life come again.

But now who believes that Christ can so easily snatch us from death and bring us to life? And we see here that he gladly wants to do that. No one asks him to do it. The poor widow's need lamented to him and he approaches unasked and makes her son alive again. Therefore, we should receive this example and not be frightened by death but rather [we receive] the Lord Christ. For this is also done for our sakes. With this he will say to us all, "I know all too well that death frightens you but don't be afraid. Let not your heart be terrified. But instead learn, so that you not only experience what you feel, so that you become afraid, but look instead to me and see what I can do and what I gladly do, namely, I can just as easily awaken you from death as you awaken someone out of their bed and their sleep. And I am ready and willing to do it. Neither my desire nor my skill and ability will fail."

So it must also be that those in the churchyard and lying under the earth sleep much lighter than we do in our beds. For you often sleep so soundly that someone can call to you ten times before you hear them once. But the dead hear a single Word from Christ and wake up as you see here of this boy and in John 11 of Lazarus.

Therefore, death is not called death before our Lord God. For us it is called, and is, a death when we die. But before God it is only a light sleep which could not be lighter.

That is how our Lord Christ would have us think so that we are not terrified if pestilence and death itself approach. Rather, we learn to say, "What can you do, death, even when you are at your worst? You have false teeth which you show to frighten me so that I do not die gladly. But I will not only regard what you do and how you draw your sword like an executioner. Rather, I will think and see what our Lord God can add to it and what he wants to add to it when you have slain me. Namely, he is concerned for me and doesn't ask about your rage and murder but he says, 'Death, I will be your death. Hell, I will be your pestilence. If you can slay my Christian I can still slay you and bring them to life again.' "

That is the comfort which Christ offers in today's gospel. Even if the Christian dies he is not dead. Rather, he sleeps and so lightly that Christ can wake him with one finger. This robs death of its little glory since even if it is at its worst it can do and accomplish nothing more than does lying in a human sleep. For Christ wakes him again from sleep with a single word as he says in John 5, "The hour is coming in which all who are in the grave will hear the voice of the Son of Man and will come out, those who have done good unto the resurrection of life, those who have done evil to the resurrection of judgment."

So Christians have comfort. The Turks and Jews do not have it and our papists also do not have it. They surely know that they will die and that the judgment and hell are approaching. But what do they do? They do not set their heart and hope upon Christ but rather they run away from him with their prayer, masses, indulgences, fasting, and the rest. And they regard Christ as nothing but a judge that is only there to curse and condemn. That is the terrible devil who makes the Christian more evil than death itself. Therefore, they must fear the last day and have a dull unbelieving heart.

Christians do not do that. They know well that on the last day Christ will judge the unbelievers who do not want to receive the Word or believe it. But then they make a distinction and say, "I am baptized and believe on the Lord Jesus Christ. He died for my sins and through his resurrection has won for me righteousness and eternal life. Then what will I fear? He is not my enemy but rather my friend and mediator with the Father. Therefore, even if that last day breaks in or I have already died, that is not important. My Lord Jesus Christ sees how death slays me for a little while. And when death thinks that I am done for and I have completely died, yet I only sleep and sleep so sweetly and lightly that even before the Lord Christ can open his mouth, I hear it and rise to everlasting life."

Hauspost. N.Y. Ausg. 435–436: Sermon on Trinity 16, Luke 7:11-17

Now I will cling forever To Christ, my Savior true;
My Lord will leave me never, Whate'er He passeth through.
He rends Death's iron chain, He breaks through sin and pain,
He shatters hell's dark thrall, I follow Him through all. (*TLH* 192: 6)

Monday

*Just as death came by one man so through one man comes
the resurrection from the dead. 1 Corinthians 15:21*

That is, just as Adam is the beginning and first-born, through whom we all must die as he died, so Christ is the first-born through whom we all shall rise again to new life as he was first raised. So these are the two people and two pictures which the Scriptures set against each other. God has ordained that just as through one man death has gone over all men, and still does, so through one the resurrection from death will come. Therefore, Adam is an image of Christ (as he says in Romans 5:14, where he treats and portrays them both more fully), yet in a way that this image (Christ) is such a much better and different sort of thing, yes, even accomplishing the opposite of what his counterpart, Adam, had done. For everyone has inherited nothing but death in common with all mankind so that both he and we must remain in it and no one can escape it. But should there be help, then God had to let another man come anew who might bring us out of death again to life.

So now St. Paul sets these two images next to each other and by this wants to say that through one man, who is named Adam, so much is accomplished that mankind must die, both he and all of us together. Even if we have not committed the transgression nor have been aware of it but only because we are born of him, we come into sinfulness and death (although after the fall and when we are born they are no longer foreign sins but rather become our own). That is a lamentable affair and a terrifying, horrible judgment of God. It would be even more horrifying if we should forever remain in death. But now God has established another man against this who is named Christ so that just as we, for the sake of another [that is Adam], apart from our own guilt, die, so on the other hand for the sake of Christ, apart from our service, we will live. As we must in Adam recompense it all only because we are his offspring, or his flesh and blood, so we also benefit in Christ alone. He is our head and a great gift and grace, so that we have nothing to boast about concerning our works and service as our monks and false saints teach. Then how could we, who are born in sin and belong to death, desire to receive

[this] also through our [monks] hoods or other works to work our way from sinfulness and death, since we are by flesh and blood from Adam? Should we who, on this account, go on living from out of straw and ashes be brighter and more beautiful than the sun and all creatures? That cannot be by human power or ability nor by all creation, also not by the angels in heaven but rather only by God himself. He must be another man who earns such things and brings them near, who is named Christ, God's Son, and Lord of sin and death, devil and all things, as St. Paul will say of him later. He is the one whom this article treats and it began with him and is given us. We also come to it through him so that we, through baptism, are enlivened by him and we are called and implanted in this article. So we are resurrected and will live through the same power and attribute by which he is resurrected and lives.

Because such things are not complete in us, since we come into both death and eternal life, we have an even stronger comfort and hope because we will have life through Christ, just as surely as we now have and feel the sins and death from Adam. For even if it were in our ability and it were told us that we could earn and receive life from sins and death through our own actions, yet we could have no peace our whole life and we would have to ceaselessly plague ourselves and be concerned with works. Even if we had been martyred to death with this and one man among all the world could be brought in this way to holiness, yet we could not be safe and sure that we had done enough and straightened so much out that God must be satisfied with it. Therefore, God has worked grace for us and staked it to one man who has earned and straightened out everything already without us and before us so that it is certain for us and cannot fail. Therefore, we also become, as far as we are concerned, completely guiltless, and it doesn't help us what we do or can do in addition to it. We receive grace and resurrection even when we do and should do good works in the same way that we also are without fault even though we are sinners and must die. For we have done nothing to add to what happened when he ate the apple in the fall, even if we also ourselves commit sins after it. And everything remains this way that concerns sins and righteousness, death and life, only in the two men, as he now describes further.

Altb. VI, 287-288: Lectures on 1 Corinthians 15, 1534; cf. AE 28

Jesus lives! And thus, my soul, Life eternal waits for thee;
Joined to Him, the living Head, Where He is, thou, too, shalt be;
With Himself, at His right hand, Victor over death shall stand. (*TLH* 188: 4)

Tuesday

*Thereafter [comes] the end when he will deliver the
kingdom of God to the Father, when he will abolish all
dominion, and all authority and power. 1 Corinthians 15:24*

What is this? The Scriptures still say unanimously that he should
remain king in eternity and his kingdom will have no end. How does this
fit with his saying he will give his kingdom over and place himself under
the Father and lay his crown, scepter and everything that is his before
him? Answer: He speaks of the kingdom of Christ now on earth which
is a kingdom of faith in which he rules through his Word, not in a visible
public manner but rather as one sees the sun through the clouds where
one surely sees the light, if not the sun itself. But when the clouds are
parted, you see together both the light and the sun all at once. So now
Christ reigns indivisibly with the Father and it is a single kingdom. The
only difference is that it is now dark and hidden, or veiled and covered
up, grasped completely in faith and in the Word because one can see no
more of it than Baptism and the Sacrament nor hear anything of it but by
the external Word which is all of his power and might, through which
he reigns and accomplishes everything.

We also already would like to see him reign in the way of kaisers
or kings with external splendor and might and by putting his foot down
on the evil ones but he will not do that now. Rather, he desires to rule
secretly and invisibly in our hearts through his Word alone and through
the same defend and preserve us under our weakness against the world's
power and might. This kingdom is here on earth just as it will be
hereafter in heaven except that it is now hidden and not before our eyes.
Just as a dollar in a purse or pocket is a true dollar and remains so if I
pull it out and have it in my hand except it is no longer hidden, so he
will draw out and publicly display before the eyes of all the world the
treasure that is now hidden. So we know nothing more about it than
what we hear and believe. Yet we have this same treasure no less surely,
just as a seller is as sure of his money as if he had it in his pocket when
he has his contract signed and sealed. So here it is only encountered by
faith through the Word and Sacrament. Because of them we undoubtedly
hold that we are God's children and of the kingdom of the Lord Christ,
and he is our king, who rules and protects us against all our enemies and
helps us out of all need, even if we do not see it, but rather feel the
opposite. Sins drown us, the devil frightens and plagues us, death slays,
the world persecutes and everything overwhelms and drowns us. But that
means that you should not see it but rather believe; not grab it with the
five senses, but rather encounter it only by hearing what God's Word

tells you as long as the time of trial lasts. There Christ will make an end of this and display himself publicly in his majesty and glory. There you will see and experience what you now believe. Sins are exterminated and drowned. Death is taken away and removed from sight. The devil and the world will lay at your feet and he will be visibly with God. Everything will be clearly in sight as an unveiled treasure just as we now desire and wait for it.

That is what St. Paul means when he says that Christ will deliver the kingdom of God to the Father. That is, he will put aside faith and the hidden manner and present his own [people] before God the Father and so publicly place us into the kingdom that he has brought about, as now he daily contends that we will see him without cover and dark Word in the clearest manner. And then he will not call it a kingdom of faith but of sight and a public operation. So it is a single kingdom, both of Christ (who, for our sake has become man, that he brings about faith in him) and of God (for whoever hears Christ, hears God the Father, himself). Yet it is now actually called the Kingdom of the Lord Christ because God is now hidden in his majesty and he has given everything to Christ so that he brings us to him through his Word and Baptism. Also, he himself is hidden in Christ so that we should seek and know God nowhere but in him.

But there it will actually be called God's kingdom, after which Christ will have brought about all that he will bring about and no longer rule under our weakness and odiousness but do away with death and sins and all that is against God. And he will bring us in so that we see him with the Father in the divine majesty and he will no longer prescribe his gospel, compel Baptism and the forgiveness of sins, exhort our learning to know him, nor frighten us more with any kind of misfortune. Rather, he will be pure God, eternal righteousness, salvation and life with us in a present visible way and deliver to us all these things so that we will become as he is.

So he himself explains and clarifies it with the Words that follow there, "When he will abolish all rule and all authority and all power, etc." That is, he will make an end of everything both of the spiritual rule that is now conducted upon the earth, which is Baptism, the seat of preaching, the sacrament, keys or absolution, etc., and also of the world with its positions and offices.

Altb. VI, 292-293: Lectures on 1 Corinthians 15, 1534; cf. AE 28

Oh, joy to know that Thou, my Friend, Art Lord, Beginning without end,
   The first and Last, Eternal! And Thou at length—O glorious grace!
Wilt take me to that holy place,   The home of joys supernal.
      Amen! Amen! Come and meet me! Quickly greet me!
With deep yearning. Lord, I look for Thy returning. (*TLH* 343: 7)

Wednesday

But he must rule until all his foes lay under his feet.
1 Corinthians 15:25

Someone might like to say, "Why didn't he do that soon after his resurrection when he had already become a Lord over everything if he desires to subject everything under his feet?" St. Paul answers: It is established in Scripture that he will rule and reign beside the world authority and command through his spiritual mandate, "The LORD says to my Lord, sit at my right hand until I lay your enemies as a stool for your feet." This is our comfort and it is good for us. For he did not so quickly, for a thousand years, beat down his enemies but rather spared them until we also could come. For they are not all yet born who belong to his kingdom. "But he must reign that he bring all of the children of God together," as Scripture says in another place. Therefore, he must make his kingdom complete, not waiting for his enemies to be exterminated, but for all who belong in it to be brought in. After that he will do away with everything altogether and strike at once. In this, he allows the preaching of his Word and rules Christianity spiritually, with Word, Sacrament, faith and Spirit, under his enemies that so plague and oppress us. He preserves and defends us against this with the sure comfort that he will some day lay them completely under his feet. For through the gospel and Christianity he spiritually strikes the sects and drives the devil back, displaces the tyrants from their thrones, drowns the world's ranting and raging, takes from sins and death their power and might, etc. That is his work by which he drives and advances until the last day, except now he does it partially and selectively. But there he will at once eliminate the last straw and make an end to it all.

So we see how he places countries and people under the gospel from the beginning of Christianity until the world shakes. He has overthrown and overturned all who have set themselves against this. Here kings are displaced. There he drives away a tyrant, as he also has made this known now in our situation and will also do more. As he begins here to seek them secretly, then he will finally completely displace them, for they also bear heavy guilt because God has given them position and authority to rule over body and goods so that they should punish and force the evil, disobedient and rebellious, preserving peace and defense for the good. But they attack God himself, misusing their appointed offices as they trouble and persecute the pious Christians. They do not desire or suffer to hear the gospel and blame God as if he brought the insurrection and the destruction of lands and people. These things truly happen. But who is to blame? No one is [to blame] but themselves because they are appointed by God and their offices are laid upon them and they do not want to punish the evil. They dare to punish God's children and become hardened and unruly against God himself.

It serves them right that by their own power they have so many starts and stops, just as God in Christ stops death and the devil which also have power to catch and ensnare the sinner with their nets, but there they fall upon Christ with their nets and think, "I have devoured so many of you that I will also devour this one." Then they are stopped and burn themselves, for he is not ashamed as if he belonged in the net and it is not permitted to catch him. Therefore, they are driven back and the net is ripped so that it can nevermore hold any Christian. "For it would be impossible," (says St. Peter in Acts 2:24), "that he could be held." So it is also impossible that he or those who are his should be allowed to be held by the world, even if they have the net thrown over them and they [the world] decide to slay them. But he goes on and rips through their might and power and everything that would hold him and makes of it a torn and holey net, for he will not be frustrated and stopped by anyone. The world will trap and hold fools and scoundrels in their net, but when they want to go further and hold Christ, himself, then he would go through it like a cobweb, ripping it away so that nothing remains of it. This is what he did first with the Jews as they have retained no land or city and are so completely torn that they cannot catch a fox, yes, not even a hound. For they would not let themselves be satisfied with the power that God had given them against evil, but rather than the good one, they let Barabbas go and want to trap and kill God's Son, himself.

Altb. VI, 294-295: Lectures on 1 Corinthians 15, 1534; cf. AE 28

Whom should I give my heart's affection But Thee, who givest Thine to faith?
Thy fervent love is my protection; Lord, Thou hast loved me unto death.
My heart with Thine shall ever be One heart through-out eternity. (*TLH* 404: 4)

Thursday

Do not let yourself be seduced. Evil talk ruins good habits.
1 Corinthians 15:33

They say that Christ and Paul are nice foolish people who say that there will be another life after this one. What is wrong with so many fine people on earth, kaisers, kings, princes and rulers, learned and wise people (as there were especially in Greece), who also know so much more than these poor beggars and unlearned people? These are immediately sure in their hearts that this is silliness and think: Who knows if what they preach is true? Should I believe them when so many more learned and wise people do not believe? Who told it to them? We must put up with and become accustomed to that kind of person. Even if we preach much [about it] we still could not prevent such useless prattle and such evil poisonous mouths from running on among us just as St. Paul himself was not able to prevent it.

So that line of talk is there and it is a truly evil line of talk. But with this you are warned for the sake of God that you do not regard it even if you must hear it. Rather, you can value God's Word all the more than all of the world's talk even if it is the most wise and highest teaching as kaisers and kings [speak], as wise and learned as they want to become. For if you do not turn your ear away and if you wanted to cling to such talk then such jolts and scandals would battle you, "Who knows, it [the afterlife] probably won't be." And when the devil brings you into that [line of thinking] he has already begun to do what he had done to Adam and Eve. For what he says is evil. In that way, he locked mankind away from the Word and stole the same from their hearts so that you do not think of it or experience it and he brings other thoughts in to take its place. That is his usual game. Therefore, you must be prepared so that you recognize this attribute or stratagem and oppose such poison. And if you should entertain such talk with a single ear, then soon hold the Word against it with all your heart.

For I myself have experienced those who knock one on the head and trouble the heart when you hear these people and smart-alek wise guys speaking so surely and definitely about such matters. They mock with complete scorn as if there were nothing so definitely false so you must think later: "So who knows?" There are so many great, learned and valiant people, the world's best core group, and also the greatest number, who say and believe otherwise. Now if it were not true, no greater deception could come upon the earth. Have I not also met and seen many that have had terrible trials over whether there will be another life after this life?

See, all of this comes from such wrong, evil talk especially where there are weak and untried hearts (for I am, God be praised, so prepared against it that if God desires, all that the world prattles about will not do me any harm). Therefore, one must always be on guard and hold to God's Word through which this article is grounded and has now stood and remained for fifteen hundred years. It has already been attacked by many ways of talking and vomit but has never been swept aside or drowned while all of them with their prattle are dead and gone, so that no one speaks of them anymore, or thinks of them.

But this article remains and still stands evermore as it was preached by the dear apostles and is believed by Adam and all the fathers and saints. It shall be preached so long as the earth remains until the time comes when it will come into action and experience. We want to remain in that and not turn away from it, even if some speak of it and mock it so poisonously. But it comforts us that they are not worthy of it and we let them be as the blind and the leaders of the blind (as Christ says of the pharisees) and let them go on blithering until they must stop. They have their portion and they could not be punished in any worse way. For if they were worthy of it, then they would believe God's Word with us. Therefore, we say to them as St. Paul says to his Jews, "Since you will not hear and consider yourselves unworthy of eternal life we turn to the Gentiles." But thank God that he has given his grace to you and has called you to this understanding and made you worthy so that you would believe. And let the rest go with their mocking, devouring, and drinking and living like pigs who lay on their slop and fatten themselves until they are ready for the final slaughter.

So you can defend and battle against all kinds of scandalous poison when you say, "I want to hear what God's Word says and stay with that." For that is better than other lines of talk, as a necessary salutary Word given by God. It also remains from the beginning of the world and will remain until the end. And I would act just like a good daughter should act when she hears an unclean mouth or would be compelled to unchastity by an evil pimp. She says, "My mother has not taught me that. I would much rather follow her than any other. She would not give me bad advice." Or as a good son who will not hear what any fool wants to say to mislead him but rather opposes it: "That is not true. For my dear father or schoolmaster has taught me . . ." As such children hold to their parents' word against such poison so that they do not harm their hearts, so should a Christian hold to God's Word so that he expel such heathen and godless talk against his faith and remain with the one upon whom he is baptized and called and with whom is the entire Christian faith and life.

Altb. VI, 310–311: Lectures on 1 Corinthians 15, 1534; cf. AE 28

Defend Thy truth, O God, and stay This evil generation;
And from the error of its way Keep Thine own congregation.
The wicked everywhere abound And would Thy little flock confound;
But Thou art our Salvation. (*TLH* 260: 6)

Friday

In their jewels go the daughters of the king. The bride
stands at his right hand in pure costly gold. Psalm 45:13

The queen, his wife, he calls the bride that stands to his right in
pure costly gold. This bride is the church and the whole body,
especially as it is taken out of the synagogue and Judaism, for St.
Paul and the other apostles converted many states and peoples among
which there were princes and kings. So Sergious, the governor was
converted. But there is only one bride, namely the Church, gathered
from all these positions of kings, princes, poor people, virgins,
married people. But this is a common usage in Scripture. Christ is a
bridegroom and the congregation is called his bride, as in Ephesians
5. For he calls her through the Word of the gospel and Baptism,
adorns and leads her with his mercy, grace, forgiveness of sins. That
is what it means when he says, "She stands at his right hand."

That is a very great love and no one could be closer to the
bridegroom than the bride. So that is the greatest honor. The church is
the partaker of all the wealth that belongs to the Lord Christ and has
become one body in common with him. That which the church is, the
same also belongs to the Lord Christ, and on the other hand, what Christ
has, the same belongs to the church. What a true treasure that no man
can sufficiently express or grasp with his heart! Yet these people were
drawn into the estate of marriage from far away to where there is the all-
surpassing love between bride and bridegroom, the love and trust which
is one body, heart, thought and temperament. Between Christ and the
church is that love of the bridegroom towards his bride, the church, to
whom he bestows and gives everything that he has honestly, permanently
and eternally. Compared to this, the love of living married people is only
a figure and inkling.

Therefore, it is the salutary pride of the Christian congregation
that she boasts not of her own wisdom and righteousness but rather
of the righteousness and wisdom of her Bridegroom, of the Lord
Christ, and all that he has. So also in the estate of marriage, when
a man and woman marry, both their bodies and goods are in
common. The children and everything else are both of theirs alike.
The woman is just as much lord over the man's wealth as the man
himself. So there is no difference between them except the man is
lord of the woman. Apart from that, no matter what the worth of the
household, the wife is just as much lord over everything as the man.
So the church also confesses Christ as her Lord and Bridegroom and
boasts before and over all people on earth who do not believe in

Christ that she partakes of all the wealth and gifts of Christ her Bridegroom and has them in common with him.

Therefore, if sins afflict her she clings upon Christ's, her Bridegroom's, righteousness and says, "I have my bridegroom's righteousness, which is my eternal wealth, therefore shut your mouth." In the same way, also, when the devil wants to frighten her and make her weep then she turns to her Bridegroom and says to the devil, "Truly you can find sins in me but in Christ you will find none. I know that well. Now he is mine and I am his and we have the same wealth. Because of that leave me alone!" So also when she is sad and troubled she says, "In Christ, my Bridegroom, is life, grace, peace, joy and holiness. All of this is mine, for Christ is mine. So why do you frighten me?" So Christ's bride is only a mighty queen and first lady over death, sins, fear and all evil to which the devil testifies. She is established with full rights in Christ as a queen of life, righteousness, grace and purity.

But while these words, that Christ is the bridegroom of the church, are common, they will be despised. For the popes, bishops and pastors have called themselves bridegrooms of the church, when they have no right or ability to brag so. St. John the Baptizer did not allow it said of himself either but rather only called himself a friend of the Bridegroom. For this reason, if the popes and bishops were also God-fearing and good they would likewise not be bridegrooms of the church but rather only his friends and servants. There is only one Bridegroom, Jesus Christ, who gives this bride everything.

So now the miserable devil has thus invented such names for the popes and the bishops, that they should be the bridegrooms of the church so that he might take these very lively Words out of our eyes, which, since they will be said of everyone and are in constant use, are not heeded. But when we focus upon them with thoughts, discourse and faith, we use them well and they are reasons for pride in us so we can have great comfort. For forgiveness of sins and the whole treasure of divine mercy could not be more wonderfully revealed and pictured than calling the church Christ's bride. From this illustration it follows that the bride has everything that is the Lord Christ's. But what kind of wealth does the Lord Christ have? Eternal righteousness, wisdom, might, truth, eternal life, joy, grace and purity. Therefore, the church is a first lady and queen over all the wealth of Christ, her Bridegroom, since they are mercy, life and holiness, etc.

Altb. VI, 408–409: Lecture on Ps. 45, 1534

Hallelujah! Let praises ring! Unto the Lamb of God we sing,
In whom we are elected. He bo't His Church with His own blood,
He cleansed her in that blessed flood, And as His Bride selected.
Holy, holy Is our union and communion. His befriending
Gives us joy and peace unending. (*TLH* 23: 2)

Saturday

Hear, daughter, give attention and incline your ears. Forget your people and your father's house. For the king's desire will have your beauty. He is your Lord, and you shall hearken to him. Psalm 45:10,11

The Holy Ghost uses very wonderful words when he says, "that he will have desire for your beauty," that is, you will attract him, through your faith so that he does what you want. He will of himself, moved by great love, run after you so that he will be with you and make his dwelling with you. For if God has given his Word, he does not let his work that he began in you lay, but rather continues so that you are defended from the devil, from the world and from your own flesh so that he makes you brave. In this way, he takes his bride into his arms with great love. For if we had no trials, we would ask nothing of him and would not learn to listen to him, look to him or incline our ears to him. Therefore, he leads us so that we ever cling more firmly to the Word and believe in him and he does the same out of great love. But such a heart being taken into his arms acts so poorly by the opinion of our flesh that our eyes overlook it and sweat from terror breaks out over us. Yet it is necessary for us.

For this reason, this is a wonderful comfort. He does not desire to remain aloof and imposing towards us. He wants us to be able to lay hold of him. Our king, Christ, not only has a desire for the Word and our faith but rather also has the kind of lively love for us that a Bridegroom has for his Bride. He is inflamed and ardent so that he himself pursues us. Additionally, we bring him [to us] when we hear his Word with desire and joy, believe on him and forget about our righteousness. But that happens with great difficulty and distaste. Therefore God, the Lord, would bestow upon us his grace that we could do the least of such things in the doctrine, Preaching Office and administration of the Sacrament. So we also, as we have begun through God's grace, completely forget monkish teaching that it remain not in the least in us as [it does] in the sacrament despisers, anabaptists and the papists' rule and reign, which had completely devoured THIS monk. For they are nothing more than shorn monks before whose abominations God the Lord will mercifully defend us. Amen.

Now this is the summary of all this. Our treasure and goodness are established not in our own powers and good works, also not in the gifts that we receive from God through which we might do good works and everything that belongs to this life and the righteousness of the law. Rather our goodness is only established when we grasp

Christ and believe in him since then we are truly and rightly good since this goodness looks only to Christ alone apart from anything else. Therefore, it is false and deceiving when one teaches that we should be good and acceptable to God through special services to God and through our own righteousness. Before people, and especially before worldly-wise people, this seems to be good and desireable but before God we must have another goodness. But this is the single treasure and goodness, that we believe in the Lord Christ. This same faith purifies us from all spots and wrinkles through the washing of water in the Word, Ephesians 5. By this he makes us acceptable before God. This faith can do anything as Christ says in Mark 9, "All things are possible to those who believe." Therefore, faith is also the most wonderful treasure and goodness, compared to which every other adornment and goodness is nothing. For apart from and outside of faith in the Lord Christ, we are lost and damned with all that we have and exhibit.

"For he is your Lord, and you should hearken to him." In the immediately preceding verse we have heard a teaching which is difficult for those who are used to the righteousness of the law and works. To them it is not enough to cling completely to this doctrine, namely, that they hope and trust only in the splendid grace of the Lord Christ and throw away their own righteousness, and not ever return again to their disposable righteousness and should not even think upon it. But it is no wonder concerning the Jews that they do not cling to or grasp this teaching. They are compelled by the law. So also the papists do not receive it, with whom we are tangling and already for many years have tangled for no other reason than that we teach that sinners become justified only by faith, not through the works of the law, much less through these works which everyone compels through their own meditations and good thoughts without a definite command of God.

The prophet established nothing to add to this very difficult teaching even when the Jews were unwilling to listen. For this reason the heretics in the church have brought great trouble. For as he taught the Synagogue and the Jews, to forget their people and their father's house, and only hold to the Word of the gospel, hear it gladly and cling firmly to it (which itself is quite difficult), he now also adds the reason why the Jews much less those who came before them didn't like it, namely that Christ is Lord and God whom they should hearken to, to whom both their people and their father's house and even the whole law should give way and make room because the law was given through Moses, who was a servant, but now the Lord, king and God himself is at hand.

Altb. VI, 420–421: Lecture on Ps. 45, 1534

I could but grieve Thee, Lord
And with my sins displease Thee;
Yet to atone for sin
My works could not appease Thee.
Though I could fall from grace
And choose the way of sin,
I had no strength to rise,
A new life to begin.

But Thou hast raised me up
To joy and exultation
And clearly shown the way
That leads me to salvation.
My sins are washed away,
For this I thank Thee, Lord;
And with my heart and soul
All dead works are abhorred. (*TLH* 417: 3–4)

Week of Trinity XVII

Sunday

And from one moon until another and one Sabbath unto another all flesh will come to worship me, says the Lord. Isaiah 66:23

So the Third Commandment concerning the Sabbath is a great boast in Judaism as a common command applying to all the world. But this jewel with which Moses adorns and dedicates his people is bestowed upon no one but the Jews alone. Just as in the First Commandment, no one but only the Jews should peculiarly believe and confess that the common God of all the world has led them out of Egypt, so the actual meaning of the Third Commandment is that they should hear and learn God's Word on that day by which both they and the day were sanctified. This is just how these have been read and preached in all previous times until this day by the Jews, concerning the Sabbath day of Moses and the prophets. But when a person preaches God's Word, it is obvious that one must rest and be still for those hours at that time and only speak and listen to what God says and teaches us or speaks with us apart from all other business.

So everything depends on a person's sanctifying this day more than rest. For God does not say, "You shall rest on the holy day, or make a Sabbath." You can see that for yourself. Rather, you should sanctify the holy day or Sabbath so that far more stress is on the sanctifying than the resting. And if one of them needed to be omitted, it would be better that the resting be left behind rather than the sanctifying. For the commandment chiefly exhorts us to the sanctifying and constructs the Sabbath not for the sake of itself but rather for the sake of the sanctifying. But the Jews regard the resting, as their own addition, more than the sanctifying. God and Moses do not do this.

Now Moses names this the seventh day and since God had created the world in six days, they should not work at all. This is the temporal jewel by which Moses adorns his people peculiarly by this commandment. Beforehand, one did not find such things written by either Abraham nor in the times of the former fathers. Rather, it is a temporal addition and adornment established only for this people who were led out of Egypt, which also will not eternally remain, so little as the whole law of Moses. But the sanctifying, that is, the teaching and preaching of God's Word, is established from the beginning and remains constantly in all the world. Therefore, the seventh day is not used among us gentiles and even in Judaism itself it is often no longer observed until the time of the Messiah. Nevertheless, the nature and need for it compels that on those days or hours when God's Word is preached, a person of himself, as said, must be still and rest or keep the Sabbath. For God's Word cannot be heard or learned when one thinks about something else at the same time or is not silent.

Therefore, Isaiah also says in Chapter 66 that this kind of seventh day, or jewel of Moses as I call it, should cease in the time of the Messiah, when the true Saints and God's Word would richly come; "It will be," he says, "a Sabbath based on other things, a new month based on other things." There will be pure Sabbath, nothing but seventh day without six days between. The Saints or God's Word will daily and richly go forth. All days will be Sabbaths.

I already know well what the Jews say about this and how they treat this text, but I cannot briefly summarize everything that I would like to present against the Jews who so scandalously treated and destroyed the prophets. Still, let no Jew tell me (treating it shortly), how it is impossible that all flesh should worship the Lord in Jerusalem every month and Sabbath as this text must clearly and definitely say, when some people or flesh live so far from Jerusalem that they cannot come there in twenty, thirty, or a hundred Sabbaths, and they themselves, the Jews, in fifteen hundred years, that is, twelve times fifteen hundred months (I will not even mention Sabbatical years) have not worshiped in Jerusalem. But I cannot respond to everything now in this brief work.

As [He is the] Jewel and declaration in the first part of the First Commandment, "who has brought you out of Egypt," Jeremiah also says in the twenty-third Chapter, "Behold, the time is coming, says the Lord, that I will raise up to David a branch of righteousness and he shall be a king who will reign well. He will administer truth and righteousness," etc. And shortly after that, "Behold the time is coming that no one will say any more, 'Truly the Lord lives, who has brought the children of Israel out of Egypt,' but rather, 'Truly the Lord lives who has brought us the seed of the house of Israel (note that it is not the whole house of Israel, but rather a seed from it is mentioned here), and brought them out of the land of darkness and out of all lands where they had been scattered so that they will dwell in their land.' "

Altb. VII, 42–43: Against the Sabbatarians; to a Good Friend, 1538; cf. AE 47

Father, Son and Holy Ghost, Praise to Thee and adoration!
Grant that we Thy Word may trust And obtain true consolation
While we here below must wander, Till we sing Thy praises yonder. (*TLH* 16: 4)

Monday

If you love me then keep my commandments. John 14:15

There are few Words like these that give a farewell from him and also a good night. He comforts and warns them so that his parting itself would not terrify or trouble them. It is as if he would say to them, "I must now depart from your eyes. Therefore, I say this to you as the last thing. This will be my worth to you, that you do not fear or become terrified, but rather believe on me and hold on to what I say to you. For I will not leave you without comfort and counsel even if you now should have no help or comfort from the world. Yes, I go just for that reason, to the Father, that I receive my power and rule and help you by that. If I bodily depart from you, in that way, I will yet send to you another Comforter from the Father who will thenceforth be with you forever. For I know that you could not remain in the world without a Comforter."

"Until now I became your Comforter through my bodily presence which has given you joy, made you safe and fearless and you still gladly would remain with me. But now, as you hear, since you will lose this comfort, it will be troubling and unsettling for you. But it will not harm you. Only remain my disciples and hold onto me for I will generously restore what is lacking. For I will ask the Father himself that he give you the Comforter who will remain with you forever. Neither the world nor the devil will take him from you even if they should become wild and crazy. He shall strengthen, comfort and make you bold more than I can now do bodily. Additionally, he is also wiser and smarter than all the world so that you shall have no lack of comfort, strength and courage, or wisdom."

That is the comfort. But he does not establish these Words for nothing, "As you have love for me, hold my commandments." For the dear Lord has already seen that when he went away he would perpetuate his activity in Christianity, especially under the preachers and teachers. He saw that they would not remain united but rather administer division and sectarianism among themselves. Now he has lifted off all of Moses from his Christians and would leave us unencumbered by the unbearable burden of the law. So it always happens where one would rule with laws, especially over the conscience, there is no end or measuring of the laws and compulsions. One law makes a hundred others and one hundred become a hundred thousand. "Therefore I lay upon you nothing more." He says, "I call for and desire nothing more than this one thing; that you faithfully preach of me and let my Word and

Sacrament be commanded and for my sake hold love and unity with one another and suffer with patience what opposes you for it."

"These are the short commands which are here called 'my commandments' which I present with no others. With these you have love for me and you gladly do them for my sake. For I do not desire to be a Moses who exhorts and plagues you with drowning and terror. Rather, I give you such commands which you could and would hold well without commands because of your love for me. For if that is not so, even this is yet done for nothing, even if I would give you many commands. Then it would still remain an annoyance. Therefore, only attend to this: If you would keep my command because you have love for me and would remember what I have done for you, it is only right that you should love me as the one who gave his body and life for you and shed my blood for you. So continue in this for my sake and remain united and friendly with one another so that you hold onto me in this manner with your preaching and bear one another with love and do not administer division and sectarianism."

"For I have also administered it honestly and well. It became sour for my heart and cost me my body and life so that I could save you. I threw myself under death and the devil's rage so that I take away your sins and death, destroy hell and the devil's might and give you heaven and everything that I have. I will also gladly preserve you for good if you sometimes err and fail, or even coarsely fall, being weak and fragile, only that you cling to me again and walk in love and also forgive one another as I do you so that the love does not become severed."

He began this warning before but he takes it further and stronger as he would have this impressed upon them to the last. For he had known well that there would be many who also would boast of his name, as Christ's disciples and preachers of the gospel, yet would rather be in their own darkness, glory and boast than to boast of Christ's body and blood. And they would not regard his grace and unspeakable love and all that he gave to save us as being so precious, but they are dangerously established in their own confidence or honor and might. [They think it better] that they should spit out their own skill and cleverness, as things that are weightier, so that they may be boasted about and regarded as clever, wise, learned. [This is regarded as more precious] than where Christ and the pure doctrine of the gospel remain.

Altb. VII, 89: Sermons on the Gospel of St. John, Chapters 14–16, 1538; cf. AE 24

Thy heavenly strength sustain our heart That we may act the valiant part,
  With Thee as our Reliance; Be Thou our Refuge and our Shield
That we may never quit the field, But bid all foes defiance.
Descend, Defend From all error And earth's terrors. Thy salvation
Be our constant consolation. (*TLH* 235: 5)

Tuesday

What troubles you my soul, and why are you dissettled within me? Wait on God. I will yet thank him for he helps me with his presence. Psalm 42:6

He wants to say, "Why do you plague me without a reason?" Turn quickly away from the sadness, cling to comfort and say, "Wait upon God, for I will thank him for helping me with his gracious presence." Your thoughts (he wants to say) are lies and false for you make out of God a terrifying judge or slave driver who is a friendly Father and comforting Lord. Away with your wrath and terror. Leave them to the godless tyrants and others who are not safe and do not ask anything of God. They belong back there, but let me be at liberty. For I believe in my Lord Christ who died and rose again for me. He both prays for me and sends me the Holy Ghost and the Comforter from the Father. Therefore, without fail, no matter what happens, even if everything collapses in a heap and thunder and lightening would strike, then let it fall, tear and break. Where my Father stays there I also stay.

It is so blessed when one can do this and know such things. Yet it never fails that the devil is still too mightily by us, the world too strong, and we see so many kinds of obstacles and scandals before our eyes that we forget this and cannot believe that God gives comfort to our hearts. Then we only feel that we are in trouble that is overpowering and this overcomes a person so completely that he cannot think of these Words. Therefore, it is a Christian characteristic to learn to rise up over every terror and sorrow, fear and trouble and say with the prophet, "Why are you so sorrowful?", etc. The feeling and trouble is there, that I know well (says Christ) and I told you it would be so, so that you might not follow such feelings or believe your own thoughts but rather my Words. For I will ask the Father and he, through my prayer, will surely give you the Holy Ghost, and he also will comfort you. By this you can be sure that I love you just as do the Father and the Holy Ghost whom he will send.

Yes, your heart says against this that you have not lived rightly and are full of sins. That is altogether too true, but what of it? "Oh, you must go to hell," says the devil. No, God doesn't want that. In this leave the devil and the evil world behind. For my Lord Christ says "No," and also that the Father is not angry with me but rather gives me the Comforter and the same comes to me as he requested. And they are one in this matter. For they do not desire me frightened and troubled, much less cast away and damned, but rather they have comforted and helped me.

See how the Lord Christ himself receives his Christians so faithfully and willingly and would gladly impress upon them such things that they will have sufficient comfort and learn both his and his Father's hearts and thoughts. He would be nothing else to them nor require anything else from them but that they should be comforted. That is because he is sent from the Father. The Holy Ghost's work and office is also nothing other than that he comfort them and tell them not to be afraid. And when they would be comforted by God's Word, they also behold and receive the same. That comfort surely comes from the Holy Ghost and it is both the comfort of God the Father and the Lord Christ.

Now that is rightly learned from the Holy Ghost for he is called a "Comforter." This is his skill, office and quality. For from his divine nature, or *substantia,* we would not argue here since the word "Comforter" is a personal word. Additionally, from this it is apparent that he is a distinct person, for he says, "The Father shall send you another Comforter." He reveals him as a distinct person that is neither the Father nor the Son. But that he is also God, or in a single nature with the Father and the Son, we will hereafter see further in the fifteenth chapter. No, it is enough that you learn and note here that he is called a Comforter and is called that for our sakes. So as to his deity, he is with the Father and Son in an indivisible divine nature: But he will be called by us a Comforter so that this name is nothing other, whether a revelation or a confession, than what one should receive from the Holy Ghost. He is a comforter. But he is no Moses or law-bearer who frightens along with the devil, death and hell when he is called a "Comforter." But rather he makes a troubled heart light and happy towards God and calls you to good courage as one whose sin is forgiven, death slain, heaven open and [with whom] God is pleased.

Whoever is able to hold this definition would already have this and would find and see nothing but only comfort and joy in heaven and earth. For because the Father sends this Comforter and Christ asks for it, then he will act out of no wrath but rather [his actions must] flow out of pure Fatherly and heart-felt love. So a Christian should eagerly learn that he make use of this title or name of the Holy Ghost so that he is a Comforter and we are the afflicted and driven ones. So he will comfort us. As he is then called a Comforter to all the driven; not only us, but all who are in the world, as he also says here that he shall be the kind of Comforter who remains eternally with Christianity.

Altb. VII, 95–96: Sermons on the Gospel of St. John, Chapters 14–16, 1538; cf. AE 24

To mine His Spirit speaketh Sweet words of holy cheer,
How God to him that seeketh For rest is always near
And how He hath erected A city fair and new,
Where all that faith expected We evermore shall view. (*TLH* 528: 9)

Wednesday

I am a true vine and my Father a Vintner. John 15:1

That is a very comforting image and a fine, loving presentation by which he does not place before our eyes an unnecessary, unfruitful tree, but the dear vine, which, while not appearing impressive, yet bears much fruit and gives the best loved, sweetest juice. Every suffering that the vine and fruit will encounter is nothing but the ready work and care that a vintner or vine keeper does to his vine and branches which are growing and bearing. He wants us to learn by this that we regard the troubles and suffering of the Christian much differently than the way we ourselves feel it and as it seems before the world. Namely, that it does not happen without divine counsel and desire. It is not a sign of wrath and punishment but of grace and fatherly love and it must serve us for our improvement.

This skill is that one believe these things and hold them as true so that what troubles us and annoys us should not be called a working of trouble or sorrow but that they rather work what is good and necessary. We consider this as when we see a vine-dresser work and hack at his vine, which, if it could speak and question it when it sees the vintner coming along to him with the sickle or hoe, hoeing at the roots and cutting the branches with the sheers or the knife cutting, would have to say, "Hey, what are you doing? Now I must be ruined and shrivel up because you came near and took my earth and set the iron teeth upon my tendrils, tore and whacked me to pieces so that I must stand in the earth naked and dry. You wouldn't do what you are doing to me to any tree or plant."

But against this the vintner would also respond saying, "You are a fool and don't understand. For even if I snap off a branch from you it is because it is an unnecessary branch which takes away your power and sap so that the other branches that you should bear would become useless. So when it is taken away it is for the best. But I am an expert in this and do it because it is good for you and you need it. It is so the foreign wild branches do not draw the others' power and sap. It is so that you could be even better and bear more and give good wine." So also when the vintner throws dung on the root or stock, he also does that for the good of the plant even if it also might complain and say, "What are you doing that for? Isn't it enough that you cut and hack me up? Must I also suffer you to soil my tender branches so scandalously with stuff that no one can even stand in the stable?"

Now Christ defines this suffering which he and his Christians will have in the world so that it not be called trouble or suffering but good and helpful to become even better and bring more fruit. Then we might also learn to think in the same way as he himself thought of it. He wants to say, "Yes it is surely true and I cannot think of it in any other way; everything is happening to me as it does to the branches. My Jews will throw dung on me and hack me apart, encumber and mock me so scandalously, martyr me in disgrace, pluck me, crucify me and execute me so that all the world will think that I must finally be ruined and come to nothing. But such dunging and hoeing that happens to me also serves me so that I bring forth even more fruit, that is, that I come through cross and death to my glory and begin my kingdom so that I am confessed in all the world and they will believe in me."

"So (he says) may it also henceforth be with you. For you must also be fertilized and pruned. The Father who makes me a vine and you my branch will not suffer the vine to lay there unfertilized and unpruned. Else it would be made a completely wild unfruitful vine and must finally be completely ruined. But now, when it is well worked, dunged, pruned and in bloom, it goes forth with full strength and not only bears much but also makes good desireable wine."

So this is surely a fine comforting image. Whoever is able to understand it and interpret this in needs and afflictions and when the death of the Christian truly knocks him on the head, the devil attacks and plagues, the world encumbers him and scandalizes him as an apostle of the devil, etc., he could say, "Behold, there I am being dunged and worked upon like a branch on the vine. Welcome, dear sickle and hoe, hack, cut and prune for I would gladly have you. For this is God's sickle and hoe which is needed and good for me. So if Christ interprets this as a master and can apply it also to himself then I will be dunged, pruned, cut and defoliated but I know for sure that it is not as the world sees it, that I will be destroyed and defeated. It is the work of my dear Father as the one who works on his vine if it would grow and bear [fruit]."

Now from this learn, whoever can, that each one think this way in his trial and temptation, "The world, the devil, death and all misfortune is nothing other than God's hoeing and pruning. So every burden and insult that the Christian encounters is God's dunging."

He says, "Good God be thanked, who can even use the devil and his evil so that everything must serve for our good, else (if it depended on the devil's evil will) he would quickly slay us with his knife and soil and make us smell with his dung." But now God takes him in his hand and says, "Devil, you are surely a murderer and a villain but I will use you wherever I desire. You will only be my hoe. The world and all that clings to it will be my dung for my dear vineyard, that it become even better."

Altb. VII, 131–132: Sermons on the Gospel of St. John, Chapters 14–16, 1538; cf. AE 24

Though earth be rent asunder, Thou'rt mine eternally;
Not fire nor sword nor thunder Shall sever me from Thee;
Not hunger, thirst, nor danger, Not pain nor poverty
Nor mighty princes' anger Shall ever hinder me. (*TLH* 528: 13)

Thursday

Every branch in me that does not bring fruit will be taken away. And every one that brings forth fruit he will purify that he bring more fruit. John 15:2

Here he makes a blunt differentiation between those who are called the branches on the vine and those who are the false Christians. He portrays both kinds as being on the vine. Now some branches growing on it are called "runners" or "wild branches" that are useless lumber and sap-guzzlers, which bear no fruit and do nothing more than consume the sap that the true fruit-bearing branch should have. "So my father," he says, "is the kind of vintner that when he sees such a branch, which is good for nothing and hinders the others, he cuts it off and throws it away." This cutting off is evil and terrible to the false branches but to the others, his cutting, pruning and purifying lets them be established. This does not harm them but is good and needed. But this is a cutting off into the fire.

It is the case now, which we also see and complain about, that in Christianity there are always also some false and unfit branches who only bear more wood so that one must throw them away. They truly come out of the vine but they do not remain in it. They are also baptized, hear the gospel and have forgiveness of sins. In summary, they are initially in Christ, as he says here, as in the vine. But when they should go forth, they become instead a wild shoot who only are Christians in name, use God's Word, praise God's glory, use and consume the alien sap, so that they grow large upon the vine, want to have the praise and glory as the best Christians, can contribute more lavishly and wonderfully than the others and have a splendor and appearance above all. But there is nothing behind it and they are found to be only lazy wood, without true sap and power. For they cannot learn the Word in the right way nor confess it and all is just a false appearance. We call them fanatics and false brothers.

The others [in this category] are the lazy Christians who surely have the Word and true doctrine yet nothing follows this in their lives. They want only to act and live as they themselves desire. These two are never far from each other for these only lack a master. For such worthless, lazy Christians allow themselves very easily to be subjected through sectarian and false doctrine, which, when they [sectarian teachers/doctrines] come find in them [the lazy Christians] true students who are, then, also easily won as those who are sated with and tired of the true doctrine. For if they were concerned to stay in right doctrine they would be fresh and hearty in right faith. This is why both of these are not far from each other. For when false teachers come to such lazy Christians they finally become one cake, that is, one sect comes from it because they cannot remain by us but rather they separate themselves and make it apparent that they are incapable.

Now Christ says that his Father is the vintner who tends his vine and is waiting. He differentiates between the false branches and the others and will not suffer them to get the upper hand and ruin the true branch. Therefore, he portrays this to us and tells us by this judgment that they must be cut off and thrown into the fire. But it seems to those seeing it to be quite different. For one sees them [the false useless branches] growing and increasing. They are much stronger, become fatter and thicker, than the others and because of this, they alone are held as the true ones that will bear fruit. But we on the other hand are poor, dried out and unfruitful. Yes, one would like to uproot and cut us out as unneeded and useless, but the others go on as if they should remain forever. The whole world thinks much of them.

But again this requires a completely spiritual understanding and outlook so that one believe it. For God always sees to it that, as many sectarians throw themselves against the Christian, yet always his true little bunch remains and the sectarians are severed. From the apostles' time, many heretics opposed and so demolished the article of Christ, of Baptism, Sacrament, the righteousness of faith, etc., as if the true doctrine and the Christian church would be decimated by it. But God has cut them all off and preserved his branches so that in spite of that we remain in the true doctrine, Baptism and Sacrament that are planted by the apostle and in the faith that has forced its way through the Word, from Abel, the first, and will remain until the last Christian. So not one of these will be cut away but rather all remain unanimously upon the vine. Thus as one has learned, believed and lived, so all of them learn, believe and live.

So from now on, one should not see or judge how big and thick such false branches appear to be but rather only about whether they are true branches in Christ. This is what Christ himself soon reveals and explains when he says, "You are pure for the sake of my speaking." That is, only see who are the people that have and hold to the doctrine that is purely and expressly grounded in the Scriptures, as the apostles and prophets have had. Then you can see and know that there are true Christians. Even if they do not appear good and are dry branches, that is not harmful. Often a dry weak looking branch can bear a beautiful bunch of grapes, where another lazy thick shoot can bear nothing at all. You know and are assured from this kind of discernment that these branches which hold onto Christ and have his Word shall remain and no one will uproot or drown them, no matter how strong or big the others are that oppose them, as if they would overgrow them. Rather, they must be cut away in time so each true one remain before him.

Altb. VII, 134–135: Sermons on the Gospel of St. John, Chapters 14–16, 1538; cf. AE 24

O God, how sin's dread works abound!   The haughty spirits, Lord, restrain
Throughout the earth no rest is found,   Who o'er Thy Church with might would reign
And falsehood's spirit wide has spread,   And always set forth something new,
And error boldly rears its head.   Devised to change Thy doctrine true. (*TLH* 292: 5–6)

Friday

You are now pure for the sake of the Word that I have spoken to you. John 15:3

That is a strange purity and seems not to harmonize with what was written before when he has spoken of suffering and cross. This is like something tossed in askew. But this is well added and gives an antidote or medicine against the poison which is called the false hope or presumption of self-righteousness, which does not let anyone think that he should stand to receive forgiveness of sins and [compels him] to become a branch before God, apart from Christ. So naturally this usually follows: When a person has done many good works or has suffered much and perceives his fruit, that he is made as something special and has brought about preaching or something else, there the sweet poison will always knock him down so that he thinks,

"Hey, I also have done something so that God will see me and be gracious to me," etc. Thus the [sinful] nature always drives such runners and wild branches that want to grow from this and takes the sap and strength from the true branches so that they cannot thrive. Because of this, the vine-tender must be lively and always battle such false thoughts and presumption through the constant exhortation of the Word.

That is why he now says, "you are not pure because of the things that you do or because you suffer or because of the fruit that you bring. For you would not even be able to do such things if you were not already pure and were not a good, rightly-made branch. But the fact that you are pure must be done through the Word, which must always be there both before and after you are made pure. Because of that, the same [that is, the Word] has power in you and will be surely grasped and held fast so that the Father gives you all kinds of suffering, danger, fear, need and affliction, through which you become humble and learn that the purity does not come out of yourself nor is it your doing. Therefore, your suffering in that way is not the purity itself, that you, for your own sake, should be declared pure before God. But yet it is of service insofar as it compels the person that he ever more deeply grasp and retain the Word. So through it, faith will be exercised. But actually, the Word itself is the purity of the heart, so that the heart clings to it and remains."

But he says definitely, "You are pure through the Word that I have spoken to you," that is nothing else than the whole preaching of Christ. For he was sent into the world from the Father that he would pay for our sins and reconcile the Father through his suffering and death. Because of that, all who believe in him shall not be damned or lost but for his sake have the forgiveness of sins and eternal life. This Word (which through faith is grasped in the heart) makes a person pure. That is, it brings forgiveness of sins and makes him acceptable before God for the sake of that same faith. Through faith alone such Word will be received and grasped. We, who so cling to it, become reckoned and regarded as completely pure and holy before God even though our nature and life have not been completely pure enough, but rather are always sinful, weak and fragile, and thus are yet to be purified and this remains with us so long as we live on earth.

So with this passage he teaches the true chief article of the Christian doctrine, how and through whom a person becomes and remains pure before God. This same purity, which God would give against sins, will not be given at all and shall not be allotted by our action or suffering, even if that happens to those who are Christians and these are called true, good, pure fruits. For he speaks altogether in the same way as do his dear apostles that were believers or Christians and says, "You are pure and yet, not because you bear good fruits but rather for the sake of my Word."

How can that be? How are you at the same time not pure and yet pure? If you are pure, then why does he say that you must always be made pure? Or why do you ask our Father: "Forgive us our trespasses?" and "Your will be done," etc., in which you confess that you still have sins and are unclean? For is one called "pure" if he asks for forgiveness of sins and complains that God's will is not done? But again, if you are unclean and yet must still become purified, how then does he call you pure? How can you reconcile the two together? Answer: As I have said, a person is first declared pure through God's Word for the sake of Christ, on whom he believes. Then through such faith of the Word, he will be engrafted into the vine, Christ, and is clothed in the purity of Christ so it will be accounted to him as if it were his own and thus complete and whole as it is complete and whole in Christ.

That all happens through the Word which is received and held by faith, by which I hear God's will and promise that he forgives my sins for the sake of Christ and enriches me purely and will preserve me. When I grasp the Word through faith, such Word (through the Holy Ghost, who works through it) makes a new heart and thoughts in me which hold fast to the same and don't doubt it whether I am living or dying. Since I cling to that, what is still impure and sinful in me will not be accounted to me. Rather, the same weak, partial, beginning purity will be considered whole complete purity and God makes the cross over it and does not consider the remaining impurity. Where such purity through the Word in faith is and proceeds, there God approaches over it and drives and exercises it through cross and suffering so that it becomes stronger and fuller. By this faith grows and the common impurity and sins decrease from day to day and are swept away until in the grave. That then is called the branch that is in the vine and is now pure through the Word, continually pruned and purified as he has said above.

Altb. VII, 138–139: Sermons on the Gospel of St. John, Chapters 14–16, 1538; cf. AE 24

As silver tried by fire is pure From all adulteration,
So thro' God's Word shall men endure Each trial and temptation.
Its light beams brighter thro' the cross, And, purified from human dross,
It shines through every nation. (*TLH* 260: 5)

Saturday

Without me you can do nothing. John 15:5

So here is concluded a terrible judgment over all life and work no matter how great, wonderful and good it might be. If it is outside of Christ it can do nothing and should be called nothing even if it is great and important before the world. There it is called an important generous work, but here, before God, in the kingdom of Christ, it is truly nothing because it is not raised out of him nor does it remain in him. For it is not his Word, Baptism and Sacrament, but rather our self-made things that we have chosen and exhorted outside of the Word. Therefore, it cannot bring forth fruit or remain standing before God but rather must, as a lazy and dried out branch without sap and strength, be rooted out and (as he says following this) be thrown into the fire. So let others prune and make what they can without him until they make a new birth and fruit out of the tree from their own works. But they will only make this passage come true (if God desires) and from all of this become a big nothing.

But who believes that this should be so far reaching and condemn so many people or that the world is so full of false Christians and saints? But this is preached to us so that we do not run and work in vain (as St. Paul warns in 1 Corinthians 9) but to see that we will be found remaining in Christ, that is holding his Word, and not let anything tear us away from it, remaining in the fruits that also follow. For it is a mighty great comfort and defiance when a person knows that he does not live and work apart from it but rather God is well pleased with his works and they are called true fruits and from the bottom of his heart he can say: "I am baptized on Christ. I didn't think of that myself or make it through my order, rule or human decision, but rather it is from my Lord Christ, himself. This I know for sure. For another thing, I know and confess before all the world that I believe on the man through God's grace and intend to remain with him and to lose both body, life and everything before I would deny him. In such a faith I stay and live. Thereafter I go out, eat and drink, sleep and wake, rule, serve, do and suffer everything in faith so that since I am baptized I also know that they are good fruits and God pleasing."

For such a person's living and acting, no matter how great or poor they are called, are thus pure fruits and he cannot be without fruits. For he is also born into a new nature in Christ so that he is full of good fruits without interruption and will be the kind of person that everything he does is easy and without sour labor or being annoyed. Nothing is so difficult or so big that he is not able to suffer and bear it. On the other hand, the others who do not have faith and would themselves make fruits, if they are martyred by enemies and do much greater work and more work than the others, in this they do not yet have such comfort. They do everything with worried hearts so that they are never happy; they will never be joyous or be sure that it pleases God and so everything that they do is in vain and lost. For it is true: What is without or outside of Christ does nothing and they are only lazy, unnecessary, nothing works. Then again, when everything is done in Christ they are only rich, complete, valuable fruits.

But the world and its false saints and sects cannot understand this. What kind of a Christian (they say) would that be? Can he do nothing more than eat and drink, work in his house, raise his children, drive the wagon, etc.? I can do that too, and better! Surely, one must differentiate between the things that a Christian does that a heathen also does and not quickly call everything fruits of the Christian life. Else the heathen would have it better than we, according to such common works that father and mother, child, servant, man or wife do. Therefore, we must have what is different and special over a common person's work, like going into a cloister, laying prostrate on the ground, wearing the hair shirt, praying day and night and night and day. So they define the works that they call a holy life and Christian fruits and thereafter they quickly conclude that it is not a holy life, leading children, doing housework, etc. For they cannot judge according to the stem or birth in this vine but rather only see the outer mask of works. But who doesn't know that the monks with their works look greater if one wants to behold them and consider them by what they make and how their hair is cut but not according to where their skill or birth comes from?

Christ says that the only good fruits are the ones done by those who are in him and remain in him. What such a person does and lives are all called good fruits even if they are poorer than a farmhand that loads and drives a cart full of manure. No one can understand that but they regard such works (as they see them before their eyes) as heathen works. But in the Christian there is a complete and utter difference between the works that they do and that a heathen or another (outside of Christ) does even if it is completely the same work. For the heathen's work does not flow and grow out of Christ, the vine. Therefore, they cannot please God nor can they be called Christian fruits. But the Christian's works, since they proceed from faith in Christ, are all purely true, useful fruits.

Altb. VII, 147–148: Sermons on the Gospel of St. John, Chapters 14–16, 1538; cf. AE 24

I build on this foundation, That Jesus and His blood
Alone are my salvation, The true, eternal good.
Without Him all that pleases Is valueless on earth;
The gifts I owe to Jesus Alone my love are worth. (*TLH* 528: 3)

Week of Trinity XVIII

Sunday

Jesus said, "You shall love God, your Lord, with all your heart, with all your soul and with all your mind."
Matthew 22:37

Christ here commends to the pharisees and teachers of the law a double lesson. First, he takes on their blindness and teaches them what the law is. In the other he teaches how impossible it is for them to keep this law. He takes their blindness away in that he teaches them what the law is, namely, that the law is love. Reason today, as with these Jews, cannot understand this. For if reason were able to grasp it, then the pharisees and teachers of the law, who at the time were the best and cleverest of the people, would truly have grasped it. But they thought that it only depended on a person's doing the outward works of the law, as given to God, whether done willingly or not. But they could not see their inward blindness, pride and their evil, hard heart. They thought they understood the law perfectly well and were fine, pleasing, holy and good people. But they now stood in the light of day. For no one is able to keep the law unless he is completely made anew.

So it is sure that human reason is never able to understand or do the law even if it knows what is in it. When do you do unto another what you would have him do unto you? Who loves his enemy from his heart? Who dies gladly? Who gladly suffers insult and scandal? Friend, show me a person that gladly has an evil rumor [said of him] or who gladly lives in poverty. For human nature and reason completely flee before these. It shrinks away, is frightened and is terrified by it, and if it could, so much as it is able, it wouldn't suffer from such things.

Human nature can never fully grasp what God demands from us in this law. Namely, that we should give over our will to the will of God so that we renounce our own understandings, our will, our might and our skills and say from the heart, "Thy will be done." Indeed, you will not find anyone who loves God with his whole heart and his neighbor as himself. It can easily happen that two are quickly friends and they live amicably with one another. But yet under that, some irritation is hidden which you ignore until sometime when you are especially bothered by it. Then you will see well how you love him and whether you are flesh or spirit. For this law would say that I should be friendly from the heart to the one who has hurt me. But when do I do that?

So Christ would show here that you rightly preach the law when one learns that we are not able to do it and that we are the devil's own. Experience teaches us this and it is revealed all over in the Scriptures, especially in St. Paul, where he says of this in Romans 8:7,8 that "Those who are of the flesh are enemies against God since it [the flesh] does not submit to the law of God. It is also unable to do so." He says soon after that, "But those of the flesh are unable to please God."

So now take before you this commandment: "You shall love God, your Lord, with all your heart," and contemplate it. Bring it forward and investigate what kind of commandment it is. Think how far you are from fulfilling this commandment. Yes, you have still not even begun to fulfill it, namely to suffer and to do from the heart what God desires to have done. It is a pure hypocrisy when one wants to crawl into a corner and think: "Oh, I want to love God. Oh, how I have loved God, who is my Father! Oh, how favorable I have been to him!" and more of the same. Yes, if he [God] does things according to what pleases us, then we could say many such words. But when he once gives us misfortune and trouble, then we no longer regard him as a God, or as a Father.

A true love of God does not act so towards him. Rather it is in the heart and says also with the mouth, "Lord God, I am your creature. Do to me as you desire. It matters not to me. I know that I am yours. And if you desire that I should die this hour or soon suffer a great tragedy then from my heart I gladly suffer. I will never regard my life, honor and wealth as higher or greater than your will, which will be good for me all my life." But you will find no such people who hold themselves completely to this commandment. For your whole life that you live in your body in your five senses, what you do with your body should all be governed so that it praises God, according to the demand of this commandment that says: "You shall love God, your Lord with all your heart and all your soul and all your mind." Christ wants to say, "Love God with your whole heart, your whole soul, your whole mind, so that you never fail to experience it in your outward life; namely, it is when everything that you do, asleep or awake, working or standing idle, eating or drinking is directed so that it is done to God from love in your heart. Likewise your mind and thoughts will also be completely directed through and through on God, that is, you would not entertain an opinion that you weren't sure was pleasing to God." Yeah, where are people that do that?

Erl. 14, 144–146: Sermon on Trinity 18, Matthew 22:34–36

It was a false, misleading dream That God His Law had given
That sinners could themselves redeem And by their works gain heaven.
The Law is but a mirror bright To bring the inbred sin to light
That lurks within our nature. (*TLH* 377: 3)

Monday

But when the time was fulfilled God sent his Son, born of a woman and made under the law, to redeem those who were under the law, that we receive adoption. Galatians 4:4,5

Christ had committed no sin, nor was any guile found in his mouth, so that he was guilty of nothing before the law. Yet, as much as he was made innocent, righteous, holy and blessed before the law, it [the law] fought against him and exerted its oppression on him much more and harsher than it attempts to do against us though we are sinners, cursed and condemned. For it had accused him as if he were the worst blasphemer and disturber and it seemed that he was guilty of all sins in the whole world against God. It also then brought about so much anger and fear against him that he had to shed his blood. Finally it condemned him through its judgment to death and not only to a terrible death but to the most shameful and scandalous death on the cross.

This could readily be called a wondrous battle. For the law, as a creature, undertook to accuse its creator and was allowed to use its might and oppression against the Son of God that it would curse him as any other sinner. Yet it had no right [to do that] as it has against us who are children of wrath. Since, then, the law had so horribly and blasphemously treated its God, it stands to rights that it must allow itself to be accused. There Christ himself marches against the law and says, "Mrs. law, you are surely both a mighty and unconquerable queen and a horrible tyrant over all human transgression and you have a right to do that. But what have I done to you that you have accused, terrified and condemned me, an innocent man, so horribly and blasphemously?" The law, which previously condemned and executed the whole world, thence stops in its tracks since to this charge it can reply and excuse nothing. It must also let itself be condemned and executed because it holds no further right or might, not only over and against Christ, since it so shamefully had sold itself out against all justice and had executed him so horribly, but also over all those that believe on him.

For Christ says to the same, "Come to me, all of you who labor and are under the yoke and load of the law. If I wanted to, I could have overcome the law with all its rights and justice without myself becoming guilty so that I would not have to suffer or die, etc., since I am the Lord of the law and so it has no right to me. But for your sake, who were under the law, I became a man and have thrown myself under the law, that is, out of pure love and mercy I have given myself and let myself come here into the same jail, oppression and slavery of the law. There you were born and must serve. I let the law govern and rule over me, whose Lord I still am. It frightened and accused me as the greatest sinner, yes, sentenced me to death on the cross though it had no right to do it. By this I have doubly overcome the law, laid it to the ground and executed it. First as a Son of God and Lord of the law; thereafter, in your person or in your place, which is as much as if you yourself had overcome the law. For my victory is truly and surely your own."

St. Paul also speaks in this way about this wonderful war in his epistles. He makes of the law a very mighty hero or giant who has attacked Christ, condemned him and put him to death. But Christ has turned around and flattened him and since he is again resurrected from the dead, he has conquered, condemned and executed him [the law]. As in Ephesians 2:16, "He has executed the enemy through his death." And Chapter 4:8 quoting from the 68th Psalm, "He has ascended on high and led captivity captive." He brings the same discussion also in Romans, Corinthians and Colossians, where he says, "He has condemned sin through sin," etc.

So now Christ has driven away the law from our conscience through his victory and overcome it so that it can no longer bring us to shame before God, neither driving nor condemning us to despair. So already sins no longer expose, accuse and terrorize us. But the conscience grasps these words of the apostle against this, "Christ has freed us from the law," and it clings to these words by faith and is comforted. Yes, it becomes so stubborn and brave in the Holy Ghost that it is able to present itself obstinately to the law and say, "I don't care so much about all your terrorizing and threatening for you also have erred and sinned much more coarsely than I have in that you have crucified God's Son and therefore have exerted might and injustice to him. Therefore, also the sins that you have done against him can nevermore be forgiven you. Yes, you have lost all rights so that you can from now on no longer attack and put me to death. Rather, you are now overcome, attacked and bound with chains so you can harm neither Christ nor me, the one who believes in Christ." Since he has received you and preserved you he has given the victory. So we are now free of the law to eternity and have become free as we remain in another, in Christ. Therefore, praise and thanks be given to our dear God, who has given us this victory through Jesus Christ, our Lord. Amen.

Altb. VI, 758-759: Lectures on Galatians, 1535; cf. AE 26 & 27

Yet as the Law must be fulfilled Or we must die despairing,
Christ came and hath God's anger stilled, Our human nature sharing.
He hath for us the Law obeyed And thus the Father's vengeance stayed
Which over us impended. (*TLH* 377: 5)

Tuesday

Since you are his children, God has sent the Spirit of his Son into your hearts who cries, "Abba, dear Father."
Galatians 4:6

The Holy Ghost is sent in two ways. In the beginning of Christianity he was sent in a visible form, Acts 2, as he also came upon Christ visibly by the Jordan in the form of a dove. He came in the form of a fire upon the apostles and a few other believers. There was a reason that the Holy Ghost was sent to Christianity in this way at first. For Christianity had to be established and attested through such visible signs for the sake of unbelievers as St. Paul shows in 1 Corinthians 14, "The tongues," he says, "are not signs for the believer but rather for the unbeliever." But after that, now that Christianity is gathered and was attested to by these signs, there is no longer any need that the Holy Ghost be sent in a visible form.

The other way [that he is sent] is this: When the Holy Ghost is sent through the Word into the hearts of believers, as it says here, "God has sent the Spirit of his Son into your hearts," etc. This happens without any visible form or sign when we hear the Word, read it, etc. Our hearts are inflamed and enlightened through such oral preaching by which we become different and new people, consider everything in a different way, conduct ourselves in a new way, and gain other thoughts, feelings and desires than we had before. Such a transformation or new understanding, thought and will is surely not a work of human reason or powers but rather a gift and work of the Holy Ghost. When the Word is preached, it at once both purifies hearts through faith and makes us spiritually minded towards God.

So there is a great difference between us and those who are enemies of the gospel or those who pervert it and confuse people. We, by God's grace, have the judgment that we can actually know and be sure from God's Word what God's intention concerning us is. We are able to set in order all kinds of law and doctrine and distinguish between our vocation and life and other peoples'. On the other hand, the papists and fanatical spirits have nothing that is a definite understanding and never actually and surely know what to make of things. For the fanatics pervert and falsify God's Word as the papists persecute and blaspheme it. But when someone doesn't have the Word, then he cannot have either a sure understanding or judgment about anything.

Though no one can observe anything about our outward appearance to prove that we have received the Holy Ghost with his gifts and are renewed in our hearts, one can nevertheless understand and note that we see everything differently, judge things otherwise than others and also speak and acknowledge other things than what we previously sought after. For, before, we were not able to regard or judge anything rightly and have also not spoken or confessed as we now, God be praised, speak and confess after the dear sun of truth has risen above us and enlightened us; namely, that all our action and nature is sinful and cursed and that Christ alone is our only merit *congrui* and *condigni*, for whose sake God is merciful to us and makes us good.

Therefore, we should ask for nothing more even if the world (of whom we show that their works are evil) regards us and proclaims us as the most shameful heretic, rebel, destroyer of all religion and common peace, possessed by the devil, from whom we speak and to whom all our affairs should lead. Against such outrage and perverted judgment of the world it should be enough for us that our conscience give witness to us that we are sure that God has not only given us faith in Christ but also the kind of faith that is free to publicly teach and confess before all the world. So as it is in us by faith in the heart, we also speak and confess with our mouth, as the 116th Psalm says, "I believe, therefore I speak, though I be afflicted."

Thereafter we diligently practice a desire for a God-pleasing life, guarding against sins, so much as we are able. But if we sin we do not do it intentionally but out of weakness and it gives us sorrow. It can surely happen that we fall, for the devil pursues the Christian constantly according to 1 Peter 5, and many remaining sins still adhere to our flesh and the whole nature. So, as far as we consider our flesh, we are still sinners, even when we have received the Holy Ghost. So there is a very small difference between a Christian and other good, worldly people if one would only see the outer appearance. For the works that a Christian does have a poor appearance outwardly because he only does what is for him to do according to his station and calling. One may administer an office in the common system, rule his house, farm his field, counsel, help and serve his neighbor. A fleshly person does not regard such things as great but considers them crude, common, poor works that are good for nothing, which even a layman or even a heathen could do.

For the world perceives nothing from the Spirit of God because it also has a perverted understanding and thoughts concerning the works of those who are saved by God and are Christians.

Altb. VI, 761-762: Lectures on Galatians, 1535; cf. AE 26 & 27

Thou highest Comfort in ev'ry need, Grant that neither shame nor death we heed,
That e'en then our courage may never fail us When the Foe shall accuse and assail us.
Lord have mercy! (*TLH* 231: 4)

Wednesday

Who cries, "Abba, dear Father." Galatians 4:6

St. Paul could well have said, "God has sent the Spirit of his Son into our hearts, who there calls out, 'Abba, dear Father.' " But he has intentionally said, "Who there *cries*," so that he would show here the affliction of a Christian who is yet weak and has weak faith. In Romans 8 he calls it an inexpressible sigh. "Because of this," he says, "the Spirit also helps in our weakness. For we do not know what we should say, what is right, but the Spirit himself pleads for us mightily with inexpressible sighs."

Now this is a very great and mighty comfort. St. Paul says here, "God has sent the Spirit of his Son into our hearts, who cries there, 'Abba, dear Father.' " And in Romans 8, "that he helps us in our weakness and pleads for us with inexpressible sighs." Whoever believes this as sure has no need in any affliction no matter how great it might be. But there are sometimes many things that hinder this faith. First, we are conceived and born in sin, ruined and deluded by the devil. Thereafter, this defect naturally gives birth to doubting so that we can never be so sure about the grace that God directs to us. [It asks] how it is proper that God should graciously be pleased with us? Above this our adversary, the devil, comes here with horrible, frightening roaring and says, "Behold, you are a sinner so that God is angry with you and will damn you eternally."

We have nothing to aid and preserve us against such great and unbearable roaring and screaming of the devil except only the bare Word which stands Christ, who has overcome sins, death and all evil, before the Christian. But at first there is great effort and work to be able to hold on fast and tight to this same Christ, when we are in such terror, fear and war. There is nothing in our minds that the Christian can experience. For we do not see him [Christ] with our eyes so the heart also feels nothing that will help in the affliction that is directly at hand. Yes, it lets itself see that he is angry with us and will completely forsake us. So a person feels in his afflictions how mighty his sins are, how weak his flesh is, how we are so fickle and doubting in faith and also we feel the fiery darts of the devil, terror before death and before God's wrath and justice. All of this in one heap cries out so mightily and horribly over us that we think that it can be no other way but that we must eternally doubt and die.

But when we are in the middle of this and are stuck most deeply in such terror of the law, where sins thunder over us, death makes us tremble and shake; the devil roars most horribly, then the Holy Ghost (as St. Paul says here) arises in our heart to cry out, "Abba, dear Father." And such crying as this is much stronger than that of the law, of sins, of death and of the devil, even when they sound so big and ghastly. He breaks through the clouds and brings this with all his might into heaven, comes before God's ears and will be heard, etc.

Therefore, St. Paul would reveal with these Words what kind of weakness in which the saved of God are yet beset. As he also says in Romans 8, "The Spirit helps us in our weakness." So since this means to us that we will experience more fear than hope, more sorrow than comfort, etc., we allow ourselves to think according to our experience, that God is more wrathful to us than merciful to us. Therefore, the Holy Ghost is sent into our heart, which does not secretly sigh and call out but rather cries with all his greatest might, "Abba, dear Father," and he pleads for us, according to God's will, with unspeakable sighs.

But how? When our conscience is rightly, seriously terrified and attacked, it soon happens that we grasp Christ and believe that he is our savior. But then the law's strength is at hand with its work and doesn't quit scaring and troubling us. For the devil also does not remain outside with his fiery darts. With all his might and power, he dares to take Christ from us along with everything that we should trust in. There a lesser man fails completely. We do not submit and doubt, for if that happens, we are as a broken reed and a smoking flax.

Yet the Holy Ghost helps us in this war in our weakness and pleads for us in inexpressible sighs, witnessing to our spirit that we are God's children. In this way, he would again help our heart so that it sighs to our savior and High Priest, Jesus Christ, overcoming the weakness of the flesh and comforting our heart so that it can say, "Abba, dear Father." Such a sigh, that we can barely feel and is truly thin, St. Paul calls a cry and inexpressible sigh by which heaven and earth are filled. So he also calls it a cry and sigh of the Spirit because the Holy Ghost awakens and directs this cry in our hearts when we are weak and in affliction.

Altb. VI, 764–765: Lectures on Galatians, 1535; cf. AE 26 & 27

Prompt us, Lord, to come before Him   With a childlike heart to pray;
Sigh in us, O Holy Spirit, When we know not what to say.
Then our prayer is not in vain, And our faith new strength shall gain. (*TLH* 226: 5)

Thursday

The Lord said to Moses, "Why do you cry to me? Say to the children of Israel that they should go forward."
Exodus 14:15

God the Lord says to Moses in Exodus 14:15 at the Red Sea, "Why do you cry to me?" And yet, Moses did not cry out. But he was trembling and quailing so much that he could surely have doubted and there was no apparent faith or courage in him, but only unbelief, fear and doubt. For he could see that the children of Israel were trapped on both sides with mountains, with the sea in front and enemies behind so that they could go nowhere. He had brought them into this situation. It was easy for good Moses to become stepped on and frightened so that he could barely rebel [against it]. But why then does Scripture say that he had cried out? In his ear there was no crying any more than there was in the ears of the children of Israel. But God took this to be a cry that he heard in heaven. So we should not judge this kind of sighing and crying according to our senses but rather according to God's Word which teaches here that the Holy Ghost will be given to such troubled hearts that are attacked by terror and doubt, so that he assists and comforts him. For they are not overcome and ruined in such affliction and other needs. Rather, that affliction, fear and need are overcome even if they bring great fear, trouble and labor.

The papists have thought, "whoever has the Holy Ghost does not feel any terror or sorrow for the sake of their sins, does not fear death but rather, is always joyful, etc." But they speak of the matter as inexperienced people, not from the Scriptures, but out of their own heads. It is just what the fanatics try to say now. But St. Paul says that the power of Christ is mighty in our weakness. So the Holy Ghost helps our weakness and pleads for us with unspeakable sighs. From this it surely follows that when we need the comfort and help of the Holy Ghost most, he then is also near and mighty in us and with us when we are weakest and doubt is at hand. Wherever one is comforted in his trouble and affliction, the Holy Ghost has done and bestowed his work. But he has to deal especially with those who are very terrified and weary and he draws near (as in the Psalms) to those before the gates of hell.

As I have just said of Moses, he was in the water and wherever he looked on all sides before his eyes, he saw the apparent certain death of all his people. Because of this, he was easily stuck in the greatest fear and doubt and especially felt doubt in his heart as mightily and horribly as if the devil had cried out against him and said, "Behold, on this day the people must all stop, miserably perish and be ruined. For it is not possible for them to escape by any way or path. You alone have brought them into such great misery, fear and need and no one else. You, you have led them out of Egypt." The cry of the people was also added to this, who said, "Were there not graves in Egypt that you had to lead us away to die in the desert? Why have you led us out of Egypt? Didn't we tell you in Egypt, stop and let us serve the Egyptians? etc." Here Moses certainly did not have the Holy Ghost *speculative* as the papists speak of him, like a blind person talks about color. Rather, [he had him] in truth, who mightily pleaded for him with unspeakable sighs so that Moses cried in his heart and said, "Dear Lord, since I have led the people out of Egypt as you have told me, so also stay with me and deliver, etc." The Scriptures call this sigh a mighty cry.

If I wanted to treat this passage of St. Paul in a fuller and richer way, then I would gladly explicate what the Holy Ghost's own work and office are and when he usually effects his office, namely, that he comforts us and helps uphold our weakness when we are in trouble, etc. Therefore, in affliction, we should certainly not judge the Holy Ghost's work and office according to our senses or according to the cry that the law, sins and the devil, etc., causes in our conscience. For if we follow our feelings and would believe the devil's cry then invariably we must quickly say that the Holy Ghost must have cancelled all help and comfort to us and that we are expelled and rejected from God's presence by everything.

But much better that instead we think as St. Paul says, namely that the Holy Ghost upholds our weakness and cries, "Abba, dear Father," that is, we should remember that the Holy Ghost at least awakens a little sigh in our hearts when we seem to be in affliction. Yet God receives that sigh as a great mighty cry and an inexpressible sigh. Therefore, learn and get used to this, that you cling to Christ in all your affliction and weakness and sigh to the one who gives you the Holy Ghost who cries, "Abba, dear Father!" To this, God the Father answers and says, "I hear nothing in all the world before this single sigh and this sigh in my ears is such a powerful and strong cry that both heaven and earth are filled with it and all the cries of the devils, etc., are drowned out."

Altb. VI, 766-767: Lectures on Galatians, 1535; cf. AE 26 & 27

Thou highest Comfort in ev'ry need, Grant that neither shame nor death we heed,
That e'en then our courage may never fail us When the Foe shall accuse and assail us.
Lord, have mercy! (*TLH* 231: 4)

Friday

*So remain in the freedom by which Christ has freed us and
do not again be taken in the servant's yoke. Galatians 5:1*

St. Paul has arranged his words because he wants to give
something common a particular meaning. So one should readily and
deeply think about these words. "So now remain," he says. As if he
would say, "Here you must truly be on guard and be on the lookout
that you remain established." In what? In freedom. In whose
[freedom]? Not the one by which the kaiser but rather by which
Christ has made us free. The kaiser had given the pope the city of
Rome along with other lands free; yes, he had to give it. On top of
that, [he] also [gave] privileges and freedoms for the pope's shorn
and anointed bunch, etc., which is also called a freedom, but a
temporal one through which the pope along with his barns are freed
of the common burdens which the other subjects of the kaiser must
bear.

Over that there is yet another freedom, namely, [freedom] of the
flesh or much more, of the devil, through which he, unfortunately,
rules mightily in all the world. For those who presume to have this
freedom belong neither to God nor a single law but rather
mischievously do everything that they desire. Everyone hunts to the
ends of the earth after that kind of freedom. The fanatic spirits and
sectarians also are drawn to this, even if they, with words, would
give another impression and put up an appearance. For they hold,
teach, believe and do what occurs to them, not considering if it is
right or not and so they want no masters or punishment. These stay
in the freedom by which the devil has freed them. We want nothing
to do with this freedom, although they, unfortunately, do! All too
strongly they customarily act this way and the world doesn't desire
or crave any other freedom. Neither do we here want to discuss
anything of the freedom that one worldly station has over and against
another, but rather of a spiritual [freedom], which is at enmity with
the devil and which he fights against with all his strength.

And that is the one by which Christ has set us free, not from a
human servitude in the prison of Babylon or the Turk, but from the
eternal wrath of God. But where? In the conscience. There our
freedom turns and it proceeds no further. For Christ has set us free,
not according to a temporal or fleshly manner, but rather by a
spiritual one. That is, he has freed us in such a way that our
conscience is free, is comforted and joyful and is not frightened of
the coming wrath. This alone is called and is the true freedom that

none could treasure or attend to highly enough. It is great and wonderful, so that if one would compare and reckon it next to the temporal or fleshly freedom that the world settles on seeking, they are barely a drop compared to the whole sea.

For who can proclaim what kind of great thing this is that one hold as sure in his heart and believe that God is not angry with him, yes, will nevermore be angry but that he is and will remain in eternity his gracious and merciful Father for the sake of Christ? Truly, it is a wonderful and ungraspable freedom that the divine majesty is gracious to one, defends him, helps him in every need, and finally will also make him bodily free. So our body, which is buried in corruption, in disgrace and weakness, again shall be resurrected incorruptible in all power and glory. Because of this freedom, namely, that we should be freed eternally from the wrath of God, it is an inexpressible freedom and much greater than heaven and earth and all creatures.

Out of this follows another freedom. We will be made free and safe from the law, sins, death, from the devil's might and hell, etc. For just as God's wrath cannot frighten us, since Christ has freed us from it, so also the law, sins, etc., also cannot charge us or condemn us. Even if we are guilty of the law and sins frighten us yet they are unable to drive us to despair and curse us. For there faith overcomes the world and it says readily, "That has no power over me. For my Lord Christ has saved me from them and made me free." So also death, even if there is no mightier or more horrible tyrant in all the world since he slays all mankind, is used by Christ to free us. It still is able to frighten you but it can do no more than that. For faith holds these or similar Words of Christ, "I am the resurrection and the life. Whoever believes in me will live even if he dies." This faith sets things right and receives comfort in all troubles and terrors of death. Therefore, one should readily consider what a great necessary thing freedom is for a Christian. Surely these words, freedom from God's wrath, law, death, etc., are easily and quickly repeated. But when it also happens that one feels the magnitude and power of this freedom in the conscience, that is, when one should be helped in the evil of death and other spiritual wars and afflictions and with this he is defended and protected, this is the single true use and the foremost fruit of this freedom. This comes home to one so dramatically that no one can say enough about it.

Altb. VI, 814–815: Lectures on Galatians, 1535; cf. AE 26 & 27

Blest be the Lord, who foiled their threat That they could not devour us;
Our souls, like birds, escaped their net, They could not overpow'r us.
The snare is broken—we are free! Our help is ever, Lord, in Thee,
Who madest earth and heaven. (*TLH* 267: 3)

Saturday

You, who would be righteous through the law, have lost Christ and are fallen from grace. Galatians 5:4

This is referred to often, "You are no longer in the kingdom of grace." For just as someone who falls out of a ship must definitely drown in the sea, so it can be no different for one who falls from grace, who must be lost and condemned. Therefore, whoever would be righteous through the law suffers a shipwreck and delivers himself into the danger of eternal death. But how can one who has lost God's grace and favor in Christ always end up committing some great folly and sin and then want to counter it with the law of Moses? He only retains it, so that he is always piling God's wrath upon himself and loads himself with all kinds of misfortune, etc.

But they that want to be justified through the law of God have fallen from grace. Friend, to where have they fallen, who want to be justified by human statutes, their vows and service? Into the deepest bottom of hell. Not so! Rather, they are led by the angels in heaven. For they have certainly taught: "All those who walk in the order, etc., after St. Benedict, Francis, etc., will have God's peace and mercy." So whoever loves to keep chastity, poverty, obedience would have eternal life. But disregard any such terrible and cursed lies and note everything St. Paul says, "You have lost Christ," and what Christ himself said, "Whoever believes on the Son has eternal life. Whoever doesn't believe the Son will not see life, but the wrath of God remains over him." So, "who does not believe is already judged," John 3.

Therefore, every Christian should consider these Words well: "You have fallen from grace." For they contain much that is weighty, namely, that whoever falls from grace, nevermore can become cleansed from his sins, that is, nevermore receives righteousness, freedom and life, all of which Christ has earned and acquired through his death and resurrection. Instead, he receives in place of this heavenly wealth God's wrath and justice, sins, death, so that he must be the devil's own servant and eternally damned.

But to those who are established fast in the freedom by which Christ has made us free, this passage is a comfort. For he maintains the doctrine of faith and the article of Christian righteousness. It comforts us in the mightiest way against the pope's raging, that persecutes and condemns us as heretics because we teach this article. This passage of St. Paul, "You have lost Christ," should justly terrify all enemies of faith and grace, that is all works-righteous people, so that they would stop persecuting and blaspheming the doctrine of faith, grace, life and eternal salvation. But they are so horribly hardened and impenitent that with seeing eyes they are blind and with hearing ears they are deaf. For even when they read or hear this terrifying judgment spoken by the apostle in opposition to them, they do not contest it. Therefore, we leave them behind for they are blind leaders of the blind.

Altb. VI, 823: Lectures on Galatians, 1535; cf. AE 26 & 27

Preserve Thy Word and preaching, The truth that makes us whole,
The mirror of Thy glory, The power that saves the soul.
Oh, may this living water, This dew of heavenly grace,
Sustain us while here living Until we see they face! (*TLH* 264: 5)

Week of Trinity XIX

Sunday

But be renewed in the spirit of your mind and put on the new man who is created according to God in honest righteousness and holiness. Ephesians 4:23,24

Just as we will take off the old man, he also desires that we then put on the new man so that day to day we become ever more new people. This happens when first we are freed from error (or the erroneous thoughts and conceits of our ruined human nature which cannot rightly know God or think of him or fear him or believe in him). And now, through God's Word, we hold right thoughts about him and trust in his grace with right faith that he desires to forgive us our sins for Christ's sake. So we implore him for that, as well as for the sake of withstanding and overcoming powers, so that he would bestow might and that faith would be preserved and increased.

First he calls it, "Being renewed in the spirit of your mind." That is to always receive and be strengthened in the right true understanding and clear confession of Christ against erroneous and false conceits. Whoever becomes so renewed (he says) is the kind of person who "is made according to God in right or true righteousness and holiness." In the old man is nothing but error through which the devil leads him to ruin. But the new man has the Spirit and Truth instead, through which his heart is enlightened, which bring righteousness and holiness with them. So this person follows God's Word and desires a good, godly walk and life, etc., instead of error which follows lust and the love of sins and every vice. Such a new person is created according to God, as an image of God, that must be different than those that live in error and lusts, without the knowledge and obedience of God. So if he is an image of God, then a true divine knowledge, thought and mind must be in him and then a godly life, or righteousness and holiness, follow, as in God himself.

Adam was originally created by God in this image, both in his truthful soul, without any error, in true knowledge of God and faith, but also, in addition to this, according to a holy and pure life. That is a life without impurity, filthy desires, greed, sexual impurities, envy and hatred, etc. His children, that is all of mankind, would also have remained so from birth if the man had not let himself be deceived by the devil and had so ruined himself. But now, through God's grace and Spirit, the Christian is again renewed to that divine image. So they shall also live, that both the soul or spirit would be right before God and would please him by faith in Christ, and also his body, or his entire outward life would be pure and holy so that it is a true holiness.

So a small or great pretended holiness and purity are only but a false appearance in which the world is clothed. This is what the heretics and monkish saints do when they establish their holiness and purity only upon outward, special works and self-chosen works. These look good and are called before people fine holiness and pure praying and fasting, being cloistered, etc. But inwardly, they are and remain proud, poisonous, greedy, hateful, full of filthy fleshly lust and evil thoughts, as Christ also says of such people in Matthew 5:29 and Luke 16:15.

Erl. 9, 310–312: Sermon on Trinity 19, Ephesians 4:22–28

Renew me, O eternal Light,	Destroy in me the lust of sin,
And let my heart and soul be bright,	From all impureness make me clean.
Illumined with the light of grace	O, grant me pow'r and strength, my God,
That issues from Thy holy face.	To strive against my flesh and blood! (*TLH* 398: 1–2)

Monday

Be angry and do not sin. Do not let the sun go down upon your wrath. Ephesians 4:26

So a Christian must not dress himself with wrath but rather extinguish and dampen the first sparks. That is proper to the new man. He can conquer wrath. He will not be made to stumble again by the devil from the faith started in him nor will he lose what he has started.

For if he would follow such an irritation of his flesh, then he would already be led by the old man again through error into damnation. He is no longer strong in himself, following his own lusts, and adorned with lies, and still wanting the right to rage and revenge, as the world does, which also chafes, "They treated me with great might and injustice. Should I put up with that? I have a just cause. I will not submit." Then he is again purchased. He himself makes his own case unrighteous both before God and the people. As the old saying also says, "Whoever hits back is wrong."

That is why it is forbidden in both divine and human law for anyone to be his own judge. For this reason, God establishes authority and the office of judge, that he [God] will punish unrighteousness for his own sake. This is called (when it is rightly used), not man's justice, wrath and punishment, but God's. Therefore, whoever strikes out against that justice strikes God himself in the mouth and commits two-fold injustice and thus receives a two-fold curse. But if you desire to have and seek justice because you are not being protected, do it in an orderly way, namely, in the place or among the people who are appointed by God to do that, those whom you can call on and receive defense. If that will help you, as the judge and authorities are responsible for it, use them. Where they won't help, then you must suffer it and summon God as is said further elsewhere.

In short, a strange verdict is here decided and set down. Whoever will not control his wrath and wants to hold onto his anger longer than a day or overnight is no Christian. Then where will those remain who perpetually bear wrath and hate one, two, three, seven, ten years? That is no longer a human wrath but rather the devil's wrath from hell, which is never satisfied or quenched. Rather, when this wrath burns inside, if it could, it would ruin everything in an instant with hell fire. Just as this devil is not satisfied that he has brought the whole human race trouble and death in the fall but cannot have peace until he leads all mankind into eternal damnation with him.

Therefore, you should rightly with all diligence defend yourself as a Christian against such a burden. God can have patience that you let your heart boil and that wrath then reigns in you, even though that is also sinful; only that it not completely overcome everything, but that you fight it in you and through the knowledge of God's Word and your faith you extinguish it and let it sink. If you are alone or you go to bed then you should say your "Our Father" and ask for forgiveness and you must remember that God has forgiven you much more, and daily forgives much more, than your neighbor could possibly sin against you.

Erl. 9, 316–318: Sermon on Trinity 20, Ephesians 5:15–21

Create in me a new heart, Lord,
That gladly I obey Thy Word
And naught but what Thou wilt, desire;
With such new life my soul inspire.

Grant that I only Thee may love
And seek those things which are above
Till I behold Thee face to face,
O Light eternal, through Thy grace. (*TLH* 398: 3–4)

Tuesday

Jesus said to him, "Truly, truly, I say to you, if you do not eat the flesh of the Son of man and drink his blood, you have no life in you." John 6:53

The Lord swears with a great effort, "Truly, truly," by which we truly heed this text. It also presents his ability. The Turks, pope and Jews and also many among us are yet far from this. It is a great thing and very difficult that one should establish his heart, faith and future on these Words, that in this flesh and blood lay eternal life. God lays us not before the divine majesty but rather [before] the man Christ. This is the most vexing thing to reason, that if I would be saved, it shall be through my soul hanging on to and bound to the flesh and blood that has died for me so I will be bound to it and enter into it and say, "I know no other life or being freed from sins, except that I plunge my soul into the flesh which dies for me and the blood shed for me."

I let that be my comfort and will hear of nothing else besides that. Now if the devil comes and says, "Oh, friend, what have you done that is good? If you were good then you could go to heaven but since you have become evil in life and are wicked, then you must go to hell." But you answer, "The pope, devil and Turks also teach that. No, I know much besides that. Even if I had done many good things, yet I would not give so much for all of them. Even if I had lived with such chastity as the Virgin Mary, yes, even if I had every holy work yet I would base nothing on that for none of it gives eternal life."

It is not as Hilarious the Hermit said as he comforted himself, "Why do you fear before death, my soul? Haven't you served God in the wilderness for seventy-three years and done many good works, etc. And yet finally I must doubt about it." The devil carries all of it away and it belongs in hell. It does not hold the assault. But rather, it should sound like this, as you should say, "It is not good that I have led such an evil life but yet for the sake of doing evil I am not conquered and troubled. Also for the sake of good works I am not measured." So do not go too far either to the left or to the right but much better remain in the middle of the road and say, "There stands one who says his flesh is our soul's food. I let him handle it."

Since, then, our good works do not stop the sting, as you also cannot, yet the flesh and blood stop every opposition. Christ cannot be weakened but my works can be weakened. If you only remain with his flesh and blood there is no need. But if you should fall from it, as the devil wants to bring about, then you have lost and you are out. You are already overcome.

Here you have the text in which you have life. If you shrink from it then you have made a mistake. With his Gospel St. John has served this up so that he portrays the article of justification of the world to the heart and would set it before your eyes. But it didn't help much when you could not see him under the papacy. It opposes this. So if we would die, then curious people would do as before. They would hold onto works as was previously done under the papacy. So they would not persevere in St. John with his mighty gospel, much less our books. Yes, the text of this gospel is also sung and read in all churches.

That is the preaching the Lord had done after the miracle when he fed five thousand men with five barley loaves and a few fish and had handed it out. He said that whoever did not eat his flesh and drink his blood does not have eternal life.

Altb. V, 676–677: Sermons on the Gospel of St. John, Chapters 6–8, 1531; cf. AE 23

Thy body, given for me, O Savior, Thy blood which Thou for me didst shed,
These are my life and strength forever, By them my hungry soul is fed.
Lord, may Thy body and Thy blood Be for my soul the highest good. (*TLH* 315: 11)

Wednesday

As the living Father has sent me, and I live because of the Father, so whoever consumes me will also live because of me. John 6:57

He said so often, "I live by and from the fact that the Father is in me and I in him. Therefore, whoever eats of me will live because of me. For I am in him. That is, whoever believes in me and is preserved will live by and from that. For he is in me and I am in him."

That is a beautiful Johannine text. For he portrays and describes Christ as not only man but also as God. He doesn't say that he has life because he thinks about the Father. Rather, "The Father is in me who is my life." So he has eternal life because the Father has begotten the Son, and not the Son the Father. Such life, as he has from the Father, and the fact that he has become a man according to the Father's will, has freed us. Since the Father is now in him, he has bestowed it [such life] upon us with these Words, "As I have life because the Father is in me, and he has given it to me, so you shall also have life by this because you are in me and I am in you." Now this is completely right except that we are not with God in a natural manner as Christ is. For the human nature and divine nature are surely not by nature a unity even though they are in the single and indivisible person, which you cannot divide from one another just as sugar water is water but so mingled with sugar that no one now can divide the sugar and water from each other, even though there are two different natures. It is not a perfect comparison but yet it shows in a small way that Christ, our true Savior, is a person that is God and man. If you grab hold of the human nature of Christ you also have caught the divine nature. Just as in sugar water you have truly found sugar, so the divine and human natures of the Lord Christ are also one cake.

As Christ is now made an inseparable person, who is God and man, so from Christ and us are also made one body and flesh that we could not divide. For his flesh is in us and our flesh is in him so that he is also truly, substantially present in us, etc. But that is a different union than a personal union. It is not so high and great as the union where Christ, true man, is one God with the Father and the Holy Ghost. Yet in this, it is settled that Christ would become the Lord through becoming one body with us through his flesh and blood so that I would belong to him just as all members of my body belong to one another. For my hand, arm, foot and mouth belong to my body and are one body with each other as every drop of my blood belongs to my whole body. What a part of the body fails to do also ruins the others. If a part of the body is given honor, evil, or good, the whole body receives it.

So we also have come and been united with Christ in one body and manner so that what happens to me for good or evil happens to him. If I strike you or make you sorrow or I honor you, I also strike Christ or make Christ himself sorrow or be given honor. For whatever happens to a Christian, happens to Christ himself. He turns up his nose at that. The tooth does not bite the tongue without the whole body feeling it. If you hurt a hand or foot then the whole body has a bad day. Even when a hair is pulled out, the whole body feels it.

In short, whoever strikes a Christian or locks him in a tower throws the body of Christ himself into a tower. For the Christians are his members. He receives them and is saddened over these things just as if it happened to him. As in the Prophet Zechariah, Chapter 2:8, "Whoever touches you grasps the apple of my eye." And in the Acts of the Apostles, the Lord Christ says to Saul who is persecuting Christians, "Saul, Saul, why do you persecute me?" And in Matthew 25:40 it is clearly established, "What you did to the least of my own you have done to me."

But this union is hidden and doesn't appear before the world. We see the opposite. For the godless bishops treat us as if they received neither God nor man among us and as if there were no union between us and Christ. But faith sees it and learns to recognize Christ in an invisible life and manner, not from reason. Faith also finds the proof because many much better people, who with all humility and gladness acknowledge Christ and God's Word, again are preaching lies and by this they let go of their life and everything else.

Altb. V, 680–681: Sermons on the Gospel of St. John, Chapters 6–8, 1531; cf. AE 23

With Thee, Lord, I am now united; I live in Thee and Thou in me.
No sorrow fills my soul, delighted It finds its only joy in Thee.
Lord, may Thy body and Thy blood Be for my soul the highest good. (*TLH* 315: 12)

Thursday

It is the Spirit who makes alive. The flesh is of no use at all. The Words I speak are Spirit and they are life. John 6:63

This is a very fine passage which for six or seven years now has suffered hard knocks as a great martyr. But I hope it is finished. The blasphemers of the Sacrament have urged this passage against the Sacrament and have further used it to abolish the presence of the living true body of Christ in the Lord's Supper, so that it is only bread and wine and that the body and the blood of Christ are given to no one in the Supper, for it is flesh. They have desired by this to establish that Christ says, "The flesh is of no use but it is the Spirit who makes alive."

Because of this, we must be prepared against this foolish and mad spirit. Christ does not say, "MY flesh is of no use." For above he has said, "My flesh is true food" and boasted that his flesh gives life to the world. But now, because they are angry at this and will not believe that his flesh is true food, he answers, "What are you doing? My Words are pure life. When I say, 'My flesh is the food,' those are Words which also belong to the Spirit so that you will understand of these Words, 'drink my blood and eat my flesh,' that this is purely a matter of the Spirit." It is incontrovertible that this text compels that he is not speaking of his flesh, that is also already a food and is truly spiritual food, full of the Holy Ghost and a divine flesh in which is found pure Spirit shocked full of grace; for it gives life to the world.

But now he sets Spirit and flesh against one another and speaks differentiating each from the other. So this passage cannot be understood as pertaining to the flesh of Christ in which is Spirit and by which he makes alive. So we should not think or let these Words, "The flesh is of no use" be used to apply to the body of Christ, since it cannot be understood as this flesh. Rather, this is the meaning. It is just as God says in Genesis 6 (where the world was ruined by the filth of sin), "My Spirit will no longer remain with man, for they are flesh." And above in John 3 Christ also says, "That which is born of the flesh is flesh and what is born of the Spirit is spirit." So he also here sets flesh and Spirit against each other and says, "The flesh is of no use and dead but the Spirit makes alive." Here Christ calls "flesh" everything that is born from the flesh, as Adam's children, and so comes from the flesh. Except for the single body of Christ which is not born of the flesh but "of the Holy Ghost." As we confess in the Symbol, "I believe in Christ, who was conceived," not from the flesh, but "by the Holy Ghost." He had taken true flesh on himself but the flesh had not begotten him. He had had no father. Rather the Holy Ghost had begotten him in the body of the virgin Mary. Our faith acknowledges this. The mother has become impregnated with him, not by fleshly power or by a human work, but by the Holy Spirit and his co-operation.

So when Christ speaks of his flesh, he says "my flesh." With this word "my" he separates his flesh from all other flesh. This, his flesh, is holy, blessed and graced with the Holy Ghost. He is also by nature Mary's child but yet he has spiritual flesh, a truly divine and spiritual body in which the Holy Ghost dwells. The one who had conceived him likewise completely "spirits through" his flesh.

Because of this, this is the summary: No flesh belongs to my Words which I speak. No one on earth will understand these Words through the flesh. They will not hold it. What is born of the flesh is flesh. All people are called flesh except for Christ and his Christians. For where there is no higher birth, which comes from the Spirit, then the fleshly birth is not capable or useful but rather all of it is cursed. So the Lord Christ's body is not referred to here but he is thinking of all people on earth: the cleverest, mightiest, most beautiful, strongest and holiest. For all wisdom that a person can discover from his head and reasoning, as "on track" as it seems, is still only flesh.

Altb. V, 688–689: Sermons on the Gospel of St. John, Chapters 6–8, 1531; cf. AE 23

Weary am I and heavy laden, With sin my soul is sore oppressed;
Receive me graciously and gladden My heart, for I am now Thy guest.
Lord, may Thy body and Thy blood Be for my soul the highest good. (*TLH* 315: 6)

Friday

No one can come to me. It is for him to whom the Lord has given it. John 6:65

You must believe. Now, while you hear, it concerns faith so you soon say, "I want to raise faith out of myself. But no, you have already let me have it." We also do this. If one would preach that you must make satisfaction for sins, then you grab onto your own works to do penance for your sins. But Jesus wants to do that and take hold of your sins. Do you want to be the man that would have such a mighty heart? Yes, first learn that faith is a gift of God and a divine might. "You will not believe in me out of yourself." Do you want to rebel against the devil? Where will you go, fool? He is too high for you. Beware, lest you fall into this presumption and think when you hear these Words that you could believe it so soon. That is what the sectarian spirits and false Christians do a lot now. But when the time comes to prove their faith, to give a reason for their false teaching, or that they should comfort themselves in times of need, then soon the praises are laid aside and no one is home.

So then you say, "I thank my God that I have learned that I will not deal with my own sins with my own penance nor begin my faith and take away my sins by my own works. Before man I can surely do that. It helps before the world and the judge. But before God is eternal wrath. I cannot make satisfaction there. I must fail. So I thank you that another deals with sins for me, bears them, pays for them and has made satisfaction. I would be glad to believe it. It seems to me also to be good, right and comforting. But I cannot surrender to it. I cannot find in my power the ability to do that. I cannot accept it as I know I should. Lord, beget me, help me and give me the power and gift that I can believe it. So sighs the prophet in Psalm 51:10, 'Create in me a clean heart, O God, and give me a new true Spirit.' I am not able to make a new pure heart. It is your creation and creature. Just as I cannot make the sun and moon that travel through and brightly shine in the heavens, so little can I also make my heart pure and that I have a true spirit, strong steadfast courage that is firm and not wavering, doubting or shaky about your Word."

A new, pure, gentle heart is one that can say, "I have a right Spirit and new thought; a courageous heart that holds fast and does not doubt. Rather, it actually believes that it wants to lay aside body and life because Christ has died for it."

Because of this, you should give these Words good attention. For Christ would say by these Words, "No one comes to me," because faith is a gift of God. He also gladly gives it; only that one ask God for it. To come to him is to believe in Christ. But whoever does not believe, is far from him. You think that believing is your doing, your might and work. By that you fall from me too quickly. It is God's gift so that you only give him the glory and no one is able to boast of a single power. It is the Father who draws us and gives that Word, the Holy Ghost and faith through the Word. It is both his gift and not our work or power. St. Paul also says in Ephesians 2:8-9, "By grace you are saved and that not of yourself or works, for no one can boast."

That is called a Christ-like demeanor, against which the world is always mad and foolish and still rages. In it no work can boast but only of my Father's drawing. For my flesh, my blood, my spirit and everything that belongs to it are his and not ours, should I have life. So everything else that we do is completely discounted.

But then you say, "Who doesn't believe that? We are Christians. Go out to the Jews and Turks to preach to them of faith." True Christians say, "Oh, God in heaven, how well and rightly it is spoken, 'Whoever eats my flesh,' etc., or: 'Who believes in me has eternal life.' Ach! How I would gladly be free from sins! O God, if I could embrace it with my whole heart, how I would love it! How gladly I would have eternal life as these Words promise me!" Christians say that they do believe but they do not say that they completely believe as they rightly should.

This is a preaching which was not invented by us. It is also taught when others preach without our ideas and additions. So faith comes into us without any of our works and might; only through God's grace. He has become so high and has this great glory that if you set your good works against him you do not pay due attention to him, like valuing a candle or lamp as if they were the sun.

Altb. V, 695–696: Sermons on the Gospel of St. John, Chapters 6–8, 1531; cf. AE 23

Draw us to Thee, Lord, lovingly; Let us depart with gladness
That we may be Forever free
From sorrow, grief and sadness. (*TLH* 215: 2)

Saturday

Jesus answered and said, "My doctrine is not my own but that of the one who sent me." John 7:16

He answers properly, announcing that he understands and notes well that they find him guilty and blaspheming as if he had this doctrine from himself or from the devil. For whoever speaks from himself speaks from the devil. Because of this he answers and says, "My doctrine is not mine." How does that work? If it is not his, why then does he preach and urge it and take it so seriously and yet refuses the honor? Why doesn't he say, "That is what I have preached."? Doesn't even a Christian say, "That is my preaching, my Baptism, my Christ, my God or my gospel."? And yet it is not his, for he did not make it. It didn't come from him. It is not his work. Yet it is also his gift, given to him by God. As I also say, "That child is mine. That man or wife is mine." Yet it is not yours for you did not create it. It is another's work who bestowed and gave it. Yet I have not poured or carved it out but it is given to me as it is. The Lord Christ says the same thing of his doctrine.

I also say the same thing, "The gospel is mine to separate me from all other preachers' doctrine who do not have my doctrine." Therefore I say, "This is mine, Luther's, doctrine." Yet I also say, "It is not my doctrine. It is not of my hand but rather God's gift. For, dear God, I have not invented it from my head, it did not grow in my garden or spring from my well, nor is it born from me. Rather, it is God's gift, and not a human offspring." So both are true. It is mine. And yet it is also not mine. For it is God's, the heavenly Father's, and so I preach and bring such doctrine.

He himself lays out this way of speaking and says, "Even if no one wants to do the will of the one that sent me, etc., they will find out if I speak from me or from God. My teaching is not mine, for it is God's and I only preach it."

This is a necessary article and a completely beautiful text. [He shows] that if one speaks in his house of field, meadow, garden, of cows, butter, calves, cheese, etc., that will not reach the soul and the coming life, as one might desire, even as these things are under the control of reason, which says, "These are mine." But in the preaching office, where the divine Word is the concern, it should go as Christ says here. No one should preach a single doctrine if he has a presumptuousness or doubt about it so that he does not preach on his own or of his own doctrine but rather that he be sure that he is called by God into the preaching office.

All the others also say they teach God's Word. No devil, heretic or sectarian spirit stands up and says, "I, devil, or heretic, preach my doctrine." Rather, they would all say, "It is not my doctrine, it is God's Word." Every one wants to have the reputation that it is God's Word that he preaches. The pope and sects also do that. So then let everyone see to it that he is sure if [the] one [they hear] is speaking of things that do not concern what is temporal but what is saving and sure so that one knows where he should trust his soul. When we have departed to another life, each preacher and listener should be able to say, "I did not invent this doctrine. It is not my gloss, meaning or interpretation, but rather it belongs to the one who sent me."

Everyone in Christendom should be sure of that, the preacher, teacher and pastor, yes, each one who presents God's Word, is sure that his preaching is not his own but rather knows for sure that it is

572

God's Word. Or when you doubt if it is God's Word, remain quiet and shut your mouth until you are sure it is God's Word. A man is a man and dies quickly. With him also die his words and all his thoughts, as stated in Psalm 146:4. When he is gone, so is his word, his teaching, works, thoughts and powers. For a mortal human word is also mortal. If a man cannot have eternal life through his preaching and teaching, then he should keep quiet and only hear God's World alone. For there is no life unless God's Word is there upon which one could say, "I do not have this from men, even if I have received it through men. For God's Word remains forever but man's word ceases. You cannot build upon it." And if one should die, he has no comfort or help from mortal word, rule, works and teaching. There, a Carthusian monk's order and other brotherhoods all cease and if God's Word is not added, that teaches him something better, then no mortal words will hold water.

Altb. V, 714–715: Sermons on the Gospel of St. John, Chapters 6–8, 1531; cf. AE 23

The haughty spirits, Lord, restrain
Who o'er Thy church with might would reign
And always set forth something new,
Devised to change Thy doctrine true.

O grant that in Thy holy Word
We here may live and die, dear Lord;
And when our journey endeth here,
Receive us into glory there. (*TLH* 292: 6,9)

Week of Trinity XX

Sunday

The kingdom of heaven is like a king who prepared a wedding feast for his son. Matthew 22:2

First you must learn what the words "heavenly kingdom" mean here. Namely, it is not a kingdom upon the earth but a realm in heaven in which God above is king. We call it the Christian Church here upon the earth. So the Lord uses this comparison to a marriage because he, the Lord Christ, the Son of the king, takes the church to himself as his bride. So you must learn to understand the heavenly kingdom as a kingdom here, underneath, upon the earth, yet not as a worldly and temporal realm but as an eternal and spiritual one. So we Christians here on earth are already more than half in the heavenly kingdom, specifically with all our soul and spirit. But that is true only according to faith. So whenever you hear talk about the kingdom of heaven, you should not only gape into heaven but stay here below and seek it among people to the ends of the world where the gospel is taught and the Holy Sacraments are rightly used. Often in good German, this heavenly kingdom is also called the kingdom of Christ, the kingdom of the gospel and of faith (For where the gospel is, there Christ is. Where Christ is, there is the Holy Ghost and his kingdom, the true heavenly kingdom). All who have the Word and Sacrament and believe and remain in faith in Christ, are heavenly princes and children of God. The only thing left is that our Lord God take away the wall that yet divides. That is, that we die so that there will only be heaven and blessedness. So now, first of all, you should learn that the heavenly kingdom means that our Lord Christ is where there is the Word and faith. In this kingdom we have life in hope and are cleansed of sins by the reckoning of the Word and faith. We are free of death and hell except that we are still deficient in this old sack, the foul flesh. The sack is not yet torn, the flesh is still not done away with. That must happen in the future. Then we shall have only life, righteousness and blessedness.

Christ says that up to the time when Christ came, our Lord God called and invited his people, the Jews, through the holy prophets, to this wedding. So their noble office is established in order to call the Jews who have waited for this wedding, that is, they comforted their people with the Son of God who would become man and pay for the sins of the world and through his resurrection from the dead would destroy the devil's kingdom and power. Thereafter, the gospel would go out to all the world and forgiveness of sins and eternal life would be preached to all men in his name. By such preaching of mercy, the holy prophets called the people to wait and to be comforted and hope in Christ for the forgiveness of sins and eternal life. But Christ says here, "You remain outside and will not come in," just as when the Jews in the wilderness desired to be back in Egypt. Then he sends out other servants. It was now time. For Christ has come and is recognized by his preaching and his miracles. Then there were John and the disciples of Jesus who said the meal is prepared and nothing is lacking. So they should let everything remain as it stands, get dressed up and appear at the wedding. But it didn't happen. Rather, they despised the invitation of the Lord, and went away; one to his field and another to his work, and so forth. They are unhappy people, who for the sake of their fields and plows despise this wonderful meal, namely the forgiveness of sins and eternal life. And yet they have the hope that it will turn out well for them. However, they will not hold the field or work so dearly when these things caused them to miss the meal.

But this always happens to the gospel when it comes to the people. At the same time this game appears that the world becomes annoyed and everyone wants to go to work. There is so much to do that you cannot wait to take care of the business which takes the priority. So everyone is only concerned about the present world, where city dwellers and farmers are so shamefully greedy and wear such pride and overconfidence. But on the other hand, when their pastors invite them to the meal, they [these pastors] are regarded in a more unfriendly and bothered manner than any of those invited would treat their own servants. I say, let no one be so annoyed with such people that he start to think that it is okay that such people go to their fields or work and so would imitate them. Not on your life! For our Lord God is a good host who, for a time, will probably allow a second of delay to some. He gives it to them, but he doesn't have to.

Hauspostile. N.Y. Ausg., 453–454: Sermon on Trinity 20, Matthew 22:1-13

Delay not, delay not! Why longer abuse The love and compassion of Jesus, thy God?
A fountain is opened; how canst thou refuse
To wash and be cleansed in His pardoning blood? (*TLH* 278: 5)

Monday

Jesus said: "My sheep hear my voice and follow me."
John 10:27

The Christian holy people of God are first recognized where God's Holy Word [is proclaimed]. But that Word can proceed wrongly. St. Paul says that some have it purely and some impurely. Those who have it pure are called those who build on the foundation with gold, silver and precious stones. Those who have it impurely are called those who build upon the foundation with hay, straw and wood that would yet be made pure with fire. Of this, what is said above is more than sufficient. This [pure Word] is the chief part and the high primary sanctuary by which Christian people are called holy. For God's Word is holy and makes holy those it touches. Yes, it is the holiness of God himself. Romans 1, "It is God's power, which makes all saved that believe on it," and 1 Timothy 4, "It makes all holy by Word and prayer." For the Holy Ghost himself carries it and anoints or makes holy the church, that is, the Christian holy people. It is not the anointing of the pope by which the pope anoints or makes holy fingers, clothes, books, cups and steins. For by these, people can never learn to love God, believe, praise or be holy. They would like to adorn the maggot sack (flesh) by them. After being ripped up and polluted by such anointing and holiness, no matter how much it is applied, it yet remains a maggot sack.

But this holiness is true holiness and the true salve that anoints unto eternal life even if you can have no pope's crown or bishop's miter but must live and die a plain, unadorned human life just as the babies (and all of us) are baptized naked and without adornment. We are referring to the external Word which is orally preached through people like you and me. For Christ has left this with us as an external sign by which you can recognize the church, or his holy people in the world. We also speak of the kind of oral Word that is believed with zeal and publicly confessed before the world, as Jesus says, "Who confesses me before the world, I will confess him before my Father and his angels." So there are many who know it well in secret but do no want to confess it (openly). Many have it but they do not believe it or act according to it. So the ones who believe in it and act accordingly are few. As the parable of the seed says in Matthew 13, it is given and possessed by three parts of the field but only the fourth part is fine, good, ground that yields fruit in patience.

Now wherever you hear or see such a Word being preached, believed, confessed and thereafter performed, then have no doubt that the same place must definitely be a true *Ecclesia Sancta Catholica*, a Christian, holy people, even if such places are also scarce. For God's Word doesn't return void, Isaiah 55. It must have even the least quarter or part of the field. And even if this [that is, true preaching] were the ONLY sign, it would be enough of a sign to know that that must be a Christian and holy people. For God's Word cannot be without God's people. Who would want to preach or hear God's preaching if God's people were not there? And what could or would God's people believe, if God's Word were not there?

This is the teaching that does all wonders; to make everything right, preserve all things, straighten everything, do everything and drive out every devil, like the pilgrimage devil, the idolatry devil, the false Church-ban devil, the brotherhood devil, the saints devil, the mass devil, the purgatory devil, the cloister devil, the priesthood devil, the orders devil, the rebellion devil, the heresy devil, and the papacy's devils and also the anti-law devils. Yet this is not without outcries and clamor as he shows the poor people in Mark 1 and 9. No, outcry and breaking off must follow if Jesus proceeds as one sees in Emser, Eck, Rotzloeffel, Schmied, Wetzel, Tolpel, Knebec, Filz, Ruelz, sow, ass and the like in their outcry and writings. Those writings are all the devil's mouth and dress by which he cries out and divides. But it doesn't help him for he must depart since he cannot stand God's Word. For they themselves confess that the Word is God's and that Scripture is holy but that one cannot have it better than from the fathers and church councils. But so be it. It is enough that we know how this chief holiness [the Word] saves, holds, nourishes, strengthens, and defends the church.

Altb. VII, 286: On Councils and the Church, 1539; cf. AE 41

Glorious things of thee are spoken Zion, city of our God;
He whose word cannot be broken Formed thee for His own abode.
On the Rock of Ages founded, What can shake thy sure repose?
With salvation's walls surrounded, Thou may'st smile at all thy foes. (*TLH* 469: 1)

Tuesday

Go and teach all nations, baptizing them in the name of the Father and of the Son and of the Holy Ghost, and teaching them to keep all things I have commanded you. And, behold, I am with you every day to the end of the world. Matthew 28:19,20

So now *Ecclesia*, the holy Christian Church, does not have mere external Word, Sacraments or offices. Satan, who apes God, also has such things and even more of them. But rather God has also commanded, established and ordered the church so that he himself (no angel) will work through these things by his Holy Spirit. Neither angel nor man nor creature shall command Word, Baptism, Sacrament or forgiveness, or office. Rather God himself commands them. Apart from these he will not bring us poor, weak, stupid people to trust and goodness. He will not do it by the revelation of his naked bright majesty for what poor sinful flesh could stand to see that even for a second? And Moses says in Exodus 33:20, *Non vivebit me homo et vivet* [no man will live, who sees me]. So the Jews could not stand to set foot on Mount Sinai because of the clouds and effects on it. How could they want to see that sun of his divine majesty with their naked eyes which had brightly illuminated Mount Sinai? But rather God wants to work through a tolerable, proper, living mediator, or means, which we ourselves could not have chosen any better than he did. For he chose that a pious, good man from among us speaks, preaches, lays on hands, forgives sins, baptizes, gives bread and wine to eat and drink. Who could be terrified before that kind of bodily form? Wouldn't you rather and much more rejoice in your heart?

Well, then, that is revealed to us stupid people as good. In this, we see how God treats us as dear children. He will not deal with us with his majesty (as is his right). Yet under [these means] he works majestically using divine working, might and power, as sins are forgiven, sins are swept away, death is removed, grace and eternal life is bestowed. This piece is missing in the devil's sacrament and church. There no one can say, "God has decreed, ordered, instituted and established this;" but he [who serves the false church] will be there and do everything himself. But one must say, "God did not decree THAT, but forbids it. Men have decreed much more than God has." Those aping God have decreed it and the people are seduced by it. So he also works nothing but what is mortal. When it is supposed to be "spiritual" it is mere deception. For he cannot forgive sins and make people saved eternally when at the same time he denies it with holy water, masses and monkery. It is as if they were letting a cow fight to keep her milk from others when they themselves had already taken it away. So when a Christian calls them [i.e., holy water, mass, etc.] whores of the devil and battles against them, as is only right, they themselves are burned with fire. But they do this not because the milk is being stolen [for there was none there to begin with] as would be right but rather for the sake of their blasphemy, so that the devil's sacraments and church are strengthened against Christ.

In short, if God would command you to lift a blade of straw or to tear a feather with such a decree, command and promise that you would be forgiven all sins and have his grace and eternal life by it would you not receive it with all joy and thankfulness, love, praise? Because of that, would you not hold that straw or feather as a high sanctuary because you are loved more than heaven and earth through them? So no matter how poor the straw or feather would be, yet you would find in them more good than what earth or heaven or even all the angels could give you. Why are we such scandalous people that we do not also regard the water of Baptism, bread and wine that is Christ's body and blood, the proclaimed Word, the laying on of a man's hand for the forgiveness of sins, as such a high sanctuary as we would hold that straw or feather? Yet in the same way we hear and know that God himself will work and they will be his water, Word, hand, bread and wine; by which he will make us holy and saved in Christ, who has given us such weak things that we might acquire them and the Holy Ghost from the Father.

So if you are equipped as they are to go to St. James (on pilgrimage) or you read from the works of the Carthusian monks, barefooted monks and preachers who tell you to mortify the flesh so that by it you may be saved, these are not commanded or instituted by God, but by the devil. You considered them [formerly] as special sacraments or as priestly orders. Even if you could carry heaven and also earth in a way that by it you could become saved, yet it would all be worthless. The one who would lift the straw (were it commanded) would do more than even a person that could lift ten worlds. Why? God desires that one should heed his Word, that one should use his sacrament, one should honor his church and by that God will deal with him graciously and gently enough; and more graciously and gently than we could desire. For it says, "I am your God. You shall have no other god," which also means, "to this one you should listen" and to no others.

Altb. VII, 294: On Councils and the Church, 1539; cf. AE 41

He who craves a precious treasure	Ah, how hungers all my spirit
Neither cost nor pain will measure;	For the love I do not merit!
But the priceless gifts of heaven	Oft have I, with sighs fast thronging
God to us hath freely given.	Thought upon this food with longing.
Tho' the wealth of earth were proffered,	In the battle well-nigh worsted,
Naught would buy the gifts here offered;	For this cup of life have thirsted.
Christ's true body, for thee riven,	For the friend who here invites us
And his blood, for thee once given.	And to God Himself unites us. (*TLH* 305: 3–4)

Wednesday

Out of the depths I have cried to you, O Lord. Psalm 130:1

He wants to say, "I am most vigorously attacked and anxious because I see my sins. I discover the frightening wrath of God. The fear of eternal death has come upon me. Therefore I do not know, within or without, where I can seek help or counsel."

That is the great fear and need in which the prophet found himself trapped. It is the weight and burden that pressured him. He did not know how he could possibly be relieved of it. You can find advice about jealousy and hate and other afflictions by which we are attacked by the world. But if you are stuck in this kind of fear and need there is no advice unless help comes from above.

For other tribulations and heartaches that afflict believers can be overcome by patience, as when our honor, money and goods are in danger. Yes, you can also fairly easily overcome the coarse sins of the flesh into which the youth are plagued to fall. In this, you can be comforted. But if these hard knocks come and the hounds from hell surround us so that you cannot experience or find anything but that you are cast away and alienated from God, then this is hard to overcome and break out of. Those who now feel that kind of affliction have this example of David encountering and suffering this, too. For such people, the affliction is even heavier when they believe they suffer alone, unlike everyone else.

So let us all learn here that almost all of the great saints also suffered this way and were frightened and brought right to death by the law and their sins. We see David calls out and cries as if he were utterly in hell, "Out of the depths I cry, Lord, unto you." But he must not be allowed to stay here with only the comfort that we are not alone, but others have suffered so. We should also learn here by the manner and ways of these same saints also stuck in such a hell, how they turned from such heartache. For he did not doubt. Rather, he called and cried out. For he knew that a definite hope of help and comfort was yet at hand. You also should believe and act this way in your sorrow.

For David was not afflicted in this matter so that he would doubt. You must also neither understand nor accept your affliction as if you will be utterly sunk and ruined in your sorrow and heartache. Rather, if you are led into the depths, you should know that you have the kind of God and Lord who will save you again and make you well. If your soul is full of grief and sorrow, then you should at the same time wait on the one who helps and on the comfort of the one who has called you. For a broken spirit is his sacrifice and he is pleased to have it. A broken and a contrite heart he will not despise. Rather, he wants to rescue the person in need and the one whose spirit is broken.

But if one is stuck in such heartache and sorrow, there is a great comfort and a priceless comfort that pious Christian people want to have with them. For God has ordered the Christian congregation that one should comfort another and make petition when two of us are assembled in his name, so that he would be the third. We also experience that nothing else can or would comfort such a broken heart. So if a person hears of a brother with this terror, he knows that this did not occur so he would be ruined but so that he should be encouraged when he is reminded of grace and receives the same with thanksgiving.

But if we could not have such words of comfort, then we must do what David does here. We call and cry to God and pray this psalm with David in which David's great fear and need are revealed. By this, then, it is easy to note that he does not use many useless words as he sometimes actually does in thanksgiving. So he not only calls out of the depths to God but he also admonishes God in his prayer as to the way in which God should hear him. But after this he is not satisfied, but repeats the same thing, yet in other words.

Altb. VII, 613–614: Lecture on Psalm 130, 1541

In God, my faithful God, I trust when dark my road;
Tho' many woes o'ertake me, Yet He will not forsake me.
His love it is doth send them And, when 'tis best, will end them. (*TLH* 526: 1)

Thursday

If you, Lord, would impute sins, O Lord, who would stand?
Psalm 130:3

No one. For if anyone could stand, then without a doubt, King David would also. He is a holy man who understood God's Word well. He was also well practiced in faith and the fear of God by much death and persecution. We would stand, too. For I do not believe anyone under the papacy was so upright as David yet no one regarded his good works and righteousness as more feeble than David did. Yet David says that righteousness would not be achieved by works, "For if you, Lord" (he says) "would impute sins, Lord, who would stand?"

Therefore, we should learn that we do not come before God out of confidence of our good works and holiness even if we already have done all that we are able and is possible to do. It is written of a saintly hermit named Agathon that he lay three days harshly afflicted in the fear of death. When some of his disciples comforted him and asked why he was so afflicted since he had led such a holy life he answered and said that he was already shaking before the judgment of God. They asked why he was so afraid. He answered that he had lived as he was able according to God's law, yet he was a man and didn't want to build on his good works. For God pays attention to other things than what mankind considers when he judges and decides. So you see how this man, when he considered himself standing before God's judgment, didn't want to be abandoned with only his good works and righteousness.

They also speak of another hermit who wanted to comfort someone who had a disease and would die soon. He advised the man that he should suffer death patiently. If he did that, it would bring him a blessed death. That's also how our monks care for and comfort people in that condition. They don't consider the service of our Lord Jesus Christ at all, or very little. But they say if the poor people would suffer the shame of death, through that they would come to eternal life. But what comfort does this hermit bring? Then if that one [the hermit] would die, as soon as the hermit would bring to mind what dismal comfort he had given his poor brother, he would be distressed and harshly afflicted himself for commending the man more to patience than to hope and trust in the service and death of the Lord Christ. By this dire grief this hermit would also be so strongly plagued that he also would die in three days.

There are also countless examples which we hear and experience daily that show that our righteousness, willing death and patience are not enough for salvation. But faith in Christ Jesus fills every need here. For he is the sacrifice for the sins of the world. But our death, even if we suffer it patiently, and even if we've done all kinds of good works, yet would be thoroughly sinful if we thought that we could stand before God's judgment by them.

So no one should dare to want to stand before the judgment of God by his own righteousness and service, as reason might contend to the contrary. I would also like to stop our opponents who say these things and understand things in this way. They also teach this and commend people to their works and reliance on their holiness. But to us, when we teach the opposite and lead and guide the congregation of God, to rely on and take confidence in the service and dying of our Savior Christ Jesus, they ban us and declare we are heretics. But isn't that a great evil that they do not do what they teach others to do, lest they themselves should rely on their own works and service in death? Yet are they compelling other people to do this or are they cursing as heretics do?

All pious hearts have experienced this. No one could stand before the judgment of God with his works and righteousness. But consider our whole nature. If you are not afflicted immediately, think of your many kinds of works and if you could atone for yourself before God by them. But here we have a clear, bright doctrine which says, "So, Lord, if you would impute sins, O Lord, who would stand?" Now if he would come before God's righteousness with his own, he would be overcome, sentenced and damned.

Altb. VII, 615–616: Lecture on Psalm 130, 1541

Lord, Thee I love with all my heart: I pray Thee, ne'er from me depart,
With tender mercy cheer me. Earth has no pleasure I would share,
Yea, heav'n itself were void and bare If Thou, Lord, wert not near me.
And should my heart for sorrow break, My trust in Thee no one could shake.
Thou art the portion I have sought: Thy precious blood my soul has bought.
Lord Jesus Christ, My God and Lord, my God and Lord,
Forsake me not I trust Thy Word. (*TLH* 429: 1)

Friday

With you is forgiveness, that man may fear you. Psalm 130:4

By this David turns from doubt to confidence and hope in divine mercy. If we look upon our sins and would turn to them, nothing is possible. We would become burdened and attacked and fall eternally into doubt. But you should not judge by turning your eyes only to your sins but also to the mercy seat, on the forgiveness of sins.

So, though we cannot deny that we are sinners, yet we nevertheless also believe in the forgiveness of sins and do not deny it. So why is the forgiveness of sins declared to us if those sins do not conquer and trap sinners? Yes, it is because of this fact. For this reason David called out and set his mind entirely upon the forgiveness of sins and the mercy seat. He would show that he is a sinner and publicly make it known and also that the mercy seat or forgiveness actually belonged to him. He had it in every need.

But this can also say to you and remind you, "I surely believe that God is merciful. But my sins make me unworthy of God's being moved to pity me. So David, Peter and Paul could hope for this forgiveness of sins, but I am a sinful person and cannot hope that way, and so forth." You should drive such horrid thoughts from your mind and flee from them. For you can and may think much more like this, "Even while I am a sinner, the forgiveness of sins also belongs to me. For those same people are also not examples of piety or righteousness but are rather called 'poor miserable sinners'. Therefore, I will not doubt or trouble and torture myself to death. Rather I turn to my dear Lord God, who announces forgiveness to me and all sinners." He bids us to hope, trust and believe, and so forth.

So now we see that in these two verses, David presents us with the sum of the whole Christian teaching and the dear bright sun which enlightens the whole Christian congregation. So when this teaching is established, then the church, the congregation of God, also stands. But if it should fall, then at the same time, the congregation and everything is leveled to the ground. That is the reason why I carry this teaching so heavily. Satan applies himself whole heartedly to rip this confession of Christian righteousness and the forgiveness of sins from hearts and eyes. I know and have experienced that. By this, he rules the world by persecution, fanatics and sects and all heartaches so that he buries this teaching to be one that is clouded and darkened to make it utterly dim.

Altb. VII, 617–618: Lecture on Psalm 130, 1541

In Him I have salvation's way discovered, The heritage for me He hath recovered.
Tho' death o'ertakes me, Christ ne'er forsakes me,
To everlasting life He surely wakes me.
[Original translation of verse in Link]

Saturday

Israel, hope in the Lord, for with the Lord is grace and much salvation. Psalm 130:7

To be sure, this is a golden verse that is worthy of learning and contemplating thoroughly. He desires to exhort all people to depend upon the sure hope of God's mercy and to persist in it. So this faith is not so poor or unworthy of respect as the papists teach. They think this faith is nothing but a poor wish or thought of the heart. Its purpose is to believe there is one God as if someone had dreamed him up so that one could speak and pray and say, "I like God" and so forth. That is how the papists speak and teach about faith. Because they do not undergo trials anymore or experience the difficult war in which faith must stand, they deride our faith if we say that faith is a divine power and strength, the only means by which we become pious and rid of our sins. As a wise man rightly said, "A fool only understands what is in his heart."

What we say now about faith, they attribute to love and prefer love to faith. But if one wants to speak and teach correctly about faith then he will go way beyond love. Then you see what faith is occupied with exclusively and what it does. Namely, faith alone battles Satan who ceaselessly troubles and torments us before God. This kind of battle does not concern itself with trivial matters but concerns death, eternal life, sins, the law. Satan convicts us against grace by which God would forgive our sins. If one holds love, which concerns itself with lesser things (such as that one serve others, help with counsel, deeds, give comfort), against such wondrous things [as life, forgiveness, etc.], then how could you not see that faith is much higher than love? So should love not act and be displayed appropriately? Should not the difference between God and man be shown? The difference is that one man can help and counsel another but where can you find one through whom eternal death is overcome?

So that is the work and nature of faith. It fights and disputes with Satan in the greatest danger before the face of God. For our enemy, as I have said above, gives us no peace night or day. But now, though love is not only a very good and rare virtue, and covers more than other virtues, yet at the same time, faith is a thousand times greater and mightier because of the things it does and also for other reasons.

For it is the use and the fruit of faith to make the heart firm and sure that death is conquered by the death of the Lord Christ. Death is taken away through grace and the forgiveness of sins and the law is lifted off. All these things are in themselves whole and true and without doubt true. But we are so weak in faith that we can not satisfactorily believe or grasp it. So neither the thought of death nor of sins frightens us. So if this confidence of God's grace with us and on us were perfect, then a believing heart could nevermore be sorrowful or afflicted. Because of this, David exhorted the nation of Israel to persevere in forgiveness after it had welcomed it and not to let her confidence in mercy be taken away.

But he observes that in the battle of the conscience, if the heart now and then begins to totter, it doubts the mercy of God when surrounded by misery and tribulation. But because we cannot hold and grasp this comfort, given in his Word, in the hour, then in such a battle the heart will fall into doubt. Against that kind of onslaught, David exhorts us all to know and remember that we have hope in the Lord and that we not weaken his Word by our flesh or entertain thoughts or interpretations against the Word. But why is that? For this reason: That grace is of the Lord.

When our flesh stands in affliction or danger, it experiences nothing but that God is purely fierce wrath and displeasure. Therefore, the Holy Ghost will comfort us completely and take this from us and displace this false thought and delusion about God. He declares this necessary testimony of the Holy Ghost publicly, to all. When we follow after our reason, thoughts and feelings, then we experience the opposite.

But we should not judge and make opinions out of our feelings and perceptions nor out of the tribulation in which we find ourselves stuck. Rather, we follow the Word of God and know definitely that everything that the Word teaches us is true and that such things belong to faith, not to experience.

Altb. VII, 624–625: Lecture on Psalm 130, 1541

The haughty spirits, Lord, restrain
Who o'er Thy Church with might would reign.
And always set forth something new,
Devised to change Thy doctrine true.

Oh, grant that in Thy holy Word
We here may live and die, dear Lord;
And when our journey endeth here,
Receive us into glory there. (*TLH* 292: 6, 9)

Week of Trinity XXI

Sunday

Your priests are clothed in righteousness and your saints rejoice. Psalm 132:9

God promises that he will govern the priests so that they are pure and holy through the Word and that they should have a good conscience. If we could hold this [truth] against their little mortal deficiencies we would bear their priesthood with greater patience.

I became a monk and lived in confusion, bound with cords of a troubled conscience. This burden of the human condition piles one sin upon another. I was bound to an impure chastity outside of marriage against nature. If someone would have told me how I could purchase the precious freedom with Christ, the great glory and prize that we now have through the Word and Spirit of God, I would have fallen on my face. I would have gladly given my life to only plead for the redemption of my conscience.

But now because we are in truth clothed with salvation by means of the majestic and public promises of forgiveness of sins and of eternal life, we forget such spiritual goods and kingdoms and complain because we are not kings in this mortal life. We hold our eternal and divine honor as no big thing.

That is the height of unthankfulness. We become so annoyed by external poverty because we don't have joy and happiness by these great spiritual goods. Who would not rather beg from house to house while possessing spiritual wealth than be Bishop of Mainz, or pope, who are enemies of the Word and are under the unfortunate salvation of the wealth of the world? For they do not have the forgiveness of Christ and everything else we have through the Word unto overflowing. Even if we are also despised, martyred, saddened, plagued, horrified and poor before the world, we would yet be comforted by those gifts we receive from the heavenly kingdom; that we are more than conquerors through faith in the Word over sin, death and Satan; that we are completely and thoroughly clothed with salvation.

How many have fallen into doubt during this wholesome and blessed time? If they had had the knowledge of grace and the consolation of the Word, wouldn't you think they would have rather lost all their worldly goods for their sake? For if one feels the wrath of God and doubt, all [worldly] wealth would melt in importance and seem feeble. For what good are art, cities, kingdoms and principalities then?

That's why Paul calls the entire fleshly heritage expendable for the sake of this knowledge. So even if we must live on beggar's bread, that will not break you for don't we eat bread with angels, the gospel, Christ and the Sacrament? But no one tastes this in the papacy if he wants to follow the papacy and seeks a cardinal's miter made on the devil's forge. I strove after other goods that those wise fellows who are either Epicurean or academics, actually despise.

But I hold it higher than all the pearls of the world and all its gold. If I, for my first 30 years, had truly understood only a single psalm, I would have thought that I would have been as God. Everything was so full of atrocious errors, horror and countless idolatries.

But now that the Lord has revealed divine wisdom and knowledge just like a flood, we do not seek unthankful people or worldly goods, and we are so gentle that we do not mind that we lack something that the world has. But Isaiah 28:20 states, the bed is narrow. Therefore both [divine and worldly things] do not both fit. We do not reject worldly goods, for they are God's gifts. But whoever is given them has them with thanksgiving and without complaint he fills the needs of this neighbor [with them]. But to those who do not approach wealth, God would have them suffer patiently, as Paul says that he could suffer anything, being fed or hungry, having enough or suffering need, and so forth. This is because we have another kingdom in heaven and an expectation of salvation. The one who has begun to give us this through the Word and Sacrament gives us the Word and the priesthood purely and surely in order that we not concern ourselves too much with other things.

Therefore, this is a wonderful understanding. The church and the Word must remain until the end of the world. That will not happen by human advice or wisdom but by God clothing his priests with salvation. If not, the world is full of idolatry as in the times of Ahab and the godless kings of his time. But there will also be true prophets through whom the Word can be obtained.

Altb. VII, 652–653: Lecture on Psalm 132, 1541

Anoint them prophets. Make their ears attent
To Thy divinest speech, their hearts awake
To human need, their lips make eloquent
To gird the right and ev'ry evil break. (*TLH* 483: 2)

Monday

So as you forgive people their sins so your heavenly Father will also forgive your sins. Matthew 6:14

This is a wonderful but also a very precious addition to the single petition "Forgive us our trespasses," so that all might marvel. He might have done the same with other such petitions and said, "Give us this day our daily bread as we give it to our children." Or "lead us not into temptation, as we also tempt no one." Yet no other petition has such an addition. It appears that the forgiveness of sins should be earned by our forgiveness. Where does our teaching then stand that forgiveness comes only through Christ and is only experienced by faith?

The first answer is that he wanted to establish this petition in a special way and bind the forgiveness of sins to our forgiveness. By that, he attaches Christians to it so that they love one another and to let that be their chief and foremost article next to faith and receiving forgiveness. They will continuously forgive their neighbor. As we have it from him in faith, we also will be disposed through love in the same way to our neighbor so we don't annoy each other and make each other sorrowful. Rather than thinking that we are always forgiven, if such sorrow is perpetrated by us [that we don't forgive] (as must also be encountered in life), we should know that it is not forgiven us. For where wrath and ill will lay in the way it ruins the whole prayer so that one can neither desire nor pray the petition. This makes a fast and strong bond by which we are held together so we do not become divided from each other and cause splintering, factions and sects, and pray and secure something before God in a different way. But rather we agree with each other through love and remain united in all things. When that happens, it is a mature Christian community because they both believe and love rightly. What is defective after that should be covered by prayer and everything be forgiven and given.

But how is it that he [the Lord] makes the forgiveness of our sins dependent on our works and says, "If you forgive your neighbor, then shall you be forgiven, and on the other hand . . ." Does this not say that the forgiveness does not depend on our faith? Answer: The forgiveness of sins, as I have often said already, happens in two ways: First through the gospel and Word of God which is experienced inwardly in the heart before God through faith. To others [it happens] outwardly through works from which Peter speaks in 2 Peter 1, where he teaches about good works, "Dear brothers, be diligent, make your calling and election sure." There he desires that we should make sure that we have faith and the forgiveness of sins. That is, that we be informed of these works so that you perceive the tree by its fruits and make apparent the good tree rather than the rotten tree. For where there is a right faith there good works surely follow. So a person is both inwardly and outwardly pious and right, both before God and people. That is the consequence and the fruit by which I make sure to myself and to others that I have right faith which previously I could not know or see.

This is the outward forgiveness. So I, indeed, reveal a true sign that I have forgiveness of sin from God. Again, when you do not show this to your neighbor, then you have a sure sign that you do not have the forgiveness of sins from God but are stuck in disbelief. See that this is a two-fold forgiveness. On the one hand it is inside the heart and depends only upon God's Word. Outwardly, it breaks out and overflows and makes us sure that we have it inwardly. So we distinguish between faith and life as an inward and outward righteousness in the same way. The inward is previously there as the trunk and root out of which good works, as fruit, must grow. The outward is but a sign of the same and as St. Paul says, *certificatio*, an affirmation that such faith is definitely there. Whoever does not have the inner righteousness does none of the outward works. Whoever doesn't display the outward sign and evidence, I cannot be sure of that one. But rather such a person deceives himself and others. But when I see and feel that I gladly forgive my neighbor then I can say with confidence that I do not do that according to my nature but I experience something different through God's grace than I did before.

Altb. V, 871–872: Commentary on the Sermon on the Mount, 1532; cf. AE 21

Make them apostles, heralds of Thy Cross;
Forth may they go to tell all realms Thy grace.
Inspired of Thee, may they count all but loss
And stand at last with joy before Thy face. (*TLH* 483: 5)

Tuesday

Dear brothers, when a person is overcome by some sin, you, who are spiritual, return him to the right with a gentle spirit. Galatians 6:1

We offer the observation that among those who love Christ and rightly learn his Word and believe, we not only keep peace and unity but also desire to suffer and bear all human weaknesses and sins with hearty pleasure and would gladly instruct with a humble spirit. St. Paul not only teaches this here but also makes it known by his deeds. He had endured the Galatians in their weakness by which they had fallen so horridly and also among other communities which the false apostles, who thought they could turn them and improve their hearts and zeal, had turned. He had also tried to restore those involved in incest in 2 Corinthians 2. He had reconciled the servant Onesimus, whom he had converted to the faith in Rome while he was imprisoned. He restored him to his master. Even so, here and in other places, he teaches through his own example how you should help others who have so fallen. So these are examples of where he wanted to counsel, that is, make their errors, sins and failures of heart known in order to improve them. But when he was opposed, he experienced the speediest attacks from the false prophets who were so hardened and defended their doctrine as if it were not erroneous, but rightly made. "Would to God," he says, "That they also would be eliminated, who are destroying you," or "Who makes you fall into error, he will bear his judgment, no matter who he is," or "even if we, or an angel from heaven . . . let him be accursed."

There is no doubt about this. There would be many who are false apostles against Saint Paul who defended themselves and said that they also had the Spirit and were Christ's servants, who taught the gospel just as Paul had. If they did not agree with him in all articles of doctrine, Paul should not for that reason speak against them with such a frightening judgment since by his being so stubborn, he only showed that he makes the congregation wander and divides their fine unity. But he doesn't let any such fine practical words stand to contest his own. Rather, he acts in freedom from them. He damns and curses the false apostles, calls them detractors of the congregation and perverters of the gospel of Christ without making a big show of it. He lifts his doctrine very high to oppose them and desires that all should yield and give way to peace so that there can be unity of love, apostelicity, angels of heaven and whatever is eternal.

So if you desire to be a true caretaker of souls [*Seelsorger*], you must learn this doctrine of Paul quickly and be concerned over those who fall in this way. Dear brothers, he says, when one is overcome in a sin, embitter and afflict him no further. Do not dismiss or condemn him but help him to restoration. Make him alive or advise him (as is contained in the Greek word), and by your humble spirit restore what the devil has ruined in him by his cunning and by the weakness of the flesh. For the kingdom into which you have been called is not a kingdom in which one's conscience is frightened and tortured, but rather it should correct and comfort them. Therefore when you see some brother who is frightened for the sake of the sins he has committed, run to him, extend your hand to him, that he can again be established after his fall. Comfort him with sweet loving words and receive him again with a mother's heart.

But those hardened in their thoughts and impenitence, who persevere and proceed without fruit in all security in sin, those you scold and punish hard. Then again, those who are overcome in some sin, whose fall is painful and causes sorrow, then you who are spiritual should aid and advise and do all with a humble spirit; not with great sharpness and severity, as some father confessors do intentionally. They were sent to refresh them with life-giving comfort and make them alive but they trample weak hearts with their feet. They give nothing but vinegar and gaul to drink as the Jews did to Christ on the cross.

Altb. VI, 871: Lectures on Galatians, 1535; cf. AE 26 & 27

Anoint them priests, Strong intercessors, they,
For pardon and for charity and peace.
Ah, if with them the world might, now astray,
Find in our Lord from all its woes release! (*TLH* 483: 3)

Wednesday

Then Jerusalem will be holy and no foreigner will wander through her. Joel 3:17

The papists have completely darkened, yes, buried and interred this passage as they have also done with the gospel or the forgiveness of sins. How will they learn what the holy Christian church is when they teach that a person should doubt if he is in God's grace or not? They say that God would be blasphemed if someone says that he is holy. But the witness of the prophet should have greater standing and credibility with us, who freely and purely says that Jerusalem, that is, the church that is on earth is holy. Truly, one should not make any article of our Christian faith commended to him by the church as uncertain and doubtful in order to rather believe an opinion of the flesh that is true neither in the flesh nor on the earth.

So that this article is understood better I must remind the reader that the Scriptures speak about the church in two ways. First, it calls the church all who are in it, even though many hypocrites and godless people are mingled under it as Christ says, "Many are called but few are chosen." Or "Who believes and is baptized will be saved, who does not believe will be damned." The last part of the passage shows that one only baptized but unbelieving will be damned because of that, as the parable of the wedding feast also teaches. For the guests are all indeed dressed but they are not all dressed in wedding clothes. These were expelled and cast into darkness. So also the parables of the fish net and of the wheat and tares portray this and place before the eyes the kind of church where there are [both] the pious and the evil. The evil are always more than the pious as also the passage says, "Many are called but few are chosen."

Yet under this mixed heap are always a few chosen, that is, people who receive and cling to God's Word with true faith and receive the Holy Ghost. The preaching office cannot act without fruit or profit. The Scripture calls this rightly made pure little heap "the church" for which reason it actually bears the name "holy." It is not because the elect are sinless. For fallen flesh and blood retain their character and nature and are never without evil lusts and thoughts. But the believing and rightly made Christians quench such lusts with the help of the Holy Ghost and do not cling to them or give them space. Yet such lusts in them are themselves still damnable sins. But they cannot damn those who fear God, since they acknowledge such impurity of their hearts and believe in Christ.

This faith is what makes the church holy. For faith grasps the one who is holy and with his grace takes and destroys our misdeeds, as a fire the stubble. If now you could see the church of the elect with your eyes (yet if you could definitely see it, you would not be able to believe it is the church), then you would see such people who are like the others, that is weak and poor sinners, as also only the elect acknowledge their weakness and pray daily without interruption for the forgiveness of sins. Therefore, Scripture calls them poor and miserable, not only in the way of common misfortune and affliction that they suffer here, but also they cry and lament with anxious and disturbed hearts for their weakness. They are also plagued and anxious with the terror of God's judgment against sins. There, along with this, is the other great heap who are always secure and are bridled by their lust which they also follow.

Altb. V, 989–990: Some Good Preaching on a Christian's Armor and Weapons, 1532

Savior, since of Zion's city I thro' grace a member am,
Let the world deride or pity, I will glory in Thy name.
Fading is the worldling's pleasure, All his boasted pomp and show;
Solid joys and lasting treasure, none but Zion's children know. (*TLH* 469: 4)

Thursday

This is my beloved Son, in whom I am well pleased.
Matthew 3:17

First we learn who this is, namely God's only Son, and how he is established as Lord (as truly born heir) over heaven and earth and all creatures. Here he is praised and proclaimed and crowned as king by the Father himself. Not with purple or gold or seated on a golden throne or anointed with oil as people do, but he is adorned with another crown and balm, namely the divine glory, teaching and voice who calls there, "This is my beloved Son, the Lord of heaven and earth; king of kings and Lord of lords," and so forth. By nature he was truly God and Lord over all creatures beforehand. He had no need for such Word and praise on his own account. But it is revealed to us, made clear and described so that we also know how to regard him. It is declared to us that we should regard him as the person upon whom lay heaven and earth, angels and men, righteousness, life, sins, death and all that man can name that is now God himself (all here exhibited in his humanity). For this reason this man is established and thereafter proclaimed, that we should believe that in him we have such a Lord and are baptized upon this, that he would be our Lord, reign for us, defend and help; that we have everything in him and nothing can harm or overcome us.

Don't let any speech talk you out of this even if it is decorated and adorned with gold or precious stones. For this teaching is too high above the crowds. God's natural Son, the Lord, is high over all creatures. A single angel alone is more wonderful and mightier than the whole world with all its splendor and might. But the Son of God is ineffably higher and wider over all the angels and all that is thought of about any creature. Yet all this is completely poured out and given us in the Words, "This is my beloved Son." But all this (as I have said) is held in faith. For according to his appearance, it is wholly unlikely that such things could be said of this man. As great and wonderful as this wonder of the natural Son of God and the heir or the Lord of all things is, just so great and much greater and more wonderful it is that all of this is placed upon this person who lay there on the lap of the virgin and stands here in the Jordan to be baptized. There you see nothing but a poor, miserable, unadorned man. No one could look poorer and so completely lacking any appearance of glory and power. Yet, he alone is called and believed in as Lord of lords, king of kings, yes, before all angels; who has both works, devil, sins, death and all things mightily in his hands.

Who could gather all this about this poor man? Who would be able to say or believe this of him if God himself had not revealed it and told from heaven who this is? That is the first part of this divine heavenly preaching.

The other is, "in whom I am well pleased." With this he also ordains him as pastor or priest. Just as Psalm 110 calls him an "eternal priest," because he stands eternally before God to atone and appear for us. For we know that we are all born in sin, condemned to death, and eternally under God's wrath, from the first person to the last. That was served up by the devil and he has led all people under calamity. Now who can restore us again to God and take the flood from us? There is no man, no prophet, no saint yet to come who had been able to walk before God and been able to still God's wrath. For they themselves had to die, by necessity. Yes, no angel had been able to take such wrath upon himself and make satisfaction for it. Yet, so that man is helped and someone saved, sins exterminated, death strangled, the devil's kingdom destroyed, hell extinguished and God's grace illumined and made known and preached; God himself must be the source of this and send a mediator and install him. Through him we pass from wrath to grace, out of sins and death to goodness and life. No one has been able to be that or do that but his only Son, himself, so that he himself came to us, bearing our nature, flesh and blood. Yet the one who should help us with sins would himself be born without sins and so, as a mediator between God and us, is truly both God and man. But in order that he would be received as such and would be believed, the Father himself here reveals it to us from heaven and says of him, "This is my beloved Son, in whom I am well pleased." As if he would say by this, "If you would be freed of wrath and damnation and seek and find grace by me, then you must come here and cling to this man, who will be the one true priest and mediator. There and nowhere else you find your reconciliation and a merciful God."

Altb. VI, 459: Sermon on Our Holy Baptism, part 3, 1535

Ye seed of Israel's chosen race, Ye ransomed from the fall,
Hail Him who saved you by His grace And crown him Lord of all,
Hail Him who saved you by His grace And crown him Lord of all. (*TLH* 339: 3)

Friday

*Owe nothing to anyone except that you love one another,
for who loves the other has fulfilled the law. Romans 13:8*

If the laws were born of love and all of them are mastered by love then it wouldn't make any difference how many commandments there were. If one wouldn't want to hear and learn all of them but would bear hearing and learning a few of them then he would learn that the same love is taught in all of them. If he heard and learned all of them and could not recognize love in any of them, even so he would acknowledge that he would rather have them in just one law.

St. Paul also takes up this rule and way of mastering and understanding the law, when he says, "Owe nothing to anyone except that you love one another," and "Who loves the other has fulfilled the law," All laws are contained in the law, "Love your neighbor as yourself," and "Love does no evil to the neighbor," and "Love is the fulfilling of the law." Every Word of this epistle concludes and says that love is the master of the law.

Then again, if one teaches and bears the law without love and outside of love, there is no greater misfortune, no greater injustice, no more miserable calamity in all the earth. Then the law itself is nothing but a plague and ruin. There the proverb becomes true: "*Summum jus, summa unjustitia,*" the strongest justice is the strongest injustice. And Ecclesiastes 7:16, "*Noli nimium esse justice,*" "Do not be overly righteous." Yes, then one leaves the beam stuck in our eye and doesn't know it and goes around with it to rip the cinder out of our neighbor's eye. That kind of person makes awkward, frightened and broken consciences, without any need or reason. Great injury to body and soul follows. All kinds of courage and work take place. Yet all is lost.

To be informed, we consider the example of someone in that condition when David was hungry in 1 Samuel 21:6. If the priest had not desired to give David the holy bread and had become so blind that he would stand upon the law and not be aware of the love, and had forbidden David the bread, what would have happened? So much depended on him yet David would have had to die of hunger. The priest would have committed murder for the sake of the law. Then it would surely have been nothing else than "*Summum jus, summa injustitia,*" the sharpest justice is the sharpest injustice. If you could look into the heart of that kind of mad priest, you would have an abominable horror because he makes sins and a troubled conscience where there is no sin and troubled conscience. For he would have held that it was a sin there to eat bread when it was love and a good work. On the other hand, he would have held that murder was no sin if he let David die but a service to God and a good work!

But who can account such a horrid, blind, perverted folly as satisfying? He would do evil by acting that way, which would not upset the devil. For by that he makes sin and a troubled conscience out of nothing; he takes man away from grace, salvation, virtue and God with all his wealth and does all of this for no reason. It is also false and deceptive when he lies about God and is cursed through and through. Then again, he makes a good work and a service of God out of death and wrong. He places the devil and his lies in the place of God and rules with the greatest idolatry that can be and thus ruins body and soul. He murders the body through hunger and the soul by the conscience. He makes a god out of the devil, heaven out of hell and hell out of heaven; out of sin righteousness and out of righteousness sin. That is called, I think, twisted, and the sharpest justice becoming injustice.

Erl. 8, 53–55: Sermon on Epiphany 4, Romans 13:8–10

Oh, draw us ever unto Thee, Thou Friend of sinners, gracious Savior;
Help us that we may fervently Desire Thy pardon, peace, and favor.
When guilty conscience doth reprove, Reveal to us Thy heart of love.
May we, our wretchedness beholding, See then Thy pardoning grace unfolding
And say: "To God all glory be: My Savior, Christ, receiveth me." (*TLH* 386: 5)

Saturday

Thus says the Lord God, "Woe to the women who sew magic charms on their sleeves and make veils for the heads of the people of every age to hunt souls! If now you have hunted the souls of my people, you are promised the same." Ezekiel 13:18

What does this say but that the blind teachers of the law terrorize the conscience and make sin and death where there is life and grace and life and grace where there is sin and death? That concerns everything worth a hand full of barley and some bits of bread. That is, they bind such laws to external things that they are concerned with the things of the hand like drink or a bit of bread. They let love be directed only by those kinds of things while loading the conscience with sins that lead to eternal death. From this the following is self-evident.

"Because you have falsely afflicted the heart of righteousness, which I have not afflicted, and have strengthened the godless in his deeds, so he does not turn from his evil if he desires to live, then you will no longer preach useless doctrine and no longer prophecy but I will rather deliver my people from your hand and you shall know that I am the Lord." See, it is afflicting good hearts when you load them with sins when they are doing good works, when you give strength to the godless, when you regard good works where there are only vain sins. He also says concerning this in Psalm 14:4–5, "You do not call upon the Lord and there is great fear." That is, you make consciences fear where they should not be troubled. And again, where they should fear and are not serving God, there they feel safe and do not fear. So Isaiah also says in chapter 29:13, "You fear me for nothing because you follow the commandments of man," and so forth. This twisted people twists all things. Call on God and do not fear where the devil is. Do not call and be afraid where God is.

See that this is the complaint and the misery of all who strike out with their works and the law. Following their blindness, they do not acknowledge the law's meaning and master love. We also observe this in the poor people, the ministers, and all who follow them. They are stuck deep and they firmly hold onto their own actions. Even if they should ruin all the world, nevertheless their ways must go and stand as the standard and not be ruined. But they do not see that the body is in an epidemic and is dying. The soul dies and is ruined. But they think that this death and ruin is a service to God. They do not fear. They do not trouble their conscience with it. Rather, they strengthen themselves in such evil so they nevermore are turned from their actions and life. Then again, because they praise those who are spiritually poor in order to save their body and soul, to eat flesh, or to become married, then there is fear, there is a troubled conscience. There is sin and law, death and hell. There he doesn't call on God or serve him even if his life should perish ten times and his soul go to the devil one hundred times.

By this you see what the world is, what flesh and blood does even when it wants to do its best. How dangerous it is to proceed and reign with the law. Yes, how impossible it is to rule and teach the soul with the law without great danger, when the Spirit and love are not there; when they have all the law in the hand with full power.

Erl. 8, 55–57: Sermon on Epiphany 4, Romans 13:8-10

My soul, no more attempt to draw
Thy life and comfort from the Law.
Fly to the hope the Gospel gives;
The man that trusts the promise lives. (*TLH* 289: 4)

Week of Trinity XXII

Sunday

Therefore, the heavenly kingdom is like a king who wanted to go over accounts with his servants. Matthew 18:23

When God desires an accounting he lets the preaching of his law go out so we learn to acknowledge what we owe. For instance God says to the conscience, "You shall have no other Gods before me, but hold me only as God. Love me with all your heart and place your trust in me alone." That is the accounting and the ledger on which the reasons for our guilt are written. He holds it in his hand, reads it to us and says, "Look. You should do this. You should fear, love and honor me alone. You should only trust in me and regard me as the best. But you do just the opposite. You are my enemy. You don't believe in me and you fix your trust on other things. In short, you see here that you have not kept one letter of the law."

Now when the conscience hears this and the law strikes it properly the servant sees that he is guilty of what he has done and what he has left undone. He becomes sure that he has not kept a letter of the law and must confess that he has not believed and loved God for a moment. So now what does the Lord do? When the conscience is led to this and acknowledges that it must be lost, it will receive only fear and trouble so it says, "Pay up! All you have is to be paid to him." That is the reason that when the law shows sins, it quickly says, "This is what you should have done and what you haven't done." So punishment belongs to those sins. One must pay. For God has not given his law so that he allow sins to pass unpunished and as if he will not put an end to them. The law is not sweet and friendly. Rather, it brings with it bitter, terrible punishment and it delivers us to the devil, throws us into hell and leaves us stuck in punishment until we pay back the last penny.

Paul has correctly presented this in Romans 4:15 where he says, "The law brings nothing but wrath," that is, when it reveals what we have handled wrongly, it brings us only wrath and disgrace. So when the conscience sees that it has done evil, then it feels that eternal death is inevitable, and so punishment follows quickly and surely. That is why this lord commands this servant to pay with all that he has. He cannot pay. What does the servant do now? The fool goes on and thinks he can still repay it. He falls down and begs that the lord have patience with him. That is the plague of all consciences when sins come and bite. They feel how they are evil before God. So they have no peace, run here and there, seek help here and there that they be free of sins. They even dare to do a lot to pay God. This is what we previously taught from which also many pilgrimages, convents, cloisters, masses and other foolish works have come. There we have fasted and whipped ourselves, become monks and nuns, all because we have the understanding that if we lead such a life and do so many works, God should behold it and allow himself to be paid by it. We thought we would quiet our consciences and make our way to freedom before God so we have acted even as this fool does.

Now such a heart which is so effected by the law and feels its need and terror, experiences true despair. That is why such a heart falls down before the Lord and pleads for grace. Without that, it still has the defect. It wants to help itself. One cannot remove this from his [fallen nature]. When the conscience feels such misery, then it may also be said that all the works of the angels in heaven are not enough [to help]. In that case, the person can easily be convinced [by someone] that he is bound to do everything that person can demand of him. Then it always becomes apparent that he still wants to pay for sins with works.

Erl. 14, 241–243: Sermon for Trinity 22, Matthew 18:22–35

My soul, no more attempt to draw
Thy life and comfort from the Law.
Fly to the hope the Gospel gives;
The man that trusts the promise lives. (*TLH* 289: 4)

Monday

So this servant lamented to the lord and he released him and forgave him his debt. Matthew 18:27

Now the gospel cure is illustrated and how God treats us. When you are so stuck in sins and are worried and desire to get yourself out of it, then the gospel comes and says, "No, it is not so, my dear friends. It doesn't help to madly martyr yourself and make yourself upset. Your works will not do it." But God's mercy acts and he allows himself [to hear] your miserable lamenting and sees that you are stuck in the kind of misery that chokes you like mud. You cannot help yourself out. He sees that you cannot pay. Thereupon he bestows unto you everything. It is great mercy. For he forgives your debt, not for the sake of your works and service, but because he laments for the sake of your cries, your grievance and your utter fall. That means that God regards a humbled heart as the prophet says in

Psalm 51:17, "The sacrifices of God are a contrite heart. A broken and a contrite heart, O God, you will not despise." Such a broken and discarded heart, he says, cannot help itself and become happy. So God extends his hand to him. That is the best sacrifice before God and the right way to heaven.

Following the way of mercy, since God allows the lamenting of misery, he also lifts away his rights in the matter. He no longer says, "Remit what you have and pay." He desired to say before, "You must pay. I have ruled so but for your sake I will not use my rights." So he is not able to punish because of his mercy. He will not deal with him according to his sentence but rather he changes the ruling by grace. He is merciful to him, gives him back his wife and child and everything he has and forgives him the debt. So because God lets it be proclaimed through the gospel, "Whoever believes, not only the debt, but also the punishment is forgiven," no work is required after that. Whoever preaches that one could lay aside his debt and punishment by works has turned the gospel into a lie. For the two will not allow each other. God's mercy and your having to purchase something are mutually exclusive. "If it is grace it is not earned. If it is earned, then it is a right and not grace." Romans 11:6. So if you pay what you owe, then he gives you no mercy. If he gives you mercy, then you do not pay. Therefore, we are exhorted to allow him to handle this matter for us and trust and believe in him. That is the gospel here.

So notice that because this servant is so humbled by the knowledge of his sins, the Word is mighty and comforting for him, because the lord declared him free and forgave him both the debt and pain. By this he reveals that the gospel does not enter the wicked heart nor those who are insolent. Rather, the gospel enters only those troubled consciences that are pressured by sins, that would like to be free. Over these God has mercy and has given everything. So this servant has been exhorted to receive the Word and becomes God's friend. Those who have not received the Word in that way, would not receive help and no relief would have been felt. Then it would not be enough that God lets us plead for the forgiveness of sins and that he proclaims a golden time full of grace, but rather it must be grasped and believed. If you believe it, then you are free from sins and all of them [the sins] are evil.

Erl. 14, 243-245: Sermon for Trinity 22, Matthew 18:22-35

Salvation unto us has come By God's free grace and favor;
Good works cannot avert our doom, They help and save us never.
Faith looks to Jesus Christ alone, Who did for all the world atone;
He is our one Redeemer. (*TLH* 377: 1)

Tuesday

Then the same servant went out and found one of his fellow servants who owed him $100; and he grabbed him and choked him and said, "Pay me what you owe." Matthew 18:28

But for faith we die hourly. Now this servant has enough. He retained his life and goods, wife and child and has a gracious lord. So he would be an even greater fool if he now went on to do everything he could to earn a gracious lord. But instead of wanting to speak well, as the lord does, he mocks his lord. Therefore, he could do no works to receive this grace that was declared to him. He could be happy then and thank the lord and also act towards others as the master had done towards him. It is also that way with us. When we believe we have a gracious God, we need nothing more so that even the time of sudden death could be welcomed. But if we yet live on earth, our life must not be ruled by the desire to gain God's favor. That would be mocking and blaspheming God (since it has already been given). It was previously taught that one must attract God's attention with good works, prayers, fasts and the same until we obtain grace. We have received grace already, not out of works, but out of mercy. Should you now live, then you must do something and be occupied somehow. Christ says all of this life must be showered upon your neighbor.

❧ The servant goes out from the lord. In what manner does he go out? Where does he end up then? He is here in faith but now he goes out. There he should show his way of life to people through love. Faith leads people from others unto God and love leads him [back] out to the people. Previously he was in faith, which is between him and God alone, for no one can see or be sure of faith and what faith and God do with each other. That is why faith is called "out of the eyesight of people," for no one but God can see or feel it and a person will only be established by faith and cannot be received through any outward work. But now the servant comes out before his neighbor. If he had remained with his master, he would have gladly died. But he must go out and live with other people and circulate with them. Now love should begin here. There he finds a fellow servant whom he stops and blocks; he chokes him, wants to be paid and will have no mercy. This is what we have said. We Christians should break out and make known with actions before people that we have a rightly fashioned faith. God doesn't need your works. He has enough in your faith. But for the sake of your faith being made known to yourself and the world, he would have you act. For he already sees your faith but the people don't see it. Therefore, you should regulate those same works that they be useful to your neighbor.

So this servant should be an example and image of all who should serve his neighbor because of his faith. But what does he actually do? He acts even as we do when we let ourselves think we believe, and we do believe after a fashion and are happy that we have heard the gospel and can talk about it a lot, but after that won't go out and live with people. We have brought that faith so far that the devil's teaching and delusions are partly laid aside and we now learn what is right and what is not right; that only through faith one must treat God and treat the neighbor with works. But after that it is difficult to bring about that love and act towards one another as God has acted towards us, as we ourselves also complain that sometimes they become much angrier with us than they used to be.

Erl. 14, 246–247: Sermon for Trinity 22, Matthew 18:22–35

Faith clings to Jesus' cross alone and rests in Him unceasing;
And by its fruits true faith is known, with love and hope increasing.
Yet faith alone doth justify, works serve thy neighbor and supply
The proof that faith is living. (*TLH* 377: 9)

Wednesday

How utterly inscrutable are the judgments of God and hidden his ways. Romans 11:33

If they were not ineffable, if we could altogether understand them, it would be because they would all be just in our eyes. What is a man compared to God? What is our might and ability compared to God's might? What is our strength and vigor next to his power? What is all our teaching and wisdom next to his wisdom? What is our nature compared to his nature? So now our reason teaches and must confess that all human might, wisdom, knowledge, all our nature and everything that is ours are nothing compared and reckoned with the divine might, strength, wisdom, nature. Is this not a great thing that we alone want to oppose the judgments and righteousness of God and we dare to judge, measure and investigate his divine judgments and the high majestic opinion? Why don't we also immediately say that our opinion is nothing when one compares it with the divine opinion? Human reason itself asks if reason must not surrender and acknowledge its own folly and presumption, that it won't let God's opinion and judgment be and remain inscrutable. So reason itself confesses that God's wisdom, strength and all that belongs to God is beyond us. But what kind of foolishness is this to me, that we confess in all other things God's wisdom and majesty and we alone [of all creatures] will oppose his opinion and judgments? And could we not, therefore, believe that he is right, even if it seems otherwise to us, yet since he has said so, we (when his coming majesty is publicly seen) shall eventually see everything and give praise that he is and remains right?

I will give an example in order to strengthen and comfort faith when we have suspiciously looked at God as if he weren't right. Behold, God the Lord acts and reigns in external things in the world so that if one should consider and judge according to reason he must say that either there is no God or else God is unrighteousness. As a former poet said, "It often occurred to me that there is no God." So see how everything goes best for the godless and evil in the world and just the opposite for those who are pious and Christian, for whom everything goes evilly. Daily this is the common wisdom and experience from which the proverbs are derived. One of them testifies: "The greater the rogue, the better the fortune." And, "The barns of the godless (Says Job 12:6) are altogether full." And Psalm 73:12 also complains that the godless of the world possess the kingdom. Now, my friend, doesn't it seem altogether unjust, as reason and understanding grasp it, that everything goes well for the godless and evil rascals? Their wishes are fulfilled. The pious are stuck in grief, lamentation, heartache and every evil. Well then, that is the public course of the world and it has continuously been that way since the beginning. With this, also the greatest people have such an excellent understanding that following it they have said there is no God. So everything happens by chance. After this everything they say is stuck in a rut. Thereafter, as the Epicurean and Pliney and also Aristotle did, when they write of the first, highest most exalted Thing of Things [God], because to them it seems unseemly and difficult that God should see so much misfortune, so much heartache of the pious and so much injustice (by which he maintained that such a high Thing is Holy at the very top), so Aristotle held and invented that the High Thing could only behold himself and nothing here on earth.

After that, the holy prophets truly believed and knew that God is the sort of God who, when he chooses to act a little, is accompanied by the greatest affliction. For he lets the godless have their wish and lets the pious have evil and receive injustice as one sees in Jeremiah, Job, David, Joseph and others.

What do you think that Cicero and Demosthenes had thought at last when they received a reward of wretchedness when they had done all that was possible, even the highest acts as judged by human reason, from good motivation? Yet countless injustices appear, for which neither reason nor the light of nature can rationalize why they occur.

Altb. III, 288: That the Free Will is Nothing, Against Erasmus of Rotterdam, 1525

What God ordains is always good, He never will deceive me;
He leads me in His own right way, and never will He leave me.
I take content what He hath sent; His hand that sends me sadness
Will turn my tears to gladness. (*TLH* 521: 2)

Thursday

"I have sworn upon myself," says the Lord. Genesis 22:16

It is truly a great and wondrous thing which the writer of the letter to the Hebrews had also noticed and valued that God swore by his own self in this passage. This is an indication of the kind of heart that burns completely and utterly with great and inexpressible love and desire for our salvation. It is as if God would say, "I crave and have so much desire that you be given my Word and believe that I not only promise but also place myself as the pledge. For there is nothing greater than myself. In short, as truly as I am God, where I do not keep my promise, then I will no longer be who I am." That is truly a high thing upon which you can easily be established. It is well worth our immediate attention. For God's truth wants to announce and say, "You, man, are fickle, wandering and inconsistent. So I will add an established and sure oath to my promise. I show that I would sooner be no God then to fail you."

If he had only spoken and sworn with these words: "I will let heaven and earth, the sun, moon and the beautiful wondrous structures of the whole world be destroyed before I will let my promise be in vain," then it would still be a great promise that would be no less wondrous. But here he does something much weightier and holy and adds, "I, who am God, who have the power to destroy heaven and earth, or to fashion it, I swear and set as a pledge not a creature, not heaven and earth, but myself, who am the creator of all things." This oath, which is so great and holy, will damn all unbelievers since he had awakened and increased the faith of the holy fathers in this wonderful way. For they also thought, "God has promised us life and salvation from death and the devil and has sworn by himself. That is our Light and Justice. If we do not believe because of that, we must be damned." So let us also learn that God makes his promise so rich and gushing that it is also above all our thoughts and faith. Then he increases and strengthens them by his majesty so that we have no reason for a single doubt or unbelief. That means it is right that you let yourself be under the promise and let it completely guide your weakness. We will have enough if he raises a finger to bring for us his Fatherly goodness. But now he presents us with his Word and not only promises us but also swears and curses himself so that we are able to say by that that he can bring us his blessing.

Altb. IX, 618–619: Lectures on Genesis, 1535

This I believe, yea, rather, of this I make my boast,
That God is my dear Father, the Friend who loves me most,
And that what-e'r betide me, My Savior is at hand
Thro' stormy seas to guide me and bring me safe to land. (*TLH* 528: 2)

Friday

Then God thought on Noah. Genesis 8:1

It is no small matter that Moses says, "The Lord thought on Noah." It has appeared that he forgot Noah, though in truth he cannot forget his saints. For we live in this thought and we also feel that God appears to forget us. A "grammarian" doesn't understand this. It must be this way for the most mature saint who can understand it and for whom God (as I said) preserves faith. Therefore, the Psalms and the Bible are full of such complaints in which they picture the Holy God as one who wants to establish you and open your eyes; he wants you to hear and resurrect you. The monks have to experience this affliction more commonly than others. For they have called these times "*suspensionem gratiae,*" that is, a halting or delay of grace, that one can also feel in "easy" afflictions. For where the lust of youth is not mitigated by God's Word and the Holy Ghost, that lust is totally unbearable. So also the impatience and lust for revenge in older people will in no way be overcome where God does not witness to their hearts. How much more easily can one speak to another in terrible afflictions, in the darkness of doubt or bonds and dangerous thoughts about providence when they feel the suspension of grace?

So one should not shamefully pass over these Words as if they were only said as a part of the grammar, as the rabbis think, but one should consider it from the standpoint of the heart and passions that Noah felt at this time. Then we would discover that he could have inexpressible comfort even while he had a glimmer of faith and the flesh was overwhelming it. For the sake of that Paul complains about Satan's messenger in 2 Corinthians 12:7. In the same way, Noah's heart felt the same thorn or prick and had also disputed with himself often, "Do you think God loves you so? Do you think that you will be endlessly preserved?" For the rains came from above without stopping and it appeared that these great clouds could never become empty. But what kind of screams, complaints and cries and what thoughts also came into the weak hearts of the poor wives? Therefore, Noah needed to comfort and rule completely opposite of what was in his own heart and conscience when he himself became weighed down and frightened to death. So it is no joke or game that they had to sit so long, blockaded in the ark. They must have seen unspeakable power in the rain and water and, in the ark, they were driven here and there and drifting. There Noah felt a forgetful God, as Moses shows when he says, "God has stopped thinking of Noah and his children," and also those who feel the same, that they have been overcome because of faith and have not been able to be overcome without great affliction of faith, as a young fellow who lives in chastity overcomes his lust, but truly not without adversity, work and pain. But the danger here is greater because all circumstances have oppressed faith. Noah must argue with himself whether God is gracious and if he would remember them. So if you also have such affliction, overcoming it does not happen without a frightening battle and pain. For the flesh that is so weak cannot endure the slightest thing, let alone such a God who does not think about us but has forgotten. For by nature, we are that way. We become inflated and proud if we think God is thinking of us, giving good fortune and favor. What is the wonder that we become discouraged and doubt when God lets it seem that he has dismissed us and lets us experience every sorrow and misfortune?

Altb. IX, 218–219: Lectures on Genesis, 1535

Thy flock, Thine own peculiar care, Tho' now they seem to roam uneyed,
Are led or driven only where They best and safest may abide. (*TLH* 530: 3)

Saturday

And Jesus spoke to the captain, "Go home, it is done unto you as you have believed." Matthew 8:13

This passage is also good to note. It is very consoling to all who want to be Christians. He establishes faith so purely and plainly and says nothing more than, "As you believe, so it is done to you." By this he says, "not only in this disaster, but rather if you also would pray for your servant, or be in greater need, and you would only believe, you will have it." So praise faith as that which is sufficient for so much that it would not only give this small thing it attends to but even if it were greater it would have all that it requests. That is the Word and also the subject proclaimed by the gospel. By faith, things are handled in Christianity. Yet no one can bring this into the people or even in our own heart.

Therefore, you should grab onto these Words as a general passage or teaching about faith. In this is contained a definite promise to each. It says, "As you believe, so it is done to you." There we would quickly take this matter in. It needs no means or mediator, no princes or lawyers, not even angels from heaven from then on. So (he says) I will teach you truly to know and trust me so that you will be helped, namely, when you believe. For God has presented and given us everything through his beloved gospel, as he himself portrays it in this illustration, the "Word of Life" as St. John calls it in 1 John 1:1, and says that we have seen him and experienced him in it. Where the Word is, he wants to say, there is my heart and will and you should look me in the face as you see it in my Word. There I picture myself for you as I truly am. In this image and in no other you see rightly how you can see me in my majesty. Now it belongs there. There you should grab onto that image well as in a good mirror, giving the undistorted reflection. For according to the quality of the mirror, so is the quality of what is seen. Therefore, only look upon it so you see me rightly. I do not fail or deceive with my image. But where the mirror is false, there I will not be rightly grasped. Therefore, as you picture me, that's how you will have me. If you fashion me rightly, you have me rightly. That means as you believe, so it shall be to you.

So this captain has informed him [that is, Jesus] that he [Jesus] is a kind and comforting man and Christ also establishes himself and teaches so. Just as he had appraised him, quickly he answers him in kind. It will be so, as you believe. There both his faith and Christ's heart sound the same, as they should. Then who also can speak and believe sees the right picture so that God must say, "That is an image that is like me. Just as I have fashioned Adam to an image that was like me because my image was put in his heart as I myself am, so he bore my image and was himself my image." So if we grasp such an image, says St. Paul in 2 Corinthians 3:18, so he mirrors or images himself in our heart, that we day by day, yes, more and more, are clarified in that same image until we are completely mature. This will happen every day. But here he must begin to mirror and fashion [himself] so that we learn more and more to understand, then, as the gospel shows, that he is a merciful Savior that gladly desires and does good. He desires and promotes nothing more than that one only believe.

Altb. VI, 464: Second Sermon on the Gospel of Matthew, Chapter 8

He that believes and is baptized
Shall see the Lord's salvation;
Baptized into the death of Christ,
He is a new creation.
Thro' Christ's redemption he shall stand
Among the glorious heav'nly band
Of every tribe and nation.

With one accord, O God, we pray;
Grant us Thy Holy Spirit;
Look Thou on our infirmity
Thro' Jesus' blood and merit.
Grant us to grow in grace each day
That by this Sacrament we may
Eternal life inherit. (*TLH* 301)

Week of Trinity XXIII

Sunday

Give unto Caesar what is Caesar's and unto God what is God's. Matthew 22:21

You should baptize children so you know how he [the child] is named. That means a lot in Germany. You want to give the kaiser what is his and what is God's has belonged to God for a long time. So you would first be a rebel against the kaiser when you take and keep what is yours from him. First ask if you should give him what you acknowledge and say is from the kaiser. Yet you don't want to give it to him. That is rightly and honestly called rebellion if you would rather take from the kaiser than give him what is his.

You should hear this truth from the master of truth. That is, if you do not want him to scold you as the kaiser's robber and thief, when you gladly take his authority and his belongings and make yourself lord against your own conscience, since you must acknowledge that it is the kaiser's coin and inscription. People who do that damn themselves because they do not give and reserve what belongs to him as if they had the right to do that. They should justly be punished in body and goods as rebels twice over. That is one thing.

The other is that just as they are the kaiser's robbers and thieves, they are also in the same way shameful thieves of God. Not only do they steal and rob God of what is his, but they also want to declare their right to do it. So these are called robbers of God as the prophet Jeremiah says in Chapter 23.11ff of those who will not rightly preach God's Word and withhold it from the people to whom it is sent, because it [that Word] is God's. But they give something else instead, robbing and stealing not from God in heaven but from the people to whom God has given and commanded it to be given. So they rob God of souls and make what is his into what does not honor him as if he had no rights to anything. Christ would censure and curse such misshapen tender fruits. Therefore, they should also heed such preaching from him so they would not be rebels and thieves of God and deserve to be struck to death by kaiser and God in many ways.

Now concerning our present hypocrites who are tender little goodies; bishops, pastors in all the parishes, vermin who also publicly acknowledge Christ in his Word and the truth of the gospel and are Christians out of vivid lust and impenitent evil and persecuting. What are they, but, as Christ here portrays, rebels and opposers of the kaiser and thieves of God. They want to obey neither God nor the Christian Church, neither the kaiser nor his authority. Rather, they want to be lord themselves and live by and follow their lusts. No one should or is allowed to resist them while they are not only disobedient but also rage and scream against the innocent Christians. They choke and murder as if they could and would gladly exterminate God's kingdom in an instant. Still, they want to have the reputation and fame as if they do what is right and are good obedient people while we must die as heretics against God and Christianity and as rebels against authority. At the same time these give neither God nor kaiser what is his and yet they make themselves shine brightly in goodness, as if they sought to bring forth a life of responsible obedience and faithfulness towards God and the kaiser and as if they teach both kinds of obedience.

But what would happen if just once the wheel would turn and the sin that they now charge us Christians with would fall on their heads? So if they would be publicly charged and condemned as the true robbers and thieves of the majesty of God and kaiser, receiving their reward as such people should, then even if the gospel and Christ do nothing, since he compels no one with a fist, but only speaks the truth, still you would want to see others come (as I fear that it will happen to them) who take them in their fists and teach them so everyone learns that they must stop persecuting the Christians. That is what one is asking for when he taunts him (Christ) with his own rights.

Erl. 14, 272–274: Second Sermon for Trinity 23, Matthew 22:15–22

Grant us hearts, dear Lord, to yield Thee Gladly, freely, of Thine own;
With the sunshine of Thy goodness Melt our thankless hearts of stone
Till our cold and selfish natures, Warmed by Thee, at length believe
That more happy and more blessed 'Tis to give than to receive. (*TLH* 442: 2)

Monday

And this is the name that you will call him; the Lord, who is our righteousness. Jeremiah 23:6

I have often said, a Christian life consists of two parts. First, that our sins we have committed are completely forgiven and removed through Christ so that we believe in him. Thereafter, that not only sins are forgiven us and a righteousness is there but also complete salvation from the remaining sins, so that they do not harm me. So Christ is purely the truest righteousness. He is completely right and pure and he also purifies me from my sins which yet adhere to my flesh. So this righteousness of Christ is mine and will justify me so I am without sins. This is not for my sake but for the sake of Christ's righteousness. Now when I believe in Christ, then Christ will walk before the face of God in heaven with his righteousness and give answer for me. So we should and must receive his righteousness as if it were our own and because of that be bold for the sake of our inheritance. So these Words that name our justifier are no joke!

Now see what a Christian has for his wealth; the one who can nevermore die. He has Christ himself. What will death or sins hold over a Christian in the desperation of death? Nothing. Death becomes a matter of laughter before him. He asks for nothing on account of his sins. So neither sins nor death, neither devil nor hell can bring anything against a Christian that has Christ with him.

When death now comes to a believing Christian, then the Christian says, "*bene, veritais,* Dear death, what have you brought? What do you seek here? Don't you know who I have with me? Christ is my righteousness. Friends, go ahead and take me along. If you would take me, then I will follow; but you will bring me what is good." So the Christian is bold in death and says with St. Paul in 1 Corinthians 15, "Death, where is your sting? Grave, where is your victory?" And, as he says in another place, Philippians 1, "Christ is my life and death my victory." I die, so I have victory, for I come after him into death. There you see what death brings to the Christian. It is only your victory. You lose nothing to it. But it bites you until death.

The same can be said of the sins that yet remain and still cling to us. They cannot hurt us and also cannot damn us. For Christ is with us who sweeps us off and purifies us so that day by day and longer and holier, we become greater enemies of sins and desire to die and are drawn to salvation and eternal life. So that names our righteousness. Therefore, because Christ is our righteousness, do not fear. Rather, he sweeps us off and purifies us so long as we remain here until we also become clean and holy as Christ is holy. But all this comes from him.

Also the prophet reveals the Office of Christ with these Words. Namely, that he is our king, our bishop or priest and he is our righteousness. By that he is also our savior from sins, death, devil and hell. He saves us from all needs and is our life, salvation and blessedness. Therefore, if I have all this by faith, then the whole world can bring nothing against me nor can anyone do me harm. For he is too great and sits on the right hand of God where he already

612

dwells before everyone, safe, and brings this down to me. He holds fast. Let us only hold fast to him and to his righteousness so we will have no need.

Erl. 41, 213–215: Lecture on a Passage from Jeremiah 23 on Christ's Kingdom and Christian Freedom, 1527

Nothing in my hand I bring, Simply to Thy cross I cling;
Naked, come to Thee for dress; Helpless, look to Thee for grace;
Foul, I to the fountain fly, Wash me Savior, or I die. (*TLH* 37: 3)

Tuesday

But I am dead to the law through the law so that I live to God. Galatians 2:19

That is, through the new law in the New Testament, I have died to the old law of the Old Testament. Moses gives me nothing anymore since I have Christ. The Old Testament says that the Jews must keep the law, which God gave to Moses on Mt. Sinai, namely, that they should keep the Sabbath or the festivals as they should remain in them and their land and regulate themselves according to it with respect to food and clothing and whatever else the law and command should be. So all their concerns were bound to person, time, state and donations. They also would have an established order as other kingdoms have their order and law even as the Saxons have their Saxon games by which they rule and preserve themselves. But such a force as the Jews were, the Christians will not maintain. For they will not be bound to any law that compells and forces them to act in such a way that they would be attached with a time, person, country or tax as the Jews had. Rather, they should be a free and unbound people with desire and love to willingly do everything. Therefore, the 110th Psalm says, "Your will is gladly done there."

What is the reason that the Christian will not be bound by the law? This is the reason: "For the king is come to distribute righteousness on earth," that is, to make the people pious. Now, if HE will make the people good, what use is the law? If the people were right and pious, then one would not need to be made either right or pious. Whoever is healthy needs no physician, as Christ says in the gospel.

Now because the prophet said that this king is a justifier and a good king not only unto himself but that he would make others right and pious also, then we are not bound to any law and don't need any law since we are under his kingdom. We become good through his kingdom. So if the world were good, then we would need no kings nor princes, nor mayors nor judges nor executioners nor lawyers nor gallows nor fire nor water nor sword nor spears. Then each would willingly, of himself, do what he should, as he now willingly and without being compelled eats and drinks. But because the world is a stall filled with evil fools, one must have laws and authority, judges, executioners, sword, gallows and whatever else is needed by which one could defend against the wicked fools. So as St. Paul says in 1 Timothy 1, "No law is given to the righteous but rather to the unrighteous and the disobedient, the godless and the sinners, the depraved and the unclean, the murderers of fathers and mothers, the murderers, the lustful." But in Christianity there are pious and right people where everyone does what he wants gladly and willingly. There is no power or Lordship of one over another. Rather, they are only brothers who serve one another. Each helps, speaks with and receives the other as his neighbor and his brother, yes, even as himself. He keeps silent lest he offend his brother. There no one needs either a judge or executioner, neither sword nor gallows, for all go as among brothers. Christ is also not ashamed to call us his brothers as he says after his resurrection to Mary of Magdala, John 20, "Return to my brothers and say: 'I go to my Father and your Father, to my God and your God.' "

Erl. 41, 216–217: Lecture on a Passage from Jeremiah 23 on Christ's Kingdom and Christian Freedom, 1527

Oh, blest the house, what-e'er befall, Where Jesus Christ is all in all!
Yea, if He were not dwelling there,
How dark and poor and void it were! (*TLH* 625: 1)

Wednesday

I called to the Lord in my trouble and he answered me. Jonah 2:2

First he begins to praise God's grace and help and to thank him for aid in his need. By this he first shows us God's mercy. After this, he shows his need out of which God helped him. He teaches us two great and necessary doctrines in this verse. First, that in all things you should run to God and cry in need to him and implore him. For God cannot permit it. He must help those who cry and call [to him]. He would not withhold his divine mercy. He must hear. It only depends upon your calling and crying to him and not keeping quiet. Only lift up your head and throw your hands up and fly [to him] crying, "Help God, my Lord, etc." Just so soon you would feel that all would be better. If you can call and cry, then you are free and have no further need. Then hell would also not be hell. Nor would the hell remain from which you call and cry to God. For that hell is because you howl and cry but at last are bitten and devoured with despair or you think the one who would help you is lost, that you do not come out of it but sink deeper. Hear what Jonah does. He also was consumed for quite a while with fear before he called as he himself would admit. He thought he was already lost. He also cries out and teaches that these things that pursue him do nothing. Rather, he is quickly assured. He has cried out and will be saved.

But no one could believe how difficult it is to do such beckoning and crying, howling and imploring. We can relate enough of the trembling and doubting that placed us in the most abominable situations. But when beckoning will not go forth, then the evil conscience and sins pull us under and choke us. Then you definitely feel a wrathful God. That is such a burden that the whole world is not so heavy as that. In short, human nature alone, or one that is godless, is not able to bear this burden and to call upon God, who is raging and punishing there. Nor can it run to any other. As Isaiah writes many times, people will not turn to God who has struck them. That [fallen] nature rather shows that it flees before God when he rages or punishes. It is silent, lest he turn to God and call to him. It seeks help elsewhere and does not desire God's help. It cannot stand him. Therefore, they also flee eternally and yet they cannot escape wrath, sin, death and hell. They must remain in them.

Here you see that a large part of hell, as experienced by sinners in this life, is that they flee God's wrath and nevermore flee to him. They still do not cry or call to him. But again Isaiah says in chapter 28, who trusts on Christ the cornerstone will not flee, as he says, "All the godless flee eternally before God and his wrath and they cannot flee to him before whom they fled frightened." The believers are safe through Christ.

[Fallen] nature cannot do or show anything but what it feels and experiences. Now if it feels God's wrath and punishment, it maintains only that God is a wrathful tyrant. It cannot propel itself above such wrath or jump over that feeling. By this it is compelled to call to God against God. So, since Jonah came so far as to call [to God], he already won. So you think and do the same. Don't throw your head back or flee. Rather stay still and rise above it so that you will experience that this verse is true: "I cried in my fear to the Lord and he answered me." To the Lord, to the Lord and to no one else; even to the one who is wrathful and punishing and to no other.

Erl. 41, 374–376: Lectures on Jonah, 1526; cf. AE 19

Approach, my soul, the mercy seat Where Jesus answers prayer;
There humbly fall before His feet, For none can perish there. (*TLH* 456: 1)

Thursday

"I cried from the belly of hell and you heard my voice."
Jonah 2:2

But the answer is that it will soon be better. Soon he would feel the wrath mitigated and the punishment softened. God leaves nothing unanswered if you can only call on him and can do nothing more than call out. So he does not call according to his service, for God knows that he is a sinner and has deserved his wrath. He does not punish. But fallen human nature cannot allow this. It wants always to bring something along that could appease God and then comes up short. For human nature does not believe or know that only crying out to him is enough to still God's wrath, as Jonah teaches us here.

All people do this. When God is neither angry nor punishing but gives plenty and treats us well, we are so insolent, daring, proud and deficient that no one can get along with us. Then no force, no tears, no example of God's wrath helps. It is all only a vain mockery and despising. But then again, if God punishes, we are so broken up and dull that no comfort, no good, no mercy is able to lift us up or strengthen us. So as God acts towards us, so we yet need nothing. Look how haughty the peasants are, how despondent the rulers were in this horrible rebellion of our neighbors. Neither imploring nor terrorizing helped the peasants. Neither consolation nor exhortation helped the rulers. Then again, there is no limit to the rulers' comforts and haughtiness since no force or terrors help until they feel God's wrath again. Nature does not forsake nature.

The other lesson is that when we also fear such wrath in our hearts so that we also cry the kind of cry that God answers, then we could also boast with Jonah, that when we call in need, God answers. Now that is nothing but calling with a true faith in the heart. For the head cannot be lifted up nor the hands raised if the heart does not first rise up. It is raised, as I have said, that through the Spirit's presence it runs to that wrathful God and seeks grace under that wrath. [Such a heart] lets God chastize and yet at the same time is comforted by his goodness. So note what a sharp face the heart must have that is presented by God with only wrath and punishment and yet it goes [to him] and feels no punishment or wrath, but grace and good things. That is, the heart will not see or feel anything without at the same time seeing and feeling the highest things. It will see and feel grace and good things even if the heart is buried in the greatest depth.

Look, it is such a great thing to come to God. You break through his wrath, through punishment and displeasure as if through a common hedge, yes, through futile spears and swords. That is the calling of faith. You must feel in your heart that you encounter God just as Christ felt it when a power went out from him when he gave peace to the woman with the flow of blood. For one feels the Spirit's Word and work. They are encountered and do not fail. But those that cry and beg into the wind as if they may or may not encounter God; that is nothing and also does nothing. This is a mere mocking and hypocrisy before God.

The other part of this verse is also of the same type as what has now been said. For it is the same thing to call to the Lord in need and battle for an answer as to cry to the Lord from the belly of hell and the voice is heard. But he announces it twice so that it is even surer. We believe even firmer that this is how things happen before God. For Scripture has a method in which it says one thing two times, one after another, so it is more certain, as Joseph in Genesis 41 explains the same meaning for the two dreams of pharaoh for the reason that it be more sure.

His saying he is in the belly of hell means he is in the belly of the fish. He calls it the belly of hell not because the fish is hell but because the belly became that to him. It became hell as Jonah had his hell therein. He might just as well have said, "From the belly of death," not that the fish is death, but that Jonah suffered his death in there. So he doesn't say here what the fish is but what came to his mind in the fish, namely, that he had thought he would go under to hell when he went into the belly of the fish. Thus he might well say, "Out of the belly of my hell, or from what had been my hell."

Erl. 41, 376–378: Lectures on Jonah, 1526; cf. AE 19

From depths of woe I cry to Thee, Lord, hear me, I implore Thee.
Bend down Thy gracious ear to me, My prayer let come before Thee.
If Thou rememb'rest each misdeed, If each should have its rightful meed,
Who may abide Thy presence? (*TLH* 329: 1)

Friday

But he will be frightened by a cry from morning to midnight. And he will be moved with great rage for the sake of the extermination and ruin of many. Daniel 11:44

Here [we see] that God's praise will become completely evil in the papacy. For blows would not be able to make the pope fall though they knock at him and exhort him to penance. But it is wasted and for nothing. But now no armor, no army, no warrior, no forces but only a voice or a cry comes over him. For that reason he is frightened. Because of that he is knocked down. Oh God, you are wonderful in your works! This horror, which tramples all kings with its feet and which God himself has knocked down from above, must fail and fall before a feeble voice. How are you frightened, a great power established upon soft soil, that you are blown over by a Word? St. Paul clarifies these words of Daniel, "The Lord Jesus will slay him with the Words of his mouth."

Now these are the last days in our time when the gospel is pure and cries against the papacy. He [the pope] doubts and does not know what he will do or how. He cannot and will not bear to call a council. He will not allow anyone to address or speak of the Light. He thinks only of attenuating the cry with might. He drives it out with great terror, says Daniel, by his armor, through his clerics, through legates, through bulls, writings and many evil books. He will ruin many and cause them to fall. He incites the kaiser, king, every devil and all evil people and whomever he can infuriate. Without fail, people act for his sake. But his end is coming and no one can help him, says Daniel. The cry is too mighty. For the pope does not return to his previous position. His own no longer can bear him. As Revelation 18 says, he must be shattered without being struck by hand or sword as was his prototype Antiochus, Daniel 9.

But that such a cry would be heard from the morning to midnight means that this gospel comes from above, from the very morning, or rising. No one can, then, truthfully say or boast that such doctrine is brought forth out of his head or by his premeditated advice or desire. We have all come to it without seeking and stumbled over it. It is shown to us, as Isaiah says, "I have been found by what I did not seek and seen what I did not request." So also I sought something much different in the beginning and in what I considered in the beginning of my writings; those beginnings being only about the abuse of indulgences and not the indulgence itself, much less the pope or a hair of the pope. I rightly understood neither the pope nor Christ. Yet this cry also comes from midnight (he says), that is, from the pope's own kingdom. So we are in the time when the papists and antichrist are much stronger than they were.

Erl. 41, 311-313: Lectures on the Prophet Daniel

Jesus, all Thy children cherish And keep them that they never perish
Whom Thou hast purchased with Thy blood. Let new life to us be given
That we may look to Thee in heaven Whenever fearful is our mood.
Thy Spirit on us pour That we may love Thee more—Hearts o'er-flowing;
And then will we be true to Thee In death and life eternally. (*TLH* 444: 4)

Saturday

Our soul escaped as a bird in the snare of the fowler. The snare is broken and we are free. Psalm 124:7

The enemies of the Word do not always let their furious, unmerciful and cruel hearts be seen. Rather, they clothe and adorn their heart, posing as one who would gladly serve everyone, seek unity and preserve every division, just as the illustration of the fowler shows. The fowler also presents himself in as kind a way as possible. He wants the bird to see his support and hopes to lure it into what looks like safety, as if he wishes the bird well. The fowler also whistles in the trap and lets himself appear as one acting in a kind way. But everyone knows that underneath the appearance of friendliness, the poor bird is prepared for misfortune. For the snare is hidden. If it lay out altogether in the open it would not seem so terrible, like a bare sword or a growling wolf's teeth. But why does the fowler prepare such things for the bird? For only one reason, that when the bird now comes into it he snares the bird's neck and kills it.

So this comparison shows well the cunning, speed, deception and insidiousness with which the enemies of the Word clothe their rage and their cruelty. In truth, they seek only to mislead and slay us. They conduct such devilish bird-driving continually and by their cruelty and great cunning they cause confusion in every way possible as they have publicly displayed. Now I do not wish to speak of my summons to Worms. Nor do I wish to think further about the Augsburg Tribunal. There the pope and his bishops, the fowler of the devil, Kaiser Karl, the precious and peaceable blood, as an owl they would use to drive the bird, summoned us up to Augsburg. Not that they would sue for peace as they pretended, but that we would be buried and put into the oil. Finally, they allowed themselves to be seen by our people when they answered, "They not only committed their authority and goods, but also their blood, to exterminating our teaching." First, that is the fowler of the devil's deception and tyranny made public. Previously, this was offset by the gentleness and goodness of the praise-worthy fowlers. So God has also now torn the snares and made us free. [In this text] The attractive description by the Holy Ghost and our experience show that the enemies are cruel and also cunning and that there is no help against them except when the Lord himself breaks the snare and frees those who fear God as the psalm says, "If God were not with us, etc."

This kind of danger and salvation are always experienced as an inconsistency. How often does it happen that people are preserved in the midst of those among whom a disease has spread? How often has it happened to you that you have experienced dangerous falls and yet did not become vulnerable? In all this, one is poorly equipped to write about the defense that angels provide under God's command against the devil's cunning. For without our knowledge we are preserved, especially when all our powers and strivings become doubtful.

Now these things are totally unbearable. But afterwards they are signs of common comfort, by which David always considers that God is at hand, who preserves us when we think that we've completely had it. So he also says in Psalm 94:17, "If God had not helped me, my soul would have dwelt in hell." So we experience this in times when we are burdened with a great misery and we would despair from the first hour but yet endless comfort appears. So in our life we must always be wary of the devil's snare and we are the foolish birds for which Satan sets the net to not only take our life, but bury us in sin and misfortune. If he can slay us, he will. But when that doesn't happen, he throws us into great danger alone. For he is the father of lies and a murderer. But it is God's gift that we are not seduced but protected from his lies and sins and are preserved in health.

Altb. VII, 537–538: Lecture on Ps. 124, 1541

Cast afar this world's vain pleasures,
Aye, boldly fight for heav'nly treasures,
And steadfast be in Jesus' might.
He will help, whate'er betide you,
And naught will harm with Christ beside you;

By faith you'll conquer in the fight.
Then sing, thou weary soul!
Look forward to the goal: There joy awaits thee.
The race, then, run; The combat done,
Thy crown of glory will be won. (*TLH* 444: 2)

Week of Trinity XXIV

Sunday

You search the Scriptures for in them you think you have
eternal life and the Scriptures witness of me. John 5:39

Christ desires to reveal with these Words the chief reason that
Scripture is given, namely, that one should study, seek and learn that
he, Mary's Son, is the one who can give eternal life to all who come
to him there and believe in him. Therefore, whoever would read the
Scriptures rightly and usefully, sees that he is seeking Christ in them
and will assuredly find eternal life. Then again, if I do not study and
learn in Moses and the prophets that Christ, for the sake of my
salvation and that of all people, came down from heaven, became
man, suffered, died, was buried, ascended into heaven so that
through him I have restoration with God, forgiveness of sins, grace,
righteousness and eternal life, then my reading the Scriptures for
salvation helps me in no way. I can become a learned man by
reading and studying the Scriptures and yet it wouldn't help me a bit.
For if I neither find nor know Christ, then I find neither salvation
nor eternal life. Yes, I find only bitter death. For it is settled by our
dear God, "There is no other name given among men through which
we can be saved, than the name Jesus." Acts 4:12

From this it is clear that whoever finds Christ in the Scriptures
and believes in him has eternal life through him, as Christ himself
says, John 3:15, "Whoever believes on me has eternal life." The
Scriptures give this wonderful witness to Jesus of Nazareth and no
other patriarch or prophet. Whoever believes on him will not be lost
or damned. Such a believing person could die, just as he will. He can
be burned to dust and ashes and have the ashes strewn to the wind,
or thrown into water, as John Huss's ashes were [disposed of], or
they can be eaten by the fish of the sea or the birds of heaven yet he
(Christ says) will be raised again and have eternal life and will be
and remain with me eternally in heaven, as he says himself in John
14:3, "I will return to you and take you to me so that you will be
where I am." So a Christian, or a believing human body, the poor
maggot sack, even if it is buried deep in the earth, should and must
be changed that it shines as brightly as the dear bright sun and stars.
As Christ says in Matthew 13:43, "The righteous will shine as the
sun in my Father's kingdom." So you must rise again on the last day
and come forth in an eternal and imperishable life, as we have many
more passages and witnesses in the Bible.

But isn't this a great comfort and a rich promise that Christ speaks here? In the Scriptures you have eternal life. Now who would not desire to read the Scriptures and seek Christ in them so that he finds eternal life? It would make sense if all the world did that. But as it happens, unfortunately, one sees (and does not grasp) God's mercy all too well. So now, briefly, this is the meaning of the passage: Who wants to rightly read and understand the Scriptures and have eternal life will seek Jesus of Nazareth, Mary's Son, in it. When he finds Jesus there and believes on him, holding him as the only true redeemer and savior, who alone can and wants to give eternal life to all who believe on him, then he is a true doctor of Holy Scriptures.

Erl. 19, 92–94: Sermon on "Search the Scriptures", John 5:39, 40, 43, 1545

Lord, open Thou my heart to hear
And through Thy Word to me draw near;
Let me Thy Word e'er pure retain,
Let me Thy child and heir remain.

Thy Word doth deeply move the heart,
Thy Word doth perfect health impart,
Thy Word my soul with joy doth bless,
Thy Word brings peace and happiness.
(TLH 5: 1–2)

Monday

Who has given himself for our sins, for he saved us from this contrary, hopeless world according to the will of God and our Father. Galatians 1:4

Friend, note and give full attention how meaningfully and intentionally the apostle places each word. He does not say, "Christ has had pleasure in our righteousness and good works." No! No! He also doesn't say that he has received from us the sacrifice commanded in the law of Moses, much less our self-chosen services to God, masses, vows, pilgrimages, etc. Instead he says what he himself has given. So what has he given, friend? Not gold or silver, nor ox nor passover lamb, nor kingdom, principality, nor world, yes, also no angel. What then? Something that is much higher and more costly than everything made in heaven and on earth. Himself. Why then? Surely not for a crown and kingdom and definitely not because of our righteousness and holiness but rather for our sins.

But aren't these Words pure, mighty thunderclaps from heaven against all people and all kinds of righteousness, disciplined and holy life, that have an appearance or name as great and wondrous as they may? These same kind of mighty thunderclaps against all human holiness and wisdom are also in John 1:29, "Behold the Lamb of

God who bears the sins of the world." So one should readily consider these Words and similar passages as being exceptional and not pass them by so carelessly and poorly. For it is an extremely rich comfort that the poor frightened and dull conscience finds therein, when these Words are grasped by faith.

Are you now distressed for the sake of your sins? Would you like to be free and have a gracious God in heaven? Do not occupy yourself with this or that by which you can secure such a treasure for it is already forgiven. Rather, hear what St. Paul says that, because of God, there is a man named Jesus Christ, who has given himself for our sins. These are, yes, rich, important, wondrous and comforting Words.

Both Moses in the law and the prophets in their writings have prophesied of this redemption and satisfaction for our sins. And all who were saved by God before Christ came had the understanding and faith that they could not be made blessed by circumcision or works commanded in the law but rather by Christ, promised to Abraham.

So this passage is one of the chief and most comforting in all of Paul's writings and a true placard, useful tool and chief teaching that will turn back to the ground and to the depths the salvation-less realm of the pope with all of its supposed religion, holiness and self-chosen spiritual vocations and services of God. For if our sins could be blotted out by our own works, services and satisfactions, then what could be the need for God's son to give himself for them? But since he has given himself for that reason, we will certainly not let them be blotted out by our works.

Erl. 19, 210–212: On Gal. 4:5, Christ has Given Himself, 1538

Thou dost the world's sin take away; Have mercy on us, Lord, we pray.
Thou dost the world's sin take away; Give ear unto the prayer we say.
Thou sitt'st at God's right hand for aye;
Have mercy on us, Lord, we pray. (*TLH* 238: 4)

Tuesday

We know that we are from God and the whole world lies in anger. 1 John 5:19

There are so many now in the world who are entirely members of sin and the devil, yes, his bond-servants. So, as it says in 2 Timothy 2:26, he has captured all people under his tyranny and power according to his every desire. So what could it help that one rules and establishes so many orders, has invented so many great and difficult works with which to take away sins and escape the devil's power? There is also the wearing of hair coats, whipping the body with whips so that blood is drawn, to march in full armor to St. James [on pilgrimage], etc. Then let things like that be, so that if you do these and even greater things then it would remain no less true that you are yet in this contrary, angry world and not in Christ's kingdom.

But if you are not in Christ's kingdom, then it is definite that you are still in the devil's kingdom, which Paul calls here the angry world. So long as you will not be redeemed out of it through faith in Christ, who has given himself for your sins, you must always stay there and, in short, no one can save you out of it. With that in mind, all your gifts that you have, whether spiritual or fleshly, as it may be, wisdom, hypocritical righteousness and salvation, skill to read, authority, beauty, kingdom and the rest, can be nothing other than a true instrument of devilish and hellish tyranny which must serve Satan and promote and increase his kingdom.

This is first. No matter how wise and good you are, without knowledge and faith in Christ, you would ever more strongly persecute the true teaching, which would burden you and curse you as a heretic and a devil's lie. For you would take error and lies as God's Word and affirm them as truth and hate and zealously become the enemy of all who teach, hear and confess God's Word purely. Yes, you would curse them as seducers and heretics and think what you were doing was right and good. Further, you dare to darken and becloud the divine truth and teaching with your lies and fraud. You seduce the people with false teaching so they cannot come to acknowledge Christ. For instance, you praise and boast of your own righteousness and holiness, but the holiness of Christ, our only means of being made holy and right, you persecute and curse with the greatest wrath as if it were, of all things, a completely godless and devilish thing. You endlessly destroy the kingdom of Christ by your power, to abuse it, to blot out and eradicate the gospel in order to pursue and murder Christ's servants along with all who hear it and have love for it, etc. Therefore, your wisdom, as long as you are outside of Christ, is a two-edged folly. Your holiness and righteousness are a double sin and blaspheme of God. Because of these, you know nothing about God's wisdom and righteousness, but rather, wherever possible, you darken, hinder, blaspheme and persecute what is completely wonderful.

For this reason, St. Paul might well call the world an angry world. For where it wants to be the most pious and best, there it is the most angry. In the works-righteous, rational and learned people,

624

the world brings forth the best and most pious people and it is even
then doubly evil. Now I will not consider the great fleshly charges
that go against the other table [of the law] by which the whole world
is lost, such as is found in disobedience to parents and rulers, all
kinds of sexual indecency, whoring, divorce, avarice, robbing,
stealing, taking advantage, scratching, clawing, hating, lying, deceit,
murder, misleading, revelry and other oppression, etc. These are
great and terrible burdens and sins. Yet they are weaker when one
considers them compared to what is said above, namely compared to
the righteousness and wisdom of the hypocrites and works-righteous
people. For they sin against the first table of the law. This is the
white pretty devil who drives the people to spiritual sins, which one
holds and defends not as sins, but as pure righteousness. He is the
one who does the great harm, much, much more than the black devil,
who only drives the people to coarse sins of the flesh which are so
recognizable that even the Turk and heathen would acknowledge
them as sins.

Erl. 19, 227–229: On Gal. 4:5, Christ has Given Himself, 1538

My Savior sinners doth receive Who find no rest and no salvation,
To whom no man can comfort give, So great their guilt and condemnation;
For whom the world is all too small, Their sins both them and God appall;
With whom the Law itself hath broken, On whom its judgment hath been spoken,
To them the Gospel hope doth give: My Savior sinners doth receive.
My Savior sinners doth receive. (*TLH* 386: 1)

Wednesday

*Now as the chosen of God, holy and beloved, put on
heartfelt mercy, affection, humility, gentleness, patience.
Colossians 3:12*

The Christian's dress is two fold: Faith and love. Just as Christ
wears a two-fold cloak which is indivisible, which refers to faith and
the other which is love. So now St. Paul speaks here of the second
coat, love, and shows us Christians what we should wear in the
world as our adornment and clothing, namely, not silk or costly gold,
as also wives are depicted by St. Peter in 1 Peter 3:3 and St. Paul in
1 Timothy 2:9. We serve well in our coat, namely, in love towards
our neighbor, by which we take care of him and his need. That is
called the Christian adornment before people.

See how highly and dearly he exhorts us. He doesn't plague us
by driving or compel us with commands and laws but rather he

charms and invites us by reminding us of the unspeakable grace of God by which he calls us "the bride of God," or "the saints," or "the beloved." By this he would woo such fruits of love out of faith that is free, happy and performed with ardent desire. For whoever believes from the heart and trusts that he is beloved, holy and chosen before God would not only think how he is satisfied by such an honor and name and hold himself, then, as made worthy but rather he would also become inflamed with desire to God so that he would gladly do, allow and suffer everything and would know enough what to do. But whoever does not believe it or doubts about it is not moved by these Words and does not experience what flames and fires these Words have in them, that we are holy, beloved and chosen before God.

So now let the holy ones go, who only exhort and love themselves. They adorn [themselves] with works of the law, fasts and punishments, uniforms and holding offices. For they do not want to be sinners before God. But we have another adornment before God that does not proceed with such phantom works but rather this adornment is earnest and rightly fashioned which does good to the neighbor and is useful, free, unbound by the laws of diet, clothing and times, etc. Therefore we are holy before God, before whom no one is holy because we are sinners and we let go of our own holiness. But everyone who is holy before himself remains always godless and a sinner before God for that reason. Therefore we are also holy before God because we hate, judge and curse ourselves and let go of our self love. But all who love and value themselves are hated and unacceptable before God because of this. For instance, we are chosen before God because we dismiss ourselves and scorn ourselves as filth. For those are chosen and God has elected them from eternity. But when each one chooses himself he must be dismissed by God as also he has dismissed these people eternally. See what St. Paul intends by these Words.

Erl. 8, 71–72: Sermon on Epiphany 5, Colossians 3:12–17

Thou holy Light, Guide Divine, Oh, cause the Word of Life to shine!
Teach us to know our God aright And call Him Father with delight.
From ev'ry error keep us free; Let none but Christ our Master be
That we in living faith abide, In Him, our Lord, with all our might confide.
Hallelujah! Hallelujah! (*TLH* 224: 2)

Thursday

Now put on. . . hearty mercy. Colossians 3:12

This is part of this adornment and a lively Christian jewel. It is better established before God than all pearls, precious stones, silk and gold are before the world, an attribute true Christians also demonstrate. He would also say, "You should not only be merciful outwardly and in appearance but from the bottom of the heart, just as a father and mother become moved to the bottom of their heart and with all their being when they see or hear of their children's needs. To this end they throw their life and body and all they have on the scale so that both courage and heart are always exuberant in the work of mercy and yet they neither see nor notice in all of this that they are merciful and doing good."

With the same Word, St. Paul condemns all hypocritical saints' ways and discipline. For these do not do away with sins and frailty. Everything goes the way of the harshness of their laws, where there is only driving and compulsion, i.e., no mercy but only punishment, scolding, judgment, blaming and rage. They will put up with nothing unrighteous but among [true] Christians many sinners and frail people are established with them. Yes, the Christians mingle exclusively with them and not with the "holy ones." Therefore, they reject no one, bear everyone, yes, they receive these so heartily, as if they themselves were such weak people. They pray for them and teach, exhort and charm them and do all that is possible to help them. That is a true Christian method as God has made us in Christ and as he still continues [to make us]. This is what Christ does with the adulteress, John 8:3ff, where he freed her from those driving and hunting her and charmed her with sweet kindly Words and deeds that brought her to repentance and released her. So we also read from St. Anthony when he said Paphonitus knew how one should save souls when he suffered at the hands of other brothers who hunted and pursued him to punish him, etc. (See *Life of the Fathers*)

For if God should deal with us according to the harshness of his law we would be lost. But now he deals with us according to his mercy and has suspended his law as he says in Isaiah 9:4, "You have averted the whip from his neck and the scepter of his oppressors and the load of his burden, etc." He practices only charm and being attractive to us.

So take note how deeply those who you now hold as great Christians and yet who will not endure or have mercy towards Christian weakness are yet stuck in the law and hypocrisy when they do not see complete holiness and special wonderworks in those who now know and have Christ and the gospel. To them no one [else] is truly established so heaven will fall and the earth go under. They can do nothing more than criticize, judge and mock. Yes, that is good evangelicalism. Yes, that is a charismatic [*schwaermer*]. But by this they show in an excellent way how blind they are and still know nothing of Christ, always bearing the beam in their own eyes.

Erl. 8, 72–73: Sermon on Epiphany 5, Colossians 3:12–17

In sickness, sorrow, want, or care,	And may Thy Holy Spirit move
Whate'er it be, 'tis ours to share;	All those who live to live in love
May we, where help is needed, there	Till Thou shalt greet in heaven above
Give help as unto Thee!	All those who live to Thee. (*TLH* 439: 5–6)

Friday

So clothe yourself in . . . kindness. Colossians 3:12

This is another part of the Christian's adornment, kindness. You find out what that is in the Epistle appointed for Christmas, namely, the loving behavior of a person who presents himself in a kind way to everyone. No one is hunted by him with a sour disposition and with hard words or wild ruining which is also described in German when one says, "If he is so kind, he can present himself and act in a kind way." Therefore, such virtue is not a single work, but a whole life. Such a person is established towards everyone so that he allows everyone's action and thus proves that he is kindly disposed towards everyone. Over and against this are the strange heads that allow nothing to happen unless they contributed it. Everyone ought to adjust their way to them and resign themselves to what they want but they will adjust to no one else. One calls them unkind people.

But this kindness is not also to be used in the area of doctrine but rather in all works of life. So now we often say that life, with all its works and fruits, does not take the place of doctrine. So it [kindness] can and will love and be kind to my neighbor whatever his life may be like. But if he will not teach or believe rightly then I will not love or be kind but rather, as St. Paul says in Galatians 1:8–9, "Hold him as banished and accursed, even if he is an angel of heaven."

So divide and distinguish wonderfully between the two: Faith and life. Life will and must be kind also to the most wrathful enemy so long as he only does not contest the doctrine and faith. Faith will and cannot suffer even father or mother and the best friend if they

628

should contest the doctrine and faith, Deuteronomy 13:6-8. Therefore, life must be ordered with its actions not upon the faith and doctrine of the neighbor but rather upon his life and with works. Then again, faith is not ordered according to works and life but according to his [Christ's] doctrine and faith.

Erl. 8, 75–76: Sermon on Epiphany 5, Colossians 3:12–17

All love is Thine, O Spirit; Thou hatest enmity;
Thou lovest peace and friendship, All strife wouldst have us flee.
Where wrath and discord reign, Thy whisper kindly pleadeth
And to the heart that heedeth Brings love and light again. (*TLH* 228: 6)

Saturday

Agree with one another and forgive one another if one has a complaint against another. Just as Christ forgave, you also forgive the other. Colossians 3:13

Note that here he describes true Christians and saints and yet he holds them to be so weak that they act to make others sorrowful and complain against one another. This should not happen among Christians and saints. But as I have said, this is why Christ's kingdom is such a mystery. It is hidden, as can never be preached and heard enough. Those who would not believe it cannot be brought to do these works, but those who believe it cannot bring themselves to such works [forgiveness/reconciliation] anywhere else. Everyone who does not want faith also does not want life.

So Christ's kingdom is come in such a way that his Christians are not altogether holy but have rather begun to be gathered. Therefore, one always finds wrath, evil lust, false love, sorrow and other evil frailty among them as they share in common their Old Adam, which St. Paul calls "The neighbor's burden, which one should bear for one's brother" (Galatians 6:2). And [he calls it] "weakness, which one should receive (or take up)," Romans 15:1, just as Christ was patient and bore these in his apostles and he daily bears his own [people].

Now if one were to tally up these "fruits of the spirit," Galatians 5:22, that the Christian should be "mild, good, patient and chaste," and considers this passage as a command and a law, then one will not believe there are Christians where there are not these fruits that exclude all weaknesses. See, he cannot believe that Christ is where he yet truly is and must then judge impiously. Such a person complains that there are Christians nowhere and rages therefore of a greater wisdom than Christ's, as they boast from Scripture that they could recognize the Christian by his fruits, as Christ also says in Matthew 7:16, "That one recognizes a tree by its fruits." Upon this such a person stands.

Now advise me, what is wrong with this? It is wrong because he understands nothing about the kingdom of God. For he grasps the passage which speaks of the Christian with this understanding: The Christians should be good and mild, that is, they should never rage and patiently bear everything and not be impatient against anyone, even against a single person. Where this is not true, then, they are not Christians, for they do not have the fruits. Friend, who compels such a judgment but such a person's own blindness? He dreams it up for himself that Christianity is a completed holy station of life in which there is no weakness as it will be in heaven among the angels. But tell me, where do the Scriptures say this of Christians?

Now whoever recognizes that Christianity is a beginning and growing station in life does not get worked up if a Christian occasionally is simply tough, unkind and impatient. For he knows this [toleration] is called by Christ "bearing a burden" and "enduring weakness."

Erl. 8, 77–79: Sermon on Epiphany 5, Colossians 3:12–17

Forgive our sins, Lord, we implore, Remove from us their burden sore,
As we their trespasses forgive Who by offenses us do grieve.
Thus let us dwell in charity And serve our brother willingly. (*TLH* 458: 6)

Week of Trinity XXV

Sunday

But, dear brothers, we do not want you to be ignorant about those who sleep so that you will not mourn as others who have no hope. 1 Thessalonians 4:13

Here St. Paul throws in some sugar and mixes some sweetness with the bitterness of such tragedies and says, "You are sad and are concerned because of those who have died. It is true. It is troubling when one looses a good friend. I do not dispute it. Rather, I praise it. For it is a sign that these are good hearts that think so much of their dead. But still, there is a great difference between your death and that of the heathen, between your sadness and that of the heathen and all who have no hope that after this temporal life an eternal life should follow. But you know that you do not die but only slumber." So as you believe that Jesus has died and arisen it is also sure that God will lead those who have died in Christ to himself and will not let them remain where we think they reside. Rather, he will bring them from there to where he is. But note that even concerning this he does not say, "So believe that Christ was slumbering." Rather, he makes it more concrete by way of Christ's very death. It is about us that he says that we will not die but rather sleep. He calls our death not a death but rather a sleep and Christ's death he calls a proper death. Christ's death is so wondrously powerful that in comparison we can consider our death a sleep. So this is true comfort, that one consider the death that we suffer and regard with our eyes, as we commonly do, as the least thing according to the Spirit and [compare that death] directly with the death of Christ. Therefore, St. Paul desires to say so much with these Words. When you contemplate your death, then consider the true death compared to which all other deaths are nothing. For these are not dead, for Christ died instead. So if we want to be troubled, we should also be troubled because of Christ's death. That is called the true death, not only in itself, where there had been bitterness, disgrace and greatness, but also for the reason that it is so mighty that it has drowned every other death so that they should not be deaths but are called sleep. So it is true, as seen in the passion, that Christ died uniquely. His is not similar to any person's who has died since the beginning of the world or will die in the future. St. Paul says to contest your sadness and troubles. Embrace your good friends and make Christ's death so great that all human death thereafter be considered as a sleep. Since this is true, then why is it that we become so troubled about another one, even if you yourself die and are buried? It is only a part of the person that dies and not the whole—only the body. But here is God's Son himself. The Lord of all creatures died. Therefore, your death and my death and whoever has Christ's death will not have such bitterness because it is immeasurably different from all other deaths by reason of the death itself and the person that died.

So St. Paul would here spring us free and in the death of Christ reveal that we should consider him so immeasurably greater so that based on this, if your heart is troubled because of a good friend who is taken by death, you should learn. If you are troubled, then, so highly by your good friend who must finally die, why are you not troubled also for the sake of this [Christ's] death? Why do you not cry and complain also concerning your Lord Christ, whose death is much greater and more miserable than that of all other people?

Erl. 18, 361-363: Comforting Sermon on the Coming of Christ and Signs of the Last Day, Luke 21:25-33

Asleep in Jesus. Blessed sleep.
From which none ever wakes to weep;
A calm and undisturbed repose.
Unbroken by the last of foes.

Asleep in Jesus, O, how sweet
To be for such a slumber meet.
With holy confidence to sing
That death has lost his venomed sting! (*TLH* 587: 1-2)

Monday

Then the Lord himself will come down from heaven with a cry of victory and the voice of the archangel and with the trumpet of God and the dead in Christ will rise first.
1 Thessalonians 4:16

These are ringing "allegorical words." He would gladly model how one must teach this to the children and the simple and employ Words which are especially used in connection with a wonderful, practical military campaign. When a lord is announced to the field in great triumph with his satellites, banner, trumpets and arms, everyone hears that he is coming. So Christ also will be announced here with a great cry and he lets blow with his trumpet which will be called God's trumpet. That will be done by the archangel with a countless host of angels who will be his forerunners and leaders and are able to make such a cry by which heaven and earth in the blink of an eye are burned, lain in a heap and changed. And the dead will be brought together from all places. That will be a different trumpet and sounds much different than our trumpets and armaments on earth. But it will be a sound

632

or a voice, perhaps in Hebrew, or if it were not a particular language, yet it will be a kind of voice by which all the dead must awaken. And it seems to me that it will be the kind of voice, "Rise, you dead," that Christ used to call Lazarus, who died, from the grave, John 11:43, "Lazareth, come forth." And to Magdalene and the young man, "I say to you, arise," and all was done with some Words, as he spoke to the blind and the lepers, "See!" "Be clean." He calls this a victory cry or the voice of an archangel, that is, the archangel will cry so that one can hear it with his ears. And it shall be called the trumpet of God, that is, God through his divine power will wake the dead by this just as he says in John 5:28-29, "The hour is coming in which all who are in the graves will hear the voice of the Son of God, and will go out from there, those who have done good unto the resurrection of life," etc. He is not thinking here of a voice, that Christ himself would speak, but rather the voice of the archangel, trumpet, which is called God's voice or trumpet. Just as now the preacher's voice, who preaches God's Word on earth, is not called the Word of man, but God's Word, so also the voice of the archangel is yet the voice of the Lord Christ as it is from his command and power.

Behold, he has wonderfully illustrated how it will happen so that we should be comforted and bold and not so frightened about those who have died, especially those who die in faith and through Christ. Hope in this: That Christ himself is coming and he will fetch you and us so that the archangel will draw near with his trumpet with so many thousand angels (as the angel, Luke 2:9, who made known to the shepherds concerning Christ's birth, was with the multitude of the heavenly host). As the victory cry sounds forth, Christ will also quickly appear. And thereafter, we will awaken and be brought to heaven, eternally singing, "Glory to God in the highest." We should regard this rightly (as St. Paul concludes) and should comfort each other with these Words. It is written so certainly, as if it were already done and he foretells those future, unexperienced events as if they were history. Upon this, he would make us just as sure as he is so that we not be terrified by death and we consider every plague, pestilence, illness as beggarly and fix a beautiful picture in our eyes of what shall follow after them. He will make a beautiful eternal summer from every winter in which everyone has died and is buried. And to the flesh that lies there buried and decayed, he will bring a much more beautiful and wonderful future than it has yet become.

Erl. 18, 383-384: Comforting Sermon on the Coming of Christ and Signs of the Last Day, Luke 21:25-33

Asleep in Jesus. Peaceful rest.
Whose waking is supremely blest;
No fear, no woe, shall dim that hour
That manifests the Savior's pow'r.

Asleep in Jesus. O, for me
May such a blissful refuge be.
Securely shall my ashes lie
And wait the summons from on high. (*TLH* 587: 3–4)

Tuesday

Death is swallowed up in defeat. Death, where is your sting? Hell, where is your victory? 1 Corinthians 15:55

He wants to say, "Death is buried and has lost its kingdom, might and victory." It surely had the upper hand and for the sake of sin all the world has been subjected to it. All people had to die but now it has lost the victory. So against the kingdom and victory of death, the Lord God, the Lord of Sabaoth, has made another victory, the resurrection from death through Christ. Death has sung, "Ho, triumph! I, death, am king and lord over all people! I have the victory and cover all!" But our Lord God himself sings again a little song that sounds like this, "Ho! Triumph! Life is king and the Lord over death! Death has lost and is buried!" Up to now death has sung, "Victory! Victory! Ho! Won! Here is only death and not life!" But God himself now sings again, "Victory! Victory! Ho! Won! Here is only life and not death!" For death is overcome and has died in Christ. Life retains the victory and has won.

This little song will be sung by us in the resurrection of the dead when this mortal life is brought to immortality. Now death chokes us people miserably and in many ways, one by sword, another by pestilence, this one by water, the other by fire. And who can count all the ways by which death throttles us people? Death lives as lord, reigns, has victory and sings, "Won! Won! I, death, am the king and the victor over all the world. I have might and right over all that lives upon the earth. I strike dead and throttle all people, young, old, poor, rich, high, low, noble and ignoble, despite those who battle me!" But death wants to demand and sing them to death. His cantata should soon lay them under. So on Easter Day, another little song exalted that sounded this way: "Christ is arisen from his tortures so we should all be glad. Christ will be our comfort." Death, where is your victory now? Where do you have the one who lay in the grave and who had been put to death on the cross now? We sing this little song in the person of Christ and in those who are arisen with Christ from the dead, as we believe and as St. Matthew announces with clear Words. So these are complete and they return victory against death. But in the resurrection we will also sing this little song in our own person. There we will also laugh over death, be bold and say, "Death, where are you? Here is only life. I am lord and victor over you. Formerly, you devoured me and lorded over me. Now remove your teeth from me. I am lord over you! Formerly, I had to fear before you but now you can no longer affect me. Before, you laid me in the grave under the worms and you painted me in a hideous form. Now I am arisen from the dead and shine, more beautiful than the sun. See how I felled you? Formerly, you frightened me. Now I spite you! Just try to curl one little hair!"

The prophet Isaiah had prophesied long ago that the Lord of Sabaoth, our Lord Jesus Christ, would lord over death and have such a victory that would last eternally. "He will," says Isaiah, "swallow death in victory," that is, he will so completely devour death that nevermore will death come to power and might but rather life will hold the victory and upper hand forever.

Altb. VIII, 407–408: Four Sermons on the Resurrection from 1 Corinthians 15, 1544

Christ Jesus lay in death's strong bands, For our offenses given;
But now at God's right hand he stands And brings us life from heaven;
Therefore let us joyful be And sing to God right thankfully
Loud songs of hallelujah. Hallelujah! (*TLH* 195: 1)

Wednesday

But God be praised who has given the victory through our Lord Jesus Christ. 1 Corinthians 15:57

Through Jesus Christ we have the victory. He has come and become a man for the sake of us men and our salvation. He has suffered death on the cross, descended into hell, resurrected from the dead and ascended into heaven. He has wiped out sins, death and hell, has fulfilled the law completely and thoroughly and stopped the law's mouth so it must stop accusing us and damning us. This is now a victory where death has lost his sting, the law no longer awakens sin, nor can sins yet give strength to death. So Christ has done penance for our sins and wiped out the handwriting (of the law) and nailed them to the cross. Colossians 2.

But God bestows such a victory to us through the Word, through the preaching of the gospel and through the service of the Holy Sacraments. The same Word we believe. Now, if the law sits on us and says, "You have done such and such," and he wants to bring us to death through sins, then we should cling to Christ and say, "Yes, I am a sinner but I believe in Jesus Christ who has suffered for me and has died, yes, who for my sake rose from the dead and sits at the right hand of God. He represents me." When death hears this he must give way. For Christ, God's Son, has shed his blood so that death, sins and the law should be dead and they can no longer accuse us nor awaken sins. Death can no longer scare us. So Christians resist the law, sins and death with a joyful spirit and fast faith and say, "I know of no sins. But if I sinned, yet I believe in Jesus Christ, God's Son, who is in heaven and neither death nor death's pain, sins, nor sin's power, the law which I feel prevail, but rather he has overcome this in me for good. If my body dies, nothing lays there. The soul does not die and the body will, in its time, also be resurrected from the grave. Therefore, I venture death joyfully and am comforted and sing with the beloved Simeon, 'With peace and joy I depart,' etc." In this life we have the victory in Word and faith and continue to sing this little song in the spirit. But every day we will have the victory. In the Revelation we will also have it bodily and visibly. Then we will complete this little song in body and soul and joyfully sing with all the chosen of God, "Where now is death's pain? Where now is the evil little dog, the bad conscience? Where now is the power of sin, the law, which on earth had gladly compelled me to doubt? Death is consumed by victory. Sin is completely destroyed and done away with. Hell is purely quenched and wiped out. God be praised and thanked forever."

Altb. VIII, 411: Four Sermons on the Resurrection from 1 Corinthians 15, 1544

Here the true Paschal Lamb we see, Whom God so freely gave us;
He died on the accursed tree So strong His love! — to save us.
See, His blood doth mark our door; Faith points to it, death passes o'er,
And Satan cannot harm us. Hallelujah! (*TLH* 195: 3)

Thursday

But I lived a while apart from the law. But then the law came and sin again sprang to life. Romans 7:9

St. Paul speaks of sins which are called true sins. That is, ones that are living, terrifying the heart and conscience. For all people are already sinners yet they do not understand all that is sin. The great heap of people in this world proceed safely, have good courage until all of a sudden they lay in hell. Such people do not feel what sin and death and their power are until they have been completely swallowed up by sin and death. For that is the method and nature of sins. At first they sleep and are still, as the Lord says to Cain, "Is it not so?

If you are pious then you are received. But if you are not pious then sin lays at your door." When a sinner is served up some foolishness and roguishness then he does not soon feel the sin and is not frightened over it but drives towards this foolishness and knavery ever more and more. That is a sleeping sin. But when the sin awakens in the heart and the conscience nails and bites him he doesn't know if he can remain. That is an awakened, living sin. Just as a snake when it lays in the grass sleeps as if it were dead, should it awaken it will strike and cling to you. So also sin lays quietly and lets the sinner feel safe a while as if it were dead. But when it becomes apparent and living in the conscience then it frightens and kills. St. Paul calls it the pain of death. But it is nothing else than the cursed sigh of the heart where the person cries, "Oh, I am lost!" When the goad sticks, a person cannot remain alive. But he must die, even if he is healthy, if he does not become saved through the comfort of the gospel.

I have known a bird trader going to Erfurt who had good courage, going in safety and heaping many sins upon himself in life. Then he became sick unto death. He cried out, "Oh, no! Have I now for this become a sow-tender (referring to the prodigal son)?" The same is said of another bird trader going to Naumberg. On his last journey he cried out, "Oh Lord God, I have always had enough money and goods and all that my heart desired. If only I also now had someone who would go to hell for me!" That is the goad when sins awaken in the conscience and make a person anxious so he doesn't know where he will remain. We call it in German "remorse." If a slayer and a murderer comes to acknowledge his sin, then the sin puts him to death from that moment on. If he would not be helped through true comfort he must die. Crude, insolent people know absolutely nothing about this goad. They go on in safety and do not feel what sin and death are until death has completely devoured and swallowed them as is seen with those two bird traders. But the Christian must daily experience and feel in himself what kind of power sin and death have. For this goad doesn't only come to this remorse by coarse sins like infidelity, whoring, slaying and murder but this also comes to those who are pious people before the world who must bite in their heart because of their sins because they have not feared God, not believed and trusted him and haven't served him. I have seen several monks in the papacy in cloisters who enter into constant misery and sigh," Oh God! Oh God! If only I already held my order!" What an especially sharp fearful heart have they who often feel death's goad. I have had to feel and taste such a goad often, in fact, so much remorse of conscience that I broke out in an anxious sweat.

Altb. VIII, 409–410: Four Sermons on the Resurrection from 1 Corinthians 15, 1544

From depths of woe I cry to Thee, Lord, hear me I implore Thee.
Bend down Thy gracious ear to me. My prayer let come before Thee.
If Thou remembrest each misdeed, If each should have its rightful meed,
Who may abide Thy presence? (*TLH* 329: 1)

Friday

And has also given him power to be keeper of judgment.
Therefore he is the Son of man. John 5:27

Heironymous writes: "I think about the day of judgment so often. It frightens my heart and my whole body. For some this is a joy in this present life and is useful to them. Yet the gravity of the coming judgment never leaves my mind or fails to be remembered." It is surely true. Whoever believes this from the heart and holds it as definite that he must die and come before the judgment will gladly pass by dissension and will not be the source of foolishness and trouble. As Sirach also says in chapter seven, "If you would consider what you do against the end, you will never do evil again." Still a human heart is terrified when it hears the terrifying history and horrifying examples of the great and earnest wrath of God, that God wiped away the godless world with the flood and has overturned and cursed the cities of Sodom and Gomorrah with sulfur and fire. How could it not be terrifying when we hear that God will summon the last world by thunder, lightening and fire to the last judgment when the heavens, as St. Peter says, pass away with fire and the elements are melted with fire. So all histories are only previews of the coming wrath and judgment of God, as also the apostle Peter says that God has made certain with these examples how it will be in the end for the godless.

Now the mercy of God will not desire that we be suddenly overcome with the day of judgment. Therefore, he acts towards us with grace and honor. He truly warns us, lets his Word be preached to us, calls us to repentance, builds forgiveness of sins on Christ for us, tells us we will be free of guilt and pain as we believe in his Son. He calls us to stay in our calling and perform our appointed office. When we do that, he grants us good that we eat and drink, have good things and joy. Though we must eat and drink, we should live differently on earth. Only we should not forget God and the coming life. Is it not a good and pious God who thinks of us truly and completely as a father does? He speaks to us in no other way than a father speaks to his children. Dear children, repent, believe in my Son, whom I sent. Be good and obedient and perform your office.

638

Then eat and drink and use the temporary goods I have given. Only see to it that you use the world and temporal goods in such a way that you wait for the last trumpet so that when it sounds and the last thunderclap peals, you are ready with a holy way of living and a saved soul. If you do that, you have no need.

Altb. VIII, 403–404: Four Sermons on the Resurrection from 1 Corinthians 15, 1544

And though it tarry till the night and till the morning waken.
My heart shall never doubt His might Nor count itself forsaken.
Do thus, O ye of Israel's seed, ye of the Spirit born indeed.
Wait for your God's appearing. (*TLH* 329: 4)

Saturday

So be glad, young people, in your youth and allow your heart good things. Do what your heart desires and your eyes behold and know that God will lead you for the sake of these things before the judgment. Ecclesiastes 11:9

That is, you youth, who do not yet know the world, if you would rightly live and do well, then hear what I teach and write to you here. Do not think that you will only have lust as the godless believe, who know nothing of God. Use joy, which God gives and be prepared if you encounter evil deception in the world so that you can look to God. The world jeers. Her evil and deception overcome you. Learn what it means that the world is scornful. Do not be like a monk, cringing in the corner, but give your heart to joy and build and trust in God. So he says now: If you would pursue salvation so you put up with the evil world, then get used to looking to God and using what is present from your youth on.

"Give your heart to good things in your youth." That is, God gives you joy, so use it. If he brings trouble, then do not be frightened and do not refuse it. You should instruct the young people from youth on. And whenever youth do not follow such advice, they will not become a rightly formed adult. For young people are hotheads and are still inexperienced in many things. Therefore, they cannot yield or bear the great evil and thanklessness of the world. So Solomon is a true royal schoolmaster. He does not build up the youth to be with the people or to be happy in the way the monks teach their students, for then they would only become wooden and blocks. As the monk, Anselm's mother also said, "A young man, so stressed and drawn away from the people is like a fine young tree that could bear fruit but is planted in a small pot." So the monks start with their youth like one sets a bird in a cage so that the people must neither see nor hear them and no one is allowed to speak with them. But it is dangerous for the youth to be alone like that, so completely cut off from people.

One should let a young person hear and see and experience all kinds of things so long as they retain discipline and honor. Nothing is accomplished in the rules of the monks. It is good for a young person to be with people but also that he forthrightly be exhorted to uprightness and virtue and be protected from burdens. To the young such tyrannical, monkish rules are completely scandalous and to them joy and delight are as necessary as eating and drinking. So they also stay in the best of health. They should have, of primary importance, personal dedication to fear and know God, hear and learn God's Word and become an honest heart. If he is god-fearing and pious in heart then his life will soon follow. Therefore, one must make sure that he not be drawn to a monastery and become completely heavy-hearted which is a result of their method and nature but only that one give good attention that he not be given to empty reason or foolishness. For revelry, games, and lovers are not the joy of heart about which Solomon is speaking. These often rather bring sadness.

"Do what your heart desires and your eyes behold and know that God will lead you for the sake of all these before the judgment." These Words give me reason to understand this text so that Solomon says *ironice*, or irony. For it sounds as though it doesn't speak in a godly way: do what your heart desires. . . But this is all to say, as it follows the text that precedes it, that when first your heart is truly instructed, then be joyful, as God gives it. Only keep your flesh from sinning as is said above.

Altb. V, 1275–1276: Lectures on Ecclesiastes, 1532

Joy to the world, the Lord is come! Let earth receive her King:
Let every heart prepare Him room And heav'n and nature sing,
And heav'n and nature sing, And heaven and heaven and nature sing. (*TLH* 87: 1)

Week of Trinity XXVI

Sunday

But when the Son of Man has come in his glory and all the holy angels with him, then he will sit on the seat of majesty. Matthew 25:31

Christ presents his exhortation in the strongest way but with his trustworthy promise of majestic, eternal reward and the turning away of frightening eternal wrath and pain for those who have attended the warning. So if this does not stir and provoke them, then surely nothing will arouse people. For he says that he himself will come visibly in his majesty on the last day with all the angels and he himself will establish those who believed on him and have displayed the life of a Christian in the kingdom of the eternal majesty of his Father. On the other hand, those who did not wish to live as Christians and that separated themselves from him and all the saints are cast into eternal hell. Now, if this were not told us, we would be craving to hear from the masses what would happen on the last day and what the Lord Christ, himself, would say or do. Now we hear it and have before our eyes first death, to which no one would run, and thereafter the day of judgment. Such a day will happen so that Christ will gather (through the resurrection) all people that have ever lived upon the earth. He will come together with them in great unspeakable majesty, sitting on his judgment seat and with him all the company of heaven soar around the judge. And all the evil and the good will be revealed, for we and everyone will stand publicly before him and no one will be able to hide himself.

This scene of such wonder and majesty will easily be the greatest terror and pain for the damned, as the epistle said. For they will suffer the pain of eternal ruin from the face of the Lord, etc. For even if there were only a single angel present, yet no one's fleeting evil conscience could remain in his presence (were it possible for that one to flee), even as a thief and criminal cannot willingly stand before a human judge. If he could leave, he would much rather do that, or even face it alone, so that he would not publicly be shamed, for in his silence, he must hear the reason that death goes over him. What kind of terrifying sight will this be when the godless will see not only all angels and all creatures but also the Judge in his divine majesty and they will hear spoken over them the reason for their eternal ruin and the eternal fires of hell? This should surely be only a fair, strong, mighty warning that we therefore make sure, as

Christians, that we are permitted to stand with honor and unafraid before this Lord of majesty at his judgment so that no fear and terror but rather only eternal comfort and joy will be there. Then, as he says here himself, the goats are soon divided from the sheep so that before all the angels, people and creatures it will be publicly seen who are his pious, rightly-born Christians and also the false hypocrites along with the whole godless world. This dividing and distinguishing cannot take place until that day (not even in the heap which is now the church of Christ). Rather, (now) the good and the evil must live under one another as in the parable of the wedding guests in Matthew 22:10. So also Christ had to endure Judas under his apostles as now it is too bad for the Christians that they must remain "with and under the undisciplined, perverted, evil people of the world" which is the devil's kingdom. Philippians 2:15.

Erl. 14, 334–335: Sermon on Trinity 26, Matthew 25:31–42

The day is surely drawing near When God's Son, the Anointed,
Shall with great majesty appear As Judge of all appointed.
All mirth and laughter then shall cease When flames on flames will still increase,
As Scripture truly teacheth. (*TLH* 611: 1)

Monday

If we are children, then we are also heirs, namely, heirs of God and co-heirs with Christ. Romans 8:17

Whoever is a child is at the same time an heir. Birth brings with it the right that whoever is a child also becomes an heir. But no one strives by his works or service to become an heir. Rather, the birth brings it. An inheritance is not earned. Rather, it will only be given. Along with this, an individual can work, sorrow and do whatever he can do and yet he cannot therewith receive an inheritance. But this makes him an heir: That he is born as a child of the estate. For plainly a child does nothing to become born but only endures it and then remains because of it with his mother. So also we come to the eternal heavenly favor, which is forgiveness of sins, righteousness, and the wondrous resurrection and eternal life, not through our service or action, but without all our works we receive them as given and they are commended to us by God through Christ. There is nothing that will bring these matters further. But our faith only grasps the extended promise, just as in the way of the world and in household a child becomes an heir only through his being born into the inheritance. Also, faith makes God's children of all who are born through His Word, which is the mother, from which we are conceived, born, birthed and brought up, Isaiah 46. Just as now through the birth, which God gives without our works, we become God's children, so we also become heirs in the same way. Now that we have become heirs we are free of death, devil, sin and have righteousness and eternal life.

But this overwhelms all human understanding when he says "You are heirs." Whose heirs? Not of the very rich and mighty kings or kaisers, not of the whole world, but God's heirs, who is almighty and the creator of all things. Therefore our inheritance is an unspeakable treasure, as Paul says in another place. Now who can believe without any doubt that it is true and surely grasps it as it is an overwhelming thing that one is God's child and heir, the same would, doubtless, consider and value all kingdoms based upon earthly power, honor and goods as only excrement and filth compared to his heavenly inheritance. Yes, all in the world that is high and wonderful would be to him as disgust and abomination and all the more as the world plagues him for it, to put him on the pilary and to mock and to become an enemy to him. In summary, what the world respects as the highest, and treasures as dearest, would stink in your point of view and offer nothing. So what is yet the whole world with all its might, kingdoms and majesty compared with God, whose heir and child the believer is? Concerning this, he would also heartily crave that he be separate from all that and would rather be by Christ, as St. Paul also wishes. To him nothing would be more desirable than that God quickly take him from this vale of tears. And if it would happen, he would receive it with joy and with Simeon he would hold this as the best freedom. For he knows and is sure that such a death is an end of all his misfortune and a way out of the devil's kingdom, which is never free. It would be entrance to the heavenly kingdom where the inheritance of which St. Paul speaks here would be eternally established.

Altb. VI, 772: Lectures on Galatians, 1535; cf. AE 26 & 27

A book is opened then to all, A record truly telling
What each hath done, both great and small, When he on earth was dwelling;
And ev'ry heart be clearly seen And all be known as they have been
In tho'ts and words and actions. (*TLH* 611: 3)

Tuesday

Bear the other's burden and so fulfill the law of Christ.
Galatians 6:2

So he would say: Do not despise or curse those who are broken and fallen under you but rather instruct with gentleness. In summary, bear one another's burdens. The law of Christ is the law of love. For Christ has freed us, renewed us, received us to be God's people, church and household. He has laid no laws on us except the single one to love one another. In John 13:34 he says, "I give you a new mandate that you love one another just as I have loved you," and verse 35, "By this everyone will know you are my disciples, that you love one another." Now love is not only doing good things for another as the philosophers dream but that one bear the other's burden, that is, that you bear what is annoying to you and what is not pleasant to bear. So a Christian must have strong shoulders and hard legs by which he could bear the flesh, that is, the weakness of the brother. For Paul says they have burdens that are weakening and annoying. So now love is friendly, kind, patient, not demanding to be complemented for its service and good deeds but rather that it produce these things for others who have not been served yet. So this love must ignore much, overlook much and endure. In the spiritual realm, pious helpers or teachers see much error and infirmity which they must bear. It also happens in the worldly realm itself that the subjects do everything and hold to what is administered by the authorities in such a way that if the ruler is not able to ignore and overlook a lot, he will seldom be able to rule well. In the household it happens occasionally that a father is displeased. But there we must also learn that since we can put up with and overlook our own sins and faults that we daily commit much, we also bear with others' sins as St. Paul teaches here, "Bear each others' burdens" and so forth and "you should love your neighbor as yourself."

Since now there is no station in life on earth in which one does not find sins and faults because no one can live without sin, St. Paul presents for the Christian the law of Christ, exhorting them through it that one bear the others' burdens. Those who do not do so give plenty of evidence that they do not understand a Word of the law of Christ, which is the law of love. "But love" says St. Paul in 1 Corinthians 13:7, "believes all, hopes all, and bears all kinds of burdens of the brother." But yet, such sins cannot be sins or errors in doctrine and God's Word. For those who commit such sins do not trample the law of Christ, that is, they do not offend either love or their neighbor but rather they oppose Christ and his kingdom, which he has earned with his own blood. But such a kingdom is not preserved by the law of love, but by the Word, faith and the Holy Ghost. Therefore, this law is not issued in a way that a single article or more of faith is overturned or falsified. Nor would such love refuse to acknowledge your sins nor thereafter defend them, nor defend those who continue in sins and always go to them, since these make Christ a liar. These burdens one is not responsible to bear but rather one should release them and all their idle talk, so that one not make himself part of their evil works. But those who believe and gladly hear God's Word and perform it, even if they fall into sin through weakness, when they are exhorted (warned), they not only hear such a warning gladly and receive it as a good thing, but they scold themselves for their past sins and apply themselves to improvement. These are the ones who become so urgently panicked and have burdens that St. Paul calls us to bear. There we should not be unmerciful or too strong and earnest. Rather, just as Christ receives and bears them, so we should also receive and bear them.

Altb. VI, 874: Lectures on Galatians, 1535; cf. AE 26 & 27

Blest be the tie that binds
Our hearts in Christian love;
The fellowship of kindred minds
Is like to that above.

We share our mutual woes,
Our mutual burdens bear;
And often for each other flows
The sympathizing tear. (*TLH* 464: 1–3)

Wednesday

. . . by our boast that I have in Christ Jesus, our Lord, I die daily. 1 Corinthians 15:31

So he would say, my dear honor and boast which I have in Christ Jesus is so high and costly, I swear. Now Christians know their boast in Christ, not that we are rich and worth a fortune, nor that we win a kingdom and principality, but that through Christ we become loosed from sins, from death and the devil and are established in hope. So to this extent, we are brought into the eternal kingdom and we boast that we have a gracious God and Father because we are baptized and believe in the man who can give us eternal life, of whom no Turk, no divisive spirit, no bishop or the pope, no prince, no teacher or false saint and, in summary, the whole world, knows nothing. I have this boast upon this article and it is established as security, as the thing that shall not and cannot fail me, for which I would not take the whole world. So I will swear so highly only upon it. But how does it sound when he says, "I die daily"? "I don't yet see," (says the world) "that anyone has placed you in a grave but you come and go, eat and drink, witness here and preach, pursue your trade; is that called dying or death?" Nevertheless, he swears to it and wants to have it held as sure. But as I have said, what he means or what sort of death he names or how it occurs is not known or understood by everyone, namely, that he always bears death around his neck and is plagued by it constantly. So he feels this death more than life and yet he says that he has an honor and a boast along with it, namely of life. Although it is weak and is often not felt at all, it thus lays constantly in the battle going on in the ring between death and life, sins and piety, good and evil conscience, joy and misery, hope and terror, faith and doubt; in short devil and God, heaven and hell. He speaks here of such a battle that he alone understands as a high apostle who is constantly haunted by it and is well exercised in it. For that reason, he must also swear to it so that people believe him as one who speaks the truth, even if others do not feel or understand it.

Why would I want to do this (he would continue to say), so that I am not only plagued, assaulted and given pain by the world, so I suffer what I encounter externally, as he enumerates in detail in 2 Corinthians 11, but I am also in such danger as I must be buried with the devil in a peculiar battle and arena day and night with death and fear with hellish anxiety? What do I get out of it? Or what does one give to me for it that I should be stuck in it for no reason so that I could well be carried away? Would I not much rather make an end of the matter and let me be put in the grave? Or should I speak of these things as the world does so that I, as a Christian and all that is Christ, could be permitted to have a good year and live as others live so that the world allows me freedom and the devil becomes my merciful lord? Yes, I could have that easily were I to justify such a life. But because I will not do that and I boast of another's life, then I must consider this and have as a reward that the world lifts me up and that the devil eats me up and torments me so I will never be happy with this life. But if he already daily throttles me and causes me such sorrow, yet I will not allow my boast to be taken from me, but rather endlessly bury him with it and preserve the victory.

Altb. VI, 306–307: Lectures on 1 Corinthians 15, 1534

Finish, then, Thy new creation;	Changed from glory into glory,
Pure and spotless let us be.	'Till in heav'n we take our place,
Let us see Thy great salvation	'Till we cast our crowns before Thee,
Perfectly restored in Thee,	Lost in wonder, love and praise. (*TLH* 351: 4)

Thursday

The Lord is my shepherd, I shall not want. Psalm 23:1

First, the prophet and every believing heart calls God his shepherd. Although Scripture gives God many human names, yet the one the prophet gives here is the most beloved name of endearment when he calls him a shepherd and says "the Lord is my shepherd." It is very comforting when Scripture calls God our confidence, our strength, our rock, our fortress, shield, hope, our comfort, savior, king, etc. For he truly, constantly makes known the truth to his own that he acts just as he is portrayed in the Scripture. But it is the greatest comfort that he is called a shepherd here and in various places in Scripture. For with this single little word, shepherd, he gives a present hope that only good and comforting things will be received from God. Therefore, the prophet speaks this word from a happy safe heart that is full of faith and overflows with great joy and comfort. And he doesn't say, "The Lord is my strength and my fortress," which is also very comforting, but rather, "He is my shepherd." So he wants to say that if the Lord is my shepherd and I am his sheep then, I am well supplied both in body and soul. He will richly nourish me, defend me and preserve me from all misfortune. He will worry about me, help me in every need, comfort me, strengthen me, etc. In summary, he will act towards me as a good shepherd should. He embraces all this charity and more by this single word, shepherd, as he himself points out when he says, "I will not want." The other names Scripture also gives to God have an aspect of wonder and majesty and bring an insight and awe with them when one hears them, as when Scripture calls God our Lord, king, creator, etc. The way of the word "shepherd" is different. It sounds like pure kindness and when those who are saved by God read or hear it, it brings safety, comfort and confidence like the word "Father" and others when they become introduced to God [in this way]. So this illustration is a most beloved and comforting one and yet it is very common in the Scripture that the divine majesty is good and true or, as Christ says, a good shepherd and it compares us poor, weak, miserable sinners to a little lamb. One cannot understand this comforting and loving picture in any better way than to learn directly from the creatures themselves what the way and proprium of a natural sheep is and what the office, work and diligence of a good shepherd is. Whoever gives attention to this cannot only understand this and other comparisons in Scripture concerning sheep and shepherds, but especially these will become the sweetest and most comforting [lessons].

A sheep must live only by his shepherd's help, protection and diligence. As soon as he loses that, there are all kinds of dangers and he must be ruined. For he is utterly unable to help himself. For it is a poor weak little animal which can neither feed himself nor make his own decisions. Nor can he find the right path or defend himself from any danger. It is by nature timid, careless and wandering. If it only strays or departs from the shepherd a little way, it is impossible for him to find the shepherd again but only runs further from him. And just as it is with other sheep and shepherds, there is nothing to help the stray for they don't know the voice of a foreign shepherd. Therefore, it flees before him and runs in his error until he is seized by the wolf or something else happens. Although it is such a weak little animal yet, nevertheless, it clings to its shepher all its zeal. It comforts itself in his help and protection and wherever he leads, the sheep follows. If he is only near the lamb, the lamb has wonderful virtue so he is completely satisfied with that (for Christ praises his sheep especially for that) and the sheep surely hears and knows the voice of his shepherd and acts according to that voice and allows himself to know nothing except what is from him. The sheep follows the voice directly. He pays no attention to the voice of a foreign shepherd and even when he [a strange shepherd] lures and praises them in the kindest way, the sheep do not receive it, much less follow him.

Altb. VI, 893–894: Lecture on Ps. 23, 1536

The Lord my Shepherd is, I shall be well supplied.
Since He is mine and I am His, What can I want beside? (*TLH* 426: 1)

Friday

I am the good shepherd. The good shepherd lays down his life for the sheep. John 10:11

It is the office of a pious shepherd to not only supply his lambs with good pastures but also, especially, that he watches them so that they come into no danger. More than that, he readily pays attention so that he doesn't lose any. But if he is missing one, he runs after him, seeks him and fetches him again. With the young, weak and sick lambs, he carefully handles them and waits with them and lifts and carries them until they become older, strong and healthy. Even so it is also with the spiritual sheep, that is, in Christendom. As little as a natural sheep can graze, lead, rule or watch and defend against danger and misfortune (for it is a weak and completely defenseless little animal), so little can we poor weak and miserable people graze and rule ourselves, keep on the right path without wandering and straying, defend ourselves against all evil by our own power or fashion help and comfort in our anxiety and need. For how will they know how to rule in a godly way when they do not know God and are conceived and born in sin (as we all are) and are by nature children of wrath and God's enemies? How should we find the right path and stay upon it, when we can do nothing besides what the prophet Isaiah says in chapter 53:6, run in error? How is it possible, since we are of the devil, who is a prince and god in this world, whom we all begin with? How should we ward him off? So we would not be able to do much even with all our skill and might to prevent even a little leaf from doing us harm or prevent one puny fly. What could we poor miserable people boast of as great comfort, help and advice against God's judgment, God's wrath and eternal death, which we ourselves and others experience in the needs of our poor bodies?

Therefore, only be sure of this. As little as a natural sheep can help himself in great need but must wait on every kindness from his shepherd, much less can a person rule himself and find comfort, help and advice in matters concerning holiness. Rather, such a person must look for everything from God, his shepherd, who is a thousand times more willing and expeditious to act for his sheep, which he always does, than any good living shepherd. But this shepherd of whom this prophet foretells is Christ, our dear Lord, who is a much different shepherd than Moses who is hard and unkind to his sheep. He [Moses] drives them in the desert where there is neither pasture nor water but rather where they find great want. But Christ is the good kind shepherd who runs after those dying of thirst and the lost sheep. He seeks it there and when he finds it, he lays it with joy on his shoulder and lays down his life for his sheep.

Altb. VI, 894–895: Lecture on Ps. 23, 1536

While He affords His aid, I cannot yield to fear;
Though I should walk through death's dark shade,
My Shepherd's with me there. (*TLH* 426: 4)

Saturday

For I have betrothed you to a man so that I present you as a chaste virgin to Christ. 2 Corinthians 11:2

The apostle shows by this that the apostolic office is nothing but the office of a friar or marriage broker, who daily governs and brings his bride to Jesus Christ, just as Abraham's servant was to fetch a wife for his son, Isaac, Genesis 24. Christ has mandated and instituted this office as if to say, "I send you that you should claim and fetch me my bride who was previously prepared or was washed from sins and became pure and holy." Now this happens daily in

Christianity through the preaching office, in which one proclaims and preaches that Christ has given himself for you, as St. Paul says. This was done when he suffered and died on the cross and on the third day was raised again. For through that he has earned grace and the forgiveness of sins for us. But if that were left there, it would not yet help us. For even if he earned the treasure for us and has done all, we would not yet receive it. But how does this same salvation which he has bestowed finally come to us? For has he now gone up to heaven and left us behind? He says it must go to us through the Word and Baptism which he has mandated the apostles to bring to us, to bring us home. Namely, that through them they should bring us forgiveness of sins in his name. So he remains above at the right hand of the Father, and yet he fetches us to himself through his apostles and preachers of the gospel, as through Paul he had brought the congregations at Corinth, Galatia, Ephesus and many others to himself. So salvation comes, earned by him, to us, through the gospel preaching office and Baptism. Where that Word is preached and heard, there one hears the friar of this bridegroom. Whoever receives it and believes and is baptized is already brought to Christ as a bride and prepared, purified, washed and made holy as Christ will have her. Because of this mandate of Christ (that all who believe the apostolic preaching of the forgiveness of sins, should be declared loosed from sin and made pure) the whole world, and also we, are finally snatched and incorporated into his bride, Christendom. For even if we do not hear the apostle himself, yet we hear the same Word and receive the same grace and salvation.

Altb. VI, 912–913: Sermon on the Passage of St. Paul in Ephesians 5:22, 1536

Hallelujah! Let praises ring!
Unto the Lamb of God we sing,
In whom we are elected.
He bo't His Church with His own blood,
He cleansed her in that blessed flood,
And as His Bride selected.
Holy, Holy Is our union
And communion, His befriending
Gives us joy and peace unending.
(*TLH* 23: 2)

Week of Trinity XXVII

Sunday

The kingdom of heaven is like ten virgins who took their lamps and went out to meet the Bridegroom. But five of them were foolish and five were wise. Matthew 25:1,2

Now Christ speaks of Christianity, which is compared with ten virgins, five being wise and five foolish. He calls all Christians "virgins." The foolish virgins are the Christians who let themselves be seen and heard as good gospel-based people. They can talk a lot about it. They praise the Word, saying, "Oh, that is a fine thing" and there can be no other way for them than following the Scriptures. Of them St. Paul says in 1 Corinthians 4:20, "The kingdom of God is not in the speaking but in power." It doesn't proceed with speaking, but with life; not with words, but with works. But now, since they can only talk a lot about these things, they are truly unwise virgins who only have the lamps, or vessels, that is, the outward apparatus but they act according to their own skills as Matthew writes in Chapter 7:22, saying, "Lord, Lord. Their mouth draws near, but their heart is far from me." The oil is not in the lamp, that is, faith is not in their hearts. They do not consider, yes, they do not know it or pause in order that their lamps be well readied. Their skill is that they gladly hear the preaching of faith so that they have heard the Word. They make and compose in themselves a thought or a delusion in their hearts that is regarded as faith and yet they persist in their habits as before. According to their old wisdom, they are just as wrathful as before, just as greedy, just as unmerciful to the poor, just as rude, etc. This faith is a creation of man so that it is foam on the sea or the head on a bad beer.

The other virgins (that are the wise) do not only carry their lamps in hand but also have oil with their lamps, that is, true faith that God created and has made in their hearts. These have been able to counsel themselves by it for they have God's Word with them, and not a composed, made-up delusion, of which not a stitch will hold, so that death blows under her eyes. These are preserved in divine promise and the Spirit of God works great things through them. Now they would rather die than live.

Now this illustration shows that it will be severe at the last judgment of God and this is how all Christians will be dealt with there. For amongst them there will be some, even the greater portion, who will turn themselves to those nearby who have true faith. Some [the believers] among them think uncompromisingly, as the Word of God has now begun [to say], that the last day is not far off. "When" exactly is up to him [Christ] and I am not concerned whether it is far or near.

The gospel, in order to cancel out [the false dreams], makes one aware that through the lamp this faith means to us an outward thing and a bodily practice. But the lamp along with oil belongs to those inwardly wealthy with true faith. So the art of faith is that God creates it and awakens in the heart a person's trust in Christ. Yes, it is so mightily grounded in Christ that it resurrects defiance against sins, death, hell, the devil and all enemies of God.

That is the skill of true faith which is completely unlike the faith of the sophists, Jews and Turks, whose hearts are astonished by one thing. They resolve that this or that is true and believe it though God had nothing to do with such dreams. It is man-made and such a dream comes from [fallen human] nature, from human free will, so that they cannot thereafter say, "I believe that God is one, that Christ has died for me, etc." And if such a faith that one has from God is beautiful, yet it is nothing if there is no oil there, since then God would not have poured in the true oil and given to the heart his Son, Jesus Christ, along with what he himself has, completely and wholly to become the heart's own [possession].

Erl. 18, 244-245: Sermon on Trinity 27, Matthew 25:1-15 On Faith & Good Works, 1522

The Bride-groom soon will call us: Come, all ye wedding-guests!
May not His voice appall us While slumber binds our breasts!
May all our lamps be burning And oil be found in store
That we, with Him returning, May open find the door! (*TLH* 67: 1)

Monday

And await the blessed hope and appearance of glory of our great God and our savior, Jesus Christ. Titus 2:3

The Christians' life should not be conducted such that they only think of living upon earth and to remain in this world (as the sows and unthinking animals do, which do not worry nor consider any further than how they can live on the earth and fill their bellies), but rather they should wait and hope for another better life. A sow and an unthinking animal has nothing better to hope for. When his belly and this life stops, then its comfort and hope are up. But a Christian has something better to hope when this temporal, passing life ceases; that he will walk in an eternal, imperishable life and in a heavenly existence in which there is only joy and blessedness.

For Christ has not come down from heaven and become man, nor was he put to death on the cross, and also he is not again arisen from the dead and gone up into heaven, so that he lets us remain down here upon earth in misery and trouble, much less to let us remain under the earth in grave and death, stench and worms. Rather, he would free us from all these and take us to his eternal kingdom in heaven. So we are also not baptized and made Christians nor do we hear the gospel so that we fill our powerless stinking bellies and that we should always stay here in this angry troubled world, but that we come into another life and existence where we no longer must eat, drink, have worry and work, suffer, be tired, die and decay.

Since now we are bought through the precious blood of Christ, through his joyous resurrection from the dead, are born again in Holy Baptism, and are called through the gospel "to a living hope, to an incorruptible and unblemished and permanent inheritance" (as St. Peter says in his first epistle, 1:3-4), that is reserved for us in heaven, then we will also happily and surely anticipate and await this same blessed hope.

St. Paul here teaches us this Christian art and this true masterpiece and exhorts us Christians that we should learn to differentiate this present, passing life from that coming imperishable life and turn our backs to this present life as passing, as what we must finally leave. We should set our face instead upon that coming life and steadfastly and surely hope for it as the life that remains forever and in which we belong. "We should wait in good works, in chastity, righteousness and divine purity," he says, "in the blessed hope that we Christians will receive a better life than this life on earth." We shall build much more strongly upon this and definitely hope for it, even if we cannot already see and feel it, more than we build and hope on this present life that we see and feel.

This is rightly taught, but not quickly learned; rightly preached, but not quickly believed; finely recommended, but not easily followed; well said, but evilly done. For there are very few people on earth that wait so surely upon the blessed hope, for the coming, imperishable inheritance and kingdom, as if it will really come, because this present life is so surely established. There are few who behold this temporal life only through a faded mirror and so blindly but behold that eternal life with clear opened eyes. The blessed hope and the heavenly inheritance is, unfortunately, all too often forgotten. The temporal life and the passing kingdoms of the earth are all too often considered. One constantly has this passing world in his face and thinks about it, worries about it and rejoices over it but turns his back on this imperishable one. One does this night and day and by this he beats at the wind.

Truly, now, it should not be that way with a Christian, but rather, it should be the opposite. A Christian should behold this temporal world only blindly with closed eyes. But he should behold the coming eternal life with completely opened eyes and with clear bright light. He should only be in this life and earth with his left hand but with his right hand and with his soul and whole heart, he should be in this life in heaven, and always wait in this same sure hope.

Erl. 19, 329–331: Sermon on Luke 12:35, 1537

Oh, glories here in this world, Thy pleasures bind me not,
My spirit heav'nward yearning For that which fadeth not,
Where I shall see my Savior There too, I'd also flee,
Where Jesus builds my dwelling There it is good to be.
(Verse translated from Link)

Tuesday

But when this begins to happen, then look up and raise your heads because your salvation is approaching. Luke 21:28

Here you might say, "Who can raise his head before such a horrible wrath and judgment?" All the world is terrified of the day and pull their heads down and stare at the ground for terror and fear. How should we then look up and raise our heads, [an action which] means, without doubt, joy and anticipation? Answer: All this is only said to the Christian, who is truly a Christian, and not to the heathen or the Jew. But true Christians are stuck in great trials and persecution from sinners and all kinds of evil that make this world sour and hateful. That's why they wait and anticipate and pray to be saved from sins and evil as, then, the Lord's prayer also says: "Thy kingdom come" and "deliver us from evil."

If we are true Christians, then we also pray the same thing earnestly from the bottom of our hearts. But if we do not pray this from the bottom of our hearts, then we are not yet true Christians. So if we would rightly pray this, then it must be sure among us that we look forward to these signs, no matter how terrifying they are, with joy and anticipation as Christ here exhorts us and says, "When you see these things then look up." He doesn't say to be afraid or to duck your head, for what we have earnestly prayed for is coming. So if we would earnestly become free from sins, death and hell, then we must have loved and anticipated this coming with greatest expectation.

So also St. Paul says in 2 Timothy 4:8, "He will give me the crown of righteousness and not only me, but also all who have loved his coming." What will he give those who hate it and hide? Without doubt hell, as his enemy. And Titus 2:13, "We shall wait for the coming of the majesty of God, which is great." And Luke 12:36, "You shall be as the people who await their master when he comes from his work."

What do those do who fear and do not want him to come when they pray: "Thy kingdom come, deliver us from evil."? Do they not walk before God and lie to him against themselves? Do they not strive against God's will, who desires to have this day for the salvation of his saints? For this reason, so much effort is made here so that hatred or dread not be found in us; for such dread is an evil sign and belongs to those that are damned. Such hard heads and hardened hearts must be broken and troubled with this kind of shock and terror if they would be improved.

But to the believers this should be comforting and dear. That day will be both the highest joy and safety for the believers and the highest terror and fear to the unbelievers, just as also in this life the evangelical truth is the sweetest thing to the good, the most hateful to the evil. Why, then, should the believers be afraid and not rejoice in the highest, since they trust in Christ and the Judge comes for the sake of their salvation and he is their portion?

But you say, "Yes, I would also await and love this coming if I were good and without sins." Answer: "Very well, but how do fearing and running help? By that you will not be saved from sins even if you were to be afraid for a thousand years." The condemned always fear for themselves and they are not freed from their sins thereby. Surely this fear only increases the sins and hinders them and makes it so they can never be without sins and yet they cannot escape the day. The fear must be put away and a desire take its place for righteousness and for this day. But it is true that if you would desire to be good and without sins, then thank God and hold on, desiring ever more to be free of sins. God would have such a desire be so rightly made and great in you that it slays you.

There is no one so well prepared on the last day than he who desires to be without sins. If you have such a desire, what are you afraid of if you have this thought about that day? He is coming so that he will free all who desire it and you also intend to be free. Thank God, remain in and go forth with this intention. Christ says that his coming is a salvation.

Erl. 10, 66–68: Sermon on Advent 2, Luke 21:25-33

Thus God shall from all evil Forever make us free,
From sin, and from the devil, From all adversity,
From sickness, pain, and sadness, From troubles, cares, and fears,
And grant us heavenly gladness And wipe away our tears. (*TLH* 67: 7)

Wednesday

*And signs will happen in the sun and moon and stars. And
on earth the people will be fearful and tremble. And the sea
and the waves will roar. Luke 21:25*

The first thing to know is that when these signs of the last day
are fulfilled, even if manifold and great, no one, or very few, will
pay attention to them or consider them as this kind of sign. For these
two things will and must accompany each other and they are both
predicted together by Christ and the apostles. First, many and great
signs will come such as were never seen since the beginning of the
world unto the time when he is before the door. So even if they
would see the signs and hear that they were signs of the last day,
they still would not believe it. Rather, they would mock it and with
great security say, "Oh, you poor fool, are you worried that the
heavens will fall and that we are witnessing that day?" Now there
must still be a few who will witness it and await it a little.

But we are advised by Christ and his apostles that such security
and despising would be among mankind. Christ says just after this in
verses 34 and 35 in this gospel, "Give attention to this so that your
hearts are not encumbered with eating and with drinking and with the
cares of this life so that this day does not come upon you suddenly
and unawares. For it will fall like a snare upon those who sit upon
the face of the earth."

From these words it is clear that the people will be occupied
with eating and drinking and with unquenchable temporal
appetites so that they are drowned in worrying about appetites and
eating and drinking, sitting and living securely in all the world,
as if it would have no end. For if there were not great security
and contempt [for this warning], then the day could not break in
quickly and unawares. But now he says, "He shall come as a
snare," as would happen to some bird or animal, even most of
them, if they were going after nourishment and had not expected
the snare. So he sufficiently explains that the world would live in
the trough, eating and drinking, building and planting, and being
drawn to temporal goods, with all of their zeal and skill, and
think that the last day hasn't come for a thousand years. So they

656

will stand in the blink of an eye before the terrifying judgment of God.

So also the Words of Christ would say in Luke 17:24, "Just as the lightening flashes over heaven and gives light over everything that is under heaven, so will the Son of Man be on that day." Notice again that the day will fall over all the world in the blinking of an eye. Further, "And just as it happened in the time of Noah, so will it happen in the time of the Son of Man. They ate and drank, they married and were given in marriage, until Noah went into the ark and the flood came and destroyed them all, in the same way as it happened in the time of Lot. They ate and drank, they bought and sold, they planted and built. But in the day that Lot went out of Sodom, there rained fire and brimstone from heaven and destroyed them all." It will also happen in this way on the day when the Son of Man will be revealed. These Words sufficiently show just how safe the people will be and how they are so deeply stuck in the concerns of this temporal life that they will not believe that the day is there.

Erl. 10, 50–52: Sermon on Advent I, Matthew 21:1-9

The day is surely drawing near When God's Son, the Anointed,
Shall with great majesty appear As judge of all appointed.
All mirth and laughter then shall cease
When flames on flames will still increase,
As Scripture truly teacheth. (*TLH* 611: 1)

Thursday

But he, being full of the Holy Ghost, gazed up into heaven and saw the glory of God and Jesus standing at God's right and said, "Behold, I see heaven open and the Son of Man standing at the right hand of God." Acts 7:55

By this, Christ revealed how near, willing, diligent he remains over us and is ready to help when we only believe on him and gladly venture our life for his sake. It is not only done for the sake of St. Stephen. It is also recorded for our sake. It is to comfort us so we should not doubt that they would also do this to us if we acted like St. Stephen.

This is comforting beyond all measure and builds a great defiance against death, that heaven stands open. What should not be open and ready if heaven, the highest creation stands open, also waiting for us and becoming glad that we come? Yes, you would also want it to stand visibly open to you. But if everyone could experience this, what need of faith? It is enough that it happened one time to comfort and strengthen every Christian's faith to make death despiseable. For as we believe, so will it happen to us, even if we do not see it.

By what likeness, of angels, of what creature, should we be prepared and steadied if the Lord himself is not ready and standing there to help? It is notably said that he saw not an angel, not God himself, but the man, Christ, who is of his most beloved and most identical nature and to mankind [this likeness] is the most comforting. For a person would rather see a man than angels and all creatures, especially in need.

Here sarcastic teachers want to measure divine works with [human] reason and measure the sea with a spoon and say, "How was St. Stephen able to see into heaven when our eyes are not able to behold it, nor is a bird when he flies at a little height; how could he even have seen Christ well enough to see that he was Christ and not another? If we see a man on our tower, he thinks we are a child and we don't recognize him." Therefore they improve the passage and say, "St. Stephen's eyes were unnaturally sharpened so that he was able to see so far and sure." But how, when St. Stephen was in the building under an arch? Let go of such human twaddle. St. Paul also heard Christ's voice from heaven on the way to Damascus and his ears were not sharpened. And the apostle on Mt. Tabor, and likewise John the Baptizer, Luke 3:22 and the people, John 12:29, heard the Father's voice and their ears were not sharpened or strengthened. But is it not much more difficult for a voice to be heard so far above than to see an image that is so high? Don't the eyes see immeasurably further than the ears hear?

When God wants to reveal himself, then heaven and all things are near. So for St. Stephen [in God's revelation to him], whether he was under the roof or under heaven, yet heaven would be nearer to him [than the roof] and he had no need to see a long way. God is at each end and has no need to leave heaven. It quickly occurs that he is such a presence that is in heaven and yet becomes seen as the nearest one without any sharpening or changing of the senses.

If we do not know how that happens or how it is possible, it makes no difference. God's wonder happens not because we can measure or catch it but rather through it we should believe and trust him. If you are so clever, fill me in on how such a great apple, pear or cherry grows from a small bud and about the other much smaller wonders. Let God work and believe and do not dare to catch and grab him.

Erl. 7, 222–224: Sermon on the Feast of St. Stephen, Acts 6:8–15 and Acts 7:54–60

Yet with truer, nobler beauty, Lord, we pray, this house adorn,
Where Thy Bride, Thy Church redeemed, Robes her for her marriage morn;
Clothed in garments of salvation, Rich with gems of heav'nly grace,
Spouse of Christ, arrayed and waiting Till she may behold His face. (*TLH* 632: 4)

Friday

Someone might say: "How will the dead be resurrected? And with what kind of body will they arise?"
1 Corinthians 15:35

Go up to the cherry tree, take a hold of a little branch at Christmas time and you will find no green leaves, no sap or life on the whole tree. Rather you find a dry, bare tree that has only dead wood. But if you come back around Easter the cherry tree begins to come alive again, the wood is full of sap and the branches win buds and shoots. Around Pentecost the buds become little stems which themselves change and out of the little stems come little white flowers. When the petals fall off, then you see a stem and out of the stem comes a seed that is harder than the tree. Inside the hard seed another seed grows, not so hard as the first seed, but somewhat softer, that serves to nourish it just as the marrow grows in bone. Outwardly, around the hard seed, grows the cherry, surrounded by its skin, like the flesh grows around the bone and is surrounded with its skin. And the cherry grows so fine and wonderfully round that no potter could make something so round.

How does it happen that through the branch in the cherry tree, which is dry and dead at Christmas time like birch branches, grows a bud and out of the bud comes a flower, out of the flower a stem and through the stem grows a seed which inwardly makes another seed and outwardly a cherry? The stem is first a small point in the flower so [small] that a needlepoint could barely stick through it. Then it grows out to a seed that has no marrow, flesh, blood or skin. Is that not a wonderful creation of God? No creature could make such a creation; no man, no king, as mighty as he may be; no doctor as learned, wise and clever as he is, can make a single little cherry. If we did not yearly see it before our eyes, then we would not believe that out of a dry branch such a beautiful lovely fruit should grow so wonderfully.

Where does the cherry tree come from? Does it not come from a dry, dead seed? When the birds eat the cherries off the tree and the seeds remain on the stem, they then become blanched and dry. They fall off under the tree or even become strewn into the garden. There people trample them under foot and pay no attention to them. Over the year, a little tree shoots out of the seed and grows from year to year until over ten, twenty years, it becomes a big tree. So out of one seed it has grown and bears many thousands of seeds. Do you say at Easter, "Ho, how will a cherry come out of a bud and out of a seed a tree?" Fool, have you never seen it done before? Let St. Margaret's Day come and I will show you the cherries that have grown from the bud. And look over one, two, five, ten years and see if a bigger tree won't stand there where now a little cherry lies.

Therefore, dear Hans Pfriem[18], open your eyes and look at the cherry tree and that will preach to you about the resurrection of the dead and teach you how life comes from death. If the cherry tree could speak, it would say to you, "Friend, see how dry and bare, how unfruitful and completely dead I am in wintertime. There you find neither leaves nor fruit, neither sap nor life. But come again around Easter and I have sap and life and am white with blooms, green with leaves. Come around Margaret's Day again and I have ripe cherries and all the world is glad of me. Whoever looks at me marvels over me and says, 'Look there how full the cherry tree is hung! What a marvelous creature of God that is!' "

"Yes," you say, "what happens with the cherry tree is such a common thing and happens ever year. Therefore, I cannot regard it as a wonder for I see it before my eyes. But that the dead shall rise, I cannot see with my eyes." I am thankful for this, Hans Pfriem, that God has hidden his wonderful works from your eyes and that you speak of his creation so coarsely and without understanding. Is it not sinful and shameful that you pass over God's creatures and works as if you were a log or stone that has no understanding? You have eyes, ears, reason, senses and yet you are still not as clever and understanding as a cherry tree. You rightly say with your mouth, "I believe in God the Father almighty, maker of heaven and earth," but you do not believe from the heart and you give no attention to his creation and work. Even if what happens to the cherry tree is a common thing and happens every year, yet it still does not happen without God's power, creation and omnipotence, that out of a dry dead branch come cherries and out of a little dead seed grows the cherry tree.

Erl. 19, 135-137: Sermon on Holy Baptism, Matthew 3:13-17, 1535

What now sickens, mourns and sighs Christ with Him in glory bringeth;
Earthly is the seed and dies, Heavenly from the grave it springeth;
Natural is the death we die, Spiritual our life on high. (*TLH* 206: 7[19])

---

[18]A pfriem is an shoe-maker's awl. He is referring to someone who is trying to "punch holes" in the core of the Christian faith.

[19]This alternate translation from verse 7 of #220 in the *ELHB*

Saturday

*But he said: "Truly blessed are they who hear the Word of
God and keep it." Luke 11:28*

I have often said one should hear God's Word with willingness
and zeal while it is available to us. The time might come that we
would gladly hear it if it were available to us. Whoever does not
desire to hear it is left behind and he will be well aware of it when
[or if] he repents of it. I do not preach to you but it is the Holy
Ghost who speaks through St. Paul. He does not desire to be
unheeded by you. If now the pope should give his three-fold crown,
or the Turkish king all of his kingdom to hear this preaching, yet
they must not hear it that way. They have not wanted to hear it when
they would have been able to. Therefore, they also shall not hear it
now even if they wanted to.

When God speaks and gives his Word, he gives it richly, hands
out his overwhelming treasure, opens heaven wide and says, "All up
to heaven, all up to heaven!" That is the time that one should open
his ears and hear. But if one does not wish to hear his Word, then he
[God] becomes silently still and takes his Word clean away. So it
happens: If we have not wanted to hear God when he speaks with us,
then we will hear the devil when God is silent. If we have not
wanted to go up to heaven while it stands open, then God can close
heaven and open hell; then we will see where we stay. To the pope
and the Turks it has gone this way. God has taken his Word from
them. They have not wanted it any other way so it has justly
happened to them. As the old saying states, *"volenti non fit injuria."*
He who wants it that way, to him it goes amiss. Choice brings
common law.

Now God also opens heaven and shuts hell. He bestows his
Word richly through the preaching of the gospel and speaks
comfortingly. But hardly anyone will hear it anymore. So it will also
happen that God will close heaven and open hell so that the people
will have to go there in a heap because now they do not want to go
to heaven while it is open. Therefore, let us listen diligently while
God speaks with us so that he does not take it away and become
silently still. If he takes his Word away and is silent, then we are
done for. If we once lose God's Word, then we will never again
receive it. I was a monk for fifteen years and would gladly have
heard a single rightly-shaped sermon but I could not have it so good.
Now we have God's Word richly but we set ourselves against it as
if it does nothing for us. Well then, we will see that we will lose

God's Word so that we will experience what we have done. It is advisable that we hear while God speaks to us and while he truly calls us and invites us as a friend would.

Erl. 19, 148–150: Sermon on Holy Baptism, Matthew 3:13–17, 1535

Oh, what blessing to be near Thee
And to hearken to Thy voice!
May I ever love and fear Thee
That Thy Word may be my choice!
Oft were hardened sinners, Lord,
Struck with terror by Thy Word;
But to him who for sin grieveth
Comfort sweet and hope it giveth.

Precious Jesus, I beseech Thee,
May Thy words take root in me;
May this gift from heav'n enrich me
So that I bear fruit for Thee!
Take them never from my heart
Till I see Thee as Thou art,
When in heav'nly bliss and glory
I shall greet Thee and adore Thee. (*TLH* 296: 2,4)

Appendix

Scriptural and Topical

Indices

666

Topical Index

680

684

688